AF775953

General and Periodic Crises of Overproduction

ECONOMIC IDEAS THAT BUILT EUROPE

Economic Ideas That Built Europe reconstructs the development of European political economy as seen through the eyes of its principal architects and interpreters, working to overcome the ideological nature of recent historiography. The volumes in the series – contextualized through analytical introductions and enriched with explanatory footnotes, bibliographies and indices – offer a wide selection of texts inspired by very different economic visions, and stress their complex consequences and interactions in the rich but often simplified history of European economic thought.

Series Editor
Sophus A. Reinert – Harvard Business School, USA

Editorial Board
David Armitage – Harvard University, USA
Steven L. Kaplan – Cornell University, USA
Emma Rothschild – Harvard University, USA
Jacob Soll – Rutgers University, USA

General and Periodic Crises of Overproduction

by Jean Lescure

Edited by D'Maris Coffman, Ali Kabiri and Nicholas Di Liberto

Translated by Nicholas Di Liberto

ANTHEM PRESS

Anthem Press
An imprint of Wimbledon Publishing Company
www.anthempress.com

This edition first published in UK and USA 2023
by ANTHEM PRESS
75–76 Blackfriars Road, London SE1 8HA, UK
or PO Box 9779, London SW19 7ZG, UK
and
244 Madison Ave #116, New York, NY 10016, USA

Part of The Anthem Other Canon Economics Series
Series Editor Erik S. Reinert

© 2023 D'Maris Coffman, Ali Kabiri, Nicholas Di Liberto editorial matter and selection;
individual chapters © individual contributors

The moral right of the authors has been asserted.

All rights reserved. Without limiting the rights under copyright reserved above, no part of this publication may be reproduced, stored or introduced into a retrieval system, or transmitted, in any form or by any means (electronic, mechanical, photocopying, recording or otherwise), without the prior written permission of both the copyright owner and the above publisher of this book.

British Library Cataloguing-in-Publication Data
A catalogue record for this book is available from the British Library.

Library of Congress Cataloging-in-Publication Data: 2023937951
A catalog record for this book has been requested.

ISBN-13: 978-1-83998-830-1 (Hbk)
ISBN-10: 1-83998-830-4 (Hbk)

Cover Credit: Produced by Di Liberto

This title is also available as an e-book.

CONTENTS

ACKNOWLEDGEMENTS

The editors have acquired many debts to colleagues over the decade that it has taken for this volume to go from conception to fruition. The editors faced several technical hurdles in producing this work, and we remain grateful to those who worked on the project in its early years. By far the largest debt of gratitude is to Catherine Wendeler, whose initial draft translation of the text showed us the challenges involved in accurately rendering Lescure's economic ideas in readable English prose. She also performed invaluable research into Lescure's biography, tracked down permission to use the image on the cover and located his archives at Bordeaux. Natalia Barrow's efforts to redraw Lescure's figures were similarly helpful and informed the eventual approach taken.

We would also like to thank Professor Roberto Scazzieri and Dr Ivano Cardinale for encouraging Professors Coffman and Kabiri to present on the Lescure translation project at a conference on 'The First Crisis Economists' that Scazzieri, Cardinale and Coffman organized at the Centro Linceo of the Accademia Nazionale dei Lincei in Rome in November 2014. At this event, Professor John Lord Eatwell offered helpful suggestions about how to approach the bibliographical challenges of multiple editions; if we did not quite realize the vision he proposed, we hope that he will be satisfied that the version we have produced has preserved Lescure's interest in and engagement with Walras. We would also like to offer a warm thank you to Professor Alberto Quadrio Curzio for encouraging this line of research during his presidency of the Accademia Nazionale dei Lincei.

More recently, we would like to thank Professor Yaacob Dweck for helping us source the image of Lescure in *Nos maîtres de la Faculté de droit de Paris* from the copy in the Princeton library. Professor David Todd and Professor Annie Lou Cot also helped point us in the right direction. Professor Jacqui Glass and Dorine Planté helped us to procure a rare copy of the second edition of Lescure's work from a French bookseller. We are grateful to Marc Malherbe for giving us permission to use material from his work on the Faculty of Law at the University of Bordeaux and for advising us on how to locate more photos and documents about Lescure in Bordeaux and elsewhere.

Professor Rui Pedro Esteves and Roshanak Safavi were incredibly generous in helping us translate some obscure technical language into English; they also helped us sense-check our rendering of idiomatic expressions.

We would like to thank Professor Sarah Van Beurden at Ohio State University for arranging access to the original bound copies of the 1938 edition of *De Crises* in the Thompson Library, which allowed the translator to produce high-resolution scans of

Lescure's original figures. Kaitlyn McKanna assisted with the reproduction and redesign of cleaner and clearer versions of Lescure's figures from the scanned images.

Finally, we would like to thank the organizations which have funded this project over the years from its inception in 2012. From 2012 to 2014, these included the Centre for Financial History at Newnham College (now at Darwin College), the Cambridge Endowment for Research in Finance, and the Economic History Society's Conferences and Initiatives Fund. In 2016, Professor Andrew Edkins agreed, as Director of the Bartlett School of Construction and Project Management, to support the completion of this project. We are thus grateful to him, to BSCPM and to its successor, the Bartlett School of Sustainable Construction (BSSC), for honouring his commitment, and especially to Helen Pascoe and Anita Treso for their administrative assistance. Professor Coffman is also grateful to University College London for the generous grant of sabbatical leave in the 2022–23 academic year during which this project was completed.

INTRODUCTION

JEAN LESCURE ON THE ROLE OF *SOLIDARITÉ* IN INDUSTRIAL ECONOMIES AND AMONG THE SOCIAL SCIENCES

Nicholas Di Liberto and D'Maris Coffman

Many readers of this first English translation of Jean Lescure's *Des crises générales et périodiques de surproduction* will have limited access to the two-volume French fifth edition, and even less so to the earlier editions of the work. A brief account of Lescure's revisions in each successive edition is a necessary beginning to any attempt to orient the reader toward appreciating Lescure's lifelong commitment to grappling with the issues he first raised in his groundbreaking and prize-winning doctoral thesis of 1906.

Lescure's doctoral thesis centred on the Crisis of 1900; the second edition (1910) contained the most information on the Crisis of 1907; the third (1923) presented the most thorough discussion of the crises before and shortly after the First World War; the fourth (1932) provided Lescure's first appraisal of the Wall Street Crash of 1929 and the first years of the global depression that followed it; and the fifth and final edition of 1938 gave a fuller account of the 1929–30 crisis and what would come to be known as the Great Depression. The fifth edition included a new section on the global recovery of 1933–37, which gave an account of the somewhat similar paths toward recovery followed by the major European states and the United States in the 1930s. Lescure also expanded the theoretical section with each new edition to include his criticism of the latest 'doctrines' and statistical methods, which were shaped not only by the changing course of events but also by the development of economics as a specialized discipline and the increasing number of statistical services that informed its research.

Incorporating new material on subsequent economic crises and including the latest statistical evidence and theoretical approaches entailed changing the balance between narrative and analysis, ultimately necessitating the reorganization of the work into two volumes. In effect, each successive edition enacts the conceptual model of crises that the early editions first described, with the aim of illustrating the analytical purchase of the author's ongoing theoretical and methodological commitments. The best-known modern example of the resulting intertextuality of successive editions can be found in Charles Kindleberger's *Manias, Panics, and Crashes: A History of Financial Crises* (1978), which is now in its eighth edition, four of which appeared posthumously.[1] There are

1. Robert Z. Aliber, Charles P. Kindleberger and Robert N. McCauley, *Manias, Panics, and Crashes: A History of Financial Crises*, 8th ed. (Cham, Switzerland: Palgrave Macmillan, 2023).

more than superficial similarities in their methodological approaches to crises and in their conceptualizations of international economic relations. Lescure appears to have anticipated the broad outlines of Kindleberger's own 'hegemonic stability theory' in his 1945 *Étude sociale comparée des Régimes de liberté et des Régimes autoritaires* ('A Comparative Social Study of Liberal and Authoritarian Regimes').[2] In this 'essay in comparative social economy', Lescure laid out the general premise that a hegemon could produce global stability and set about making the somewhat risible argument that a free-market hegemon would be desirable, in part because it had produced an Allied victory. Yet unlike Kindleberger, whose opinions held interest for his readers partly because he had enjoyed a significant career as an architect of the post-war international economic order, Lescure led a life of relative obscurity, isolated both professionally and personally from the main currents of post-war French economic thought.[3] As such, Lescure is primarily remembered today, when at all, as the first author to define 'crisis' as the inflection point of Juglar's commercial 'cycle' in the 1907 edition of this work.[4] By offering the first English translation of *Des Crises*, the editors hope that modern readers will see that there is much more Jean Lescure's economic theories and methodological approach can add not only to our understanding of economic crises and business cycles but also to the history of economics at this critical juncture in its development as a modern discipline.

Early Biography

Jean Lescure was born on 3 July 1882 in Bergerac, a canton in the *département* of Dordogne, in the southwest of France. He attended the University of Bordeaux, the primary institution serving the region, where he completed the PhD in economics with the thesis, 'Des crises générales et périodiques de surproduction', which was submitted to the Faculty of Law on 30 June 1906. It was published in 1907 in slightly corrected form by the Paris publishers Larose and Tenin. At Bordeaux, Lescure worked under the supervision of François Sauvaire-Jourdan, who at the time was regarded as a key representative of the new liberal political economy and best known for his translation of

2. *Étude sociale comparée des régimes de liberté et des régimes autoritaires: Essai d'économie sociale compare*, 2nd ed. (Paris: Domat-Montchrestien, 1945). For a review that criticizes the superficiality of Lescure's comparative analysis of capitalist, fascist and socialist economies, while nonetheless noting Lescure's preference for a single global hegemon, see H. W. Singer, review of *Étude sociale comparée des régimes de liberté et des régimes autoritaires*', by J. Lescure, *Economic Journal* 56, no. 224 (1946): 647–48.
3. See Daniel Altman, 'Charles P. Kindleberger, 92, Global Economist, Is Dead', obituary, *New York Times*, 9 July 2003.
4. Daniele Besomi, 'The Fabrication of a Myth: Clement Juglar's Commercial Crises in the Secondary Literature', *History of Economic Ideas* 19, no. 3 (2011): 91; and see section 2 in Alain Raybaut, 'Jean Lescure et l'analyse des fluctuations économiques', in *Les traditions économiques français*, ed. Pierre Dockès et al. (Paris: CNRS Éditions, 2000), OpenEdition Books, https://books.openedition.org/editionscnrs/43937.

Alfred Marshall's *Principles of Economics*.[5] International political economy had recently found a more sympathetic reception in France among Sauvaire-Jourdan's generation – a generation that was, incidentally, the first to take the new *agrégation* in political economy in 1899.[6] Although Lescure spends very little time and attention on Sauvaire-Jourdan's work, the open-mindedness of his thesis advisor in teaching the work of non-French theorists – not just Marshall and the Cambridge School but also the so-called 'marginalists' represented by Léon Walras in France and William Stanley Jevons in Britain, as well as the Historical School of National Economy in Germany and the Austrian School – may explain the exhaustive international body of literature that Lescure draws upon in *Des Crises*. Sauvaire-Jourdan, moreover, clearly believed in comparative analysis of capitalist economies, and he encouraged his students to travel extensively abroad and study foreign languages, believing, as Lescure would later argue, that theory had to draw from the direct experience of economic life in the societies one wished to compare.[7]

After completing his doctorate at Bordeaux and the publication of the first edition of *Des Crises* in 1907, Lescure taught as a lecturer (*chargé de conferences*) in the Faculty of Law at the University of Paris. He completed a second doctoral thesis in law at Bordeaux with the work, 'Le marché à terme de bourse en Allemagne: Titre IV de la loi du 22 juin 1896', which appeared in 1908. Both of Lescure's doctoral theses earned first place in the Bordeaux law faculty's annual competition, an unheard-of achievement at the time. The following year Lescure took up a lectureship at Dijon, and then in November 1910, he earned first place on the *agrégation* (civil service examination serving as the principal prerequisite to obtain permanent employment in higher or secondary education) in political economy and was posted to Poitiers. The second edition of *Des Crises* appeared in the same year, and its author had added substantial new material that took into account the Crisis of 1907. Lescure followed up in 1912 with a comparative study of the financial effects of the Franco-German political crisis of 1911.[8] At the end of July 1913, Lescure was posted back to the University of Bordeaux, where he was to become assistant professor (*professeur adjoint*) in March 1918.

When war broke out in the Summer of 1914, Lescure was drafted into the infantry, but in light of his poor health and intellectual abilities, he was assigned to the press office of the Ministry of War, and then to the office of the 18th Military Region. His perfect German was naturally a great asset, and from March 1915 he served as

5. *Principes d'économie politique*, trans. Françoise Sauvaire-Jourdan, 2 vols. (Paris: Giard & Brière, 1906–9). By 1898, Marshall's *Principles of Economics* was in its fourth English edition, and at least one colleague wrote admiringly of Sauvaire-Jourdan's sacrifice to the field in undertaking such 'a difficult task, requiring so much voluntary reluctance to pursue his own ideas'. Charles Rist, obituary for François Sauvaire-Jourdan, *Revue d'économie politique* 52, no. 6 (1938): 1611.
6. Rist, obituary for François Sauvaire-Jourdan, 1609.
7. 'Comptes-rendus des travaux des Facultés', in *Rapport du Conseil de l'Université de Bordeaux* (1946–47): 28, https://1886.u-bordeaux-montaigne.fr/files/original/352383ca2d0eb5fd982269c0a7c879899aee60f7.pdf.
8. Lescure, *Les marchés financiers de Berlin et de Paris et la crise franco-allemande de juillet–octobre 1911* (Paris: Larose & Tenin, 1912).

a German-language interpreter for the rest of the war. He was awarded the *Croix d'or* for his service. Demobilized on 30 March 1919, in June he was named full professor at Bordeaux, which one later commentator viewed as an unreasonable delay, given Lescure's talents, caused by the rigid apportionment of chairs in economics at the time. In any case, Lescure was to remain in Bordeaux only until the start of the 1923–24 academic year, at which point he became professor of social economics at the University of Paris in the Faculty of Law, a post which allowed him to 'avoid the tumult of undergraduate courses, which his temperament would not have tolerated, and he was able to spare the time necessary for his written work'.[9]

The First World War and the Globalization of Crises

Like many of his generation, Lescure's military service and his impressions of the war itself, particularly its economic and political aftermath, had a lasting effect on his work and, as we shall see, on his understanding of the global scope of economic crises. In the war's immediate aftermath, Lescure found supply disruptions and unprecedented disequilibrium not only in the availability of consumer versus producer goods but also in wholesale and retail prices. Lescure placed emphasis on the disequilibrium in supply caused by governments which had borrowed heavily and artificially distorted production, particularly in heavy industries, to meet the requirements of the war. The transition from such a massive effort directed at the production of weapons and supplies for war to a peacetime economy faced with increasing demands for consumer goods (clothing, shoes, etc.) of soldiers returning from the front, was to have a lasting impact on the European economy and its place in the world.

The position of the United States as a supplier of goods and credit increased dramatically in the 1920s, even as US politics seemed to veer toward isolation. Moreover, the war had caused European belligerents to import more from abroad, particularly from areas like Latin America, and to depend more on the resources of their colonial empires, in the case of France and the UK – even as their political hold upon these areas had become more tenuous. This had the effect of causing not only supply-chain disruptions but also an intensification of crises and the alternating movements of growth and decline that had characterized the business cycle since before the war. Hence, by the fourth and fifth editions of Lescure's book, the crisis of 1929–30 and the ensuing global financial disorder become consequences of the economic disruptions and destruction of the war and the long road to reconstruction and recovery in its aftermath. The transition from war to peace had caused a disequilibrium of production and consumption, government borrowing and foreign debt, exchange rates, currency and a trade imbalance between Europe and the rest of the world. Lescure observed, 'the disorder in this respect was universal. And the world had stopped advancing at the same pace: the solidarity and uniformity of the past had disappeared.'[10] Thus, in the years following

9. 'Comptes-rendus des travaux des Facultés', 29.
10. Lescure, *Des crises générales et périodiques de surproduction*, 5th ed. (Paris: Domat-Montchrestien, 1938), 1: 293. Hereafter all citations to the fifth edition are given in brackets in the text, as

the war, Lescure found a global situation in which national economies emerged more interdependent than ever, but, in many ways, out of sync.

In 1922, Lescure published a critical appraisal of war reparations, which was in part a response to the arguments made by Keynes and others who questioned the consequences of the terms imposed on Germany under the Treaty of Versailles. Lescure clearly saw the international consequences of the 1914 war for Europe's standing in the world, its new status as net debtor, with the United States as the principal creditor, and its unfavourable balance of trade with non-European nations. Moreover, the reparations question also brought into sharp focus a key factor in the *global* crises which had occurred since the appearance of the first edition:

> The economic interdependency [*solidarité*] of nations demands, moreover, the collaboration of all the countries of the world so bound together by the close ties of economic and financial relations. Solving the economic and financial problems posed by the war indirectly concerns all countries. All must share in the common burden.[11]

The economic interdependencies that connected all industrialized nations by way of trade and finance, as well as all 'other countries', or colonies, which during the war had supplied Europe with agricultural products and raw materials, meant that future crises could spread like a global contagion, and that preparing for them and acting to mitigate their worst effects were the shared tasks of all nations.

In the preface to the third edition of *Des Crises*, Lescure described the global implications of these deepening connections in similar terms: 'Not only is the entire economic organism affected, the crisis reaches nearly every other country; an ever-closer economic interdependency [*solidarité*] unites the economic markets, transforming the crisis into an international or global phenomenon. The most recent crises, in 1907, 1913 and 1920, have been global' (Lescure, 1: ii). The two metaphors, interdependency (*solidarité*) and contagion, occur frequently throughout *Des Crises* but figure more prominently in the discussion of crises in the latter half of the nineteenth century and the early twentieth century, and most often when Lescure seeks to explain how a crisis beginning in one sector or industry spreads to the others, becoming generalized. For Lescure, interdependency referred to the nearly organic linkages that had grown between the sectors of the industrial economy in the evolution of capitalist society. Contagion, on the other hand, was a long-standing metaphor in political economy, which derived from the tendency in the eighteenth and early nineteenth centuries to describe speculative bubbles and financial panics in moral and pathological terms. Medical metaphors, along with those referring to psychology, health or disease, have been common in Western discourse on the economy since the seventeenth century. The term crisis itself refers to the decisive turning point in the course of an illness, after which the patient either improves and recovers or continues to worsen until death. Speculation has been the

---

Lescure, followed by volume and page number in the French edition.

11. Jean Lescure, *Le problème des reparations: Comment le résoudre* (Paris: Plon, 1922), 8–9.

target of moral criticism since at least the early eighteenth century; following the South Sea Bubble in particular, this critique placed financial investment alongside the moral questions raised about insurance and speculation about human mortality.[12]

In the nineteenth century, speculation in the stock market for joint-stock ventures was also described in pathological terms and was often referred to as 'feverish', mad or irrational.[13] Likewise, we find the leading industries for speculative investment, like the railways, also described in terms of fever and panic, particularly at moments like the Crisis of 1847, which, as Lescure reminds us, was also exacerbated by the Bank Charter Act of 1844, a measure designed to address the role of speculation in financial crises by regulating the Bank of England's issuance of banknotes (Lescure, 1: 25, 36).[14] We must accept, too, that these descriptions by political economists, government officials and the public at large also fed and were nourished by palpable fears about the moral and physical costs of industrialization, the loss tradition, the restructuring of the experience of time and labour, industrial accidents, psychological manifestations of traumatic injuries suffered in railway accidents and so on.[15] Industrialization dramatically structured or restructured spaces, cities and urban centres as industrial labour concentrated in and around them. This geographic reorganization also occurred in the countryside, as agriculture became more specialized and concentrated, and as the measure and experience of time and the organization of space were dramatically altered by resource extraction and by the transport and communication lines needed to direct raw materials and commodities domestically or bring them to the point of export.

In this sense, that political economy would use these metaphors is hardly surprising, since the practical effects of industrialization and modern economic life were already associated with illness, anxiety, malaise and other strong emotions. In Lescure's time, not just political economists but also sociologists and historians became interested in the emotional and psychological registers of the problems of social and economic

12. On the similar moral vocabulary used in reference to insurance and speculation, see Edward Gillin, 'Babbage's Age of Speculation: Calculating the Value of Life After the Repeal of the Bubble Act', in *The Bubble Act: New Perspectives from Passage to Repeal and Beyond*, ed. Helen Paul, Nicholas Di Liberto and D'Maris Coffman (Cham: Palgrave Macmillan, 2023), 221–41.
13. For the paradigmatic example, see Charles Mackay, *Memoirs of Extraordinary Popular Delusions*, vol. 1 (London: Richard Bentley, 1841).
14. Suffice it to say, Lescure rejected the 'currency principle' on which the Bank Charter Act was based and supported Thomas Tooke's position 'that by inflaming public opinion, the Act of 1844 further aggravated the difficulties in times of economic crisis' (Lescure, 2: 458–59). See also Raybaut, 'Jean Lescure et l'analyse des fluctuations économiques', para. 11, https://books.openedition.org/editionscnrs/43937; and for a recent appraisal of the classic debate, see Charles Read, 'The Repeal of the Bubble Act and the Debate Between the Currency School and the Banking School', in Helen Paul et al., eds., *The Bubble Act*, 243–65.
15. On how the experience of rail travel and railway accidents shaped understandings of the costs of industrialization, see Wolfgang Schivelbusch, *The Railway Journey: The Industrialization of Time and Space in the 19th Century* (Berkeley: University of California Press, 1986), esp. 113–49. On the similar shifts in the experience of time with the advent of industrial labour, see the seminal article by E. P. Thompson, 'Time, Work-Discipline, and Industrial Capitalism', *Past & Present* 38 (Dec. 1967): 56–97.

development. The historians of the *Annales* school in particular turned to these emotional manifestations of cultural experiences and social relations. The drama of this evolution is recorded in the history of economic crises, and Lescure adopts its language and narrative structure. But the regularity or periodicity of crises and the cycles of growth and depression they demarcate is in fact the good news: if they recur, they can be predicted; if they are at the same time unavoidable, then the goals of preparedness and mitigation appear as the logical basis for the contribution of modern economics and political economy.

Crisis itself contained political, juridical and medical/pathological connotations that derived from its Greek and Latin lineages, and in each of these areas, the term evoked the sense of a decisive turning point (e.g., in the course of an illness or military campaign), a judgement or critique.[16] An impressive body of work has been done on the transmission of medical and epidemiological metaphors into modern political economy.[17] The conceptual historian Reinhart Koselleck traced the extension of the concept into economic discourse to the early nineteenth century, and in particular to the period following the Napoleonic wars. More suggestively, Koselleck identified the crisis of 1856–57 as the event which elevated the concept's economic application to a new level: 'What made it altogether new was its conceptualization in international terms extended to commercial and political interactions, as well as to the conditions of capitalist production.'[18] Koselleck referred in the German context to Max Wirth's *Geschichte der Handelskrisen*, the first edition of which appeared in 1858.[19] Lescure relied heavily on Wirth's second edition of 1874 for anecdotal and statistical information on crises up to 1873; however, in the introduction to the first edition, Lescure described Wirth's study as 'an incoherent book, without any guiding principle'.[20] However, the appearance of Clément Juglar's *Des crises commerciales* in 1862 was to be the most significant example of the broadened economic meaning of the term in French, and the most influential for Lescure's own usage.[21]

---

16. On the last sense in which the crisis concept comes to contain the tension of the moral critique of the Enlightenment aimed at the absolutist state, see Reinhart Koselleck, *Kritik und Krise: Eine Studie zur Pathogenese der bürgerlichen Welt* (Frankfurt am Main: Suhrkamp, 1973). On historians' use of the crisis trope, see Randolph Starn, 'Historians and "Crisis"', *Past & Present*, no. 52 (Aug. 1971): 3–22.
17. See Daniele Besomi, 'Crises as a Disease of the Body Politick: A Metaphor in the History of Nineteenth-Century Economics', *Journal of the History of Economic Thought* 33, no. 1 (2011): 67–118, and the more exhaustive treatment in Daniele Besomi, ed., *Crises and Cycles in Economic Dictionaries and Encyclopaedias* (London: Routledge, 2012).
18. Reinhart Koselleck, 'Crisis', trans. Michaela Richter, *Journal of the History of Ideas* 67, no. 2 (2006): 392.
19. Max Wirth, *Geschichte der Handelskrisen* (Frankfurt am Main: Sauerländer, 1858).
20. Lescure, *Des crises générales et périodiques de surproduction* (Paris: Recueil Sirey/Larose & Tenin, 1907), 12; and Lescure, preface to the first edition, in *Des crises générales et périodiques de surproduction*, 2nd ed. (Paris: Recueil Sirey, 1910), 12.
21. Although the first edition of Max Wirth's *Geschichte der Handelskrisen* appeared before the first edition of Clément Juglar's *Des crises commerciales et de leur retour périodique en France, en Angleterre et aux États-Unis* (Paris: Guillaumin, 1862), Juglar had written about commercial crises as early

Lescure and Aftalion on Interdependencies in the Economy and the Possibility of General Overproduction Crises

Lescure uses the term 'interdependency' (*solidarité*) as the main conceptual tool for understanding how general, or generalized, overproduction crises can occur in modern economies. The term is difficult to translate into English, where 'solidarity' can evoke the connotation of comradery, instead of Lescure's intended meaning, which in this English translation has been rendered most often as 'interdependency', 'linkages' or 'connection', as the context requires.[22] Lescure not only employs the term to characterize the growing dependencies of countries, as in the passage quoted above; he more often invokes the term when explaining how related industries or industrial sectors experience similar cyclical changes, either at the same time or in close succession. His specific use of the term in reference to the linkages between related industries was already present in the doctoral thesis of 1906. Here we find, in grander form, Lescure applied the 'great law of economic *solidarité*' to explain how the crisis, or the prosperity, could be 'communicated from one branch of production to another'.[23] Elsewhere in the first edition, he refers to the '*solidarité des entreprises*', when explaining how the reciprocity between closely related industries, like the metal and electrical industries, created the possibility for crisis to spread from one to another.[24] Lescure even posed the 'principle of the *solidarité* of productive forces' to Say's Law of Markets (*Loi des débouchés*); for if indeed all production was consumption, then the linkages between the industries that stood in this synergistic consumer-producer relationship explained the possibility of generalized overproduction resulting from partial overproduction. Lescure would return to the distinction between general and generalized overproduction in an important article of 1909, which was in part a criticism of Albert Aftalion's celebrated articles on 'La réalité des surproductions générales' in the *Revue d'économie politique* in 1908 and 1909, the basis for latter's 1913 book *Les crises périodiques de surproduction*, which is often compared to Lescure's similarly titled work.[25]

---

as 1856; see Juglar, 'Des crises commerciales', *Annuarie de l'économie politique et de la statistique* 13 (1856): 555–81, and the more detailed treatment in Juglar, 'Des crises commerciales et monétaires de 1800 à 1857', 2 pts, *Journal des économistes*, 2nd ser., 14, nos. 41–42 (April–May 1857): 35–60, 253–266. Juglar's usage of crisis and characterization of its periodicity did, however, have antecedents: see Daniele Besomi, 'Clément Juglar and his Contemporaries on the Causes of Commercial Crises', *Revue européenne des sciences sociales/European Journal of Social Sciences* 47, no.143 (2009): 17–47. There were of course numerous examples of articles devoted to the word in French and German lexica.

22. Lescure's use of the term is not unlike the notion of 'intersectoral linkages' employed in input-output modelling or in theories of economic growth and development. *Solidarité*, applied in this sense, was also quite common in the works of French social scientists and in Lescure's field of social economy in this period. See Laurent Duchesne, 'La solidarité', *Revue d'économie politique* 22, no. 2 (1908): 109–12.
23. Lescure, *Des crises générales et périodiques* (1907), 609.
24. Ibid., 231.
25. Jean Lescure, 'Surproduction générale ou surproduction généralisée?' *Revue d'économie politique* 24 (1910): 157–62. Aftalion's four-part article was reprinted as *La réalité des surproductions générales* (Paris: Larose & Tenin, 1909).

In Lescure, the formation and growth of these interdependencies are historically contingent, developing organically on decadal or even century-long time scales, in a dynamic manner not unlike those postulated in modern evolutionary economic geography.[26] Lescure's use of 'interdependency' is thus broader than the narrower conception of intersectoral interdependencies to be found in Aftalion's *Les crises périodiques de surproduction*, which is closer to Lescure's '*solidarité des entreprises*', particularly when applied to supply chains. Aftalion accepted the premise that general overproduction could result from a localized, sectoral shock, but questioned whether this insight could really explain the possibility of general overproduction. Each felt the other's analysis of the causes of overproduction crises did not adequately address Say's Law of Markets and failed to provide a complete theory that could account for all the facts. The stakes of their 'debate' are difficult to pin down in hindsight as anything more than a difference over which aspects of the production process should be emphasized as the primary cause of overproduction. Without mentioning Lescure, Aftalion argued that while the generalization of a partial overproduction crisis could be accepted as a descriptive hypothesis, it still fell short of a complete theory that could explain each part of the cycle:

> If we leave it at that, we are merely providing an empirical description of the beginnings and subsequent ramifications of the crisis, not a true theory of crises. All crisis theories could and probably do admit this way of thinking. The generalization, thanks to the economic interdependency [*solidarité*] of an initially less extensive movement, is a truth that can serve as a common basis for all theories. *In this respect they are all theories of generalized partial overproduction.*[27]

Although a detailed discussion of this debate is beyond the scope of this introduction, the Lescure–Aftalion encounter does help us understand an important moment in the development of the nascent discipline of economics. Moreover, it is important to remember that while Lescure would revise his work on crises in three more editions after the war, Aftalion had by then moved on to more focussed quantitative research on money and exchange-rate theory.[28]

The relationship between their formulations of economic interdependencies and their politics – Lescure's Liberalism and Aftalion's Reformism – is worth passing mention, as both believed that cycles were a feature of economic life generally and thus common to capitalist, communist, corporatist and social democratic systems and societies. In the 1920s and early 1930s, Lescure published several short works on Russian society and the course of its economy after the Bolshevik Revolution and then under Stalin.[29]

---

26. For example, see Martin Henning, 'Time Should Tell (More): Evolutionary Economic Geography and the Challenge of History', *Regional Studies* 53, no. 4 (2019): 602–13.
27. Albert Aftalion, *Les crises périodiques de surproduction*, 2 vols. (Paris: Rivière, 1913), 1: 279.
28. Albert Aftalion, *Monnaie, prix et change: Expériences récentes et théorie* (Paris: Sirey 1927); and see Bertrand Blancheton, 'Albert Aftalion, précurseur de la théorie moderne du change', *Revue d'économie politique* 108, no. 5 (1998): 711–28.
29. Jean Lescure, *Les origines de la Révolution russe: L'ancien régime et le problème social* (Paris: Tenin, 1927); *La Révolution russe: Le bolchevisme, communisme et N.E.P.* (Paris: Gamber, 1929); and *Le Bolchevisme de Staline: Le régime des plans* (Paris: Domat-Montchrestien, 1934).

As early as the late 1930s and certainly at the end of the Second World War, Lescure became a vocal critic of totalitarian regimes, first in *Étude sociale comparée des régimes de liberté et des régimes autoritaires* (1939, 1945) and subsequently in *Principes d'économie rationnelle* (1947), framing liberal capitalism (as distinct from modern 'neoliberalism') as most conducive to the laws of economic life. Aftalion, by contrast, was a proponent of 'small-state' socialism or technocratic capitalism, characterized above all by aggressive collection and monitoring of intersectoral interdependencies in a managed economy.[30] While both Lescure's and Aftalion's formulations of interdependencies could fit within a broad construction of modern, mainstream economics, they will appeal more widely today to its critics, especially those concerned with understanding intermediate or meso-levels of economic analysis, whether regional or industrial.[31] Modern mainstream economics with its mechanistic general equilibrium models and its micro-foundations leaves little room for theorizations of the interdependencies that animate Lescure's work, which in a narrow sense inform multi-sectoral growth models and in their broader conceptions are more compatible with various strains within institutional economics.[32]

Although the question of the possibility of general overproduction crises formed the basis for the exchange between Lescure and Aftalion in the pages of the *Revue d'économie politique*, the differences between them on this question were quite superficial. However, their debate does reveal a fundamental shift in thinking about industrial crises and an important moment in the methodological development of the nascent discipline of economics. For two economists with such similar professional trajectories, writing about the same phenomenon in the same period, their understanding of what the scientific method in economics should look like was very different. Aftalion clearly recognized this difference: while he recognized the contribution of a 'mainly historical and descriptive study', like Lescure's, with its 'lively, colourful presentation of events' and notes the usefulness of the 'narrative approach [...] for recognizing the unique traits of each cycle, everything that gives it its particular physiognomy [...] [and] for everything that does not lend itself to being expressed in numerical and statistical data', Aftalion nonetheless argues that 'it is not the best research tool for getting at what is common to the various cycles, what is identical, what is essential to the rhythm of economic life, for identifying the relationships of correlation, causality and dependence between the various phenomena'. And although what he called the statistical method had against it 'a dryness

30. The first edition of Lescure's *Étude sociale comparée des régimes de liberté et des régimes autoritaires* appeared in 1939; and Lescure's *Principes d'économie rationnelle: Essai de perspectives économiques* (Paris: Domat-Montchrestien, 1947) appeared shortly before the author's death. For more on Aftalion, see D'Maris Coffman and Roberto Scazzieri, 'A Re-appraisal of Albert Aftalion's Theory of Structural Transformation in an Era of Decarbonisation' (working paper).
31. Jan G. Lambooy, 'Meso-Economics and Organizational Ecology', in *Infrastructure and the Space-Economy: Essays in Honor of Rolf Funck*, ed. Karin Paschel (Berlin: Springer, 1990): 254–73.
32. For a typical exposition of this link, see Philip Mirowski, *Against Mechanism: Protecting Economics from Science* (Lanham, MD: Rowman & Littlefield, 1992). For a modern account that focuses attention on the micro-foundations, see Yuan Gao, 'A Reflection on Post-War Neoclassical Economics: The Shift from General Equilibrium Theory to the New Microeconomic Theories', *Modern China* 48, no. 1 (2022): 29–52.

of exposition', Aftalion concludes, 'we must accept that science becomes less attractive as it becomes more rigorous and gets closer to the truth'.[33] Lescure, on the other hand, would have likely considered Aftalion's separation of the historical, descriptive study of economic events from 'scientific', quantitative analysis far too rigid and artificial – a methodological position that was more in line with the views of many other prominent figures in the social sciences at the beginning of the twentieth century.

Methodological Pluralism and Interdependencies in the Social Sciences

In the first edition of *Des Crises*, Lescure also used the term *solidarité* to express a relationship between the disciplines which studied crises and their social effects. After the classic statement, defining the crisis as 'the point at which a period of expansion intersects with a period of depression', Lesure extended the metaphor of 'interdependency' to the social realm and, more suggestively, to the social sciences that studied it:

> From the social point of view, [...] the crisis, as it is marked by numerous bankruptcies, limitations of production and unemployment, has painful repercussions in all aspects of human activity: the curves of marriages, suicides, criminality, sometimes even the political state reflect very exactly the state of crisis or prosperity within a country. The idea of the interdependency of economic and social phenomena, that of the interdependency of the social sciences, appears nowhere more evident and undeniable.[34]

At least in 1906, Lescure emphasized the need for consilience among the disciplines which studied social and economic life. He meant above all history, sociology, geography and, of course, political economy. Leading figures in each of these disciplines had already been pursuing such connections. In sociology, François Simiand and Maurice Halbwachs developed an economic sociology that responded critically to the orthodox representatives of past disciplinary paradigms in political history and political economy, and what they perceived as too narrow a focus on political events, abstract economic theory and the sterile accumulation of facts. Durkheim had of course already engaged not only with the French tradition of political economy (and political history) but also with that of the German Historical School, where he encountered one of the main fronts in the great *Methodenstreit* or 'methodological dispute' between the disciplines over what constituted the best approach to social science.[35] By the fin de siècle, the 'German Historical School of National Economy' had found a lively reception in France among sociologists and economists of the new generation. Lescure relied heavily on the work of

33. Albert Aftalion, 'Le rythme de la vie économique', *Revue de métaphysique et de morale* 28, no. 2 (1921): 251–52.
34. Lescure, *Des crises générales et périodiques* (1907), 9.
35. Philippe Steiner, 'Durkheim's Sociology, Simiand's Positive Political Economy and the German Historical School', *European Journal of the History of Economic Thought* 10, no. 2 (2003): 249–78.

the Historical School's leading figures: from Wilhelm Roscher to the younger generation represented by Gustav von Schmoller, whose *Jahrbücher für Gesetzgebung, Verwaltung und Volkswirtschaft im Deutschen Reich* became a leading journal in the field, known simply as '*Revue de Schmoller*' among French political economists, and by Werner Sombart and the Verein für Socialpolitik (association for social policy), which by the time of Lescure's dissertation research had published over 100 volumes of statistical research and survey data, including *Die Störungen im deutschen Wirtschaftsleben* (disturbances in German economic life), a seven-volume series on the repercussions of the Crisis of 1900 on key sectors of German industry and finance and the social impact of the crisis on the trades and industrial labour in particular.[36] Like the younger generation of the German Historical School, Lescure emphasized the historical study of detailed primary research and statistical evidence over the largely deductive theory of classical political economy. Lescure also believed that academic economic research needed to be informed by and speak to the practical experience and interests of business leaders and policymakers, a point of view shared by the Verein für Socialpolitik under Schmoller and Sombart and the Institut für Konjunkturforschung in Berlin under Ernst Wagemann, whose *Vierteljahrshefte zur Konjunkturforschung* was an important source of statistical information used by Lescure from the third edition of *Des Crises* onward.[37]

Although a more exhaustive consideration of this encounter between German historical economics and French social sciences is well beyond the scope of this introduction, this intellectual and disciplinary context is essential to understand Lescure's methodological pluralism and unique approach to economics and its reception – not just by other economists, but by sociologists as well. Lescure's work was innovative in including richer detail and analysis of the social consequences of crises, and in having perhaps consciously or indirectly absorbed Durkheimian imperatives to resist the tendency of traditional political economists to abstract their subject matter from its social and historical context and to treat economic events and processes as part of the social, and the sociologist's, domain.[38] Thus, while he relied on the German Historical School

36. *Die Störungen im deutschen Wirtschaftsleben während der Jahre 1900 ff.*, 7 vols. Schriften des Vereins für Socialpolitik 105–111 (Leipzig: Duncker & Humblot, 1903). Nearly all of the statistical evidence on the German crisis of 1900 used in Lescure's 1906 dissertation came from this source.
37. On Schmoller's influence and continued relevance see Jürgen G. Backhaus, ed., 'Essays on Gustav Schmoller', special issue, *History of Economic Ideas* 1/2, no. 3/1 (1993/94), and Clark Nardinelli and Roger E. Meiners, 'Schmoller, the Methodenstreit, and the Development of Economic History', *Journal of Institutional and Theoretical Economics/Zeitschrift für die gesamte Staatswissenschaft* 144, no. 3 (1988): 543–51; on the Verein für Socialpolitik, see Irmela Gorges, 'The History of the Verein für Socialpolitik: An Unintended Contribution to the Pre-History of the Institutionalization of Sociology', in *Handbuch Geschichte der deutschsprachigen Soziologie*, vol. 1, ed. Stephan Moebius and Andrea Ploder (Wiesbaden: Springer, 2018), 791–808; and on Wagemann and the Institut's role in the 1920s, see J. Adam Tooze, 'Ernst Wagemann, the Reich's Statistical Office, and the Institute for Business-Cycle Research, 1925–1933', *Economic History Review* 52, no. 3 (1999): 523–43.
38. Steiner, 'Durkheim's Sociology', 254–56.

for empirical data, like Durkheim and the economic sociologists, Lescure rejected the notion that the tasks of accumulating empirical evidence and analysing its meaning were mutually exclusive. Indeed, the structure and organization of *Des Crises* through all of its editions embodied this commitment.

In Lescure's historical account of crises, one is struck by how, with each new crisis and depression, Lescure returns to the social impact of economic crises and details their ill effects on the working classes in particular. Unemployment statistics are usually given first, sometimes followed by the statistics on crime, marriages and suicides, generally among the working classes engaged in industrial labour; although he occasionally discusses unemployment affecting the more traditional trades and vocations, as in the Crisis of 1873. Unemployment clearly takes precedence as the cause of all other social ills, and especially in the fourth and fifth editions of *Des Crises*, Lescure argued that unemployment insurance (assurance), the funding of public works by the state and the organization of labour into trade unions were remedies to the worst effects visited upon workers during periods of economic stagnation and decline.[39]

Dealing with the social effects of economic crises and depressions was certainly not novel. There were of course key figures in French liberal political economy of the nineteenth century, who discussed the impact of crises and depressions on the working classes. And Lescure clearly stood in tradition of nineteenth-century liberal political economy, from J.-B. Say forward. In the historical sections devoted to the crises of the nineteenth century, Lescure often draws upon the liberal *Journal des économistes*, which appeared at the end of 1841, from the liberal publisher of Say and others, Gilbert-Urbain Guillaumin, and coincided with the founding of the Société d'économie politique in 1842. The informal group of French liberal economists focussed on Say's idea of competition and the market, as well as limited government in the French republican tradition. For these public intellectuals, it was the duty of the citizen-economist to inform the practice of (limited) government and educate practical men of affairs. In this way, they 'did not regard political economy as a theoretical type of knowledge that was reserved for experts; they continuously upheld the idea that the practical side of their science took precedence over the theoretical'.[40] The editors of the *Journal des économistes*, Guillaumin and Joseph Garnier, produced the companion publication *Annuaire de l'économie politique et de la statistique*, which embodied this practical application of the science to financial and

39. Even before the war, Lescure wrote an annual report on issues affecting industrial labour: 'Chronique des questions ouvrières', *Revue d'économie politique* 25, no. 2 (1911): 219–51; 26, no. 1 (1912): 84–110; 27, no. 2 (1913): 210–40; and 28, no. 2 (1914): 199–223. See also, after the war, Lescure, 'Le movement ouvrier depuis l'armistice jusqu'en mars 1920', *Revue d'économie politique* 34, no. 3 (1920): 337–57.
40. Philippe Steiner, 'Competition and Knowledge: French Political Economy as a Science of Government', in *French Liberalism from Montesquieu to the Present Day*, ed. Raf Geenens and Helena Rosenblatt (Cambridge: Cambridge University Press, 2012), 193. See also P. Steiner, *Sociologie de la connaissance économique: Essai sur les rationalisations de la connaissance économique (1750–1850)* (Paris: Presses Universitaires de France, 1998), 230–44.

industrial matters, and took the form of a useful compendium of statistical observations. In the first issue, the editors declared:

> Each of the main branches of human knowledge has its own annual. Henceforth, POLITICAL ECONOMY will also have one of its own. – The time has come for this science, a true *social physiology* [emph. added], to popularize its principles and teachings. [...] The main purpose of this publication is therefore to note annually the progress of economic theories, to follow the oscillations of the population, the state of [public] finances and the progress of the budget, the progress of the savings banks, pensions and charitable institutions, the expansion of French domestic and foreign trade; the growth of channels of communication, such as roads, canals and railways; the movement of public credit, the improvements of public education, and so on.[41]

Lescure regularly cites this source in *Des Crises*, where it appears as '*Annuaire de Block*', after Maurice Block, who became the managing editor after 1856. It was under Block's direction, then, that an essay appeared in the fourth part of the *Annuaire* that year, titled 'Des crises commerciales', which contained the first practical statement on the subject by Clément Juglar.[42] The timing could not have been more appropriate.

Of course, the focus on social issues and even the practical application of theory and evidence were central concerns for Marx and the socialist economists, as well as for the institutionalist '*Kathedersozialisten*' (socialists of the lectern) represented by Schmoller,[43] but they naturally differed with the liberal tradition over which elements in society their work was to inform and educate. Juglar's *Des crises commerciales* included a brief section on 'mouvements de la population', which considered variations in the demographic statistics on births, marriages and deaths in France as a whole, during periods of crisis and prosperity.[44] The *Journal des économists* also paid particular attention to social and demographic changes in relation to economic trends. Yet Juglar's account gave priority to commercial and financial causes, especially the abuse of credit in the lead-up to the crisis. Lescure, too, tended to emphasize financial and business history; however, he followed the tendency among social economists, historians and economic sociologists at the beginning of the twentieth century to consider the evidence of everyday life

41. Editorial, *Annuaire de l'économie politique et de la statistique* 1 (1844): 2. For a full explanation of the rationale and organization of the annual over its first 24 years, see 'Avis des éditeurs', in *Annuaire de l'économie politique et de la statistique: Table générale alphabétique et analytique des matières contenues dans les vingt-quatre volumes parus de 1844 à 1867* (Paris: Guillaumin, 1867), v–xii.
42. 'Des crises commerciales', *Annuarie de l'économie politique et de la statistique* 13 (1856): 555–81. The essay's full title spoke directly to the publication's areas of interest and practical approach: 'On commercial crises considered in their relation to bank discounts, population, imports and exports, and the prices of cereals'.
43. Werner Plumpe, 'Gustav von Schmoller und der Institutionalismus: Zur Bedeutung der Historischen Schule der Nationalökonomie für die moderne Wirtschaftsgeschichtsschreibung', *Geschichte und Gesellschaft* 25, no. 2 (1999): 252–75.
44. Clément Juglar, *Des crises commerciales et de leur retour periodique en France, en Angleterre, et aux Etats-Unis* (Paris: Guillaumin, 1862), 232–36.

in the study of economic life, whether in agricultural societies of the *ancien régime* or in industrialized nation states of the late nineteenth century. Unemployment among the working classes was not only an important factor in understanding the business cycle, for Lescure; by the later editions of *Des Crises*, and in light of the European experience of the 1920s (increased output with unemployment), unemployment statistics for key industries had become an important index of the course of the economy in general. For the experience of the war and the unprecedented economic disruptions and political unrest in the decade that followed frustrated older methods of economic forecasting that relied primarily on price statistics,[45] which meant the crisis that erupted in the United States at the end of 1929 'was not preceded by a period of growth similar to those which had been experienced before the war. It struck like a bolt of lightning, taking the keenest observers by surprise; for the barometers had been unable to detect the gathering storm' (Lescure, 1: 288–89). In this way, the loss of world '*solidarité*' in the 1920s presented a distinct methodological challenge for the more traditional liberal political economy rooted in the nineteenth century.

But unlike this tradition of liberal political economy in France, Lescure's 'social economy' could draw upon a more multidisciplinary approach because, by the fin de siècle, the disciplines of history, sociology and geography increasingly sought to include the systematic study of the economic causes, context and consequences in their analysis of historical and contemporary social processes. Lescure operated in the same scientific culture and professional circles that produced the new sociology represented by Émile Durkheim, Marcel Mauss, Maurice Halbwachs and François Simiand and featured in the leading journal *L'Année sociologique*, where Halbwachs and Simiand would review the first edition and third edition of *Des Crises*, respectively.[46] Lescure's social economy also had a similarly profound institutional presence in the leading French economic journal, *Revue d'économie politique*, whose long-time editor Charles Gide shared Lescure's commitment to developing methodological connections (*solidarité*) between the social sciences.[47]

45. For a contemporary analysis of the link between commodities futures prices and inflation from 1929 to 1932, see Rasheen Saleuddin and D'Maris Coffman, 'Can Inflation Expectations be Measured Using Commodity Futures Prices?' *Structural Change and Economic Dynamics* 45 (June 2018): 37–48.

46. Maurice Halbwachs, review of *Des crises générales et périodiques de surproduction* by Jean Lescure, *L'Année sociologique* 11 (1906–1909): 576–81; and François Simiand, review of *Des crises générales et périodiques de surproduction*, 3rd ed., by Jean Lescure, *L'Année sociologique*, n.s., 1 (1923–24): 802–6. Lescure's work was reviewed in *L'Année sociologique* along with other key French and international works on economic crises published at the time. See, for example, Halbwachs' reviews of *La réalité des surproduction générales: Essai d'un théorie des crises générales et périodiques* by Albert Aftalion and *Le crisi economiche* by Camillo Supino, in ibid., 585–90 and 581–85, respectively.

47. On the various ways Gide's career and his intellectual and political commitments embodied this '*solidarité*', see William Oualid and Roger Picard, 'L'économiste social', *Revue d'économie politique* 46, no. 6 (1932): 1725–42.

This intellectual milieux also constituted the 'prehistory' of the *Annales* School of History.[48] Although sociologists like Simiand disagreed with the approach of traditional French political historians and political economists, and the more orthodox representatives of the German Historical School which had influenced them, the founding figures of the *Annales* School, Marc Bloch and Lucien Febvre, would each emphasize the need to combine the findings of the disciplines of sociology, history and economics in the new historical approach they inaugurated. Long-term analysis of economic life, trade, prices and cyclical phenomena was essential to understanding the social and cultural impact of the transition from the *ancien régime* to the modern period. Although the second generation of the *Annales*, represented by Fernand Braudel, was to produce a greater body of work integrating economic history and economic analysis into the study of the pre-modern transition to capitalism, they not surprisingly differed from the sociologists and economists over the meaning and scale of the long term – '*la longue durée*' – over which such processes unfolded and were to be analysed. Whereas political economists like Lescure or Aftalion invoked the *longue durée* in their study of crises, particularly when observing price variations,[49] these political economists measured the long term in decades rather than centuries, they remained at the surface level of events, or, as Braudel would observe, economic history only reached the halfway point between the short term of political events and the long-term, structural history of the *longue durée*. The economist's 'history of conjunctures' certainly appeared interested in repeating cycles, the rhythms in the life of the economy and the systems they connected. However, Braudel argued, economists' view of structural change remained confined to that medium timeframe; while this was an important step toward the *longue durée*, it tended to overemphasize cycles of growth and contraction and the periodic, structural crises demarcating their alternation over a span of years and decades. Economics, and sociology for that matter, relied on synchronic models that remained restricted to the timeframe in which these cycles tended to recur. When the timeframe was extended to centuries, or even millennia, these momentary structures and cycles that characterize a historically specific system – the capitalist regime, for instance – could be viewed against the almost glacial time of their environment.[50] This point may seem trivial to professional economists; for they must operate in the short term to study economic dynamics in any detail. Yet, they also wish to predict the disturbances that affect the systems they study and suggest remedies to avoid or mitigate them. These coalesce as models which they apply in their efforts to understand increasingly complex global systems and dynamics. Lescure, on the other hand, tried to locate his synchronic understanding of the immediate drivers

48. See François Dosse, *New History in France: The Triumph of the* Annales, trans. Peter V. Conroy, jr. (Urbana and Chicago: University of Illinois Press, 1994), 7–41.
49. See, for example, Jean Lescure, *Hausses et baisses des prix de longue durée*, 2nd ed. (Paris: Domat-Monchrestien, 1934), which looked at long-term price movements to demonstrate the limitations of monetary theories that focussed on short-term variations in the money supply.
50. See Fernand Braudel, 'Histoire et Sciences sociales: La longue durée', *Annales: Histoire, Sciences sociales* 13, no. 4 (1958): 725–53.

of economic cycles within the diachronic processes of the medium timeframe, through which he practised his 'complex historical method'.

Historical Narrative and Statistical Evidence in Lescure's 'Complex Historical Method'

Lescure's methodological commitments come into sharper focus in the fourth and fifth editions of *Des Crises*, as he reorganized his treatise into two volumes. The publisher may have intended each volume for different readerships: the first volume presenting a historical account, followed by concise explanations or 'theoretical outline' (*schéma théorique*), which summarized much of the author's own theories in a form accessible to non-specialists; and the second, offering specialists a more detailed technical analysis of the latest theories, remedial policies and statistical methods, followed by a more thorough discussion of his own theory of periodic, generalized crises that concludes by detailing the author's approach to statistical evidence, as a means of forecasting crises and mitigating their worst effects.[51]

Lescure's heroic effort to expand this text after each new global crisis of the early twentieth century introduced inevitable problems of continuity and consistency, particularly within the work's nearly 1,000 footnotes. The revised notes and bibliographies of this English edition can nonetheless serve as a compendium of the principal scholarly work being done at a time when not only economics but also sociology, history, geography and related statistical research were taking shape as modern, specialized disciplines. And even if we find Lescure's history of crises or his approach to statistical evidence somewhat imprecise or naïve by today's standards, the work nonetheless represents an important primary source, one which through its many iterations allows us to trace the formation of the disciplines we know – or, rather, don't know – today. For while quantitative, statistics-based research in economics has become more rigorous and prolific since Lescure's time, the same cannot be said of economists' general knowledge of their own discipline and its historical development. Lescure, on the other hand, considered his work as part of this history, and it would have been unthinkable at the time for a political or 'social' economist to begin to propose remedies to contemporary crises without first gaining insight into how these repeating, if not periodic, 'conjunctures' and cycles had been theorized and dealt with in the past. His approach was multidisciplinary and transnational as a matter of course – that is, in a time before such distinctions needed to be made. What Lescure calls the 'complex historical method' is complex and nuanced *because* it is historical: it proceeds inductively from richly detailed historical analysis as the necessary precondition of proposing a theoretical framework for understanding cyclical phenomena, which are considered not in isolation but 'organically', as endogenous elements within a dynamic whole.[52]

51. Cf. vol. 1, chap. 1, sections 2 and 3, with vol. 2, chap. 3 and conclusion.
52. On the organic and inorganic, endogenous and exogenous distinctions, see section three in Raybaut, 'Jean Lescure et l'analyse des crises et des fluctuations économiques', in *Les traditions économiques français*, https://books.openedition.org/editionscnrs/43937.

Likewise, Lescure sought to present his historical account and theory of crises in a way which reflected the 'facts' of how businesses and the economy actually operated, then and in the past. In this, he was closer to the American economists Wesley Mitchell and Edwin R. A. Seligman in the emphasis on operating and production costs, capitalization versus returns in relation to profits, and conceptually in how he understands the limited applicability of 'periodicity' and 'cycle' when applied to complex historical processes. While Mitchell noted 'The chief merit of Lescure's discussion is its realistic air, its effort to look at business cycles from the standpoint of the man of business. In this effort, however, the French economist has been anticipated by an American.'[53] The 'American' was of course Mitchell's teacher, Thorstein Veblen, who had indeed observed how

> With a fuller development of the modern close-knit and comprehensive industrial system, the point of chief attention for the business man has shifted from the old-fashioned surveillance and regulation of a given production process [...] to an alert redistribution of investments from less to more gainful ventures, and to a strategic control of the conjunctures of business through shrewd investments and coalitions with other business men.[54]

Mitchell described the general framework for his own theory of crisis and business cycles as a synthesis of the two: 'Lescure's theory of variations in prospective profits combined with Veblen's theory of the discrepancy between prospective profits and current capitalization'.[55]

Again and again in his narrative, Lescure stressed the importance of the statistical evidence on production costs, orders and profits, which had only recently been made available by the industrial firms themselves. These elements constituted the driving force behind the 'spirit of enterprise';[56] as such, observing their movements offered the economist, the policymaker and the entrepreneur the most reliable means of anticipating the onset of a crisis and depression and the eventual recovery and return of growth. Lescure not only framed his discussion in terms the entrepreneur, the 'capitalist', or policymaker could comprehend but also weighed their expectations as an important variable in economic analysis.[57] While his insertion of social statistics and discussion of social factors can at times be a bit mechanical, Lescure treats them as co-determining, endogenous

53. Wesley Clair Mitchell, *Business Cycles* (Berkeley: University of California Press, 1913), 14.
54. Thorstein Veblen, *The Theory of Business Enterprise* (1904; reprint, New York: Scribner, 1932), 24–25.
55. Mitchell, *Business Cycles* (1913), 580. For more on Veblen's views in this area, see Sophus A. Reinert and Francesca Lidia Viano, 'Capitalising Expectations: Veblen on Consumption, Crises and the Utility of Waste', in *Thorstein Veblen: Economics for an Age of Crises*, ed. Erik S. Reinert and Francesca L. Viano (London: Anthem, 2012), chap. 16.
56. Emphasis on the development of 'the spirit of business enterprise' also occurs in Veblen, *Theory of Business Enterprise*, 24.
57. One later commentator has suggested that Lescure's belief in the limited usefulness of index numbers and the importance of descriptive statistics on costs, orders and profits anticipated the need to 'bring into play what would later be called the expectation of entrepreneurs'. See Lucette Le Van-Lemesle, 'Les économistes français face à la crise des années 1930: La remise en cause des politiques économiques', *L'année sociologique*, 3rd ser., 36 (1986): 42.

factors alongside the practical considerations of entrepreneurs; and these concerns were at least shared by more well-known contemporary economists like Keynes.

Nevertheless, for Lescure, the critical turning point occurred at the end of growth periods, when new businesses in leading industries failed to produce the expected returns and tended to collapse before well-established firms. Lescure's position was closer to the views of Seligman, who, like Veblen and Mitchell, similarly emphasized the tendency, during periods of growth and prosperity, to overcapitalize new or existing enterprises based on unrealistic expectations of the projected returns:

> Crises, therefore, are not necessarily the result of increased technical production. The important point is not production, but capitalization. There may be overcapitalization, without overproduction. Overproduction of particular things may indeed accompany overcapitalization, but the stress must be laid, not on the relation between production and consumption, as the older writers assumed, but on the discrepancy between the investment and its returns.[58]

Although Lescure does not place as much emphasis on the difference between investment and returns, the concept is certainly present in his discussion of how the decline in profits, and the frustration of profit potential, anticipates the onset of the crisis.

Lescure's methodological approach to economic crises began with a study of the history of crises and the periods of growth and depression which precede and follow them in periodic, alternating cycles. And yet, this notion of periodicity had its limitations. Lescure observes that although crises appear at the transition between expansion and contraction periods, this does not justify calling them cyclical or even, as we read later, strictly periodic. The term 'cycle', Lescure argued in his entry on 'Crises' in the *Encyclopaedia of the Social Sciences* in 1930,

> labors under the disadvantage of exaggerating the regularity of the phenomenon under consideration. Economic life, like life in general, can hardly be confined within equations and statistical curves. One may speak of cycles, but with the reservation that not all the years of the period before the crisis are prosperous years and not all those after the crisis are years of depression. It is undoubtedly more correct to speak of industrial fluctuations or of alternations of expansion and contraction.[59]

Lescure's article in the *Encyclopaedia*, edited by Seligman, owed much to Mitchell's views on business cycles:

> Any analysis which traces the general course of the processes bringing about prosperity, crisis, and depression, inevitably leaves a misleading impression of uniformity among

58. Edwin E. R. Seligman, *The Crisis of 1907 in the Light of History* (New York: Columbia University Press, 1908), xv.
59. Jean Lescure, 'Crises', in *Encyclopaedia of the Social Sciences*, ed. Edwin R. A. Seligman, vol. 3 (London: Macmillan, 1930), 595.

> business cycles. As a matter of fact these cycles differ widely in duration, in intensity, in the relative prominence of their various phenomena, and in the sequence of their phases.[60]

For Lescure, history was above all an empirical record, 'the facts', against which any economic theory was to be measured. Perhaps tellingly, Lescure's historical narrative comprises more than two-thirds of *Des Crises*, nearly all of volume one of the fifth edition. Although his largely event-based historical narrative is necessarily linear and diachronic, Lescure's focus remains on the periodicity of alternating periods of expansion and depression, which lends a cyclical form to his history of the key moments that marked each historic recurrence of growth, crisis, depression and recovery. This form also creates the sense of the inevitability of crises, as almost naturally recurring phenomena inherent in the development of modern industrial economies, especially during the extensive and intensive growth of international industry and finance in the latter half of the nineteenth and early twentieth centuries. Although not strictly periodic, general crises of overproduction were the result of recurring cycles of growth and recession in the evolution of industrialized, capitalist economies. As Mitchell described it, prosperity breeds crisis due to the rising costs which frustrate the expectations for potential profit at the end of periods of expansion. Mitchell's description of the 'critical point' in the cycle shared all the same points of reference repeated throughout Lescure's endogenous account of the cycle: 'The very conditions which make business profitable gradually evolve conditions which threaten a reduction of profits. [...] After these processes have been running cumulatively for a time, it becomes difficult to advance selling prices fast enough to avoid a reduction of profits by the encroachment of costs.'[61]

Lescure's analysis does suggest that the growth witnessed at the end of the nineteenth and beginning of the twentieth centuries could not be sustained without the great social and political upheavals that accompanied it. Much like Keynes, Lescure argued that economists and policymakers needed to understand the social consequences of general crises and intense depressions, namely unemployment and the various threats to the social order that were its consequence. To make sense of this relationship and propose remedies by which limited government intervention could mitigate these effects, Lescure invoked an analogy to medicine:

> States and governments cannot remain indifferent in the face of violent crises capable of threatening public order. However, their policies must resemble doctors' prescriptions and be preceded by a thorough examination and a proper diagnosis. Government policies ought to be inspired by the maxim: help nature. This must proceed from a theory of crises and, for us, from a conception that views crises as the consequence of a disruption of the equilibrium between costs and prices. Effective policies will seek to remedy the imbalance by acting rationally on costs and prices. [...] Yet recovery *must* follow depression. The crisis cannot justify a total overhaul, which would be the surest way of worsening the disorder and unemployment. (Lescure, 2: 579)

---

60. Mitchell, *Business Cycles* (1913), 581.
61. Ibid., 502.

Lescure's Liberalism and the Role of Government in the Recovery of the 1930s

Because Lescure believed that crises were inevitable in both market and command economies, he also held their onset and consequences were predictable with the help of more detailed production statistics which had become newly available at the time. Observation of corporate profits, the margin between cost and selling price, provided the means to predict crises and assess their impact, not only on industry and trade but also on the working classes who suffered unemployment and the resulting social ills – criminality, declining marriage and birth rates, homelessness, suicide, etc. – which as we have seen brought Lescure closer to the economic sociology developed by Simiand and Halbwachs, as well as the liberal political economists of the nineteenth century, like Juglar. Although he remained sceptical of government intervention in the form of '*dirigiste*' monetary measures, and lauded the successes of industrial concentration in reducing costs and weathering crises, Lescure admitted the state's role in the recovery of the 1930s in mitigating unemployment through social insurance schemes and investment in public works.

The managed recovery in the United States, which Lescure calls a 'partial success', while untraditional in terms of the level of government intervention, was in his view completely traditional in its result. It simply restored economic equilibrium: 'Here again', Lescure observes,

> it was necessary to restore the equilibrium between town and country, between agricultural and industrial prices. In doing so, America prepared the way for the global recovery that we have benefitted from for the last three years: by correcting agricultural overproduction, it has prepared the way for growth in that half of the world whose livelihood depends on agriculture, and consequently, it has stimulated growth in the entire world. (Lescure, 1: 382–83)

Roosevelt's policies, in other words, were the exception, or 'experiment', that proved the rule:

> he has re-established a common price level for all products, agricultural and industrial, and he has restored profit margins. He thus laid the foundations for a healthy currency, prepared the way for the decline in interest, the revival of the spirit of enterprise and the growth of securities issues. *His policies prepared the ground on which private enterprise would be able to build.* Arms production played an insignificant role here. The same is not true for public works. (Lescure, 1: 384, emphasis added)

Lescure suggests that Roosevelt's policies succeeded because they used public initiative, in the form of public works construction, as a means of spurring the return of private initiative. In this way, Lescure declared,

> The growth has silenced the grotesque fantasies of the "technocrats", the society builders, the reformers who proclaim that to produce means very little and that the most important

thing is to redistribute – hence the need for government assistance, substantial pensions for all, ever-higher salaries and ever-shorter working days. (Lescure, 1: 384)

Lescure largely rejected the 'doctrine of high wages' in favour of policies that would restore the equilibrium between costs and prices, raising profit margins and spurring the spirit of enterprise. Moreover, Lescure argued,

> In this return to equilibrium, the systematic devaluation of the dollar does not seem to be of prime importance. Relief for the unemployed, too, played only a secondary role: the president aimed to give work to the unemployed by recovering economic prosperity. Government assistance was incidental. The thought of receiving welfare is repugnant to the American worker. (Lescure, 1: 385)

Government initiatives were financed with borrowings at low interest rates made possible by the 'open market' policy, whereby the US Treasury placed government bonds with the banks at 'ridiculously low rates'.

Roosevelt's policies were not unlike those pursued by some European states like Germany, but the German 'planned recovery' was shaped according to the political goals of the National Socialist state. While the German recovery also relied to a large extent on public works construction and creative financing of government spending, Lescure clearly differentiates the German 'authoritarian' case from the American, British and French. German rearmament fuelled the growth in heavy industry, and the measures of the German state achieved a massive reduction in unemployment, which relied more on the government's re-allocation of labour to the countryside and the policy of mandatory military service. In contrast to the United States, the Nazi state's control of the economy in the form of plans was an end in itself, not a means to restore private initiative – at least not in a way that would allow private firms involved in heavy industrial production to determine their own course, unless it coincided with the aims of the state.[62]

Although Lescure showed a clear but guarded enthusiasm for the form of planning practised in Britain and France, and felt the jury was still out on the many 'experiments' in government-managed recovery, represented above all by the New Deal in the United States, his account suggests that while the orders delivered to industry by virtue of government spending on public works and armaments had succeeded in spurring growth and reducing unemployment, this kind of recovery was nonetheless artificial, which, Lescure argued, influenced the economist's ability to predict its course.

> The recovery was not spontaneous everywhere. State intervention was necessary. We live in a time of 'experiments'. Massive rearmament in the European states has largely absorbed

62. Lescure's comparison of the New Deal and National Socialist recoveries anticipated the debate among later economic historians, who likewise found differences in ideology and levels to which each government could exert institutional and psychological pressure, while nonetheless finding a degree of similarity in how their results were achieved. See, for example, John A. Garratry, 'The New Deal, National Socialism, and the Great Depression', *American Historical Review* 78, no. 4 (1973): 907–44.

> capital and supplied heavy industries with orders. It would be most imprudent to not take this into account when formulating prognoses, the prerogative of any scientific inquiry, whose role is to enable us to know in order to predict [*savoir pour prévoir*]. (Lescure, 1: 372)

He was not surprisingly wary of the 'planned economy' or 'plans approach', the 'autarkic' aims of which directed Soviet industrialization, on the one hand, and the grand public works schemes of Fascist Italy and Nazi Germany, on the other. German re-armament, too, hung like spectre over the discussion of the recovery of the mid- to late 1930s; and while Lescure details the successes of the Nazi's 'gigantic experiment' in eliminating unemployment, increasing industrial orders and realizing gains, as well as the creative financing of these achievements, he suggested the growth could not continue without increasing Germany's national debt and that such expansion favoured heavy industry at the expense of social well-being: 'Germany's prosperity finds greater expression in the activity of its factories, the intensity of labour and the disappearance of unemployment than in the comfort and well-being of its population, who are told by their government that guns must come before butter, that a strong people is better than a fat one.'[63]

Here, the difference between the managed recovery in the United States and that of the command economy of Nazi Germany was particularly clear:

> The German recovery was so managed [*dirigée*] that it is impossible to regard it as a traditional kind of recovery. It was the first recovery in economic history entirely brought about and maintained by the state. Whereas in the United States the government confined its ambitions to ensuring smooth transitions [to private initiative], in Germany, the government dominated and directly intervened in the economy. Considerations of cost, price and profit were secondary. Profits were regulated and limited. The impetus no longer came from private initiative. The state played the essential role with its industrial orders, financial policy (which imitated the policy practised during the war of 1914) and two five-year plans. (Lescure, 1: 390)

Lescure's Complex Historical Method and the Use and Misuse of Statistics

Lescure's historical narrative also includes analysis, which most often takes the form of statistical observations derived from a variety of economic indexes, annuaries and journals – sources which were becoming more numerous and comprehensive by the turn of the century when he was researching the dissertation, and much more regular, professional and specialized over the thirty years in which he revised the work through five editions. His approach to statistics was unique, and here again, Lescure drew inspiration and useful metaphors from other disciplinary vocabularies. In the preface to the

63. Lescure, 1: 401. This was likely a reference to a well-known radio address by Hermann Goering, in which he put the rhetorical question to the German public: 'Would you rather have guns or butter? Preparedness will make us powerful; butter will only make us fat.'

fourth edition, Lescure makes explicit the genre of metaphors he prefers as that most comparable to the work of the political economist:[64]

> For even though new statistical methods have provided us with valuable additional information, we have sometimes abused these figures. Their misuse has been particularly careless. The spirit of geometry has tried to eliminate the need for finesse; here too, reasoning has tried to ignore intuition and the imponderables that influence economic phenomena, as they do man himself. Political economy would be more successful if we appealed to the methods of biology rather than to the still very precarious procedures of meteorology. The failure of the so-called barometer method is no longer contested today. Facts have shattered the barometers. The use of statistics should not be mechanical. (Lescure, 1: x)

This also foreshadows his approach to statistics throughout the work. Lescure chose to conclude the expanded fifth edition with a detailed discussion of the development of statistical services and indexes over the thirty years since the first edition. Here Lescure outlined his own approach to statistics, as part of the 'complex historical method', which applied as much to the use of statistical evidence, or 'observations', as to the historical analysis of modern capitalist economies. Although Aftalion and others raised concerns about the lack of scientific rigour in Lescure's method, the latter hardly neglected to provide ample statistical evidence, with nearly two-hundred statistical tables and eleven graphs included in chapter one, section one, on the historical background of crises alone.[65] Yet, when it came to statistical evidence, Lescure clearly believed that quality was more important than quantity. Thus, he tended to favour descriptive statistics to index numbers, particularly when the methods by which these index numbers were established remained opaque or too complicated to reproduce.[66] Indexes often also failed to incorporate vital information. For example, the production index was hardly adequate if it did not take into account the statistics for profits and orders, and monthly production and consumption statistics were preferably to annual figures, or even to the quarterly figures used to report corporate profits. Moreover, Lescure argued that monthly figures needed to be analysed, not just month to month, but by comparing the corresponding months or quarters in successive years, both to account for seasonal or quarterly variations and to measure a rise or drop in real terms (Lescure, 2: 674). This practice, for Lescure, would result in a much more accurate diagnosis of the 'economic

---

64. Here, Lescure may have drawn indirectly – via Sauvaire-Jourdan – on Alfred Marshall's classic statement: 'The Mecca of the economist is economic biology rather than economic dynamics.' Alfred Marshall, 'Distribution and Exchange', *Economic Journal* 8, no. 29 (1898): 43.
65. Aftalion, 'Le rythme de la vie économique', 250–51.
66. In fact, Aftalion expressed similar reservations at outset of *Les crises périodiques de surproduction*, 1: 4, noting that 'the economist must exercise great caution when using index numbers and the data used to compile them.' For a similar debate about the validity of index numbers, which nonetheless 'contrasted two opposite conceptions of economics as a science', see Victor Cruz-e-Silva and Felipe Almeida, 'The Making of Index Numbers in the Early 1920s: A Closer Look at the Fisher-Mitchell Debate', *History of Political Economy* 54, no. 4 (2022): 655–86.

organism' than the so-called 'barometer method' prevalent at the time, which more often looked for month to month price variations in key sectors in the leadup to a crisis or recovery. Lescure argued that

> establishing good indexes for orders in the various industries is the most useful improvement for the observation of business life. The movement of orders, or if one likes, the acceleration of orders, is the most significant indicator of the vitality of an economy and its growth. Likewise, the elements which enable us to estimate the potential for and possibility of profit are no doubt more decisive than the production indexes. (Lescure, 2: 663n6 *bis*)[67]

For Lescure, economics derived its scientific rigour from the historical and statistical study of the facts, and not, as is so often the case in economics today, in the elaboration of theory and statistical formulae without any such regard for the historical study of longer-term trends and cycles. Moreover, Lescure believed that the field of business-cycle research – or *Konjunkturforschung*, its German variant – had reached a level of maturity that would allow for a synthesis of competing approaches and theories grounded in evidence.[68] He concluded volume one with the following statement:

> Even today, new theories arise independent of any positive study of the phenomenon. They do not deserve to be taken into consideration. A theory of crises must be preceded by a historical and statistical study of the facts. Otherwise, it is worthless, or has at most the value of a hypothesis. There is, however, broad agreement on our understanding of the phenomenon; and the differences between theorists are no longer such that a synthesis of the main positive explanations of crises cannot be successfully attempted. (Lescure, 1: 437)

With his lengthy fact-based, event-driven narrative complete, Lescure's 'complex historical method' took on the synthetic task of weighing the leading crisis theories against the comprehensive historical account. In the second volume, Lescure divided the competing theories of general overproduction crises into those that treated them principally as a monetary phenomenon and those that treat them as crises of what we today call the 'real economy', or rather of 'production, distribution and consumption' (Lescure, 2: 453).

Lescure groups explanations of crises as monetary phenomena into three main categories – those that focus on the excessive supply of banknotes, those that identify mounting abuses of credit in prodromal stages, and those that focus on a lack of sufficient credit – dismissing each in turn with recourse to the evidence he presents in volume one. Lescure's classification of theoreticians of financial crisis who principally focus on the real economy turns on a distinction between 'organic' and 'inorganic' theories,

67. For an alternative but compatible view of the limitations of index numbers, see W. C. Mitchell, 'The Making and Using of Index Numbers', *Bulletin of the United States Bureau of Labor Statistics*, no. 656 (Washington, DC: Government Printing Office, 1938).

68. Lescure's goal of synthesis in economic science was shared by more well-known figures, like Schumpeter. See Joseph Schumpeter, 'The Explanation of the Business Cycle', *Economica*, no. 21 (Dec. 1927): 286–87.

depending upon whether these crises are regarded as general, quasi-mathematical theories of economic life (inorganic) or those which regard the phenomena as endogenous to capitalist economies and societies. In Lescure's depiction of inorganic theories, the quantitative mechanisms of overproduction and underproduction, overconsumption and underconsumption are to be understood as coordination problems in the wake of innovation, globalization and increasing international trade; whereas the qualitative mechanisms are generally understood as distributional issues, resulting primarily from changes in government policy, especially taxation and public expenditure. Lescure allows that these theories have some analytical purchase, which he regards as nevertheless fairly limited in view of the high levels of generalization and willingness to ascribe causality to accidental correlations.

Organic theories from David Ricardo and Henry George through Jean-Baptise Say, Malthus and Lauderdale, Sismondi, May, Proudhon, Rodbertus, Bouniatian, Hobson, Tugan- Baranowsky, Marx, Spiethoff, among others, all receive careful consideration, but ultimately Lescure concludes that these writers are better at describing crises than they are at explaining them:

> From this collection of recent ideas and theories, a single one emerges: the development of capitalist economies through alternating periods of growth and depression stems from the irregular production of means of production and the ebb and flow of savings, sometimes toward industry and sometimes away from it. Yet, observing this phenomenon is not the same as explaining it. (Lescure, 2: 511)

Lescure sees more potential in theories advanced by Bouniatian and Aftalion, who focus on mismatches or time-lags between production and consumption, but Lescure finds limited empirical support for their explanatory models.[69] Likewise, he sees inadequate empirical support for theories that turn on uneven production across industrial sectors or variations in potential profits, especially when considered through a series of global comparisons of modern capitalist economies and their industries.

At the very end of chapter two, Lescure at last presents his own account, which relies upon his conception of interdependencies, stating, 'overproduction is not general; rather, partial overproduction becomes generalized through the play of interdependent economic sectors [*solidarités économiques*]' (Lescure, 2: 571). In Lescure's account, if Say's Law is reformulated in terms of an exchange of values rather than products as such, then it becomes possible to explain how 'overproduction causes a generalized rupture of equilibrium'. In direct response to Aftalion,[70] he explains how

69. In fact, Schumpeter was to group these thinkers together, particularly Lescure and Aftalion, 'for [their] strict adherence to Juglar's methodological principles'. Joseph A. Schumpeter, *History of Economic Analysis* (Abingdon: Routledge, 1954), 1129n14.
70. This section of *Des Crises* is titled 'Surproduction générale ou surproduction généralisée?' and reproduces the argument Lescure advanced against Aftalion in the article with same title, published in the *Revue d'économie politique* 24 (1910): 157–62.

> A crisis of overproduction becomes conceivable. But it should be noted that this is only a partial crisis, due to a particularly sharp drop in values in one branch of production. Yet, because of their interdependence, the crisis will be passed on to the other branches of production – suppliers of raw materials and industries from which the overproducing industry used to purchase after having sold its production. The crisis is not general, but it is *generalized*. By placing ourselves on the firm ground of equilibrium in value, and by abandoning the notion of equilibrium in quantity, the theory of generalized overproduction is in our view more sustainable and preferable to the theory of general overproduction. Of course, values are exchanged against values, but only a particularly sharp decrease in the values within one branch of production can explain a break in equilibrium, a crisis. This partial crisis becomes generalized. [...]
>
> This theory has the advantage of conforming better to reality and the genesis of economic crises. Born in a given branch of production, the crisis gradually spreads to the others. (Lescure, 2: 572–73)

While Lescure strongly believes his own account of crises in the real economy best accords with the evidence he has assembled, he concedes that objections may be levelled against it, namely that it would appear to predict crises on occasions where none have occurred. We invite his readers to form their own judgements.

Are Crises Inevitable and Forecastable?

Lescure's final chapter three provides an assessment of the various remedies that proposed to prevent or alleviate economic crises and their attendant social and political effects. Before doing so, he asks what may at first appear a strange question: 'Is the crisis an evil?' (*La crise est-elle un mal?*). Lescure describes the results of the development of modern societies through repeated alternations of growth and decline as a great 'waste of energy' and violation of the 'principle of the economy of forces'. If there is an upside to the crisis, it lies in the correction of the various excesses and wasted energy that characterize periods of growth. The crisis leads to a reduction of production costs, the shedding of less-productive labour and outmoded equipment, technical improvements to and better organization of the production process, and the elimination of overcapitalized and under-performing firms. Although the depression may initially appear to be 'a period of the application of the least effort', its ill effects and waste soon become apparent, as 'even the equipment with the latest improvements sits idle [and] [w]orkers of average productivity are condemned to unemployment' (Lescure, 2: 577–78). As we have seen repeated again and again in Lescure's historical account, the many social ills that arise with unemployment lead to the misery of the working classes, and the resulting political unrest can threaten the social order itself.

Crises thus result in evils which justify limited measures taken by governments, business leaders and workers themselves to remedy the worst effects. Lescure classifies these remedies as preventative and curative, taking each in turn. In terms of prevention, the creation of technocratic statistical services with the aim of helping to manage the economy and informing legislative regulation, while promising, is not always feasible, and more activist banking policies can have unintended consequences, exacerbating the problems they were designed to correct.[71] Curative remedies are also considered in detail, with public works projects having the benefit of addressing unemployment; whereas customs and tariffs policies and currency devaluations can cause 'beggar-thy-neighbour' politics and thus sub-optimal outcomes for the global economy as a whole. Lescure identifies a consensus in favour of 'managed monetary policy' (*monnaie dirigée*), while also delineating where it has failed to deliver as promised. Similarly, action by financial institutions themselves to restrict credit or curb its abuses can at best deliver only mixed results.

Moreover, Lescure does not see much promise in attempts to suppress economic crises through state intervention, taking particular time to ridicule proposals such as those by Eisler and Fisher to replace the gold standard with an index standard (Lescure, 2: 614), or May and Rodbertus' schemes to deliver to workers a higher share of the social surplus (Lescure, 2: 615–16). Lescure gleefully debunks what he takes as Marxist notions of an impending collapse of capitalist economies, and likewise corporatist notions that cartelization will produce better management of economic crises, even if he is rather sanguine about how cartels and trusts had historically weathered crises by cutting costs and maintaining stable prices. While Lescure accepts that planned economies come in different varieties, from Communist to Corporatist to Social Democratic, he distinguishes between economic planning which aims to promote economic development or to ensure wartime self-sufficiency and that which seeks to suppress economic crises. Yet taken as a whole, he sees little value in economic planning for remedying crises, except in the promotion of public works, which he regards as possible in more market-driven economies as well.

Lescure concludes that what he calls a 'levelling of production' and combatting unemployment are the most important and realistic remedies, especially as the ills attendant to crises fall primarily on the working classes. Of these solutions, he points to strong union activity and managerial efforts to preserve payrolls by cutting hours or by offering workers relief as the most promising, but he recognizes these are not necessarily compatible approaches. He criticizes compulsory unemployment insurance as being 'only a palliative', favouring instead programs designed to find work for the unemployed as the 'true remedy' (Lescure, 2: 650).

In the final section of his treatise, Lescure returns to the question of how to forecast or predict economic crises, suggesting a number of possible improvements over existing methods. Eighty-five years after the publication of the fifth edition, both these problems still obtain, despite fleeting and ill-placed optimism from Alan Greenspan that his monetary policy machinations (the so-called 'Greenspan put') would smooth business cycles and even prevent future crises.[72] Lescure would not have been surprised to learn that the consequences of such interventions have only served to increase macroeconomic

71. Though Lescure does agree with the separation of merchant and deposit banks as legislated in the Glass-Steagall Act (see Lescure, 2: 586).

72. Dwight D Murphey, 'Greenspan's Bubbles: The Age of Ignorance at the Federal Reserve', *Journal of Social, Political, and Economic Studies* 33, no. 4 (2008): 521.

inequality in the United States over the last 40 years.[73] Widening inequality globally within national economies in the wake of pressure on public sector balance sheets after the successive Great Financial Crisis of 2007–8, the Eurozone Sovereign Debt Crisis of 2011–12, and the COVID–19 crisis suggests there is little political will to mitigate the welfare effects of economic crises.[74] By the same token, while economic forecasting has become vastly more sophisticated with the growth of increasingly complex computational models, approaches that derive their leading indicators from comprehensive survey data can significantly outperform more sophisticated methods for forecasting GDP and hence the downturns that mark economic crises.[75] In effect, predicting economic crises remains an occult science. We could do much worse than to return to the reflections of Jean Lescure, in whose magisterial treatment we can see one of the earliest formulations of our modern understanding of these phenomena.

---

73. Lance Taylor, *Macroeconomic Inequality from Reagan to Trump: Market Power, Wage Repression, Asset Price Inflation, and Industrial Decline* (Cambridge: Cambridge University Press, 2020).
74. Lea Elsässer, Florian Fastenrath and Miriam Rehm, 'Making the rich pay? Social Democracy and Wealth Taxation in Europe in the Aftermath of the Great Financial Crisis', *European Political Science Review* (2022), First View, open access, https://doi.org/10.1017/S1755773922000510.
75. Johanna Garnitz, Robert Lehmann and Klaus Wohlrabe. 'Forecasting GDP All Over the World Using Leading Indicators Based on Comprehensive Survey Data', *Applied Economics* 51, no. 54 (2019): 5802–16.

TRANSLATOR'S NOTE

The text that follows is a complete English translation of the fifth edition of Jean Lescure's *Des crises générales et périodiques de surproduction*, published in two volumes by Éditions Domat-Montchrestien, Paris, 1938.[1] Volume one of the original French text presents an interpretative account of the economic history of Europe and the United States from the crisis of 1815 to the recovery of 1933–37; while volume two contains a comprehensive, critical commentary on theoretical approaches to the causes, explanations and remedies of industrial crises. Lescure's magnum opus is a flawed masterpiece of political economy, which carries the marks and irregularities of a text that went through five editions, each of which added substantial new material and many more references to the original doctoral thesis of 1906. In practice, Lescure's updates meant paring down the discussion of past crises from his historical account in order to include lengthy analysis of the crisis, or crises, most recent to each new edition. Two bibliographic appendices have also been included, one containing the works referenced by Lescure in the book and the other a comprehensive list of the author's own publications.

Many of Lescure's sources have been digitized and are available on the web in curated historical collections, like that of the Federal Reserve Bank of St. Louis' FRASER digital library, which contains the archives of important serial publications on the United States referenced in the French text.[2] Most of the French, English, German and Italian monographs, and some of the journals, published before 1929 are available in less carefully curated form from Google Books or the Hathi Trust; while the majority of scholarly journals of economics, statistics and political economy referenced by Lescure exist in digital form from the Biblothèque nationale de France, Jstor, or other scholarly repository. Thus, today, we enjoy a level of access to original sources and statistical evidence that the author himself did not possess, and this has allowed a level of editorial intervention which was impossible at the time. Whenever practicable, Lescure's references have been corrected and missing source information supplied for the modern English reader. Although one could argue that this heavy-handed revision risks presenting an English text that does not fully, or perhaps faithfully, represent the original French edition, these

1. This translation was produced from the version digitized by the Bibliothèque nationale de France and downloadable in two parts: volume 1, NUMM-3351370, and volume 2, NUMM-3351201, accessed 1 Oct. 2022, http://ark.bnf.fr/ark:/12148/cb32377605p. Figures were reproduced directly from the bound copy in the Thompson Library at Ohio State University.
2. Above all, the *Commercial and Financial Chronicle* (1829–1963), the *Federal Reserve Bulletin* (1914–2009) and the *Statistical Abstract of the United States* (1878–1950).

corrections and additions enable the reader to use the work more effectively as an entry point into the debates at this critical juncture in the economic history of the West.

Lescure's use of statistics, both in the text and in the book's many tables and figures, has its limitations and presents certain challenges to the translator. At least one reviewer of the fourth edition pointed to inaccuracies and misprints, some of which had persisted since the first edition.[3] Many of these issues remained unaddressed in the fifth edition. Clear cases in which such inconsistencies could be verified by the translator are indicated by '*sic*' in square brackets in the English translation, and in certain cases, editorial notes have been inserted to alert and inform the reader. Likewise, the units Lescure employed were very inconsistent, even by the standards of the time.[4] Monetary values were often given in thousands to express millions or billions, sometimes followed only by '(000)' to indicate their magnitude. Where Lescure gave weights in *tonnes*, it is often unclear whether metric tonnes or English long tons or North American short tons were meant; these are simply given as 'tonnes' in the English translation, unless they specifically appear as 'tons' in the original French text. Lescure sometimes gave weights in 'lbs.' or '*livres*' but also used *livres* to refer to the pound sterling. Units of weight and measure have been clarified in cases where it has been possible to trace the sources of Lescure's data or to determine the units from the context; otherwise, units and amounts have been left as they appear in the French edition, which the diligent reader can pursue further, using the augmented source information provided in the notes.

Inexplicably, Lescure often failed to provide complete source information for directly quoted material, giving only the authority's last name or a source title. Whenever possible, full source information has been provided by the translator. However, there remain several cases in which Lescure has (rather loosely) translated passages from foreign-language works which could not be located within them. These problems have been indicated in editorial notes. Lescure also neglected to provide the sources for many of his tables and figures; most likely, he may have assumed any economist of the time knew where this data could be found. In these cases, the table or figure has the label 'no source given', and when possible, the translator has supplied information to assist the reader in finding at least some of the author's data. Clear cases in which proper names – persons, places, companies and so on – were misspelled or spelled inconsistently have been corrected and/or made consistent with contemporary usage. Finally, in translating technical terminology relating to specific industries – mining, metals, textiles, banking and so on – the translator has consulted period-specific technical dictionaries and English-language works covering the same material. Here again, Lescure's usage was often inconsistent. In cases where the translation of terms and phrases has proven particularly difficult, or may otherwise cause confusion, the original French has been given in square brackets.

---

3. R. G. Hawtrey, review of *Des crises générales et périodiques de surproduction*, 4th ed., *Economic Journal* 44, no. 173 (1934): 111.
4. Ibid.

Editorial notes have been included to provide further clarification of period-specific terminology or other helpful information to the reader. These notes are numbered with Roman numerals so that they may be easily distinguished from the author's footnotes, which use Arabic numerals. Editorial endnotes follow each of Lescure's three chapters. In some cases, editorial insertions within the author's own notes are placed in square brackets and also preceded by 'Ed. – '. Although every effort has been made to correct and clarify these mistakes, they are, in the end, indigenous to the original French work. Nonetheless, the translator assumes responsibility for the inconsistencies that have undoubtedly been introduced through the course of its translation.

Nicholas Di Liberto

GENERAL AND PERIODIC CRISES OF OVERPRODUCTION

by Jean Lescure

Παλαίφατος δ΄ ἐν βροτοῖς γέρων λόγος
τέτυκται [...]
ἐκ δ΄ ἀγαθᾶς τύχας [...]
βλαστάνειν ἀκόρεστον οἰζύν.

Aeschylus, *Agamemnon*, 750–756.

CONTENTS

LIST OF FIGURES

LIST OF TABLES

Tables are listed by chapter and table number. Titles have been supplied in the many cases where no title was provided in the original French text. In some cases, dates and other descriptive information have been added to titles or given in brackets to assist the reader.

Chapter 1

Chapter 2

Chapter 3

Annexes

PREFACE TO THE THIRD EDITION

For the past twenty years, the problem of periodic crises has retained the special attention of economists. Many works have been published and official commissions named. A price research service – a kind of observatory for the economic world – has been created by the Statistique générale de France. Thanks to the concerted efforts of science and administration, the analysis of the curious periodic mechanism that characterizes our modern societies has gained in detail and precision.

From here on, the crisis appears as a point in the evolution of capitalist society. In order to understand it, one must study the period of growth that precedes it and the period of depression that follows. And the study of crises is concerned with alternating periods of prosperity and depression, with the crisis placed at the junction of the two – so much so that one speaks of economic cycles in the United States and of industrial fluctuations in England when identifying the phenomenon we seek to study here.

Points of view have changed, and horizons have broadened. The entire economic system is influenced by these pendulum swings [*balancement*]. During the growth period, the production of goods, consumption and credit develop; incomes (wages, dividends, interest) rise. Unemployment diminishes or even disappears. Savings increase. Prices rise. After a number of years (three to five), we note an inversion in the curves. It is a drop all down the line: production, consumption and incomes sag; unemployment reappears. Business prosperity is followed by stagnation.

Not only is the entire economic organism affected, but the crisis also reaches nearly every other country; an ever-closer economic interdependency [*solidarité*] unites the economic markets, transforming the crisis into an international or global phenomenon. The most recent crises, in 1907, 1913 and 1920, have been global. And now the observations are numerous and precise enough and cover a sufficiently long period of time (almost a century) for there to be no appreciable divergence of opinion among economists about the phenomenon itself or about its scope. This consensus allows us to affirm the scientific nature of these observations.

Yet, after having established the phenomenon, one is tempted to search for its causes. Herein lies the disagreement. For some economists, these cycles [*alternatives*] may occur because production is sometimes lower and sometimes greater in relation to demand. If supply falls below demand, prices rise and with them profits. New businesses are created. But before they can produce, these firms need to be organized: new equipment must be manufactured. During the time needed to manufacture the new equipment, the metal industry enjoys full prosperity, as does industry in general: supply remains lower than demand. As soon as the additional machinery comes on line, however, the situation is reversed: supply exceeds demand, and there is overproduction. And it is general overproduction because additional equipment will have been installed everywhere. Everywhere supply exceeds the intensity of demand.

This theory of general overproduction collides with the law of markets. *General* overproduction is scarcely conceivable where products are traded against other products. Moreover, it cannot explain why all industries expand at the same time, nor why they all enter a crisis simultaneously. Some economists will say this can be explained by the lengthening of the production process. Yet this lengthening is not the same for all industries: the time required to build a forge is not the same as the time needed to build a weaving mill. So why does overproduction appear in nearly all industries in the same year? A common cause must be found that can explain the extent of the crisis, one that takes into consideration the interdependencies [*solidarité*] of industries.

Walras' theory of economic equilibrium has demonstrated the close relationship [*solidarité*] between the market for products and the market for services. Let us elaborate and clarify this further: services paid for by one industry are used to buy the products of other industries. The crisis in one industry reverberates in other industries to varying degrees. The more important the industry affected, the more profound the repercussions.

In our modern societies, profit remains the driving force behind the spirit of enterprise. Profit is the margin between the cost of production and the selling price. If profit diminishes, the creation of new businesses will slow down. But the decrease in profit may be due either to a reduction in the selling price through overproduction or to production costs increasing faster than selling prices. In fact, the spirit of enterprise declines *before* the drop in the selling prices of goods. Orders for production equipment decrease before the selling prices of consumer goods or railway traffic. For the railways, the decline in net returns precedes that of gross receipts. Why? Because their operating cost, their cost price, rises faster than the selling price. And this is so because, in our modern societies, the demand for some goods increases faster than the demand for others in times of industrial expansion: coal, cast iron, steel, copper – in short, all the raw materials used to create modern machinery. During the boom, too, wages rise, even as labour productivity diminishes. Interest rates rise. No businessman would ever suggest that the interest rate does not exert a major influence on the state of business, or that excess or insufficient equipment would be the only factor to consider. In fact, history demonstrates that all crises are preceded by the collapse of new enterprises that do not yield the expected results for their investors. The profit potential declines. And this decline is due to the fact that start-up costs have exceeded projections – that the operating costs of the last firms created have increased between the moment the enterprise was conceived and the time when it begins operating. This was the case for European railway construction in the nineteenth century and, in the nineteenth and twentieth centuries, for railway construction in the United States. The history of crises is punctuated by railway bankruptcies. More recently, the electrical industries in Europe have signalled the coming of crises: new companies created at the end of a period of prosperity prove disappointing. Hence the slowdown of orders placed with the metal industry, and the fall in the prices of cast iron, steel and copper, constitutes the best indicator of the onset of a crisis. Crises that begin in this sector will spread and affect others.

During the depression, the opposite phenomenon occurs: the prices for equipment, wages and interest rates decrease. After a few years, this drop is sufficient for one to think about creating new businesses and building railways again. But this process of decline takes time to complete. Economic life, like real life, does not proceed by leaps alone. We shall see why later.

At present, this approach to explaining crises is shared by Wesley Mitchell, professor at Columbia University in New York, who has recently written the most well-documented work on the subject; by Edwin R. A. Seligman, a professor at the same university; by George Hull, an American industrialist and author of *Industrial Depressions* [...] *or, Iron, the Barometer of Trade* (New York, 1911); and in many respects, by D. H. Robertson, professor at Cambridge University, to cite only a few authors who have devoted specific studies to the subject. This is our preferred approach.

But whatever the differences may be about the causes of crises, the phenomenon is now sufficiently studied in every country for the theory of crises to allow predictions to be made. When a crisis occurs, we can safely predict that a depression will accompany it. This period of depression will be followed by a period of prosperity, and then a crisis. The statistical observation of certain indexes enables us to predict whether a growth period is about to end, or if, conversely, an economic recovery is taking shape. As such forecasts concern future prices of goods, wage rates, unemployment, interest rates, dividends and the course of securities on the stock exchange, and their future over the next several years, they undoubtedly have some use.

But in order to present the results of these statistical observations to the reader, two methods are possible: either to study these alternating periods, one after another, in the course of history, or else, to consider successively the statistics for production, then prices, then wages, then profits and so on, in order to highlight the cycle [*alternatives*] of rise and fall.

The first method has the advantage of providing a more faithful picture of real life. For once the crisis erupts in one country, it soon affects others. Born in one industry, it spreads from there to neighbouring industries. In each crisis there is a country and an industry that leads the way. The crisis may be violent here and benign there. After having erupted in industry, the crisis strikes the stock market or affects the banks. Such observations are important for any science that aims to predict. A disease is, in its essence, the same in all individuals. But, according to their age group and temperament, the consequences vary considerably from one individual to the next. The same is true of economic crises: young people and new countries are particularly exposed to troubles of this kind. Some industries are particularly vulnerable and are struck first.

The second method, on the other hand, highlights with more evidence and rigour the periodicity of the phenomenon and its characteristic features. But it does not allow us to grasp reality as closely. By isolating the phenomena under scrutiny and studying them over fifty or sixty years, one runs the risk of neglecting the links that bind them together. One tries to explain a crisis by looking at factors specific to one industry, when the cause lies in the state of a neighbouring industry. The history of crises demonstrates that in every crisis there is a focal point, a country or industry. At its onset, a crisis is not general. Little by little it spreads like an epidemic. The accompanying credit crisis is a powerful factor in its spread. The second method does not allow such observations: by studying crises in yearly succession, it fails to follow the development of the crisis day by day and step by step. Monthly statistics are valuable here. Also, the two methods are not mutually exclusive and may complement each other. Mitchell has successfully combined the two. We will do the same. But we will limit ourselves to giving the results of our observations and research, referring the reader to the original sources so as not to overload our presentation with figures and avoid duplication of well-known and easily accessible statistical yearbooks.

There is still a lot to be said on these matters. A new branch of statistics still needs to be developed in which observations will be more closely compared. Big businesses (trusts and others) will have to co-operate with this endeavour. In the United States, monthly statistics already allow for a more focussed observation of events: statistics on the net returns of the railways, on gross receipts, cast-iron production, wagons loaded, orders received by the steel trust, on foreign trade and so on. In France, we have similar statistics, but they are neither gathered systematically nor published on a regular basis. It is the same in England and Germany. By embarking on this path, the theory of crises – that is, of alternating periods of prosperity and depression – is bound to make further progress. We will understand more clearly the origin of this phenomenon and its causes. The results obtained in the United States are already very interesting.

The monthly observation of the fluctuations of economic activity, if collected in France and in Europe as has already been done in the United States, will enable us to reach more precise and, at the same time, more pragmatic conclusions. In ten years or so, it will be even more accurate to maintain, together with Clément Colson, that: 'This is one case in which the scientific observation of the facts has produced the most useful results in practice.'

April 1923

PREFACE TO THE FOURTH EDITION

Since the publication of the third edition of this book, the problem of alternating periods of growth and depression has been the subject of numerous publications. Efforts have been made to observe, explain, prevent and cure. Statistical, theoretical and therapeutic work on this topic has covered considerable ground. Yet the sheer scale of this work entails an inevitable imperfection.

But the facts themselves place the problem of crises at the forefront of our concerns. In 1929, a period of very brilliant growth gave way, in the United States, to a depression of rare intensity. The world has suffered this contagion ever since, in 1930 and 1931.

In the field of observation of the general flow of business, economic cycles and the economic conjuncture, we note that everywhere specialized services for statistical research have been created: the Harvard Economic Service, the Institut für Konjunkturforschung in Berlin and Vienna, the London Economic Service and others. Following the example set by France already in 1908, other countries have now surpassed its efforts. The economist and the businessman now enjoy an impressive number of indexes and graphs to adapt, superimpose and compare. We are almost tempted here to speak of overproduction!

For even though new statistical methods have provided us with valuable additional information, we have sometimes abused these figures. Their misuse has been particularly careless. The spirit of geometry has tried to eliminate the need for finesse; here too, reasoning has tried to ignore intuition and the imponderables that influence economic phenomena, as they do man himself. Political economy would be more successful if we appealed to the methods of biology, rather than to the still very precarious procedures of meteorology. The failure of the so-called barometer method is no longer contested today. Facts have shattered the barometers. The use of statistics should not be mechanical.

In the realm of theory, the same reservations apply. The monetary implications of crises have inspired numerous important works. Quantities of money and credit are meant to constitute the driving force of the economic world. For variations in the quantity of money provokes corresponding movements in profits. We certainly do not deny that profit is the engine of the modern economic world, acting in its variations as both an accelerator and a brake. But we doubt that quantities of money, through their influence on prices, are sufficient to explain variations in profit. We would willingly turn the statement around and say: price fluctuations determine variations in the quantities of money.

In the recent period, science has made significant progress in the field of quantitative theory. Today, it is unanimously accepted that the quantitative equation is self-evident. A given quantity of trade at a given price level corresponds to a quantity of money circulating at a given speed. It remains to be seen whether in the equation the pulse function is given by P itself or by MV+M'V'. Both theses are supported. But the facts seem to establish that price fluctuations precede the movements of the factors MV+M'V'. The rise in prices leads to a greater reliance on credit (M'), while economic growth activates the circulation of money (V'). The research is now moving in this direction, and the progress here is undeniable. Price fluctuations clearly seem to determine movements in the quantities of money. If this is the case, profit variations determine the alternation of growth and depression; however, the variations in costs and prices must be studied and explained. The solutions become far more complex. The quantitative theory no longer suffices.

Yet, the alternating periods of growth and depression, the synchronicity established between price variations, incomes (profit, interest and wages), quantities produced and the value of domestic and foreign trade cast doubt on many classical theories, in particular the doctrine which claims that an increase in production (supply) is accompanied by a drop in prices, that a fall in prices is accompanied by a rise in demand, that wages and interest grow at the expense of profit (Ricardo, Marx), or that lowering the interest rate provokes a greater demand for capital, by applying the theory of marginal productivity or, more simply, the law of supply and demand.

While classical political economy tries to give a definition of profit and an explanation of variations in wages, the existence of alternating periods of expansion and depression singularly complicates all of these problems. If we define profit (correctly) as the margin between the cost price [*prix de revient*] and the selling price, this margin may be the result of variations in one of the two factors, and, depending on the timing or moments in which they are observed, it may have different explanations: overhead costs, raw materials, wages – each have their own laws of variation at different times within the alternating movements. Profit may be explained differently at these various moments. There is no single explanation for profit, there are several. The same goes for wages. Certainly, wages are influenced by the output of the workforce or by the movement of profit. Yet at the various stages of economic fluctuations, this or that factor plays a dominant role. There is no single law of wages, there are many. In order to give one theory of wages, this theory must be extremely complex and contingent. The same applies to price theory.

The statistical evidence accumulated thus far seems to indicate the need for a reworking of economic theory. Now and in the future, our efforts must be focussed upon the revision of economic theory in light of the most fruitful of these observations. Many classical theories no longer stand the test of experience. Just as there is a Euclidian and a non-Euclidian geometry, there needs to be a static and a dynamic political economy.[1]

1. Adolf Löwe, 'Wie ist eine Konjunkturtheorie überhaupt möglich?' *Weltwirtschaftliches Archiv* 24 (1926): 165–97; and see François Divisia's and Clément Colson's comments on 'L'eternelle

The diverse elements of economic equilibrium, the prices of goods and services, have their own laws of variation. These laws lead prices to move in the same direction, but to differing degrees. The elasticity of demand causes very different price variations. Wages and interest rates have their own laws of motion, as do wholesale and retail prices. There are also variations in the magnitude or velocity of supply that are specific to various goods. Variations in the same direction but of unequal magnitude are capable of producing ruptures of equilibrium. If economic equilibrium appears to us as an equilibrium in value, if *values are exchanged against values*, then a lack of harmony in the increase of the prices of goods or services is capable of causing a disruption of equilibrium and a crisis. This kind of disruption appears to us – after the 1929 crisis, even more than before the war – to be reflected in an anaemia of probable and possible profit, which is the driving force behind circulation and production par excellence.

However, in terms of prediction and mitigation, suggestions have been made and experiments have been tried.

The proponents of the monetary explanation have looked to managed monetary policy [*monnaie dirigée*] as a means of preventing or curing crises. Having rejected the monetary explanation, we have strong reservations about these new doctrines. Discount policies coupled with credit controls are capable of moderating or accelerating price movements. However, they are more effective at moderating than at speeding up. And price is far from being the only element we have to consider. The United States has failed to stimulate the recovery of economic activity by increasing the availability of credit. Although prices were very stable from 1925 to 1929, this stability was not enough to prevent the crisis of 1929. The depression persisted into 1930 and 1931, despite an unprecedented drop in the discount rate.

It is fair to note that the 1929 crisis occurred in a period of profound economic upheavals: Europe was rebuilding itself after the devastation of the war, reconstituting its production, currencies and public finances. The distribution of wealth was profoundly disrupted, particularly by budgets that had doubled, tripled or quadrupled during the war. Public debt reached unprecedented levels. Also, the synchronicity that had existed in the past between general price movements, production and trade by and large disappeared. Last but not least, European production, now more efficient and better organized, struggled to find new outlets, as it combined with a world production that had been stimulated by the war. Thus, the 1929 crisis occurred in an already depressed world plagued by overproduction. We must go back to the end of the nineteenth century, to the period between 1873 and 1896, to find similar phenomena, albeit on a much smaller scale. The problem of overproduction is more complex than ever before. Hence the numerous publications it generates, adding to the already abundant literature.

This fourth edition, which is a completely revised and, in this regard, a new book, has been updated, completed and reshaped. It aims to demonstrate general trends without neglecting the original features of periodic overproduction crises. It studies new

question des crises', at the meeting of the Société d'économie politique, 5 June 1931, in *Journal des économistes*, 15 June 1931, 350–53.

methods of observation, theories and remedies. The most recent events confirm the explanation that we already proposed in 1906: profit variations determine the general course of economic activity. We might add that in the recent past this view has earned more and more adherents among economists in France and abroad.

We would like this book to be viewed as a synthesis of theories, and a synthesis is not to be confused with eclecticism.

PREFACE TO THE FIFTH EDITION

Recently, and for the first time in history, the interval between the periodic crisis and the recovery has been filled by an unprecedented monetary and credit crisis as a distant consequence of the 1914 war. We cannot deal with this in any detail without going beyond our subject. However, we have tried to state the essential and to show in particular that it cannot be considered as a crisis of the capitalist system: it is the logical, inevitable result of the massive recourse to credit and resulting overproduction which prevented mankind from running out of food, equipment, arms and munitions during and after the war, until the end of reparations. Here we have situated the role of the United States, explaining the violent crisis to which it fell victim. Understanding this crisis, its antecedents and causes, is of great consequence. The crisis has been resolved, and if humanity can maintain the benefits of peace, it will not be repeated. It did not prevent the traditional recovery from taking place. This recovery is most original, at times spontaneous and at times managed [*dirigée*] by the state. We have described it in some detail. It was marked by the decrease in interest rates, induced everywhere, and achieved in England and in the United States thanks to the open-market policy and elsewhere (in Germany and Belgium) by other methods.

Currency devaluations have also preceded and primed the recovery, restoring profit margins that had declined as a result of the world disruption.[1] And here we have found new empirical confirmation of the method of explaining alternating periods of growth and depression through profit variations.

Massive gold movements and capital migrations have posed unprecedented problems for central banks and exchange stabilization funds: countries will have to be protected against large and sudden variations in discount rates likely to hinder the economic recovery or stem the prosperity.

Finally, the literature devoted to the 'planned economy' is far too abundant, with recovery plans occupying too large a place for us to remain silent on the topic. The managed monetary policy [*monnaie dirigée*] of the planned economy has retained our attention, without gaining our support.

On numerous other points we have made revisions, corrections and updates.

In this preface, we have limited ourselves to indicating the essential new findings. We hope that this summary will justify in the eyes of our readers the publication of this fifth edition.

---

1. In this sense, see *Rapport officiel belge* on the economic and financial policies of the Van Zeeland cabinet.

Note: Thanks to the remarkable but as yet insufficient progress of statistics (notably with regard to orders and profits), the description of alternating periods of growth and depression has become much more schematic, more precise and more rigorous. The monthly supplement of the *Economist* (*Economist Trade Supplement*) is one such example. It makes the mistake of neglecting profits in its otherwise comprehensive and convenient tables. An index of orders would have also been valuable and would have made it a pioneering effort.

March 1938

Volume I

THE PHENOMENON

Chapter One

THE PHENOMENON

The good years alternate with the bad, and the often-quoted parable about fat cows and lean cows has lost none of its vivid meaning. However, the evolution of contemporary societies toward capitalism has had an impact upon the phenomenon of alternating years of crisis and prosperity.

Until the eighteenth century, production remained largely agricultural; thus, crises were almost always agricultural. As fickle as the seasons and the harvest, famine is its most sinister form. Nowadays, thanks to the means of transport and communication, famines have disappeared, but industrial and commercial crises have become more frequent.

We shall distinguish between crises of production, consumption, circulation and distribution.[1] However, if we encounter these different crises in isolation, we also encounter them together as general crises of production, consumption, circulation and distribution.

In his *Cours de philosophie positive*, Auguste Comte writes, 'Strictly speaking, the progress of civilization does not run along a straight line; rather it moves through a series of unequal and variable oscillations around a mean which always tends to prevail.'[2] Nothing is truer even from an economic point of view.

During the nineteenth and twentieth centuries, economic growth has ceaselessly followed depression. In very general terms, we could say that the world economy went through a period of growth between 1845 and 1873, followed by a period of decline between 1873 and 1894, followed by a new period of growth between 1895 and 1920 and a new period of decline starting with the crisis of 1920. In more specific terms, we note periods of depression between 1845 and 1873 and between 1895 and 1920; while periods of growth occur from 1873 to 1874 and from 1920 to 1931.

---

1. As an example of a production crisis, we would cite the crisis in the trades faced with the growth of large-scale industry, or the crisis of iron with the rise of steel. As an example of the consumption crisis, we would offer the frequent crises suffered by the textile industry as a result of the whims of fashion. Among the circulation crises, we would include all those arising from monetary disorders, from the excessive issue of banknotes or paper money. Among the distribution crises, we would rank all of the speculation crises, the effect of which is generally to transfer the ownership of either securities or goods; stock market crises are basically distribution crises.
2. Auguste Comte, *Cours de philosophie positive*, 5th ed., 6 vols. (Paris: La Société Positiviste, 1892–1894), 4: 325. (Note: page numbers in this edition differ from those of previous editions.)

The general overproduction crisis occurs at the point where a growth period lasting three to five years intersects with a depression of a similar duration. It is moreover a periodic crisis.[3]

The study of crises implies the examination of periods of growth and periods of depression and, as these crises are general, the examination of production, consumption, circulation and distribution in periods of growth and of depression. A historical study will help us demonstrate the identity of the phenomenon in time and, subsequently, its scientific validity. A theoretical part will enable us to describe the characteristic features of the economic phenomenon.

3. This definition was adopted if not literally then at least in spirit by the commission on crises appointed by the Ministère du Travail. See 'Rapport sur les indices des crises économiques', *Journal Officiel de la Républic français*, no. 238, 3 Sep. 1909, 1151–62. The periodicity is not mathematical. However, dictionaries provide definitions of periodicity that clearly correspond to the repeating, periodic phenomenon under investigation here. Notably in medicine, the term periodic is understood in this sense. See *La Grande Encyclopédie: Inventaire raisonné des sciences, des lettres et des arts*, ed. André Berthelot and Ferdinand-Camille Dreyfus et al., 31 vols. (Paris: Société anonyme de La Grande Encyclopédie, 1886–1902), 26: 386, s.v. 'périodicité'.

Section One

A Historical Study of Economic Crises

The lack of sufficient material prevents us from going back further than the 1810 crisis, and even then, we shall only give quite succinct information on the crises of 1810, 1815 and 1818. The sources available to us allow us at most to presume that the crises in 1810 and 1818 were truly general crises of overproduction.

§1. – The crisis of 1810

At the beginning of the nineteenth century, the emancipation of the Spanish colonies, the continental blockade (21 November 1807), the opening of Russia to European trade and above all to English trade, the great discoveries like steam and the power loom, the construction of canals and bridges, the development of lace making and the organization of insurance companies greatly stimulated production. Production developed with the formation of joint-stock companies, and savings were employed in the work of production through the issuing of shares. The 12 January 1808 issue of *Monthly Magazine* notes that between 1806 and 1808, in the space of only two years, 42 joint-stock companies were created in England. In addition to these, England also founded holding companies abroad; it also exported more extensively, particularly to South America.

Circulation developed along with production and consumption; the quantity of money in circulation increased, particularly in the form of paper currency. Credit expanded dramatically. Banks multiplied. The number of country banks in England increased from 600 in 1808 to 720 in 1810, and their note circulation represented £30 million. The Bank of England's circulation, which had represented only £15 million in 1805, reached £24 million in 1810.

Prices rose.[4] Workers could find work on a frequent basis. Merchants and industrialists made large profits.

Around 1810, the situation suddenly shifted. Many canals and textile mills were being built, the export trade was advancing, and then, all of a sudden, factories were no longer being built, exports slowed and hardly any joint-stock companies were being created.

The increase in banknote circulation, absorbed by the trade activity during the period of growth, now became excessive, and the banknotes depreciated.[5] Prices soon decreased. Banks, merchants and industrialists went bankrupt. According to a contemporary English newspaper, half of the merchants were swept away in the storm. The Bank of England suspended its payments, and on 11 April 1811, Parliament had to advance £6 million in Exchequer bonds to spare it an even worse fate. These measures were sufficient to calm the panic and improve the situation.

---

4. See Clément Juglar, *Des crises commerciales et de leur retour périodique en France, en Angleterre et aux États-Unis*, 2nd ed. (Paris: Guillaumin, 1889), 314.
5. It was then that Ricardo wrote his pamphlet: *Du haut prix des lingots de la dépréciation des banknotes* [*The High Price of Bullion, a Proof of the Depreciation of Bank Notes* (London: John Murray, 1810)].

§2. – The crises of 1815 and 1818

The crisis of 1815 was in fact more agricultural than industrial or commercial, and that of 1818 was more of a circulation crisis than an actual general crisis.

In 1811, the political situation in Europe had brought about a rise in the price of corn in England from 156 to 180 shillings. This had resulted in uncontrollable land speculation to which the banks had lent unlimited support in the form of inordinate issues of banknotes.

The Spanish colonies continued to provide a great outlet for goods and available capital. The Russian retreat and the expulsion of French troops from Spain opened up new ports and new opportunities for trade. This was all it took to unleash a wave of optimism. The prices of various products rose in fantastic proportions. Banks continued to lend their support to the bullish speculation by issuing banknotes. In the autumn of 1814, disaster struck. The larger markets that had been hoped for had not materialized: prices dropped; the banknote circulation, which could only be explained by the imprudence and blindness of country banks, depreciated rapidly. Two hundred and forty of these institutions failed between 1814 and 1817. Little by little circulation returned to normal levels. In 1817, better times were anticipated, when large cereal imports[6] and German and Austrian loans intended to improve currency circulation in these different countries drained gold from England. The Bank of England's reserve shrank so much that it had to suspend its payments in 1818, and once more the government had to intervene by lending it £28 million [*sic*].[i]

Should the 1818 and 1815 crises be called general overproduction crises?[7] They appear rather to have been circulation crises caused by the excessive issuing of banknotes in 1815 – by the related effects of abnormal imports of corn and exports of gold in 1818. In the first case, we are dealing with a domestic credit crisis; in the second case, with a foreign credit crisis or exchange crisis [*crise de change*]. But let us move on to the first proper general overproduction crisis, that of 1825.

§3. – The crisis of 1825

The 1815 crisis was essentially an English crisis. On the continent, we had enough to deal with repairing the damage caused by the wars of the First Empire. As early as 1822, England, less impacted by war and more entrepreneurial, resolutely set about fabricating the machinery needed for capitalist production; it offers us the first example of a general overproduction crisis deserving of the name.

6. Cereal imports in England grew from £11,306,000 to £23,119,773 in 1818. See Émile de Laveleye, *Le marché monétaire et ses crises depuis 50 ans* (Paris: Guillaumin, 1865), 12.
7. In this sense, see de Laveleye, *Le marché monétaire*, 11; and Juglar, *Des crises commerciales*, 321–32.

A.) Growth

Capitalists chastened by the successive panics of 1810, 1815 and 1818 took some time to abandon their distrust of industrial and commercial investment, which they had gradually abandoned in favour of somewhat less rewarding but more secure investments (government securities in particular). In 1822, English Consols crossed the threshold.

The English government, faithful to its debt conversion policies introduced by Robert Walpole in the eighteenth century, converted its £152,422,143 from 5 per cent (nominal capital) to 4 per cent.[8] This operation was a brilliant success: only £2,794,318 had to be reimbursed. However, investors [*rentiers*] were now looking for a favourable opportunity to abandon the government securities. Such an opportunity presented itself with the discovery of silver mines in Mexico, and at the same time in England, with the development of shipyards, factories and mines and with the digging of canals. On the other hand, the railway was beginning to appear. In 1825, the first line open to the public was unveiled.[9]

South America was quickly winning the favour of the English public.[10] The high profits that could be earned there made it fashionable, and South American bonds issued in London reached £48,480,000 in 1825.

British exports to South America increased considerably, doubling between 1821 and 1825 from £2,942,000 to £6,426,000. Domestic growth was no less impressive. English imports rose from £30 million in 1822 to £44 million in 1825. Subsequently, 20 railway companies were created as well as 22 canal companies, 22 banks, 27 factories and 11 gas companies, not counting breweries or shipbuilding companies. According to de Laveleye, the known subscriptions exceeded £100 million in nominal capital.[11] However, this was part of the speculation and proof that it existed; since the paid-up capital actually amounted to only 5 to 10 per cent of the sums subscribed, one can estimate that only £13.5 million of the capital was tied up in industry and commerce. This already represented an enormous sum for the time.[12]

Circulation, too, had to increase. True, the Bank of England followed a very moderate policy, but the country banks, forgetting the lessons of the past, increased their banknote circulation from £4.5 million to £11 million. Commodity prices rose: Georgia cotton prices rose by 109 per cent, silk from China by 20 per cent, tobacco by

---

8. See Paul Leroy-Beaulieu, *Traité de la science des finances*, 6th ed., 2 vols. (Paris: Guillaumin, 1899), 2: 505.
9. The Darlington to Stockton railway line. However, locomotive traction still remained very deficient. It was only with the improvements to the steam boiler and to rail traction, made by Stephenson in England and Seguin in France between 1825 and 1839, that the age of the railway really opened up.
10. Henry Dunning MacLeod, *Theory of Credit*, 2nd ed., 2 vols. (London: Longmans, Green, 1893–1897), vol. 2, pt 2: 992.
11. De Laveleye, *Le marché monétaire*, 16.
12. For further details, see Max Wirth, *Geschichte der Handelskrisen*, 2nd ed. (Frankfurt am Main: Sauerlaender, 1874), 115.

33 per cent, sugar by 34 per cent and cast iron by 77 per cent from December 1824 to June 1825.

Discount rates nonetheless remained more or less unaffected by the general upward movement of prices, and the Bank of England at least maintained its rate at 4 per cent until 17 December 1825.

On the other hand, the stock exchange allowed itself to indulge in the most extravagant optimism. Anglo-American mining shares on which just £10 had been paid were trading at £43 on 10 December 1824 and at £150 on 20 January 1825. Real del Monte stock, purchased at £70 per share, increased from £550 in December 1824 to £1,350 in January 1825.[13] The increase in dividends justified to some extent this really inordinate rise in stock market prices. Yet such an abnormal state of production, consumption and foreign trade prices could not be sustained for long.

B.) Crisis and depression

In 1825, imports exceeded exports. Newly built canals were not earning the anticipated profits, and money was not flowing as abundantly from the Andes as one might have hoped. Industry and commerce paused for a time. Prices fell: cotton by 60 per cent, silk by 39 per cent, tobacco by 23 per cent, sugar by 38 per cent, coffee by 27 per cent, cast iron by 27 per cent and lead by 24 per cent. English commercial exports reflected the general slowdown of trade: exports fell from £38.9 million in 1825 to £31.5 million in 1826 and fluctuated between £35 and 38 million from 1827 to 1832, at the time of the full resolution crisis.

Credit and circulation soon showed signs of serious trouble: the drop in prices had rendered a host of products unsaleable, and goods purchased dearly during the speculation period when prices were increasing now cluttered the warehouses and shops of merchants, who were obliged to liquidate their imprudent speculations either by selling at a loss the products purchased during the growth period or by resorting to credit. But the growing demand for credit was faced with an increasingly limited supply. Banks failed in large numbers. In October, five local banks went bankrupt, and their banknotes suddenly dropped from par to nil. Even the strongest banks were threatened. Only the banknotes from the Bank of England had not depreciated. But not having increased its discount rate since the beginning of the crisis, the Bank of England saw its available resources and means of credit reduced to such a degree that it soon had to refuse credit even to strong businesses. It had to protect its gold reserve against a double danger: first, against an exchange crisis [*crise du change*], as imports were exceeding exports to the point that remittances to the continent had to be made in gold; and second, against a domestic credit crisis that had resulted from the bankruptcy of the country banks. The Bank of England's gold reserve fell from £13,900,000 on 27 March 1824 to £1,300,000 in December 1825 under the following circumstances.

13. See Macleod, *Theory of Credit*, vol. 2, pt 2: 994; de Laveleye, *Le marché monétaire*, 15; and Wirth, *Geschichte der Handelskrisen*, 118–19.

From 28 August to 24 September 1825, the unfavourable exchange in Paris had led to significant gold exports to France. In October, the exchange crisis was further complicated by the domestic crisis of the country banks, and the £3.5 million gold reserve of 24 September 1825 had fallen to £3.2 million on 29 October. In December, the situation had grown so critical that it was decided to raise the discount rate. On 17 December, it was raised from 4 to 5 per cent. Exchange rates immediately improved. The demand for credit became less urgent. However, for more security, on 27 December the Bank of England bought 300,000 gold sovereigns from the House of Rothschild: it was receiving relief from Holland and France. Thus fortified, it was able to energetically support stable businesses and honest banks. The credit crisis entered its resolution phase; the Bank of England's gold reserve recovered, and in 1826, it had already reached £10.2 million.

A stock market crisis of extreme severity had been developing alongside the exchange crisis of the country banks. According to Tugan-Baranowsky, it was even one of the most essential characteristics of that year of industrial and commercial distress.[14] Just as unbridled speculation had been responsible for the exaggerated price rises in 1824 and at the beginning 1825, the panic was equally disastrous. The Real del Monte Company, with capital of £1 million, whose shares had risen so sharply, was sold for £27,000.[15] English capitalists lost more than £10 million in outside investment; they had paid £13.5 million; following the crisis at the stock exchange, the £13.5 million was not worth more than £3 million.[16]

The working class was hit just as hard as the capitalists. Unemployment and the fall in wages claimed many victims, so many in fact that the outraged workers smashed their machines, believing them to be the source of all their ills. 'Workers turned away from trade union action to the larger aims and wider framework of the radical and socialist movements of the time.'[17]

Thus 1825 saw the beginning of a long and intense depression during which capital could not hope to find profitable investment in industry. Existing factories found it difficult to hang on, and to avoid bankruptcy, they had to resort to technical improvements, to cutting overheads – in short, to any means necessary to reduce their production costs. It was as a result of the crisis of 1825 in particular that the steam-powered loom was more generally adopted and that all obsolete equipment in the foundries was thoroughly eliminated. Thus, little by little, a more vigorous industry formed that waited impatiently for the moment when its services would be called on once again.

---

14. Mikhail I. Tugan-Baranowsky, *Studien zur Theorie und Geschichte der Handelskrisen in England* (Jena: Fischer, 1901), 69. (First published in Russian in 1894 and translated into French as *Les crises industrielles en Angleterre* in 1913).
15. Leone Levi, *History of British Commerce* (London: John Murray, 1872), 179, quoted by Tugan-Baranowsky in ibid., 81.
16. James Wilson, *Fluctuations of Currency, Commerce and Manufactures Referable to Corn Laws* (London: Longman, Orme, Brown, Green and Longmans, 1840), 46.
17. Sidney and Beatrice Webb, *Histoire du trade unionisme*, trans. A. Métin (Paris: Giard & Brière, 1897), 115.

§4. – The crises of 1836 and 1839

By 1830, the 1825 crisis had by and large been liquidated. The interest rate had reached a new low. In 1830, the English government converted its rate of 4 per cent into 3½ per cent. The operation was an impressive success: out of the £153,671,095 of capital only £2,649,399 had to be reimbursed.[18] John Bull, regretting this decrease in revenue, was willing to lend a sympathetic ear to the promoters of industrial enterprises.

The railway had made enormous progress since 1825; the locomotive traction problem having been resolved and the engine perfected, mechanical force would permanently replace animal power. A lack of capital was the only remaining barrier to railway development, one that would soon be resolved.

A.) Growth

The railway was moreover not the only opportunity for the capitalists; the network of navigable waterways was far from being completed, and new mines were far from being fully exploited. At last, the United States, a new country of infinite wealth, was opening itself up to the European spirit of enterprise. From 1832 to 1836 all over England, a veritable deluge of new railways and canals could be seen: first, the London to Birmingham line was opened, followed by the Liverpool to Manchester line, and after this initial success, a whole series of other lines were opened; it was the same with new canals. Yet coal was needed to build these railways and to run them once they were built. Hence, new mines had to be exploited.

According to Leone Levi, in just the two years from 1834 to 1836, the nominal capital of newly created joint-stock companies would have reached £105.2 million (2,624 million francs).[19] Of that this sum, railway companies took in £69.6 million; banks, £23.8 million; insurance companies, £7.6 million; and finally mines, £7 million, and canals, £3.7 million. The taste for luxury had become so general that ten- and even five-pound notes were issued.

Production in England did not only find domestic outlets; the growing economic potential of the United States, which was already working out new forms of production and exchange, digging mines and building railway lines, played an important role in the prosperity of England at that time. British exports to the United States between 1832 and 1836 grew from £5,468,000 to £12,426,000. Capital was not the only export;[20] the workforce was also being exported, and the arrival of new immigrants and the increase in the urban population created new demand for housing. The building industry was overwhelmed. In New York, for example, no less than 1,518 houses were built between 1 January and 1 September 1838. This burgeoning population also had to be fed, and

18. See Paul Leroy-Beaulieu, *Traité de la Science des Finances*, 2: 506–7.
19. Levi, *History of British Commerce*, 229.
20. The capital involved in these diverse enterprises was valued at $300 million.

finding new land to accommodate immigrants became a priority. Arable land sales by the government increased from $4 million in 1833 to $24.8 million in 1836.[21]

In response to this trade activity, prices rose, especially in 1835 and 1836. By July 1835 and July 1836, prices had risen since July 1833, respectively:

	1835 (%)	*1836* (%)
for cotton by	25	31
for silk by	17	40
for lead by	32	95
for sugar by	23	80
for tobacco by	22	44

English iron ore prices increased from 61 in 1831 to 86 in 1836. At the same time, the number of bills of exchange drawn was increasing, banks were being created in response to the growing need for discounts, the issuing of banknotes resumed, and country banks were created in large numbers: in 1836, there were 42 new ones which, together with their branches and the other credit institutions associated with them, constituted 670 counters issuing banknotes.

The Bank of England, regulated by the new Bank of England Act of 1833, which made its banknotes legal tender and raised in its favour the limit on the interest rate to 5 per cent,[22] saw its discount grow from £3.8 million in 1833 to £6.4 million in 1834, £7 million in 1835 and £19.5 million in 1836. This did not stop the joint-stock banks. The legality of joint-stock banks which had until then been contested was now recognized in the same act regulating the Bank of England; this did not stop them from greatly increasing in number and from contributing in large measure to the industrial and commercial growth. Their number grew from 220 in 1835 to 280 in 1836, while their circulation grew from £2.7 to £3.5 million.

In the United States, the development of credit was no less significant. While at the beginning of 1834 the banks' capital in the United States only represented $200 million, loans and discounts $324 million and banknotes in circulation $95 million, on 1 January 1836, its capital reached $251 million and its banknotes in circulation $457 million.[23] Under the statutes and acts of concession, the banks could only discount or lend up to three times their capital; nevertheless, some banks issued notes of up to 20 times that number. As is well-known, these discounts and issues of notes were most often disguised as long-term loans, relying on the appearance of short-term credit. However, there is nothing so dangerous as this practice, by which banks may show profits for a time,

21. Tugan-Baranowsky, *Theorie und Geschichte der Handelskrisen*, 88; Arthur H. Cole, 'Cyclical and Seasonal Variations in the Sale of Public Lands, 1816–60', *Review of Economic Statistics* 9, no. 1 (Jan. 1927): 41.
22. See Andréas Andréadès, *Histoire de la Banque d'Angleterre*, 2 vols. (Paris: Rousseau, 1904), 2: 17.
23. Wirth, *Geschichte der Handelskrisen*, 145–46.

particularly during a period of increasing prices when it is as easy to sell as it is to buy, as was the case from 1834 to 1836.[24]

The stock exchange also benefitted from the growth period, but speculation had developed so feverishly that in 1835 a crisis occurred; although this crisis left English production and consumption unscathed. It occurred following the issue of a series of loans, in particular Spanish and Portuguese, in 1833 and 1834. After having been very sought after by the public, they ended up being abandoned for industrial investments. A crash followed in which the market dropped, but commodity prices, production and consumption continued to rise, and the stock market soon regained confidence. The value of London to Liverpool railway shares soon exceeded par value; the success of the Liverpool to Manchester line excited the public's enthusiasm; capital investments were directed toward industry, the railways in particular, at a frantic pace; and all railway shares ended over par.

B.) Crisis and depression

The rapid upward trend was short lived. The first symptoms of the disruption of economic equilibrium were manifest in the balance of trade. In the United States in 1836, imports had exceeded exports by $50 million. To resolve this deficit, silver or gold metal had to be exported. On 10 July 1836, a letter by President Jackson authorized the sale of land against metal currency. The government presented the banknotes in its coffers for reimbursement. Gold immediately became an incredibly sought-after commodity. Banknotes depreciated, sometimes by 10 to 20 per cent. Frightened clients withdrew their deposits. Prices dropped; bankruptcies followed relentlessly; and as a result, exporters in England lost $5 to $6 million.[25]

Thus, the crisis had repercussions in England, where the discount rate had to be raised to stop its gold from fleeing to America. In May 1836, the exchange rate with the United States, hitherto favourable to England, became unfavourable. English gold beat a path to New York. In August, the Bank of England raised its discount from 4 to 4.5 per cent, and then in September, to 5 per cent. By November gold exports had stopped. Nevertheless, gold continued to flow from the coffers of the Bank of England. An 'external drain' was followed by an 'internal drain'. In England, the increase in production, consumption and prices and the expansion of credit were followed by an extremely serious depression. Not only were there fewer *exports* to the United States – English exports dropped from £12 million in 1836 to £4.7 million in 1837 – but *less was being produced* in England. The ensuing price debacle began in November1838, increased in severity by the end of 1836 and continued through the course of 1837. In November 1836 and July 1837, prices had dropped compared to those of July 1836 (see tab. 1.1).

---

24. Arthur H. Cole, 'Statistical Background of the Crisis of 1837–1842', *Review of Economic Statistics* 10, no. 4 (Nov. 1928): 182.
25. Wirth, *Geschichte der Handelskrisen*, 161.

Table 1.1 Percentage Decrease in Commodity Prices Since July 1836

	By Nov. 1936 (%)	*By July 1837* (%)
Cotton	26	45
Lead	11	33
Cast iron	13	44
Copper	7	29
Sugar	11	20
Tobacco	11	31

No source given.

This drop in prices signalled many bankruptcies or suspensions of payment in the commercial and industrial world.[26]

Under these circumstances, a credit crisis emerged that encouraged the 'internal drain' by 9 November 1836. On 7 November, the Ulster and Belfast Bank suspended their payments; on 9 November, so did the large Agricultural and Commercial Bank of Ireland; and little by little, the panic spread to the other Irish banks. They could not cover the ever-growing requests for the reimbursement of banknotes and the parallel withdrawal of deposits. Faced with this constriction of the money market, they quite naturally turned to the most stable institution: the Bank of England, which found itself in demand from all sides. Learning from the experience of 1825, the Bank of England came to the rescue of banks and merchants in need as much as possible; at the end of November in particular, it rescued the Northern and Central Bank, whose demise would have been a real disaster liable to engulf the Bank of England itself in its wake. However, if the Bank of England was very generous in dispensing credit, it was very strict in demanding payment for its services. For the first time, it resorted to the policy of raising the discount rate with the now very clear intention of protecting its cash on hand, which reached a low point of £3.9 million on 6 December 1836.

A depression of such magnitude could not happen without a reduction in profits and incomes in general.

The working class was severely affected, particularly in the iron industry, where the percentage of unemployed in the foundries rose from 5.4 and 5 per cent in 1835 and 1836, respectively, to 12.4 per cent in 1837.[27] The crisis was the occasion for bitter strikes: in 1836, the Staffordshire strike involved 40,000 workers; at Preston, 15,000 were involved; and it was the same at Lancashire and Yorkshire.

However, as early as 1837, the crisis was entering its final phase, which was proceeding normally when the fall of three great banking houses involved in American speculation renewed the crisis's intensity. This new collapse of the international market came as the result of the mistakes of a financier who has since become famous – Nicholas Biddle – the director of the Bank of the United States. Two things had concerned him:

26. The number of bankruptcies in England and Wales, which had diminished between 1831 and 1836, reached 1,950 in 1837, a 64% increase on the figure for 1836.

27. Webb, *Histoire du trade unionisme*, 178–79.

the fall in prices, especially that of cotton, and the flight of gold; and for him, these were the cause of the whole crisis. The remedy was therefore simple: raise prices, bring back the gold.

In order to trigger a rise in cotton prices, Biddle secured a monopoly on the product through a large issuing of notes from the Bank of the United States. He bought the crops of his countrymen at high prices, and then, with the might of his monopoly behind him, he stood before the Europeans, threatening to deprive them of the raw materials if they did not consent to the terms of sale arbitrarily set by him. French and English manufacturers submitted to his demands, leading Biddle to believe for the moment that he had won: in 1837, £37 million in European gold was on its way to the United States.

Cotton, it is true, was not the only claim the United States had on Europe. Biddle had also used the stock market crisis of 1836 to build up a portfolio of depreciated securities: bank shares, mining shares and so on. Then, thanks to skilful manoeuvres, he moved them to the London Stock Exchange. From there, a new claim was made on England.

But such dealings were far too artificial to have remained useful in the long term. Confidence reappeared only for a moment before giving way to a marked mistrust.

The increase in cotton prices had led to higher prices for manufactured goods, and the rise in textile prices had limited consumption. Stocks of imported cotton piled up in the warehouses of French and English ports; soon manufacturers were able to hold firm in the face of Biddle's demands. Prices dropped again, particularly at Le Havre. Facing the weakness of the cotton market, the Hottinger firm of Paris, in business with Biddle, refused to continue its dealings with him; it even objected to Biddle's signature, and its example was followed by the Hope firm of Amsterdam.

This was the sign of a terrible debacle, first in the United States, then in London. In America, the paper money that had gone into circulation was at saturation point and depreciating, losing up to 20, 25 and even 30 per cent of its value. The prices of products and securities collapsed. And, as London had a large stock of them in its portfolio, the London Stock Exchange was suddenly inundated with unsaleable paper. Some $150 million worth of European capital perished in the storm. The total loss was estimated at $400 million, and 33,000 businesses went bankrupt. On 1 January 1839, the cash on hand at the Bank of England was still £9 million; by 3 January, it was no more than £2.4 million. Feeling threatened, the bank did not hesitate to raise its discount rate. For the first time, the bank used the privilege granted by the Bank of England Act of 1833 to exceed the legal rate of interest and increased its discount rates from 5 to 6 per cent, and its situation immediately improved.

Once the storm had passed, the resolution of the crisis proceeded slowly and painfully.

The working class was especially hard hit by the resurgence of the crisis, and in 1840, the percentage of unemployed men in the foundries, after having dropped from 12.4 in 1837 down to 10.5 in 1838 and 11.8 in 1839, suddenly rose again to 14.8 in 1840 and 18.5 in 1841. Tempers ran high among the working class, and serious disturbances broke out, as well as bloody conflicts in the streets. The economic malaise provoked a violent, almost revolutionary political movement.

The English people, in the depths of misery, demanded political rights and universal male suffrage, a secret ballot, the suppression of tax quotas for voting rights, equality in conscription and the yearly re-election of members of the House of Commons.[28] In short, they called for a charter which, by giving political power to the working class, would allow it to make laws in its favour. Hence the name Chartism was given to this movement. One social reform in particular was called for loud and clear: the abolition of the Assistance Act of 1834. The 1834 law, passed under the influence of Malthusian theories, had treated poverty almost as a crime to be atoned for in workhouses that strikingly resembled prisons. Chartists held meetings that became public events; they organized massive demonstrations in the streets, where long lines of demonstrators marched together, holding banners with revolutionary slogans.

In the light of this distress of the working class, it was not surprising to note a decline in the number of marriages and an increase in the number of crimes, particularly between 1840 and 1842 – that is, during the most extreme years of the depression. According to the statistics established by Tugan-Baranowsky for industrial counties, the number of marriages dropped from 192 per 10,000 inhabitants in 1836 to 157 in 1842; while the number of criminals rose from 152 per 100,000 inhabitants in 1836 to 239 in 1841 and 265 in 1842. In these same counties, public assistance saw its expenditures increase. The sums dispensed went from £0.135 per inhabitant in 1836 to £0.216 in 1842.

§5. – The crisis of 1847

The depression that followed the 1836 crisis had revealed the need for a general revision of production costs. On the other hand, significant technical progress had been made thanks to new discoveries. The process of using coke to produce cast iron became widespread for the first time. Thanks to the steam hammer, it was now possible to forge parts of considerable size, such as very powerful drive shafts. The construction of rolling mills had been improved, and the moulding of cast iron was perfected, so much so that cast iron could be used for floors, frames, iron and sheet metal structures, railway pipes and cast-iron bridges. All this pointed to a bright future for the iron industry.[29]

However, in 1842 and 1843, the capitalists were still regrouping. A conversion of the interest rate drew them out of their reserve. English Consols at 3½, representing capital of £248,759,627, or more than 6.2 billion francs, were lowered to 3¼ not convertible for a 10-year period. Only £103,352 was submitted for reimbursement; the operation was an admirable success.[30]

---

28. Tugan-Baranowsky, *Theorie und Geschichte der Handelskrisen*, 309–11; Edouard Dolléans, *Le Chartisme*, 2 vols. (Paris: Floury, 1911); and Eugène Buret, *Essai sur la misère des classes laborieuses en France et en Angleterre*, 2 vols. (Paris: Chez Paulin, 1840), and the abundant bibliography by Buret (awarded the memorial prize by the Académie des Sciences morales et politiques).
29. Adolphe-Gustave Blaise, 'Exposition nationale de l'industrie agricole et manufacturière', *Annuarie de l'économie politique et de la statistique* 7 (1850): 204; 'Statistique de l'industrie minérale', *Annuaire de l'économie politique et de la statistique* 3 (1846): 241–42.
30. Paul Leroy-Beaulieu, *Traité de la science des Finances*, 2: 507–8.

Annuitants, however, were less taken in, and they soon looked for better returns on their capital investments, which they found in the railway industry. From 1844 to 1847, this industry experienced remarkable growth in France and in England.

A.) Growth

Since 1838, when the French government had granted concessions to three railway lines that all had performed poorly, France had stayed away from such undertakings.[31] No concession was sought from 1840 to 1842. The law of 11 June 1842 intervened, combining the efforts of the state, industry and local authorities. In 1845, 2,000 km had already been conceded, and 750 million francs had been committed or spent; nevertheless, concessions for new lines were granted: the Bordeaux to Cette line, 326 km; Dijon to Mulhouse, 300 km; and the Western network, 1,067 km. In total: 1693 km. In 1847, 1,247 km of railway lines had been constructed, and another 2,433 km were under construction, under concession or awarded.[32]

The metal industry followed a parallel course of development. The number of newly constructed factories grew, particularly in 1846 and 1847.[33] In 1846, Hayange founded a subsidiary plant with three blast furnaces at Forbach; at Decazeville and Le Creusot, formerly decommissioned blast furnaces were reopened; at Montluçon, the number of blast furnaces increased to four. Denain doubled its production from 6,000 to 12,000 tonnes. In Alais, workshops were expanded, and the number of rolling mills increased. New factories were being built. Rails were being produced at Pont-Audemer and Marquise with English coal. All of a sudden, a factory with six blast furnaces, colossal for that period, was erected on the coalfield at Commentry.[34] Unfortunately, efforts to fill the deficit in metal production had to some extent produced the opposite effect, at least for the time being. The deficit, according to Léon Faucher, reached 140,000 tonnes in 1846–47 for rails alone.[35] It was again with the help of iron production in particular that the grandiose extension projects would be realized.

This new industry was created from scratch by means of issuing shares. On 30 December 1847, 2,491 million francs of shares were issued, and the railways represented real capital valued at 1,232 million francs.[36]

Quite frequently, only part of the nominal capital had been paid. This practice quickly became an instrument of speculation. The first companies had shown very favourable results, and their share prices increased. Railway shares were issued, and

31. Adolphe-Gustave Blaise, 'Le chemins de fer en 1845', *Annuaire de l'économie politique et de la statistique* 3 (1846): 266–67; and Blaise, 'Les chemins de fer et le crédit', *Journal des économistes* 18, no. 69 (Aug.–Nov.1847): 46.
32. Adolphe-Gustave Blaise, 'Le chemins de fer en 1846', *Annuaire de l'économie politique et de la statistique* 4 (1847): 109.
33. Blaise, 'Exposition nationale', 205–6; and Blaise, 'Les chemins de fer et le crédit', 46.
34. Léon Faucher, 'Du monopole des fers', *Journal des économistes* 14, no. 56 (July 1846): 317.
35. Ibid., 345.
36. J. Lobet, 'Les chemins de fer', *Annuaire de l'économie politique et de la statistique* 5 (1848): 290.

railway companies were created for the sole purpose of realizing capital gains on the stock market. This was speculation's role in the boom.

England had followed an identical course, with the same craze for the creation of new railways and a similar deluge of shares and joint-stock companies.[37] According to Wirth, the railway mania started in 1844; that is, as we have noted above, in the same year the great conversion from 3½ to 3¼ took place. In a single session in 1844, Parliament authorized the construction of 85 lines covering 1,795 miles (2,385 km), and 1844 marked the beginning of a veritable construction fever.[38] Given the handsome profits realized by the first railways, capital flowed toward such investments; and 1845 surpassed even 1844 with 1,800 miles conceded.

In 1846, the work begun in 1844 continued; 519 bills of concession were requested, and 213 were granted. A further 5,800 miles of railway remained to be built.[39] Completion was eagerly anticipated within three years. Construction of all the proposed lines would have required £40 million per year.[40]

The mining and metal industries benefitted greatly from this boom. Liverpool, Manchester, Leeds and Lancaster were experiencing an unprecedented period of prosperity.[41]

Table 1.2 Railway Concessions Granted by Parliament, 1844–1849 (millions of £)

	Value of Concessions	*Amounts Actually Paid*
1844	20.4	6.7
1845	60.5	16.2
1846	131.7	37.8
1847	44.2	40.7
1848	15.3	33.2
1849	3.9	29.6

No source given.

The brilliant growth of the railways and the mining and metal industries was accompanied by great prosperity in the textile industry. In 1846, however, the latter was suffering from the high cost of cotton, and this slowed down the industry's development. Nevertheless, cotton consumption was increasing: it went from 274,790 in 1845 to 278,377 in 1846 in England; and in France, it grew from 58,892 (1,000s of kg) in 1844 to 64,227 in 1846.[42]

37. Wirth, *Geschichte der Handelskrisen*, 203–5.
38. Blaise, 'Les chemins de fer en 1846', 122–23.
39. 'Les chemins de fer anglais', *Annuaire de l'économie politique et de la statistique* 4 (1847): 296.
40. Léon Faucher, 'La crise financière dans la Grande-Bretagne', *Journal des économistes* 18, no. 72 (1847): 315.
41. 'Les chemins de fer anglais', 295.
42. See the table, 'Situation des manufacturiers du Royaume-Uni en 1850 et en 1856', *Annuaire de l'économie politique et de la statistique* 16 (1859): 405. For France, see 'Consommation du cotton

Agriculture, on the other hand, contrasted with industry, and in 1845–46, England and France suffered one of their worst harvests; poor crops necessitated a reliance on imports. Stimulated in England by industrial growth and the abolition of tariffs, cereal imports rose from 2,162,644 quarters in 1845 to 3,614,466 in 1846; flours increased from 953,258 to 3,356,823. In France, the importation of foodstuffs rose from 187.6 million francs in 1845 to 254 in 1846 and to 364.4 in 1847.[43]

In the presence of such pressing demand, a price increase was inevitable. In general, though, it did not affect all products in the same way and affected the products of the metal industry in particular.

In France, where the increase in demand for the products of the metal industry had been strengthened by the artificial limitation of supply by means of an almost prohibitive customs tariff, the price rise had an enormous impact. Faucher, an economist of that period, estimated the deficit of our metal production, compared to the demand for rails alone, at 14,000 tonnes.[44] Hence our need to import iron, whether raw or manufactured; however, the duties in force from 1841 to 1847 amounted to 70 per cent of the value of the product for cast iron and 110 per cent for iron. The increase in the price of rails was enormous. Whereas in 1845 factory owners or farmers of factories were happy to sell their rails for 320 francs per tonne, by 1846 the Compagnie de Dieppe and that of Nantes were paying 385 francs for theirs, and soon rails were valued at 400 francs per tonne.

In England, the price increase was no less strong; Sauerbeck's statistics are very convincing in that respect (see tab. A1). In the presence of this increase in the quantity and value of trade activity, a parallel development of the instrument of exchange was inevitable. The demand for discounting became more pressing, and along with demand, the discount rate rose at the Banque de France, the Bank of England or on the open market. The 1836 and 1839 crises had directed the attention of the British Parliament toward the practices of banks of issue. Some theorists had claimed that crises arose from excessive banknote issuance: a crisis was the drop in prices following an excessive rise, and the excessive rise in prices resulted from excessive banknote issuance, according to the application of the quantitative theory. The remedy for crises was therefore to be found in an intelligent organization of banknote issues and in the suppression of the abuses to which the [excessive] issuance had hitherto given rise. The Bank Charter Act of 1844 consequently demanded an almost rigorous equation between the metal reserves and the banknotes in circulation. Despite this reform, the industrial boom led to greater reliance on the Bank of England, and its portfolio steadily swelled between 1843 and 1847. But alongside the healthy, normal credit resulting from increased trade activity, there quickly developed another form of credit that was, if not outright dishonest, at least reckless. The Royal Bank of Liverpool, with capital of £600,000, had found a way

---

en France, de 1830 à 1859', *Annuaire de l'économie politique et de la statistique* 18 (1861): 172–74; and see the second edition of the present work, p. 48.

43. Horace Say, 'Crise financière et commerciale', *Journal des économistes* 20, no. 77 (April 1848): 23.

44. Faucher, 'La crise financière dans la Grande-Bretagne', 315.

of advancing to a single firm the nearly equal sum of £500,000.[45] Others resorted to no less dangerous practices: they locked up [*immobilisaient*] the capital their depositors had entrusted to them in investments. This is how Scottish banks lent their depositors' money to the railways. The operation was so profitable as to be contagious. New banks were created in Glasgow, Edinburgh, Aberdeen and Dundee to engage in this particularly lucrative kind of operation, at the same time, moreover, that they were discounting commercial paper.[46]

The stock exchange was also experiencing a period of great prosperity and feverish activity. Naturally, speculation was in the mix and, as early as 1845, produced a crash, though this was only an isolated stock market crisis. In 1844, many shares had been issued, all of which had yielded strong capital gains; so many had been issued that the number of brokers had risen from 12 in 1844 to 300 in 1845 in the city of Leeds alone, and the number of transfers reached 1,500 to 2,000 daily; that was more than half a million pounds in stock exchange transactions alone.[47] When in October 1845 the number of speculative purchases was such that sellers outnumbered buyers, a crash ensued. Stock prices fell, at least for a while. Not for long, however, because railway profits were still satisfactory, and despite the rapidly expanding network, profits per mile continued to increase profits, rising from £3,280 in 1844 to £3,470 in 1845 and remained quite satisfactory at £3,300 in 1846.[48]

Under these conditions, profits were rising, and in England the ratio of earnings to capital invested increased from 8.2 in 1842 to 8.8 in 1844 and to 9 in 1845 and 1846.[49] In France, the progression was similar, if not greater, and in 1847, the net earnings per kilometre rose from 8,857 francs in 1842 to 22,735 in 1847.

The capitalists were not the only ones to benefit from increased incomes: the working class experienced increased demand for its labour, and with greater demand came higher wage rates. In France, the number of workers employed in the construction of railways was estimated at 780,000 in 1847.[50] The number of workers employed in the production of cast iron, iron and steel increased from 32,083 in 1841 to 37,997 in 1846.

B.) Crisis and depression

This brilliant economic growth would not last long.

45. Wirth, *Geschichte der Handelskrisen*, 214.
46. Thomas Tooke and William Newmarch, *Die Geschichte und Bestimmung der Preise während der Jahre 1793–1857*, vol. 2, trans. C. W. Asher (Dresden: Rudolf Kunze, 1859), 178. The original six-volume English edition of this work, which had become very rare, was reprinted in 1928 by P. S. King, London.
47. Armand Audiganne, 'La crise commerciale et la Banque d'Angleterre', *Revue des deux mondes* 18, no. 1 (April 1847): 164.
48. Thomas Tooke and William Newmarch, *A History of Prices and the State of Circulation from 1793 to 1856*, vol. 5 (London: Longman, Brown, Green and Longman, 1857), 352.
49. 'Les chemins de fer anglais', *Annuaire de l'économie politique et de la statistique* 4 (1847): 295.
50. Blaise, 'Les chemins de fer et le crédit', 53.

From 1843 to 1847, still more kilometres of railways had been built. Work commenced in 1848, but by 1849 the depression was serious, and the years 1848 to 1851 saw a production depression in the mining and metal industries.

Why did railway construction cease?

In France as in England, the reason was twofold: first, government policies toward the railways and, second, the increased cost of doing business and the errors in the forecasts and estimates.

The law of 11 June 1842 anticipated in effect the financial and technical collaboration of the French state in the construction of railways, and from 1843 to 1844, the French state stayed true to its promises, granting its support to the new companies. But as soon as the latter appeared to be self-sufficient, the government increased the companies' outlays and diminished its own. The state imposed free services and proposed the construction of often improvised new spur lines in the middle of a discussion, without even knowing if the projects were likely to be carried out.[51] It withdrew first partly then totally the assistance it had previously granted them; it reduced the duration of the concessions and lowered tariffs,[52] so much so that as early as 1846, Adolphe Blaise could write:

> The government has introduced such strict clauses into its new specification and, at the same time, placed such restriction on the duration of the concessions that, unless there is a parallel development of rail traffic, for which no line has yet provided an example, and of discoveries *capable of reducing operating costs by half*, the great majority of railways left to be conceded will be enterprises beneficial to the country but disastrous for those in charge of them.[53]

Prophetic words, especially since a second factor strengthened the action of the first: the rise in prices, wages, discounts and interest skewed (quite seriously) the estimates contained in industry forecasts. In 1847, Blaise estimated that the cost projection based on the prices paid two years prior had to be increased by a proportion of at least one-third.[54] And as prices rose, it was becoming increasingly more difficult to find the money needed to continue the work; a company in this situation would resort to subterfuge to circumvent the law limiting the interest rate to 5 per cent and issue bonds at 6 per cent.

Despite all these symptoms of crisis, the public remained confident. In France, news of the suspension of work on the Paris to Lyons line opened its eyes. The same company, after having actively pressed on with its work, almost completing the stretch from Paris to Tonnerre, suddenly announced that it was stopping work. The total cost, originally estimated at 200 million francs, would in reality rise to more than 300 million.[55] A

51. Ibid., 46.
52. The average rate per tonne per kilometre was 21 francs in 1843, 11.51 in 1844 and 11.12 in 1845. An increase to 11.39 was reported in 1846, a figure lower than that of 1844, which was to remain stable until 1851. *Annuaire statistique de la France* (1903): R., p. 68.
53. Blaise, 'Les chemins de fer en 1845', 268.
54. Blaise, 'Les chemins de fer en 1846', 121.
55. André Cochut, 'De la crise des chemins de fer', *Revue des deux mondes* 18, no. 5 (June 1847): 932–33.

dividend of 6 to 7 per cent had been anticipated at the company's creation; the concession project report even hinted at the hope for 14.5 million in earnings, which for a capital investment of 200 million francs would represent a dividend of 7 to 8 per cent.[56] Suddenly, shareholders were alerted to the need for a new loan of 100 million francs and a reduction of their dividend to 4 per cent.[57] A debacle ensued that little by little spread to all lines and all railway securities. Not only did the shareholders refuse to respond to the calls for funds, but they also rushed to the stock exchange to sell the now suspect shares at all costs. Whether they had been undertaken safely or unsafely, based on exact or inaccurate estimates, all of the railway companies fell into the same disrepute.[58]

No new concessions were granted in 1848, 1849 or 1850. During those three years, several railways even had to be placed in receivership or bought by the state. On 30 November 1848, the Bordeaux to La Teste line was placed in receivership, as were the Marseilles to Avignon line, on 21 November, the Paris to Orléans line, on 4 April, and the Paris to Sceaux line, on 29 December.[59]

England was also experiencing similar accounting errors. In the face of public enthusiasm for railways, Parliament expanded on the clauses of the rules governing concessions; it stipulated the lowering of transport prices as soon as profits reached a certain figure; it was stricter and more meticulous in its examination of projects submitted; it demanded of new projects, not a simple first draft, but a complete financial plan, with sketches and estimates supporting it. These precautions proved useless. The fulfilment of these magnificent projects did not go without causing severe miscalculations, however. For the 107 railways authorized by the English Parliament, the capital budgeted was 1,040,570,350 francs; however, an additional 404,140,750 francs were needed to complete their construction – an excess of nearly half of the projected cost. One can easily imagine the effect that such surprises had on the profitability of English companies, on the minds of their shareholders and on the public at large. Not only did construction costs increase but the returns per mile were decreasing, as less productive rail lines were undertaken. The profit per mile dropped from £3,300 in 1846 to £2,780 in 1847, to £2,460 in 1848 and even as low as £2,080 in 1850.

The railway crisis soon had repercussions for the mining and metal industries, and the latter were all the more profoundly affected by the loss of their best customer at a time when they had considerably increased their production capacity.

Steel production dropped in colossal proportions in France as well as in England. In order not to overload our analysis with numbers, we will only provide the figures for

56. Michel Chevalier, 'Des forces alimentaires des états et de la crise actuelle', *Revue des deux mondes* 18, no. 5 (June 1847): 911.
57. Cochut, 'De la crise des chemins de fer', 930–31.
58. Thus, the lines linking Montereau to Troyes, the two branches on the Paris to Le Havre line, at Dieppe and Fécamp, the forecasted costs of which had not been exceeded, appealed in vain for funds on the shares already subscribed.
59. M. Magne, 'Situation des chemins de fer en 1854', *Annuaire de l'économie politique et de la statistique* 12 (1855): 634–42.

France. The reader may easily supplement these with the ones for England, an industrial country par excellence, where the railway fever had been more intense than in France.

The output of the coal mines fell from 51,532,000 metric quintals (q.m.) in 1847 to 40,004,000 in 1848 and to 40,492,000 in 1849. Imports of 25,487,000 q.m. fell to 21,437,000 in 1848 and rose slightly to 23,939,000 q.m. in 1849.[60]

In 1847, coal consumption had been 78,488,000 q.m., and of this figure, two-thirds had been consumed by industrial factories, around one-fifth by the transport industries (railways, steamboats, etc.) and one-fifth by domestic consumption. In 1848, consumption was a mere 60,952,000 q.m., which was 15,535,700 [*sic*] less than that of 1847, and almost all of the decline in demand had been for the types of coal needed in industrial factories and for domestic heating; thus, industry and the working classes were most affected. No doubt the Revolution played a role in this drop in coal consumption, the best proof of which was its recovery to 64,054,800 q.m. in 1849. Still, this figure remained less than that of 1847, and industrial factories only accounted for an insignificant share of this increase.

The depression hit the mining industry hard and the iron industry even harder. Coal is of course necessary for the production of rails and wagons, and so it will keep the railway as a customer. In 1849, the transport industry accounted for the increase in coal consumption. Iron, on the other hand, mainly necessary for railway construction, ceases to have the latter as a significant customer after the work is completed. There is a great difference between the initial expense of construction and that of maintenance.

It was thus that the iron ore mines' production dropped suddenly from 34,636,940 q.m. in 1847 to 17,664,004 q.m. in 1849. In 1850, production recovered slightly to 18,211,698 q.m. before dropping again to 17,743,737 the following year. The mines employed fewer miners, whose numbers dropped from 15,069 in 1847 to 10,214 in 1849, with only a small increase to 10,386 in 1850. It is nonetheless remarkable to see a smaller decrease in the number of workers than in production levels; this was due to the fact that the bosses, instead of sacking their workers, were having them work shorter hours.

The production of cast iron and of iron in particular also declined by enormous proportions. The production decrease mainly affected the most expensive forms of cast iron and iron, that is, cast iron and charcoal iron. The crisis had the effect of accelerating a process that had already begun during the growth period: a shift toward the growing use of coke in the production of raw materials of the metal industry. Any period of crisis marks the beginning of a general revision of cost prices [*prix de revient*].[ii] Similarly, rolling mills and iron casting were being improved to such an extent that Blaise, commenting on the years 1848 and 1849, could conclude 'that they had not been totally unproductive' and that 'if national production had suffered severely, it had drawn from this ordeal an energetic resistance that had led to often successful improvements and cost-saving measures'.[61]

60. 'Industrie minérale de la France, 1847–1852', *Annuaire de l'économie politique et de la statistique* 10 (1853): 225, 227.

61. Blaise, 'Exposition nationale', 204.

Steel itself, at that time still a long way from securing the pre-eminent position it enjoys today, was experiencing hard times.

The depression in the iron industry would have been even more sudden and more intense if, at the onset of the crisis, the fulfilment of long-term contracts concluded during the boom had not given the forges a semblance of activity. The *départments* of Moselle and Côte-d'Or in particular fulfilled a considerable number of rail orders for the Lyon to Strasbourg railway after the outbreak of the crisis; as a result, their factories maintained almost complete employment. But everywhere else, there was total unemployment: new orders were completely lacking. In 1847, France produced 887,464 q.m. of rails; in 1848, 412,426; in 1850, 230,873; and in 1851, 271,980. Thus, in 1850, rail production was one-quarter that of 1847.

The consumption and production of consumer goods were affected: the textile industry, already depressed in 1847 by the high price of cotton, continued to decline from 1848 to 1850. In France, after gradually increasing to 64,227 (1,000s of kg) in 1846, cotton consumption fell to 45,542 in 1847 and to 44,904 in 1848.

The year 1847 was a good one for agriculture, and 1848 would have been equally favourable, at least for agriculture, had it not been for the Revolution. That agriculture can remain prosperous in the midst of an industrial depression is a fact worth remembering.

The crisis of 1847 was characterized by a decrease in production and consumption, as well as by the fall of prices and, in particular, the fall in the prices of cast iron and iron. The price for iron cast with coke (100 kg) went from 14.20 francs in 1847 to 10.80 francs in 1850; and the price of coke iron went from 36 francs to 25.30 francs in the same years.[62]

If the metal industry had been hit especially hard, it was not alone in this predicament, and the period from 1847 to 1850 was characterized by a general decline in prices. Alongside this slowdown in trade, in the number and value of exchanges, a most severe circulation crisis was unfolding in France and in England. In fact, we might even call it a double circulation crisis; for in truth, the year 1847 was marked by two distinct circulation crises: one at the beginning of the year and the other in the autumn.

The first currency crisis [*crise monétaire*] of 1847 occurred due to circumstances independent of industrial growth. The second, on the other hand, was the normal crisis that always accompanies a general economic crisis.

The years 1845 and 1846 had been bad from an agricultural point of view; the price of corn had risen in enormous proportions, as had the price of cotton. England and France had to appeal more widely than usual to the outside world and pay higher prices. Hence, a disequilibrium occurred in the balance of accounts. By January 1847, gold began to flow from England and France. The Bank of England and the Banque de France witnessed a gradual decrease in their cash holdings relative to the growth of their portfolio. Based on its success in 1837, raising the discount rate appeared to be

62. 'Industrie minérale en France, 1847–1852', *Annuaire de l'économie politique et de la statistique* 12 (1855): 258.

the appropriate remedy for the exchange crisis. The experience of 1847 provided vivid confirmation of these ideas.

In January 1847, the Banque de France and the Bank of England simultaneously raised their discount rate, the former, from 4 to 5 per cent on 14 January, and the latter, from 3 to 3.5 per cent on the same day, and then to 4 per cent on 21 January. From 2 January to 10 April 1847, however, the portfolio grew from £15,071,000 to £18,127,000, while the cash on hand shrank from £14,952,000 to £9,814,000. The decrease in cash holdings was even greater than the growth of the portfolio. A particular circumstance added to the bank's embarrassment: railway companies, already lacking the funds necessary to continue their construction work, proceeded to gradually withdraw their deposits from the Bank of England as early as February.[63] Also, on 10 April the discount rate was increased to 5 per cent. The effect of this measure was almost instantaneous: cash on hand [*l'encaisse*] recovered immediately, and by 5 June, it had already reached £10.2 million, and then, £10.4 million by 3 July. The reserve [*La réserve*] was also growing, and after having dropped to £2.7 million on 1 May 1847, it rapidly rose to £5.1 million by 5 June and to £5.2 million by 2 July.

In France, the exchange crisis had been less persistent, and even though between 1 July 1846 and 15 January 1847 the Banque de France's cash position had fallen from 252 million to 78 million francs (corn imports, primarily from Russia, had reached 209 million francs), the situation improved rapidly from January under the influence of the increased discount rate and because of the purchase by the emperor of Russia of 50 million francs worth of French government securities. The cash on hand recovered, reaching 110 million francs by 16 March. The monetary crisis had ended. In July, the situation seemed reassuring with the announcement of an excellent harvest. The situation would deteriorate again in October, as a new crisis emerged. After the liquidations of some bullish corn buyers, gold was again leaving the coffers of the banks of issue bound for the United States, but mostly the gold was taken out for domestic markets. As we have already seen in 1825 and 1837, the 'external drain' was followed by an 'internal drain'.

The 1847 crisis, like those that preceded it, precipitated a withdrawal of deposits, the classic 'run' on the banks and an enormous demand for credit. The discount rate on the open market in London reached up to 9, 10 and 12 per cent in October 1847.[64]

Panic ensued. The Royal Bank of Liverpool with capital of £620,000 had advanced £520,000 to a single client; it fell on 19 October, followed by the Liverpool Banking Company on 26 October. Soon after, the bank failures spread to Manchester, Newcastle and the entire West of the country; the North and South Wales Banking Company, the Union Bank of Newcastle and a whole host of other provincial banks fell successively into bankruptcy.

---

63. A Parliamentary enquiry on the 1847 crisis in England: *Extraits des Enquêtes Parlementaires anglaise sur les questions de banque, de circulation monétaire et de crédit*, vol. 4, *Enquête 1848 sur la crise commerciale de 1847*, ed. and trans. Paul Coullet and Clément Juglar (Paris: Furne and Guillaumin, 1865), pt 2, no. 3304.

64. Juglar, *Des crises commerciales*, 350.

In the midst of the universal ruin, the Bank of England remained the one undisputed lending institution.[65] When called upon, the bank responded in the broadest way to requests for credit. James Morris estimated that, from 15 September to 15 November 1847, the Bank of England lent sums totalling £2.3 million to firms in distress.[66] Confined by the Bank Charter Act of 1844, however, it had to raise its discount rate or even limit credit. On 23 September, it raised its discount rate to 6 per cent and suspended its advances on Consols and government securities [*fonds d'État*]. Nevertheless, its portfolio was still growing; its cash on hand and reserves [*son encaisse, sa réserve*] diminished. On 23 October, it was feared that the bank would be forced to cease its operations because its excessive issuing of banknotes against its stock of gold was about to reach the figure set by the Act of 1844. Public opinion was getting nervous when, on 25 October, the Chancellor of the Exchequer wrote to the director of the Bank of England about increasing the number of discounts and advances, without, however, consenting to any at a rate of less than 8 per cent. In the event of a violation of the 1844 act, the chancellor agreed to obtain a bill of indemnity from Parliament.[67] The letter's effect was immediate. One could be confident about obtaining credit, all the credit necessary, even if it meant paying dearly for it. Little by little, the crisis was entering its final phase. The Bank of England did not even need to use the option it had recently been given by the Chancellor of the Exchequer's letter. The bank's portfolio gradually deflated, the cash on hand and the reserve [*l'encaisse et la réserve*] increased, and by December 1847, the discount had fallen to 6 per cent.

In France, the evolution of the crisis followed an identical path. From the end of August, the situation in France was influenced by the same causes that had affected England: withdrawal of deposits, immobilization of deposits, insolvent customers, industrial losses and an intense, internal credit crisis. The Caisse de Commerce et de l'Industrie, the largest French bank, which had been a joint-stock company since 1830, failed. A host of other provincial banks suspended their payments. The government and the Banque de France came to their rescue.

The government extended the due dates for payments and authorized the adjustment on normal paper without imposing fines for lack of stamp; finally, a *Comptoir National d'Escompte* was created in every town with the aim of extending credit. This measure helped to ease the statutory obstacle faced by the Banque de France in providing aid to commerce and industry: the need to discount exclusively on paper with three signatures. The newly founded *Comptoir National* overcame this difficulty by adding its signature to those of the payer and payee: the trader discounted his paper with the *Comptoir National*, which in turn re-discounted it [*réescomptait*] at the Banque de France.[68]

In addition to the re-discount, the crisis of 1847 led to the organization of the collateral loan. In France, the warrant and the receipt had no legal standing until 1848:

65. James Morris, quoted in *Enquête parlementaire anglaise*, vol. 4, *Enquête 1848 sur la crise commerciale de 1847*, pt 1, no. 12, p. 5.

66. Ibid., pt 2, nos. 2645–46, pp. 9–10.

67. *Annuaire de l'économie politique et de la statistique* 5 (1848): 395.

68. Say, 'La crise financière et commerciale', 19.

the government authorized 'merchants to deposit goods in customs warehouses and to receive a receipt which the English call warrants' (Decree of 21 March 1848); by special dispensation, the warrant would be equivalent to a signature at the counter of the *Comptoirs Nationaux d'Escompte.*

The Banque de France was thus able to lend French industry and commerce the strength of its aid and its credit. Its portfolio swelled considerably, rising from 224 million francs in April 1847 to 302 million in May 1848. Under the influence of the high discount rate, the cash on hand recovered, little by little, rising from 92 million in July 1847 to 169 million in December 1847. At the end of 1847, the situation had improved significantly. But in the meantime, the February Revolution intervened; the cash holdings diminished once again and in such proportions that the Banque had to ask the government to provide a fiat rate [*cours forcé*] for its banknotes. Banknote issuance grew rapidly from 242 million francs in December 1847 to 432 million in December 1848. By that point, the revolutionary storm had passed, and the crisis had entered its end phase. Cash holdings grew without interruption, reaching 626 million francs by 2 October 1851.

Circulation diminished with the needs of commerce, and the fiat rate could be abolished on 6 August 1850. The portfolio was reduced, dropping to 99 million francs in June 1850 and to 93 million in November 1851. In 1851, the crisis was over.

The stock exchange had also suffered an assault; the drop in railway shares had been colossal. The banks involved in railway share trading suffered the repercussions of the stock market crisis.

Tugan-Baranowsky estimated that, in England, the loss incurred by the capitalists as a result of the drop in railway shares was £180 million in December 1849. His reasoning was as follows: in December 1845 the cost of railways built was £100 million and, in 1849, £230 million. Yet in December 1845, the value of the railways on the stock exchange was £160 million, £60 million more than what they had actually cost. In December 1849, their value was only £110 million at their construction, so their shares had not only lost the added value of 1845 (that is, £60 million) but also represented £120 million less than had actually been spent; they therefore lost £120 million + £60 million = £180 million.

Table 1.3 Share Values of Several Railway Lines Listed on the London Stock Exchange

	London and N. Western	*Great Western*	*South Western*	*Midland*
1846	215	195	150	150
1847	196	150	180	130
1 Jan. 1848	150	105	120	107
1 July 1848	121	93	94	100
1 Jan. 1848	125	93	80	85
1 Jan. 1850	109	58	61	45

Source: Tooke and Newmarch, *Geschichte und Bestimmung der Preise*, 2: 175.

The same was true for France. The *Journal des économistes* estimated the loss suffered by the capitalists on railway shares at 488,307,500 francs: 'Thus, in 22 months, railway speculation had lost in total the enormous sum of 488,307,500 francs on 2,491,000 shares forming an equity capital of 1,239,900,000 francs.'[69] Such figures are self-explanatory (see tab. 1.4).

Table 1.4 Share Values of Several Railway Lines Listed on the Paris Stock Exchange

	Stock Market Price on 30 July 1846	*Difference in Decrease of 1847*
Saint-Germain	800	360
Orléans	1,248.75	18.25
Rouen	961.25	131.25
Marseille	562.50	482.50

Source: *Journal des économistes* 18, no.69 (Aug. 1847): 76–77.

Profits, wages and interest declined. 'Profits changed into likely, if not certain, ruin for its shareholders.'[70] Yesterday's rich man was today's poor man, and chance had worked to abruptly drop the great capitalists of yesterday back into the middle classes, or even into the ranks of the destitute. Hence the case of the English count, who gave all his assets to his creditors in return for an annuity, preferring life on £500 a year to suicide.[71]

The working classes were very hard hit too, so much so that the crisis was the signal for popular movements to advance a little in most countries: in England, there was a renewal of Chartism; in France, there was the Revolution of 1848, whose character was clearly working class and socialist.

In England from October 1847, unemployment was colossal, and the cost of living was still very high. At the end of October, the owners of the North Western railway line dismissed 2,500 workers and were preparing to make further cuts. In Lancashire, 10,000 workers were dismissed at once, and those who were still employed were only working half of the week and on a 'short-time' basis.[72] During the winter of 1847–48, 100,000 new workers were admitted to the workhouses, and the poor tax had to be increased to £1 million.[73]

In France, Blaise estimated that 780,000 workers were kicked to the curb when railway construction ground to a halt, and although the operation of the lines built before the crisis had created a new market for the workforce, its labour requirements could not be compared with that required by the previous work of excavation, ballasting, laying railway tracks and constructing their equipment.

Thus, unemployment, diminished working hours and the drop in wages hit the working classes hard, especially the workers in the mining and metal industries. The

69. *Journal des économistes* 18, no.69 (Aug. 1847): 76–77.
70. Blaise, 'Les chemins de fer et le crédit', 47.
71. Wirth, *Geschichte der Handelskrisen*, 223.
72. Gustave de Molinari, 'Crise financière et commerciale en Angleterre', *Journal des économistes* 17, no. 67 (June 1847): 275.
73. Wirth, *Geschichte der Handelskrisen*, 218; Tugan-Baranowsky, *Theorie und Geschichte der Handelskrisen*, 271.

number of workers in the iron mines went from 15,000 in 1847 to 10,200 in 1849; in the coal mines, from 34,800 to 32,000.[74]

For England, Tugan-Baranowsky's statistics for industrial areas are particularly conclusive: the number of marriages dropped from 211 to 200 per 10,000 inhabitants in 1845 and 1846, to 169 in 1847, 177 in 1848 and 189 in 1849. The number of criminals per 100,000 inhabitants, after having decreased from 265 in 1842 to 159 in 1845 and to 169 in 1946, suddenly increased to 187 in 1847 and to 205 in 1848.

In France, crime increased in 1847 compared to the previous year, especially the number of property crimes. The number of people accused of theft on the public roads increased by 52 per cent; that of robberies other than those on public roads or domestic theft, by 31 per cent. In 1847, 530 men were charged with stealing grain and flour; whereas the average annual number accused of such crimes had never been higher than 20 from 1841 to 1846.[75]

The crisis of 1847 exerted an enormous influence in the political domain.[76]

In Paris, 100,000 workers were unemployed.[77] Thus, the first decisions of the provisional government were as much economic as they were political. After proclaiming the Republic, the creation of the national workshops was immediately announced, and when on 25 February Lamartine read the declaration announcing this double reform to the people, it was the second reform that met with immense approval.[78] A whole series of measures followed animated by the same desire to relieve the suffering of the workers. A February decree stipulated that: firstly, 'items that had been pawned at the Mont-de-Piété since 1 February 1848, such as clothes, household linens, rags, etc., whose value was under 10 francs would be returned to the depositors'; and secondly, 'the Tuileries Palace would from now on be used as an asylum for disabled workers'.[79] Prison labour was banned. A decree on 28 February created a government commission for the workers based on Louis Blanc's proposal. The provisional government organized the national workshops, which opened on 9 March. By 15 March, their membership already numbered 6,000 workers; by 31 March, they had 30,000; and by the end of April, the number reached 100,000! The circumstances under which they were abolished by the National Assembly on 23 June 1848 are well-known.

Yet the most interesting trait of this working-class movement was its co-operative character. Under the influence of the theories by Buchez, Fourier and Proudhon, the

---

74. 'Industrie minérale de la France', *Annuaire de l'économie politique et de la statistique* 12 (1855): 246.
75. 'Compte rendu général de l'administration de la justice criminelle en France', *Annuaire de l'économie politique et de la statistique* 5 (1848): 125; 6 (1849): 155; and 7 (1850): 112–13.
76. Émile Levasseur, *Histoire des classes ouvrières et de l'industrie en France de 1789 à 1870*, 2nd ed., 2 vols. (Paris: Rousseau, 1901), 2: 340. See also: Anton Menger, *Le Droit au produit intégral du travail: Étude historique*, trans. Alfred Bonnet (Paris: Giard & Brière, 1900), 32; Karl Marx, *Die Klassenkämpfe in Frankreich, 1848–1850* (Berlin: Verlag der Expedition des *Vorwärts*, 1895), reprinted from *Die Neue Rheinische Zeitung*, 1850; and Édouard Dolléans, *Histoire du mouvement ouvrier, 1830–1871* (Paris: Colin, 1936).
77. Levasseur, *Histoire des classes ouvrières*, 2: 32, 456, 457.
78. Ibid., 2: 343.
79. Ibid., 2: 340.

co-operative idea made rapid progress, and the triumphant working-class revolution asked the government for a subsidy designed to fund production co-operatives. The government allocated three million francs, without achieving the desired results. Many working-class associations were created, and while some were successful, such as the pavers' co-operative, many failed. The moment was not right for such an experiment.

In England, the Chartist movement witnessed a revival. From 1843 to 1846, during the period of prosperity, Chartism had been eclipsed, only to be resurrected again with the return of the economic crisis. Beginning in the autumn of 1847, strikes, violent demonstrations and armed conflict with the army erupted across all the industrial regions of England. In the factories of Manchester, 18,516 workers were still fully employed; however, 12,198 were only working 'short time', and a further 10,341 remained unemployed. In Wigan, the situation was even worse: out of 20 factories, only one was operating as usual. Hence, everywhere workers held meetings and organized demonstrations against the new economic order. In Glasgow, the demonstrations took on a revolutionary tenor with chants from crowds of unemployed workers demanding 'Bread or Revolution'. Shops were looted, and clashes with the police were a common sight. On such favourable ground and with the added example of the February Revolution in France, Chartism was reborn in England. The Chartists held their congress on 4 April 1848 in an atmosphere of popular enthusiasm. The speeches from delegates were marked by extreme violence. Stephenson, the delegate of North Lancashire, spoke of the starving people who had to survive on charity in a general context of excessive wealth; other speakers reiterated the same 'leitmotiv' of unemployment, poverty and death for the working classes.[80] The situation was so serious and the distress of the people so great that even the *Times* itself was moved to confirm their claims. However, it offered a penetrating analysis of the causes of the Chartist renaissance, writing in an editorial of 24 April 1848: 'One can recognise as an axiom of English politics that every important political movement reveals a lack of work among the masses.'

On 10 April, O'Connor, one of the leaders of Chartist movement, had filed a new national petition with Parliament, the third measure of its kind. It announced that a Chartist demonstration of 100,000 people would follow. Immediately, troops from all the districts of England were called to London; batteries were set up in Woolwich. More than 150,000 people frightened by the demonstrations offered to join the police force. Revolution was in the air, and there was fear that the contagion of revolution would spread from France to England. Nothing of the sort took place, however, and Chartism soon devolved into the ridiculous. The 100,000-person demonstration that had been announced in the petition with so much noise barely gathered 10,000 individuals, who marched in peaceful procession careful to avoid any clashes with the troops. Meanwhile, a parliamentary commission was examining the petition more closely and found among the 5,700,000 signatures names such as Queen Victoria and the Duke of Wellington. Little by little Chartism was losing ground. Nonetheless, Chartist meetings and demonstrations lasted as long as the depression.

---

80. See Tugan-Baranowsky, *Theorie und Geschichte der Handelskrisen*, 347–49.

Thus, the brilliant growth period from 1844 to 1847 came to an abrupt halt in both France and England. A period of growing production and consumption, stemming from a veritable fever for railway ventures, was suddenly replaced by one of decline, which, in England and France, was complicated by a serious political crisis.

But by 1850, prices had diminished significantly; production had reduced its overheads, perfected its machinery, speeded up the replacement of charcoal cast iron by coke cast iron; and a series of small businesses were thrown overboard because their production costs were too high, making them unable to withstand the decline in prices. Capital was cheap and abundant, and the workforce numerous. All the conditions were present for a new period of expansion.

§6. – The crisis of 1857

From 1850, it was not long before people recognized the very clear recovery that was taking shape.[81] It would be marked by a double character: it would be global, affecting the old world as it did the new, unfolding in the United States just as it did in France, England, Holland and Germany. It occurred as a result of the most unprecedented precious metal production in history. In the space of a few years, from 1848 to 1856, production exceeded the value of the world's existing gold and silver reserves by one-sixth.[82] The study of this growth period thus involves an examination of the economic development of a great number of countries; it requires careful observation of the phenomenon of circulation.

A.) Growth

First, we shall discuss gold production because here we will find, if not the origin and foundation of the new period of growth, then at least the cause of the relatively short period of depression that followed the crisis of 1847. As early as 1850, the English economy was again taking off. Meanwhile France, delayed by grave political troubles, had to wait until 1851 and 1852 before ushering in a period of true prosperity.

Classical theory holds that an increase in the stock of precious metals has the effects of lowering the interest and discount rates, increasing the value of securities and, consequently, stimulating trade, industry and the spirit of enterprise in general. This was the case after the discovery of gold in California in 1849 and Australia in 1851. Because these discoveries occurred in societies that lacked the means of production and technology of all kinds (railways, steamships, mines, blast furnaces, etc.) and were thus incapable of meeting their growing needs on their own, these discoveries had an even greater impact on the old nations, France and England, which had already adapted to the new modes of production. Gold production, which had represented 54,759 kg and 188.6 million francs from 1841 to 1850, suddenly rose to 199,388 kg and 686.7 million francs

81. Hans Rosenberg, *Die Weltwirtschaftskrisis von 1857–1859* (Stuttgart: Kohlhammer, 1934).
82. Émile Levasseur, *La question de l'or: Les mines de Californie et d'Australie* (Paris: Guillaumin, 1858).

from 1851 to 1855.[83] Under the pressure of this rapid development of production, prices jumped sharply, according to Sauerbeck's Index, from 74 in 1849 to 95 in 1853. The interest rate was falling, and the discount was at 1½ on the open market in England in 1852.

The opening of new markets as a result of the discovery and exploitation of gold fields stimulated the export of capital and even labour, hence the active demand for freight, soon followed by the rise in shipping rates. Tooke estimated the increase at 100 per cent for American freight.

The shipbuilding industry soon felt the effects of this increase in freight: shipyards were producing an increasing number of ships each year. In England, as early as 1851, new shipyards were opening up everywhere.[84] America followed suit.

If shipbuilding was prosperous, railway construction was no less so, and the railway played an infinitely more important role than maritime construction in the boom, particularly in France.

The railway crisis in England was the result of the excessively high operating costs. But with the fall in prices, interest and wages, and the savings to general operating costs, it was once again possible to undertake new railway projects. The net income per kilometre was growing, and the ratio of profits to invested capital increased from 7.3 in 1855 to 7.5 in 1856 and 7.7 in 1857. The railway benefitted from the renewed favour of capitalists, not only in England but also in the United States: in 1851, the United States had only 10,900 miles of railway; by 1857, it had grown to 24,500 miles. According to Schäffle, railways had absorbed $1.09 billion, $736 million of which was earned in the single year 1855–56. Later, the scandalous manoeuvring of corrupt officials came to light. Members of Congress used their authority to grant railway concessions to the highest bidder.[85]

In France, the year 1852 also saw the railways gaining serious momentum. The government tried to revise the strict rules for concession contracts in place prior to 1847 by modifying the state's involvement in the construction and the duration of concessions for the new lines. A long-term concession replaced a short-term one; the government's material involvement in part of the construction work was replaced by its financial participation in the form of subsidies. A rational merger of the various railway companies was carried out which allowed them to significantly reduce their operating costs, at the same time as it provided the state with a greater means of exerting control over them.[86]

83. Gold production figures follow Levasseur, in ibid., 40–41, 55.

84. Wirth, *Geschichte der Handelskrisen*, 253–58.

85. See Albert Schäffle, 'Zur Lehre von den Handelskrisen', pt 1, *Zeitschrift für die gesamte Staatswissenschaft* 14, no. 2 (1858): 446–48 and 446–47n1.

86. Mergers included: that of the Compagnies du Centre, the Orléans to Bordeaux line and the Tours to Nantes lines; the merger of the Compagnies Lyons to Avignon line, the Marseilles to Avignon line, the Arles to Beaucaire line, the Arles to Mines de Grande-Combe line, the Montpellier to Cette line, the Montpellier to Nîmes line, the Rognac to Aix line and the Marseilles to Toulon line.

It is curious to observe this concentration of the railways in France by means of governmental authority, whereas the play of natural economic laws was sufficient to realize this in England.

Lower prices, interest rates and wages made the construction of new lines possible and advantageous. Beginning in 1852, a whole series of new concessions were applied for, and as Joseph Garnier concluded in his 'Coup d'œil sur l'année 1852' [1852 at a glance], the new constructions would be the starting point for the recovery of the railway industry.[87] The road ahead was not smooth, however, and the French government, learning from experience, was preoccupied with sparing the country another 'railway fever' of the kind that had preceded the crisis of 1847. In 1855, the government decided to refuse any new concession: the French rail network, which had increased by 590 km in 1854 and 890 km in 1855, grew just 665 km in 1856. However, opinion soon shifted in the country and the chambers of Parliament, and in 1856, the government granted concessions for another 4,025 km! Construction increased to 1,263 km in 1857.[88] From 1852 to 1856, France spent 1,270 million francs on its railways:

1852–1854	250 million francs
1855	500 million francs
1856	520 million francs

The situation was similar in Germany: within three years the construction of railways absorbed over one billion francs.

This revival of the railway, combined with the great prosperity in the merchant marine and in maritime construction, was sufficient to trigger a very lively boom in the iron and mining industries. New ironworks were created, new mines were dug. England,[89] France[90] and the United States[91] were all caught up in the fever for new construction and extraction. Enormous quantities of capital were injected into industry. In table 1.5, the production figures for cast iron in these three major countries give us an idea of the fever driving the construction of their capital equipment.

Table 1.5 Cast-Iron Production in the 1850s (in tonnes)

	England	*France*	*United States*
1850	2,250,000	406,000	—
1855	—	—	784,178
1857	3,629,000	992,000	798,157
1858	3,456,000	872,000	705,094

Sources: For England, see Johannes Conrad et al., eds, *Handwörterbuch der Staatswissenschaften*, 2nd ed., 7 vols. (Jena: Fischer, 1898–1901), vol. 4, s.v. 'Eisen'; for France, *Annuaire statistique*; for the United States, *Annuaire de l'économie politique et de la statistique* 33 (1876): 388, tab.

87. *Annuaire de l'économie politique et de la statistique* 10 (1853): 493.
88. Wirth, *Geschichte der Handelskrisen*, 240.
89. Ibid., 300–301.
90. Ibid., 303.
91. Ibid., 317; and Arthur H. Cole, 'Statistical Background of the Crisis of 1857', *Review of Economic Statistics* 12, no. 4 (Nov. 1930): 170.

The boom was no less evident in the consumer goods-producing industries.

England built new textile mills in Lancashire; in 1851 alone, 81 new mills sprung up, 73 of which were cotton mills, using 2,866 horsepower.[92] In the United Kingdom as a whole, the number of textile businesses rose from 4,600 in 1850 to 5,117 in 1856; that of spindles, from 25,638,716 to 33,503,510; and that of power looms, from 298,916 to 369,205. The number of workers grew from 596,082 to 692,497.[93] In the silk industry, the number of spindles increased by 36 per cent.

In France, the textile industry developed along similar lines: cotton consumption increased, and silks from Lyons and Saint-Etienne were in particularly high demand at very lucrative prices.

Moreover, the prosperity of the textile industry was as much the result of foreign demand as it was of domestic consumption; and French and English exports were developing rapidly. In England, silk exports grew from 24,958,000 francs in 1849 to 74,051,080 in 1856 and to 72,246,000 in 1857;[94] and in France, they grew from 1,799,000 kg and 240 million francs in 1851 to 2,649,000 kg and 350 million francs in 1855.[95]

The building industry also shared in the general prosperity. Not only were new factories and railway structures being built, but the towns themselves were also being developed and embellished. In Paris and all the major cities of France, new wide avenues were constructed.[96] In the United States, large cities sprang up on all sides, while others expanded at a dizzying rate; land speculation followed. In New Orleans, $1 million worth of parcels of land were sold; in Chicago, $300,000; in Toledo, on the banks of Lake Erie, an acre that had been worth $1.50 in 1834 was valued at $100 in 1857, before the crisis.[97] Speculation was not only concentrated on building sites but also on the immense lands that the government granted to immigrants or nationals for a fee, and that the railways had now rendered accessible and exploitable. The American government sold these lands for $1.66 million in 1852–53, $8.47 million in 1853–54, $8.91 million in 1855–56 and $11.49 million in 1856.

In summary, the growth period from 1852 to 1857 was reminiscent of previous periods of prosperity, although the discovery of gold in California and Australia added to the renewed sense of optimism in the industrial and commercial world.

A novel kind of bank played a crucial role in this new influx of capital into industry. The operations of the first major bank of this kind, the 'Crédit Mobilier',[98] made such a noise that the term 'credit mobilier' has now become a common expression, used not only in France but also in Germany and England to refer to merchant banks. In

92. Wirth, *Geschichte der Handelskrisen*, 240.

93. *Annuaire de l'économie politique et de la statistique* 16 (1859): 403–7.

94. *Annuaire de l'économie politique et de la statistique* 18 (1861): 335.

95. Louis Reybaud, 'Des ouvriers qui vivent du travail de la soie', pt 5, *Journal des économistes*, 2nd ser., 19 (Aug. 1858): 221.

96. Ambroise Clément, 'Des crises commerciales', *Journal des économistes*, 2nd ser., 17 (1858): 185–87.

97. Schäffle, 'Lehre von den Handelskrisen', 444.

98. Founded in November 1852.

1854 alone, our 'Crédit Mobilier', then under the direction of the Péreire brothers, arranged the merger of La Société du Gaz with the Omnibus de Paris; the creation of the railway company Saint-Rambert-Grenoble; a loan to the railway company of the Ardennes; the extension of the Paris-Soissons line to the Belgian border, with an eye toward exploiting the rich coal deposits of the North; the joining of the Pyrenean railway network to the west-central one; the building of the canal on the Ebro River, from Saragossa to its mouth; the creation of a navigation company; and the Austrian railway company. In 1855, the Crédit Mobilier's activity was no less impressive: it created the Société des Hôtels et des Immeubles on the Rue de Rivoli in Paris, sponsored the Western-Southern railway and the François-Joseph railway, founded the Spanish Société de crédit, loaned 780 million francs to the French state, granted loans to railway companies, as advances on the shares and bonds of the various companies. In short, the Crédit Mobilier was at the head of all new enterprises. Keen to imitate the brilliant results of our Crédit Mobilier, Germany founded the Bank für Handel und Industrie and the Wiener Creditanstalt, which also offered credit transactions on production. Wirth estimated the share capital assembled thanks to the intervention of these German banks at 200 million thalers, of which the railways alone absorbed 140 million.[99]

In the face of this widespread expansion of the world economy, prices rose.

Yet, the price rise from 1852 to 1857, as well as industrial development in the same years, had a unique character. Instead of a slow and gradual price rise, we witness a sudden jump on Sauerbeck's Index, from 74 in 1849 to 95 in 1853 and 102 in 1854. This phenomenon, at first glance strange, can nevertheless be explained: in 1850–53, manufacturing not yet had time to develop, when it suddenly became the object of a pressing demand on the part of gold producers. Under such circumstances, it was natural for prices to climb. By contrast, at the end of the growth period, this factor was no longer important, once a new equilibrium had been established on account of the increase in the money stock; hence, prices rose more slowly. The industrial boom was now the only factor exerting an influence in the direction of a price rise. As usual, demand was mainly focussed on the products of the mining and metal industries and the machine industry; the price rise benefitted these types of goods in particular. However, consumer goods, also in high demand, largely took part in the boom.

Alongside this increase in the quantity and value of exchanges, the discount and the discount rate were increasing. The average portfolio of the Banque de France rose from 115.6 million francs in 1851 to 565.9 million in 1857. The same was true of the Bank of England. The New York banks, which listed $95,863,000 on 5 January 1851 in the loan and discount entry on their balance sheets, recorded the figure of $106,898,000 on 6 December of the same year and $120,139,000 on 22 August 1857.

In Germany and Austria, paper circulation had increased significantly. In Prussia it increased from 23 million thalers in 1855 to 51 million in 1856; in the rest of Germany, it grew from 13 to 30 million thalers.

---

99. Paul Cauwès, *Cours d'économie politique*, 3rd ed., 4 vols. (Paris: Larose & Forcel, 1893), 2: 387n1.

General wealth was increasing, and so was everyone's share in it. Capitalists saw their interests, their dividends, rise rapidly. The Crédit Mobilier, whose dividends can be used as a barometer, recorded successively: 13 per cent in 1853, 12 per cent in 1854, 40 per cent in 1855 and then only 24 per cent in 1856. In France, a miner in the mineral fuel mines could earn 700 francs per year in 1857, compared to 600 francs in 1853; a miner in an iron ore mine, 440, compared to 361; and a metal worker, 504, compared to 364. But, according to Levasseur, wages did not rise as rapidly as prices: he estimates that men's wages increased by14 to 19 per cent, and women's wages, by 7.97 per cent; whereas the prices of agricultural products increased by 25 per cent.[100]

B.) Crisis and depression

The crisis broke out in 1857. The gold mines had not performed as expected, causing much disillusionment, while the recently built railways had not yielded the expected results. As always, the projections had been overly optimistic, and estimates for production costs had been lower than the real costs.

As for gold production, the high cost of wages and the costs of transporting labour to the mines and of even basic equipment greatly affected the new mining operations' chances for success. Among them, some won, many barely got back their original investment, and others lost.[101] Gold production slowed.

Railway construction was curtailed for similar reasons; lines had been built on estimates that were too optimistic from the outset or had become so following the rise in prices. The most recent lines gave the least return per kilometre, and as a result, the returns per kilometre for the entire rail network diminished in France from 45,259 francs in 1857 to 41,398 in 1858. The performance of the new lines was especially disappointing: on the recently built Carmaux to Albi line, the returns per kilometre were 13,846 francs; on the Graissessac to Béziers line, returns per kilometre were 1,740 francs.[102] Also, the number of kilometres built declined from 1,263 in 1857 to 1,199 in 1858. In 1859, the government had to come to the aid of the railway companies to allow them to continue their construction (based on the Conventions of 1859, which established a guaranteed rate of interest).

It was the same in the United States, where between 1856 and 1857 the network expanded from 21,440 miles to 24,500 miles, an extension of 3,060 miles; by 1858, the US network was 26,210 miles, an extension of only 2,020 miles. In 1859, the increase was even smaller, only 1,647 miles. The same was true of 1860.

As had been the case in France, the returns revealed serious miscalculations: the New York Central Railroad saw its returns decrease from a maximum of $8,027,000 in 1857 to $6,528,000 in 1858 and 6,201,000 in 1859; the New York and Erie Railroad,

100. Émile Levasseur, 'Influence de l'or sur la condition des personnes', *Journal des économistes*, 2nd ser., 5, no. 5 (15 May 1858): 216–38, see esp. the detailed tables on pp. 230–33.

101. Wirth, *Geschichte der Handelskrisen*, 241.

102. A. Systermans, 'Des chemins de fer en France et à l'étranger', *Annuaire de l'économie politique et de la statistique* 16 (1859): 205 tab.

from $5,743,000 in 1857 to $4,395,000 in 1859; the Baltimore Ohio, from a maximum of $4,617,000 in 1857 to $3,618,000 in 1859; and so on. Thus from 1858 onward, there was a significant decline that continued through 1859, reaching up to 25 and 30 per cent. According to Block's *Annuaire*, the New York Central Railroad was the only railway able to pay a dividend in 1859.[103]

In England, the feverish railway construction had also slowed down. In 1857, 4,808 miles still remained to be built, and of this total, over half (2,590 miles) were not to be completed. Permits for the expropriation of land were allowed to expire.[104] In effect, their profits were falling, just as they had in France and the United States, going from £24,100,000 in 1857 to £23,300,000 in 1858.[105]

The iron and coal industries were naturally hit very hard by the backlash from this universal railway crisis. In France in particular, production had dropped drastically from 1858.

Table 1.6 Coal and Iron Industries in France, 1857–1859 (in tonnes)

	Mineral Fuel Mines		*Iron Ore Mines*	*Cast Iron*	*Iron and Steel*
	Production	*Number of Workers*			
1857	7,902,000	69,856	3,074,000	158,570,000	586,000
1858	7,353,000	64,336	2,790,000	124,750,000	553,000
1859	7,483,000	67,361	2,740,000	116,658,000	556,000

No source given.

But the industries in America and England were no less affected. In the United States, 120 blast furnaces were extinguished; as a result, 40,000 workers were kicked to the curb. In Manchester and Birmingham, they worked only short time – only 36 hours a week – in November 1857. Factories for semi-finished products, employing some 30,000 workers, were obliged to suspend work. On 31 December, according to the *Staffordshire Advertiser*, 68 blast furnaces were extinguished, leaving 18,000 workers unemployed. On the same day in Scotland, a further 41 were extinguished, and another 16,000 workers were dismissed. In South Wales, a quarter of the blast furnaces were completely abandoned, and wages declined by 20 per cent. In Yorkshire and County Durham, £5,000 less in daily wages were being paid.[106]

Under these circumstances, consumer goods industries followed a similar evolution. Cotton consumption in Great Britain fell from 403,777,000 kg in 1856 to 374,170,000 in 1857, and at the same time, the available stock decreased from 88,778 kg on 31 December 1856 to 95,900 kg on 31 December 1857 and to 104,306 kg on 31 December 1859. Such reduction in the English textile industry was due, moreover, not only to the decline in

103. *Annuaire de l'économie politique et de la statistique* 19 (1862): 329–30.
104. *Annuaire de l'économie politique et de la statistique* 16 (1859): 402.
105. Juglar, *Des crises commerciales*, 383.
106. Wirth, *Geschichte der Handelskrisen*, 356.

domestic consumption but also to the decrease in exports. The export of cotton fabrics (calico, muslins and mixed fabrics) decreased from 2,035,274,969 kg in 1856 to 1,784,459,137 kg in 1857. It was the same with sewing threads, cotton thread, canvases and linen thread, but to a lesser degree.

In France, the same phenomenon: cotton consumption went from 84,231,000 kg in 1856 to 73,062,000 kg in 1857. Its real value was still 148,400,000 francs in 1857 but only 145,500,000 francs by 1858.[107] The silk industry was no less hard hit, at Lyons and Saint-Etienne.

This general decline of industry and commerce was reflected in the number of bankruptcies: in France that number grew from 3,983 in 1857 to 4,430 in 1858. In the United States, bankruptcies reached the impressive number of 4,937 in 1857, representing liabilities in the enormous amount of $291,750,000.

On the other hand, all the banks that dealt closely or more loosely with industrial production, railway construction and the creation of new factories saw their situation decline rapidly. Our Crédit Mobilier had to decrease its dividend from 24 per cent in 1856 to 5 per cent in 1857. The banks in Scotland that had been tempted by such transactions suffered severe losses. The Darmstadt Kreditbank, based on the model of our Crédit Mobilier, saw its shares fall by 50 per cent.[108]

This abrupt halt in industrial and commercial expansion was followed by the traditional decline in prices. The coal and metal sectors played a large part in this decline, but this time, textiles were also seriously affected. As we have seen, the exploitation of new gold deposits had stimulated additional demand for consumer goods; the crisis, by drying up or at least severely reducing this market, had caused a significant fall in prices. And, just as the increase in the stock of precious metals had intensified the price rise, the disappearance of this factor led to a worsening of the decline.

Prices began to fall between May and August 1857, depending on the country, and this soon had an impact on circulation, both internationally and nationally. A foreign exchange crisis and an unusually intense and widespread internal credit crisis suddenly shook the great industrial and commercial centres of the world: New York, London, Paris, Hamburg, Bremen, Leipzig and Copenhagen were hit in succession.

Under the influence of a strong demand for credit and the decrease in the value of railway shares on the stock exchange, as early as July 1857, the American bank Ohio Life Insurance and Trust Company suspended its payments with liabilities of $5 million; it was soon followed by the Mechanics' Banking Association. These were the prelude to a real storm.

On 22 August 1857, the day the crisis exploded in New York, the sum of loans agreed to by the banks exceeded their total resources (cash on hand, banknotes in circulation) by $12 million, and a large part of this portfolio consisted of irregular or fraudulent commercial paper [*cavalerie*]. The situation became so critical in the end that the banks, together with the traders, temporarily suspended their operations.

107. *Annuaire de l'économie politique et de la statistique* 18 (1861): 172–73, tab.

108. Wirth, *Geschichte der Handelskrisen*, 265.

Despite this moratorium, the crisis was still raging at the beginning of September. Unexpected news brought the panic to its peak: the *Central America*, a ship loaded with gold bound for the United States, had sunk. Immediately the banks in Maryland and Pennsylvania ceased operations, taking with them 109 of the most important firms in Baltimore, Boston and Philadelphia.

The demand for credit was so intense and the supply so limited that the discount rate reached 30 and even 40 per cent in New York, according to de Laveleye. But European capital, attracted by the high interest rates, soon went to the New World, and gold started to return to its country of origin. From 3 to 24 October, 68,000 sovereigns left the coffers of the Bank of England bound for the United States.

The New York crisis spread to Europe. The Bank of England's reserve dropped from £6.1 million on 5 September to £3.2 million on 17 October, and its cash on hand dropped from £11.5 to 9.5 million. A similar trend affected the Banque de France: its cash on hand fell from 291 million francs on 20 June 1857 to 212 million francs by 20 October, while its portfolio swelled to 622 million francs on 20 October, up from the 569 million francs on 20 June. The Bank of England's portfolio went from £7.7 million on 5 September to £9.7 million on 17 October.

Despite a rise in the discount rate at the Bank of England, from 6 per cent on 8 October to 7 per cent on 10 October, and a similar rise at the Banque de France, from 6.5 to 7.5 per cent over the same period, gold continued to flow out. The exchange crisis was becoming more complex and was soon to become a domestic credit crisis. The drop in prices had suddenly interrupted the movement of goods, and dealers had to resort to credit. However, the crisis had precipitated the ruin of quite a large number of reckless banks. Thus, the Borough Bank collapsed on 27 October; next came the Western Bank of Scotland, which, with capital of £1,500,000, had nonetheless advanced £1,604,000 to four businesses that had since gone bankrupt; the City Bank of Glasgow followed shortly thereafter; and on 11 November, the powerful Sanderson exchange house ceased operations. Within the space of a single week, from 4 to 11 November, £1,060,000 in gold had passed from England to Scotland.

On 11 November, the Bank of England's cash on hand dropped to £7.2 million, and its reserve fell to 0.96 and then to 0.3 on 12 November. In a letter dated 12 November, the Chancellor of the Exchequer wrote to the governor of the Bank of England, promising the bank a bill of indemnity in the event it breached the provisions of the Act of 1844. A veritable assault on the bank's cashiers immediately followed, initially and until 18 November, to get gold and sell off imports to which exports no longer corresponded as a result of lower prices (gold reserves were at their minimum point at £6.5 million on 18 November), and then, beginning on 20 November, to obtain banknotes, the issuance of which was £928,000 in excess of the number set by the Act of 1844. Following a drop to £84,000 on 25 November, banknotes rose sharply to £243,000 on 26 November and to £342,000 on 27 November. The situation had already improved by the end of November; by 30 November, the extra-legal issuing of banknotes barely accounted for more than £15,000. Before 18 November, metal was primarily in demand because there was an exchange crisis requiring an international currency. From 19 November onward, the focus was on resolving the domestic credit crisis, so banknotes sufficed.

This recourse to credit most often took the form of a discount on bills of exchange,[109] and the Bank of England's portfolio was rapidly swelling; for the first time, the rate of discount reached 10 per cent.

In France, the financial crisis followed a similar pattern, and cash on hand at the Banque de France hit its lowest point at 181 million francs on 20 November, with a banknote circulation of 575 million francs. Domestic credit, however, was healthier than in England, and as soon as the exchange crisis was over, its balance sheets showed an immediate recovery. On the other hand, in England the flight of gold had stopped by 25 November, but the demand for credit was more pressing than ever before. It was not until 2 December that Bank of England's portfolio reached its maximum of £17.8 million.[110]

But from this period onward, in France as well as in England, the worst of the fever had subsided: the portfolio was deflating, metal was rapidly flowing into the bank's

---

109. These bills of exchange often did not correspond to a previous exchange; yet the collateral demanded by the Bank of England to allow a bill of exchange to be discounted was a guarantee of its subsequent repayment, even though we are dealing with an accommodation bill [*papier de complaisance*: i.e., what is informally known as kite flying].

110. This essentially global credit crisis had repercussions in Germany and especially in Hamburg, the focal point for commercial exchanges between Germany and Russia on the one hand, and with the New World, England, Scandinavia and France on the other. De Laveleye estimates the number of bankruptcies at 145, with a combined liability of half a billion francs.

On 23 November, the merchants of Hamburg had decided to form a 10-billion-mark banco guarantee fund intended to settle all regular claims. Ten per cent had to be paid immediately. One hour after opening, the subscription had already reached 22 million, one-tenth of which had to be paid straight away. But the funds were quickly exhausted, and the state was called upon to intervene. The government took the following three steps:

1. On 27 November, the Wahren-Vorschuss-Casse was created; the finance department was allowed to issue notes against goods deposited, as a kind of warrant-receipt, or against solid bills of exchange up to two-thirds the value of its deposits. However, the demand for credit was such that the 15-billion-mark banco thus issued was soon absorbed.
2. On 6 December, a discount fund (*Diskontocasse*) was created with an available capital of 15 billion, one-third of which was provided by the state in the form of railway shares.
3. Finally, a special procedure was instituted in cases of bankruptcy: the *Administrationsverfahren* [administrative procedures]. It was possible for the merchant debtor, who had to suspend his payments but who nonetheless hoped to make his creditors lose interest in him over a more or less long period of time, to refer to the *Administrationsverfahren.* The administration of his assets was then transferred to administrators charged with resolving the situation. His honour was safe until he had to be declared insolvent. Out of the 135 firms that had to suspend payments until 5 December, 65 had submitted to the *Administrationsverfahren.* See J.-E. Horn, 'Le commerce extérieur et la crise à Hambourg', *Journal des économistes*, 2nd ser., 5 (17), no. 2 (Feb. 1858): 215–53. Wirth, *Geschichte der Handelskrisen*, 384–89. Thanks to all these expedients, the financial crisis was resolved without too much trouble. By December 1857, calm had returned.

Leipzig, Stettin, Berlin, Magdeburg, Stuttgart and Cologne all registered numerous bankruptcies.

coffers, and as early as 1858–59, the Banque de France and the Bank of England were ready to support new industrial growth.

The crisis had been no less severe on the stock exchange than it had been for the banks, and quite often, the failed banks bore the just consequences of their speculations on the stock market. *Crédits mobiliers* of all kinds and from all countries – France, Germany, Austria – suffered as a result of the decrease in the value of their securities. Figures borrowed from several stock exchanges around the world will help us appreciate the intensity of the financial crisis.

In France, the drop in the value of railway shares was particularly significant. Government securities, on the other hand, performed much better: they became the refuge for investors' savings.

Table 1.7 Railway Shares and Government Securities in France in 1857

	June 1857	*September 1857*	*December 1857*
	Increase	*Decrease*	*Increase*
Banque de France	4,600	2,720	3,250
Paris to Orléans	1,490	1,307.50	1,377.50
Nord	990	840	955
Ouest	785	687.50	685
Midi	780	629	570
4½ (1852)	92	93.50–90	93.50

No source given.

Crédit Mobilier shares, which were listed at 1,982 in March 1856, hit their lowest price of 670 in December 1857.

Similarly in New York, we notice a real debacle for the value of railway shares and a rise in government securities.

Table 1.8 The New York Stock Exchange

	Government Securities, New York 6%	*Railway Shares*	
		Baltimore and Ohio	*Cleveland and Pittsburgh*
Last week of Dec. 1855	114	54	63
Last week of Dec. 1856	114	87	57
Last week of July 1857	107.25	59	38
13 October 1857	89	27	7.50
Last week of Dec. 1857	105	44	10.50

No source given.

In Sweden, the government borrowed 15 million thalers in order to create a loan fund that would make advances to merchants on goods or mortgage loans. See *Annuaire de l'économie politique et de la statistique* 15 (1858): 579.

Finally, on the Vienna Stock Exchange, which represented *the* stock exchange for German securities, we register a similar crisis, particularly for asset-backed securities and the railways between May and October 1857.

Table 1.9 The Vienna Stock Exchange

	1856	*May 1857*	*Oct. 1857*	*Dec. 1857*	*Jan 1858*
Darmstadt Kreditbank	400–420	270	241	204	233
Crédit Mobilier	1,980	1,300	900	590–720	870
Franz-Joseph-Orient-Bahn	108	60¾	44	48¾	52

No source given.

The recovery, moreover, was not long in coming, and from December 1857 to January 1858, the recovery was general. The public was regaining confidence and making clearer plans for the future. In France, a specific policy was developing in this direction: there was growing talk of introducing a special interest-guarantee clause in railway concession contracts, which would soon become reality under the Conventions of 1859.[111] Hence, the interest-guarantee system originated with the 1857 crisis.

Such severe troubles could not fail to influence the distribution of wealth. The dividends of the railway companies and the banks fell significantly. Wages also fell. In Scotland, foundry workers, instead of earning 5 sh. as they had in 1956, were now earning only 4 to 3 sh. 6 in 1857 and 3 sh. 6 to 3 sh. in 1858. In America on 24 October, according to *Express* of New York, 24,000 workers were unemployed; in Philadelphia, there were 2,500; in a number of other cities, the number of unemployed was 17,000. In total, about 43,000 families were deprived of resources. In other parts of the Union, the situation was the same, although there are no precise statistics concerning these.[112]

In English coal mines, the crisis had an interesting consequence. The crisis led to the creation of a large trade union in Yorkshire. The bosses, after having attempted in vain to maintain selling prices by an agreement, a sort of cartel, and having failed due to intense competition, tried to make their workers bear the brunt of their losses by reducing their wages. They threatened their workers with a general lockout, to which the workers responded by creating a coalition of their own. Thus, the first great professional miners' trade union was created in Yorkshire. A compromise was reached: wages were cut, but the workday was reduced to eight hours as the union had demanded.[113]

111. Alfred Picard, *Les chemins de fer français*, 6 vols. (Paris: Rothschild, 1884), 2: 169.
112. Maurice Block, 'Coup d'œil sur l'année 1857', *Annuaire de l'économie politique et de la statistique* 15 (1858): 584.
113. Tugan-Baranowsky, *Theorie und Geschichte der Handelskrisen*, 287.

§7. – *The crisis of 1866*

We begin with the description of the economic boom from 1861 to 1866, which is one of the most obscure periods that history has to offer. It was dominated by two essential facts: the advent, or more precisely, the consecration and accentuation of free trade in France and England, and the outbreak of the American Civil War. The latter event exerted considerable influence on the economic development of Europe by depriving it not only of orders from the United States but also, more importantly, of cotton.

This abrupt cessation of trade between Europe and the United States and the need to obtain cotton at any cost, often in distant countries inexperienced in its cultivation, caused serious economic unrest, especially in the money markets. In 1861 and 1864, we even find the symptoms of a general economic crisis. Hence the error of some economists. De Laveleye recorded a commercial crisis in 1861 and another in 1864. Juglar placed the crisis of the decade from 1860 to 1870 in 1864. But an examination of production figures and the statistics on issues of industrial shares lead us to qualify the years from 1861 to 1866 as years of growth, although the years 1861 and 1864 were marked by monetary difficulties.

After the resolution of the 1857 crisis, however, capital not only flowed back into the French railways but also and principally toward foreign railways.

A.) Growth

The great intermediary of the time between savings and industry, the Crédit Mobilier, took advantage of favourable economic conditions to export, with French capital, the products of the French industry. It undertook a series of railway lines in Spain (from Seville to Xeres), Russia, Austria and Italy (in Lombardy and Rome). The Crédit Mobilier was equally interested in maritime shipping companies (the Compagnie Transatlantique was founded in 1861), as well as real-estate companies. The number of newly created companies in France was proof of the renewal of the spirit of enterprise: their numbers grew from 108 in 1861 to 239 in 1865.

With the renewal of the spirit of enterprise came an active demand for machinery and raw materials, and the mining and metal industries experienced an era of prosperity. Not only the production statistics but also the statistics for selling prices, the number of employed workers and wages were proof of this revival.

Table 1.10 Coal, Iron and Steel Production in France, 1861–1866 (1000s of tonnes)

	Coal Mines	*Iron Mines*	*Cast Iron*	*Iron and Steel*
1861	9,423	3,198	967	669
1862	10,290	3,366	1,091	781
1863	10,710	3,278	1,157	807
1864	11,243	3,137	1,213	832
1865	11,600	3,011	1,204	811
1866	12,260	3,162	1,260	868

No source given.

England experienced the same prosperity; however, the course of the recovery was more pronounced there than in France. A law of 1862 created a new type of company: the limited liability company. These companies were created in large numbers, with the most varied goals. The nominal capital of English companies reached £140 million in 1863, £237 million in 1864 and £205 million in 1865.[114]

Many of these companies were involved in the railways. In the years 1864 and 1865, 640 miles were built, an average of 320 miles per year. This favour shown to the railways by capital investors can also be explained by the earnings they received. The gross returns per mile were increasing.

Around the same time, mines, insurance companies and banks saw capital flock to them: they absorbed £8,875,000 in 1863 and £12,548,000 in 1864.[115] The English mining and metal industries raised their prices, enlarging their profits from increased production. The production of cast iron increased by almost 40 per cent, from 3,943,000 tonnes in 1862 to 4,768,000 in 1864, 4,819,000 in 1865 and 4,524,000 in 1866.

In contrast to France, however, the growth in England was internal, and this particular characteristic triggered an interesting phenomenon: a decrease in the exports of iron bars, rails and large sheet metal in 1865, despite the expansion of production. Moreover, this domestic boom was not always free of speculation, and although England had no Crédit Mobilier, its discount banks were providing similar services to those of the Crédit Mobilier, lending capital to industry. To this end, they even resorted to practices that were, if not outright dishonest, at least dangerous. They disguised long-term lending in the form of short-term loans and renewals of bills of exchange [*traites renouvelées*]. Railway companies in particular used the latter practice to the greatest extent, which was criticized as 'financiering':[116] if a company needed £50,000 to complete the building of a railway line or to improve its equipment, it would pledge as collateral the portion of the line that had already been built and the equipment already in use and then would draw on the bank up to the agreed sum.

However, this practice was not without the drawback of high interest payments that could jeopardize a company's profits. Banks, moreover, were obliged to be demanding; for they ran great risks and were themselves sometimes giving out 3, 4 or 5 per cent on their deposits.

Among the large banking firms that had committed great sums to industrial enterprises, let us take the example of Overend, Gurney & Co., which had mostly used its own capital. Whereas another bank, the National Savings Bank Association created in 1856, had relied mainly on its depositors' funds and, using £100,000 of their capital, had managed to increase the number of its branches to 174 by 1866!

However dangerous these practices were in themselves, they had nonetheless contributed to stunning industrial growth in England, particularly in 1865 and 1866, and

114. Figures follow Conrad et al., eds, *Handwörterbuch der Staatswissenschaften*, vol. 1, s.v. 'Aktiengesellschaften'.
115. De Laveleye, *Le marché monétaire*, 153; and Tugan-Baranowsky, *Theorie und Geschichte der Handelskrisen*, 140.
116. See Macleod, *Theory of Credit*, vol. 2, pt 2: 1058–65.

England was indebted to these banks for the rapid success of its limited liability companies, for their feverish multiplication – in short, for the general growth of public wealth.

The consumer goods industry was no less prosperous than that of producer goods. The construction industry in particular achieved most favourable results in England as well as in France. In England, houses, hospitals and bridges were built. In France, Paris continued with improvements, clearing new avenues and building new residential districts, and other cities followed suit. The Société Immobilière of the Boulevard du Temple was created in 1862 with a capitalization of three million francs. In Marseilles, similar companies were created as the city expanded. The Compagnie Immobilière of Paris resulted from the merger of the Société des Immeubles de la rue de Rivoli with the Société des ports de Marseille in 1858, and in 1863, it became the Compagnie Immobilière, chaired by E. Péreire.

The cotton industry was the exception, suffering between 1862 and 1864 from an unfavourable situation. As a result of the American Civil War, it was forced to obtain its raw material from faraway countries, where cotton production had previously occupied only a secondary position and where its annual harvest had served only to supplement the American harvest, increasing prices. The cotton industry, working with a more expensive raw material, had to increase the prices of its products – in other words, restricting consumption and limiting its markets. These effects were not felt immediately: in 1860, at the time of the outbreak of the American Civil War, English industrialists and merchants still had cotton stores that had accumulated in their warehouses at the time of the crisis of 1857; so at first, the increase in prices was favourable to them. This was no longer the case by 1862, and in 1863–64, the situation became very critical: cotton was not only expensive; it also had to be paid for in silver. Fortunately, imports of American cotton, which had dropped from 2,580,000 bales in 1860 to 71,000 bales in 1862, recovered rapidly, to 197,000 bales in 1864, 441,000 bales in 1865 and 1,162,000 bales in 1866.[117] In 1864, the textile industry resumed its forward march, and by 1865, Tugan-Baranowsky reported that it was prosperous once again.[118] The figures for imports further confirmed this observation, rising from 1,495,000 bales in 1862 to 3,749,000 bales in 1866.

Thus, except for a slight depression in 1864, the statistics for production, shares issued, industrial companies created and the consumer goods industry all reflected a satisfactory situation of the world economy. Indeed, as the *Economist* rightly pointed out, there was no lack of capital in 1864, but there was a lack of cash.[119]

In these circumstances, it was not surprising that a price rise occurred and lasted from 1862 until 1866. Sauerbeck's general index no doubt shows prices reaching their peak in1864, but cotton prices decreased a great deal at the end of 1864, and if we examine the causes of the slump in the index numbers, we realize that it had much more

117. *Annuaire de l'économie politique et de la statistique* 21 (1864): 325, tab., combined with *Annuaire de l'économie politique et de la statistique* 26 (1869): 413, tab.

118. 'The Causes of the Existing Depression', *Economist*, May 1867, quoted in Tugan-Baranowsky, *Theorie und Geschichte der Handelskrisen*, 330.

119. Quoted in de Laveleye, *Le marché monétaire*, 156, 159.

to do with this latter phenomenon than with a general depression of prices. However, Soetbeer's Index also reached its peak in 1864 for mining and semi-finished products, the production and prices of which represent the barometer of industry, the means of production and the spirit of enterprise.[120] If we look into this fall in the index in greater detail, we notice that it was due more to the drop in the prices for metals such as silver, copper, zinc and lead, and even products such as Chilean saltpetre, than to fall in coal, raw or rolled iron, or steel. Table 1.11 makes this abundantly clear.

Table 1.11 Prices of Coal, Raw Iron and Rolled Iron, 1861–1868 (marks per tonne)

	Coal	*Raw Iron*	*Rolled Iron*
1861	15.93	6.18	18.42
1862	16.03	6.30	18.44
1863	15.08	7.32	19.50
1864	16.11	7.56	22.14
1865	16.35	7.38	21.54
1866	16.31	7.08	21.00
1867	16.02	6.96	20.22
1868	15.58	6.72	18.72

No source given.

In fact, the decisive drop did not take place until 1866.[121]

No doubt, we see a slight decline either in 1864 or 1865, but the enormous rise in the discount rate and the precarious situation of the cotton industry were bound to have an influence on the other branches of production, especially on the production of new machinery and the means of production. But if there was a pause in production in 1864, a pause in the price rise, it was soon followed by a recovery, particularly in 1865 and 1866. The period from 1865 to 1866 was indeed a period of growth, both on the continent and in England.

Thus, this quite naturally leads us to mention the rise in the discount rate, the fluctuations in the discount and the cash portfolio in the major banks of issue from 1860 to 1866.

During this period, two exchange crises affected circulation: the first crisis occurred in 1861, after the outbreak of the Civil War, as a result of the United States' calling in all of its claims on Europe; the second crisis came in 1863 and especially in 1864, as a consequence of the need to purchase cotton from other countries that would only accept specie payment in silver.

Thus, in 1860–61, we witness a phenomenon, strange at first sight, in which the cash on hand at the Banque de France and the Bank of England decreased while the

120. Adolf Soetbeer, *Materialien zur Erläuterung und Beurteilung der wirtschaftlichen Edelmetallverhältnisse und der Währungsfrage*, 2nd ed. (Berlin: Puttkammer & Mühlbrecht, 1886), 108.
121. As for agricultural products, they follow an absolutely independent course, as capricious as the seasons and the harvests.

portfolio simultaneously swelled, without a corresponding increase in trade. This phenomenon can be explained thus: in order to meet the costs of the war, America settled all of its accounts with Europe; while at the same time, it did not incur any new debts to Europe, as it imported little or no goods from Europe. The normal equilibrium between American claims and its debts to Europe was broken, and Europe was forced to free itself with money drawn from the cash on hand of the Banque de France and the Bank of England. In order to discourage the recourse to the discount or to advances, the central banks raised their discount rates, or the interest rates on their advances. Hence, by 1861, rates had reached 8 per cent at the Bank of England and 7 per cent at the Banque de France. As soon as the remittances were made, the crisis was resolved; cash holdings increased, the portfolio was reduced, and by 1862, the discount had already returned to 2 per cent in England and to 3.5 per cent in France.

Table 1.12 Movement of Precious Metals in France in 1861

	Gold	*Silver*
Imports	244,036,749	172,179,787
Exports	267,770,439	233,993,067
Deficit	– 23,733,690	– 61,813,280

Source: De Laveleye, *Le marché monétaire*, 157, tab.

One crisis was resolved only for another to appear. By 1863 and 1864, the money market was again showing symptoms of dysfunction. This was not, however, the normal exchange crisis that accompanies a general crisis of overproduction, as Juglar and de Laveleye have claimed.

Certainly, this crisis had an impact on production, consumption and prices; yet it remains an isolated exchange crisis resulting from the need to export metal in order to pay for cotton imports from India and Egypt. The best proof of this lies: first, in the rapid resolution of the crisis, coinciding with the resumption of trade relations with America; second, in the fact that in 1864 Paris alone saw its portfolio diminish, whereas at its subsidiary branches, it continued to rise; and third, in the fact that in 1865 and 1866, England and France experienced a new period of prosperity that did not reach its peak in the period from 1862 to 1866, either at the Banque de France or at the Bank of England, until 1866.

Let us go into greater detail. American cotton imports had gradually declined after 1860 and dropped to next to nothing by 1862. Conversely, cotton imports from India, Brazil and Egypt followed an uninterrupted upward trend. Normally, England and France could have offset their cotton imports with their exports of manufactured goods. But in 1863–64, their new Hindu and Egyptian suppliers would only accept silver in exchange for their cotton. England and France were reduced to paying for their cotton imports in silver. However, the necessity of obtaining its cotton from India and Egypt increased imports from India to England from £15 million in 1860 to £52 million in 1864, and imports from Egypt, from £10 million in 1860 to almost £20 million by 1864. In France, silver exports during the first quarter of 1864 reached 104,280,316 francs, compared to 79,299,270 francs during the corresponding quarter in 1863.[122] The two major European issuing banks, the Banque de France and the Bank of England, saw their cash holdings diminish respectively: at the Banque de France, from a maximum of 431 million francs in 1862 to a minimum of 151 million francs in 1864; and at the Bank of England, from a maximum of £18.4 million in 1862 to a minimum of £12.4 million in 1864, and its reserve fell to £4.8 million. The Bank of England's portfolio swelled from a minimum of £17 million in 1862 to a maximum of £25.3 million in 1863, before reducing again to £23 million in 1864. The portfolio at the Banque de France continued to grow between 1862 and 1864, reaching its peak in 1864 at 791 million francs.

Under these circumstances, the discount rate was raised to 8 per cent in 1863 and 9 per cent in 1864 at the Bank of England, and to 8 per cent in 1864 at the Banque de France. The situation improved as a result of this energetic policy and the resumption of trade relations with America. The portfolio was unburdened of all the paper, that corresponded only to monetary needs, and the discount rate was lowered in 1865, although it remained high. Shortly thereafter, under the influence of the industrial boom, which had been momentarily disrupted by the upheavals of the money market, the portfolio grew again, reflecting new and very real trade activity. In the period from 1860 to 1866, the Banque de France and the Bank of England saw their portfolio peak in 1866.

The crisis of 1864 was therefore an isolated currency crisis. The American Civil War had disrupted international trade to such an extent that the exchange crisis was more or less chronic between 1860 and 1864. But we should not conclude, with de Laveleye and Juglar, that a periodic general crisis broke out in 1864.

On the stock exchange, the boom had been neither as clear nor as continuous as in the years leading up to the crisis of 1847 and 1857. Bullish speculation in particular had been curbed by the high rate of discount and of deferrals [*reports*][iii] in 1864. Already in November 1864, the Paris Stock Exchange had experienced a real crisis; though this was not the first isolated stock market crisis that we have encountered. Between 29 September and 25 November 1864, the [government's rate of] 3 per cent dropped by 1.90, the Crédit Mobilier by 128.75, Société Générale by 63.75, Orléans by 57.50 and Paris-Lyons by 56.25; but they recovered almost immediately, and by 1866, they reached a higher rate than in 1864. On the other hand, the fall of the 3 per cent proves that this was a credit crisis and not a general crisis; for government securities increase in times of crisis. Similarly, in early 1866, the railways not only resumed trading on the stock exchange but also saw their revenues increase steadily each week, from 1864 to 1866.[123]

Profits and wages had increased particularly in England. In the United States, according to the *Bulletin of the Department of Labor* (1902), the nominal wage (with the year 1846 = 100) rose from 72 in 1850 to 81 in 1866, and the real wage went from 86 to 93 over the same years. In France, the number of workers employed in the mines

122. De Laveleye, *Le marché monétaire*, 305 [see also 156–58].

123. See the daily column, 'Marine, commerce, industrie', in the newspaper *La Gironde*, edited by Gustave Gounouilhou, 1866.

increased from 76,450 in 1861 to 91,225 in 1866, and then increased by almost 4,000 from 1864 to 1865. Hence, 1864 was not a year of crisis.

B.) Crisis and depression

The crisis broke out in 1866.

The statistics on the issuing of industrial shares are particularly conclusive. While England had created 997 companies in 1864 and 1,034 in 1865, no more than 762 were created in 1866 and only 479 in 1867. The total nominal capital of £237.2 million in 1864 and £205.4 million in 1865 decreased to 76.8 in 1866 and 31.5 in 1867.

In France, the number of new companies founded fell from 239 in 1865 and 225 in 1866 to 187 in 1867 and 191 in 1868. By the end of 1866, the disappearance or at least the weakening of the spirit of enterprise was unquestionable. Which branches of industry did the crisis affect and why?

In France, as always in times of crisis, we note a slowdown in the expansion of the railway network. In 1865, 865 km had been built; in 1866, no more than 688 km were constructed. In England it was the same: only 173 new miles were opened in 1866, compared to 283 in 1865 and 357 in 1864.

However, in France the 1866 crisis was not so much a national railway crisis as it was one of foreign railways, the construction of which had been undertaken by French banks and industry. The French railway crisis, which took the form of a late and rather feeble decline in its returns from 1866 to 1867,[124] was more likely a consequence of the crisis that had affected foreign railways and, consequently, the French industry responsible for their construction. French involvement in the construction of foreign railways had grown in the years from 1862 to 1866. The Paris Stock Exchange had experienced an influx of Portuguese, Italian, Austrian and Russian railway stocks and bonds. Yet the returns, which had been satisfactory at first, often suffered considerable losses, declining by 13 to 20 per cent in 1866 compared to 1865. Once again, we see initial cost estimates being exceeded, followed by the disappointed expectations of investors. Portuguese railway companies, with equity capital of 35 million francs and bond capital of 59 million francs, reported most unfavourable results at the annual general shareholders' meeting: construction work had exceeded initial estimates by 72 million francs; earnings had failed to meet expectations; the gross product for the first nine months of 1866 rose to 4,311,000 francs, and costs reached 57 per cent; the net product therefore was only 1.7 to 1.8 million francs. And the company expected to have to borrow further.[125] Shares fell under 100 francs, after they had been at 200 francs in January 1866. Shortly before, news came that the Turin to Savone railway line had suspended interest payments on its bonds. Then in October, the bankruptcy of the Granollers to

124. From 1866 to 1867, the net product per kilometre fell from 23,937 to 23,730.

125. See *La Gironde*, 4 Dec. 1866: 'The embarrassing situation remains unchanged', the report stated, 'the Company finds itself unable to meet its expenses completely through its ordinary resources.'

San Joan de Les Abadesses Company was announced in Madrid. Finally, the Seville-Jerez railway was in negotiations with its shareholders in order to reduce its capital by 50 per cent. Little by little, all these enterprises, which were almost always headed by the Crédit Mobilier, had, if not collapsed, then at least shown unfavourable results on their balance sheets during the course of 1866. The Société Générale Maritime had been liquidated; the Russian railways, the Nord de l'Espagne and many other companies had given poor returns.

Under these circumstances, the Crédit Mobilier, which was still paying dividends at 61.51 in 1864–65,[126] announced in May that it could only give 5 per cent statutory interest per share.[127] By mid-December 1866, it announced that the portfolio's losses had overtaken profits, and it was no longer able to distribute advances on the dividends of old shares. Its shares immediately collapsed by 500 francs.

In these circumstances, French industry suffered the intense aftershock of the railway crisis. Mining and metal industry production declined significantly (tab. 1.13). Production from the iron mines, blast furnaces and steel mills had diminished, but the crisis was as moderate as the preceding period of growth. Coal production even experienced an increase, but whereas it had increased 660,000 tonnes between 1865 and 1866, in 1867 the increase was only 479,000 tonnes, compared with 1866.

Table 1.13 Production of Metals in France, 1865–1867 (1,000s of tonnes)

	Iron Mines	*Iron and Steel*	*Cast Iron*
1865	3,011	811	1,204
1866	3,162	868	1,260
1867	2,772	835	1,229

No source given.

In England, the crisis began in May, with the bankruptcies of the Great Western Railway Company and the London and Dover Railway Company.[128] The firm Morton Peto, Betts and Co. followed in June by suspending its payments, after having undertaken overly ambitious projects and agreeing to borrow at a rate that made any profit unlikely.[129] Instantly the construction fever stopped, and instead of the 283 miles in 1865 and 357 in 1864, a mere 173 miles were built in 1866, because the returns per mile were dropping. Thus in May, when the railways began to fall, the banks soon followed.

Overend, Gurney & Co. was the most notable bankruptcy. The firm had been dealt two fatal blows: first, the bankruptcy of the Atlantic and Great Western Railways and the London Chatham and Dover Rail Company in which it had a large interest; and second, the loss of the pending lawsuit against the Mid-Wales Railway. News of the

126. *La Gironde*, 31 March 1865.
127. *La Gironde*, 12 May 1866.
128. Tugan-Baranowsky, *Theorie und Geschichte der Handelskrisen*, 143.
129. According to the *Economist*, cited in Gounouilhou, 'Marine, Commerce, Industrie', *La Gironde*, 22 June 1866.

latter came on 9 May; by 10 May it had to suspend its payments, the victim of a 'run'. Its liabilities were £10,000,000. It was soon to be followed by the Agra and Masterman's Bank, the English Joint-Stock Bank and so on.[130]

In light of this decline in the spirit of enterprise and capital reserves,[131] the mining and metal industries came to a halt. Production of cast iron in England dropped from 4,819,000 tonnes in 1865 to 4,524,000 tonnes in 1866 and remained at 4,761,000 tonnes in 1867, even lower than what it had been in 1865.

The consumer goods industry also experienced a decline. In France, cotton consumption dropped from 120,036,066 kg in 1866 to 95,903,069 in 1867. The construction industry also experienced a crisis: the Société Immobilière in the Boulevard du Temple in Paris was liquidated in 1866. It was the same for certain similar companies in other French cities, notably in Marseilles. The fall in prices was inevitable. It started in May and June 1866. The Scottish cast-iron market, after a very lively start in 1865 and at the beginning of 1866, suffered a crash at the end of May[132] and the beginning of June.[133] In January, the price of cast iron rose from 50 sh. a tonne to 65 sh. At the beginning of June, a collapse of its prices was announced.[134]

The French money market experienced little more than a domestic credit crisis, and even then, it was not that serious. For although its portfolio grew to the point of surpassing, in 1866, the highest figures reached since its creation, it deflated normally in 1867–68, and its cash holdings continued to increase. Increased banknote circulation followed. The credit crisis was domestic, as was the demand for a domestic means of payment; however, the banknote was worth gold domestically. The Banque de France, anxious to protect its gold reserves in anticipation of possible contingencies, fulfilled its customers' demands by means of banknotes, and since the banknote enjoyed the same confidence as gold, it was not presented for reimbursement.

Table 1.14 Annual Balance Sheets of the Banque de France, 1865–1868 (millions of francs)

	Cash on Hand	*Portfolio*	*Note Circulation*	*Discount Rate (%)*	
1865	439.6	4,734,997	839.3	5	3
1866	588.3	5,097,730	637.1	5	3
1867	845.0	5,001,881	1,081.5	3	2½
1868	1,174.3	5,054,337	1,233.2	2½	2½

No source given.

As for the exchange rate, it never ceased to remain favourable to France, which, having undertaken investment abroad, remained a creditor, without becoming a debtor

130. See MacLeod, *Theory of Credit*, vol. 2, pt 2: 1062.
131. The *Economist*, 1 Dec. 1866, observed that capital was not lacking, but that the spirit of enterprise was dormant.
132. Juglar, *Des crises commerciales*, 389.
133. Cf. *La Gironde*, 4 June 1866.
134. Ibid.

to the outside world. Moreover, the exclusively domestic crisis itself was like the boom: moderate, and a rise of the discount rate to 5 per cent was enough to cause the liquidation of bullish buyers.

The evolution of the credit crisis in France, which MacLeod called 'a remarkable and unprecedented phenomenon', contrasted strangely with the serious difficulties of the English money market.[135]

On 10 May, the firm of Overend, Gurney & Co. fell. The following day, a storm raged on Lombard Street.[136] On this same Friday, the Bank of England had advanced £4,000,000 and saw its reserve reduced from £5,727,000 to £3,000,000; the demands on the bank were such that, for the third time, the Chancellor of the Exchequer had to suspend the Act of 1844. The effect was instantaneous, and the future looked less bleak on the memorable evening of Black Friday. The advances approved by the Bank of England were considerable: within the space of six days, from 18 to 24 May, the Chancellor of the Exchequer estimated the advances at £12,225,000.[137] The portfolio had grown particularly large: from £19 million on 9 January, it swelled to £33.4 million on 30 May; while the cash on hand and the reserve dropped from £13 million to £11.8 million and from £5.2 million to £400,000, respectively. In May 1866, the Bank of England took its discount to 7 per cent, and then to 10 per cent. This energetic measure was sufficient to assure the swift resolution of the crisis and of the panic itself, so that by December 1866, the Bank of England had returned to normal. As of 30 November, the cash on hand had already reached £18.1 million, the portfolio had fallen to £19.1 million, the reserve had risen to £9.6 million and the discount had finally decreased to 4 per cent and, soon after on 20 December, to 3.5 per cent.

The stock exchange, particularly the railway shares market, reflected the general economic crisis. In London, from 30 December 1865 to 26 December 1866, the decline was as follows:[138]

Great Eastern	14%
Great Northern	10%
London Brighton	17%
North British	21%

In Paris, the effects of the crisis were just as clear, and none of the usual characteristics were missing from the general crisis of 1866. On 30 May 1866, the recently issued shares of the Société Générale du Crédit in Spain were worth only 72.30, a loss of 29,925,000 francs. Shares of the Cavour Canal (with capital of 25 million francs) purchased at 500 francs were now at 220, a loss of 14 million francs. Nearly all mining and industrial stock values suffered losses. Santander shares held at 500 francs were now

135. Macleod, *Theory of Credit*, vol. 2, pt 2: 1063.
136. See Louis Wolowski, 'La crise financière de l'Angleterre', *Revue des deux mondes*, 2nd ser., 64, no. 4 (Aug. 1866): 927–56.
137. Macleod, *Theory of Credit*, vol. 2, pt 2: 1063.
138. See Juglar, *Des crises commerciales*, 387.

worth 200, those of Belgian coal, 385. The 1,000-franc Nouvelle-Montagne shares were at 725; those of Centre Flein fell to 200, losing 80 per cent of their value; and finally, shares of the Mouraia copper mine were at 100 francs.[139]

Moreover, the effects of the crisis were no less intense on the stock values of foreign railways and *crédits mobiliers* (tab. 1.15).

Table 1.15 Stock Values of Foreign Railways and *Crédits Mobiliers*, 1866–67

	Crédit Mobilier *of Spain*		*Seville-Jerez*	*Portuguese*		*Romanian*	
3 Jan. 1866	471.25	475	52.50	200	195	160	168.75
16 July 1866	330	332	30	70		55	
29 Dec. 1866	305	310	34.25	90	100	83	95
27 June 1867	255		32	76.25		77.50	

No source given.

On the other hand, annuities and the French railways, which were values as safe as annuities since the implementation of the interest guarantee, looked good to many in the midst of the general panic. In January 1867, the losses on foreign securities were estimated at 1,369 million francs. *La Finance*, a newspaper at the time, estimated that, on 6 January 1867, the losses suffered by French investors on securities sponsored by the Crédit Mobilier were 591,229,850 francs.[140] The Crédit Mobilier share price fell from 880 in January 1866 to 420 in June; no dividend had been distributed. Having lost half of its capital, the Crédit Mobilier, according to article 61 of its statutes, went into liquidation. Our first great merchant bank had collapsed.[141]

§8. – The crisis of 1873

Up to the crisis of 1866, industrial crises had essentially been French and English crises. Starting in 1869–70, a change occurred: the evolution toward 'industrialization', until then a primarily French and English phenomenon, spread to the United States and Germany, and with this change, the focus of crises shifted, leaving the latter two countries particularly susceptible. France and England were to encounter infinitely calmer periods of growth and depression because they were already equipped with advanced machinery.

139. *La Gironde*, 30 May 1866.
140. *La Gironde*, 25 April 1867.
141. By 31 August 1867, a large part of the Crédit Mobilier's securities portfolio was comprised of 62,000 shares of the Spanish Crédit Mobilier, whose prices are given in our text. Jean B. Vergeot, *Le crédit comme stimulant et régulateur de l'industrie* (Paris: Jouve, 1918), 178.

A.) Growth

Immediately after the end of the Civil War, the United States resumed the task of creating a great national industry that had begun before 1857. Germany followed an identical course beginning in 1869; it benefitted greatly from its success in 1870 and from the war indemnity paid by the French after their defeat in the Franco-Prussian War.[142] Thus, the two main focal points of crises were Germany and the United States.[143]

In America, the end of the Civil War had given industry a decisive boost. No sooner had New York been connected to San Francisco than a new railway line was built linking the North to the South. The most audacious railway expansion projects took shape. In 1860, the United States still had only 49,311 km of railways. In 1873, they had 106,516 km.

In Europe, the fever of railway construction was no less impressive: according to Wirth, their length had increased from 42,000 miles in 1865 to 70,000 miles in 1873.[144]

Shipbuilding also played a large part in the boom. The opening of the Suez Canal facilitated trade relations between the Far East and Europe, greatly stimulating the progress of navigation and maritime construction.[145]

Mining and the iron industry responded to this new demand for the means of production. This period of growth served as the cradle for the great German metal industry. German cast-iron production, which was only 143 million kg in 1840 and still just 592 million kg in 1861, suddenly reached 1,114 million kg in 1867, 1,264 in 1868, 1,413 in 1869, 1,564 in 1871, 1,988 in 1872 and 2,241 in 1873.[146]

It was the same in the United States: cast-iron production suddenly rose from 1,666,000 tonnes in 1870 to 2,561,000 in 1873, a nearly twofold increase in less than three years.

England followed suit, albeit more slowly, and English cast-iron production increased from 5,964,000 tonnes in 1870 to 6,566,000 tonnes in 1873.

However, it is worth noting that this increase in the production of cast iron in England was due less to the development of domestic consumption than to the increase in its exports to the United States. English iron and steel exports to the latter rose from £17.7 million in 1870 to £37 million in 1872.

In the presence of such an upsurge in capital production, the entire economy was invigorated.[147]

---

142. Maurice Block, 'La crise économique', *Revue des deux mondes*, 3rd ser., 32, no. 2 (March 1879): 435–36.
143. Yet German industrial growth had started before the war. In this regard, see Erhard Hübener, *Die deutsche Wirtschaftskrisis von 1873* (Berlin: Ebering, 1905), 39.
144. Wirth, *Geschichte der Handelskrisen*, 440.
145. Ibid., 442 (and quoted statistics).
146. We note that the growth of the German iron industry happened before 1870 and coincided rather more with the strengthening of the *Zollverein* [Customs Union] than with the Treaty of Frankfurt [ending the Franco-Prussian War on 10 May 1871].
147. In Vienna, one paid 200, 300 or even 500 florins to see a performance by Adelina Patti. The great actress undoubtedly attributed this success to her amazing talent, when in fact it depended in large part on a favourable economic situation.

The creation of large industrial centres, the concentration of the population from the countryside into the cities had created a considerable need for new housing. Around the mines, workshops and factories of all kinds, villages and sometimes even entire towns suddenly sprung up.[148] Big cities such as Berlin and Vienna were enlarged and improved.[149] Companies with diverse names like *Bau-und Verkehrsgesellschaft* [Construction and Transport Company], *Stadtgesellschaft* [City construction company] and so on were created, which turned construction into a real business. They were building for resale. Speculation intervened, and Schäffle reports that a premiere construction company bought a house for 400,000 florins, which at this price could return about 2.5 per cent. It found a buyer for 550,000 florins, who then sold it to another for the sum of 700,000 florins.[150] In Vienna, the year 1873 began in an atmosphere of excitement aroused by the opening of the World's Fair, which for a time sustained the golden age of Viennese construction.

The textile industry did not lag behind the construction industry: the silk industry experienced especially brilliant growth that was stimulated by improvements in the dyeing process and by the discovery of aniline. In the United States in particular, French engineers and workers were in demand to found silk mills; their national production grew from $23,904,000 in 1870 to $39,880,000 in 1871 and to $36,448,000 in 1872.

Cotton fabrics were also in high demand, and American agriculture benefitted greatly from the increase in cotton consumption. The total area planted in cotton expanded from 7,811,000 acres in 1871–72 to 8,867,000 acres in 1872–73.

Numerous companies were created. In the United States, in just the period from 1868 to 1873, $1.7 billion was spent on railways, $121 million of which was spent in 1873 alone. Projectors quite often resorted to dishonest practices to attract capital. The most common form was to create a company with reasonable nominal share capital, and only 10 per cent of this capital was paid in before bonds were issued.[151] The public readily subscribed to these pseudo-bonds.

In Prussia, the law of 11 June 1870 greatly encouraged the creation of joint-stock companies by lifting the requirement of government authorization.[152] The number of new companies in Prussia increased from 41 in 1870 to 225 in 1871 and 504 in 1872, and they represented capital of 177.07 million marks, 1,018.14 million marks and 1,495.78 million marks, respectively. See table 1.16 for more detail.

148. Wirth, *Geschichte der Handelskrisen*, 460.
149. For the complete details and circumstances, see ibid., 528–33.
150. Albert Schäffle, 'Der "grosse Börsenkrach" des Jahres 1873', *Zeitschrift für die gesamte Staatswissenschaft* 30, no. 1 (1874): 16.
151. H. M. Hyndman, *Commercial Crises of the Nineteenth Century* (London: Swan, Sonnenschein, 1902), 109.
152. Wirth, *Geschichte der Handelskrisen*, 534; Wilhelm Oechelhaeuser, *Die wirthschaftliche Krisis* (Berlin: Springer, 1876), 31, 138–39; Hübner, *Die deutsche Wirtschaftskrisis*, 103.

Table 1.16 Creation of New Companies in Germany, 1870–1874 (Capital in millions of marks)

	Semi-finished Goods; Salt Mines		*Metal Work; Construction of Machines*		*Textile Industry*		*Banks*		*Railways*		*Construction*	
	Number	*Capital*	*Number*	*Capital*	*Number*	*Capital*	*Number*	*Capital*	*Number*	*Capital*	*Number*	*Capital*
1870	4	2.88	4	2.25	2	6.45	5	22	2	50.04	4	76.56
1871	15	68.43	34	103.87	8	15.75	42	424.16	2	222.45	15	35.62
1872	60	224.87	86	91.86	24	42.64	49	345.61	8	183.98	66	290.02
1873	11	76.86	8	30	2	1.92	6	45	7	273.75	14	83.10
1874	3	21.90	1	3	2	1.92	1	1.50	5	47.82	3	1.33

No source given.

The aims of these different companies were extremely varied: mining, metalwork, banking, railways, textiles and construction. But the largest share of the capital went to the mines, factories producing semi-manufactured goods and the railways. From that time on, large lending banks financing production were at the forefront of this movement. Gelsenkirchen, nowadays one of the largest integrated enterprises in the Ruhr basin, dates from this period; its shares are issued by the Diskonto-Gesellschaft. Similarly, the Laurahütte mining and metalworks corporation was created in 1871 under the auspices of the Bleichröder investment firm.[153]

In Austria, companies had to obtain governmental approval for their incorporation; hence, we have precise statistics at our disposal. The number of new companies created rose from 32 in 1868 to already 141 in 1869 and to 376 in 1872, with a paid-up capital of 936.2 million florins in 1869 and 1,798 million in 1872.[154]

England also contributed to the economic growth, though indirectly; for it was primarily thanks to its exports, either to Germany or to the United States, that its production achieved prosperity.[155] The number of new companies grew significantly, from 595 with a nominal capital of £38.3 million in 1870 to 1,234 with a nominal capital of £152.1 million in 1873.[156]

In light of such a pressing demand for the means of production and for consumer goods, prices increased; in no time, prices rose to unprecedented heights. The products of the mining and the metal industries led the way in the upward movement of prices (see tab. A1). The portfolio of the banks, particularly of the banks of issue, was expanding rapidly (tab. 1.17).[157]

---

153. Hübener, *Die deutsche Wirtschaftskrisis*, 103.
154. For further details on the creation of new companies in Germany and in Austria, refer to Wirth, *Geschichte der Handelskrisen*, 461–513; and Hübener, *Die deutsche Wirtschaftskrisis*, 58–86 and 135–36.
155. Exports from Great Britain grew from £28.3 million in 1870 to £43.1 million in 1872. The greatest increases were to exports of iron, steel and coal (*Statistical Abstract*, 1873).
156. This spirit of enterprise in Germany had been actively stimulated by the French war indemnity payments. This indemnity had a twofold purpose: first, to reimburse the different German states for their war debts; and second, to introduce gold monometallism, as well as to demonetize silver.

    The first of the two operations had quite naturally brought an influx of capital seeking investment; as a result, interest had diminished. Industry seized this opportunity without hesitation, and new joint-stock companies were created. German industry benefitted from all these new orders; but as it could not meet all of them, foreign industry, and particularly English industry, benefitted as a result. A large part of the war indemnity was paid in goods, thanks to the system in which Germany bought the products either in France or England. The French state paid them off by borrowing. This explains why French gold did not leave the country in larger amounts. Franz Gutmann, *Das französiche Geldwesen im Kriege (1870–1878)* (Strasbourg: Tübner, 1913).
157. Cash on hand did not diminish even during the growth period, which was unusual. This was probably the case because the war indemnity payment had brought gold into Germany. On the other hand, the boom was largely domestic, and domestically the growth in banknote circulation equalled the increase in the stock of metallic currency.

Table 1.17 Balance Sheets of the Preussische Bank (later the Reichsbank), 1870–1874

	Cash on Hand	*Portfolio (millions of marks)*	*Loans and Advances*	*Banknote Circulation*
1870	86.29	143.20	28.22	163.26
1871	120.73	121.68	23.62	202.35
1872	172.87	194.29	31.67	253.18
1873	223.61	207.44	30.66	290.49
1874	228.81	127.43	22.67	277.47

Source: Conrad, et al., eds, *Handwörterbuch der Staatswissenschaften*, vol. 2, s.v. 'Bank'.

With the influx of billions of francs into Germany, the Berlin Stock Exchange believed stock prices, particularly industrial stocks, would continue to rise indefinitely. More and more, government securities were abandoned. Shares of the Bochümer Bergwerkgesellschaft [Bochum Mining Company] were listed at 109 in 1869 and valued at 377 by 1873; the Cologne-Minden railway line shares, worth 119 in 1869, reached 169.5 by 1872. Speculation was fierce in Berlin and especially in Vienna.

Table 1.18 Share Prices on the Berlin Stock Exchange, 1869–1873

	Cologne-Minden (Railway)	*Hüttenverein (Ironworks)*
1869	114	106
1870	133	111⅞
1871	164	117
1872	169½	137½
1873	142½	115

Source: Wirth, *Geschichte der Handelskrisen*, 604–6.

According to Schäffle, one would have to go back to the times of [John] Law's system or the tulip speculation in Holland to find levels of dizzy speculation similar to those witnessed on the Vienna Stock Exchange from 1872 to 1873.[158] The most prominent personalities were involved in the most indecent manoeuvres, lending their names to joint-stock companies in order to win the public's confidence. Banks had been created with the singular purpose of playing the stock market and exploiting the small savings: the so-called *Raten- und Rentenbanken*. Stocks and bonds were sold on credit and payable in instalments, so much per month, and very often, the seller did not have, and would never have, these securities in their portfolio. The sole purpose of the *Maklerbanken* [i.e., broker or investment banks] was to make it easier for the public to play the stock market, and they were primarily involved in financing the purchase of the securities of newly created industrial companies with call money.[iv] However, this speculation was also based upon genuine consideration of the rising dividends.[159]

158. Schäffle, 'Der "grosse Börsenkrach"', 7–8.
159. Oechelhaeuser, *Die wirthschaftliche Krisis*, 70–71, provides interesting statistical analysis of the dividends of several German companies.

Table 1.19 Average Dividends of German Firms, 1870–1874

	*Railway Companies**	*Banks and Lending Institutions*		*Mines and Factories*	
		Created before 1870†	*Created after 1870*‡	*Created before 1870*§	*Created after 1870***
1870	6.34	7.30	—	7.08	—
1871	6.61	9.80	11.28	9.58	8.33
1872	6.05	10.75	10.46	15.69	10.80
1873	5.38	7.15	2.52	19.23	7.02
1874	4.76	6.83	2.89	9.96	2.91

* The number of railway companies was 383; † 48 companies with paid-up capital of 847 million marks; ‡ 95 companies with capital of 570 million marks; § 26 companies with capital of 187 million marks; ** 58 companies with capital of 344 million marks.

No source given. [Lescure's figures were likely adapted from Oechelhaeuser, *Die wirthschaftliche Krisis*, chap. 2.]

Wages increased, according to Wirth, by 25 to 30 per cent. Workers enjoyed Saturdays and Sundays off. Workers' productivity declined. Oechelhaeuser provides the truly typical example of the masons: in Berlin, masons' wages had doubled; while at the same time, the number of stones laid by each mason per day had diminished by half.[160]

In the United States and Great Britain, we find the same phenomenon, the same rise in wages: in the United States, according to Block, wages doubled; in Scotland, where wages were fixed according to the prices of raw cast iron, the wage rate increased from 7 sh. 3 in 1872 to 8 sh. in 1873.

European immigration to the United States increased, reaching 346,938 in 1871, 404,800 in 1872 and 422,545 in 1873.

B.) Crisis and depression

At the beginning of 1873, Germany, Austria and the United States all presented with the symptoms of a general crisis of overproduction. The crisis erupted in Germany and Austria in May 1873 and in September in the United States. The two sensational episodes were, in Europe, the Vienna Stock Exchange crash in May 1873 and, in the United States, the bankruptcy of the large firm of Jay Cooke and Co. But let us be careful not to mistake these simple episodes for the deeper causes of the crisis.

From the beginning of 1873, bad news arrived. The most recent companies were not performing as expected, and the balance sheets for the 1872 fiscal year, which were only drawn up in March–April 1873, revealed the miscalculations. The new railway lines, instead of paying an average dividend of 11.28 as they had done in 1871, only gave their shareholders 10.42 starting in 1872. The last railway line undertaken registered the worst results. Thirty-seven recent railway companies, representing capital of 159 million marks, fell into bankruptcy or liquidation. The initial cost estimates had been exceeded by 50 to 100 per cent as a result of the rise in prices, the poor quality of

160. Ibid., 71–81.

labour and the use of defective materials. One kilometre of railway cost 208,000 marks in 1865 and 237,000 marks in 1873.[161]

The same was true in the mines, the machine industry, the steelworks and the blast furnaces. The newest companies were the most seriously affected. The same could be observed in the textile industry, construction and breweries.[162]

Whereas in Prussia 500 new companies with capital of 1,495.7 million marks had been created in 1872; in 1873, there were only 72 with capital of 538.23 million marks and, in 1874, only 19 with capital of 77.59 million. Prussia spent 273.75 million marks on railway construction in 1873; by 1874, it was only spending 47.82 million. The railways pulled the iron industry and mining down with them. Cast-iron production within the *Zollverein* (Germany and Luxembourg) dropped from 2,241 million kg in 1873 to 1,906 million in 1874 and to 1,846 million in 1876.

The crisis followed a similar pattern in the United States. The newest railway lines caused bitter disillusionment among their investors. On the whole, the American railway network never gave the appearance of a branch of industry in distress, neither in 1873 nor in 1874. In 1874, the American railways' gross returns did diminish, but only from $526 million to $520 million. Certain lines were still showing favourable results in 1874 (the Central Pacific, Chicago and North Western, and the Erie); however, the gains of these old lines failed even to compensate for the capital losses of the newer lines recorded in the overall statistics.[163] The economic crisis began with the receivership of the New York and Oswego Midland Railroad.[164] Then at the beginning of September, the Northern Pacific collapsed, taking the firm of Jay Cooke and Co. with it; the latter had $500,000 of this railway's shares in its portfolio. Thus, from September to November, one witnessed a veritable bloodbath of the railways. By 15 November, the number of railway lines that had suspended their payments was already at 15.[165] The other lines fared no better, and it was only by cutting production costs, either their operating expenses or their employees' wages, that they managed to avoid bankruptcy. For example, the Harlem New York Central and the New York Harvey Hatford cut their workers' wages by 20 per cent; while the Atlantic and Pacific Saint Louis, the Kansas City and the Northern lines cut wages by 10 per cent.[166]

Needless to say, given the circumstances, capital was increasingly diverted from the railways. Thus, the iron, cast iron and rail-producing industries soon entered a phase of acute depression. Cast-iron production plummeted from 2,561,000 tonnes in 1873 to 1,869,000 tonnes in 1876. Imports of rails into New York dropped by half between

161. Hübener, *Die deutsche Wirtschaftskrisis*, 57.

162. Oechelhaeuser, *Die wirthschaftliche Krisis*, 38–50, clearly highlights the fact that new businesses were the first to be hit by the crisis.

163. Clément Juglar, 'Les recettes des chemins de fer pendant la crise des États-Unis', *Économiste français*, 20 Dec. 1873, 1012.

164. Hyndman, *Commercial Crises*, 116.

165. Wirth, *Geschichte der Handelskrisen*, 643–46, provides extensive details on the various American railway bonds in default.

166. Ibid., 646.

1873 and 1874, from 307,413,233 to 159,649,112 lbs.[167] The distress was extreme: the Pennsylvania ironworks, which until then had been quite prosperous, was forced to restrict production and dismiss 25,000 workers. In the eastern regions, three-quarters of the factories had to dismiss their personnel: one after the other, the Stillman Manufacturing Company in Westerly County; the metalworks in Troy, New York; and the factories of the Atlantic DeLanic Company had to completely suspend production. The same occurred in the central and western states of America. In Jersey City and Hoboken, 5,000 workers were sacked. In New York alone, 182,000 union members were out of work.

Other industries like textiles and construction suffered the repercussions of this crisis.

The wool industry was particularly hard hit. Imports of raw wool into New York decreased by 1,105,655 lbs from 1873 to 1874. Some cotton mills, such as Harmony Mills in Cohoes, had to suspend production.

In the construction industry, 'The enormous costs of doing business', writes Wirth, 'severely limited the construction industry's appeal for investors, and capital was diverted to other branches of industry.'[168] But it was in Germany and Austria that the construction crisis was most acute. With the crisis in full swing, many workers left the cities, incomes diminished, and fewer houses were needed, especially the less luxurious ones. Rich capitalists who had been attracted to Berlin or Vienna during the period of growth returned to their '*Rittergut*' [country estates]. The enormous increase in construction costs compounded the effects of the reduction in demand.[169] Construction companies and mortgage lending were seriously affected.

Poverty was widespread, and the demand for luxury and consumer goods decreased. The retail trade suffered greatly from this consumption crisis.[170]

Bankruptcies were numerous: in the United States, their number rose from 2,915 with liabilities of $85,252,000 in 1871 to 5,183 with liabilities of $228,199,000 in 1873.[171] In Austria-Hungary at the beginning of March 1874, bankrupt joint-stock companies represented capital of 26.7 million francs, and liquidated companies, capital of 29.5 million francs. Instead of creating new companies or issuing new shares, the talk was only about capital reduction and mergers. Thus, nine banks were merged in Austria.

The drop in prices was enormous. We do not find a similar collapse of the markets for coal, cast iron or iron in 1847, 1857 or 1866. The price rise had been intense, and the decrease was no less so (see tab. A1).

By May–June, the decline was clearly discernible across the board in Germany.[172] The factories complained about the lack of orders and had to grant their buyers more and more substantial price reductions.

---

167. *Annuaire de l'économie politique et de la statistique* 34 (1877): 444.
168. Wirth, *Geschichte der Handelskrisen*, 647.
169. 'But the housing shortage had been such that wages and the cost of building materials had increased considerably. Hence, construction costs were higher than normal.' Ibid., 533.
170. Oechelhaeuser, *Die wirthschaftliche Krisis*, 88.
171. Wirth, *Geschichte der Handelskrisen*, 653.
172. *Économiste français*, 21 May 1873, 158.

In America, the crisis came a little later; it would not begin until October, and the repercussions were felt in England by November.[173] This price drop that began in 1873 was to be extremely long, lasting until 1879.[174]

Circulation had an influence, but we see no exchange crisis; we record a domestic credit crisis. Although the cash holdings of the large banks of issue did not diminish, their portfolio and note circulation grew in enormous proportions.

In Austria, the national bank's cash position hardly varied: from 142.6 million florins on 31 March, it reached its minimum on 23 April at 142.5, and by 7 May, it had already gained almost 1 million at 143.1. The portfolio, on the other hand, swelled rapidly, from 153.8 million florins on 31 March to 187.7 million on 28 May 1873. Advances also followed this trend, increasing from 26.3 million on 31 March to 46.1 on 30 June. In Vienna, 22 banks succumbed, 17 of which were recently created.[175]

A similar pattern occurred at the Preussische Bank (soon to become the Reichsbank): an increase in the portfolio, note circulation and cash holdings, which undoubtedly was due to the influx of French gold.

We see the same phenomenon in the United States, where there was no exchange crisis, despite a credit crisis and one of overproduction. The exchange rates from London and Paris to New York experienced insignificant variations. The speculation had been domestic, and so had been the crisis. Traders in difficulty were paying in banknotes or specie: banknote circulation and the portfolio were increasing; while the cash on hand remained more or less constant.[176] The credit crisis was intense, however. The firm Jay Cooke and Co. succumbed on 18 September. The firm Fisk and Hatch soon followed, driven by the failure of the Central Pacific and the Chesapeake and Ohio railways. Thus began a long series of bankruptcies, which included the Bank of the Commonwealth, the Union Trust Company and so on. The panic was such that the stock exchange had to be closed. The discount had reached up to 25 per cent. Faced with the lack of means of payment, a remedy was devised that would remain the conventional response until 1913: the issuing of clearing-house certificates. The clearing house issued certificates of deposit in denominations of $5 to 12,000, which were accepted as compensation at the clearing house. It advanced traders and industrialists up to 70 per cent of the titles or goods put up as collateral. Thus, during the crisis of 1873, $26,565,000 in certificates were issued.

In addition to the issuing of certificates, we also find the usual withdrawal of deposits. Deposits in the New York banks fell to £240,206,400 on 19 July 1873 and to £167,967,200 on 22 November.

---

173. *Économiste français*, 8 and 15 Nov. 1873, 861.

174. The year 1873 was in fact the origin of the phenomenon known as the price depression – that is to say, a slow decline in prices that was to last from 1873 to 1893–94, or thereabouts. We shall see a little later how the price decrease was interrupted in 1879–1882, 1883 and 1888–1890. See Hector Denis, *La dépression économique et sociale et l'histoire des prix* (Ixelles-Brussels: G.-J. Huysmans, 1895).

175. Wirth, *Geschichte der Handelskrisen*, 600.

176. 'Cours des changes', *Économiste français*, 6 Dec. 1873, 952–53.

Once the panic had passed and liquidation was completed, a phase of slow depression set in, characterized by the reduction in the portfolios of banks in Austria and in Germany, as it had been in the United States. The portfolio of the Preussische Bank shrank from 207.44 million marks in 1873 to 127.43 million in 1874; banknote circulation diminished from 293.49 to 277.47 million marks. At the same time, the cash on hand was growing.

It was the same in the United States, where the New York banks' portfolios had already fell to $248,067,300 on 22 December 1873, which represented a sudden reduction of almost $30 million compared to that of 20 November.[177]

However, the salient feature of the 1873 crisis was its intensity, represented by the stock market crisis in Berlin, Vienna and New York. Share values plummeted. Government securities remained resistant.

Table 1.20 The Vienna Stock Exchange in 1873

	6 April	*30 April*	*25 May*
Government Securities			
Pensions (Paper)	70.70	70.70	68
Pensions (Silver)	72.40	72.40	71.50
Banks			
Anglo-Austrian Bank	309	284	265
Construction:			
Wiener Baugesellschaft	313	302	142
Baugesellschaft Leopoldst	116	105	60
Railways			
Eisenbahnbaugesellschaft	114	100	70
Eisenbahnwaggon-Leih-Anstalt	115	117	80

Source: Wirth, *Geschichte der Handelskrisen*, 574–76.

Table 1.21 The Berlin Stock Exchange in 1873

	15 April	*15 July*	*4 October*
Disc-Commandit	300	216	195
Prov. Disconto	174	128	111
Berlin Bankverein	154	113	103
Laurahütte	254	175	180

No source given.

177. Credit in England was infinitely less affected than it had been in preceding economic crises, and if the Bank of England's balance sheets registered a credit crisis characterized by a sudden increase in its portfolio, this was soon to be followed by a reduction, and the trend was slow and moderate. The average portfolio, for example, of £27 million in 1872 grew to £28.8 million in 1873, only to fall to £26.4 million in 1874 and to £25.1 million in 1875. At the height of the American crisis, its discount rate was at 9 per cent on 10 November and at 8 per cent on 20 November; but its cash on hand and its reserve experienced insignificant variations.

In Berlin, and in Germany and Austria generally,[178] all the *Maklerbanken* and the *Raten- und Rentenbanken*, which had specialized in stock market transactions or similar, closely connected transactions, succumbed one after the other. The crisis broke out on 9 May in Vienna; a rescue committee was immediately created with the aim of offering credit on speculation papers but was refused by the national bank and other serious credit establishments. Instead, the largest firms created a fund guaranteeing 20 million florins for the same purpose. A deadline was agreed upon for settling up the contracts for difference [*opérations sur différences*], and a compensation rate was fixed for securities. On 15 May, the deadline expired. Suspensions that had been avoided for a while now took place – in particular, that of the celebrated firm Placht and Fels, which had been able to attract small savers' confidence. Then followed a string of scandals: the collapse of shares in credit institutions presided over by high-ranking officials, who succumbed in the face of the decline in value of the paper in their portfolios. The failures included the Boden-Kreditanstalt Bankverein, whose director von Hopfen was the former president of the Parliament; the Vereins- und Frankobank Union, presided over by the former minister Giskra; the Anglo-Bank headed by Count Eugene Kinski and so on.[179] The panic culminated on 9 June with the bankruptcy of the Wechslerbank, which was deeply involved in railway companies. Losing all its capital, it pulled other credit institutions down with it and claimed victims as far away as Berlin and Breslau.[180]

On 13 June, a new rescue committee was formed in Vienna that soon found many imitators in the provinces, as well as in Hungary. From that time forward, the crisis entered its resolution phase. By December, the situation in Vienna had improved significantly. In Berlin stock market prices had recovered some stability by August and September.

Wirth estimates that the losses on the Berlin Stock Exchange for the 90 principal share values listed at the time reached 131,138,000 marks.[181] In Vienna, losses reached 4,903,106 florins on railways and transport companies, 2,030,400 on industrial shares and 3,307,000 on banks.[182] The losses were particularly severe for shares of new companies that were unable to distribute reasonable dividends.[183]

In New York, the stock market crisis, like the crises of production and credit, had struck a little later, in August 1873. Panic was such that the New York Stock Exchange was forced to close on 20 September and remained closed for ten days. When it reopened, the drop in prices was enormous, and liquidation involved colossal sums of money. However, liquidation was completed fairly quickly, and beginning in December 1873, the stock exchange resumed its normal volume of trade.[184]

178. Hübener, *Die deutsche Wirtschaftskrisis*, 87–101.
179. Schäffle, 'Der "grosse Börsenkrach"', 8.
180. Wirth, *Geschichte der Handelskrisen*, 582.
181. Ibid., 599.
182. For further details, see ibid., 600–601.
183. Oechelhaeuser, *Die wirthschaftliche Krisis,* 39–45, 50.
184. For further details, see Wirth, *Geschichte der Handelskrisen*, 635–38.

The stock market crisis led to a complete upheaval in the securities market: panic sellers went bankrupt, buyers became rich. In 1873, those with small savings sold their stock *en masse* after the crisis exploded. Moreover, this panic was justified by falling dividends. The average dividend for railway companies dropped from 5.38 in 1873 to 4.76 in 1874; that of banks, from 10.75 in 1872 to 7.15 in 1873 and to 6.83 in 1874. For new companies, however, the fall in dividends was particularly enormous, from 10.46 to 2.52 and 2.89. A host of companies no longer distributed any dividends in 1874. According to Oechelhaeuser, in 1874, out of 389 new shares introduced on the Berlin Stock Exchange, 210, or 55 per cent, did not pay dividends at all. A few typical and sometimes amusing facts were recorded, such as the once happy speculator who, having lived in a mansion during the boom period, now had to content himself with a modest flat after the onset of the crisis; or the millionaire who was seen walking through the city dressed in summer clothes during the winter of 1874; or the domestic servant who, after having become rich enough through lucky speculations to be master and owner of his own household, was now reduced to his former condition. Some could not resist the blows dealt by fate: the number of suicides rose. Some suicide attempts were faked, like the insolvent speculator who pretended to kill himself by leaving old clothes on a bridge parapet before fleeing.

The working class was not spared from the crisis. Not only did wages drop (in Pittsburgh, wages at the blast furnaces had been reduced by 10 per cent in 1873, and in New York, brick masons were earning $4 less daily) but also the number of unemployed workers and the number of days of unemployment per week increased considerably. In Vienna and the suburbs, there were 18,380 unemployed workers at the beginning of February, and if the *Wiener Tageblatt* is to be believed, 14,000 workers had already left the city at that time. Manufacturing could count 5,600 unemployed workers, the ironworks lost 4,300, and another 3,400 were lost from the construction industry. In Germany, according to the *Times*, with the exception of Krupp, the number of workers employed in the 22 largest factories had decreased, from 27,700 in April 1873 to 14,600 by April 1877.

Still, it was hard to find, even in the most unexpected trades, those who were not at least touched by the crisis: in Vienna there were 860 unemployed bakers, 280 unemployed shoemakers and so on.[185]

Together with the arrival of the depression and unemployment, an opposite phenomenon to that observed during the growth period was in operation: an increase in worker productivity. In fact, unemployment allowed employers to keep only their most skilled and experienced workers; on the other hand, the reduction in the number of hours worked per day and the number of workdays per week had the effect of increasing the intensity of workers' labour and, as a result, its utility. According to Neumann-Spallart, a coal miner's output grew from 248 tonnes in 1873 to 279 tonnes in 1878.[186]

185. Ibid., 679.

186. Franz von Neumann-Spallart, *Übersichten der Weltwirtschaft, 1883–1884* (Stuttgart: Julius Maier, 1887), pt 2: 329.

Hector Denis reached a similar conclusion in more general terms: 'An examination of the diagram reveals that efficiency always tends to vary in inverse proportion to coal prices', and using his field observations of the Liège coal fields as evidence, he shows how miners' productivity decreased between 1859 and 1872 and then increased between 1873 and 1876.[187]

The crisis exerted an influence on certain social phenomena: marriages, suicides and crime.[188] Couples married less frequently, and suicides were on the rise, or more precisely, increased at an accelerated rate. Crime reflected the economic situation: theft and vagrancy developed, especially in the United States, where vagrancy took the usual form of organized gangs who exploited and extorted the rural population.[189] Immigration to the United States was decreasing as well: from 422,545 in 1873, it fell to 373,339 in 1874 and to 191,231 in 1875.

§9. – The crises of 1882 and 1884

In 1877, the depression had already reached its culmination in the United States. In Europe, the recovery did not take place until 1878–79. Nevertheless, the period of prosperity, arriving late, would not last over the long term. Crisis intervened, starting as soon as 1882. It remains of interest to us, however, because the growth of this period was essentially happening in France.

It was at this moment that the Freycinet plan was approved and implemented.[190] It was also at this time that the law of 11 June 1880 on local railways came into force.[191]

In the other great countries of Europe, such as England and Germany, the progress was much slower. Germany lacked capital; England was looking for a profitable use of its own capital, turning more and more toward foreign investments, especially in America.

A.) Growth

In France, the growth period was characterized by the increase in the figures for industrial shares issued [*émissions industrielles*]; starting at 350 million francs in the first half of

187. Denis, *La dépression économique et sociale*, 84.
188. We will not mention births; for if poverty can reduce their number, so can higher wages. According to some economists, poverty may even have a tendency to increase the number of children born, more so than prosperity.
189. Block, 'La crise économique', 441–42.
190. The costs for the project were estimated at 5 billion francs, of which 3.5 billion was allocated to the railways, 1 billion to navigable waterways and 500 million to ports. The expenditure was to be divided between the budgets for the years 1878 to 1890. The national railway network [*chemins de fer d'intérêt general*] was to be extended by 18,000 km, 10,000 km of waterways built or improved, and almost all maritime ports enlarged or transformed. See *Économiste français*, 10 Jan. 1880, 42; and Hyndman, *Commercial Crises*, 130.
191. Henry Vergé, 'Des chemins de fer d'intérêt local et des chemins de fer à voie étroite', *Économiste français*, 16 June 1883, 729–31.

1879, it grew fivefold, to 1,748.4 million francs in the first half of 1880; and in 1879–80, it reached the enormous sum of 4 billion francs, not counting the loans from Belgium, Austria-Hungary and Russia, which were not directly issued on the Paris market. In 1891, 430 new companies were created in Paris with share capital of 1,929 million francs.[192]

However, the growth took on an original appearance as a result of the completion of great public works projects, and apart from industrial output, orders came from the state's budget for public utilities. In order to complete the Freycinet plan, the French government spent 60 million francs in 1878, 130 million francs in 1879 and 200 million francs in 1880. By 11 November 1882, public works had absorbed 1,367 million francs. In accordance with the plan's projections, these funds were used for the construction and improvement of railway lines. The increase in the French national railway network reached 1,814 km in 1879, 810 km in 1880, 1,169 km in 1881 and 1,327 km in 1882, for a total expansion of 5,120 km.

Under the influence of the law of 11 June 1880, the local railway network was also developing rapidly: in 1879, only 69 km had been built; in 1880, 219 km had already been built; and in 1881, another 2,716 km were added.

In fact, profits justified the extension of the railways: the net income per kilometre for the French national rail network increased from 20,362 francs in 1879 to 22,687 francs in 1881.

The French mining and metal industries greatly benefitted from the expansion of the railways: production in the mines, blast furnaces and steelworks grew rapidly. The number of factories increased as new ones were built near Bayonne (Boucau), St Nazaire, in the Pas-de-Calais region, where English coal and mineral ore from Spain were imported at very cheap prices; or else in the East, where the cheap coal from the Ruhr valley and Lorraine had become useable thanks to Thomas' discovery. In 1882, orders which a few years earlier had been divided up between nine factories were now shared by sixteen factories. The flow of capital toward industry continued in France following the creation of a number of banks that put shares into the public domain in return for up to a quarter, making an appeal to small savers (peasants and the lower middle class). Quite often they sent salaried agents into the countryside with the task of placing these third- or fourth-rate papers; in return for a payment of 125 francs, the agent provided a lavishly printed title, with 500 francs in large print. One of these institutions, the most important one, the Union Générale would remain famous in economic history because of events which we will soon examine in greater detail. But it was not the only bank to get involved in this type of transaction: the Crédit de France, the Crédit de Paris, the Banque Nationale, the Société nouvelle de Banque et de Crédit, the Crédit Provincial, the Caisse Industrielle and so on were all for a time also supporters and facilitators of our national trade and industry. Under their patronage, the new Compagnie départementale d' Eau et de Gaz [County Water and Gas Company], the Omnibus company

192. See Neumann-Spallart, *Übersichten der Weltwirtschaft*, pt 1: 57, figures according to the *Revue des Banques* (1885): 345.

in Marseilles, the Entrepôts Libres de Paris-Lyon-Méditerranée [Free Warehouses of Paris-Lyons-Mediterranean], the Compagnie Générale du Gaz, the Société Générale de Navigation à Vapeur [Steam Navigation Company], the Entreprise Générale de Construction de Travaux Publics [Company for the Construction of Public Works], the electro-metalwork plant in Auteuil, the blast furnaces in Balaruc, the coal companies of Vernet and of Augits.[193]

Table 1.22 shows a similar trend in the United States.

Table 1.22 US Railway Construction, 1878–1881 (in miles)

1878	2,687	1882	11,596
1879	4,721	1883	6,735
1880	7,171	1884	3,977
1881	9,789	1885	3,131

Source: Neumann-Spallart, *Übersichten der Weltwirtschaft*, pt 2: 502.

Issues of securities naturally followed a parallel course. In the state of Ohio in particular, the issued railway share values followed the progression below.[194]

1880	$25,580,000
1881	$40,460,000
1882	$71,580,000
1883	$36,120,000
1884	$4,560,000

Simple tramways also enjoyed the capitalists' favour: issues of tramway securities grew rapidly, reaching their highest point in 1882.

At the same time, the mining and metal industries were expanding considerably, particularly rail production, which increased from 780,000 tonnes in 1878 to 1,305,000 tonnes in 1880, 1,647,000 in 1881 and 1,508,000 in 1882. Despite the development of national production, however, imports also grew from 153,000 tonnes in 1878 to 302,000 in 1881 and 296,000 in 1882.[195]

The production of cast iron, iron and steel naturally followed that of rail. Thus, industries supplying the means of production, both in France and the United States, experienced a phase of great prosperity,[196] which was shared by the consumer goods-producing industries.

193. See Paul Leroy-Beaulieu, 'La liquidation de la crise de 1882 et l'état présent du marché financier', *Économiste français*, 20 Sep. 1884, p. 345.
194. Conrad, et al., eds, *Handwörterbuch der Staatswissenschaften*, vol. 1, s.v. 'Aktiengesellschaften'.
195. Ibid., vol. 4, s.v. 'Eisen'.
196. These industries in France and even in Germany benefitted greatly from French and American growth, but only as a side effect, and if one compares the statistics for shares issued in England and especially in Germany and Prussia before the 1873 crisis and before that of 1882, we arrive at the same result: the flow of capital toward industry was very

In France, the number of active spindles increased from 4,383,140 to 4,716,897 in 1882. Instead of 50,028 in 1876, there were 71,977 looms in operation in 1882.[197]

Similarly in the United States, the national textile industry developed rapidly, as did foreign imports. Imports of woollens grew from $24,356,000 in 1878–79 to $44,275,000 in 1882–83.[198]

The demand for luxury goods expanded with rising incomes, and silk consumption in France went from 3,717,000 kg in 1879 to 4,413,539 kg in 1881.[199] In the United States, imports of raw silk progressed from 1,889,776 lbs in 1878–79 to 3,253,270 lbs in 1882–83.[200]

The railway opened up new, unexploited territories to capital and culture. Immigrants in particular flooded into the United States. Sales organized by the Land Office in Washington grew from 8,950,219 acres in 1879 to 9,166,916 in 1880 and to 10,579,107 in 1881.

World trade reflected this general prosperity, either with imports or with exports.[201] Prices rose in response to increasing demand (see tab. A1).

With the increase in the quantity of goods produced and traded, and the rise in their prices, the portfolio of large banks, particularly that of the Banque de France, grew. The discount rate increased.

The stock exchange experienced one of those periods of rising prices in which speculation becomes exaggerated. The Union Générale's share value increased from 1,280 francs in May 1881 to 2,880 francs by December 1881.

Finally, progress was made in the distribution of wealth.

In France, the demand for labour was such that one even had to resort to employing mediocre workers at very high wages. The implementation of the Freycinet plan was affected by this, and the projected cost estimates were soon exceeded. In the United States, in the states situated east of the Mississippi, the average monthly wage for agricultural workers increased by $3 from 1879 to 1882, and in the industrial states of the Northeast, the wage rise reached up to $6.40.[202] The wage increase was even greater for mine and factory workers.[203]

Moreover, the capitalists were no worse off, as dividends followed an upward trend: the Union Générale, for example, distributed 16.25 francs on 125 francs paid per

---

feeble. While the maximum value of Prussian shares issued during the growth period preceding the 1873 crisis was at 1,495.8 million marks, during the growth period preceding the 1882 crisis, it stood at 199.2 million marks. Cf. the first edition of the present work, p. 162, and Conrad, et al., eds, *Handwörterbuch*, vol. 1, s.v. 'Aktiengesellschaften'.

197. Neumann-Spallart, *Übersichten der Weltwirtschaft*, pt 2: 358.
198. Ibid., 369.
199. Ibid., 379.
200. Ibid., 383.
201. Ibid., 546.
202. Ibid., 49.
203. *Économiste français*, 20 April 1882, 49.

500 francs share; so, 13 per cent gave 40 francs in 1880, or 32 per cent. In 1881, with a paid capital of 12.5 million francs, the net profit reached 11.5 million francs.[204]

Other investment firms also announced very satisfactory dividends (tab. 1.23).

Table 1.23 Percentage Dividends for French Investment Firms

	1879 (%)	*1880 (%)*	*1881 (%)*	*1882 (%)*	*1888 (%)*
Banque de France	11	15	25	29	14.6
Industrial and Commercial Credit Company	14	14.8	15.3	14.8	10.8
Creusot	11.1	16.6	25	25	16.6

No source given.

In the United States, dividends followed an equally ascending curve, particularly those of the railway companies. However, although dividends were increasing, net profits were not rising as fast as gross profits; construction costs rose together with the prices of rails and wagons, wages and interest, and net returns suffered as a result.[205]

B.) Crisis and depression

In France the Union Générale crash – the interruption or at least the slowdown of public works – signalled the onset of the crisis.

Beginning in 1882, capital stopped flowing toward industry. We have already described above the often risky activity of the banks during the period of growth: the Crédit de France, Crédit de Paris, Banque Nationale and so on collapsed one after the other, dragged down by the bankruptcy of the multiple industrial and commercial firms that they had helped create. Whereas in Paris 430 companies with capital of 1,929 million francs had been created in 1881, only 338 were created with capital of 798 million francs in 1882; and in 1883, it dropped to 230 with capital of 251.2 million francs, and then to 143 with a capital of 92.9 million francs in 1884.[206] The Crédit Lyonnais lost 62 million francs from its title portfolio. The public withdrew nearly half of the deposits entrusted to this institution. From then on, its director Germain abandoned financial transactions, the expansion of branches and the transformation of credit companies into banks dealing exclusively with deposits and discounts. All shareholding interests, long-term advances and the firm subscription for industrial shares and securities were to be left to the investment banks.

As in previous crises, the 1882 crisis was marked by the resounding collapse of a large bank: in 1866, it was Overend, Gurney & Co., in 1873, Jay Cooke & Co., and in 1882, it was the Union Générale. However, the French state, after having stimulated production

204. Émile Struck, 'Zur Geschichte des Pariser Börsenkrisis von Januar 1882', *Jahrbuch für Gesetzgebung, Verwaltung und Volkswirtschaft im Deutschen Reich*, n.s., 7, no. 1 (1882): 255.

205. Adalbert-Frout de Fontpertuis, 'Le mouvement économique aux États-Unis', *Économiste français*, 12 Aug. 1882, p. 194; and the *Railway Age*, cited in Fontpertuis, p. 165.

206. Neumann-Spallart, *Übersichten der Weltwirtschaft*, pt 1: 57.

through its many industrial orders, suddenly suspended work on the railways. To the embarrassment of French finances, the unforeseen expenses, which exceeded estimates, necessitated a slowdown of civil engineering and war-related works.

According to Fougerousse, who did a survey of various industries, the first cause of the crisis was 'the overproduction in our factories coinciding with a sudden halt in public works and construction'. A second additional element was 'the almost sudden replacement of iron by steel in rail construction'. Therefore, 'the metal industry appeared to be [...] the sector of our national industry hardest hit at this time'.[207]

Table 1.24 Rail Consumption in France, 1879–1882 (1,000 tonnes)

	Iron	*Steel*
1879	39	231
1880	38	262
1881	28	290
1882	27	350

No source given.

Table 1.25 Metals Prices and Production in France in the 1880s

	Cast Iron (1,000 tonnes)	*Price of Cast Iron (francs)*	*Iron and Steel (1,000 tonnes)*
1882	2,039	91	1,531
1884	1,872	75	1,380
1887	1,568	57	1,265

No source given.

Construction, especially in Paris, suffered an intense crisis: the returns from the excise duty on construction materials dropped from 19,273,000 francs in 1882 to 14,811,000 in 1883. On the other hand, all trades – masons, joiners, locksmiths, carpenters, painters, plumbers and roofers unanimously deplored the lack of work and the workers' miserable situation. 'Last year we employed 1,100 workers, and now, only 250', commented a masonry entrepreneur.[208] Bankruptcy also struck numerous victims in the construction industry: from 25 in the second half of 1882, the number rose to 135 for the year 1883, and 15 occurred within the first eight weeks of 1884 alone. With the coming of the crisis, many capitalists left the cities. Unemployed workers did the same; and on 8 July 1883, we see the end of small tenancies, with 6,795 moving out compared to 4,599 moving in: it is estimated that 2,196 workers had left Paris by that date.

207. Auguste Fougerousse, 'La crise industrielle en France', *La Réforme sociale* 7 (1884): 200–26, 257–69, 306–20, 402–14 [*sic*, quoted material occurs on pp. 260, 261 and 257, respectively].
208. Ibid., 214–220 [*sic*, quoted material occurs on p. 215].

Luxury consumption had drastically diminished, affecting the silk industry in particular: raw silk consumption in France fell from 3,506,942 kg in 1881 to 2,692,132 kg in 1882, and it only increased to 3,306,100 kg in 1883 because of the influence of the demand from the United States, which still enjoyed full prosperity before falling to 2,626,627 kg in 1885.[209]

In general, the textile industry shared the same fate as the silk industry: cotton wares suffered from overproduction, which was further aggravated by the increase in the price of the raw material,[210] the cotton crop having been bad in the United States.

In the latter country, the effects of depression were more delayed. However, if prices, production, consumption and issuing still point to a state of real prosperity in 1882, a slowdown in economic activity was already beginning in 1883. Thus, railway construction diminished from 11,596 miles in 1882 to 6,735 in 1883, to 3,977 in 1884 and 3,131 miles in 1885.

In the state of Ohio alone, the United States had issued $71.98 million worth of shares in 1882 and $31.12 million in 1883 but did not spend more than $4.56 million in 1884.

In 1884, 37 companies, operating 11,838 miles of railway (with share capital and bonds of $714 million), were handed over to receivers for liquidation. In 1885, there were 44 companies with capital of $385 million operating 8,836 miles.[211]

Cast-iron production in the United States decreased from 4,623 (1000 tonnes) in 1882 and 4,956 in 1883 to 4,098 in 1884 and 1885. Rail imports, which had reached 302,000 tonnes in 1881, 296,000 in 1882 and already 118,000 in 1883, collapsed to 8,000 in 1884 and to 4,000 in 1885.[212]

At the same time in the mining and iron industries, instead of the $32.2 million spent in 1882 and the $19.3 million in 1883, no more than $2.8 million was spent in 1884, and $500,000 in 1885. The same was true for the different workshops producing finished goods, where the value of shares issued fell by more than 50 per cent from 1882 to 1885,[213] with 36.2 for 1882 and 13.1 for 1885. Steel and iron experienced a similar collapse.[214]

The usual trends were present: blast furnaces were extinguished, workers were dismissed, and operating and production costs were revised. Thus, alongside the increased number of extinguished furnaces,[215] we find an increase in the average output of the

209. Neumann-Spallart, *Übersichten der Weltwirtschaft*, pt 2: 379.

210. 'Principaux pays étrangers', 4th booklet, *Annales du commerce extérieur: faits commerciaux*, no. 5 (1890).

211. *Statistical Abstract of the United States* 43 (1920): 355, tab. 249.

212. Neumann-Spallart, *Übersichten der Weltwirtschaft*, pt 2: 347. Conrad et al., eds, *Handwörterbuch*, vol. 4, s.v., 'Eisen'.

213. Conrad et al., eds, *Handwörterbuch*, vol. 1, s.v., 'Aktiengesellschaften'.

214. Ibid., vol. 4, s.v., 'Eisen'. Iron exports from England: 4,042,000 tonnes in 1883, 3,497,000 in 1884 and 3,128,000 in 1885. See Neumann-Spallart, *Übersichten der Weltwirtschaft*, pt 2: 340.

215. From 270 in 1882, the number increased to 433 in 1884.

blast furnaces still in operation, from 15,032 tonnes in 1882 to 15,827 in 1884; by reducing the number of pourings [*coulées*], the production cost was also reduced.

Under the influence of the general depression in a whole branch of American production, we see a reduction in textile consumption. This reduction translated into a drop in national production, and in particular, into a reduction of foreign imports: cotton wares imports decreased from $36.85 million in 1882–83 to $27.19 million in 1884–85;[216] and raw silk imports fell from $3,253,009 in 1882–83 to $3,222,546 in 1883–84. Lyons and Saint-Etienne, still struggling to recover from the 1882 crisis, saw a reduction in their American market. The silk industry was not the only one to be affected. Porcelain exports from Limoges suffered a blow, as did champagne exports from Rheims.[217]

The combined reduction in production and consumption inevitably meant the disappearance of a number of producers: hence the number of bankruptcies.[218] The export and import values declined in the different counties.[219]

These economic troubles of production and consumption soon caused a reaction in prices. In France, the price fall took shape beginning in 1882.

In the United States, MacLean Hardy's index[v] (at 100 for the year 1860) was at 106.9 in 1880, at 105.7 in 1882 and at 106 in 1883; a deep collapse occurred in 1884 with the index at 99.4.[220] From 1882, the banks attempted by artificial means to maintain high prices, and they were successful for a time. But the depression in production and consumption felt as early as 1883 necessitated a drop in prices that the most skilful financiers could at best defer.

The circulation statistics also reflected very faithfully the general slowdown of trading: the Clearing House of New York, the Banque de France and American national banks witnessed a progressive decline in their portfolios. However, just as the crisis and depression in France showed a certain moderation, the resolution of the credit crisis also produced no serious effects that could not be mitigated by an increase of the discount rate to 5 per cent. After having reached a maximum of 1,724 million francs in 1882, the portfolio was reduced, reaching its minimum of 797 million francs in 1884. As for an

216. Neumann-Spallart, *Übersichten der Weltwirtschaft*, pt 2: 357.
217. *Annales du commerce extérieur: Faits commerciaux*, 11th booklet, no. 113 (1888): 4, 46–48.
218. In 1882, the number of bankruptcies in France reached 7,061, with liabilities of 243.9 million francs, and in 1884, there were 7,719 bankruptcies and a loss of 284.4 million francs.

   In the United States, the number of bankruptcies increased from 6,738 with liabilities of $101.5 million in 1882 to 10,968 representing $226.3 million in 1884.
219. See *Annales du commerce extérieur: Faits commerciaux*, 11th booklet, no. 113 (1888): 4 for statistics on France; and Neumann-Spallart, *Übersichten der Weltwirtschaft*, pt 2: 549, for statistics on the United States.

   Germany and England also experienced a depression of their foreign trade, while the situation of their domestic markets remained relatively favourable. After having benefitted from the period of growth, they suffered the effects of the depression in France and the United States. See Neumann-Spallart, *Übersichten der Weltwirtschaft*, pt 2: 549.
220. See *Annuaire de l'économie politique et de la statistique* 53 (1896): 692.

exchange crisis, there can be no question: as growth had remained internal to France, so the credit crisis and cash on hand showed rather feeble variations.[221]

In the United States, where speculation had been more intense and the recourse to credit accommodations [*crédit de complaisance*: i.e., credit kiting] extremely frequent, the credit crisis was more severe. By 1883, railway construction had begun to slow down, prices were following a downward trend, and even the profits of large joint-stock companies had even begun to fall. Nevertheless, the general state of the economy remained satisfactory. Thanks to multiple expedients, the crash had been postponed. At least in May 1884, it was still possible to hope that the periodic economic crisis that had befallen Europe in 1882 had been averted. The storm broke out suddenly and was all the more intense because one had attempted to avoid it. A whole series of credit abuses, such as the immobilization of demand deposits, were employed to give the appearance of an upward trend in demand. Suddenly, cracks appeared in the fragile façade that would soon collapse entirely. It started with the bankruptcy of the firm Grant and Ward, which was soon to be followed by Nelson, Robinson and Co. on 14 May, and the firm Goffle and Randle. The news of the Hutch and Foote Bank and the Metropolitan Bank closing their counters brought the confusion to a head. Suspensions continued one after another, as did bankruptcies. Out of the 3,261 national banks, 404 had to go into liquidation, thereby ceasing operations, and 70 did so with a view to re-establish them on new basis; 100 went bankrupt.[222]

From 14 May, a procedure was used that had already proven effective during the 1873 economic crisis: the issuing of clearing-house certificates up to 75 per cent of the amount of the assets deposited as collateral.[223] This decision restored confidence; as early as 15 May, the Metropolitan Bank had reopened its doors, and prices were rising on the stock exchange. Purchase orders from Australia had even seriously calmed anxieties when news of the bankruptcy of Dimock and Co., with liabilities of $1.5 million, caused trouble on the market. At 2.45 p.m., it was announced that the firm Fisk and Hatch had stopped payments, and at 3 o'clock, the stock exchange closed in an atmosphere of general consternation.

The situation had not improved by the following day, when the list of bankruptcies continued to grow with its first victims; among them was Hardy and Son, a bank and discount firm of the first order. The crisis was approaching its climax; and on 17 May, it had entered its resolution phase. The portfolios of the New York banks had reached their maximum in March 1884, with $357 million on 15 March, at a time when banks under threat were beginning to refuse the discount. Following the great panic of May 1884, portfolios shrank rapidly, reaching $293 million on 1 July 1884 (see tab. 1.26).[224] The banks' cash of hand experienced insignificant variations.

---

221. Juglar, *Des crises commerciales*, 400.
222. Adalbert-Frout de Fontpertuis, 'Le mouvement économique aux États-Unis', *Économiste français*, 7 Feb. 1885.
223. 'La crise de la spéculation à New-York', *Journal des économistes*, 4th ser., 26 (June 1884): 436.
224. See Clément Juglar, 'La crise de New-York', 2 pts., *Économiste français*, 16 Aug. 1884, 191–92 and 13 Sep. 1884, 315–17.

Table 1.26 Balance Sheets at the Banks of New York on 1 July (millions of dollars)

	1882	*1883*	*1884*
Circulation	18	15	14
Portfolio	332	328	293
Deposits	305	324	286
Metal Reserve	56	64	55

Source: Juglar, 'La crise de New-York', pt 2, *Économiste français*, 13 Sep. 1884, 316.

The crisis was also raging on the stock exchanges. In France, the stock market crisis was felt on the Lyon and Paris exchanges; and in the United States, the crisis broke in 1884 on the New York Stock Exchange.

In France, the two most prominent episodes were in Lyon, with the debacle of the Banque de Lyon et de la Loire shares, and in Paris, with the debacle of the Union Générale shares. On 3 January 1882, shares in the Banque de Lyon et de la Loire had already fallen from 1,500 francs to 800 francs. This sudden fall immediately put the Paris Stock Exchange on alert; in the meantime, the rumour of the refusal of a concession for a maritime bank in Trieste was confirmed, causing the first collapse. Bank failures erupted in Bordeaux and in Lyons, and by 10 January, the decline was confirmed all down the line: shares in the Banque de Lyon plummeted to 550 francs after an initial rise to 920; they even remained unsaleable for a while. Finally on 18 January, the Banque de Lyon suspended its payments in the face of legal proceedings; its shares slumped to 425. The panic then gripped Paris. The Union Générale's share price, which had jumped from 450 francs at the end of 1878 to 2,280 in December 1881, also collapsed on 12 January to 1,250. It was soon to be followed by other credit institutions, major French industrial firms and even the Banque de France (see tab. 1.27).[225]

Table 1.27 Share Prices on the Paris Stock Exchange, 1881–82

	End of May 1881	*End of December 1881*	*End of January 1882*	*End of March 1882*
Rente 4%	104	103½	103¼	103
Banque de France	5,750	5,725	5,500	4,900
Crédit Lyonnaise	895	895	800	785
Société Générale	725	825	800	785
Comptoir d'Escompte	1,055	1,045	1,020	1,017
Union Générale	1,280	2,880	950	—
Cail	278¾	125	80	50
Châtillon-Commentry	1,055	1,045	977½	1,000
Fives-Lille	640	605	550	580

No source given.

225. Speculation had been so intense in France, and in particular there had been so much abuse of the provision in our companies act allowing shares to be traded with only a quarter paid up, that Mr Humbert, the justice minister, reassured the Chambers, which were stirred by these financial abuses, in the following terms: 'The attention of the government will focus on the legislation with the utmost care, and we will manage, I hope, to present ways to

Table 1.28 Share Prices on the Vienna Stock Exchange in January 1882*

	14 Jan.	*23 Jan.*
Austrian Notenrente (paper denom. bonds) 5%	94.45	75.23
Hungarian Goldrente (gold denom. bonds) 6%	119.60	115.75
Austrian Kreditanstalt	332.79	327
Austrian Bodenkreditanstalt	273	195
Austrian Nordwestbank	249	188

* One of the interesting features of this crisis was its repercussions on the Vienna Stock Exchange. The Union Générale and the Banque de Lyon were at the head of many Austrian firms; hence, the collapse of these two institutions seriously affected the course of shares on the Vienna Stock Exchange.
Source: Struck, 'Zur Geschichte des Pariser Börsenkrisis', 268.

The stock market crisis was no less severe in the United States, and the crash, having been deferred for a time, was all the more intense. The decline began as early as 1883, but the collapse did not take place until 1884. The crisis was preceded by a tournament of billionaires, as frequently happens in the United States. The two opponents involved were Jay Gould and Villard. Jay Gould supported the Union Pacific, and Villard, the Northern Pacific. The two railway companies had been in competition and were engaged in a tariff war. The fight was not just confined to tariff rates; it also spread to the stock exchange, where the respective owners of the two railways were both determined to drive down his adversary's share value. At the beginning of 1884, it appeared that Jay Gould was winning; then in May, the firm suddenly collapsed, and with it, the shares of the Union Pacific, which dropped from 84 at the beginning of January to 40. The debacle was soon universal: not only were all of Jay Gould's supporters, large and small, ruined, but the slump had also become general. The share values of other railway companies were severely hit (see tab. 1.29).[226]

reconcile the many different interests.' See 'La crise de bourse de Lyon et de Paris en 1882', *Journal des économistes*, 4th ser., 17 (Jan. 1882): 347.

It was also at this time that the discussion on the regulation of the futures market and the gaming exception began. See Mattieu Rodet, 'Le marché à terme et les jeux des Bourses', *Journal des économistes*, 4th ser., 17 (Jan. 1882): 361–83. On 6 February 1882, Mr Naquet took up a bill that had already been formulated twice, in 1875 and 1878, by Mr Audrian, demanding the recognition of the futures market and the abolition of the gaming exception. Since then, the law of 28 March 1885 has been in force, enshrining this principle. Crises even have an influence on legislation.

226. Many banks dragged down by the crisis had concluded many 'puts' (option trading [*opérations à prime*]). They were hard hit by the drop in stock exchange prices. An interesting detail: before taking up the securities, the put had to be endorsed at the bank. Russel-Sage, a large financier heavily involved in these sorts of operations, got so tired of endorsing puts, on which he was losing 50 per cent, that one day he closed his counters at 3 p.m., giving the long queue of impatient clients appointments for the next day. See 'La crise de spéculation à New-York', 444–45.

Table 1.29 Share Prices of the Principal Railway Lines on the New York Stock Exchange, 1881–1884

	1881	*1882*	*1883*	*1884*
Central Pacific	100	82	61	30
Union Pacific	130	98	70	28
New York Central	151	125	111	37
Northern Pacific	88	100	49	37

Source: Juglar, 'La crise de New-York', *Économiste français*, 16 Aug. 1884, 317.

Dividends and wages dropped. In France, however, some companies, thanks to their large reserves, managed to defend their dividends. But the workers engaged in railway construction, mining and the metal industry were affected.[227] Instead of the 1,100 francs he had earned in 1882, a coal miner was only earning 1,072 francs a year in 1884; a miner in iron ore mines earned 1,010 francs in 1882 and 971 francs in 1884. The number of employed miners decreased from 120,456 in 1882 to 110,410 in 1884. In the metal industries (cast iron and steel), 13,547 workers were dismissed between 1882 and 1884.

In the United States, nearly the same situation existed at the end of 1884. However, wage reductions were the rule, and they were greater in the United States because the crisis was more intense there than in France. By the end of 1884, wages had been cut by 25 to 30 per cent in the wool and cotton industries, and by 15 to 22 per cent in the metal industry (iron, cast iron and steel). In the latter industry, we find the largest number of workers organized into unions, which meant their wages were cut more slowly. The wage reductions did not prevent workers from losing their jobs. From February 1884, various firms in the Pittsburgh area dismissed 3,000 workers. The anthracite mining companies of the Pennsylvania basin, with the exception of the Pennsylvania Railroad Company, agreed to limit their extraction in 1885. The companies in Lehigh and Lackawanna and in Delaware, Reading and Hudson dismissed 10,000 miners.[228]

Crime increased with poverty and unemployment, especially petty crimes, like vagabondage, begging or petty theft. In France, after having gradually decreased between 1877 and 1881, crime increased significantly in 1882 and especially in 1883. The number of convictions for vagrancy rose from 12,452 in 1881 to 13,583 in 1882 and 15,071 in 1883. Those convicted of begging went from 7,569 in 1881 to 7,771 in 1882 and 8,470 in 1883. Finally, the number of convictions for petty theft, after having reached 35,747 in 1881, rose to 35,930 in 1882 and 35,959 in 1883.[229]

227. There were also some wage reductions in the textile industry, mainly silk and wool, which were a result of amicable agreements concluded between bosses and the workers. *Annales du commerce extérieur: Faits commerciaux*, 11th booklet, no. 113 (1888): 9. See also: *Enquête Réforme sociale* [Social Reform Survey].

228. *Économiste français*, 7 Feb. 1885.

229. See *Annuaire de l'économie politique et de la statistique*, 1880–1885.

In England, the very high unemployment rate in the years 1885–1887 provoked a resurgence of the socialist movement.[230]

§10. – *The crises of 1890 and 1893*

With the crisis of 1873, we already encountered an interesting phenomenon: the long duration of the depression that followed it; with the crisis of 1882, we observed another: the feeble intensity and short duration of the period of growth. The crisis of 1890 presents us with a similar characteristic: a brief and altogether moderate period of growth.

In total, from 1873 to 1884, the years of depression outnumbered the years of growth; and the years of prosperity revealed, at least in Europe, only a very relative prosperity. Are we not then confronted with a long period of depression that contradicts our so-called law of the development of capitalist societies through alternating periods of economic growth and depression? We think not. The existence of more general movements – upward and downward trends overlapping those which are the specific and exclusive objects of the present study – is undeniable. Yet, far from invalidating our theory, the existence of long periods of depression[231] demonstrates the contrary: it explains the peculiarities presented by the periods of growth and depression at that time.

In Europe, the growth was characterized by the flood of European capital toward faraway business ventures. The European market contracted, and capital continued to turn toward new countries that lacked modern machinery, particularly railways.

Thus by 1886–87, English capitalists had taken an interest in the South American republics of Uruguay and Argentina.

France remembered the crisis of 1882 and would not commit similar excesses. Repairing the damage done to its vineyards by 'phylloxera' absorbed a good part of its savings.

Germany, on the other hand, having recovered from the harsh experiences of 1873, resumed its triumphant march toward 'industrialization', profiting in no small measure from the economic boom in the United States.

The United States was far from having reached the peak of its development and would suffer a crisis.

---

230. G. D. H. Cole, *British Trade and Industry, Past and Future* (London: Macmillan, 1932), 95.

231. On the distinction between crises and depressions, refer to Carroll D. Wright, *The First Annual Report of the Commissioner of Labor, March 1886: Industrial Depressions* (Washington, DC: Government Printing Office, 1886), 11; Edward D. Jones, *Economic Crises* (London: Macmillan, 1900), 5; and Magnus Biermer, 'Die letzte deutsche Wirtschaftskrise und ihre Ursachen', in *Sammlung nationalökonomischer Aufsätze und Vorträge*, vol. 1 (Giessen: Roth, 1905), 171–212.

A.) Growth

Hardly had the crisis of 1884 been liquidated than American industry experienced a vigorous recovery, in 1886. As early as 1886, in the 14 southern states, 1,575 new firms were launched with a capital of $129 million, and in 1887, another 1,430 with a capital of $246 million. On the other hand, the depressed prices of American stocks – especially railway shares – soon attracted European capital. And in 1888–89, prosperity again reigned in industry, trade and on the stock exchange. Confidence had been restored.

The railways and their construction were, as always, the most significant part of this growth. From 1885 to 1892, the American network was extended by 46,863 miles; in 1889, a further 8,348 miles were opened to traffic; and in 1890, only 4,287. In 1891, as a result of more or less artificial measures, this figure rose to 6,386 miles and still reached 6,245 miles in 1892. Capitalists' keenness for the American railways was also explained by the gradual increase in returns per kilometre.[232]

Cast-iron production also increased in the United States by 127 per cent between 1885 and 1890 (tab. 1.30), surpassing that of England for the first time; and while in 1888 the exports of rails from England to the United States were still 24,277 tonnes, they decreased from 250 to 134 in 1889 and 1890, as American domestic industry developed. It was the same for cast iron imported from England, which decreased from 418,919 tonnes in 1886–87 to 81,916 tonnes in 1890–91.

Table 1.30 Production of Metals in the United States (1,000 tonnes)

	Cast Iron	*Iron*	*Steel*
1885	4,110	1,473	2,604
1890	9,348	2,558	3,439

No source given.

The state of the American iron industry at this time presents us with an interesting peculiarity. Struck by alternating periods of feverish production and slack production, it had attempted to regulate production by means of agreements between producers. Since the demand for iron and steel was mainly due to railway construction, the great American industrialists headed by Andrew Carnegie believed that they could achieve this result by regulating rail production. In 1888, they created a rail 'pool' that divided production among the 13 largest rail producers in the United States at the time. Their participation in the cartel was the only condition fixed by the contract; prices were determined by verbal agreement. Initially, there were no fines for violating the pool. It was not until 1891, when demand was particularly pressing, that a fine of $1.50 per tonne produced in excess was established. As long as the economic growth lasted, the pool worked. However, the confusion it brought with expanded production encouraged

232. *Économiste français*, 25 Aug. 1894, 243. Statistics from the *Statistical Abstract of the United States* fail to provide a comparable series of figures for this period.

most of its members either to buy the factories of other pool members or to merge their factories in order to secure a dominant position in the pool. It was thus that Carnegie's stake rose from 13.5 per cent in 1888 to 25.9 per cent in 1892, and that the North Chicago Rolling Mill Company merged with the Joliet Steel Company and the Union Steel company in 1889 to form the Illinois Steel Company. By 1890, Carnegie and Illinois represented 51.8 per cent of rail production. The dominant position of the large producers had the effect of reducing the share of production allocated to smaller factories to the benefit of the large ones. After their merger in 1890, Lackawanna and Scranton only obtained a 14.3 per cent share in 1892; while between them they had 10.0 + 13.3 = 23.3 per cent stake in 1890. On the other hand, Carnegie and Illinois obtained 51.8 and 58.6 per cent in the same years.[233] This situation could not last.

Great Britain, deprived of the American market, turned to Australia, Canada, Argentina and Uruguay. Certain banks played a crucial role here, the firm Baring Brothers and Co. in particular. Baring issued corporate stocks or bonds and government securities. These companies, these states, were thus credited with the amount of the sums subscribed by English capitalists, who in exchange for their payments to the bank received shares, bonds or annuities. These companies, these states (in the case of Baring Brothers, Argentina in particular), obtained open credits [*crédits ouverts*] from the bank in the form of acceptances in the amount of their loans; with the help of these acceptances, they could pay for the coal, cast iron, machinery and rails that they were buying from English factories.[234] By the beginning of 1890, the Baring Brothers firm had issued 2.5 billion francs worth of Argentine securities, 700 million of which were issued in 1888 alone.[235] Under these conditions, English exports to Argentina grew rapidly, from £4.7 million in 1885 to £10.7 million in 1889.[236]

In particular, much had been borrowed for the construction of railways, and the Argentine network was rapidly extended from 5,484 km in 1885 to 10,244 in 1890.[237] In Uruguay we find a similar, albeit smaller, increase: 500 km in 1885 and already 1,127 km in 1890.

Finally, in Australia the length of the railway went from 6,126 miles in 1885 to 10,234 in 1893.[238] More generally, however, all the metal parts were exported from the mother country. English exports to Australia were growing rapidly.

233. L. Glier, 'Zur neuesten Entwicklung der amerikanischen Eisenindustrie', pt 1, *Jahrbuch für Gesetzgebung, Verwaltung und Volkswirtschaft im Deutschen Reich* 27, no. 3 (1903): 241–44 (1025–28).
234. 'The Crisis of 1890', *Economic Journal* 1, no. 1 (Mar. 1891): 192.
235. Arthur Raffalovich, 'La crise de Londres en novembre 1890', *Journal des économistes*, 5th ser., 4, no. 12 (Dec. 1890): 324; and see Hyndman, *Commercial Crises*, 148, 153–55.
236. Tugan-Baranowsky, *Theorie und Geschichte der Handelskrisen*, 163.
237. Some lines were undertaken by the government, others by the provinces; still others, and by far the most numerous, were undertaken by private companies.
238. For further details, see F. X. von Neumann-Spallart and Franz von Juraschek, *Übersichten der Weltwirtschaft, 1885–1889*, with additions by F. von Juraschek up to 1895 (Berlin: Verlag für Sprach- und Handelswissenschaft, 1896), pt 2: 674.

This increase in England's foreign trade meant that it needed to develop its merchant fleet. According to *Lloyd's Register*, 743 ships with tonnage of 1,594,705 were built in 1890, compared to 378 ships with tonnage of 455,856 in 1885.[239] Under these circumstances, the demand for cast iron, iron and steel was extremely lively, and cast-iron production in England increased from 7,122,000 tonnes in 1886 to 8,456,000 in 1889; iron production, from 1,643,000 tonnes to 2,290,000; and steel production, from 2,301,000 tonnes to 3,617,000.[240]

Germany continued its evolution toward big industry to the extent that its capital would allow. The number of joint-stock companies created and the amount of their capital increased rapidly from 1886 to 1889 (tab. 1.31).

Table 1.31 New Joint-Stock Companies Created in Germany, 1886–1890

	Number of Companies Created	*Share Capital (mill. marks)*
1886	113	103.94
1887	168	128.41
1888	184	193.68
1889	360	402.54
1890	236	270.99

Source: Neumann-Spallart and Juraschek, *Übersichten der Weltwirtschaft*, pt 1: lxxxv.

Germany constructed 778 km of railways in 1886, 1,115 km in 1887, 926 km in 1888 and 912 km in 1889. Under the influence of an energetic protectionist policy, Germany built its national iron industry. The number of blast furnaces went from 215 in 1886 to 222 in 1890, and their output increased from 19,427 to 23,114 tonnes in the same years.

Once again, steel production quickly outpaced that of iron, and while iron production grew by about 10 per cent, steel production increased by almost 60 per cent. Thomas' discovery, which allowed the use of phosphorous iron ore from Lorraine, was widely applied in Germany.

Thanks to this growth, the need for more residential housing was keenly felt, new cities were created, and others were expanded. For instance, Buenos Aires entrusted one company with the task of organizing its water and sewage service. In Australia, banks were responsible for providing entrepreneurs with capital, thereby encouraging land and real-estate speculation.

The textile industry also experienced a period of prosperity. The consumption of cotton wares, in particular, provided a large outlet for the abundant cotton harvests of

239. It is interesting to note the replacement of iron by steel. In 1885, 260 iron ships with tonnage of 290,429 tonnes were constructed; in 1890, only 106 with tonnage 36,031 tonnes were built. See ibid., pt 2: 407.

240. Ibid., pt 2: 393–99. Production per blast furnace had decreased, which tends to indicate the use of outmoded equipment. The sudden increase in demand was satisfied as much as was possible.

1886, 1887 and 1888. But already in 1889, the cotton harvest was poor, which made the raw material expensive, causing many difficulties for the textile industry.

Like cotton wares, woollens and silk were in high demand in the years 1888–1890, and raw wool and silk imports were growing rapidly in the different countries.[241]

Finally, agriculture itself was no stranger to the general economic prosperity, at least in the United States. In the face of the growing demand for cotton, the number of acres of land planted in cotton increased from 18.5 million in 1886 to 19.05 in 1888 and to 19.5 in 1890.[242]

Prices rose because of the general development of demand and trade. As usual, the mining and metal industries saw the prices of their raw, semi-manufactured and manufactured products rise quite sharply. Textiles themselves, despite good cotton harvests, followed this trend, and agricultural products did not remain unaffected.

However, while in Europe the upward trend in prices transformed into a downward one as early as 1890, in the United States prices remained high until 1893. This particular aspect had two causes: the United States artificially increased the demand for its products and artificially restricted supply and competition in its domestic market. It then increased demand by means of the Sherman [Silver Purchase] Act, which raised the required monthly silver purchase of the US Treasury to four million ounces per month.[243] In 1890, the highly protective McKinley tariff came into effect, squeezing out foreign competition.

The discount rate increased with the growth in trade. The portfolios of the Bank of England, the Reichsbank and the New York banks reflected the increasing use of the discount. The average rate rose from 3.30 per cent in London in 1887 to 4.51 per cent in 1890; and in Berlin, from 3.41 to 4.52 per cent over the same period.

The stock exchange also experienced a period of increasing prices. In Berlin in particular, the Bochümer Verein's share increased from 197 on 31 December 1888 to 284 on the same date in 1889; the share value of the Dortmunder went from 98 to 137, and that of the Gelsenkirchen, from 134 to 217, in the same years. In London and New York, it was the same. South American securities in London and North American railway securities found an ever more favourable reception among capitalists and investors.

Rents, interest, profit and wages increased. First, rents: in Melbourne on Collins Street, a plot of land that sold for 24,000 francs per English foot was sold for 50,000 francs soon after.[244] Interest followed suit. Argentine and American railways had to pay an increasing interest rate on their bonds. Dividends and wages also showed gains. For America, we rely on a valuable statistical document: the *Bulletin of the United States Bureau of Labor Statistics*. In the January 1902 issue, we find two wage indexes, one for

241. Ibid., pt 2: 439, 481, 507.

242. Ibid., 428.

243. The Bland Act of 1878 had fixed it at 2.4 million. See Costantino Ottolenghi, *Delle perturbazioni economiche* (Torino: Fratelli Bocca, 1901), 16–20. [Ed. – In fact, the Sherman Silver Purchase Act raised the monthly aggregate amount to 4.5 million ounces.]

244. See Pierre Leroy-Beaulieu, 'L'Australie et la Nouvelle-Zélande', *Revue des deux mondes*, 4th ser., 137, no. 2 (15 Sep. 1896): 433.

the nominal wage and the other for the real wage. While the nominal wage index rose from 151 in 1886 to 161 in 1892, the real wage index increased more rapidly, rising from 157 to 174. Here we encounter an interesting phenomenon: an application of the principle according to which upward or downward movements are not instantaneously passed from one branch of industry to another. In fact, the more rapid increase in real wages indicates that the prices of the workers' consumer goods did not increase as rapidly as the nominal wage rate.

In England, another country that enjoyed real prosperity from 1888 to 1890, wages also rose by 30 to 40 per cent. The increase was particularly noticeable in the mining and metal industries.[245]

The general prosperity exerted an influence on various social phenomena, such as the number of marriages, crime and emigration. In England and in Prussia, the number of marriages increased, while crime diminished. The economic boom in the United States and Argentina had the effect of increasing the number of immigrants to these countries. For the United States, the number of immigrants rose from 490,109 in 1886–87 to a maximum of 623,084 in 1891. For Argentina, there were 93,116 in 1886 and 260,909 in 1889.

In Germany, industrial prosperity tied the people to the national soil; the number of emigrants diminished from 104,787 in 1887 to 97,103 in 1890.[246]

B.) Crisis and depression

England owed its economic growth to its foreign investments and faraway business ventures. Losses on these investments signalled the crisis of 1890.

This crisis has often been referred to as the Baring crisis, after the firm that was its first and main victim; however, we should not conclude from this that the fall of the Baring firm was the cause of the crisis. In fact, the opposite is true.[247] In Argentina, the first companies to be established had been successful, while those created later were less so, in particular the Buenos Aires Drainage and Waterwork Company. Founded with capital of £10 million, the issue of its shares failed completely, as 90 per cent had remained in the hands of the issuing firm Baring Brothers. Baring's representative in Argentina, S. B. Halle, had drawn on Baring Brothers for £8 million in bills of exchange which Baring had accepted. When the last £4 million came due in November 1890, Baring succumbed. This was just one episode in a more general crisis. The rising cost of interest and wages resulted in losses for Argentinian companies. Raffalovitch wrote, 'firms that employ many workers and consistently use many raw materials earn large industrial profits mainly at the beginning of the recovery, but their profits then diminish

245. Neumann-Spallart and Juraschek, *Übersichten der Weltwirtschaft*, pt 1: lvx.
246. Conrad, et al., eds, *Handwörterbuch der Staatswissenschaften*, vol. 1, s.v.: 'Auswanderung'. This example contradicts Neumann-Spallart and Juraschek's contention that every prosperity period signals an increase in emigration from Europe.
247. In this sense, see 'The Crisis of 1890', 192.

with the increased costs of labour and production'.[248] This purely economic cause was compounded by a political one. The Argentine revolution depressed Argentine securities in general and government securities in particular.

A period in which the spirit of enterprise had been too lively gave way to one of general mistrust. Railway profits fell, and with them, the construction fever. Many lines remained unfinished, and many were unproductive and threatened to remain so for a long time.[249] The import of iron products and manufactured goods in Argentina collapsed from $24,726,113 (paper) in 1889 to $9,566,752 in 1890 and $4,517,420 in 1891; that of railway equipment, telegraph and so on, went from $24,173,749 in 1889 to $36,273,503 in 1890 and $3,545,625 in 1892.[250] England suffered a severe backlash from the Argentine crisis: its exports fell from £10,681,879 in 1889 to £4,246,700 in 1896, almost £2 million of which were in iron exports and almost £1 million in machinery.[251] Thus, the number of shares issued on the English market was down from 238.76 million in 1890 to 95.53 in 1893. The depression in England was mainly reflected in the reduction of its exports. However, the crisis in Argentina was not the only culprit.

England was suffering from an increase in the American national metal and mining production, as well as from the worsening of its customs tariffs. Germany was affected too. Yet the 1890 crisis in Germany was more of a domestic crisis than an export crisis. German industry continued to produce heavy machinery which had given it pride of place among the great industrial nations. A quieter period ensued. The German iron industry suffered a depression until 1895.[252]

On the other hand, the United States sustained its economic growth well beyond 1890, postponing for a while its decade-long crisis. Thanks to its strong protectionism and the expansion of its mint,[253] the American economy triumphed over the repercussions exerted by the European crisis. Moreover, the year 1891 had not been a very successful one, as is demonstrated by the statistics for production, prices, credit and the clearing house; but by 1892, prosperity had fully returned. It seemed that the crisis had passed. It had only been postponed.

The crisis began with the railways. From the beginning of 1893, certain lines showed significant miscalculations; in particular, the shares of the Reading Company collapsed in February from 76 to 23.5.[254] Yet the optimism remained until the events that took place between April and July finally opened everyone's eyes. From April to

248. Raffalovitch, 'La crise de Londres', 324n1.
249. W. H. Bishop, 'The Argentine Crisis', *Economic Journal* 1, no. 3 (Sep. 1891): 537.
250. *Statesman's Yearbook*, 1890–1894.
251. *Journal of the Statistical Society of London* (1894): 329 [*sic*].
252. Theodor Vogelstein, *Die Industrie der Rheinprovinz, 1888–1900: Ein Beitrag zur Frage der Handelspolitik und der Kartelle* (Stuttgart: Cotta, 1902), 56–58.
253. Ernst von Halle, 'Die wirtschaftliche Krisis des Jahres 1893 in den Vereinigten Staaten von Nordamerika', *Jahrbuch für Gesetzgebung, Verwaltung und Volkswirtschaft im Deutschen Reich* 18, no. 4 (1894): 158–60 (1188–90), provides interesting details of the consequences of the Sherman Act. See also Ottolenghi, *Delle perturbazioni economiche*, 10.
254. Von Halle, 'Die wirtschaftliche Krisis', 163, 197 (1191, 1227).

July, 35 blast furnaces had closed down, 24 of which were extinguished in the last half of June. In July it was worse: bankruptcies, factory closures and worker dismissals were the order of the day. The railways formed by far the largest contingent of its victims: at the end of May, the Northern Pacific line suspended payments, followed on 25 July by the New York-Lake Erie.[255] In 1893, only 2,630 railway miles were built, compared to 6,245 miles in 1892, and the slowdown in construction was even more pronounced in the first half of 1894.[256] Returns were in fact showing capital losses, as many of the newly opened lines had ended up being unproductive. In July, the average gross returns per week declined, for the Denver-Rio Grande, from $236,000 to $101,000, and for the Missouri-Pacific, from $593,000 to $292,000. On the whole, after a period of continuous increase, gross returns showed capital losses for the first time in July 1893. In January 1894, the decline was 12.25 per cent, when compared to the profits for the same month in 1893, and in June, the figure rose to 21.80 per cent. This was a real debacle for the railways.[257] From 1893, the length of the railways that went into liquidation reached the enormous figure of 36,000 miles, representing equity capital of $900 million and bond capital of $1,500 million. During the first half of 1894, 23 new lines, 2,968 miles long with equity capital of $138,258,800 and bond capital of $121,143,000 also fell into the hands of liquidators.[258] Suspensions of payment had been so numerous that the 'receivers' (trustees) were overwhelmed. Their number was increased.[259]

The carnage of the railways was naturally accompanied by a severe crisis in the mining and metal industries. Already in the first half of 1893, some blast furnaces were beginning to be extinguished; however, it was only in the second semester of 1893 that this decline in production of the metal industry became a significant drop.

Table 1.32 Cast-Iron Production in the United States (1,000 tonnes)

	Annual Totals	*First Half-Year*	*Second Half-Year*
1892	9,157	4,770	4,387
1893	7,124	4,563	2,562

Source: von Halle, 'Die wirtschaftliche Krisis des Jahres 1893', 195 (1225) and 197 (1227).

255. Ibid., 171 (1201).
256. *Économiste français*, 25 Aug. 1894, 243.
257. Von Halle, 'Die wirtschaftliche Krisis', 193 (1233).
258. *Économiste français*, 25 Aug. 1894, 241.
259. *Économiste française*, 8 Sep. 1894, 370. Deposition of Mr. [Thomas W.] Phillips, transcribed in *Hearings before the Industrial Commission on the Subject of Trusts and Industrial Combinations* (Washington, DC: Government Printing Office, 1899), 68–69.

In 1892, American cast-iron production exceeded that of England for the first time. The crisis returned it to second place.[260] The mining[261] and metal industry as a whole recorded results similar to those of the blast furnaces. The rail industry in particular was very hard hit. Thus, we see the fall of the rail pool. Following some disagreements among its members, the pool collapsed in 1893. Small members benefitted as their share of the effective output grew, in 1893, compared to the share that had been apportioned to them by the pool in the previous year. Carnegie's percentage dropped in 1893 compared to 1892, from 25.9 to 22.7 per cent; and that of the Illinois, from 32.7 to 25.9 per cent. Conversely, the small producers' share increased: Cabria's share of production went from 6.9 to 8.9 per cent; Lackawanna's, from 14.3 to 18.1 per cent; Maryland's, from 7.0 to 12.6 per cent; and Pennsylvania's, from 4.0 to 5.3 per cent. Efforts to reconstitute the pool failed. Hardly had it been restored when it dissolved again, and from 1893 to 1895, a series of rail pools were created only to be quickly dissolved.

Thus, the large factories sought to protect themselves from the crisis by other means: instead of forming pools to support prices, they created trusts in order to lower production costs and prices. Thanks to the price decrease, demand was revived. Giant production concerns were formed, which included mines, blast furnaces, steel works, not to mention merchant fleets and railway companies.

Thanks to the celebrated Rockefeller-Carnegie 'deal',[262] Carnegie became the largest steel producer in the United States and, at the same time, the one with the lowest production costs. He took the opportunity to lower prices so much (rail prices collapsed from $28 to $18 per tonne in April 1897) that the remaining pools in the metal industry had no option but to dissolve. The other large producers in the United States had to merge in order to resist the competition. The Illinois Steel Company merged with the Minnesota Iron Company in 1898 to form the Federal Steel Company. The other steelworks were also combined with the blast furnaces and the mines.

From 1891, the textile industry in England was in a shaky position, its exports having been drastically diminished, especially those to Argentina, which imported $17,189,797 in textiles in 1891 compared to $30,024,966 in 1890. A few mills suspended production. In 1892, the situation remained unfavourable; demand was weak, and exports were reduced. It was not until 1893, however, that true overproduction manifested itself, as

260. In 1892, US production surpassed it by 2,540,000 tonnes. In 1893, it outproduced it again, but by only 195,000 tonnes. In 1894, English production was again lower. 'L'industrie de la fonte en Angleterre', *Rapports commerciaux des agents consulaires français*, 1895, no. 223.

261. Von Halle, 'Die wirtschaftliche Krisis', 197 (1227).

262. First, Rockefeller agreed not to produce steel. Second, Carnegie acquired the Rathburn and Mountain Iron mines and paid Rockefeller $600,000. Third, Carnegie paid Rockefeller $0.25 per tonne extracted. Fourth, Carnegie had to allow a minimum of 1,200,000 tonnes to be transported by the Rockefeller, Duluth, Missabe and Northern railways. Fifth, Carnegie agreed not to sell the mineral ore exploited by Oliver (Carnegie owned five-sixths of its shares). He could only use it in his own steelworks. Sixth, Carnegie had to transport all of his mineral ore by means of Rockefeller's fleet (Bessemer Steamship Company).

a consequence of both the American crisis and the crisis that had just broken out in Australia, a British colony.

It was in Australia, in fact, that we encounter the most clear and characteristic construction crisis at that time. Private individuals and banks had been involved in reckless land speculation thanks to the concentration of formerly rural populations in Australia's large cities. The banks in particular had purchased houses and plots of land with part of the deposits obtained by the veritable teams of savings trackers who stalked the Australian colony in all directions.[263] In the end, too many buildings were built on land that was too expensive. Construction activity was suspended, workers were dismissed, and soon a whole section of houses was without tenants. A house that was rented for 130 francs in 1890 brought in only 30 francs in 1893. Some owners even offered free use of their house in exchange for taking care of the maintenance.[264] Banks that had recklessly tied up their deposits collapsed one after the other. In April and May 1893, 14 had already suspended their payments,[265] unable to reimburse the 1.8 billion francs in deposits which they had received.[266] However, an ingenious remedy was found by the first victim of the crisis, the Commercial Bank of Australia, and it saved the country from a terrible panic. Depositors were offered, and accepted, the chance to convert their deposit debts into equity and bond capital. The Bank of Australia exchanged deposit certificates against £6.5 million in bonds, 4.5 reimbursable at the bank's discretion, and against £3 million in preferred stock at 5 per cent. Thanks to this combined scheme, the bank resumed payments only a few days after they had been suspended. This ingenious procedure proved very helpful at first. Subsequently, however, it did not always produce the anticipated results; notably in 1894, new arrangements had to be made.[267]

In England, the number of bankruptcies, which had decreased from 5,310 in 1887 to 4,383 in 1890, rose suddenly to 4,590 in 1891, 5,003 in 1892 and 5,257 in 1893; yet, the sum of the liabilities for these different bankruptcies is much more significant. After having dropped to £9 million in 1887 and to £6.18 million in 1890, it rose to £8.60 million in 1891 and £8.84 million in 1892. A similar phenomenon was recorded in Germany, with 7,623 bankruptcies in 1891 compared to 5,396 in 1890.[268] However, bankruptcy found the most victims in the United States: from 10,344 in 1892, the number rose to 15,242 in 1893, with liabilities of $114,044,167 and $346.779,889, respectively.[269]

263. On the Australian bank agents, see 'The Late Australian Banking Crisis', *Economist*, 17 March 1894, 331.
264. See Pierre Leroy-Beaulieu, 'L'Australie et la Nouvelle-Zélande', 436.
265. Arthur Raffalovitch, 'La crise et le protectionnisme en Australie', *Journal des économistes*, 5th ser., 15 (1893): 88.
266. Pierre Leroy-Beaulieu, 'L'Australie et la Nouvelle-Zélande', 435–36; *Économiste français*, 1 July 1893, 73, and 21 Oct. 1893, 222.
267. 'Commercial History and Review of 1894', *Journal of the Statistical Society of London* (1895): 122.
268. Neumann-Spallart and Jurascheck, *Übersichten der Weltwirtschaft*, pt 1: lxxxvii and xc.
269. *Statistical Abstract of the United States* 43 (1920): 228, tab. 145.

The general slowdown of economic activity also affected foreign trade. Exports from England in particular decreased from £328.2 million to £273.8 million in 1894.[270]

Prices fell, under the combined pressure of an increase in supply and a decrease in demand. In Europe, prices of iron, cast iron, steel, coal and textiles began to decline from 1890. In America, the specific circumstances mentioned above delayed the crisis until 1893.

In England, as we have seen, the prosperity of the growth period was due in large part to foreign enterprises. When the crisis struck, exchange rates were disrupted. On 7 November, the Bank of England raised its discount rate to 6 per cent, and by 9 November, it was borrowing gold from the Banque de France. On 14 November, immediately after receiving news of Baring's collapse, the bank assumed responsibility for all the firm's liabilities. As soon as the Baring Brothers' default was made public, a meeting of the major banking houses in London took place at the Bank of England. It was decided that the Bank of England would handle the liquidation of the Baring firm's business. It would be covered by a guarantee fund underwritten by the different major firms in London; by the evening of 14 November, the fund reached £5 to 6 million and, a few days later, £18 million.[271] At this point, the crisis entered its resolution phase; as usual, the portfolio shrank, gold flowed back into the Bank of England's coffers, and the discount could be lowered.

In the United States, bad money had chased out the good, ever since the Sherman Silver Purchase Act came into force in 1890; and from 1890 to 1893, while the stock of silver had increased by $158 million, the stock of gold had been reduced by $98 million. When the crisis struck, the flight of gold abroad reached worrying proportions. Gold exports exceeded imports, from 1 July 1892 to 31 June 1893, by $87.5 million, $60 million of which was exported in the first six months of 1893.[272] The discount rate also increased considerably; in March, the money 'at call' was paid out at 60 per cent.[273] Moreover, means of payment were lacking, both abroad and domestically: 161 national banks with commitments of $6 million closed in 1893; of these, 46 had voluntarily entered into liquidation. Two hundred government banks also went bankrupt, as well as 241 private banks. In light of this debacle, the banks once again had recourse to the expedient of clearing-house certificates, lending at 6, then 7.5 per cent of the amount of the deposited guarantees. As early as June, the procedure was being used in New York, and then, in July and August, Boston, Philadelphia, Baltimore and Pittsburgh followed suit.

---

270. While England's exports (excluding its colonies) decreased by £5,604,060 from 1892 to 1893, the decrease in exports to the United States alone reached £3,107,000.
271. 'The Crisis of 1890', 195. Arthur Crump rightly draws our attention to the solidarity demonstrated by the London banks. See Crump, 'The Baring Financial Crisis', *Economic Journal* 1, no. 2 (June 1891): 391–92.
272. F. W. Taussig, 'The Crisis in the United States and the Repeal of Silver Purchase', *Economic Journal* 3, no. 12 (Dec. 1893): 734.
273. Von Halle, 'Die wirtschaftliche Krisis', 164 (1194).

Excellent results were obtained. Thanks to the initiative of three New York banks, the exchange crisis and the flight of gold were successfully remedied. In August, the metal reserves in banks of New York had fallen to $53 million. Gold had to be imported at any cost. Three banks in New York devised a plan to send a portfolio of clearing certificates valued at $5 million to London, thereby obtaining gold from England in return. The success of the first attempt encouraged new ones, and as a result, $48 million in gold had returned to the United States by the end of August 1893. From that moment on, gold reserves were rebuilt, reaching $96.5 million on 28 October 1893 in the New York banks. The portfolio shrank, and that of national banks went from $903 million in 1893 to $750.7 million in 1894.

Table 1.33 Cash Holdings of the New York Banks in 1893 (millions of $)

	Specie	*Legal Tender Notes*
Week ending on 27 May	70.7	64.0
on 12 Aug.	53.6	22.9
on 28 Oct.	96.5	60.5

Source: Taussig, 'Crisis in the United States', 737.

Times had not been easier on the stock exchange. In London, the slump had mainly affected Argentine and South American share values. The *Economist* estimated the losses to English capitalists on South American shares at £58,545,000, as a result of their devaluation between 1890 and 1895; and of this total, Argentine government securities alone represented £21,850,000, and Argentine railways, £18,785,000, for a total of £40,635,000.[274]

In Germany, shares in the banks and industrial companies, more specifically, metal and mining companies, had depreciated considerably, sometimes by over 50 per cent. The railways also lost value: the Lübeck-Buchen line and the Wessabahn were down by 16 and 20 per cent, respectively; the Diskonto-Gesellschaft, by 16 per cent; the Berliner Handels-Gesellschaft, by 45 per cent; and the Dresdner Bank, by 38 per cent. Among the industrial stock values, Gelsenkirchen lost 40 percent, Laurahütte 35 per cent and AEG 65 per cent.

But in New York, above all, the stock exchange debacle was complete in 1893. Von Halle has compiled an interesting statistical table that allows us to follow step by step the evolution of the crisis on the New York Stock Exchange.[275] For a while there was talk of closing the stock exchange. The most difficult period was during July and August, when

274. 'The Depreciation of North and South American Securities', *Economist*, 23 March 1895, 381–82. The remainder of the losses can be attributed thus: £4,450,000 on Brazilian railways, £4,500,000 on Uruguayan government securities and £1,630,000 on other South American share values.

275. Von Halle, 'Die wirtschaftliche Krisis', 200 (1230).

bullish positions were liquidated. But beginning in September, calm was restored, and the stock exchange regained its usual appearance; as the fever of the crisis subsided, the calm of stagnation ensued. The credit crisis was also reflected in the statistics for the clearing houses.

Table 1.34 The Credit Crisis at the Clearing Houses, 1890–1893

	Clearing House of London	*Clearing House of New York*
1890	£7,801,050,000	[$37,458,608,000]
1891	£6,847,510,000	[$33,749,322,000]
1892	[£6,481,560,000]	$36,662,469,000
1893	£6,478,010,000	$31,261,038,000

Sources: Neumann-Spallart and Juraschek, *Übersichten der Weltwirtschaft*, pt 2: 610; and von Halle, 'Die wirtschaftliche Krisis des Jahres 1893', 183 (1213). For more details on other American clearings (quarterly results, etc.), see the tables in von Halle, 181–85 (1211–15). [Lescure's figures have been completed and corrected using original sources.]

Beginning in 1890, England and Germany saw unemployment claim numerous victims. Wages were down, and the increase in poverty caused the number of marriages to fall and suicides to rise.[276] On the other hand, emigration from Germany, which had slowed down for a time, quickly resumed its forward advance: the number of emigrants went from 96,070 in 1889 to 120,089 in 1891 and 116,336 in 1892. This increase in German immigration was felt above all in the United States, where their numbers increased from 84,424 in 1889 to 108,611 in 1891 and 107,823 in 1892.[277]

In 1892–93, the Independent Labour Party was founded.[278]

Crime too was influenced by the crisis: in Germany, the number of crimes against persons, which had remained constant between 1882 and 1890, rapidly increased from the end of 1890. The number of those convicted of simple theft rose from 70,495 in 1890 to 82,751 in 1882. Von Lindenberg considers breach of trust to be the crime that best reflects the state of the working classes in poverty or relative prosperity; and it is covered under section 289 of the German Penal Code (such as the sale by the tenant of property belonging to the landlord). The number of those convicted of that particular crime rose from 1,507 in 1890 to 2,150 in 1891 and 3,137 in 1892.[279]

276. See Neumann-Spallart and Juraschek, *Übersichten der Weltwirtschaft*, pt 1: x.
277. Conrad, et al., eds, *Handwörterbuch der Staatswissenschaften*, vol. 1, s.v.: 'Auswanderung'.
278. Cole, *British Trade*, 95.
279. G. Lindenberg, 'Die Ergebnisse der deutschen Kriminalstatistik', *Jahrbücher für Nationalökonomie und Statistik*, 3rd ser., 8, no. 5 (1894): 719, tab.

Table 1.35 Prices of the 25 Principal Stocks on the New York Stock Exchange (in dollars)

Shares	*Highest in 1890*	*Lowest in 1890*	*Lowest in 1891*	*Highest in 1891*	*Highest in 1892*	*Lowest in 1892*	*Highest before May 1893*	*May*		*June*		*July*		*Aug.*		*Sep.*		*Oct.*	
								Highest	*Lowest*	*Highest*	*Lowest*	*Highest*	*Lowest*	*Highest*	*Lowest*	*Highest*	*Lowest*	*Highest*	*Lowest*
Chicago, Burlington and Quincey	111	30	75	110	105	95	103	92	81	88	82	87	69	80	71	87	76	87	77
Chicago, Milwaukee and Saint Paul	79	44	50	82	84	75	83	76	66	70	65	69	46	58	50	63	57	68	66
Chicago, Rock Island and Pacific	98	61	63	90	94	75	89	81	68	73	66	92	51	62	54	67	60	72	63
Chicago and North Western	117	98	102	118	121	110	116	111	105	108	100	105	84	99	90	101	96	107	98
Atchison, Topeka and Santa Fe	50	23	24	47	46	32	36	31	23	26	19	22	12	18	13	22	17	23	16
Denver and Rio Grande	21	15	13	21	19	15	18	15	13	14	10	15	8	10	9	11	9	10	9
Northern Pacific	39	16	20	30	26	15	18	16	12	14	12	12	7	9	3	9	5	3	6
Union Pacific	68	50	32	52	50	35	42	36	20	30	23	26	15	22	15	24	19	21	15
Lake Shore and Michigan Southern	114	101	105	127	140	120	134	128	118	125	119	121	104	119	109	123	117	129	119
New York Central	111	94	98	117	119	107	111	106	99	105	99	102	92	102	96	104	100	104	100
New York, Lake Erie and Western	29	16	17	33	34	23	26	20	17	18	15	17	7	15	10	16	12	16	13
Central of New Jersey	128	90	105	122	145	111	132	114	104	110	99	104	84	102	89	112	99	120	106
Delaware, Lackawanna and Western	149	123	130	145	167	138	156	142	134	149	137	147	127	140	132	150	135	171	146
Delaware and Hudson	175	120	118	141	149	122	149	127	120	130	119	121	102	114	108	121	111	131	119
Philadelphia and Reading	48	26	25	43	65	38	53	26	16	18	12	15	12	18	12	21	14	23	16
Illinois Central	120	85	90	109	110	95	104	100	92	93	87	92	86	93	89	94	91	98	91
Louisville and Nashville	92	65	65	83	84	64	77	72	64	68	42	66	47	58	52	58	49	53	43
Norfolk and Western Preferred	66	48	46	57	56	37	39	30	26	28	20	20	16	21	20	24	23	22	20
American Cotton Oil	34	13	15	35	47	32	51	44	30	37	33	35	24	33	25	36	32	39	33
Tennessee Coal and Iron	89	28	24	41	50	31	37	20	16	18	12	16	10	15	10	16	14	17	14

Source: von Halle, 'Die wirtschaftliche Krisis des Jahres 1893', 200 (1230).

In the United States, the working class was even more affected. The crisis was even the starting point of an actual revolt by American workers. In August 1893, the number of unemployed was already estimated at one million. It grew subsequently. Wages were considerably reduced. In the mining, metal and textile industries, the reduction reached 20 to 25 per cent,[280] despite the strong resistance of the trade unions. In the bituminous coal mines of the West, a powerful labour movement looked for a while as if it would bring revolution to the United States. Strikes ensued. Miners from the East joined in solidarity with the miners from the West. The number of strikers reached 200 to 250,000. Armed struggles occurred in Colorado. Some workers were killed, and others were wounded. Communications were eventually disrupted throughout the West, and the railways ran out of fuel. In the midst of the general confusion, Coxey, a horse trader from Massillon, Ohio, became the promoter of the Industrial Army of the Commonweal of Christ, an association of unemployed workers organized like an army, which was to march on Washington to demand from Congress the bread that they could no longer earn through their labour. The idea was an unexpected success among the working classes, and whole regiments of unemployed were formed with Washington as their objective. They requisitioned supplies en route. Trains were stopped and pillaged; in the event that a train hid police troops, real battles were fought that always ended in bloodshed. Public opinion was eventually stirred, and a lively movement hostile to 'Coxeyism' appeared. A commission of conciliation was appointed, and by the end of June, it had succeeded in bringing an end to the strike; the workers gave way all down the line. It took some time before calm could be restored. Although the strike theoretically ended in June, it was not actually over until July.

In light of such events, the flood of immigrants to the United States had decreased: from 502,917 in 1892–93, their number had dropped to 314,467 in 1893–94 and 279,948 in 1894–95.

By about 1895, the elimination of poorly equipped or weak producers had been achieved. Interest rates and wages were lowered. Production costs were significantly revised and reduced. In the United States and Germany, new economic forms – trusts and cartels – had become more common. The economic world was ready for a new period of expansion.

§11. – The crisis of 1900[281]

A.) Growth

The growth was above all in Germany.

280. Von Halle, 'Die wirtschaftliche Krisis', 205 (1235).

281. For a more detailed study of this crisis, see the 1906 edition of the present work.

1.) France and Great Britain

But France and Great Britain were prosperous, too. The statistics on stock issues showed an influx of capital toward industry, and the total for industrial shares issued grew from 386.1 million francs in 1895 to 2,295.2 million in 1900, of which 595.8 million were for shares in 1889 and 1,298.4 million, for shares in 1900. In England, the total shares issued went from £152,807,000 in 1890 to £165,499,000 in 1900. What is more, in France, one must take into account the issues of Russian annuities [*rente*], which to a large extent resulted in orders to our national industry.

Thus, production, and more specifically the production of cast iron, went from 2,004,000 tonnes in 1895 to 2,714,000 tonnes in 1900 in France, and in England, from 7,827,000 tonnes in 1895 to 9,103,000 in 1900.[282] Foreign trade and profits from the railways also reflected the satisfactory state of trade and industry. At the same time, the portfolios of the banks of issue swelled, and the total figures for their business reflected the growth of trade and industry (tab. 1.36).

Table 1.36 Average Cash on Hand and Portfolio at the Bank of England and Banque de France

	Cash on Hand		*Portfolio*	
	Bank of England (mill. £)	*Banque de France (mill. francs)*	*Bank of England (mill. £)*	*Banque de France (mill. francs)*
1895	38.9	3,291.6	22.1	543.6
1899	32.3	3,062.1	32.6	828.3

No source given.

Dividends, business profits and wages were increasing. In England, Bowley's salary index (1900 = 100) went from 94 in 1895 to 100 in 1900.[283]

2.) Germany

In Germany, the electrical industry, local railway construction, soon to be followed by the mining and metal industries, the building industry and, to a certain degree, by the textile industry, showed the signs of economic recovery. Even German agriculture felt the consequences, sometimes happy, sometimes harmful, of this mostly industrial boom.

282. *Annuaire statistique de la France.*

283. A. L. Bowley, 'The Statistics of Wages in the United Kingdom during the last Hundred Years (Part VIII): Wages in the Building Trades – Concluded', *Journal of the Royal Statistical Society* 64, no. 1 (1901): 102–12; and especially, A. L. Bowley and George H. Wood, 'The Statistics of Wages in the United Kingdom during the Nineteenth Century (Part XIV): Engineering and Shipbuilding', *Journal of the Royal Statistical Society* 69, no. 1 (1906): 192–93.

Discoveries such as long-distance transport of electric power, high-frequency currents, and the increased use of electricity as motive force or as a means of lighting brought about the rapid development of the electrical industry.[284]

Up until 1895, there were only 32 electrical companies in Germany with capital of 156,085,800 marks. In 1900, there were 131 with capital of 891,344,800 marks.[285] The large electricity concerns, such as the Allgemeine Elektrizitäts-Gesellschaft (AEG), the Union-Elektrizitäts-Gesllschaft (UEG), Schuckert & Co. and so on, got involved in transactions that had hitherto been reserved for the banks.[286]

The director of AEG thought to create subsidiaries (*Tochtergesellschaften*). These subsidiaries received all the necessary capital, machinery and equipment from the parent company and paid the latter in shares. The parent company held the shares of the new company in its portfolio for about a year, after which, they were put on the market, where the announcement of a handsome dividend attracted buyers at high prices. In this way, the electric companies' business profits were doubled through speculative gains.[287]

Such issues of shares required the confidence of capitalists. From there, two methods were devised: the *omnium* (*Massenunternehmung* [mass enterprise]), which involved bringing together a bloc of tramway companies or electrical plants under one corporate name; and the trust (similar in name only to the trust in America), a true investment bank for the industry, subscribing and placing the electric companies' shares.[288] These trusts, created with a share capital of 10.20 to 30 million marks, issued bonds at a fairly low interest rate, or in any case, lower than the rate that would have been required of a small company.

In order to speed up production, night overtime was introduced, and unqualified workers (tailors, labourers) were hired. Cartels were created to regulate prices. In 1898, on the initiative of Siemens and Halske, all of the large companies agreed to a price increase on manufactured goods proportional to the increased cost of raw materials.

Means of transport, by both land and sea, also developed.

The law of 18 July 1892 gave a strong boost to local railway construction. In Prussia, on 1 October 1892, according to data from the Ministry of Public Works, there were only 90 rail lines with 1,034.8 km of track. By 31 March 1901, their length had grown to 8,454.9 km.[289] One of the most active companies in this sector was the Allgemeine Kleinbahnes. From 1893 to 1900, it distributed handsome dividends.

However, maritime construction played an even more decisive role (tab. 1.37). From 1893 to 1896, Germany had no major shipyards. In 1893, the Hamburg-Amerika still

284. On these technical advances, see Josef Loewe, 'Die elektrotechnische Industrie', in *Die Störungen im deutschen Wirtschaftsleben während der Jahre 1900 ff*, 7 vols. Schriften des Vereins für Socialpolitik 105–111 (Leipzig: Duncker & Humblot, 1903), 3: 79–81; Emil Kreller, *Die Entwicklung der deutschen elektrotechnischen Industrie und ihre Aussichten auf dem Weltmarkt* (Leipzig: Duncker & Humblot, 1903), 1.

285. See Loewe, 'Die elektrotechnische Industrie', in *Störungen*, 3: 77–78.

286. Kreller, *Die Entwicklung*, 77–78.

287. Loewe, 'Die elektrotechnische Industrie', in *Störungen*, 3: 120.

288. For a list of the trusts belonging to the various major German electric companies, see ibid., 124. Siemens & Halske had two trusts, one founded in 1896, and the other in 1897; AEG had one, founded in 1895; and UEG had four, created between 1894 and 1896.

289. D. Erler, 'Die vorgänge im Gebiete des Kleinbahnwesens', in *Störungen*, 4: 205.

ordered two large ships from the Harland and Wolf shipyards in England. From 1896, large, well-equipped German shipyards were facilitated by the exemption of customs duties and the lowering of transport tariffs on their raw materials.

Table 1.37 Merchant Ships Built in German Shipyards, 1895–1899 (in tonnes)

1895	59,621	1898	131,165
1896	41,179	1899	189,000
1897	86,169		

No source given.

The equity or debenture capital of the major shipyards increased from 42,674,400 marks in 1896 to 54,128,000 marks in 1900. In 1898, the military construction plan came into effect. Labour was in great demand and had to work overtime. From 1897 to 1900, some shipyards even had to refuse orders for lack of workers.[290] The wage rate increased: in the northeast, the average annual wage rose from 934 marks in 1897 to 989 marks in 1900; in the northwest, it went from 812 marks to 914 marks. Dividends also increased.[291]

Table 1.38 Percentage Dividends of German Shipyards, 1898–1900

	Vulcan (Stettin) (%)	*Neptun (Rostock) (%)*	*Germania (%)*
1898	14	4	4.5
1899	12	8	4.5
1900	14	9	4.5

Source: Schachner, 'Seeverkehr und Reederei', in *Störungen*, 4: 169.

The mining and metal industry in Germany followed the same trend. At the time, Germany had two important 'coal basins': the Ruhr and Upper Silesia. Both enjoyed great prosperity from 1895 to 1900.

Table 1.39 Quantity and Value of German Coal Production and Average Number of Workers Employed in the Mines, 1894–1899

	Coal Production (1,000 tonnes)	*Value (1,000 marks)*	*Average Number of Workers Employed*
1894	76,741	509,100	299,627
1895	79,169	538,845	303,937
1896	85,690	592,976	316,513
1897	91,055	648,939	336,174
1898	96,309	710,233	357,695
1899	101,639	789,449	478,575

Source: *Statistisches Jahrbuch für das Deutsche Reich* (1902): 25.

290. Notably Johannsen & Co. See Robert Schachner, 'Seeverkehr und Reederei', in *Störungen*, 4: 173.

291. Ibid., 169.

In 1895, the output of the Ruhr coal basin was still very mediocre. A noticeable improvement occurred in 1896: production increased, and profits rose as a result of a moderate increase in prices. From this moment on, the increase in production and prices continued uninterrupted until 1900. In 1897, the coal cartel imposed no limitation on production; demand was so pressing that in May, generally a less active month for production, merchants were complaining about delays in fuel delivery. The Hoesch steelworks was even receiving contracts for a period of two years at prices five marks higher than the quoted price. The workers also did not hesitate to demand wage increases. In the Hibernia mine, the average daily wage for a miner rose from 3.50 marks in 1895 to 4.30 marks in 1889.

Upper Silesia experienced neither the same level of prosperity nor any real prosperity until 1898. At that time, English coal, the most formidable competitor of Silesian coal, found a local consumer. Silesian fuel became the master of the northern German market and contributed to the development of the mining industry.[292]

The strike in the mines of Saxony, Bohemia and Austria and the severity of the winter further complicated these initial factors of prosperity. Upper Silesia was overwhelmed by orders that it could not always satisfy; in Bavaria, Saxony and central Germany, factories had to close due to fuel shortages. Deliveries to factories and even railways were limited. No doubt, production was extended as much as possible, but demand progressed more rapidly still. On the other hand, any extension of production had to face the labour shortage and the necessity of employing inexperienced workers, which too often required wage increases and no work on Mondays.[293]

Iron ore mines could be found in the Lorraine and Siegerland regions, but above all, in the part of Lorraine annexed by Germany. Ever since the introduction of Thomas's process of dephosphorization had made it possible to produce pure, strong steel from the ore of Lorraine, mining there had made rapid progress. Iron ore production in Lorraine increased from 8,135,000 tonnes in 1895 to 13,914,000 in 1900. In 1895, it represented only 65 per cent of Germany's total output, but by 1900, it accounted for 73.35 per cent.[294] Daily wages went from 3.70 marks in 1895 to 5.20 in 1900.[295]

A similar phenomenon can be observed in the metal industry.

In Lorraine, the development of the metal industry, particularly blast furnaces and steel mills, was to a certain extent comparable to that of the iron mines. An entirely new

292. In 1908, the miners' strike in Wales caused a reduction in English coal production of 1.7 million tonnes. In addition, the Spanish-American War, by stimulating the demand for freight, triggered an increase in the demand for coal; in 1899, the Boer War had the same effect; and Russia, moved by the depletion of its forests, substituted mineral fuel for plant-based fuel and became an increasingly important buyer of German coal. Lastly, the national domestic boom reached its peak.

293. F. Kuh, 'Die Hüttenindustrie Oberschlesiens', in *Störungen*, 2: 145. Kuh estimates the loss in production due to this voluntary unemployment at 10 per cent.

294. Note that French capital successfully challenged German capital in this industrial zone.

295. Otto Bosselmann, 'Erzbergbau und Eisenindustrie in Lothringen-Luxemburg', in *Störungen*, 2: 35.

industry appeared in the form of large, and quite often, integrated factories.[296] These companies were themselves organized into cartels, and Lorraine had one cartel for cast iron and one for steel.

Despite the need to transport Westphalian coke, the enormous growth of German production and the increase in competition, the share of the Lorraine-Luxembourg region in Germany's total production increased from 27.8 per cent in 1895 to 29.2 per cent in 1900.[297]

Facing this expansion of production, the demand for labour increased rapidly, and with it, the number of workers at the blast furnaces went from 3,878 in 1895 to 7,795 in 1900; and in the steelworks, from 1,044 to 4,050. But the new workforce (from Germany, Italy or Hungary) was less productive;[298] hence the rise in the number of workplace accidents[299] and the regrettable discord among the workers, who were unable to organize themselves into trade unions. The Italians in particular were known for their nomadic instinct. It was estimated that no more than 20 per cent of the total number of workers were permanent residents in the Lorraine region.

In the provinces of Rhineland-Westphalia from 1894, the crisis of 1890 had been definitively resolved. By 1895, orders began to pour in and continued to grow from 1896 to 1899.

The expansion of the mining and metal industry encountered an obstacle: the remoteness of coal and iron mines and the high transport costs of both coal and mineral ore. The industry responded by making technical and economic improvements, as well as by resorting to integration and the formation of cartels.

Thus, from 1896, the German metal industry purchased coal and mineral ore mines. The Phoenix and Dortmunder Union bought the Westende and Adolf mines in 1896. The movement spread so rapidly that the share of production for the mines with attached coking plants (*Hüttenzechen*) in the Ruhr basin increased from 10.66 per cent in 1893 to 17.81 per cent in 1900.[300] Steel mills built or annexed blast furnaces in order to produce their own cast iron, and rolling mills were combined with steelworks; as early as 1895, the Hoesch steel mill was producing its own cast iron. Around the same time, the *Gewerkschaft*[301] Deutsche Kaiser joined its coal pits and Martin steelworks with blast furnaces and a Thomas steel mill. The only incomplete (*reinige* [i.e., 'pure', or non-integrated]) steel mill in the Ruhr basin had even collapsed in 1894, a victim

296. See Wilhelm Jutzi, *Die deutsche Montanindustrie auf dem Wege zum Trust* (Jena: Fischer, 1905), 3–4; Bosselmann, 'Erzbergbau und Eisenindustrie', in *Störungen*, 2: 23; Kuh, 'Die Hüttenindustrie Oberslesiens', in *Störungen*, 2: 202–3; and see Lescure, 'Aspects récents de la concentration industrielle: L'intégration dans la métallurgie', *Revue économique internationale* 6, no. 3 (Aug. 1909): 256–94.

297. Bosselmann, 'Erzbergbau und Eisenindustrie', in *Störungen*, 2: 35.

298. Ibid., 6–11, 32–36.

299. See ibid., 14.

300. Hans Gideon Heymann, *Die gemischten Werke im Grosseisengewerbe: Ein Beitrag zur Frage der Konzentration der Industrie* (Stuttgart: Cotta, 1904), 110–17.

301. A *Gewerkschaft* is a specific type of company, the definition of which can be found in Conrad et al., eds, *Handwörterbuch*, vol. 3, s.v.: 'Gewerkschaft'.

of the onerous conditions demanded of it by the blast furnaces. Rolling mills merged with steelworks, such as the Westfällische Union, one of Germany's largest rolling mills of rolled wire, sheet steel and iron bars, which merged with Phoenix, one of the largest steel mills. Finally, factories fabricating metal products bought or built rolling mills and steelworks.[302]

Thanks to integration, German industry reduced its production costs; by means of the cartel and price and production controls, it also stabilized the market.[303] At least in the beginning, the cartels showed restraint in raising prices.

At the end of the growth period, the 'bulls' finally prevailed over their 'bearish' opponents at the cartel's general meeting. They even appeared to regret their previous moderation and went so far as to imagine, in 1899, a price policy, known as the merger policy [*politique de fusion*], which was to prove fatal to their clients and, soon after, to themselves. (See below.)

In the Dortmund basin from 1894 to 1900, daily wages increased by 1.02 marks, or 33 per cent, while the yearly wage increased by 371 marks, or 38 per cent.[304]

The shareholders' dividends rose in greater proportion to wages. The Bochumer Verein gave a dividend of 16⅔ per cent in 1898–99 and 1899–1900, up from the 5 per cent it had given in 1894–95; the Hörder Bergwerke- und Hüttenverein yielded 14 per cent, up from 3 per cent; the Phoenix Company, 15 per cent, up from 10 per cent; the Gute-Hoffnungshütte, 20 per cent, up from 4; and so on, for an increase that varied from 50 to 300 per cent.

Such was the boom in the metal industry in Rhineland-Westphalia.

In Upper Silesia, the growth was less clear cut. Iron ore came from Grönsberg and Gerlivara in Sweden. Its largely foreign market allowed it to benefit only marginally from the German Empire's customs policy. However, from 1895, it did benefit from the creation of a national industry in Russia. German exports, following the end of the tariff war with Russia, went up from 194 million marks in 1894 to 372 million in 1897 and 359 million in 1900, and Upper Silesia received a significant share of this amount.

Table 1.40 Metals Production in Upper Silesia (1,000 kilos)

	Cast Iron	*Steel and Iron*
1896	615,419	604,339
1898	678,840	743,326
1900	747,163	788,713

Source: Kuh, 'Die Hüttenindustrie Oberschlesiens', in *Störungen*, 2: 216, 219.

302. Heymann, *Die gemischte Werke*, 154–55.
303. See Leopold von Wiese, 'Die rheinisch-westfällische Eisenindustrie in der gegenwärtigen Krisis', *Jahrbuch für Gesetzgebung, Verwaltung und Volkswirtschaft im Deutschen Reich* 26, no. 1 (1902): 302–6.
304. Theodor Vogelstein, 'Die rheinisch-westfällische Montan- und Eisenindustrie', in *Störungen*, 2: 89.

Just as in the Ruhr basin, we find integrated enterprises and cartels. Here, however, the integrated businesses did not present with the same features as the giant enterprises in the Ruhr basin; the integration in Upper Silesia was more generalized by comparison. Whereas in the Ruhr the blast furnaces and steel mills were the focal points of concentration, in Upper Silesia, it tended to be the rolling mills.[305] During the growth period from 1895 to 1900, the self-consumption of cast iron by the steel mills grew from 377,908 tonnes, representing 71.06 per cent of total consumption, in 1895 to 563,294 tonnes, or 75.40 per cent of total consumption, in 1899.

The Silesian cartel thus offers us an interesting example: it is comprised of integrated factories. Hence, according to Kuh, the great moderation of the expansion of the Silesian cartel.[306]

Table 1.41 shows the trend of the number of workers employed, the total wages paid, and the average wage per worker in the metal industry; and table 1.42 shows dividends rising in equal measure.

Table 1.41 Number and Wages of Metal Workers Employed in Upper Silesia

	Number of Workers	*Total Annual Wages (marks)*	*Average Wage per Worker (marks)*
1896	27,104	20,780,697	781
1898	31,654	25,678,476	875
1900	34,352	29,993,815	937

Source: Kuh, 'Die Hüttenindustrie Oberschlesiens', in *Störungen*, 2: 224–28.

Table 1.42 Dividends of Metallurgical Firms in Upper Silesia

	Donnemarck Hütte	*Königs- and Laurahütte*	*Ob. Eisenindustrie AG*
1896	9	10	8
1900	16	14	10

Source: Kuh, 'Die Hüttenindustrie Oberschlesiens', in *Störungen*, 2: 216–17.

In the machine industry,[307] the very lively growth was mainly domestic,[308] and domestic consumption absorbed 75 per cent of production.

Around 1895–96, production could no longer satisfy demand. In all probability, overall production increased on average by 25 to 30 per cent from 1896 to 1900.[309]

In the steam engine industry, which was almost exclusively concentrated in Saxony and in Westphalia, average production grew by 50 per cent from 1895 to 1900; the number of workers employed increased from 1,805 in 1895 to 2,875 in 1900; and the total

305. Kuh, 'Die Hüttenindustrie Oberschlesiens', in *Störungen*, 2: 193.
306. Ibid.
307. Paul Steller, 'Die Maschinenindustrie Deutschlands', in *Störungen*, 3: 10.
308. The machine industry had headquarters in different parts of Germany, particularly in Westphalia, in the Saar basin, Saxony and Upper Silesia. Ibid., 6.
309. Ibid., 10.

value of engines produced rose from 6,630,000 marks to 15,600,000 marks. (Domestic orders increased to 11,551,000 marks in 1900, compared to 3,397,000 marks in 1895.)[310]

The boiler industry was in the same situation,[311] receiving numerous orders from the German navy; as was the industry for extraction machinery used in mining (in the Rhineland, Westphalia and Saxony) and the machine tooling industry.[312]

Gas engine[313] factories in particular benefitted from recent discoveries that enabled the use of gas from the blast furnaces as drive force.

Locomotive and passenger-carriage factories were also enjoying great prosperity.[314] In 1895, Germany had only 20 carriage factories; by 1900, 38 new factories had been created. Banks played a very important role in the growth of the machine industry. Despite the deliberate silence of the banks' reports,[315] it was well known that the Diskonto-Gesellschaft had significant interests in Aschersleben Machinenbau AG created in 1898, as did Deutsche Bank in the Mecklenburgische Wagonfabrik AG of Gustrow, and that Dresdner Bank founded the Kontinental-Eisenbahnbau- und Betriebsgesellschaft in 1896.

Integration and cartelization were less developed in the machine industry than they were in the forges, steelworks and rolling mills. Even though we may cite some machine factories integrated with blast furnaces, steel mills and rolling mills, such as the Königs- and Laurahütte, the Bochumer Verein or the Dortmunder Union, these were in fact the exceptions.

The diversity of its products, their quality, weight and mode of production (the very large factory rubbed shoulders with the humble craftsman), and the often-decisive importance of management, presented nearly insurmountable obstacles to the introduction of the cartel form into this category of production. Even in the instances where a cartel managed to form, this union of producers resulted in a simple agreement for the fixing of prices, which, in the absence of effective sanctions, remained completely unnoticed. Thus, for example, there was an agreement on railway carriages, which established the Norddeutsche-Wagenbau-Vereinigung, and another one for steam engines. But these remained exceptions, and steam engines, gas engines and the machines needed for mine extraction were produced and sold under a system of free competition.

The workforce in the machine industry was particularly well paid because workers needed to possess a degree of technical knowledge and skill. From 1895 to 1900, the increase in the daily wage reached 20 to 30 per cent, and that of the annual wage was 50 per cent, due to the longer working day and the reduced number of holidays (see tab. 1.43).[316]

---

310. Ibid., 22–30.
311. Ibid., 32–35.
312. Ibid., 43–50.
313. Ibid., 39–43.
314. Ibid., 35–39, 66–70.
315. See Otto Jeidels, *Das Verhaeltniss der deutschen Grossbanken zur Industrie* (Leipzig: Duncker & Humblot, 1905), 3 and 11–13.
316. Steller, 'Die Maschinenindustrie', in *Störungen*, 3: 20–21.

Table 1.43 Average Daily Wages in the Machine Industry in Germany, 1895–1899

	1895	*1896*	*1897*	*1898*	*1899*
Fitters	4.50	4.40	4.70	4.80	5
Smiths	4.70	5	5	5	4.90

Source: Steller, 'Die Maschinenindustrie Deutschlands', in *Störungen*, 3: 20–21.

A 50 to 100 per cent increase in dividends was the norm.[317]

The rapid and brilliant development of German industry caused the population of the empire to concentrate around the mines, factories and mills. The cities, large and small, and even villages were enlarged. Construction companies were formed all over Germany and were energetically supported by a particular form of mortgage lending.

The organization of mortgage lending [*crédit foncier*] in Germany differs from its French counterpart. Instead of there being one large bank with a semi-monopoly, one finds a whole host of mortgage-lending institutions (*Hypothekenbanken*) in Germany. By issuing shares and mortgage bonds (*Pfandbriefe*), these banks find the capital they then lend to private individuals, developers and construction companies. The profit margin for these companies results from the difference between the interest rate paid to the bond holders and the rate paid by the borrowers. In 1895 the interest rate was very low. The necessary conditions were met for a boom in the building trades. Unfortunately, unhealthy and often dishonest speculation developed. Land that was worthless one day yielded enormous capital gains on the next. Developers purchased land and built houses with the pure and simple intention of reselling them. To enter the competition, one only needed to possess capital equal to the difference between the purchase price of the property and the sum that a mortgage bank agreed to lend on the first mortgage of that property.[318] Better still, if the first operation was successful, the gains would increase the speculator's means, and the operation would be repeated on a larger scale. The capital of the Prussian mortgage banks went from 15 million marks in 1895 to 21 million in 1899, while the amount of their obligations increased from 244 million to 356 million marks.[319] In light of such abuse, mortgage lending was regulated in Germany by the law of 13 July 1899, according to which, mortgage loan companies had to obtain authorization from the *Bundesrat* before they could be created. The new companies were placed under state control and only allowed to lend from three-fifths to two-thirds of the value of the mortgaged properties.

---

317. See the many tables and details for the different branches of the mechanical engineering industry in ibid., 26–28.
318. On the rapid rise in mortgages during this period, see F. Kühnert, 'Die Hypothekenbewegung in Preussen während der Rechnungsjahre, 1895 bis 1900', *Zeitschrift des Königlich Preussischen Statistischen Bureaus* 43 (1903): 324–402.
319. Ernst Kritzler and Felix Hecht, 'Die Sanierung notleidender Hypothekenbanken: Die deutsche Treuhand-Gesellschaft', in *Störungen*, 7: 55–57.

The boom in the construction industry was accompanied by the rapid development of related industries, such as concrete and brickmaking. The concrete industry in particular was organized into six cartels.[320]

The textile industry felt the effects of the general prosperity. But here, the expansion of production required too little capital for production not to adapt quickly to consumption.

Thus, the number of spindles used in the cotton industry rose from 6,260,424 to 8,434,610, and that of looms, from 170,533 to 211,818.[321] But except for 1899, which had been a very favourable year, the growth in the market had not been offset by a corresponding increase in production. The same applies to the woollens industry.[322] On the other hand, the textile industry suffered the effects of the increasing demand for labour in other industries, which deprived textiles of its own workforce. In order to fix the labour shortage, textile manufacturers were obliged to raise wages (tab. 1.44).

Table 1.44 Textile Industry Wages in Rhineland-Westphalia (in marks)

	Cotton Spinning	*Wool Spinning*	*Wool Weaving*
1895	585	517	806
1897	517	546	827
1899	654	578	882

Source: Richard Calwer and Ignaz Jastrow, 'Gewerkschaften, einzelne Gewerbe', in *Störungen*, 5: 186.

Dividends increased little, sometimes not at all, or remained nil. The Aachen Tuchfabrik (cloth factory) gave 5 per cent in 1895, 4 per cent in 1896 and 5 per cent in 1898 and 1899; the Bautzener Tuchfabrik und Kunstmühle gave 4, 6, 6½, 7 and 7½ per cent over the same years; and the Neue Tuchmanufaktur (Bischweiler), 7, 6, 6 ,7 and 6 per cent.[323]

As for agriculture, there were good harvests from 1895 to 1900, but the industrial expansion had a dual impact. Industrial growth led to an increase in the consumption of agricultural products, such as bread, meat, beer and so on. The prices of agricultural goods rose. Yet, because the agricultural workforce had been drained by the labour needs of industry, agricultural workers had to be replaced by machines. According to Steller's survey of German manufacturers of agricultural machinery, in some factories the number of workers had risen by 100 per cent, and production had tripled or quadrupled.[324]

320. See Richard Calwer, ed., *Handel und Wandel: Jahresberichte über den Wirtschafts- und Arbeitsmarkt*, 2 vols.: Jahrgang 1900 and 1901 (Berlin: Edelheim, 1901–2), 121.
321. Heinrich Sybel, 'Die Baumwollindustrie', in *Störungen*, 1: 143.
322. Kurt Kuntze, 'Die Wollindustrie', in *Störungen*, 1: 175.
323. For woollens, see Kuntze, 'Anhang 1: Die Wollindustrie', in *Störungen*, 1: 260–71, tab.; for cotton wares, see Sybel, 'Die Baumwollindustrie', in *Störungen*, 1: 149, tab.
324. Steller, 'Die Maschinenindustrie', in *Störungen*, 3: 63.

Table 1.45 shows gross profits of the railways increased until 1900 and net profits, until 1899.

Table 1.45 Profits of the German Railways (millions of marks)

	Gross Receipts		*Expenditures*	*Net Returns*
	Passengers	*Goods*		
1895	421.1	1,011.1	852.1	645.6
1897	472.8	1,124.0	951.6	725.6
1899	533.7	1,258.2	1,198.0	750.7
1900	573.0	1,309.1	1,293.2	740.9
1901	571.4	2,251.0	1,316.6	662.8

Source: 'Die deutschen Eisenbahnen in den Jahren, 1885–1901', in *Störungen*, 4: 181.

Maritime shipping showed brilliant results, especially European transport and the Anglo-German lines delivering English coal and iron to German industry. Coal freight between these countries increased from 3/9 shillings in 1897 to 7/9 in 1900. German trade with the United States, which had been affected for a while by the Dingley tariff in 1897, was also satisfactory.

German navigation companies also increased their capital and perfected their machinery, thereby improving their equipment. The average tonnage of each ship increased, while steam was replacing sails. The five largest German navigation companies (Hamburg-Amerika, Norddeutscher-Lloyd, Hansa, Kosmos, and Hamburg-Sudafrikanische G. (*sic*))[vi] were assured a dominant position (tab. 1.46).

Table 1.46 Tonnage and Capital of the Five Largest German Shipping Companies

	Tonnage of the 5 Largest Shipping Companies (Br. R. T.)	*Total Tonnage of German Steam Shipping (Br. R. T.)*	*Percentage of Total Tonnage of the 5 Largest Companies*	*Capital of the 5 Largest Companies (1,000 marks)*
1896	606,790	1,319,060	46	142,368
1900	955,202	1,863,524	51	267,582

No source given.

Their dividends were also increasing; those of the Hamburg-Amerika were at 8 per cent in 1896 and 1898 and at 10 per cent in 1900, while those of the Norddeutscher-Lloyd went from 4.7 to 8.5 per cent over the same years.

The number of German sailors on sailing vessels went from 14,487 in 1896 to 13,268 in 1900, while the number on steamships increased from 25,139 to 31,027.[325]

325. Schachner, 'Seeverkehr und Reederei', in *Störungen*, 4: 75.

Table 1.47 German Special Foreign Trade (millions of marks)

	Imports	*Exports*
1895	1,580.4	1,385.4
1897	1,873.0	1,626.4
1899	2,260.2	1,949.3
1900	2,515.8	1,922.9

No source given.

The need for metal currency increased, which mainly reflected the need to pay wages, the needs of the retail trade and the payment of dividends and interest. During the growth period from 1895 to 1900, gold from the Transvaal arrived in Germany via London. The German market was still receiving gold, but less of it was coming from the United States. Germany's stock of gold grew from 37 million marks in 1895 to 47 million in 1896, 53 million in 1897, 126 million in 1898, 154 million in 1899 and 148 million in 1900.

From 1895 to 1900, the Reichsbank saw its portfolio swell. In December 1899, its discount was raised to 7 per cent; nevertheless, its portfolio and advances continued to grow. Its banknote circulation increased to meet this more active demand for credit.[326]

German banks, both investment and commercial banks, played a leading role in the general economic expansion. Beginning in 1895, Deutsche Bank set up five branches, one in Frankfurt am Main, one in Munich, Bremen, Hamburg and London. The Dresdner Bank, which already had branches in Berlin, Dresden and Hamburg, now created subsidiaries in London and Bremen. The Bank für Handel und Industrie [Bank for Commerce and Industry] followed their example.[327]

On the stock exchange, the influx of capital toward industry was depressing government securities. Imperial Germany and Prussia, having waited until 1897 to convert their annuities, saw their enterprise, if not fail, then at least achieve only mediocre success. On the other hand, industrial values were rising. Gelsenkirchen's share price increased from a minimum of 154.30 in 1895 to a maximum of 199.05 in 1900; Harpener went from 103.25 to 244.40; the Dortmunder Union, from 97.50 in 1896 to 111.02 in 1900; Königs- und Laurahütte, from 120 in 1895 to 284 in 1900; AEG, from 206 to 261.80; the Hamburg-Amerika, from 81.50 to 132.40; and Deutsche Bank, from 170.25 to 213.75. Thus, despite the *Börsengesetz* [stock and commodity exchange law] of 21 June 1896, the rise in values and the speculation it caused advanced during this period.

Lastly, the effects of the expansion period, and particularly of industrial development and the rise in wages, on certain sociological phenomena, such as marriages, welfare, emigration and crime, need to be retraced.

326. Karl Helfferich, 'Der deutsche Geldmarkt, 1895 bis 1902', in *Störungen*, 6: 48, and statistical tables of the bank balance sheets.

327. Ernst Loeb, 'Die Berliner Grossbanken in den Jahren 1895 bis 1902 und die Krisis der Jahre 1900 und 1901', in *Störungen*, 6: 85–86.

Fewer emigrated from Germany as agricultural workers were transformed into industrial labour. Emigration diminished during the expansion period from 1895 to 1900, as it had done in the period preceding the crisis of 1890; the number of emigrants went from 37,498 in 1895 to 24,631 in 1897, 22,221 in 1898 and 22,309 in 1900.[328]

While the population of Germany increased from 52,279,901 inhabitants in 1895 to 56,367,178 in 1900, an average increase of 1.5 per cent per year, that of municipalities with over 2,000 inhabitants (i.e., the village or urban population), rose from 26,859,511 to 30,633,075, an average annual increase of 2.63 per cent. The agricultural population on the other hand only grew by 0.25 per cent, rising from 25,400,390 to 25,734,106.[329]

Despite this increase in population, the use of foreign labour became indispensable. From 1897 in the Rhineland-Westphalian basin (Recklinghausen, Ost-Dortmund, Nord-Bochum, Herne, Gelsenkirchen, Wattenscheid, Essen and Oberhausen), there was an influx of workers from Bohemia and Galicia. In 1897, the number of these new workers was estimated at 20,000. The movement continued into 1898–99, and by 1900, the labour shortage was such that special agents were employed in Hungary, Styria and even Lower Silesia to speed up immigration. Also at that time, in one of the newly opened mining districts of the Ruhr basin, the Oberhausen district, out of 16,682 miners employed, 6,731 were foreigners, mainly Poles, Italians, Dutch, Hungarians and Austrians who spoke languages other than German.[330] Germany was transformed from a country of emigration into one of immigration.

The number of marriages was also positively influenced by the rise in wages (see tab. 1.48).

Table 1.48 Number of Marriages in Germany, 1895–1900

	1895	*1896*	*1897*	*1898*	*1899*	*1900*
Berlin	17,238	18,642	19,330	19,580	19,946	20,756
Cities of 200,000 + inhabitants	34,154	35,804	39,457	41,085	43,365	44,935
Cities of 100,000 + inhabitants	16,637	18,239	19,019	20,434	21,277	22,430
Cities with fewer than 100,000 inhabitants	9,016	10,706	10,206	10,733	11,165	11,455
Total	77,045	84,391	88,012	91,832	95,753	99,576

Source: A. Heinecke, 'Eheschliessungen', in *Störungen*, 5: 234. However, the statistical analysis must be corrected by taking into account the concentration of the urban population.

The crime rate declined.[331] There was a reduction in all petty crimes, like begging, vagrancy and simple theft, which are the result of poverty and unemployment. The number of convictions for simple theft fell from 72,446 in 1898 to 69,154 in 1899. The number of those convicted of simple theft as a second offence went from 12,312

328. A. Heinecke, 'Auswanderung', in *Störungen*, 5: 227.
329. A. Heinecke, 'Ab- und Zuzüge', in *Störungen*, 5: 197–225.
330. Calwer and Jastrow, 'Gewerkschaften, Einzelne Gewerbe', in *Störungen*, 5: 156–57.
331. W. Bloch, 'Bettel, Kriminalität', in *Störungen*, 5: 265–80; Ludwig Cohn, 'Obdachlosichkeit', in *Störungen*, 5: 249–58. See also *Vierteljahreshefte zur Statistik des Deutschen Reichs* 4: 76.

to 11,950; for armed robbery, from 9,619 to 9,290; and for armed robbery as a second offence, from 2,824 to 2,564.

Finally, the economic prosperity made the recourse to assistance much less frequent, and despite the concentration of the less fortunate working population in the cities, the per capita expenditure on public assistance was falling.[332] The average dropped from 0.98 in 1896 to 0.67 in 1899. The reduction was particularly noticeable in cities where industrial growth had been especially brilliant; in Dortmund, for example, the coefficient fell from 0.99 in 1896 to 0.67 in 1899.

Thus, this growth period was exactly the same as those we have already encountered. It was a crisis in the making.

3.) The United States

Once again, the United States did not advance at the same pace as Europe; the former's period of growth lasted until 1903.

Good harvests beginning in 1897 gave industry the necessary momentum to recover completely from the 1893 crisis. Issues of shares and bonds increased. The great iron and coal industry, enriched by the discovery of prodigiously rich coal fields at ground level in Mesabi in 1890, enjoyed an era of unprecedented prosperity. While in 1890, England could still challenge the United States for first place in cast-iron production, by 1902, cast-iron production in the United States exceeded that of both England and Germany combined.

We note two particularities from this parallel growth in American and European industry: the long duration of the growth period and its continuation, after 1900, into 1901 and 1902[333] and the policies of the great American iron and coal industries.

That American industry still experienced several years of prosperity in 1900, 1901 and 1902, after the outbreak of the crisis in Europe, should come as no surprise. We have already noted a similar pattern in 1882 and in 1890. Two interesting peculiarities may explain the prolonged boom in the United States: the concentration of American industry and a new policy that changed how corporations used their profits.

The policies of American joint-stock companies. – Up to this point, periods of growth had been characterized by the introduction of machinery that was more or less obsolete and lacked the latest advances in technology. As a result of the increase, this equipment was put back into service. After 1898, America broke with this policy. In 1898, all newly opened blast furnaces were equipped with the latest technology; it was the same in 1901. A blast furnace producing 1,270 tonnes per week, which would have been exceptional in 1898, had become the norm in 1901. Instead of taking advantage of the higher prices

332. Landsberg, 'Armpflege', in *Störungen*, 5: 259–64.

333. Wesley Clair Mitchell, *Business Cycles* (Berkeley: University of California Press, 1913), 64–66.

of their products and distributing large dividends to their shareholders, American joint-stock companies used the income to improve their operations and lower costs.[334]

Without going into detail, we shall concentrate on the evolution of one of them, the Republic Iron and Steel Company.

Created in 1898, it had not seen an increase in its capital nor issued any bonds since that time; nevertheless, from 1 May 1899 to 30 June 1903, it spent $6 million on the expansion of its equipment. In the years from 1899 to 1903, it realized $15,009 million in profits, using $6,066 million in new construction, $3,248 million to create a reserve fund and only $5,694 to distribute as dividends. Under these conditions, in 1903, its factories were equipped with the most advanced machinery. It produced 2.5 million tonnes of iron ore and 1.5 million tonnes of coal in 1898 and 20 million tonnes of ore and 14 million tonnes of coal in 1903; its blast furnaces were now able to produce 600,000 tonnes of cast iron in 1903, compared to 400,000 tonnes in 1898.

Concentration of industrial enterprises. – Yet the concentration of production and the evolution of the trust have played a more decisive role in the United States.

In 1899, thanks to William Henry Moore's efforts,[335] the great American iron industry was in the hands of a very small number of producers, 10 at the most. The market for semi-finished goods was almost completely monopolized by the Carnegie Steel Company, Federal Steel Company and the National Steel Company. Rail production had two major producers: Federal Steel and Carnegie, who established a cartel for five years. The production of tinplating was completely monopolized under the power of a great trust: the American Tin Plate Company. The wire industry was similarly organized into a powerful trust: the American Steel and Wire Company, which bought the steel it could not produce by itself from Carnegie and the Federal. Finally, the pipe industry was represented by two companies: the American Steel Hoop Company and the National Tube Company.

By 1899, only fine sheet steel was produced by multiple companies. Moore set about lowering prices to such an extent that the recalcitrant companies were soon running at a loss; threatened in their very existence, they were forced to give in; and on 14 February 1900, the fine sheet steel trust was born: the American Sheet Steel Company.

Each of these trusts was asked either to produce its own raw materials, if it was a trust for manufactured goods, or to process its own products in the case of a trust for semi-finished goods.

At the beginning of 1900, there was fear of an era of competition such as the world had never seen before. The trusts' formidable power had the competitors retreating;

---

334. On these considerations about America, we refer to L. Glier's very well-documented, three-part article in Schmoller's review, where Glier, out of theoretical considerations, explains the evolution of this powerful industry in the United States: see L. Glier, 'Zur neuesten Entwicklung der amerikanischen Eisenindustrie', 3 parts, *Jahrbuch für Gesetzgebung, Verwaltung und Volkswirtschaft im Deutschen Reich* 27, no. 3 (1903): 229–99 (1013–83); 27, no. 4 (1903): 43–127 (1223–1307); and 28, no. 1 (1904): 149–278. Here, see Glier, 'Zur neuesten Entwicklung', pt 3: 250.
335. Ibid., pt 1: 281 (1065).

they preferred conciliation to open struggle. The US Steel Corporation emerged from this agreement, and although it did not enjoy an absolute monopoly, it nevertheless controlled 50 to 70 per cent of the production of iron in America if we include its various subsidiary branches.[336]

This trust followed the same policy as the joint-stock companies; it lowered its production costs. To this end, it closed the less-profitable factories, leaving only the factories equipped with the best machinery in operation. The trust revised its operating costs, dismissed inefficient workers, secured favourable tariff rates from the railway companies by being a valuable customer and even acquired railway lines of its own.[337]

Nevertheless, sales had to be made. American industry benefitted from the moderate policies of the cartels (pools).[338] Unlike the cartels in Germany, the American cartel would group together four or five firms, the same ones in different cartels. Thus, the oligarchy easily transforms itself into a monarchy in which one company gains supremacy. The four American cartels of heavy manufactured goods (rails, construction materials, large metal plating and cast iron bars) were in the hands of the Steel Corporation.

It was thus easy for the American cartel to effectively regulate production and prices, and even consumption, by raising or lowering prices according to the circumstances. The American cartel, far from abusing its power by raising prices disproportionately, replaced the old policy of price increases with one that maintained a stable market with a stable price. From May 1901 onward, the Steel Corporation opposed any price increase.

Despite the price rise for cast iron and semi-manufactured goods, the prices of manufactured goods (rails, sheet metal, etc.) were even lowered.[339] Consumption increased, and the growth continued. Railway consumption will give us a better idea of the situation (tab. 1.49).

Table 1.49 Consumption of Goods and Equipment by the US Railways (1,000s of $)

Fiscal Year	*Maintenance of Railways and Structures*	*Equipment*	*Replacing Rails*	*Bridges, etc.*	*Fence and Cattle guard*	*Ties*	*Freight Wagons*	*Locomotives*
1894	143,669	112,894	8,207	16,673	3,970	22,016	43,329	38,318
1900	211,220	181,173	10,517	24,963	5,697	27,985	70,909	62,156
1901	231,056	190,299	16,590	27,017	5,020	31,070	73,595	66,253
1902	248,382	213,381	10,952	28,888	6,968	31,617	82,813	88,753

No source given.

336. Ibid., pt 3: 150–217.
337. Industrial Commission, *Preliminary Report on Trusts and Industrial Combinations*, vol. 1 of the Commission's reports (Washington, DC: Government Printing Office, 1900), 32–33; and see Etienne Martin Saint-Léon, *Cartels et Trusts* (Paris: Lecoffre, 1903), 144–78.
338. Glier, 'Zur neuesten Entwicklung', pt 3: 264.
339. See ibid., pt 3: 220–21.

Therefore, the trust, far from being an instrument of exploitation and speculation, appears to us on the contrary to be a strong regulator of production and prices.

B.) Crisis and depression

1.) France and Great Britain

Unlike the United States, France and England experienced a crisis in 1900, followed by a period of depression in the years that followed; but both the crisis and depression were moderate, just as the growth had been. Events abroad in Russia signalled its onset. Once the great Russian railway lines such as the Trans-Siberian and Trans-Manchurian lines had been completed, Russian industry lacked further orders.[340] From there, the crisis spread to the whole of Europe.

In France, the total value of shares issued decreased from 1,298.4 million francs in 1900 to 499.7 million in 1903, and in England, the issues of industrial shares dropped from £79,227,000 in 1900 to £31,385,600 in 1904.

Cast-iron production in France went from 2,714,000 tonnes in 1900 to 2,389,000 in 1901; in England, from 9,103,000 tonnes in 1900 to 8,055,000 in 1901. However, the figures for foreign trade and railway profits showed only a slight depression.[341]

The Banque de France's average portfolio fell from 875.2 million francs in 1900 to 546.3 million in 1902; that of the Bank of England, from £29.494 million in 1900 to £26.7 million in 1904.

In the face of such a shrinking demand for the discount, the average discount rate gradually decreased: in London, it was lowered from 3.96 in 1900 to 3.01 in 1905; and in Paris, from 3.25 in 1900 to 3 in the years 1901 to 1905.[342]

The coal mining and metal industries' dividends diminished. The naval steelworks distributed dividends of 50 in 1901 and 45 in 1902, compared to 65 in 1900. Wages were reduced. In the coal mines of France, this decline in wages was accompanied by a violent general strike in 1902.

In England, the indexes by Bowley and the diagrams by Bowley and Wood already cited above are particularly conclusive.[343]

---

340. Georges Afanassiev, 'La crise actuelle des capitaux en Russie', *La Réforme Sociale*, 4th ser., 10 (40) (Oct. 1900): 577–86.
341. For more precise figures, see *Annuaire statistique de la France* (1907); and *Statesman's Yearbook* (1905): 94.
342. *Volkswirtschaftliche Chronik*, Jahresübersicht [yearly overview] (1905): 816, tab. 1.
343. *Journal of the Royal Statistical Society* 64, no. 1 (1901): 102–12; and 69, no. 1 (1906): 192–93.

2.) The German Crisis

The same industries that had been the first to signal the period of growth (the electrical industry, the machine industry, railway construction and the building trades) were the first to show signs of the coming depression.[344]

The debacle of the electrical industry was essentially caused by the insufficient prices for electrical products when compared to the generally high production costs and by the industry's involvement in projects unlikely to make a profit.

As early as 1899, some electrical companies were beginning to complain about competition. In 1900–1901, reports from various factories were unanimous in their criticism of the drop in prices of electrical goods, and this period of declining prices lasted through to 1901–2, when it reached 25 to 30 per cent compared to 1900–1901.

Alongside this drop in the prices of electrical products, we see an increase in the costs of the industry's raw materials, such as coal, coke, copper, lead and rubber. Copper prices in London rose from £70 1 sh. 15 d. to £78 17 sh. 6 d. in 1900, as a result of the formation of the Amalgamated Copper Co. Some electrical companies worked at a loss.

Also contributing to the crisis were companies that carried out ill-advised projects. For instance, a city of 40,000 inhabitants has one electric tramway. In Germany in 1900, 17 towns, each with a population of less than 40,000, possessed this means of transport. In the fever to produce, they had agreed to specifications that were infinitely too burdensome and costly.[345]

Many factories had to suspend work – the Vereinigten Elektrizitätswerken and the Watt-Akkumulatorenwerken, for example. In June 1901, Kumer and Co. collapsed following the difficulties caused by the Murmau to Oberammergau railway line; it had promised profits but was showing a deficit. Hélios A. G. followed, unable to 'digest' Félix Singer and Co., which it had recently absorbed. Others reduced their share capital after the decline in their profits: the Bayerische Elektrizitätsgesellschaft, for example, reduced its capital by a ratio of 4 to 3.[346] Other firms were less affected, notably Siemens & Halske; but by the end of 1901, they too were experiencing a slump in business.

As they were producing less, firms needed fewer workers. All the unqualified electricians who had been hired during the growth period were sent home. The number of workers employed by AEG went from 17,316 in 1899–1900 to 14,644 in 1900–1901 and 14,897 in 1901–2; that of the workers at Schuckert and Co., from 7,413 to 6,868 and 5,365 in the same years. After that, working hours were reduced. As early as 1900–1901, Schuckert E. G. agreed to the workers' request to introduce the eight-hour workday, and by the autumn of 1902, a third of the other firms had followed its example.[347]

---

344. See G. Blondel, 'Les faits économiques et le mouvement social en Allemagne et Autriche', in *La Réforme sociale*, 5th ser., 1 (51) (1901): 641–42, 978–80; 2 (52) (1901): 360–62, 603–5, 922–26, 929–31; 3 (53) (1902): 328–35; 4 (54) (1902): 600–610; and 5 (55) (1903): 598, 911.
345. Loewe, 'Elektrotechnische Industrie', *Störungen*, 5: 118.
346. Ibid., 103–4.
347. Ibid., 90–92.

The financial firms that we have referred to as 'trusts' were also affected. Loewe gives us the following description of their experience. In the first year, a railway or a factory is built, and investors have the greatest expectations for these new enterprises. By the second year, the project runs into difficulties related to construction; nevertheless, it is hoped that the line or the factory will soon be opened, which does indeed happen in the third year so that, by the fourth year, profits are made, and dividends are distributed at 3 to 7 per cent. In the fifth year, the situation has already become less favourable, and the dividend drops by 1 per cent. Finally, in the sixth year, the results are a complete disappointment to the shareholders. Capital gains give way to capital losses and the usual trail of bankruptcies and reductions in capital. The large electrical companies associated with these trusts had to assume responsibility for either their liquidation or their transformation.[348]

In order to do this, they increased their capital and proceeded to exchange the trusts' depreciated securities against private shares. Thus, the crisis of 1900 became the basis for the merger of electrical firms.[349]

The main electrical enterprises, which numbered seven before the crisis, formed two groups in 1902 and 1903; one of which dealt more specifically with transport, and the other, with the instruments and means of electrical production. Heading the first group was AEG and UEG; heading the second was Siemens & Halske and Schuckert and Co. of Nuremberg, which merged into the limited liability company Schuckert-Siemens Werke, with capital of 90 million marks. The trust formation (in the American sense of the term) had positive consequences: it enabled a better distribution of markets, a more advantageous price policy and a healthy regulation of production. On 1 July 1903, the AEG and the Union dismissed over 1,000 redundant workers.

Profits dropped considerably, however.

348. For further details, see ibid., 128–29.

349. Already in 1897, a proposed merger of AEG with UEG and the firm Loewe and Co. ended in failure. A second plan to merge AEG and Schuckert also failed in October 1901. It was not until December 1902 that an association of mutual interest (*Interessengemeinschaft*) was arranged between AEG and UEG. The association involved an exchange of supervisory board members between the two firms. On certain questions, they agreed to nominate a delegation council (*Delegationsrat*), whose decisions would be binding for both companies. Nevertheless, each company retained its autonomy, drawing up its yearly balance sheets and calculating its profits in the usual manner. These profits were combined and distributed between the two companies in proportion to their share capital calculated based on the share prices at the time of the contract; and in our estimation, according to this arrangement, AEG would receive profits at a ratio of 15:19, and UEG, at 4:19. In February 1903, Siemens and Schuckert merged. For further details, see Kreller, *Die Entwicklung*, 28, and Loewe, 'Elektrotechnische Industrie', in *Störungen*, 5: 144, as well as the 1906 first edition of the present work.

Table 1.50 Dividends of the Major German Electrical Firms, 1900–1902

	AEG	*UEG*	*Schuckert*	*Siemens*
1900	15	16	15	10
1901	12	10	—	8
1902	8	6	0	4

No source given.

Although Erler would disagree, the crisis also affected local short-line railways.[350] In 1900, 163 million marks had been spent on railway construction, yet 35 lines, representing 47 million marks in capital, failed to return a profit. In 1902, the statistical evidence registered worse results. Errors in the cost estimates brought great disillusionment. A cost of 20 to 30,000 marks per kilometre had been anticipated, and satisfactory profits were projected, even for lines established in sparsely populated areas. The cost per kilometre after completion amounted to 74,000 marks for the standard-gauge lines (*Vollspur*) and 43,000 marks for the narrow-gauge ones (*Schmalspur*). Expenditures often exceeded revenues starting in 1900. It was the same in 1901 and 1902.[351] In 1902, a reorganization of the Allgemeine Kleinbahn-Gesellschaft was planned, whose prosperous activity from 1895 to 1900 we have already explained above.

Maritime shipbuilding also suffered a crisis due to the depression of foreign trade and the decline in inland river navigation, particularly on the Rhine.[352] But as it took two to three years to build a ship, the crisis was not fully felt until 1901 and 1902, and even then, only in the shipyards building merchant ships. The navy continued to place numerous orders.

The shipyards for inland waterway transport were severely affected, at least those on the Rhine, by competition from Dutch shipyards that were able to purchase their raw materials from Germany at reduced prices, lower than those demanded of Germany's domestic industry.[353]

Table 1.51 Merchant Liners and Naval Vessels Built in German Shipyards, 1900–1902

(tonnage in R.T.)		*For Germany*		*For Foreign Orders*		*Warships*	
		Number	*Tonnage*	*Number*	*Tonnage*	*Number*	*Tonnage*
1900	Total	245	210,624	37	31,738	10	7,064
	Steam	145	194,300	24	29,123	10	7,064
1901	Total	213	204,106	20	28,750	21	19,372
	Steam	147	190,593	20	28,750	21	19,372
1902	Total	272	190,412	30	21,440	10	21,898
	Steam	154	157,619	22	21,205	10	21,898

Source: Schachner, 'Schiffbaugewerbe', in *Störungen*, 3: 165 and 185, tabs.

350. Erler, 'Vorgänge', in *Störungen*, 4: 204.
351. Ibid., 205–10.
352. See Peter Stubmann, 'Die Rheinschiffahrt', in *Störungen*, 4: 216.
353. Robert Schachner, 'Schiffbaugewerbe', in *Störungen*, 3: 184.

The steam engine, boiler and gas engine industries, as well as the machine tooling industry, were severely affected by the crisis from 1900 onward. The Benz factory producing gas engines in Mannheim yielded 4 per cent dividends in 1901–2, compared to 8 per cent in 1900–1901. Berliner Werkzeug, a machine tool factory, after having distributed dividends of 12½ per cent from 1895 to 1900, was only giving 4½ per cent in 1900–1901 and 0 per cent in 1901–2.

The same phenomenon can be seen in the locomotive and railway-car industries. Little information is available on the evolution of the crisis in the locomotive industry because factories were privately owned. But in the railway-car industry, the decrease in profits led to a reduction in the share capital of several share companies (*Sanierung* [restructuring]).[354]

The mining and metal industries did not suffer the crisis of 1900 crisis immediately or as deeply as the other industries mentioned above.

The year 1900 was not even strictly speaking one of crisis for the coal mines. Never had demand been so pressing, nor prices so rewarding. This was the year of the '*Kohlennot*' [coal shortage]. Coal has the dual property of being essential to the building of machines and also to their operation. Yet the year of the crisis also marked the culmination of the period of prosperity, and it was the year in which the greatest number of machines were built and put into operation. We might add that the special circumstances in 1900 acted in the same direction. The lack of railway cars and the inability to navigate on the Rhine at the end of 1899 prevented the adequate and complete exploitation of the Ruhr coal basin. Quite often, the cartels that had concluded long-term agreements during the economic growth period categorically refused to settle these contracts and lower prices.

But in 1901, and especially in 1902, the crisis intervened.[355]

In the Ruhr coal basin, the depression raged from the beginning of 1901. The Rheinisch-Westfällische Kohlensyndikat first reduced its members' production output by 10 per cent, then in July, by 15 per cent and, in October, by 20 per cent. At the beginning of 1902, production was still being limited by 20 per cent. Despite these radical measures, however, the inventory of syndicate producers increased to 270,371 tonnes by the end of 1901, compared to 79,056 on 31 December 1900; their stocks increased to 346,817 tonnes in January 1902, only to decline gradually to 304,530 tonnes in the course of 1902.

What was true for coal was also true for coke and charcoal briquette production, which was organized into two separate cartels. The Bochum coke syndicate reduced its members' shares of production by 5 per cent in January and February, by 10 per cent in March, by 10 then 16 per cent in April, by 20 per cent in May, by 15 per cent in June and, from July onward, by 31.5 per cent. Shipments were down 952,780 tonnes compared to 1900, with a total weight of 6,883,567 tonnes.

By 1902, the situation was getting worse; the reduction was kept at 35 per cent of the original participation figure. Nevertheless, the participants' inventories kept expanding.

354. Steller, 'Die Maschinenindustrie', in *Störungen*, 3: 26, 34, 48, 68–70.

355. Iron ore was hit sooner and more severely, as it was less ubiquitous than coal.

The working class suffered unemployment, fewer working days per week and a reduction in the number of hours per workday, which went from eight to six hours.[356]

Yet the cartels managed to contain the fall in prices. (See table 1.52.)

Table 1.52 German Coal Prices

	1901	*1902*
High-grade bituminous, or 'fat' coal (*Fettkohlen*)	9.75–10.75 marks	9.50–10 marks
Coking coal	10.50–11	9–9.75
Low-grade coal	9–10	8–9

No source given.

As for coke, in 1901 it reached prices even higher than those in 1900, but for a rather special reason that we will soon learn.

In the Upper-Silesian coal basin, the crisis did not actually happen, nor was it felt, until 1902. It also exerted an influence mainly on coking coal and coke. As a result of special circumstances, coal itself suffered very little.

In fact, the Silesian mining operation had the Prussian railway as its main customer. Consumption varied little, and long-term contracts gave prices a fairly high degree of stability. On the other hand, Silesian industry had to struggle in general against external competition. After the onset of the crisis, a reduction in imports followed the fall in demand. Bohemian industry in particular felt the repercussions of the crisis in Germany. In 1901, it employed 33,000 miners compared to 37,000 in 1900 and reduced its production by 20 per cent. In 1902, it employed only 30,000 workers.[357] In these circumstances, fortified by a very intense cold and a very favourable sugar season, the Silesia operation, instead of shrinking, increased slightly in 1901 compared to 1900, going from 24,815,041 tonnes in 1900 to 25,251,625 tonnes.

In 1902, however, with a milder winter, the ever more intense crisis in the metal industry forced the Silesian mining industry to limit its production and lower its prices; yet on the whole, the situation remained favourable, especially when compared to that of the Ruhr basin[358] or to that of coke producers.[359]

Little by little, the crisis spread to the metal industry, where it first hit the manufactured product (rolled steel), then steel and cast iron.

In the Lorraine region from 1899 onward, rolling mills had to resort to exporting their products in order to sell off their inventories, and under the increased competition,

356. *Der Arbeitsmarkt*, 15 April 1902.

357. 'Böhmische Braunkohlenindustrie', in *Die Störungen im deutschen Wirtschaftsleben während der Jahre 1900 ff., in ihrem Rückwirkungen auf die industriellen, Effekten- und Geldmarktsverhältnisse Österreichs*, Schriften des Vereins für Socialpolitik 112 (Leipzig: Duncker & Humblot, 1903), 9.

358. Kuh, 'Die Hüttenindustrie Oberschlesiens', in *Störungen*, 2: 159–72.

359. At Königin Louise-Grube, the price of coke dropped from 8 marks on 1 July 1900 to 6.50 on 1 Jan. 1902. Ibid., 175–80.

prices soon fell on the foreign markets. Trade and buyers in general had shown more reserve, and by the fall of 1900, cast-iron production was being limited, and shortly afterwards, that of the steel mills as well. In 1901, production decreased by 10 per cent compared with 1900, and cast-iron prices dropped by 30 to 40 per cent.

However, industry in the Lorraine region was to some degree guaranteed against too sudden a drop by the policies of its cartel. The cast-iron syndicate in particular had concluded long-term contracts with the producers of semi-manufactured goods, and the latter did the same with the manufacturers of finished products. Thus, it was easy for some to shift the responsibility for the crisis onto others. However, Lorraine's cartels granted price reductions to their buyers.

In the provinces of Rhineland-Westphalia and the Ruhr basin, things were different.

At the beginning of 1900, the situation was again favourable, and optimism prevailed. But from April onward, the rolling mills began to experience a shortage of orders. Firms that had remained independent from the cartels consented to price reductions; money was expensive. In May, these symptoms of the crisis became clearer: raw materials and semi-manufactured goods were still in demand, whereas bar iron was in very low demand, and the price of tinplating was even falling. Nevertheless, in July production restrictions and unemployment were still rare exceptions, but if we examine things more closely, we arrive at some troubling conclusions. If the market for iron itself was becoming increasingly unfavourable for some of its products, the demand for iron ore held up well, and cast iron was easily sold off at high prices; yet, the market for semi-manufactured products was just satisfactory, and the rolling mills were already suffering from the crisis. On the other hand, in areas where prosperity still prevailed, new orders were lacking. By August, the situation was getting worse, and by autumn, there was no longer any doubt that the crisis was at hand. The price for bar iron, which had been 220 marks just a short while before, fell to 170–180 marks;[360] as the periodical *Stahl und Eisen* commented, 'although current orders are sufficient for a long time to come, many firms are suffering from a shortage of new orders'.

The cartels gave the downward trend that was to last until 1903 a distinctive feature.

In the manufactured goods industry, the cartel's influence proved very decisive: either because the crisis was more intense, or because the cartel's situation was less severe, or because it was inspired by different principles, the cartel consented to price reductions for its buyers as soon as the crisis arrived. Even better still, the cartel revised in the buyers' favour contracts that had been concluded during the period of prosperity. Delays were granted, and orders were reduced.[361] In the raw-materials industry (coke, cast iron), the cartels were less flexible. They imposed an extremely strict policy for buyers, the so-called merger policy [*politique dite de fusion*].[vii] Instituted by the coke cartel,

360. Von Wiese, 'Die rheinisch-westfällische Eisenindustrie', 308.

361. See the depositions of Moser and Weil, in *Kontradiktorische Verhandlungen über deutsche Kartelle*, 5 vols., commissioned by the Reichsamt des Innern (Berlin: Siemenroth, 1903–6), 3: 595, 663.

the policy was then adopted by coke buyers – that is, by cast-iron producers.[362] At the beginning of 1900, sometimes even as early as 1899, the raw-materials cartels proposed, or we should say insisted,[363] that their buyers contract for 1901 and that they agree to combine [*fusionner*] the contracts already concluded in 1900 with those to be concluded for 1901. The prices for 1901 were raised. They then arrived at the adjusted prices [*les prix de fusion*] valid for 1900 and 1901 by adding the 1901 prices to those stipulated for 1900 and dividing the total by two. Thanks to this procedure, the cartel was assured an outlet for two years at extremely lucrative prices. The buyers had to consent somewhat against their better judgement; however, because prosperity was still prevailing, they had agreed. The crisis erupted almost immediately after the contracts were signed. The buyers demanded that the contracts be terminated to no avail. They filed lawsuits but lost their cases. Their signatures were ruled legally binding, and the cartel proved unyielding in its demand that their commitments be fulfilled.

A real debacle unfolded in the manufacturing industry, which was the first to feel the crisis and suffer its worst effects. Subject to the greatest reduction in prices, it had to pay higher prices for its raw materials. Rolling mills in particular suffered one of the worst periods in their history and were having to pay exorbitant prices for their raw materials and to compete both domestically and abroad with integrated firms that produced their own raw materials. The German cartel investigation is full of the claims made by independent (*reine*) rolling mills.

However, the adjusted prices were only valid for 1900 and 1901. By 1902, the depression was intensifying. The price for no. 1 cast iron fell from 102 marks in 1900 to 63 marks in 1902, and Thomas cast iron went from 90.5 to 58 marks. In 1903 and 1904, the decline continued, without however affecting the sudden pace it had taken on in 1902.

The cartel policy of limiting production is no less interesting than their price policy. Some cartels were endangered by it. It had an effect on the concentration of firms.

In the face of restricted markets and a fall in prices, everyone was inclined to regain their independence. On the other hand, cartels did not enjoy an absolute monopoly, and as Gothein, a member of the *Reichstag*, remarked, it was the outsider who really benefitted; selling a little cheaper than the cartel, they were enjoying a large outlet. Finally, the integrated enterprise, either as a result of its own requirements or individual advantages, made the situation very difficult for incompletely integrated enterprises in

362. However, there is far less agreement on this point. The coke cartel claims that cast-iron prices rose before those of coke. Cf. the two theses in the report by H. Voelcker, Regierungsrat, in *Kontradiktorische Verhandlungen*, 1: 640–41; and see the depositions of Kirdoff and Schleifenbaum in ibid., 1: 664–65 and 3: 276, respectively. According to Bertram's very precise testimony, the cast-iron cartel would have raised its prices as early as May 1899, and the coke cartel would not have resorted to the merger policy until October 1899, ibid., 3: 278; on the same point, see the depositions of Springmann and Menne in ibid., 3: 278–79, 284, 287 and 3: 315, 317.

363. The coke cartel, while proposing this combination, warned its customers that if they refused, it could not guarantee the supply of coke in 1901. See Voelcker's report and the depositions of Gothein and Plehn in ibid., 3: 640–41, 653–54, 660, respectively.

the cartel.[364] For a time, there was fear of a general collapse of the cartel in the Ruhr basin, but it never materialized. Apart from a few small cartels of manufactured products, the others survived and were renewed: the pig-iron cartel (*Roheisensyndikat*) in 1902, the coal cartel (*Kohlensyndikat*) in 1904 and the steel cartel (*Stahlwerksverband*) in 1904. The latter two were not only renewed but enlarged. The coal cartel absorbed the coke and briquette cartel. The steel cartel was the result of the merger of the cartels for semi-manufactured products, rails, girders, sheet metal and others still.

The concentration of enterprises was progressing in the form of integration[365] and mergers. By merger we mean the acquisition of the small, syndicated enterprise by the large factory so that the latter could take advantage of the small factory's share of production in the cartel: the small factory would then be closed, which allowed the large factory to produce the small factory's share of production in addition to its own. The overheads decreased in the large factory because of the greater efficiency of its machinery. In the construction of bridges, Weil estimated that 10 firms had been bought by larger companies.[366] Yet the cartel's role was not only to regulate production and prices domestically; it also encouraged exports through 'dumping'.

The *Roheisensyndikat* [pig-iron cartel] and *Halbzeugsverband* [semi-finished product association] sold off a large portion of their production at ridiculously low prices so that the exports of cast iron and semi-finished products exceeded, from 1900 to 1905, the figures of the growth period from 1895 to 1900.[367] Part of these exports sold at a loss went to England. Hence, it was at this moment that Joseph Chamberlain chose, rightly or wrongly, to embark upon a protectionist campaign.[368]

But German industry was also supplying foreign competitors, particularly the Dutch and English shipyards, at the expense of the Rhine shipyards.[369]

Wage rates were not lowered, but the number of workers, workdays per week, and hours in the working day were reduced; in total, the reduction in annual wages could be estimated at 17 per cent. However, thanks to this reduction in working hours, the

364. See Lescure, 'L'évolution du cartel dans la grande industrie allemande de la houille et du fer', *Revue d'économie politique* 20, no. 5 (1906): 368–86.
365. Heymann, *Die gemischten Werke*, 155.
366. *Kontradiktorische Verhandlungen*, 3: 686.
367. See Vogelstein, 'Die rheinish-westfällische Montan- und Eisenindustrie', in *Störungen*, 2: 126.
368. According to the trade journal *Stahl und Eisen*, 14 Nov. 1903, imports of semi-manufactured goods from Germany in the Newport harbour alone would have reached 20,000 tonnes in 1902. The price difference between the products of Germany and those of its English competitor would have reached 10 to 12.5 sh. per tonne at the place of consumption.
369. The director of a shipbuilding firm in Newcastle, the Palmers Shipbuilding and Iron Company, stated that, in the years 1900–1903, he purchased his raw materials 30 per cent cheaper in Germany, which allowed him to sign contracts that he would not otherwise have been able to make. See the deposition of Schmieding, in *Kontradiktorische Verhandlungen über Deutsche Kartelle*, 3: 515. See Gothein's comments in the debates section, in *Verhandlungen der Generalversammlung in Hamburg, 14, 15 und 16 September 1903*, ed. Verein für Socialpolitik, Schriften des Vereins für Socialpolitik 113 (Leipzig: Duncker & Humblot, 1904), 193–94.

number of unemployed, while not negligible, was moderate. Foreign workers, or those from East Prussia, were returning to their countries of origin.[370] Dividends decreased more sharply than wages (tab. 1.53.).

Table 1.53 Dividends in the Mining and Metal Industry

Years	*Bochumer Verein*	*Hörder Bergwerks Hüttenverein*	*Phoenix*
1899–1900	16⅔	14	15
1900–1901	13⅓	10	4
1901–1902	7	0	0

No source given.

In Upper Silesia, industry was heading toward depression after having been deprived of its Russian customers since 1899, and its German customers in 1900. Yet the reduction in production and the fall in prices were slower and more moderate here than in the other regions of Germany. In 1901, cast-iron production was only 100,000 tonnes less than that of 1900.

In the field of construction, the number of empty houses increased from 3 November 1900 to 3 November 1901: in Essen, from 1.2 to 3.4 per cent; in Mannheim, from 1.8 per cent in May 1900 to 6.1 per cent in March 1901;[371] in Magdeburg, from 0.18 per cent in 1900 to 0.49 per cent in 1901 and 1.21 per cent in 1902;[372] in Dresden, from 4.39 per cent in 1900 to 6.70 per cent in 1902.[373] This increase in empty houses applied to either small dwellings or luxury mansions. While the working classes were pushed back to the countryside,[374] the great capitalists affected by a loss in income could either look for cheaper rents in the city or return to their estates in the country. In Munich, the need for small lodgings did not decrease, but it was otherwise for luxury apartments and houses.[375] The same was the case in cities such as Halle, Chemnitz, Dresden, Elberfeld, Frankfurt am Main, Posen and Danzig.

The crisis in the construction industry was a result of both the general crisis that had discouraged new construction everywhere and the industrial crisis that put an abrupt end to industrial construction.[376] These primary causes have already been examined above. But a whole series of other causes, though not as significant as these first two, were nonetheless important: the high cost of credit, materials and wages deserve our

370. Calwer and Jastrow, 'Gewerkschaften, Eizelne Gewerbe', in *Störungen*, 5: 140–41.
371. Franz Eulenburg, 'Die gegenwärtige Wirtschaftskrise: Symptome und Ursachen', *Jahrbücher für Nationalökonomie und Statistik*, 3rd ser., 24 (79), no. 3 (1902): 371.
372. Heinrich Silbergleit, 'Zur Bodenentwicklung Magdeburgs', in *Störungen*, 7: 205.
373. Felix Hecht, 'Dresden und die Grundstückskrisis', in *Störungen*, 7: 242.
374. Silbergleit, 'Zur Bodenentwicklung', in *Störungen*, 7: 205.
375. Ludolf Maass, 'Die Entwicklung der Bodenverhältnisse in München', in *Störungen*, 7: 416. Calwer, ed., *Handel und Wandel*, vol. 2 (1901): 154.
376. Calwer, ed., *Handel und Wandel*, vol. 2 (1901): 155.

attention.[377] We have already seen the important role played by credit in the development of industrial cities in Germany. As credit became more expensive, construction slowed – all the more since the costs of materials and wages had increased. As long as the economic growth lasted and the rise in rents offset the higher interest rates, the price of goods and wages, all was well. This situation changed after 1900.

Mortgage loans, after responding to the ever-livelier demands for credit, now found fewer and fewer borrowers. However, the rate of interest on the *Pfandbriefe* [mortgage bonds] had risen. Several mortgage banks collapsed.[378] Construction companies reduced their dividends. Many craftsmen in the building trades went bankrupt, victims of their clients' fraudulent practices. By the end of 1900, the level of unemployment exceeded that of the preceding years, and by 1901, the number of workers employed in the construction industry was declining rapidly. Yet the wage rate declined only a little, or not at all.[379] In October 1900, Calwer estimated that 7,000 masons were unemployed in Berlin alone.[380]

The cement industry, on the other hand, was experiencing marked overproduction. During the growth, it had doubled its production. Once the crisis struck, orders practically disappeared.[381] The crisis hit it so hard that cartels collapsed, and by 1905, the industry was still far from having regained its normal production levels.[382] In 1901, for example, the *Syndikat der Nordwest-Mitteldeutschen Fabriken* [cartel of the Northwest and Central German Factories] collapsed as the result of a 50 per cent limit placed on the production of its members. Efforts to reform the cartel failed.[383]

In the brick industry, where there was already a rudiment of organization in the form of *Verkaufsvereine* [seller associations], the crisis had the opposite effect. After fierce competition at the beginning of 1900, the brickworks sometimes managed to found powerful cartels. Thus, the *Verkaufsvereine* in Dortmund, Essen, Gelsenkirchen, Herne, Recklinghausen, Hamm, Hagen, Oberhausen and Witten succeeded in forming a cartel in February 1900 that was to last for five years.[384]

The impact of the crisis on the textile industry was not very pronounced. Cotton and wool prices, which had increased significantly in 1899 and 1900, declined in the second

377. Eulenburg, 'Die gegenwärtige Wirtschaftskrise', 859. Calwer estimates the rise in production costs to be 22 to 33 per cent. Calwer, *Handel und Wandel*, vol. 1 (1900): 118.
378. Raoul Giraud, *Des banques hypothécaires allemandes* (Paris: Rousseau, 1904), 85–128, and Kritzler, 'Preussische Hypotheken-Aktien-Bank', in *Störungen*, 7: 3, argue that this crisis was due to the manoeuvres of its directors alone. It does not seem so to us. For all of the mortgage banks were more or less caught off guard by the crisis. The most poorly administered ones collapsed. However, it was the crisis that revealed their mismanagement. On this topic, refer to the first edition of the present work, pp. 332–33.
379. Calwer and Jastrow, 'Gewerkschaften, Eizelne Gewerbe', in *Störungen*, 5: 171.
380. Calwer, *Handel und Wandel*, vol. 1 (1900): 117.
381. Ibid., vol. 1 (1900): 120; and vol. 2 (1901): 157.
382. On the difficulties of the cement industry in December 1905, see the *Berliner Tageblatt*, no. 649, 21 Dec. 1905, and no. 658, 28 Dec. 1905.
383. Calwer, ed., *Handel und Wandel*, vol. 1 (1900): 122–23.
384. Ibid., vol. 2 (1901): 162.

half of 1900, at the moment when the crisis was beginning to have a clear impact. The unemployed workers from the iron industry, on the other hand, sought work in the textile industry which could in turn lower its wages.

Nevertheless, the crisis affected the textile industry. In the linen industry in particular, the crisis had led to a return of buyers of everything from linen fabrics to cheaper cotton wares. Wages had been reduced by 20 to 23 per cent in the lingerie industry. In 1901, the manufacture of false collars and cuffs employed 10 per cent fewer workers than it had in 1900.[385] During the winter of 1901–2, many craftsmen were without work. In the cotton industry limited production in 1900.[386] At first, it only affected various isolated factories, but in 1901, production limits were extended to a majority of enterprises in weaving and spinning. The wool industry suffered a lack of outlets. Workers in the iron industry consumed a lot of woollen cloth in their work. After having increased in 1899, dividends dropped from 1900 to 1902.[387] Here, the effect of the crisis on the cartel was the opposite of what it was in the cotton industry, as it signalled an increase in the number of outsiders.[388] The number of workers employed either in the wool or cotton industries fell from 660,024 in 1900 to 651,772 in 1901. Dividends were reduced, often to nothing; out of 44 mills with shares, 25 in 1900 and 33 in 1901 were not paying any dividends.[389]

Breweries, butcheries, cobblers, perfume makers, hat makers and clock makers were also hit by the crisis. The number of bankrupt craftsmen increased from 3,994 in the first trimester in 1900 to 4,690 in the corresponding term in 1901. Thus, the master craftsman increasingly tended to replace the well-paid adult workforce with an adolescent workforce, the journeyman with the apprentice. A social movement developed within the ranks of trade-guild members, whose claims were heard by lawmakers. A law was passed regulating apprenticeships and limiting their number.

As a result of the increase in their operating costs, the railways' net profits decreased as early as 1900, despite the increase in their gross receipts. But in 1901, gross and net receipts were down: total gross receipts dropped from 2,034.1 million marks in 1900 to 1,976.2 million in 1901; while net receipts went from 740.9 to 662.8 million marks.

Maritime shipping was similarly affected by the crisis. However, the export policy followed by the cartels allowed maritime shipping companies to withstand the first shock. It was only in 1901–2 that the depression was really felt in this sector. Net income dropped, and with it, dividends: from 10 per cent in 1900 to 6 per cent in 1901 and 4.5 in 1902 for the Hamburg-Amerika and from 8.5 to 6 per cent and 0 per cent for the Norddeutscher-Lloyd. Small shipping companies with less capital, inferior machinery,

385. Heinz Potthoff, 'Die Leinenindustrie', in *Störungen*, 1: 97–101.
386. Sybel, 'Die Baumwollindustrie', in *Störungen*, 1: 136.
387. Ibid., 149.
388. Kuntze, 'Wollindustrie', in *Störungen*, 1: 249.
389. Ibid., 237.

less credit and overburdened by high-interest loans taken out during the growth lost out to the larger companies.[390]

Meanwhile, large maritime shipping companies integrated mines, shipyards and repair shops. Norddeutscher-Lloyd together with Krupp bought the Emscher-Lippe coal mine, concluded a financial agreement with the Stettiner Vulkan-Werft shipyards and the firm John Elder and Co., expanded the repair workshops of the Bremer Reparaturwerkstätte in 1901 and acquired a share in the Norddeutsche Maschinen- und Armaturenfabrik [North German machine and fittings factory] in 1902. The Hamburg-Amerika shipping company followed the example of Norddeutsche-Lloyd, albeit more timidly, and was content to handle the interior design of its liners and the necessary repairs, but it did not acquire any coal mines or shares in the workshops.[391]

Lastly, agreements were concluded to moderate the ruinous competition and form a business association (*Betriebsgemeinschaft*). The simple agreement constituted a fairly innocuous means of concentration in which two or more companies agree to share the field of action where previously they had been competitors. We might mention the International Mercantile Marine Company which rejected all competition from England or the United States in favour of German companies in the ports of Hamburg and Bremen; in return, German companies conceded certain advantages to the American or English companies. Sometimes a business association was negotiated with the aim of organizing the lines more adequately and adjusting the tonnage to the movement of traffic. This saved considerably on the cost of transport. The back and forth was reduced to a minimum, and ships were always fully loaded.[392]

The crisis finally had an impact on the money market. Despite the increase in the stock of gold circulating around the world, gold was in high demand in 1900 and even as early as 1899.

However, Germany's economic growth had been mostly domestic. The rupture of equilibrium was also felt domestically. Banknotes made it possible to satisfy the demand for credit. Gold was less sought after in Germany in 1900 than it had been in London in 1890, for example, where despite the low intensity of the growth preceding the crisis, much gold had to be exported because the growth had been mainly external.

The Reichsbank, and in general the whole German money market, experienced their most critical situation at the end of 1899 and the beginning of 1900. As soon as war was declared in the Transvaal, England realized its claims on the foreign markets and on Germany in particular. Table 1.54 shows Germany's gold exports exceeding its imports.[393]

390. While the tonnage of the 5 largest maritime companies represented only 46 per cent of the total tonnage of the German navy in 1896, 44 per cent in 1897, 46 per cent in 1898, 49 per cent in 1899 and 51 per cent in 1900; by 1901, it represented 58 per cent, that is, a 5 per cent increase per year during the period of depression, compared to a 1 per cent increase during the period of growth. Schachner, 'Schiffbaugewerbe', in *Störungen*, 3: 75.

391. Ibid., 162.

392. Ibid., 155, 158–60.

393. *Volkswirtschaftliche Chronik* (1901): 611, tab. 8b.

Table 1.54 Amount by which Germany's Gold Exports Exceeded Its Imports (millions of marks)

1899	October	8,305
	November	1,893
1900	January	22,849
	February	25,023
	March	8,954

Source: *Volkswirtschaftliche Chronik* (1901): 611, tab. 8b.

The Reichsbank's cash position dropped from 804.6 million marks on 30 January 1900 to 743.7 million marks on 31 March, and after rebounding to 860.3 million marks on 31 July, it hit its low point of 725.4 million marks on 29 September. The portfolio reached 789.3, 973, 737.8 and 971.0 million marks, respectively, on the same dates.

The discount rate was increased from 4 to 5 per cent on 7 August 1899, to 6 per cent on 3 October and to 7 per cent on 19 December 1899.

Yet, domestically it was possible for banknotes to play a role that they could not fulfil in settling international exchanges. The increase in the Reichsbank's portfolio corresponded to an increase in the circulation of banknotes: from 1,099.7 million marks on 30 January 1900 to 1,310 million on 31 March and, after various fluctuations up or down, it reached its highest figure on 31 December 1900 of 1,409.9 million marks. Its variations were far more considerable than those of the cash on hand and paralleled the demand for a discount. After oscillating between 700 and 900 million marks, the portfolio reached its maximum of 1,088.3 million marks on 31 December 1900.[394] The same was true for the other banks in Germany. As usual, the liquidation of inflated positions was deferred by means of the extensive use of credit. Once the liquidation had occurred, however, the decrease in the number of bills of exchange issued in Germany reflected the general slowdown in trade. The rate of discount was cut. On 12 January 1900, it was lowered to 6 per cent; on 27 January, to 5.5 per cent; on 13 July, to 5 per cent; and on 11 February 1902, it was at 3 per cent. The value of the bills of exchange circulation in Germany as a whole was 20,937 million marks in 1899, 23,304 million in 1900, 22,966 million in 1901 and 21,505 in 1902.

We also note the return of a phenomenon frequently observed in times of crisis: the sudden withdrawal of deposits. The large banks could resist it, while the small and medium-sized ones collapsed. In Berlin, newer banks, such as the Berliner Bank and the Breslauer Bank, fared much worse than Deutsche Bank or the Diskonto-Gesellschaft. While the overall business of the latter two firms was still growing in 1901, that of the others diminished. The increase in deposits flowing into the large banks is of particular significance here. The ground had been prepared for the broad concentration of the banking business.[395] In some cases, the small banks asked the large ones for help, thereby giving up, more or less totally, their independence. In the case of others, when a

394. *Volkswirtschaftliche Chronik* (1900) (Monthly balance sheets at the Reichsbank); and (1904): 947.

395. See Edgard Depitre, *Le mouvement de concentration dans les Banques allemandes* (Paris: Rousseau, 1905), 104–5. Hermann Schumacher, 'Die Ursachen und Wirkungen der Konzentration

formerly prosperous bank collapsed, a large bank would create a subsidiary branch in its place.[396] Regional banks in the Rhineland and Westphalia were gradually absorbed by the large banks of Berlin. Sometimes this was a matter of absorption, pure and simple; other times it was an 'association of common interest'. The crisis suffered by the German banks from 1900 onward was the result of their close ties to industry. The Lepiziger Bank's collapse was brought on by an industrial firm, the Trebertrocknungsgesellschaft [a company for the drying and industrial use of spent grains]. For other banks, the write-offs on current accounts receivable went from 3,085,000 marks in 1900 to 4,765,000 marks in 1902; write-offs on investments [*participations*] and sponsorships [*commandites*], from 4,477,000 marks to 5,214,000 marks. Dividends dropped from 116,277,000 marks in 1900 to 97,256,000 in 1902.

However, German banks were also hit by the stock exchange crisis. The write-offs on securities reached 1.5 million marks in 1900 and 3.5 million in 1902.

A stock exchange crisis signalled the industrial crisis that would arrive a short time later. The decline in securities began in April 1900. It first affected the share market of the electrical industry. By the end of 1900, share prices, with the exception of those in preferred industries (chemicals), were lower than at the beginning or the middle of the year (see tab. 1.55).

Table 1.55 Average Prices on the Berlin Stock Exchange

	3% Empire	*Gelsenkirchen*	*AEG*	*Hamburg-Amerika*
1895	96	154	206	81
1899	87	182	243	117
1900	84	176	189	117
1901	86	153	169	104
1902	90	162	163	96

No source given.

From 1901 to 1903, the liquidations continued, and in 1902 and 1903, the average prices of the various shares still remained lower than those of the previous year. In 1904, there were very clear signs of an improvement.[397]

The rise in government bonds and fixed-income securities in general contrasted with the drop in shares.

Finally, the crisis had repercussions for certain social phenomena, such as emigration and immigration, marriages, public assistance, crime and politics.

im deutschen Bankwesen', *Jahrbuch für Gesetzgebung, Verwaltung und Volkswirtschaft im Deutschen Reich* 30, no. 3 (1906): 36 (918).

396. Such was the case for the Leipziger Bank. See Felix Hecht, 'Die Katastrophe der Leipziger Bank', in *Störungen*, 6: 373–90; Jakob Riesser, *Die deutsche Grossbanken und ihre Konzentration*, 3rd rev. ed. (Jena: Fischer, 1910).

397. A full table of the stock exchange rates can be found in the second edition of the present work, p. 288.

Domestically, we find agricultural populations returning from industrial centres to the countryside, and the return of foreign industrial workers, who had been attracted to production centres by higher wages, to their country of origin. It was the same outside Germany: foreign workers were being repatriated, and German emigration resumed.

Beginning in 1901, the excess of departures in Chemnitz was 1,850; in Crefeld, 833; in Danzig, 435; in Duisburg, 2,049; and in Görlitz, 319. In places where the crisis had not yet produced all of its effects, the number of arrivals in excess of departures had decreased considerably: in Berlin, that number fell from 59,515 in 1900 to 29,480 in 1901; in Bochum, from 2,247 to 1,933; in Breslau, from 8,673 to 5,160.[398] The labour inspectorate (*Gewerbeinspektion*) reports provide us with details about the fate of these emigrants: they returned to farm labour and are employed, as in the Wiesbaden area, in agricultural or forestry work;[399] others returned to their country or region of origin, as did those who quit the Ruhr coal basin to return to Upper Silesia.[400] Foreign workers returned to their country of origin either by paying their own way or at the state's expense; Galatian workers returned home from the Oppeln district, as did Dutch and Italian workers from Cologne.

Nonetheless, with the declining demand for industrial labour, German emigration resumed, and their numbers increased from 22,307 in 1900 and 22,073 in 1901 to 32,098 in 1902. Most of this emigration was directed toward the United States; there, the number of German immigrants grew from 19,912 to 29,211.[401]

The number of marriages had declined in 1900 compared to 1899, and it dropped further still in 1901 compared to 1900. The proportion of newlyweds per 10,000 inhabitants decreased from an average of 168 in the years 1896–1900 to 165 in 1901 and to 158 in 1902.[402]

Public assistance spending in the various cities, which had progressively diminished until 1900, was again following an upward trend. In Barmen, the number people receiving assistance rose by 20 per cent in 1901 and 0.2 per cent in 1902; in Breslau, it increased by 8.8 per cent in 1901, and in Elberfeld, by 15 per cent. The assistance spending per capita was rising rapidly, especially in the industrial cities such as Dortmund, Dresden and Düsseldorf.[403]

The impact of the crisis on crime rates was no less apparent, and the German courts saw an increase in defendants charged with vagrancy, petty theft and robberies. The number of home burglaries increased from 22,218 in 1900 to 23,596 in 1902, and cases of embezzlement, from 20,030 to 22,185. But the most striking increase was in thefts: the number of petty thefts rose from 69,154 to 76,426 in 1902; that of petty theft as a

398. Heinecke, 'Ab-und-Zuzüge', in *Störungen*, 5: 198–99, tab. 50.
399. Calwer and Jastrow, 'Gerwerbeinspektion', in *Störungen*, 5: 104–5.
400. Ibid., 99, 105.
401. Heinecke, 'Auswanderung', in *Störungen*, 5: 229.
402. *Annuaire statistique de la France* (1904): R., p. 126. See also: Heinecke, 'Eheschliessungen', in *Störungen*, 5: 234–35.
403. Landsberg, 'Armpflege', in *Störungen*, 5: 262–63.

repeat offence, from 11,950 to 13,102; and that of burglary, from 9,213 in 1900 to 11,363 in 1902.[404]

The crisis of 1900 also had political repercussions. Although the crisis of 1900 did not cause social unrest as serious as that seen from 1835 to 1837 in England, or in 1848 in France, the enormous increase in votes obtained by the German Social Democratic Party in the 1903 elections was due in large part to the impact the crisis had on the working classes, for whom the crisis represented a confirmation of Marxist theories. Trade unions saw their situation worsen as a result of the high unemployment compensation distributed to their members.[405] The theory of the trade union as a political organization increasingly prevailed over the theory of the union as an instrument of economic struggle and resistance against the syndicate boss in his powerful cartels. During the 1907 elections, in the midst of a period of prosperity, the Social Democrats would lose if not votes, then at least many seats.

In conclusion, the crisis of 1900 was more clearly the starting point for a process of concentration than any crisis before it. Competition was particularly fierce in the electrical industry, the machine industry, the metal and mining industries and the banks. It was also in these industries that concentration made the fastest progress. This process had taken many forms: sometimes that of the hostile takeover, where the small rolling mill folds before the integrated factory; sometimes it was the merger, where the large company annexes the small one at a set price, the mining company purchases the small mine, or the very large bank absorbs the large, medium or small bank; and sometimes it was an association of mutual interests, where two companies would acquire interests in each other's business.

3.) The United States

It remains for us to describe the unique evolution of the United States. Its growth period had continued beyond 1900, the year the crisis began in Europe. Yet, in the United States, the 1884 and 1893 crises had also occurred two to three years after these crises had hit Europe. America experienced a simple depression during the second half of 1903 and the first half of 1904 that undoubtedly was characterized by all the usual symptoms: the restriction of production, especially metal production, a fall in railway profits, a drop in prices, a decreased stock of gold, a rise in the discount, a decrease in the portfolio of the banks and stock exchange crises which were the consequence of the fall in prices, reduced production and decreased dividends, particularly the trusts' dividends. But by the second half of 1904, the economy in the United States was recovering. We may consider 1904 to be quite favourable and 1905, by all accounts, to be a year of great prosperity.

---

404. *Vierteljahreshefte zur Statistik der Deutschen Reichs* 4 (1904): 73–76.

405. Parvus, *Handelskrisis und Gewerkschaften: Gesetzentwurf über den achtstündigen Normalarbeitstag* (Munich: Ernst, 1901), 45–46. From 1900, travel allowances paid by the unions to their members rose from 313,321 to 641,028 marks; their unemployment relief, from 304,607 to 501,078 marks.

By the second half of 1903, the iron market was showing weakness. After a period of astonishing growth during which cast-iron production leapt from 13,620,703 tons in 1899 to 18,009,252 in 1903, it slumped to 16,497,033 tons in 1904. The downturn was apparent in the second half of 1903.

Table 1.56 Cast-Iron Production in the United States, 1902–1904 (in tons; 1 ton = 1,016 kg)*

	First Semester	*Second Semester*
1902	8,808,874	9,012,733
1903	9,707,367	8,301,885
1904	8,173,438	8,323,595

*Here and in the preceding paragraph, Lescure evidently uses the long ton (1,018 kg), which was more common in the Imperial System than in the United States, where the short ton (907 kg) is used.
No source given.

The mining industry followed, and in 1904, the production of mineral fuel fell from 283 million to 250 million tonnes for bituminous coal mainly used in industry, and from 59 to 57 million tonnes for anthracite, more commonly used for domestic heating.

As for the iron ore mines, the effects of the depression were even more pronounced. In the iron mines of Lake Superior, which represented four-fifths of US production, only 21.5 million tonnes were extracted in 1904, compared to 24.5 million in 1903 and 27.5 million in 1902.[406]

In the same period, the textile industry was greatly affected by the high price of its raw materials.

The depression in the steel industry had a detrimental effect on the railways. Gross profits, after having increased from $1,133 million in 1897 to $1,721 million in 1902, that is by 70 per cent, only grew by 1 per cent in 1904.[407]

Prices, circulation and distribution equally reflected the critical economic situation, which was reflected in the trend of index numbers in *Dun's Review* (tab. 1.57).

Table 1.57 Index Numbers in *Dun's Review*, 1902–1905

	1 January	*1 July*
1902	101.59	101.95
1903	100.36	99.46
1904	100.14	97.19
1905	100.32	—

Source: Pierre Leroy-Beaulieu, 'Le mouvement économique et social aux États-Unis', *Économiste français*, no. 25, 24 June 1905, 906.

406. Pierre Leroy-Beaulieu, 'Le mouvement économique et social aux États-Unis', *Économiste français*, no. 3, 21 Jan. 1905, 79.
407. Pierre Leroy-Beaulieu, 'Le mouvement économique et social aux États-Unis', *Économiste français*, no. 10, 11 March 1905, 326–27. The railways in industrial regions were most affected by the decline.

The decline was, as always, particularly hard on the prices of iron products, which were already down by around 30 per cent in 1903, and this trend continued into 1904. Notably in September 1904, American forges decided to lower the price of steel billets from $24 per tonne to $19. Following an excellent cotton crop in 1904, cotton prices also fell. After climbing to 17 cents per pound (2,000 francs per tonne) in 1903 under the pressure of speculation, it collapsed to 7 cents per pound (800 francs per tonne) in February 1904.[408]

Circulation faithfully reflected the slowdown in the volume and value of trading. The banks of New York limited their operations considerably in the second part of 1903. From 26 September to 19 November, the portfolio shrank from $917.1 million to $878.7 million, then reached its minimum at $841.6 million on 28 November 1903. The traditional exchange crisis finally came to strike the decisive blow on the American economy. The bank coffers were depleted of gold, especially in the last week of October and the first week of November. Cash on hand lost $17 million until 5 December, dropping to $151.6 million, but by 25 December, it had already regained $9.6 million, rising up to $162.2 million,[409] and on 29 August 1904, it reached the unprecedented height of $279.2 million.

A stock market crisis of great intensity ran parallel to the credit crisis, affecting the shares in the metal industry in particular, and especially those of the steel trust, which suffered a dilution of its capital.[410] After having distributed only 4 per cent of the dividend on its common shares in 1902, it was drawing up a report of insolvency by the fourth quarter in 1903. Gross receipts were down by $92,167,441 in 1904 compared to 1903. Despite measures taken to reduce overheads and costs (eliminating the special fund for construction and improvements reaching $10 million in 1903, reducing operating expenses by $55,641,284 and overhead costs by $2,062,456), the dividends distributed to shareholders fell from $12,707,563 in 1903 to zero in 1904 for common shares, and preferred stocks decreased by $5,184,496, going from $30,404,173 in 1903 to $25,219,677 in 1904. Already in the last quarter of 1903, ordinary shares had received no dividends, and by the end of 1903, their value had collapsed to 10 (par being at 100). Share prices reached their minimum in May 1904, at the moment when industry was experiencing the worst part of the depression, trading at 8¾. Preferred shares held at 7 per cent fell below 50 and bonds at 5 per cent dropped to 65.[411]

Not only were dividends dropping but the working class affected by unemployment saw its resistance weaken in the face of the bosses. The 1903 convention regulating wages in the coal industry was revised.[412] The bosses removed the clause requiring

408. Pierre Leroy-Beaulieu, 'Le mouvement économique et social aux États-Unis, *Économistes français*, no. 3, 21 Jan. 1905, 78.

409. Pierre Leroy-Beaulieu, 'Le mouvement économique et social aux États-Unis, *Économistes français*, 17 Oct. 1903, 536.

410. *Volkswirtschaftliche Chronik* (1904): 571–73.

411. Pierre Leroy-Beaulieu, 'Le mouvement économique et social aux États-Unis', *Économistes français*, no. 14, 8 April 1905, 479.

412. The return to this convention triggered off the miners' strike in Pennsylvania in May 1906.

them to employ only unionized workers. This allowed 1,500 companies once again to employ non-union workers. As a result of unemployment, immigration diminished from 857,046 in 1902–3 to 812,870 in 1903–4.[413]

Thus in 1903–4, the United States exhibited all the characteristic traits of a general economic crisis. But any attempt to follow its classical evolution and normal transformation into a slow economic depression would be in vain. By the summer of 1904, barely a year after the onset of the crisis, the American economy was picking up and thriving more than ever. Cast-iron production in 1905 exceeded all previously recorded figures. Undeniable prosperity was reflected not only in cast-iron production but also in industrial output, railway receipts, foreign trade, prices and in the improved situation of the banks and on the stock exchange. No sooner had prices dropped in September 1904 than consumption, stimulated by the lower prices, recovered immediately.

How do we explain this phenomenon? In describing the American growth period from 1897 to 1903, we have focussed on the policies of American stock companies and the evolution of American industry toward trusts, on its organization into cartels comprised of a small number of very large producers. The speed with which the crisis was overcome in the United States may be explained by the considerable fall in production prices (costs) during the growth period that in turn enabled the American economy to absorb a price fall, even a severe one, which reanimated demand and the spirit of enterprise.

In addition to these essential factors, we note the role of secondary factors such as the Russo-Japanese War, the low price of capital goods in Europe and the fall in wages in America.

§12 – The crisis of 1907

It was, however, the United States that was to become the focus of the general and periodic overproduction crisis in 1907.[414]

A.) Growth

1.) France

By 1905, there were very clear signs of recovery in France, as well as in England and Germany. The statistics for the issuing of shares showed a significant recovery in France from 1904. The amount of the shares issued grew from 499.7 million francs in 1903 to 1,361.7 million francs in 1904, 1,907.2 million francs in 1905 and 1,617.1 million francs in 1906. Bond issues followed the same upward curve, increasing from 201.8 in 1904 to 674.3 in 1905 and 1,062.5 in 1906.

---

413. Jean de Kergolay, 'L'émigration aux États-Unis', supplement, *Journal des débats*, 12 April 1905.

414. For more detailed study of the 1907 crisis, see the second edition of the present work.

By February–March 1906, order books were so overloaded that during auctions for the Indochina and the Ivory Coast railways, several lots of rails, splices and accessories could not be auctioned. Micheville and Longwy, who together took 1,195 tonnes of rails, granted a rebate of only 2 per cent. In May 1906, no contractor could be found to renovate the bridge in Asnières at the price given in the project estimates. The metropolitan rail companies ordered 100 million francs worth of wagons in 1906, after having ordered only 6 million francs the year before. Factories were also rapidly modernizing their equipment. Cockerill built a Thomas steel mill and rolling mill machinery. Ougrée was building blast furnaces; Angleur, a steel mill with four retorts; and La Providence, a fourth blast furnace in Marchienne. Marcinelle and Couillet completed the installation of blast furnaces; Sambre-et-Moselle built blast furnaces in Montigny and completed construction on its steel mill. L'Espérance Longdoz constructed a third blast furnace and a steel mill; the Nicaise and Delcuve steelworks and La Crayère's rolling mills were expanded.[415] Under these conditions, French production increased, particularly that of coal, iron ore, cast iron and steel.[416]

Prices rose with demand, and from November 1905, the coke markets were renewed with increases of 0.50 and even 2 francs. Mines refused to commit themselves after 30 June 1906, blooms brought 105 at export, and billets, 112.50, compared to 96 and 101, respectively, on 10 October, and the International Girders Syndicate decided on a new increase of 2 sh. 6, the fifth rise since 1 September, which brought the price to £5 per tonne for this product.

Imports of raw materials went from 2,865,273 francs in 1904 to 3,687,126 francs in 1906 and 3,878,446 in 1907. Exports of manufactured goods grew from 2,208,706 francs in 1904 to 2,699,461 in 1906 and 2,852,387 in 1907. The returns of the French railways increased from 1,514,656,000 francs in 1904 to 1,577,218,000 in 1905 and 1,619,315,000 in 1906.

This growth in trade translated into an increase in the circulation of bills of exchange.[417] The portfolio of our credit companies was swelling. The Banque de France recorded an increase in its portfolio and a decrease in its cash holdings.

This industrial prosperity brought increased activity on the stock exchange; fixed-income securities were decreasing. The decline of the French 3 per cent provoked much discussion; and we wrongly looked for political explanations (the Moroccan Affair, a proposed tax on pensions) rather than economic ones; for the drop was not limited to government securities but affected those of every country and all fixed-income securities.

Share prices were rising. (See table 1.58.)

---

415. *Revue hebdomadaire des valeurs régionales de la Banque Renauld et Cie*, 4 Dec. 1905, 19 March 1906 and 28 May 1906.

416. See *Annuaire statistique de la France.*

417. Alfred Neymarck, 'Les établissements de crédit depuis cinquante ans', *Journal de la société de statistique de Paris* 50 (1909): 122–34. Gaston Roulleau, *Les règlements par effets de commerce en France et à l'étranger* (Paris: Dubreuil, Frèrebeau, 1914).

Table 1.58 Prices of Select French Securities

	Variable-Income Industrial Shares		
	Denain-Azin	*Longwy*	*Transatlantique*
7 Jan. 1904	1,145	920	—
5 Jan. 1905	1,480	1,088	158.75
4 Jan. 1906	2,045	1,180	199
3 Jan. 1907	2,275	1,195	225
2 Jan. 1908	1,919	1,030.50	204

Average Values of the French 3%

1904	96.61	1906	97.40	1908	96.67
1905	99.23	1907	94.97	1909	97.50

No source given.

2.) Germany

In Germany, issues of industrial and banking securities resumed their growth after a momentary interruption (tab. 1.59).

Table 1.59 Values of German Industrial and Banking Securities from the *Deutsche Ökonomist*, 1904–1908 (millions of marks)

	Issue of Industrial and Banking Shares and Securities of Germany and Others		*Issue of German Industrial Securities*	
	Nominal Amount	*Market Value*	*Nominal Amount*	*Market Value*
1904	496.71	697.75	234.27	359.80
1905	619.07	915.32	309.18	552.09
1906	809.03	1,196.02	390.94	653.80
1907	583.04	783.00	284.14	431.32
1908	689.90	1,048.97	262.33	599.81

Source: *Deutsche Ökonomist*.

Beginning in 1905, electrical companies noticed a considerable improvement in demand: to the degree that electricity was used as a source of power by factories, forges, railways and tramways, by the merchant marine and the navy, and as a lighting source, the demand for steam turbines became more pressing.[418] Thus in February, the Schuckert-Siemens company requested its common shares capital to expand its factories.[419] On 14 May 1906, AEG proceeded to issue 7,116,000 marks in bonds at 4 per cent.[420]

Local railways entered a new phase of their development after 1905. Born in 1900 from the reorganization of the *Kleinbahnfinanzgesellschaft*, the *Deutsche Kleinbahnfinanzgesellschaft*

418. *Kölnische Zeitung*, no. 1234, 27 Nov. 1905.
419. *Berliner Tageblatt*, no. 84, 15 Feb. 1906.
420. *Berliner Tageblatt*, no. 237, 11 May 1906.

[German Local Railway Finance Company] released very favourable projections in its report for 1905 and was distributing 3 per cent dividends, compared to 2 per cent in1904.[421]

The metal and mining industries soon followed, as the large German cartels for coal, cast iron and steel invited their members to increase their production from 1905 to 1907. They were also raising prices. This increase, which was already taking shape at the end of 1905, continued into 1906, and by May 1906, it had become generalized.

Coal production increased from 169,194,320 tonnes in 1904 to 193,537,493 in 1906; imports grew from 14,968,141 tonnes to 17,684,152 tonnes in the same years, while exports remained more or less stationary at around 18 million tonnes. What was true for coal was also true for cast iron, the production of which rose from 10,987,000 tonnes in 1905 to 13,045,000 tonnes in 1907.

However, the most interesting statistics are provided to us by the steel cartel (*Stahlwerksverband*), which records its shipping figures on a quarterly basis (tab. 1.60). The cartel's products are grouped into three basic categories: semi-finished steel, profiled iron and railway equipment; instead of using quarterly statistics, which would take us too far afield, we will confine ourselves to reproducing the annual figures.

Table 1.60 Shipments of the *Stahlwerksverband*, 1905–1908 (1,000 tonnes)

	Semi-finished Steel	*Railway Equipment*	*Profiled Iron*
1905	1,910	1,631	1,673
1906	1,861	1,935	1,936
1907	1,557	2,327	1,698
1908	1,390	2,070	1,302

No source given.

In October 1905, the cast-iron cartel in Düsseldorf had already decided on an increase of 3 marks per tonne for the first term of 1906. From 1 May 1906, it further increased its prices by 5 marks per tonne for hematite and no. 1 cast-iron mouldings.[422] The example was soon followed by the wire cartel, which raised its prices from 132.50 to 138 marks[423] and, by combining with strip rolling mills, increased its prices by a further 7.50 marks per tonne; and then, once combined with light iron sheets, it brought its prices up to 145 marks.[424]

What applied to the mining and metal industries also applied to the textile industry. The statistics for consumption, the price of wool and of cotton in Germany are relevant in this regard (tab. 1.61).

421. *Berliner Tageblatt*, no. 195, 18 April 1906; no. 214, 28 April 1906.
422. *Berliner Tageblatt*, no. 36, 16 Feb. 1906.
423. *Berliner Tageblatt*, no. 195, 18 April1906.
424. *Berliner Tageblatt*, no. 198, 20 April 1906. For further details on the pace of cast iron prices in 1905, 1906 and 1907, see *Volkswirtschaftliche Chronik* (1907): 771.

Table 1.61 Consumption and Prices of Cotton and Wool in Germany

	Consumption		*Prices (marks per dozen)*	
	Cotton (doz.)	*Wool (doz.)*	*Cotton (Middling)*	*Wool (Buenos-Aries)*
1905	3,943,131	1,645,980	97.21	389.79
1907	4,500,527	1,689,760	121.53	437.48
1908	4,205,281	1,665,187	107.21	375.92

No source given.

Foreign trade and railway profits clearly reflected the increase in exchanges.

The number of ships being built in Germany was rapidly increasing, rising from 381 ships with a tonnage of 211,307 Br. Reg. T. in 1904 to 673 ships with a tonnage of 308,034 Br. Reg. T. in 1907.[425]

From then on, the circulation of bills of exchange experienced a parallel increase. For Germany, we possess an overall statistic that is very characteristic. (See table 1.62.)

Table 1.62 Circulation of Bills of Exchange in Germany, 1904–1908 (millions of marks)

1904	23,201	1907	30,766
1905	25,507	1908	30,114
1906	28,062		

No source given.

The Reichsbank's portfolio swelled, while its metal reserve shrank. The discount rate at the Reichsbank in 1906 reached the already high average rate of 5.15, following a rate of 3.81 in 1905. By 1907, it was at 6.03.

However, the German stock exchange responded to this economic prosperity with great reserve. The crisis of 1900 was beneficial for the German public. Kept informed by the economy pages in the daily newspapers and the different indices allowing one to forecast the coming of crises, both the public and the market were already on their guard in 1906. In table 1.63, we see the rise in share values was nonetheless very clear.

Table 1.63 Average Prices for Select German Securities, 1904–1907

	3 ½% Imperial Bonds in Berlin	*Gelsenkirchen*	*AEG*	*Hamburg-Amerika*
1904	90.02	198.50	198.14	133.26
1905	90.08	224.84	217.80	161.64
1906	87.33	230.21	234.23	156.38
1907	84.15	219.18	219.64	111.85

Source: *Volkswirtschaftliche Chronik*, Jahresübersicht [yearly overview] (1907): 850–51, tab. 5–6.

425. *Volkswirtschaftliche Chronik* (May 1908): 255, tab.

The number of workers seeking employment in industry was now much lower than the number of available jobs.

With the industrial recovery, the curious movements of populations, already observed during the growth period from 1895 to 1900, resumed in 1905. Agricultural workers from eastern Germany flocked to the industrial regions in the west,[426] and foreign immigration was on the increase. Thus, migrant workers from Croatia, Bohemia, Serbia and Galatia returned to the Ruhr coal basin.[427]

Emigration from Germany was again decreasing.

3.) England

In 1904, 3,831 companies with nominal capital of £92,526,000 had been created.[428] In 1905, 4,358 were created with nominal capital reaching £119,179,000. In 1906, a further 4,840 were created, and their capital reached £136,736,249. All branches of the economy, or almost all, were becoming interesting, but the shipbuilding and textile industries led the growth, followed by the iron industry. Railways had for a long time ceased to play the leading role in England.

While in 1904, 749 ships weighing 1,322,327 tonnes had been launched, in 1905, 823 ships were launched weighing 1,752,969 tonnes. But, more significantly, this increase in construction was mainly in commercial vessels. In 1905, 795 commercial vessels weighing 1,623,168 tonnes had been launched; while in 1906, the number rose to 886 ships weighing 1,823,343 tonnes.

The great prosperity in shipbuilding partly contributed to the growth in the coal, iron and steel industries. Cast-iron production reached 9,08,086 tonnes in 1905 and increased to 10,109,453 tonnes in 1906.[429] What was good for cast iron was also good for iron ore and, *a fortiori*, for coal.[430] The textile industry also shared in the industrial growth in England. In 1903, there were only nine new companies representing capital of £740,000, putting about 3,529,000 spindles into operation. In 1904, 15 new companies were created with capital of £3,350,000 and 1,840,000 spindles. Although it is true that in 1906 their number dropped to 22 companies with capital of £1,710,000 and 1,840,000 spindles, the notable increase in 1904–5 could easily explain the interruption in the development of textile production. The production of cotton wares, which was just 5,169,361 yards valued at £55,186,000 in 1903, expanded to 5,479,553 yards valued at £62,983,000 in 1904, 6,156,000 yards at £70,339,000 in 1905 and 6,284,383 yards at £75,476,000 in 1906.[431]

In 1904, the profits realized by the textile factories were £31,729, which represented 2.5 per cent of their capital. In 1905, they reached £693,000, representing 7 per

426. *Berliner Tageblatt*, no. 196, 19 April 1906.
427. *Berliner Tageblatt*, no. 658, 28 Dec. 1905 and no. 619, 21 Dec. 1905.
428. *Économiste européen* 30 (1906): 505.
429. *Économiste européen* 31 (1907): 505.
430. *Statistical Abstract*.
431. *Économiste européen* 33 (1908): 441–42.

cent of their capital.[432] In 1906, 65 cotton spinning companies, with share capital of £ 2,529,667 and bond capital of £1,257,121, showed a profit of £423,277, or 12¾ per cent of their capital.[433]

The statistics for foreign trade and railway receipts clearly reflected this general increase in exchanges. The exports of the United Kingdom were as follows:[434]

(in 1,000s of £)

1905	14,495	19,912	3,919
1906	17,618	26,348	3,968

Railway receipts were also increasing, but the rise in net profits was hindered by the rapid rise in fuel prices and the increased cost of materials, from the first half of 1906 onward. For every 3.8 per cent increase in gross receipts, the cost of materials increased by 5.2 per cent. For the second semester in 1906, the ratio was 2.5 per cent to 5.2 per cent.

Thus in 1904, 1906 and even 1907, economic prosperity in England was complete; and its impact on circulation and on the clearing house and the Bank of England can be clearly seen. The sums offset by the London Bankers' Clearing House are of particular interest because they reflect the expansion in commodity trading and securities – that is, the boom on the stock and commodity exchanges (see tab. 1.64).

Table 1.64 Amounts Cleared at the London Bankers' Clearing House, 1904–1908 (millions of £)

	Totals for the Year	*Amount Cleared on the 4th of Each Month*	*Amount Cleared on Consols Settling Days*	*Amount Cleared on Stock Exchange Account Days*
1904	10,564	445	597	1,536
1905	12,287	497	638	2,070
1906	12,766	524	644	2,031
1907	12,730	542	631	1,822
1908	12,120	542	631	1,822

No source given. [Ed. – Note: although the original French column labels for the table clearly follow the practice of the *Statistical Abstract for the United Kingdom* for its yearly table on the London Bankers' Clearing House, Lescure's figures only partly match those given in the *Statistical Abstract* for these years. The repeated figures from 1907 and 1908 seem to indicate typos.]

The Bank of England's portfolio was growing. (See table 1.65.)

432. *Économiste européen* 29 (1906): 87.

433. *Économiste européen* 31 (1907): 23. For further details, see *Économiste européen* 29 (1906): 87, 279; 30 (1906): 311, 504; 31 (1907): 87, 504, 569; and 32 (1907): 87, 727.

434. *Statistical Abstract of the United Kingdom.* [Ed. – Note that columns in the original French edition have no labels, and the figures listed could not be found in the *Statistical Abstract of the United Kingdom*, covering 1905 and 1906.]

Table 1.65 Bank of England's Annual Averages (millions of £)

	Cash on Hand	*Portfolio*
1904	34.4	76.2
1907	34.87	85.96
1908	37.26	62.73

No source given.

On the stock exchange, the rise in industrial values contrasted with the drop in fixed-income securities (government securities). (See tab. 1.66.)

Table 1.66 Course of Select Shares and Securities on the London Stock Exchange, 1904–1908

	Iron and Coal				*Shipping Companies*				*Gov. Consolidated 2½*	
	Cammell Laird		*Vickers Sons and Maxim*		*Cunard*		*P. & O. Steam Navigation*			
	+Incr.	*+Decr.*	*+Incr.*	*+Decr.*	*+Incr.*	*+Decr.*	*+Incr.*	*+Decr.*	*+Incr.*	*+Decr.*
1904	8¾	6⅜	2⅝	$1\frac{11}{16}$	$13\frac{9}{16}$	11¾	131	125	91¼	85
1905	$10\frac{27}{32}$	$8\frac{3}{16}$	$2\frac{25}{32}$	$2\frac{9}{32}$	15	11¾	135	126½	$91\frac{13}{16}$	87½
1906	11⅛	8⅜	$2\frac{27}{32}$	$2\frac{11}{32}$	15⅝	13½	131¾	126½	91	$85\frac{9}{16}$
1907	$9\frac{3}{10}$	4	$2\frac{19}{32}$	$1\frac{31}{32}$	15¾	13⅛	128½	119	87⅜	80¾
1908	5	$2\frac{9}{16}$	2⅙	$1\frac{17}{32}$	15½	12⅝	126¾	120	88⅜	$83\frac{5}{16}$

Source: *Investor's Monthly Manual*, n.s., 39, no. 12 (Dec. 1909).

In table 1.67, we see wages also took part in the general increase, but only by a small margin.

Table 1.67 Change in Weekly Wages, 1904–1907 (+ rising; – dropping)

	Coal Mines	*Other Industries*
1904	– £31,000	– £8,000
1905	– 13,000	+ 11,000
1906	+ 27,000	+ 31,000
1907	+ 174,000	+ 27,000

Source: *Labour Gazette*.

On the other hand, industrial growth was immediately reflected in the unemployment statistics (tab. 1.68); the unemployment rate began to diminish compared to the figures from the previous year in January 1905.

Table 1.68 Monthly Percentage of Workers Unemployed in Great Britain, 1904–1909

Yr.	*Av.*	*J.*	*F.*	*M.*	*A.*	*M.*	*J.*	*J.*	*A.*	*S.*	*O.*	*N.*	*D.*
1904	6.0	6.6	6.1	6	6	6.3	5.9	6.1	6.4	6.8	6.8	5	7.6
1905	5.0	6.3	5.7	5.2	5.2	4.7	4.8	4.7	4.9	4.8	4.6	4.3	4.5
1906	3.6	4.3	4.1	3.4	3.2	3.1	3.2	3.1	3.3	3.3	3.9	4.0	4.4
1907	3.7	3.9	3.5	3.2	2.8	3.0	3.1	3.2	3.6	4.1	4.2	4.5	5.6
1908	7.8	5.8	6	6.4	7.1	7.4	7.9	7.9	8.5	9.3	9.5	8.7	9.1
1909	7.7	8.7	8.4	8.2	8.2	7.9	7.9	7.9	7.7	7.4	7.1	6.5	6.6

Source: *Labour Gazette.*

The number of paupers per 1,000 inhabitants dropped from 26.8 on 1 July 1904 to 24.8 in 1907. An increase in the number of marriages was also noticeable. After having dropped from 259 in 1901 to 258 per 10,000 inhabitants in 1904, it rose again to 261 in 1905, 270 in 1906 and 276 in 1907.

4.) The United States

The growth period that preceded the 1907 crisis was essentially no different from the one that had preceded the 1893 crisis or from the European growth periods in the middle of the nineteenth century; and even if the new electric industry lent an original aspect to this growth period, as it had the German prosperity before the 1900 crisis, this remained just about the only feature worthy of comment. The American growth period was essentially one of railway expansion.

As in Europe, the growth period in America was characterized by the flow of capital toward industry and an increase in the issuing of securities. Thus, if we deduct from recent issues the amounts of conversions, we arrive at the figures shown in table 1.69 on issuance in the United States.

Table 1.69 New Issues of Securities and Conversions in the United States, 1904–1906 (in dollars)

	Total	*Conversions*	*Net Demand for New Capital*
1904	2,785,138,525	353,445,223	2,431,693,302
1905	3,688,124,622	323,487,879	3,364,636,743
1906	5,126,000,000	2,001,000,000	3,125,000,000

Source: *Journal of Commerce and Commercial Bulletin*, 2 Jan. 1908.

But what is more important to consider than the statistics for issues in general are the statistics for industrial issues.

Unfortunately, we can only consider general statistics on this topic. The figures from the New York Stock Exchange can, however, give us a sufficiently accurate idea about industrial issues. Despite the federal character of the United States' political organization, Wall Street is unquestionably the United States' stock exchange. The statistics for industrial issues on Wall Street during the period from 1904 to 1906 will allow us to get an idea of the influx of capital toward industry for the period under consideration. It also allows us to see the preponderant role played by the railways and tramways (see tab. 1.70). In the first half of 1907, the demand for capital was such that the best borrowers had to borrow at 5 and 6 per cent.

Table 1.70 Security Listings on the New York Stock Exchange, 1904–1908

	Bonds (1,000s of $)			*Stocks (1,000s of $)*		
	Railways	*Tramways*	*Diverse*	*Railways*	*Tramways*	*Divers*
1904	343,036	17,118	174,925	120,915	—	54,951
1905	538,584	29,650	411,792	176,922	58,274	298,237
1906	305,727	126,231	139,940	248,186	188,210	226,372
1907	267,192	16,072	136,749	146,750	20,443	408,837
1908	506,160	65,076	301,722	200,502	2,417	34,007

Source: *Commercial and Financial Chronicle* 88, no. 2274, 23 Jan. 1909, 194; and 89, no. 2301, 31 July 1909, 259–61.

Thus, an original type of security was used: short-term notes and loans (short-term bonds). This then allowed the possibility of converting them at the first opportunity.[435] The New York Central issued 50,000,000 of these reimbursable notes on the same date. In the first semester in 1907, $296,210,000 worth of these notes were issued in New York, out of which $286 million were for the large and small railways.[436]

Like the growth that had preceded the 1893 crisis and the growth that had announced and prepared the depression of 1903–4, it was indeed the railways that were at the forefront of industrial development in the United States. In 1905, 9,700 miles were constructed; in 1906, 10,300 miles; and in 1907, 10,000 miles.[437] This was far from the figure of 2,900 miles built in 1897. The expansion of the American metal industry must be attributed to the fever for new railway construction. The production of rails, wagons and locomotives grew in proportions roughly equal to this lengthening of the railway network. The 36 main railway wagon construction companies and the 12 major locomotive construction companies published an annual report that provides very exact figures for wagon and locomotive production. Just as 1905 had seen a resumption of railway construction, so too did it mark the beginning of a new boom in the wagon and locomotive industry. From 1904 to 1905, the number of constructions had fallen considerably; yet in 1905, the production figures showed signs of a recovery that would continue unabated into 1906 and 1907.

435. Over 2 billion francs worth of these bonds were converted in 1909. *Moniteur des intérêts matériels* (1910): 1444.
436. 'Listings on the New York Stock Exchange during the Half-Year', *Commercial and Financial Chronicle*, 85, no. 2193, 6 July 1907, 14.
437. *Statistical Abstract of the United States* 43 (1920): 334, tab. 228 (includes all lines of one, two, three and four tracks).

Table 1.71 Number of Wagons and Locomotives Built for the Railways in the United States, 1903–1908

	Freight Wagons	*Passenger Wagons*	*Total Wagons Built*	*Locomotives Built*
1903	153,190	2,007	155,202	5,152
1904	60,806	2,144	62,950	3,441
1905	165,455	2,551	*168,006	*5,491
1906	240,503	3,167	*243,670	*6,952
1907	284,188	5,457	*289,645	*7,362
1908	76,555	1,716	78,271	2,342

* Includes Canada

Sources: *Économiste européen* (1909): 573; and *Commercial and Financial Chronicle* 88, no. 2276, 6 Feb. 1909, 338.

Rail production followed a parallel course. It is interesting here to compare the tonnage of rails produced with that of steel. Although we know the number of wagons produced, we do not know their exact weight. However, by multiplying the number of wagons by 20 tonnes, and that of locomotives by 60, we are still likely underestimating the real figures. We can then approximately account for the role played by the railways in the growth of the metal industry.

Let us first give the figures for the production, import and export of rails, and then determine the figures for American consumption (tab. 1.72).

Table 1.72 Steel Rail Production and Consumption in the United States, 1904–1908 (in tons)

	Production		*Imports*	*Exports*	*Consumption*
	Totals	*Bessemer*			
1904	2,284,711	2,137,000	37,776	416,250	1,906,237
1905	3,375,929	3,192,000	17,278	295,023	3,098,184
1906	4,005,642	3,791,000	4,943	328,036	3,682,654
1907	3,633,654	3,380,000	3,752	338,906	3,298,500
1908	1,921,611	1,354,000	1,719	196,510	1,727,820

Source: *Commercial and Financial Chronicle* 84, no. 2177, 16 March 1907, 602; and 88, no. 2276, 6 Feb. 1909, 338.

If we compare steel production with the tonnage of rails, wagons and locomotives, calculated as indicated above, we arrive at the figures shown in table 1.73.

Table 1.73 Steel Production in the United States, 1904–1907 (1,000s of tons)

	Steel		*Rails, Wagons and Locomotives*
	Bessemer	*Totals*	
1904	7,859	13,859	3,749
1905	10,941	20,023	7,064
1906	12,275	23,398	9,295
1907	11,667	23,362	10,108

Source: *Commercial and Financial Chronicle* 88, no. 2280, 6 March 1909, 600–601.

These figures clearly show the major part played by the railways in the expansion of the steel industry. Coal and cast-iron production figures followed a symmetrical progression.

A synthesis of these results can be found in the steel trust's balance sheets. The concentration of production allows us to observe the movements of expansion and depression. In the past, the prosperity of a factory had at most limited significance. Observing a period of growth was a difficult task. Price statistics remained the best indicator and means of forecasting. This is a very imperfect index, however, because prices are susceptible to the influence of external factors, beyond those of production and consumption, especially speculation. Thanks to the concentration of production, however, we can measure supply, production and demand. For the first time, we believe somewhat more precise statistics on demand may be established.

The statistics for orders allow us to focus our observations, making them completer and more precise. A surge in orders is the clearest indicator of economic recovery. The statistics from the steel trust enable us to determine that the growth period extends from the fourth quarter of 1904 into the third quarter of 1907 (see tab. 1.74).

Table 1.74 Orders of the Steel Trust in the United States, 1904–1909 (1,000s of tons)

	1904	*1905*	*1906*	*1907*	*1908*	*1909*
1st Quarter	4,136	5,597	7,018	8,043	3,765	3,512
2nd Quarter	3,192	4,829	6,809	7,603	3,313	—
3rd Quarter	3,027	5,865	7,936	**6,425**	2,421	—
4th Quarter	**4,696**	7,605	8,489	4,624	3,603	—

No source given. [Ed. – Boldface figures represent the beginning and end of the growth period.]

From the third quarter in 1907, the figures were lower than those for the corresponding quarters in 1906. The trust also provides us with statistics for its monthly net profits. Thanks to these statistics, we can specify not only the quarter but also the month in which the industrial recovery occurred. We can measure both the intensity of the growth and its exact duration. From then on, we note a curious correlation between orders and net profits. However, the decrease in the number of orders *precedes* the drop in net profits.

Whereas the growth in the number of orders dropped in the third quarter in 1907, net profits continued to rise until November 1907 (cf. tabs. 1.74 and 1.75).

Table 1.75 Monthly Net Profits of the Steel Trust in the United States, 1904–1909 (1,000s of $)

	1904	*1905*	*1906*	*1907*	*1908*	*1909*
January	2,868	6,810	11,856	12,838	5,052	7,226
February	4,540	6,629	10,958	12,145	5,709	7,669
March	6,036	9,585	13,819	14,137	7,466	7,989
April	6,863	9,037	12,581	14,600	6,761	—
May	6,256	10,602	14,041	16,056	6,021	—
June	6,370	10,665	13,501	14,846	7,482	—
July	6,344	9,035	12,242	13,804	8,599	—
August	6,202	10,986	13,158	15,279	9,152	—
September	6,226	11,218	12,713	14,720	9,354	—
October	7,250	12,400	14,984	17,042	9,415	—
November	7,117	11,827	13,482	**10,467**	8,756	—
December	7,099	10,988	13,282	5,034	8,053	—

No source given. [Ed. – Boldface figure indicates the reversal of the rise in net profits.]

The iron industry, moreover, was not the only one to prosper, nor did it owe all its prosperity to the railways. The expansion of the electrical industry, and consequently of copper mining, the construction industry, and the textile industry also contributed to the boom in the iron industry.

Cast iron, and nowadays even more so steel, is used to a large extent in the manufacture of dynamos.[438] Yet, what was true of dynamos was even more so for electric tramway cars, and especially for rails. Certainly, a new metal, copper, played a considerable part here; nevertheless, iron retained its own very important share of production in the period from 1904 to 1907. The American electrical industry was no less prosperous than the metal industry. The electric railway, along with the telephone and lighting, played a role in the electrical industry somewhat similar to that of the national railway vis-à-vis the iron and steel industry. Here again, our observations are made possible by the existence of large companies.

American periodicals have shown little interest in the evolution of the recent crisis in the field of production. Hence, we must rely on a method of piecing together fragmentary observations and consulting companies' balance sheets.

The period from 1901 to 1907 had been marked by the development of electric tramways. First, old horse-drawn trams were replaced by electric tramways. Second, new urban and suburban lines were created. Third, local short-line electric railways were sometimes built, and even some interstate lines were electrified.

The length of tramway lines grew annually. While in 1904 the network had reached a length of 29,820 miles, it grew to 32,517 miles in 1905 and 36,212 miles in 1906. The gross and net profits justified the extension, and although we do not possess overall

438. Ministère de l'Industrie et du Travail, *Construction des machines et appareils électriques* (Brussels: Office du Travail et Inspection belge, 1908), 48–51.

statistics for electric tramway profits, as we have for the railways, the *Commercial and Financial Chronicle* has provided a summary of gross and net receipts for 468 electric railways, which gives us a clear idea of the great prosperity in this branch of industry. Net profits followed more or less the increase in gross profits, albeit at a slower pace (see tab. 1.76).

Table 1.76 Gross and Net Returns of 468 Electric Tramways in the United States

	1905	*1906*	*Increase*	*%*
Gross	$269,595,550	$300,567,453	+ 30,971,902	+ 11.49
Net	$114,024,076	$126,580,195	+ 12,556,119	+ 11.01

Source: 'Growth of Electric Railway Operations', *Commercial and Financial Chronicle* 84, no. 2181, 13 April 1907, 840–43 and 842, table.

Moreover, electricity had other applications. In the absence of overall statistics for telephones and telegraphs, we must consult the report on American (Bell) Telephone and Telegraph Co.[439] Its statistics on net incomes, construction expenses and length of lines in operation are indicators of the development of the industry in the United States. Net profits went from $11,275,702 in 1904 to $16,269,388 in 1907. The construction of new lines represented $33,436,700 in 1904, $50,780,906 in 1905 and $79,366,949 in 1906; and by 1907, construction had already fallen to no more than $52,921,400. Its share capital as of 1 January 1908 was $179,595,355 and its bond capital reached $186,000,000. The length of its toll lines went from 1,121,228 miles on 1 January 1905 to 1,265,236 miles on the same date in 1906 and 2,727,929 in 1907. Finally, the number of employees grew from 59,451 in 1905 to 74,418 in 1906 and 90,324 in 1907.[440]

If we were to consider the various companies incorporated into the telephone trust, we would arrive at identical results. Bell telephone companies in Philadelphia, Chicago and New Jersey were increasing their capital to match the growth in their net revenues. They also expanded the number of telephone stands.[441]

It was natural that electrical construction companies would prosper. Here again, our observations are aided by the existence of a large company, whose development can be considered as a barometer of the industry: the General Electric Company. It publishes very detailed reports that provide information not only on the amount of its capital but also on its deliveries and orders, as well as on the number of workers it employs. All of these figures enable us to follow closely the boom in the United States (tab. 1.77).

439. *Commercial and Financial Review* 82, no. 2126, 24 March 1906, 699.

440. American Telephone & Telegraph Co., 'Annual Report for the Year Ending December 31, 1907,' *Commercial and Financial Chronicle* 86, no. 2230, 21 March 1908, 733–37.

441. See their reports in the *Commercial and Financial Chronicle* 84, no. 2191, 22 June 1907, 1484–86; 87, no. 2246, 11 July 1908, 93; 87, no. 2247, 18 July 1908, 162–65.

Table 1.77 General Electric and the Growth of the US Electrical Industry, 1904–1909

On 31 Jan.	*Share Capital*	*Profit*	*Deliveries**	*Orders†*	*Workers Employed*
1904	$43,866,700	$7,789,370	$41,699,617	$39,060,038	17,000
1905	48,247,943	6,719,546	39,231,328	35,094,807	18,000
1906	54,286,750	7,119,160	43,146,902	50,044,272	22,500
1907	94,353,550	8,427,843	60,071,883	60,483,659	28,000
1908	65,167,400	6,586,653	70,977,168	59,301,040	20,000
1909	65,178,800	4,802,253	44,540,676	42,186,917	—

* Includes installation work, freight, transportation, supplies, boilers, machinery, etc., and copper wires.

† The orders category includes only what is manufactured by General Electric.

Source: *Commercial and Financial Chronicle* 84, no. 2185, 11 May 1907, 1088–89; 86, no. 2237, 9 May 1908, 1157, 1164–65; 88, no. 2288, 1 May 1909, 1100, 1125.

On 6 December 1905, the company issued $19,500,000 in shares, and then $9,260,000 on 10 December 1906. The statistics for orders in particular, compared with those for deliveries, show the degree to which demand was far exceeding production. At least until 1907, the figures for deliveries always remained lower than those for orders.

The expansion of the electrical industry had repercussions on copper mining. Consequently, copper production also increased rapidly from 391,600 tonnes in 1905 to 409,500 in 1906 and 399,600 in 1907. The prosperity of the copper industry was expressed on the balance sheet of the Amalgamated Copper Company, the copper trust, whose entire capital of $153,887,900 was invested in copper mines, copper factories and rolling mills. Its net income rose from $9,161,637 in 1906 to $14,154,400 in 1907, and its dividend, from 5¾ to 7¾.[442]

This prosperity had an impact on other branches of production such as construction and the textile industry. The geological commission in the United States estimates the value of buildings erected during the course of each year (see tab. 1.78). This assessment includes the 17 most important cities in the United States.

Table 1.78 Value of New Construction in the United States (1,000s of $)

1905	640,555
1906	624,009
1907	651,773
1908	581,821

No source given.

The increase in construction caused the rapid growth of the cement industry. Reinforced concrete offers the right technical qualities at a cheap price, which means a great future for the construction industry.[443] Thus cement production

442. *Commercial and Financial Chronicle* 86, no. 2243, 20 June 1908, 1526.

443. Reinforced concrete is also used in the construction of railway bridges. Thus, the bridge in Maumee, Ohio, 360 m long and 4.80 m wide between its parapets and consisting of 12 arches that span 22 to 25 m, was built in reinforced concrete. *Le Ciment*, Dec. 1908.

expanded extremely fast. It was still at 8,482,000 barrels in 1900; however, between 1904 and 1908, it would almost double, from 26 million in 1904 to 48 million in 1907 (see tab. 1.79).

Table 1.79 US Cement Production, 1904–1907 (barrels)

1904	26,505,881
1905	35,246,842
1906	45,610,822
1907	48,785,390

No source given.

The textile industry also experienced this growth, only moderately. The number of spindles in operation went from 23,214,000 in 1904 to 25,924,000 in1907 (tab. 1.80).

Table 1.80 Number of Spindles in Operation in the United States, 1904–1907

1904	23,214,000
1905	23,687,000
1906	25,811,681
1907	25,924,000

No source given.

American cotton consumption, which had been at 3,603,000 bales in 1900 and 4,523,000 in 1904, rose to 4,877,000 in 1905 and to 4,974,000 in 1906. It diminished a bit in 1907.[444]

It was the same in the wool industry, where we can follow the wave of prosperity thanks to the existence of a trust, the American Woollen Co. of Boston. Its profits increased along with its sales, from $4,781,158 in 1905 to $4,809,397 in 1906 (see tab. 1.81).

Table 1.81 American Woollen Co. and the Growth of the American Wool Industry, 1905–1908 (in dollars)

	Sales and Other Incomes	*Costs and Expenses*	*Net Profits*
1905	48,660,449	43,879,291	4,781,158
1906	51,420,696	46,611,299	4,809,397
1907	47,377,846	43,951,240	3,426,606
1908	29,986,978	28,706,273	1,280,705

No source given.

444. *Statistical Abstract of the United States* 43 (1920): 554, tab. 312.

But the United States did not hold the top position in textiles as it did in the metal industry. It satisfied its own need for textiles largely through imports. Table 1.82 shows the exports from France to the United States.

Table 1.82 French Textile Exports to the United States, 1905–1908 (millions of francs)

	Silks	*Cotton Fabrics*	*Woollens*	*Clothing and Linens*
1905	41.3	59.6	14.2	11.4
1906	64.8	78.9	17.8	17.5
1907	84.2	72.9	18.8	7.9
1908	57.1	54.4	12.1	6.6

No source given.

All these growth trends in production and consumption were also reflected in the increase in the gross and net returns of the railways and the statistics on foreign trade. And, through the often-observed phenomenon of economic interdependency [*solidarité*], railway construction was stimulating the spirit of enterprise in the railway industry itself.

In table 1.83, the figures from the portfolios of the national banks and clearing-house statistics inform us of the state of credit and money circulation.

Table 1.83 Portfolios of the National Banks in the United States, 1904–1908

	New York (millions of $)		*Clearing House*	*Banks in other Cities (millions of $)*	
	*Demand Paper [*papier à vue*] (with one or more signatures)*	*Short-Term Paper [*papier à terme*] (with two or more signatures)*			
1904	7.5	149.1	$122,872,359	272.3	1,167.6
1905	11.4	135.7	143,909,448	308.7	1,246.6
1906	10.7	138.0	159,808,641	364.0	1,366.0
1907	16.3	161.1	145,175,733	411.9	1,487.7
1908	6.8	146.2	132,262,067	389.1	1,436.2

Source: Gaston Roulleau, 'L'abus du crédit aux États-Unis et la théorie des crises', pt 1, *Journal de la Société de statistique de Paris* 49, no. 3 (1908): 97, tab.

We possess concise statistics for the New York Stock Exchange. The three columns shown in table 1.84 make it possible to follow both the development of speculation and the rise in prices.

Table 1.84 Number and Values of Stocks on the New York Stock Exchange, 1903–1908

	Number of Stocks (1,000s of shares)	*Approximate Value (100,000s of $)*	*Average Value*
1903	161,102	11,004	73.2
1904	187,312	12,061	69.9
1905	263,081	21,295	87.3
1906	284,298	23,393	94.2
1907	196,438	14,757	85.8
1908	197,206	15,319	86.6

Source: *Commercial and Financial Chronicle*, 88, no. 2274, 23 Jan. 1909, 191.

Table 1.85 Wages in the United States, 1905–1907 (1890–1899 = 100)*

	Workers Employed	*Hourly Wage*	*Retail Price of Items for Family Consumption*	*Purchasing Power of Hourly Wage Relative to Retail Prices*
1904	125.7	117.0	111.7	104.7
1905	133.6	118.9	112.4	105.8
1906	142.9	124.2	115.7	107.3
1907	144.4	128.8	120.6	106.8

* For a critical analysis of these statistics, see the second edition of the present work, p. 341.
Source: From the *Bulletin of the United States Bureau of Labor Statistics*.

While nominal wages had increased throughout the period from 1904 to 1907, real wages increased only up to 1906. By 1907, the rise in the prices of commodities had already neutralized and negated the rise in nominal wages. Real wages dropped slightly in 1907.

Finally, unemployment was reduced. Although we lack the overall statistics, let us nonetheless consider those for unemployed trade union members in the state of New York. The percentage of unemployed union members shrank by half from 1904 to 1906 (tab. 1.86).

Table 1.86 Percentage Unemployed in New York State, 1904–1908

1904	*1905*	*1906*	*1907*	*1908*
13	8.3	5.9	12.6	27.7

Source: 'Unemployment in the United States', *Economist*, 22 May 1909.

Table 1.87 Number of Immigrants to the United States, 1905–1908

1905	1,055,968
1906	1,215,439
1907	1,334,166
1908	410,319

No source given.

On the whole, the growth period from 1904 to 1907 had the usual characteristics. One feature distinguished it, however: it occurred at a time when two great peoples in the Far East were at war, the conduct of which demanded enormous sums of capital. Thus, capital was not only in demand by industry but also by the belligerent powers. From 1904 to 1907, issues of Japanese government securities reached the enormous sum of 4,980,400,000 francs. The issues of Russian securities even exceeded this figure, with around 10 billion in capital being absorbed by the war. Consequently, the interest rates rose very rapidly. From December 1906 onward, the discount at the Reichsbank was at 7 per cent. It was very high in all the great countries of Europe, except France (tab. 1.88).

Table 1.88 Average Discount Rates at European Central Banks of Issue in 1906

	Berlin	*Bern*	*Vienna*	*London*	*Brussels*
1906	5.15	4.76	4.33	4.72	3.84

No source given.

B.) Crisis and depression

The periodic crisis of 1907 broke out prematurely, just as the crisis of 1873 had occurred after the Franco-Prussian War of 1870–71, seven years after the 1866 crisis. With the benefit of more precise statistics, we can see it occur in almost all the countries simultaneously. In October 1907, the panic in America led one to believe that the crisis had arrived. However, the rupture of equilibrium between production and consumption, the halt in demand and in the rise in prices would have been unmistakable to the astute observer as early as July 1907.

1.) United States

Up to this point, the most conclusive evidence we have had at our disposal to discern the onset of the crisis was the statistics on industrial output. From here on, we will have the more informative statistics on the steel trust's orders. This index enables us to identify the starting point of the crisis and follow its development. These are preferable to production statistics because orders are placed in advance, and production only starts to stagnate after the crisis has already been apparent for some time. And orders are preferable to price statistics because trust and cartel prices are fixed by those in authority and will remain the same despite the decline in demand. The crisis is no longer, according to Juglar's often-quoted definition, the halt in the price rise; rather, it is the *halt in demand*, which does not always find immediate expression in a drop in prices.

We have already noted the dominant role played by the railways in the expansion of American industry. This remained the case during the crisis.

In March 1907, E. H. Harriman declared in an interview with the *New York Times* that it was impossible to organize the administration of the railways more economically than it was already. Nevertheless, the American railway industry was sinking under the weight of the cost of its raw materials, interest and wages.[445] Railways that would have normally been able to borrow at 3.5 or 4 per cent were having to pay 5 and 6 per cent in 1907.

In April 1907, several hundred Chicago firms issued a public statement which said:

> We do not object to the regulation of the railroads by the National Government in the proper manner, but we do object to going through a period of hard times similar to that between 1893 and 1897 in order to accomplish alleged railroad reform. The situation is serious. Immediate action is necessary, or business will diminish; bank accounts will be reduced, profits will disappear, salaries will be cut, wages decreased, men discharged and thousands will be looking for work. Every labouring man, every business man, every professional man – in fact, everyman – is and will be affected.[446]

And in fact, from this moment on, railway construction was suspended.

In July 1907, the steel trust declared: 'the market for cast iron has weakened in all countries, and prices must fall'; and it added that this was not merely a momentary pause, but rather a turning point in the development of the consumption of steel products and a halt in industrial business. In September, this news was confirmed with a further clarification: old orders were to be honoured, but no new orders could be accepted.[447]

The explanation for how the crisis unfolded in the United States can be found in the reduction of the railways' net earnings, despite the increase in gross receipts, and confirmed by the statistics on orders from the steel trust. (Cf. table 1.74 and figure 1.1.)

---

445. 'The general level of freight rates has not been advanced in recent years, notwithstanding that prices in the industrial world have been almost steadily rising, and notwithstanding that the roads have been obliged repeatedly to raise wages and to pay higher prices for everything entering into their operating accounts'. 'Limits on Economy in Railroad Operations', *Commercial and Financial Chronicle* 84, no. 2178, 23 March 1907, 660.

'Mr. Harriman's purpose in these statements was to show first that the railroads in handling the increased volume of traffic under present conditions, or anything approximating them, must do it at an ever-increasing ratio of expense, that will tend some day to become prohibitive if existing rates are to be maintained or fair returns realized for their shareholders'. Ibid., 661.

446. *Commercial and Financial Chronicle* 84, no. 2183, 27 April 1907, 963.

447. *Commercial and Financial Chronicle* 85, no. 2203, 14 Sep. 1907, 624. See also the well-documented pamphlet by Laurent Dechesne, *La panique financière aux États-Unis, fin 1907* (Paris: Larose & Tenin, 1908), 9–10.

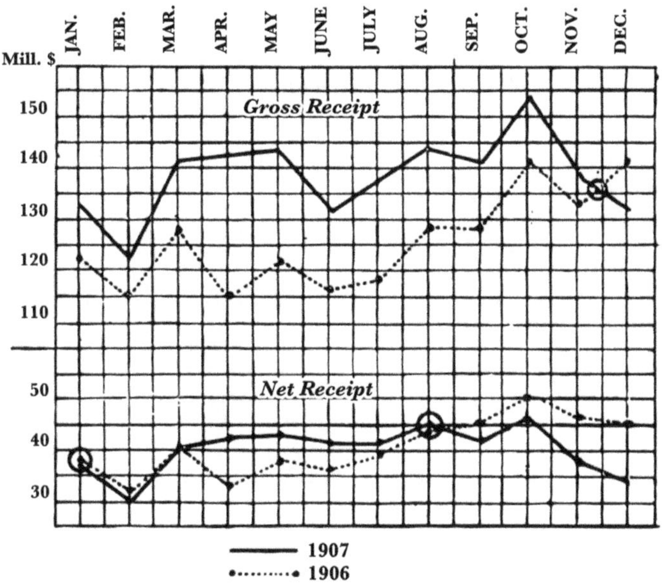

Figure 1.1 Railway Profits in the United States, 1906–7

These statistics reveal the existence of a crisis in the iron industry from the second quarter of 1907. It would be tempting to suggest the beginning of 1907 as the starting point, that is, the very date of the first decline in the railways' net returns. In fact, the number of orders received by the trust decreased from 8,489,000 tonnes in the last quarter of 1906 to 8,043,000 tonnes in the first quarter of 1907. Orders decreased further in the second quarter of 1907 to 7,603,000 tonnes, then to 6,425,000 tonnes in the third and 4,624,000 in the fourth. Yet one observation demands our attention. The statistics show a constant decline in the number of orders in some quarters and a constant rise in others. If we rank the quarters, we notice that the most favourable quarter is always the last one, then comes the third, then the first, and finally the second. It is therefore not surprising that the first quarter of 1907 shows a figure lower than that of the last quarter of 1906. The figures to be compared are therefore in fact the quarterly differences between the two years 1906 and 1907.

We are thus led to note that the reduction in orders for the first quarter in 1906 compared to the last quarter in 1905 was 587,000 tonnes, while in 1907 it was only 446,000 tonnes. The first quarter in 1907 does not indicate the beginning of the crisis. In the second quarter of 1907 orders were down by 440,000 tonnes, compared to 209,000 tonnes in 1906. There was thus a 50 per cent greater reduction. The crisis was already apparent, becoming more evident in the third quarter: an increase of 1,127,000 tonnes in 1906, against a corresponding reduction of 1,178,000 tonnes in 1907. Orders increased by 1,740,000 tonnes in the fourth quarter of 1906, against a corresponding decrease of 1,801,000 tonnes in 1907. These statistics therefore corroborate in all respects the figures for the railways' net receipts, Harriman's statements and those of the steel trust. It was only in July, when it seemed the halt in order would be both decisive and long lasting, that the trust sounded the alarm. But the crisis preceded this decision.

The national railways were not solely responsible for the crisis in the metal industry. The electric tramways played their part as well. The electrical industry was organized into large companies, which were charged not only with the technical aspects of electric tramway construction but also with its financing: in France this fell to the Thompson-Houston company; in Germany, AEG; and in the United States, General Electric. However, General Electric experienced a reduction in orders after the first quarter of 1907 (tab. 1.89).[448]

Table 1.89 Orders Received by General Electric (1,000s of $)

	1906	*1907*	*1908*
1st Quarter	14,639	18,602	10,003
2nd Quarter	14,326	16,493	9,624
3rd Quarter	16,428	14,581	10,387

Source: *Commercial and Financial Chronicle* 86, no. 2240, 30 May 1908, 1346; 87, no. 2252, 22 Aug. 1908, 482; and no. 2265, 21 Nov. 1908, 1360.

All long-term orders were terminated as a result of the rising cost of raw materials, especially copper.[449] Tramway construction was abandoned. This stop in electric railway construction was examined in an article published in the supplement edition of the *Commercial and Financial Chronicle* devoted to electric railways. In 1907, 1908 and 1909, railway developers had not realized the expected profits: earnings were insufficient to meet costs and fixed expenses. Profits did increase, but less than construction and operating costs.[450]

Cost of equipment had increased anywhere from 20 to 98 per cent, depending on the case. Wages were much higher. However, transport prices remained at 5 cents. In many instances, through the development of the correspondence system, it had even dropped so much that the average cost of transport was only 3½ cents. We shall also add an additional factor about which the *Commercial and Financial Chronicle* remains silent: the rise in interest. When consulting the balance sheets of the electric railways, one notices that the drop in net income was often linked to the rise in interest.

Thus, when we consider the examples of Massachusetts Electric and Co. (Boston) and the Milwaukee (Wisconsin) Electric Railway and Light Co., the rise in interest is an essential factor (tab. 1.90). Despite a more rapid increase in gross receipts than in operating costs, the income available for dividends was diminishing by 1907 as a result of the increase in interest charges.

448. Raphaël-Georges Lévy, 'La crise économique en 1907 et les États-Unis d'Amérique', *Revue des deux mondes* 42, no. 4 (Dec. 1907): 805–28.

449. Ibid., 814.

450. See 'Street Railway Fares', in 'Electric Railway Section', supplement, *Commercial and Financial Chronicle* 88, no 2279, 27 Feb. 1909, 1–3.

Table 1.90 Balance Sheets of Massachusetts Electric and Co. (Boston) and the Milwaukee Electric Railway and Light Company

	Massachusetts Electric (1,000s of $)		*Milwaukee (Wis.) Electric (1,000s of $)*	
	1907–8	*1906–7*	*1907*	*1906*
Receipts	7,809	7,758	3,823	3,523
Expenses	5,001	5,000	2,204	1,945
Net Income	2,087	493	1,619	1,573
Other Income	—	—	183	155
Total Net Income	—	—	1,802	1,733
Reserve Funds for Depreciation	—	—	382	352
Interest	1,784	1,702	572	509
Shareable Income	1,023	1,055	1,847	871

Source: *Commercial and Financial Chronicle* 87, no. 2257, 26 Sep. 1908, 806; and no. 2267, 5 Dec. 1908, 1475.

The halt in demand for the electrical industry would soon have repercussions for the copper industry and for copper mining in particular. The second key phenomenon that signalled the American crisis and preceded the October panic by three months was the drop in orders for the steel trust and the decrease in the price of copper by the United Metals Selling Co. This price drop reflected the decrease in copper orders that had begun in June.[451] The United Metals Selling Co., which was responsible for selling off the output of the copper trust, Amalgamated Copper, and of another copper producer, Phelps, Dodge and Co., announced in July a price reduction of 3 cents per pound, bringing the price of electrolytic copper to 22 cents. Yet despite this price reduction, orders were still lacking. In the first week in September, the price was lowered further to 18 cents, which in the space of five months represented a reduction of 7 to 8 cents, or almost 40 per cent. Yet stocks of copper continued to grow to such an extent that they could be seen when crossing the copper regions by rail.[452] The situation worsened in the month of September. The Calumet & Hecla Mining Co., a company independent from Amalgamated Copper, announced a dividend of $15, which was down from $20 for the preceding quarter, and $20 for the corresponding quarter in 1906. Similarly, the Quincy Mining Co. lowered its dividend from $4.50 to $2.50. Finally, it was announced that the Wolverine Mining Co.'s dividend would decrease from $10 to $7.50, and that of Utah Consolidated Mining, from $1.50 to $1.0. The crisis in the copper industry was quite general. On 14 September, the United Metals Selling Co. further lowered its prices to 16½ cents. Despite the repeated drops in prices, demand was limited: within a few weeks, the stock of copper grew from 150 to 200 million pounds.[453]

451. Henry Germain-Martin, 'Chronique sur les questions monétaires et le credit: La crise américaine', *Revue d'économie politique* 22, no. 3 (1908): 205; *Commercial and Financial Chronicle* 84, no. 2192, 29 June 1907, 1515.
452. *Commercial and Financial Chronicle* 85, no. 2202, 7 Sep. 1907, 552.
453. *Commercial and Financial Chronicle* 85, no. 2203, 14 Sep. 1907, 623 and no. 2204, 21 Sep. 1907, 687.

From September 1907 onward, copper production and consumption were in the midst of a crisis in the United States. When comparing the evolution of the crisis in the electrical or metal industries, we see that the transition from the period of expansion to that of depression was not abrupt, sudden or general in consumption and production. The monetary phase of the crisis during which all industrialists and traders are affected can be an illusion. However, the monetary crisis is often preceded by a gradual disruption of the equilibrium between production and consumption in certain industries. Thus, the American crisis did not enter its monetary phase until October 1907. And if this phase in particular attracted the public's attention and if in the minds of many the monetary crisis appeared to signal a periodic crisis in October, then this was an illusion. But why did the rupture of equilibrium between supply and demand, between production and consumption, only manifest itself in circulation in October? Nowadays, producers do not work on the basis of daily orders, but on contracts to be fulfilled in the future. The absence of new orders in no way implies the absence of deliveries to be made, and a crisis may very well exist without any interruption in the circulation of wealth. We find proof of this in the statistics on deliveries of certain large companies like General Electric, for example, or in the profit statistics of the steel trust. General Electric did not see a decrease in its deliveries until 1908; whereas its orders began to decline from the first quarter in 1907. The profits of the steel trust did not begin to decline in comparison to those of the previous year until November 1907, despite the fact that its orders started to decline in July 1907. On the other hand, and although this applies less to the United States, deliveries are often payable within a fixed term of three months. The crisis in circulation could therefore only have occurred sometime after the onset of the disequilibrium between supply and demand and even between purchases and sales.

This then explains why the crisis did not appear immediately. But why did it erupt in October in particular? Moving the harvest requires a lot of money and means of payment. But the crisis is reflected in circulation by an abnormal need for money and an abnormal need for means of payment. Thus, the two factors compound and aggravate one another.

A crisis in circulation consists in the buyer's inability to resell. By failing to resell, industrialists and merchants have to pay with their own money, instead of paying with the money owed them by the buyers. An abnormal need for money appears. Merchants and industrialists withdraw their deposits. If the banks have not kept enough metal money in their coffers to cover their repayments, they have to resort to suspending their payments because of 'runs'. The classic features presented themselves in the 1907 crisis with particular intensity, in a time before the existence of reserve banks.[454]

454. On the monetary phase in the American crisis, we have very detailed and well-documented studies: Martin, 'Chronique sur les questions monétaires'; Hermann A. Schumacher, *Le marché financier américain et sa récente crise monétaire*, trans. Jean Lescure (Paris: Giard & Brière, 1909); Edmund Théry, 'La crise américaine et la question de l'or', *Économiste européen* 32, nos. 830–31, 6 and 13 Dec. 1907, 710–13, 742–46; Arthur Raffalovitch, 'Les relations de l'état et du marché financier aux États-Unis', 2 pts., *Économiste européen* 32, nos. 823 and 825,

Suspensions followed, one after another, all over the United States, from 16 to 26 October. On Wednesday, 16 October, Augustus Heinze suspended payments after the failure of the copper corner. Heinze had to resign from the Mercantile National Bank.[455] Yet on Monday, 26 October, after closing time on the New York Stock Exchange, news came that the National Bank of Commerce would refuse to admit the Knickerbocker Trust Co. as compensation from Tuesday, causing its president, Charles T. Barney, to resign. The following day the Knickerbocker was besieged by depositors, and after having reimbursed $800,000, it was forced to suspend payments. These events had repercussions on the stock exchange, where first-rate securities dropped six points. In the afternoon, the brokerage firm Mayer & Co. was summoned because it was no longer able to meet its commitments. On Wednesday, after a report by a morning newspaper that there had been an advisory meeting the night before about the business of the Trust Company of America, one of the most influential trust companies, a run was unleashed which continued for the next two days, but which could have been averted with the help of J. P. Morgan and other financiers. On the same day, more serious news arrived from Pittsburgh that the various Westinghouse companies were in trouble and that trustees had been appointed for the Westinghouse Electric Manufacturing Company and the Securities Investment Company, which had been created by George Westinghouse as a pure 'concern'. On the same day, at the request of the Pittsburgh Clearing House, the Pittsburgh Stock Exchange suspended trading. It remained closed on Thursday and Friday. In the afternoon, the Iron City Trust Co. of Pittsburgh was placed in the hands of the trustees. On Thursday, the Hamilton Bank and the Twelfth Ward Bank were forced to close their doors, and the Empire City Savings Bank announced that it now required six days' notice before deposits could be withdrawn. Huge sums were withdrawn from the Lincoln Trust Co. and the Fifth Avenue Trust Co.

On Friday came new suspensions: the Union Trust Co. of Providence, after having resisted a run which had lasted all day on Thursday, was forced to suspend payments. In New York, the United States Exchange Bank closed its doors. The International Trust Co. remained closed, as did its subsidiaries in Brooklyn known as the Brooklyn Banks. In Brooklyn, the Borough Bank, the First National Bank of Brooklyn, the Jenkins Trust

---

18 Oct. and 1 Nov. 1907, 489–90, 553–55; Raffalovich, 'Le drame de New-York', *Économiste européen* 33, no. 824, 25 Oct. 1907, 521–23; Raffalovich, 'Notes sur la crise américaine', *Économiste européen* 33, nos. 826–32, 8 Nov.–20 Dec. 1907, 585–87, 617–20, 650–51, 676, 680–84, 713–15, 746–47, 778–79. (These articles constitute a day-to-day history of the American crisis, considered primarily in its monetary phase.) See also the weekly accounts in the *Commercial and Financial Chronicle* in 1907; 'Le discussion de la Société d'économie politique', *Économiste français*, 28 Dec. 1907, 920–22 and 25 Jan. 1908, 117–19; Pierre Leroy-Beaulieu, 'Le mouvement économique et social aux États-Unis', *Économiste français*, 21 Sep. 1907, 406–8, 2 Nov. 1907, 621–23, and 21 Dec. 1907, 877–79; A. Piatt Andrew, 'Substitutes for Cash in the Panic of 1907', *Quarterly Journal of Economics* 22, no. 4 (Aug. 1908): 497–516; and O. M. W. Sprague, *History of Crises Under the National Banking System* (Washington, DC: Government Printing Office, 1911).

455. See the bankruptcy statistics for national banks in the *Annual Report of the Comptroller of the Currency*, 1907, 19–20.

Co. and the Williamsburg Trust Co. followed its example. On Saturday, Charles Morse, Heinze's partner in the copper speculations, resigned from all the banks for which he served as director: the National Bank of North America, the New Amsterdam National, the Garfield National, the Fourteenth Street Bank, the New York Produce Exchange Bank, the Mercantile National and the Van Norden Trust Company. This led to a deluge of new presidents, vice presidents and bank directors being brought in as replacements for former presidents and, in particular, for former presidents belonging to the group of Heinze, Thomas and Morse.[456]

Table 1.91 List of American Banks Having to Suspend Payments in 1907

	Capital ($)	*Deposits ($)*
United States Exchange Bank	100,000	641,548
Borough Bank of Brooklyn	200,000	4,000,000
Williamsburg Trust Co.	700,000	8,000,000
First National Bank of Brooklyn	300,000	3,500,000
Fenkins Trust Co.	500,000	4,391,000
Union Trust Co. of Providence	500,000	25,000,000
Industrial Trust Co. (Providence)	3,000,000	43,000,000
Iron City Trust Co. (Pittsburgh)	2,000,000	2,033,000
Bath Trust Co. (Maine)	100,000	500,000

No source given.

The week from 21 to 26 October 1907 had been one of those 'black' weeks for which the history of previous crises has already given us many examples. The repeated and successive suspensions of payment were the consequences of the policies of the banks, particularly those of the trust companies. In the United States, the connection between the banks and stock market speculation is much closer than it is in Europe. Most banks were subservient to industrial firms. The former supported not only the value of shares but also the price of products. The fall of Heinze illustrates these policies. However, the repeated suspensions were a product of the very organization of the American banking system itself. The monetary crisis was characterized by an abnormal need for means of payment, resulting from a halt in exchanges. The organization of American banks did not allow this abnormal need to be met, whether that need was for specie payments abroad, or for domestic means of payment, banknotes or metal.

Today, the American banking system has been reorganized. It would be superfluous to dwell on past mistakes.[457] However, in New York during October 1907, money was valued at 22 per cent; it reached 75 and 125 per cent at the height of the crisis. The secretary of the United States Treasury placed the revenue at the disposal of the banks, at the very moderate interest rate of 2 per cent, sometimes less. Thus, on Thursday,

456. For more details, see the *Commercial and Financial Chronicle* 85, no. 2209, 26 Oct. 1907, 1058–60.

457. See the second edition of the present work, pp. 358–61.

24 October 1907, the US Treasury put $25 million into the banks; by 11 November, the total advances to the banks reached $226,836,237.[458]

Financial assistance also came from private individuals: on the same day that Secretary Cortelyou lent $25 million to the banks, the J. P. Morgan group formed a monetary pool that advanced the same sum; and finally, again on the same day, John Rockefeller placed $10 million at the disposal of the Union Trust Co. in an attempt to aid the trust companies, and he declared that he would be prepared to advance additional funds if the situation demanded it. The day before, money had been valued at 100 and 125 per cent.[459] Europe was also contributing its capital to the United States, even though the exchange rates were unfavourable. The Banque de France agreed to re-discount a portfolio of first-rate English bills, as well as to deliver in exchange 75 million francs worth of American money to the Bank of England. The Banque de France affirmed its position as the premier issuing bank in the world at the time.

Such were the extraordinary measures taken by the United States to satisfy its need for metal money. Once again, the United States resorted to the clearing-house certificate. At that time, the United States did not yet have the Federal Reserve Banks; so, they relied on the certificate.

On 26 October, a group of bankers decided to issue some in New York. The example was soon followed in Boston, Philadelphia, Baltimore, Louisville, Pittsburgh, Cleveland, Cincinnati, Detroit, Indianapolis, Chicago, Milwaukee, Kansas City, Topeka, St. Louis, San Francisco, New Orleans and so on.

Despite all these measures, the intensity of the crisis was such that 'legal holidays', or moratorium periods, were introduced, during which payments were suspended. Banks reduced the amount of the cheques presented at their counters by 4 and 5 per cent. Finally, some banks placed daily limits on the sums of money they were prepared to reimburse.[460]

Little by little, the monetary crisis subsided. Banks that had been put to the test by the crisis could again think about reorganization. Many of them reopened their doors, among them, the one whose collapse had been the most resounding: the Knickerbocker Trust Company.[461]

In the United States, more so than in any other country in the world, there is a closer relationship [*solidarité*] between deposit banks and the stock exchange. In Europe, and especially in France, our banks use their deposits in discount operations. In the United States, deposits are put to profitable use in call money transactions [*opérations de report*] on the stock exchange. The futures market [*marché à terme*] is unknown on Wall Street, or more precisely, only overnight transactions [*opérations à échéance du jour suivant*] are used. Hence, during the same trading session on the stock exchange, speculators buy, sell, buy

458. Schumacher, *Le marché financier américain*, 76.
459. *Commercial and Financial Chronicle* 85, no. 2209, 26 Oct. 1907, 1051.
460. Schuhmacher, *Le marché financier américain*, 45; G. Martin, 'Chronique sur les questions monétaires', 208.
461. On the improvement in the trust companies' situation, see the 'Bank and Quotation Section', supplement, *Commercial and Financial Chronicle* 85, no. 2210, 2 Nov. 1907.

back and so on. The next day, they pay the differences or get carried over [*se font reporter*]. Banks use their deposits in these call money transactions that are carried over to the following day; and in order to know the state of the credit market in the United States, we must observe, not the discount rate of an issuing bank or some large credit company, but the discount rate of the call money – that is to say, of the deferrals on Wall Street. Only then can we comprehend the repercussions that mass withdrawals can have on call money and speculation on the stock exchange.

The monetary crisis triggered a violent crisis on the stock exchange (see tab. 1.92). Not only were securities being sold to obtain money, but the high cost of money was making upward speculation difficult. When prices collapsed on the stock market, the brokers succumbed.

Table 1.92 Stock Prices on Wall Street in 1907

	At Highest Value		*12 October*	*25 October*
	Date	*Price*		
Amalgam. Copper	5 Jan.	121	52	44
Amer. Car	14 Jan.	45	28	25
Amer. Locomotive	15 Feb.	75	44	36
General Electric	22 Jan.	163	113	101
U.S. Steel	7 Jan.	50	23	23
New York Central	10 Jan.	134	100	98
Union Pacific	5 Jan.	183	118	104

No source given.

Thus, we reach the end of the convulsive phase of crisis and enter a period of depression.

If we consider the number of rails produced, wagons and engines built, the decline is enormous. Production was reduced, sometimes by over 50 per cent. In the United States, the length of newly constructed railways dropped from 10,300 miles in 1906 and 10,900 in 1907 to 5,700 in 1908. Steel rail production decreased from 4,005,642 tonnes in 1906 to 3,633,640 in 1907 and 1,921,611 in 1908. If one considers the movement of imports and exports, consumption fell to new lows in 1908 that had not been seen since 1896. Rolling mills in Pennsylvania were producing 315,563 tonnes of Bessemer steel rails, compared to 1,093,932 tonnes in 1907 and 1,298,409 tonnes in 1906.[462] When we multiply the figures for the decrease in production by the price of steel rails, $28 per tonne, we arrive at the value of $57,122,092, or nearly 300 million francs.

The depression within the wagon and locomotive industry was no less intense. Yet whereas the depression could be seen in rail production and in the parallel halt in the construction of new railway lines, the average intensity of traffic remained fairly great in 1907. The crisis did not assert itself here until 1908. In 1907, 284,188 freight wagons and 5,457 passenger carriages were produced, compared with 76,555 freight wagons and 1,716 passenger carriages in 1908; the number of locomotives built dropped from 7,362 in 1907 to 2,342 in 1908.

462. 'The Country's Small Rail Output in 1908', *Commercial and Financial Chronicle* 88, no. 2276, 6 Feb. 1909, 338.

The depression in production was reflected in the performance of the large firms such as the American Locomotive Co. and American Car and Foundry. The net profits of the first decreased from $6,771,165 for the 1906–7 fiscal year (30 June) to $1,986,790 for the 1907–8 fiscal year.[463] Net profits for the second firm were also down, from $9,347,084 in 1907 to $8,961,380 in 1908.[464]

Bessemer steel production declined from 11,667,000 tonnes in 1907 to 6,116,000 tonnes in 1908, the lowest figure recorded since 1897. Steel production in general fell to 23,372,000 tonnes in 1908. Likewise, cast-iron production fell to 6,918,000 tonnes in the first half of 1908, compared to 13,478,000 in the first half of 1907, and annual production fell from 25,270,000 tonnes in 1907 to 15,936,000 in 1908. The American crisis paralysed the metal industry. The Tennessee Steel and Coal Co., which was being severely affected, came under the control of the steel trust. But the policy of an immediate and deep drop in prices, which had averted a long depression in 1903–4 in the United States, was replaced by the opposite policy of resisting any drop in prices. Until February 1909, the trust refused to reduce prices, which fuelled its buyers' reservations.

In the electrical industry, the drop in prices was a little less extreme than in the iron industry. The decrease in orders at General Electric was not comparable to that of the steel trust. At General Electric, orders dropped from $60,483,659 for the year ending on 31 January 1907 to $59,301,040 for the year 1908 and to $42,186,917 in 1909. American Telephone extended its network of wires of all kinds (on poles, on houses, underground or underwater) by 1,493,048 miles for the year ending on 31 March 1907, by only 938,781 miles for the year ending on 31 March 1908 and by 1,152,168 for the year ending on 31 March 1909.[465] The number of workers employed went from 104,646 in 1907 (March) to 100,884 in 1908 and 98,533 in 1909. But profits, whether gross or net, were still increasing in fairly significant proportions. The same did not apply to the profits of a whole series of competing telephone companies mentioned in the American Telephone fiscal report of 1908. These companies experienced a situation similar to that of General Electric, whose net profits were dropping before any decrease in total receipts, as a result of the increase in expenses of all kinds (see tab. 1.93).

Table 1.93 General Electric's Profits and Expenses in 1907 and 1908

	Net Profits	*Receipts*	*Expenses*
On 31 March 1907	$8,427,843	$61,608,832	$53,106,594
On 31 March 1908	$6,586,653	$72,484,988	$65,536,305

Source: *Commercial and Financial Chronicle* 86, no. 2237, 9 May 1908, 1157.

The effects of the crisis on the electrical industry can be found in the annual balance sheets of the copper trust Amalgamated Copper, whose net profits dropped from

463. *Commercial and Financial Chronicle* 87, no. 2255, 12 Sep. 1908, 675–76.
464. *Commercial and Financial Chronicle* 86, no. 2244, 27 June 1908, 1586.
465. *Commercial and Financial Chronicle* 88, no. 2283, 27 March 1909, 829.

$14,154,400 in 1907 to $6,680,557 in 1908 and $3,663,980 in 1909.[466] Copper production, however, had decreased little overall. It fell from 407,500 tonnes in 1906 to 399,600 in 1907, only to rise again to 435,200 in 1908.[467] Stocks of copper swelled and weighed on the market: American speculators tried to hide their significance by dumping them in Europe. But the price of copper fell in Europe.

It was the same for cotton and wool prices. In the United States, the textile industry saw its production and profits diminish. The net profits of the American Woollen Co. dropped from $4,809,507 in 1906 to $3,426,606 in 1907 and $1,280,705 in 1908. Its sales figures were down by almost half, from $51,420,696 in 1906 to $29,986,978 in 1908. In the silk industry, the crisis was reflected in a reduction of imports from Europe (Lyons, St. Etienne).[468] French exports of silk fabrics to the United States went from 84.3 million francs in 1907 to 57.1 million in 1908. Cotton fabrics, clothes and lingerie were similarly affected.

In the construction industry, the value of new construction decreased from $651,773,000 in 1907 to $581,821,00 in 1908. In the large industrial cities, the drop was even more considerable, especially if one compares the figures for 1908 with those for 1906. Whereas in 112 cities the decline in construction had been 11.9 per cent in 1908 compared to 16 per cent in 1906, the drop in Brooklyn was 37.9 per cent. In New York, it was impossible to secure money on a second or third mortgage; rents dropped by 20 per cent, and some landlords were offering two months' rent free.[469]

In response to the decline in the construction industry, the cement industry greatly reduced its production. The *Wall Street Journal* estimated production at 35 million barrels in 1908, compared to 48 million barrels in 1907.

The crisis even found expression in the bankruptcy statistics. The hardest hit companies had been those which were the least concentrated, that is, the banks; the number of failed banks grew by 14 per cent, and their liabilities, by 110 per cent.[470]

The figures for foreign trade also clearly reflected the depression: exports fell from $1,923,426,000 in 1907 to $1,752,833 in 1908, and imports, from $1,423,169,000 to $1,116,449,000. But more significantly, the difference between exports and imports continued to grow to the advantage of exports: the export surplus grew from $500,256,000 in 1907 to $636,382,000 in 1908. The United States looked abroad for markets that they could no longer find at home.

466. *Commercial and Financial Chronicle* 88, no. 2295, 20 June 1909, 1526.
467. However, when we consider some companies, we notice production limits reminiscent of those of the steel trust. The production of the Anaconda Mining Co. fell from 94,963,835 lbs. in 1906 to 63,055,000 lbs. in 1907 and 64,869,675 lbs. in 1908.
468. From this last point of view, the American crisis soon had far-reaching consequences. Such grand hotels in Paris, which had been built to provide accommodations for rich Americans, now found themselves almost deserted. The value of precious stones imported from Europe by the United States, which stood at $43,575,000 in 1906, dropped to $31,713,000 in 1907. Facts of this nature abound. G. Martin, 'Chronique sur les questions monétaires', 211.
469. 'Building Construction in 1908', *Commercial and Financial Chronicle* 88, no. 2273, 16 Jan. 1909, 132.
470. 'Failures in 1908', *Commercial and Financial Chronicle* 88, no. 2274, 23 Jan. 1909, 190.

Likewise, railway profits, both net and gross, were declining in 1908 in comparison to 1907.

The circulation of wealth was less lively; the portfolio of the national banks decreased considerably in New York, from $16.7 billion in 1907 to $6.8 billion in 1908 for forward papers [*papier à terme*]. In other cities the drop was not as deep. The on-demand portfolio [*portefeuille à vue*] dropped from 411.9 in 1907 to 389.1 in 1908, however, and the forward portfolio [*portefeuille à terme*] decreased from 1,487.7 in 1907 to 1,436.2 in 1908. The clearing-house statistics reflected this slowing down of trade. From 1907, the amounts cleared dropped to $145 billion against $159 billion in 1906, and they fell to $132 billion in 1908.

The stock market, too, could no longer find in production and trade the necessary basis for any upswing, and it tried in vain to anticipate the normal return to prosperity with waves of speculation. These attempts led to crises on the stock exchange of the kind seen in February 1909, when the steel trust's shares dropped by 10 points in the space of a few days. The overall statistics published by the *Commercial and Financial Chronicle* confirm this (see tab. 1.84).

Government bonds and fixed-income securities were the only exception, in contrast to variable-income industrial securities. Their value increased, while that of the latter was dropping.

As for the trusts' dividends, those of the copper and steel trusts were dropping in very significant proportions. We have already mentioned the drop in profits. That of dividends would follow. Thus, Amalgamated Copper's dividends dropped from 7¾ per cent in 1907 to 4 per cent in 1908 and 2 per cent in 1909. The steel trust did not distribute any dividend on common shares, and for the moment, there was the fear that it would be unable to pay the interest on its obligations. As for the workers, they were severely hit by unemployment and wage reductions. Unemployment figures are less complete for the United States than for England and Germany. However, the *Bulletin of Labor* for the state of New York publishes unemployment statistics, based on information provided to it by trade union members, for the percentage of unemployed workers among union members. If we consider that unionized workers are in general the best workers, this statistic gives us an idea of the severity of unemployment (see tab. 1.94).

Table 1.94 Monthly Percentage Unemployed Among Union Members in New York

	Jan.	*Feb.*	*Mar.*	*Apr.*	*May*	*Jun.*	*Jul.*	*Aug.*	*Sep.*	*Oct.*	*Nov.*	*Dec.*
1907	19.0	17.4	15.5	8.5	7.7	6.2	5.4	7.7	9.7	16.1	20.0	30.5
1908	35.1	35.9	35.9	32.2	30.6	28.7	25.2	22.2	23.0	21.5	20.9	25.9

Source: 'Unemployment in the United States', *Economist*, no. 3430, 22 May 1909, 1078.

Note: On 9 January 1909, the number of unemployed workers in New York was estimated at 125,000, *Labour Gazette* (1908): 42.

However, the rise in unemployment was not limited to the state of New York. On 9 and 11 January 1908, the British consulate in Philadelphia telegraphed that 4,000 workers had been dismissed from one of the largest locomotive factories and that working hours were to be reduced from 10 to 8 hours per day. On 27 January, a new dispatch announced that the same factory had further reduced the number of workers from 19,500 to 11,000.[471] In Chicago, a rolling mill that produced sheet metal for machines and employed 1,200 workers closed its doors in January 1908. A railway company that employed 1,000 in its workshops reduced the number of workdays per week to two.

Things were no different in the construction industry. At the end of February 1908, 40 to 60 per cent of carpenters were without work in Chicago, and the *Massachusetts Labor Bulletin* recorded 21 per cent unemployment among unionized workers in the building industry. On 14 December 1908, there were 120,000 unemployed in Chicago alone.[472] Wages were also being reduced, notably in the railway industry, and here one witnessed the opposite phenomenon to the one observed during the growth period: a reduction in operating costs.[473]

Thus, the New York Central realized savings of $10,384,249 on its expenses in 1908. And the largest part of this savings, $7,236,547, came from the savings on wages: workers' performance improved, and wages had been reduced.[474]

Wages were reduced in the metal industry. From February 1908 onward, the steel trust proceeded with wage reductions of 15 per cent on average; although for some workers, wage cuts reached 40 per cent. A coal miners' strike failed in March–April 1908. During the same period, the textile industry was reducing wages. At Lowell and other cities in Massachusetts, New Hampshire and Maine, wages were cut by 10 per cent after 31 March 1908. This affected 120,000 workers. In New England and New York, the situation was similar, with a 10 per cent reduction beginning on 13 April 1908 that affected 153,000 workers (144,000 employed in New England and 9,500 in New York State). At Fall River in Massachusetts, the fall in wages was greater at 17.9 per cent, and one worked 'short time'; however, these measures impacted just 45,000 workers.

The labour commission of the state of Missouri instructed the English consul to discourage the emigration of workers from England to the United States.[475] Overall, immigration in the United States decreased by two-thirds (see tab. 1.95).

471. *Labour Gazette* (1908): 42.

472. *Labour Gazette* (1908): 73, 109, 372; and (1909): 13.

473. *Labour Gazette* (1908): 109.

474. 'The New York Central in a Year of Depression', *Commercial and Financial Chronicle* 88, no. 2282, 20 March 1909, 718.

475. *Labour Gazette* (1908): 73, 109, 176, 372.

Table 1.95 Immigration to the United States, 1906–1908

	1906	*1907*	*1908*
January	51,123	65,417	27,220
February	68,346	65,541	23,381
March	133,245	139,118	32,517
April	150,397	145,256	41,274
May	150,917	184,886	36,317
June	119,900	154,734	31,947
July	84,403	97,132	27,570
August	81,592	98,825	27,782
September	95,331	98,664	38,238
October	99,974	111,513	40,994
November	94,721	117,476	37,076
December	80,000	65,574	46,060

Source: *Économiste européen* 35, no. 892, 12 Feb. 1909, 221, table.

2.) Germany

Germany was also suffering greatly during the 1907 crisis. The cast-iron cartel in Düsseldorf was disbanded. The monetary crisis in October and November 1907 raised fears that the Reichsbank would suspend operations.[476] But the outbreak of the crisis in Germany, as in the United States, did not date from 1907 but preceded it. The large German cartels already lacked orders from the end of July,[477] and cast-iron prices were beginning to fall from this moment on.[478] From the start of 1907, the building trades experienced a full-blown crisis that affected construction, as mortgage-backed securities could no longer find any subscribers. On 1 July 1907, the amount of maturing mortgage debts that remained unpaid reached up to 100 million marks. Construction ceased. For a three-month period (from September to November 1907), the steel cartel delivered 332,000 tonnes of girders, compared to 474,000 for the corresponding period in 1906. In 1908, the situation grew worse.[479]

In addition, the statistics for industrial output showed a very noticeable drop in 1907 when compared with those of 1906. Coal production did not decline immediately, however. Yet in contrast, coke production fell to 9,944,000 tonnes in 1908, down from 10,069,000 tonnes in 1907.[480] The cartel reduced its prices and limited production.[481] The price of cast iron was reduced from 12 to 10 marks per tonne, and that of steel, from 5 to 4 marks per tonne, depending on the type. The price fall was accompanied by a decrease in production: that of cast iron went from 13,045,000 tonnes in 1907 to

476. Bankenquête [bank enquiry] (Berlin: Reichsdruckerei, 1909), see esp. the speech by the governor of the Reichsbank, p. 168.
477. This information was confirmed for us by the representative of a large cartel during a period of residential study in Germany.
478. See *Volkswirtschaftliche Chronik* (1907–8).
479. Arthur Feiler, *Die Konjunktur-Periode, 1907–1913, in Deutschland* (Jena: Fischer, 1914), 25, 42.
480. *Bulletin du Comité des Forges de France*, circular no. 309 (1909).
481. See the *Volkswirtschaftliche Chronik* (Nov. 1908): 674–75, which provides price details.

11,813,000 in 1908. The outlets of the steel cartel contracted significantly. However, the drop in prices was particularly steep for cast iron, as a result of the dissolution of the cast-iron cartel.

The conflict within the cartels between integrated factories and incomplete factories represents one of the most interesting characteristics of the economic depression.[482]

The machine industry was also affected, with the exception of wagon and engine factories, which were filling orders placed during the growth period, when there was a shortage of materiel. By 1909, these industries, too, were being affected, and orders were becoming increasingly rare in 1908 and 1909. The motor and cycle industries suffered a similar fate.[483]

Table 1.96 Shipments of the *Stahlwerksverband*, 1907–1909 (1,000 tonnes)

	Semi-finished Products			*Railway Equipment*			*Profiled Iron*		
	1907	*1908*	*1909*	*1907*	*1908*	*1909*	*1907*	*1908*	*1909*
Jan.	134	101	118	188	214	159	148	67	131
Feb.	141	108	105	183	207	166	124	104	124
March	147	132	144	208	198	204	158	155	171
April	142	104	109	173	141	123	166	126	131

No source given.

The depression equally affected the maritime shipping industry.[484] In 1908, Norddeutscher-Lloyd paid no dividend, and its April 1909 balance sheets showed a loss of 17,650,000 marks. Hamburg-Amerika was experiencing such difficulties that it had to call for the intervention of an important person to save it. The shipyards also experienced a significant reduction in orders, and the tonnage of the ships built in Germany's shipyards dropped from 329,856 British tonnes in 1906 to 308,034 tonnes in 1907.[485]

The crisis had a similar impact on the textile industry, though only in 1908. According to Feiler, 'The decrease in the workers' purchasing power influenced the textile industry. The decline started at the beginning of 1908 and affected all branches of the industry: spinning, weaving and manufacturing.' In June 1908, the cotton mills decided to reduce production by 14 per cent.[486]

Imports and exports and railway receipts also reflected the crisis and economic depression. The monetary phase was interesting. The discount rate at the Reichsbank

482. Integrated factories suffered little from the crisis. Statistics for 14 of the major integrated firms in Germany show an insignificant reduction in profits: 108.61 million marks in 1906–7, as opposed to 100.66 million in 1907–8. Similarly, production in these factories decreased very little and even increased for coal as Germany increased its production, and also for cast iron, despite the reduction of production in Germany.
483. Feiler, *Konjunktur-Periode*, 45, 66.
484. Léon Hennebicq, 'La crise des frets', *Revue économique internationale* 6 (May 1909): 396.
485. *Volkswirtschaftliche Chronik* (1908): 225.
486. Feiler, *Konjunktur-Periode*, 44.

increased to 7.5 per cent, and that of advances, to 8.5 per cent. The Reichsbank's cash on hand reached its lowest recorded level since 1885, at 621 million marks on 30 November 1907; it concealed a banknote circulation of 1,510 million mark and a portfolio of 1,289 million marks.[487] Once the crisis had been resolved, the portfolio shrank, and cash holdings were reconstituted.

The onset of the crisis had been so carefully anticipated on the stock exchange with effective levels of discount that the decline in values was moderate. The drop in industrial share values followed their rise, and fixed-income stocks performed more favourably (see tab. 1.97).

Table 1.97 Prices on the Berlin Stock Exchange

	8 Nov. 1907	*10 Nov. 1908*	*10 July 1909*
3% Govt Bonds	82.10	84.40	85.60
Norddeut. Lloyd	106.90	88.10	89.60
Hamburg-Amerika	120.25	111.20	116.75
Gelsenkirchen	189.50	189.25	177.75
Harpener Bergwerk.	192.00	194.25	189.50
Stettiner Vulcan	239.75	237.50	225.50

No source given.

Dividends were falling if they had not already dropped to zero (see tab. 1.98).[488] Wages were also affected by the crisis, but workers suffered above all from unemployment, which rose by 30 to 40 per cent for the whole of Germany (tab. 1.99).

Table 1.98 Drop in Corporate Dividends in Germany

Industrial Firms				
	Hoesch Stahlwk.	*Bochumer*	*Rh. Stahlwk.*	*Phoenix*
1906–7	18	16⅔	15	17
1907–8	14	15	11	11
Banks				
	Deutsche Bank	*Dresdner Bank*	*Diskonto-Gesellschaft*	*Darmstädter Bank*
1906	12	8½	9	8
1907	12	7	9	6

No source given.

487. See Hermann Schumacher, 'Die deutsche Geldverfassung und ihre Reform', *Jahrbuch für Gesetzgebung, Verwaltung und Volkswirtschaft im Deutschen Reich* 32 (1908): 1257–1388.

488. According to the *Kölnische Zeitung*, no. 706, 3 July 1909.

Table 1.99 Percentage Unemployed Among Union Workers in Germany, 1904–1909

1904	2.1	1907	1.4
1905	1.6	1908	2.9
1906	1.1	1909	2.8

No source given.

3.) England

England had long since built up its equipment; its industry was stationary, or nearly so. England sought out new markets for its capital and its products throughout the world, in its colonies and in South America and China. In the event of a crisis, England would suffer above all in her exports, merchant fleet and shipyards. But England no longer witnessed the periods of feverish securities issue that it had experienced between 1840 and 1870, periods of crisis and depression, as well as those of growth, had lost the intensity of former times.

Following the crisis of 1907, the most affected industry was shipbuilding. During the growth period, the shipyards had too much work, as their production was stimulated by the nearly ubiquitous prosperity and by the orders from the Russian and Japanese merchant navies as the two countries armed for war. The tonnage under construction in the third quarter beginning on 30 June 1907 was 50,000 tonnes less than that of the first quarter and 150,000 tonnes less than that of the second.[489] The decline in construction continued into the next two quarters, and in total, in 1907, 742,360 long tons less were built than in 1906. On 4 February 1908, there were 978,830 long tons under construction against 1,166,889 the year before.[viii] The decrease in naval construction was enormous in 1908, reaching 45 per cent. Several shipyards had to slow down their production considerably, and some were even forced to close due to the lack of orders (tab. 1.100).

Table 1.100 Percentage Reduction in English Shipyards in 1908 Compared to 1907

Clyde	*Tyde*	*Wear*	*Tees*	*Hartlepool*
43.3%	38.3%	71%	58%	65%

Source: *Comité des Forges de France*, circular no. 300 (1909): 9.

Also, since maritime construction represented the leading industry in England, the crisis in the shipyards soon had serious repercussions on the production of iron ore, cast iron and steel (see tab. 1.101). Coal was less affected. Prices dropped. The year 1908 saw a slow and steady decrease in prices, of 2 sh. 6 d. for steam coal and 3 sh. for coke.

489. *Économiste européen* 39 (1911): 88.

Table 1.101 Coal, Cast-Iron and Steel Production in Great Britain (in tonnes)

	Coal	*Cast Iron*	*Steel*
1907	267,812,852	5,194,712	6,522,748
1908	261,506,379	4,633,353	5,295,642

Source: *Comité des Forges de France*, bulletin nos. 2819, 2847 and 2865 (1909).

The textile industry suffered a decrease in its exports. The consumption of cotton per week in English factories decreased from 75,842 pounds in 1907 to 66,392 in 1908, and total consumption, from 1,971,883,770 pounds in 1907 to 1,726,185,930 in 1908.[490] Exports of cotton wares decreased from 6,297,707,900 yards in 1907 to 5,532,413,000 yards in 1908.[491] Moreover, the reduction in foreign trade was general. Imports went from 157,137,000 tonnes in 1907 to 129,882,000 in 1908; while exports dropped from 137,359,000 to 125,740,000 tonnes. The exports suffering the greatest reduction were those to Germany, which dropped from 41,377,000 tonnes in 1907 to 33,374,000 in 1909; to the United States, which fell from 30,910,000 to 21,189,000; and those to Chile.

Shipping companies suffered from the contraction of foreign trade. The large European companies concluded an agreement intended to support freight shipping and to reduce the number of trips between England and the continent, on the one hand, and between England and the United States, on the other.[492]

Table 1.102 Decline in Railway Profits in Great Britain (millions of £)

	Gross Profits	*Operating Expenses*	*Net Profits*
1907	121,549	76,609	44,940
1908	119,891	76,392	43,449

No source given.

The British money market was shaken by the impact of the American crisis on London; the Bank of England was forced to keep its discount at 7 per cent. The portfolio shrank. Clearing-house compensations declined. On the London Stock Exchange, share prices dropped for the large mining and metal companies, as well as for the maritime shipping companies; English Consols picked up.

For the 24 industrial firms surveyed by the *Economist*, net profits had dropped from £16,471,692 to £14,480,523. For the 100 cotton manufacturers surveyed by the same journal, net profits collapsed from £1,321,157 in 1907 to £586,511 in 1908, with average dividends dropping from 15⅞ to 11¾.[493] After an initial increase of £199,605 in weekly wages paid in 1907, a reduction of £61,897 followed in 1908. These changes to

490. 'Commercial History and Review of 1908', supplement, *Economist*, no. 3417, 20 Feb. 1909, 17.
491. *Économiste européen*, 35, no. 889, 22 Jan. 1909, p. 120; *Economist*, 17 April 1909, 816, 908.
492. 'L'armement et la crise économique', *Revue économique internationale* 6 (May 1909): 256 and Hennebicq, 'La crise des frets'.
493. *Economist* 68, no. 3424, 10 April 1909, 767.

work contracts met with energetic resistance from workers. The number of strikes did not increase; there were 382 in 1908 against 601 in 1907. However, these were gigantic strikes involving millions of workers, and despite the drop in the number of strikes, the number of strikers doubled, from 147,498 in 1907 to 291,046 in 1908, and the number of workdays lost as a result of the strikes in 1908 rose fivefold compared to 1907. The number of days out of work rose from 2,162,151 in 1907 to 10,783,000 in 1908. This increase was mostly localized in the branches of industry hardest hit by the crisis: coal mining, shipbuilding, machine shops and textiles (cotton). These branches of production accounted for 166,000 of the workers on strike, or 57 per cent of the total number, and 8.25 million lost days of work, or 77 per cent of the total number.[494]

The percentage of unemployed workers almost doubled in 1908 compared to 1907. From November 1907, the unemployment curve begins to rise. This period of intense unemployment saw the streets of London filled with a procession of unemployed workers, wandering through the rich parts of the city.[495] The government preoccupied itself with the conditions of the working classes. At the beginning of 1909, a voluminous Parliamentary report appeared on the remedies to address the unemployment.[496]

4.) France

Our observations on England could be repeated in our study of France. We no longer see the periods of feverish expansion followed by sudden depression experienced in the past. The field of enterprise had narrowed. The concentration of credit was complete, and that of production and trade was sufficiently advanced; the economic equilibrium was more secure.

Nevertheless, France was affected by the depression. Cast-iron production was 3,391,150 tonnes in 1908 compared to 3,588,949 in 1907. The production of iron ore declined from 10,981,000 tonnes in 1907 to 9,000,000 in 1908. Steel production decreased by 19,156 tonnes in 1908, a decline of 1.4 per cent compared to 1907.[497]

Lyon, St Etienne and Limoges (porcelain) suffered the repercussions of the American crisis. In Limoges, a mutual agreement between bosses and workers reduced the working day to 3 hours in order to avoid the dismissal of 14,000 workers.

The situation was the same for the French automotive industry, where exports had grown from 50,000 quintals in 1903 to 144,000 in 1907 but dropped to 127,000 in 1908.

Foreign trade also sagged, though only slightly. Imports decreased from 6,223 million francs in 1907 to 6,091 million in 1908, and exports fell from 5,596 to 5,272 million.

The Crédit Lyonnais stated in its report for 1908 that

> The creation of commercial bills of exchange has involved reduced sums, and the discountable material has been significantly reduced, which has made it more difficult to

494. *Labour Gazette* (Jan. 1909): 4.
495. *Times* (London), Jan. and Feb. 1909.
496. *Report of the Royal Commission on the Poor Laws and Relief of Distress*, 3 vols (London: HMSO, 1909), Cd. 4499 (unemployment insurance).
497. *Comité des Forges de France*, nos. 2838, 2839 and 2846 (1909).

> recruit funds for our commercial portfolio; the interest rate on deferrals and discounts has remained low; all these circumstances are unfavourable for an institution [...] which must seek to use its important resources in the service of a great liquidity.

The Banque de France, which had proven to be the support for the world's credit during the monetary crisis, experienced a reduction in its portfolio in 1908. The discount rate fell from 4 to 3 per cent. Its cash holdings increased.

The crisis caused a drop in industrial values and a rise in fixed-income securities. But the drop was not very significant. The most interesting part of the phenomenon was the rise of the rate of the 3 per cent government bonds. In spite of the vote in the Chamber on the rent tax and the success of the plans for the income tax, the French 3 per cent rate has continued to rise since 1907.

Dividends were diminishing, and unemployment was increasing. In 1908 at St-Etienne, the unemployment rate among lace workers was 70 per cent; Calais lacked outlets for its silk netting [*tulles*]. Some Parisian hotels waited in vain for their usual clientele.[498]

§13. – The crisis of 1913–1914

The depression that followed the 1907 crisis was short-lived. From 1909, the general curve of prices was rising for goods other than mineral materials and metals. However, we do not find real growth until 1911–12. On the other hand, growth arose at a time of serious political troubles (Agadir, 1911, the Balkan war, early signs of the 1914 war), and from 1913, the growth curve is inverted. The period of prosperity was very brief, and the transition between the period of growth and the period of depression occurred without serious incident.

A.) Growth

By 1910, capital was returning to industry. The issue of industrial shares in France, which had declined to 983 million francs in 1907, rose to 2,274 million in 1910, 1,655 in 1911, 2,847 in 1912 and 2,314 in 1913.

It was the same in England, yet the figures lead us to believe that the phenomenon of expansion and of contraction only affected England on a smaller scale. Industrial values were at £111 million in 1910, 77 million in 1911, 107 million in 1912 and 77 million in 1913.

In Germany, industrial shares continued to make rapid progress: 284 million marks in 1910, 315 million in 1911, 457 million in 1912 and 286 million in 1913.

We possess an interesting statistic for the electrical industry which regrettably only concerns the first half of each year and shows that public appeals for savings investment in the electrical industry increased from 1910 to 1912. In 1913, the figure fell to 10 million marks, as opposed to 32 million in 1912.

---

498. G. Martin, 'Chronique sur les questions monétaires', 211.

What was true for Europe also applied to the United States with one difference: the United States made a false start in 1909–10, and true prosperity did not return until 1911 and became particularly noticeable by 1912–13.

France developed its local railways and tramways. In Paris, electrical power was replacing steam or animal power. The Nord-Sud line was being equipped, and construction was completed on the Métropolitain. The statistics on the tramways clearly show that this lengthening of the tramlines was justified by the net returns per kilometre.

In this period, France was also developing its automotive industry. The number of vehicles increased from 45,000 in 1909 to 91,000 in 1913. Exports were picking up from 1909, rising to 262,000 quintals in 1913, compared to 127,000 in 1908.

Finally in the East, the development of the metal industry was gaining strength. Cast-iron production went from 3,574,000 tonnes in 1909 to 5,200,000 in 1913.

Great Britain lagged somewhat behind the same trend. However, shipyards experienced a period of prosperity in 1912. On 1 October 1912, construction began on 500 new vessels with a tonnage of 1,850,000 tonnes under construction, or 400,000 tonnes more than the previous year on the same date. Cast-iron production and prices were increasing. An old product, oil, played an increasingly important role in this growth thanks to the development of the automobile and the discovery of the diesel engine. Its production rose from 44 million tonnes (29 million in the United States) to 53 million in 1913 (33.7 million in the United States). It was thus primarily for the transport of oil that new ships were being built in England. Out of the 108 ships under construction on 30 December 1912, 40 were 'tankers'.[499] The price of oil, quoted at 6 d. per gallon in 1910 (May), rose to 9 d. per gallon in March 1912.

In Germany, on the other hand, the growth was much clearer. The electrical industry had weathered the 1907 crisis without suffering too much damage. New markets were opening up: as tramways were built, the use of electrical power was expanding each day and now gained the shipyards, mines and steel mills as customers. The era of large electric power stations had begun. By 1910, the dominance of the great consortium AEG, Siemens-Schuckert and Felten-Guilleaume-Lahmeyer was assured. Exports of electrical products were increasing. In 1910, AEG increased its capital from 100 to 130 million marks in order to join with the firm the Felten-Guilleaume-Lahmeyer. In 1912, it was the Bergmann-Elektrizitätswerke's turn to be absorbed by Siemens & Halske. In 1911, the order books for AEG reached 362 million marks by 30 September against 270 million the previous year.

The machine industry, so powerful across the Rhine, had plenty of orders (with the exception of the factories producing railway equipment, which lacked adequate labour, and factories making machinery for the textile industry). The recently established automotive industry was very prosperous, and the number of vehicles in Germany increased from 27,000 in 1907 to 78,000 in 1913.[500]

499. Dennis Holme Robertson, *A Study of Industrial Fluctuation: An Inquiry into the Character and Causes of the so-called Cyclical Movements of Trade* (London: P. S. King, 1915), 158n3.

500. *Frankfurter Zeitung*, no. 120, 1914.

From 1910 to 1913, the metal industry enjoyed a period of true prosperity and also proceeded to reorganize itself by means of integration, the use of gas in its blast furnaces, the renewal of cartels (the cast-iron cartel was reorganized), or the consolidation of existing cartels (the steel cartel survived the difficulties that had threatened it in 1912; the taxes of the coke and coal cartels were joined in 1912). Beginning in 1910 and 1911, the large firms realized great profits: Hoesch (integrated forge) paid 18 per cent dividends in 1909–10 against 14 per cent the previous year; then 20 per cent in 1911–12 and 24 per cent in 1912–13. Phoenix did the same, paying 15 per cent (up from 9 per cent), then again 15 per cent, 18 per cent and again 18 per cent. Harpen (coal mine) yielded 7 per cent in 1909–10, then 8 per cent, 9 per cent and 11 per cent in subsequent years. Cast-iron production increased from 12.9 million tonnes in 1909 to 19.2 million in 1913.

Deliveries for the steel cartel show the following figures: for semi-manufactured steel, 1,554,000 tonnes in 1910 and 1,680,000 tonnes in 1913; for railway equipment, 1,887,000 tonnes in 1910 and 2,879,000 tonnes in 1913; and for profiled iron, 1,614,000 tonnes in 1909 and 2,181,000 tonnes in 1912. Yet prices did not actually rise until 1911, and the increase was significant.

Schmitz has calculated the price index for Germany, and he provides both a general index and one for the price of metals, which we reproduce in table 1.103.

Table 1.103 General Price and Metals Indexes for Germany, 1909–1913 (1879–98 = 100)

	General Index	*Metals Index*
1909	111	121
1910	113	127
1911	118	140
1912	130	154
1913	127	152

Source: O. Schmitz, 'Statistische Übersichten', quoted in Feiler, *Konjunktur-Periode*, 186–87, tab. 15.

On the other hand, the textile industry only participated to a very limited extent in this expansion. For cotton spinning and weaving, 1910 was one of the worst years ever. The year was also bad for the jute industry, and it was just satisfactory for the wool and linen industries.[501]

While the metal and electrical industries were enjoying full prosperity, in 1911 the situation remained disappointing for cotton weaving and spinning. During the first half of 1911, there was overproduction, buyers waited for a fall in prices and production was reduced. In July, news of a good crop in the United States caused cotton prices to drop further. In the fourth quarter of 1911, orders were growing in the weaving and spinning mills. However, out of the 49 major share companies in spinning and weaving surveyed by the *Frankfurter Zeitung*, 27 showed losses for the year 1911.

501. Feiler, *Konjunktur-Periode*, 84–85.

For the linen industry, the year was unfavourable as a result of the increased price of raw materials. The situation was better but far from good in the wool industry, as its markets did not expand sufficiently: at the beginning of 1911, the Silesian wool industry was complaining that the high cost of living prevented the working classes from spending more on their clothing. In the autumn, the complaints were about the consumption of the rural population.[502]

It was only in 1912 that the textile industry experienced real improvement: the cotton wares industry was prosperous, while the linen industry left much to be desired. The wool industry still had much to complain about at the beginning of 1912,[503] which was confirmed by its dividends. For the years 1908 to 1913, the dividends for the Concordia Spinnerei (spinning) were at 0, 7½, 8, 7½, 7½ and 4½; for the Gladbacher Spinnerei und Weberei (spinning and weaving), dividends were 9, 8, 0, 0, 0, 0; and for the Norddeutsche Wollkämmerei (carded wool), they were 8, 12, 10, 10, 10, 10.[504]

The construction industry picked up again with the drop in interest rates and the greatest latitude for investment in mortgage bonds. After the 1907 crisis, construction had come to a nearly complete halt. In the autumn of 1909, a marked recovery was taking place: by 1908, mortgage banks were able to resume issuing bonds. In 1909, the price of materials had dropped considerably. Houses whose foundations were above ground or which had been left unfinished above the first floor were now being completed.

For the United States, it is possible to focus more closely on the alternatives of growth and depression thanks to monthly statistics for production, orders and net and gross railway receipts. In the period from 1909 to 1913, we will find features identical to those which announced the crisis of 1907, albeit in an attenuated form. The close relationships between railways, their net receipts, the orders sent to the metal industry, the prices of steel, and production appear once again with remarkable clarity.

After attempting to resist the fall in prices, the steel trust decided to give in by 1909. The drop caused orders to return. In January 1908, factories in the trust were operating at 13 per cent of their production capacity; by June 1909, they were producing at 80 per cent; in September 1909, 95 per cent of the blast furnaces were reopened. In November, the trust announced it was expanding its operations.

Table 1.104 Unfilled Orders of the Steel Trust at the End of Each Quarter, 1908–1913 (1,000 tonnes)

	1908	*1909*	*1910*	*1911*	*1912*	*1913*
1st Quarter	3,765	3,542	5,402	3,447	5,304	7,496
2nd Quarter	3,313	**4,057**	4,257	3,261	5,807	5,807
3rd Quarter	3,421	4,796	**3,158**	**3,611**	6,551	**5,004**
4th Quarter	3,603	5,927	2,675	5,084	7,932	4,282

Source: Mitchell, *Business cycles* (1913), 419 and 424. [Figures in boldface indicate the quarters in which the trend reverses.]

502. Ibid., 91.
503. Ibid., 105.
504. Ibid., 191.

The railways had reduced their orders to a minimum as a result of the crisis of 1907; in response to the growth in their net profits, orders picked up again from 1909 onward, thanks to the reduction in the railways' operating costs (tab. 1.105).

Table 1.105 Operating Costs, Gross Receipts and Net Income of US Railways, 1908–1910

	Length (100 miles)	*Gross Receipts (millions of $)*	*Operating Expenses (millions of $)*	*Net Operating Income (millions of $)*
1908	3,336	2,440	1,710	720
1909	3,424	2,473	1,650	823
1910	3,518	2,812	1,882	930

No source given.

Gross receipts per mile were reduced, while the net product per mile rose thanks to the decrease in general overheads and operating costs per mile.

Business was also picking up in the construction industry, as well as in the electrical and textile industries.[505] For 45 cities in the United States, the cost of construction projects subject to building permits was $535 million in 1908, $733 million in 1909 and $675 million in 1910.[506]

This recovery did not last long: in 1910, the government proceeded with antitrust regulations. The wage increases obtained by the railway workers as a result of many serious conflicts caused a drop in net profits despite the increase in gross profits. Capital was scarce and expensive: the United States had to issue railway bonds in Europe (in Great Britain, France and Germany), which turned out to be very difficult operations. Railway orders to the metal industry sagged; prices dropped once again. Cast-iron and steel production declined. The gross profits of the railways were dropping. By 1911, this decrease in railway profits, combined with the dissolution rulings against the trusts, strengthened the depression. By the end of 1911, however, a recovery was already taking shape. It was to last until 1912, with an uninterrupted rise in orders, prices and production.

An increase in foreign trade and railway receipts accompanied the boom in global production. Sometimes even, in Germany, the development of the electrical industries' exports was at the root of the boom itself. The same was true of the French car industry.

Banks' portfolios swelled. The shares went up on the stock exchange. Again, no regrettable excesses were being recorded anywhere. The drop in fixed-income securities and the rise in variable-income securities occurred without any incident.

From all the above figures a conclusion may be drawn: before the war, the whole world seemed to be entering a period of progress that was slower than those that had taken place from 1890 to 1913, when the United States led the industrial nations and Germany led Europe.

505. Ibid., 59.
506. Mitchell, *Business Cycles* (1913), 421.

Many useful lessons had been drawn from the 1907 crisis. From the beginning of 1913, the German press was unsparing in its advice to German industry. Finally, the international political situation in Europe, the state of budgets and the increase in armaments manufacturing could not leave the economic world untouched. Government bonds were fierce competition for industrial shares.

B.) Crisis and depression

Thus, the transition from growth to depression was slow enough from 1913 for some to doubt the presence of a real periodic crisis. All the characteristic symptoms were manifesting themselves, however.

Germany was showing the symptoms of a crisis from the start of 1913. No longer able to find the funds necessary for expansion, the construction industry had to compete with national and foreign loans on the capital market.[507] The issuance of mortgage bonds went from 515 million marks in 1911 to 204 million in 1912 and 44 million in 1913. Besides, industrial issues were following the same curve with 692 million marks in 1912 and 367 million in 1913. Government bonds themselves comprised 810 million marks (on the 2,494 million marks of issued securities). It was moreover less the overall figure for issues which sagged than it was the overall figure for *productive* issues and industrial output. If we also examine the shipments of profiled iron produced by the steel cartel, we find the first traces of the crisis: starting in March 1913, the shipping figures for 1913 were significantly lower than those of 1912, at 178,000 and 250,000 tonnes, respectively. Semi-finished products were also in less demand; whereas railway equipment enjoyed a strong market for the whole of 1913.

The machine industry also fell victim to the crisis. But it was hit *after* the iron and steel industries. Still enjoying a good situation at the beginning of 1913, it would soon suffer the same fate:

> the large backlog of old orders was still being processed, and new ones were coming in at an increasingly slower pace because the political turmoil and the high cost of capital frightened buyers [...] Some branches of the machine industry held up better, particularly locomotive and wagon factories, which benefitted from the great needs of the local railways and which consolidated their position by forming a German wagon cartel.

But elsewhere the reduction in dividends was enormous: the Koppel factory in Chemnitz reduced its dividends from 28 to 10 per cent.[508]

The car industry saw its outlets contract: incomes had declined, and the expenses of arming for war weighed heavily on the wealthy classes, whose capital was subject to an extraordinary levy.

The ancillary industries related to construction, such as brickworks, glassworks, joineries and wallpaper factories, were gravely affected. Furniture and earthenware factories were similarly affected.[509]

---

507. Feiler, *Konjunktur-Periode*, 162.
508. Ibid., 145.
509. Ibid., 146.

On the other hand, the electrical industry held out quite well until the autumn of 1913. AEG released an annual report, for the period from 1 July 1912 to 30 June 1913, that was more favourable than the previous one. It was a record-breaking year.[510] On 3 December 1912, it had increased its capital from 130 to 155 million marks, and it still distributed the same dividend of 14 per cent as the preceding year. However, the statistics for the issue of electrical industry securities left an unfavourable impression, and the figure for orders reported by AEG at the general meeting in October was 318 million marks, down from 362 million marks in 1911.

Tonnage under construction in the shipyards (naval and commercial) was greater than all previous figures.

On the other hand, the textile industry was all the more affected because it had benefitted little from the period of growth. This weakened its resistance. At the beginning of 1913, the cotton mills still had work; however, soon there were complaints about competition from Austrian spinning mills and the loss of their markets in the Balkans. By the summer, the domestic market was shrinking, and production was reduced. At the end of 1913, weaving mills in the South decided to cut one workday per week starting on 1 January 1914

During the first months of 1914, the situation worsened. The metal industry reduced production even further.

Only the coal mines, on the strength of their monopoly, were able to refuse to reduce their selling prices. And yet, the cartel began to slow down coal production in July and coke production in August 1913; and the quantities to be produced (percentage of participation) were down on the same month in 1912 and on the preceding month in 1913.[511]

Railway profits, at first unaffected by the situation in the other industries, also declined, once the crisis became general. In November 1913, the profits per kilometre for freight transport were less than those for November 1912 and October 1913.[512]

In Germany, monthly statistics enable us to follow step by step the progress of the 1913 crisis. Semi-manufactured steel and profiled steel were the first to be affected because of the crisis in the construction industry. Then followed the blast furnaces, the machine industry, the car industry and finally the textile industry.

In France, monthly statistics by the *Comité des Forges* enable us to understand, from August–September onward, the repercussions of the German crisis on the French metal industry. Ingot production was in crisis in Germany from the beginning of 1913, while in France it began in August. Production for August 1913 (342,000 tonnes) was less than that of August 1912 (351,000 tonnes) and that of July 1913 (368,000 tonnes). It was the same for girders and profiled steel from August 1913, for rails and track materials from June 1913 and for sheet metal and large metal plates from August 1913. Cast iron would

510. *Volkswirtschaftliche Chronik* (Oct. 1913): 680–82.
511. See the monthly statistics in Feiler, *Konjunktur-Periode*, 182–83.
512. Ibid., 186.

follow in September 1913. From then on, metal factories complained of a lack of orders. Prices were in decline.

The decline in the issues of industrial shares can also explain the slowdown in orders sent to the metal industry. Yet we tend to accord the greatest influence to the German crisis and its impact on French steel markets. The German steel industry retained a dominant position until 1914.

It was the same in England: in June 1913, a debacle occurred in Glasgow on the cast-iron market that caused the bankruptcy of the very old firm of James Watson. The warrant prices for cast iron fell from 70.6 shillings at the end of May to 54.6 shillings on 13 June. On the Belgian market, the price of Thomas cast iron went from 85–86 francs at the end of May to 74–76 francs on 20 July 1913.

The crisis which had started in Germany from the beginning of 1913 spread little by little to the whole of Europe.

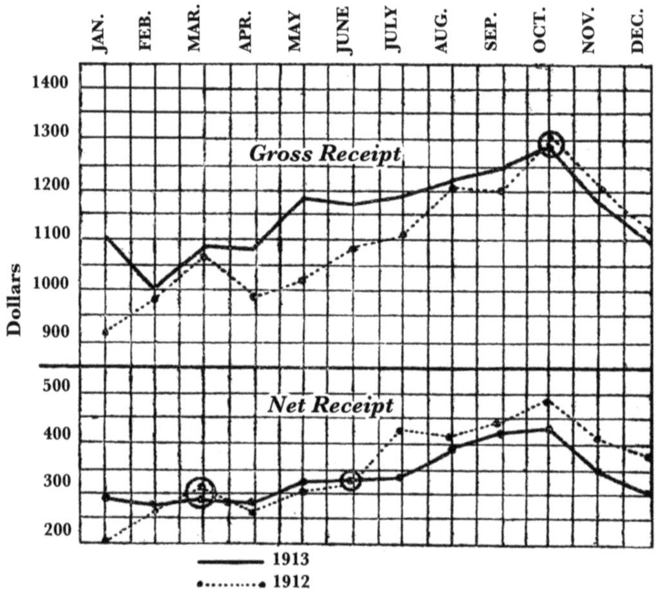

Figure 1.2 Monthly Gross Profits and Net Product Per Mile for US Railways in 1912 and 1913. Source: N. Mondet, 'Les chemins de fer des États-Unis en 1913', *Journal des économistes*, 6th ser., 42 (April 1914): 83, fig.

In the United States, the situation was analogous to that of Europe. From the spring of 1913, the net profits of the railways were down despite the increase in gross receipts (see fig. 1.2). The railways reduced their orders to the metal industry. Cast-iron production and unfulfilled orders of the steel trust were declining. For the second quarter in 1913, the steel trust's orders were equal to those of the corresponding quarter in 1912. But, whereas in 1912 there was an increase in the second quarter compared with the first, in 1913 there was a decrease. In the third quarter, the difference was 500,000 tonnes in favour of 1912. (See table 1.104.)

However, until October 1913, cast-iron production did not decrease in comparison to the corresponding month in 1912. But from that date onward, production was declining rapidly. In the first quarter of 1914, cast-iron production in the United States reached 6,121,000 tonnes against 8,145,000 for the corresponding quarter in 1913.

Moreover, heterogeneous factors were aggravating the situation of the railways. The railway companies, particularly in the East, demanded the authorization to raise their tariffs by 5 per cent. In order to justify this request, they argued that the increase in their charges was necessary to offset the 7 to 8 per cent rise in the prices of goods consumed by them. But by the end of 1913, the Interstate Commerce Commission declared that an inquiry would be necessary before any increase in tariffs.

Yet the three attempts at arbitration in the conflicts between railway workers and management further increased the cost of wages for 1914 by $14,500,000. In addition, various measures which had been passed in 21 states imposed the 'full crew' system on the railway companies, increasing the personnel on each train. This resulted in an additional cost of $6,800,000. In total, $21,300,000 in added labour costs were paid in 1914. In order to compensate, companies reduced to a minimum their orders for rails and locomotives, suspended work of all kinds and phased out some trains altogether. The crisis was worsening. Cast-iron prices declined: in September 1913, the price was already lower than the price for September 1912. In December, the price dropped significantly to $15.71 per tonne against $18.15 in 1912.

Just as Germany had shown the first symptoms of the crisis, the German money market was particularly shaken. In March and June 1913, the private discount rate was getting closer to the official rate. The Reichsbank rigorously held to its discount practices by strictly enforcing the three signatures rule and by excluding renewed or financial drafts that hid overdrafts on long-term advances. Its discount rate was increased from 5 to 6 per cent until 27 October 1913. In August, the bank's balance sheets were already showing more satisfactory results. On 27 October, the discount rate was decreased to 5.5 per cent and then to 5 per cent on 12 December 1913. The most critical stage was over. The portfolio had reached its maximum by the end of June (1,505 million marks). For political as well as economic reasons, cash reserves were continually reinforced throughout 1913.

France herself was also experiencing mild monetary stress. Until the beginning of May 1913, the rate of discount on the open market reached 4 per cent (equal to the rate of the Banque de France). From May 1913, that rate was decreasing. By the end of 1913, it had reached 3⅞ to 3½ per cent. Whereas the maximum portfolio of the Banque de France was 1,394 million francs in 1912, it dropped to 2,153 million francs in 1913. The discount rate remained fixed at 4 per cent all year. Yet the Banque de France reinforced its reserves on a continual basis. Juglar's index was faulty by omission, as were the German indexes and for the same reasons.

More sensitive to the global repercussions of the crisis, the Bank of England carried its discount rate from 4.5 to 5 per cent on 2 October in order to defend its gold reserves, which Egypt then put to good use. The financial situation was worsening in Brazil, where it was feared that a rate of 6 per cent would be necessary by the end of 1913. This did not materialize. The portfolio hit its maximum of £46 million on 26 March, if we disregard the £52 million figure for the year ending on 31 December 1913. Throughout the year 1913, cash holdings showed slight variations.

The stock exchanges, particularly the Bourse de Paris, suffered the aftermath of the crisis (see tabs 1.106–8). One mistake was made. In Paris, in August 1913, it was believed that the growth period would continue. Thus, on 23 May 1914, when it became clear that there was a crisis, a mild panic was recorded.

Table 1.106 Share Values on the Paris Stock Exchange

	2 Jan. 1913	*28 June 1913*	*14 Aug. 1913*	*23 May 1914*
Crédit Lyonnais	1,624	1,625	1,675	1,600
Banque de Paris	1,770	1,715	1,739	1,548
Lens	1,760	1,485	1,690	1,300
Navy Steelworks	1,896	1,774	1,929	1,748
Jeumont	497	449	490	393
Thomson-Houston	763	772	767	690
Transatlantique Co.	204	163	169	132

No source given.

Table 1.107 Securities Prices on the Berlin Stock Exchange in 1913–14

	2 Jan. 1913	*16 May 1914*
3½ % (Imperial bonds)	88	86
3 % (Imperial bonds)	78	77
Deutsche Bank	254	239
Diskonto	187	187
Gelsenkirchen	197	181
Phoenix	261	234
Hamburg-Amerika	162	127

No source given.

Table 1.108 London Stock Exchange: Lowest and Highest Values During the First Half of the Years 1913 and 1914

	1913		*1914*	
	High	*Low*	*Low*	*High*
Consuls	75¾	72½	72⅜	72½
Great Eastern	63⅜	57	47⅓	48½
Great Western	119¾	112½	112¾	113½
Midland	60¼	56¼	56½	57
Underground	5 $^{3}/_{16}$	3¼	3¾	4
Armstrong	52/6	39/9	£2	£2 $^{1}/_{16}$
Guest, Keen	68/9	63/0	£3 $^{1}/_{16}$	£3 $^{3}/_{16}$
Cunard	35/9	28/0	33	34
P. and O.	350	270	288	290

No source given.

The situation was the same on the New York Stock Exchange: concerning the price of 60 railway shares, *Dun's Review* index showed 90.37 in 1913 against 103.05 in 1912. Stock trading, according to the *Commercial and Financial Chronicle*, represented $7,446 million in 1913 compared to $11,836 million in 1912.

The net profits for the steel trust were at $17,994 million for the first quarter of 1914, compared to $34.426 million for the first quarter of 1913. The decline in net profits dates from the fourth quarter of 1913 ($23 million against $35 million in 1912).

On the other hand, foreign trade did not show an immediate drop. The German cartels' practice of dumping was stimulating exports. The war in the Balkans encouraged emigration from Europe. Exports rose from 9,099 million marks in 1912 to 10,182 million in 1913, and imports, from 11,017 to 11,127 million marks over the same years. It was the same in France and England. Yet, the effects of the crisis were being felt at the beginning of 1914. During the first three months of 1914, exports diminished in France, especially exports of manufactured products. Railway profits declined from 1 January to 30 June 1914 on the Northern, the State and the Orléans lines. In Germany exports reached 841 million marks in April 1914 against 872 million in April 1913; imports also dropped from 972 million in 1913 to 951 million in 1914. In England, exports were down by £3,106,000 in April 1914 in comparison to 1913, and imports, by £1,329,000.

The crisis of 1913 was accompanied by wage reductions and increased unemployment (tab. 1.109).

Table 1.109 Unemployment Rates in Great Britain

	Jan.	*Feb.*	*March*	*April*	*May*
1913	2.2	2.0	1.9	2.1	1.9
1914	2.6	2.3	2.2	2.1	2.3

No source given.

From the beginning of 1913 in Germany, the percentage of unemployed union workers was increasing in comparison to 1912. In the second half of 1913, it was again as high as it had been in 1908. The year 1913 had clearly been one of crisis, which marked the transition from a period of expansion to one of depression. The depression was to be short-lived.

The war of 1914 was to give a very distinct look to economic life, one in which the usual alternating periods of growth and depression gave way to a continuous rise in prices and to the progress of industrial labour, just as the political war was transformed into a war for resources. However, the end of the war was to signal a swift reappearance of the phenomenon of overproduction which presented characteristics analogous to those we have studied so far. We must now examine these more closely.

§14. – The crisis of 1920[513]

In many respects, the war period resembled a period of industrial prosperity. Prices of goods went up, together with profits, wages and interest rates. Unemployment disappeared, and a feverish level of activity was observed everywhere.

Yet some major differences separate this period from an ordinary period of prosperity; whereas a growth period is usually characterized by a rapid development in production, the war period in Europe, and more particularly in France, saw a general slump in production that intensified with the mobilization. Thus, the price rise was itself the consequence of the restriction of supply, as well as the intensity of demand. Demand had an impact, however, because the war turned the majority of goods into basic necessities for which buyers had to pay the asking price without question. When the buyer is the state, price is discussed even less since the government pays with paper money. To be an *effective* buyer (one with means of payment), the state needs only to print more banknotes.

In a normal period of expansion, imports and exports develop simultaneously. During the war, Europe was importing without exporting. It was purchasing on credit. Domestically, the government borrows by means of the forced exchange note [*le billet à cours forcé*]. Abroad, the state borrows by issuing government securities or by means of advances from one treasury to another. The British Treasury, and later the US Treasury, offered credit to their allies. Wartime credit skewed and exaggerated the normal increase of prices, profits, interest and wages. It created the illusion and appearance of wealth by creating effective, unlimited demand at any price. The end of the war brought us back to reality, where the basis for all wealth would again be production. The end of the war marked the beginning of an exceptionally violent crisis.

In other words, the crisis of 1920 should not be confused with a periodic crisis. It was essentially the result of the return to a more normal situation after four years of artificial conditions caused by the war. With the return to normality, Europe stopped importing without exporting, as credit became more and more limited, if not outright refused. Products were once again being exchanged against other products. And the crisis began with the exporting countries, such as Japan, the United States and Great Britain, which had to slow down their sales to European countries (France and Germany, and even

513. Here our study will be based primarily on evidence drawn from the *Labour Gazette* (in a month-by-month breakdown) for England; and from the monthly economic circular published by the National City Bank of New York, for the United States. See also: the *Revue économique Internationale* (Nov. 1920); Henry Germain-Martin, 'La crise industrielle en France', speech given at the meeting of the *Société d'économie politique de Paris*, 4 Dec. 1920; André Liesse, 'Vues sur le crédit dans la crise actuelle', *Économiste français* 29 Jan., 19 Feb., 4 June, 9 July and 30 July 1921; Baron Mourre, 'La crise de 1920–1921 et ses causes', *Revue d'économie politique* 35, no. 5 (1921): 545–67; Mourre, 'Les crises et leurs signes caractéristiques aux États-Unis de 1882 à 1921', *Journal de la Société de Statistique de Paris* 63, no. 1 (1922): 5–24; a series of articles in the *Revue d'économie politique*, May–Aug. 1921 and March–April 1922, by Louis Baudin, Jean Lorin and Marcel Bourbeau; and the monthly economic indexes, as well as the 'Circulaire mensuelle de la French-American Banking Association' in the *Revue politique et parlementaire.*

more so to Poland, Russia and the Balkans), as they no longer had the means to pay. Yet, one might ask, how was it that the crisis did not follow the signing of the Armistice? Why, after a slight depression of economic markets at the end of 1918 and at the beginning of 1919, did prosperity and the increase send up one last flare?

After the conclusion of the Armistice, those in industrial and commercial circles feared the outlets for their products might be reduced. Cotton would no longer be used to make explosive powder and return to being the humble textile of the past; wool would clothe mere civilians instead of the soldiers, thereby becoming less of a necessity. Civilians also consume less, while soldiers consume a lot. In short, we can believe that a period of crisis opened with the end of the war. Prices fell until March 1919; yet soon after, the price rise resumed everywhere.

From May 1919 to March 1920, the world went through one last period of rising prices and feverish activity in industry and commerce. However, the activity presented the same features as those met during the war: insufficient production and stockpiles in a whole part of Europe, more imports than exports and buying on credit.

The reasons for this were as follows: the demobilization and the end of the war revealed an exceptional need among all the belligerents. Soldiers who had become civilians again had to find winter and summer clothing. The merchant fleet was partially being rebuilt. Stocks needed to be replenished. Battlefields had to be rebuilt. Everywhere railways overworked during the war were in need of maintenance. Everywhere wartime factories also had to be transformed into peace-time factories. The Armistice was not the same as the demobilization, just as the demobilization by itself did not bring a return to normal levels of production. Supply was believed to be greater than demand when it was the other way around. Needs seemed almost unlimited, as the war had caused so much damage. Also, a general increase in prices occurred with exceptional intensity. But even if needs were unlimited, the means with which to satisfy them were not. Products were again being traded for other products, since sales on credit were replaced by the exchange of goods against goods. The crisis would appear as soon as a somewhat more normal situation returned, one characterized by the resumption of production in Europe, by the stop or slowing down of American or English sales on credit, and by the satisfaction of exceptional needs after the end of the war (for clothing, ships, replenished stocks and the reconstruction of accumulated of ruins). Yet the limitation of credit in the United States and Great Britain was to play an essential role. Thus, the crisis of 1920 took on a very unique appearance. It looked like a general periodic overproduction crisis, but differed from latter in the very short growth that preceded it, in the intensity of the crisis that followed it and in the reasons that provoked it, which we will now explain in greater detail.

A.) The period from May 1919 to March 1920

After the Armistice, as before, the supply of goods remained markedly lower than the demand. The workforce was still partly mobilized, and wartime factories sat idle. Industrial production was insufficient, and agricultural production would not feel the effects of demobilization until 1920, at the time of the harvest that followed this demobilization.

In addition, before resuming production, Europe needed to replenish their stocks which had been depleted by the war. A good portion of Europe lacked sufficient food stores; it had to resort to importing food. The countries possessing raw materials (the United States, Great Britain), those possessing foodstuffs (the United States, Argentina), or those whose industries remained intact (the United States, Great Britain) were able to find enormous outlets for their production.

However, their potential customers were still unable to pay for their imports with their exports. Rich countries that had not been destroyed by the war were selling on credit. No doubt, as early as spring 1919, the US and English Treasuries were suspending advances from treasury to treasury. Private credit replaced credit from the treasuries. The Americans and the British were selling their products in France and Germany in francs and marks. This built up an enormous foreign debt in francs. Germany was exporting marks by the billions.

This substitution of private credit for treasury credit proved a crucial turning point. While a government may have almost unlimited credit at its disposal, a private person does not; he either consents to loans with his own capital or borrows from a bank in order to sell on credit. But there is a limit to this kind of operation; the industrialist's capital would soon prove insufficient, and banks, deposit banks in particular, could not engage in these long-term credit transactions on a large scale. Indeed, this was a kind of long-term credit, which the French customer would repay in francs. And the American exporter would recover his dollars who knows when. He would not repay his bank immediately. But as long as selling on credit functioned, great prosperity prevailed in all branches of production, agricultural and industrial. The European continent lacked everything: food, raw materials and manufactured products. The rise in prices would still be general. Demand for all products remained intense, and this intense demand remained efficient as long as credit was extended to the foreign buyer.

Thus, production and prices achieved dizzying progress within a few months. In the countries with depreciated exchange rates that still lived in large part by imports, the increase in prices was even more sensational; the depreciated exchange rate then compounded the prices on imported goods.

It would be superfluous to quote figures: in the United States and Great Britain, factories were overwhelmed by orders at rising prices. In France, where the US and English Treasuries ceased supplying dollars and pounds at a fixed rate in the spring of 1919, the rise in the exchange rate intensified the rise in prices.

Yet in addition to this very specific cause of economic growth and rising prices and the shortages in Europe, other factors were at work for certain products: the end of the war brought an exceptional demand.

In the clothing industry, demand was most active: with thousands of men returning to civilian life needing summer and winter clothes and summer and winter shoes. Woollens and cotton wares were in great demand. The French textile industry remained for the most part in a state of paralysis, having been ransacked by the enemy. German industry itself lacked raw materials, and the '*ersätze*' (substitute products) were barely useable. Shops in Germany were a sorry sight on the day after the Armistice.[514]

The merchant fleet, which had been very hard hit by the submarine war (having lost 2,835 ships and 9,600,000 tonnes), was partially rebuilt. However, its services were in great demand, repatriating the American army (May–September 1919), bringing raw materials, foodstuffs and manufactured goods back to Europe from the United States and transporting mainly manufactured products from Great Britain. Often the outgoing or the return freight was lacking. Freights were upped in enormous proportions. The Cardiff-Rouen freight went from 47 shillings at the end of 1918 to 70 shillings at the end of January 1920. Maritime construction was stimulated (see tab. 1.110).

Table 1.110 Shipbuilding in Great Britain and the World

Vessels under Construction in Great Britain (tonnes)		*Vessels Built in the World (tonnes)*	
End of Dec. 1913	1,956,000	1913	3,333,000
End of June 1919	2,523,000	1919	7,144,000
End of Dec. 1919	2,994,000		

No source given.

Worldwide, the maximum number of ships under construction reached 2,195, weighing 7,720,000 tonnes, at the end of June 1920 (*Lloyd's Register*).

The railways had also been overburdened during the war and were now proceeding with repairs. As a result, the coal and steel industries received an overabundance of orders. Oil, whose importance as a fuel was growing, saw its production rise from 69 million tonnes in 1918 to 87 million in 1920. Oil production in Mexico made the most rapid progress, recording 8 million tonnes in 1918 and 20.8 tonnes in 1920.

We must add that the end of the war, far from signalling the return of a rigorous economy and an intense production effort, was often accompanied by excessive consumption, which was encouraged by the liberal policies of governments and the joy of finally achieving peace. A wave of laziness overcame a people overworked by the immense effort required by the war and anaemic production.

Finally, let us remember that unscrupulous merchants did not hesitate to hoard goods, further increasing the rise in prices and reducing the already insufficient supply. And this concludes our observations on the economic situation from May 1919 to January 1920. From the beginning of 1920, the situation reversed itself. At this point, we witnessed one of the most violent crises in history. It recalled the crises of brutal speculation that had at times accompanied general crises in the past, and which regularly tended to follow the abuse of credit. More than a simple crisis, the one in 1920 was a general crash.

514. We were able to see this first hand at the beginning of 1919 in the vicinity of Aachen.

B.) Crisis

It has been commonly claimed that the crisis originated in the Far East. But this has been somewhat exaggerated. In reality, starting in November 1919, the American Federal Reserve Board urged the banks to remain cautious. At the beginning of 1920, flour and cereals suffered a drop in prices in the United States. In April 1920, it was mainly exports of cereals, meat and dairy products that were being affected. Argentina resumed its shipments to Europe. From January, exports from Buenos Aires to Europe for the period from 1 January to 26 February reached 1,005,000 tonnes for wheat (against 141,000 in 1919) and 640,000 tonnes for corn (against 210,000). European markets still remained partially closed to products from North America. Yet soon afterwards, other symptoms appeared. In February 1920, the price of metals began dropping for copper, lead and zinc. In March 1920, a collapse occurred on the Japanese silk market. This crash caused the suspension of two banks. The stock exchange had to close. Silk had reached very high prices: the consumer was forced to show restraint by first limiting luxury purchases. Silk was valued at $18 per pound in the United States during the winter of 1919–20; in October, it was only $7 or less. The United States was the principal buyer of Japanese silk.

Silver began to depreciate at the end of March, which also affected the purchasing power of the Far-Eastern countries; lacking goods to trade, they used silver as a means of payment. The value of silver dropped because the Far East imported less (its exports had shrunk) and because production (in Mexico in particular) had increased. In Europe, silver money was being melted. The drop in the purchasing power of the Far East was being felt in Lancashire in May 1920; for the crisis was about to evolve very rapidly in the United States and in Great Britain.

Domestic consumers refused to pay very high prices. Their needs had in part been fulfilled from April 1919 to March 1920. Europe no longer had the means to purchase because the United States and Great Britain practised a policy of restricting credit.

From May 1920, demand in the textile industry declined in the United States for woollens and cotton wares. Prices dropped. Manufacturing was all the more severely affected since the price of cotton remained high, reaching its maximum on 23 July at 43.30 cents, the highest price since the Civil War. A poor harvest was expected. Yet in August the price dropped to 26.25 and to 18.50 in October, after a satisfactory harvest.

The domestic consumer was not the only one refusing to buy. From May 1920, American exports were down compared to the corresponding month in 1919, and the preceding month in 1920. The retailers further aggravated the crisis by refusing to lower their prices: they claimed that goods bought at high prices were to be sold at high prices. This led to a glut on the markets.

What was true for textiles also applied to the shoe industry (tab. 1.111). From March 1920, we see the same collapse in the prices of hides in the United States, which dropped by 50 per cent, as well as a drop in exports.

Table 1.111 Pairs of Shoes Exported from the United States

8-mo. period ending Aug. 1920	11,912,000	August 1920	1,045,000
8-mo. period ending Aug. 1919	13,972,000	August 1919	1,719,000

No source given.

From this date onward, the facts accumulated, revealing a developing crisis characterized by falling prices and a reduction of production and exports in the textile industry, in manufacturing and in the wholesale and retail trades.

In Great Britain, events were similar: cotton wares were first to suffer a decline. From the beginning of May, orders from India dropped. By the end of May, a large number of mills were closed in the Blackburn district. From June 1920, exports of cotton wares were sagging, and in July, that of spun threads. The situation then gradually worsened. The wool industry experienced growth until the end of June in Great Britain. And still, the situation was worse in June than it had been in May, simply because less overtime was being worked. In July, however, the decline intensified and was to continue unabated. Starting in June, exports began to sag, after they had increased from January to May without interruption.

In the shoe industry, the decline began in March 1920. Until then, the situation had remained uncertain because of the shortages of labour and raw materials. The industry had to slow production. But in March, it was the market that faltered; working hours were reduced. Exports declined without any interruption, after having reached a maximum of 119,000 pairs in December 1919. By April 1920, the figure was 74,000 pairs.

The prices of cotton, wool and leather decreased. Unemployment increased, and the number of employed workers decreased from month to month without interruption.

In France, the phenomenon was a little different. Textile production recovered little by little through the course of 1920. The textile industry was initially less affected by unemployment than by the fall in prices. The consumer resisted and refused to pay very high prices, which were all the higher because the exchange rate intensified the increase. In the summer of 1920, there was a shortage of orders. All in all, agriculture, copper, zinc and lead were the first to be affected. In the United States and Great Britain, the decrease in exports worsened the contraction of domestic markets.

Yet the reduction in exports also meant a reduction in freight. Since the Armistice, on the other hand, feverish work was undertaken to rebuild the merchant fleet. In July 1920, American maritime shipyards began to reduce their workforce, and the demand for steel plating shrank. Also, in August, cast-iron production experienced its first decline that continued uninterrupted thereafter.

In Great Britain, the situation was identical. In September 1920, the decrease in freight would cause a slowdown in shipbuilding. In October, the situation worsened, and the coal miners were on strike. But in November, we find the surest indicator of a crisis: orders for new vessels were being cancelled at every major port in Great Britain.[515]

515. *Labour Gazette*, Dec. 1920.

In the iron and steel industries, the shortage of orders was beginning to be felt in September, and in the cast-iron industry, eight blast furnaces were shut down; by the end of December, only 248 furnaces remained open, compared to 270 at the end of September. In the steel industry, there were continual complaints about the lack of orders; and factories were closing by the end of December. Elsewhere, workers were on short time. Unemployment developed. The crisis then grew worse by the month.

The mechanical engineering industry was partly responsible for this crisis in the forges and steel mills. Already in July, this industry felt the repercussions of the industrial depression. In the car industry, the crisis intensified by the end of July, and it was the same in the boiler industry. In August, the factories of Tyne and Wear County were affected. From this point onward, the crisis pervaded all the branches of the mechanical engineering industry. The unemployment spread.

On the other hand, the coal mines initially escaped the crisis that from September had been spreading, little by little, to all the other industries. The phenomenon was not unprecedented. Coal was generally one of the last to be affected by a crisis. In 1920, however, some specific factors intervened: the French coal mines had been destroyed by the enemy. Germany, the other great centre of production, was still politically unstable. Only the United States and Great Britain maintained normal mining operations. But in February 1921, coal mining was being affected in Great Britain. Production declined, and then unemployment grew uninterrupted.

Beginning in February 1921, oil prices dropped in New York from a maximum of 25 cents per gallon in January 1921 to a maximum of 11.5 cents in August 1922.

In the United States, the crisis finally struck the construction industry in July: the cost of construction was too high. Without a doubt, the need for housing was enormous. But the cost of materials was too dear, and the interest rate too high. Renting would not earn any interest on one's money. Construction stopped.

This, in broad strokes, was the genesis of the 1920 crisis. Far from affecting all industries at once, we can see that it spread gradually. Agricultural products were affected first, then textiles and footwear; exports dropped; the merchant marine was affected; maritime construction and mechanical engineering also, and the metal industry; and later on, the coal industry.

The crisis of 1920 was to be particularly severe for a country living mainly by its exports. The overproduction of 1920 presented a novel feature: the overproduction in some countries was caused by the underproduction in others. So, whereas a large country that was more or less economically self-sufficient such as the United States could survive on its own and recover through its own efforts, the case was different for Great Britain.

From 1920 onward, goods were no longer sold against paper money or other credit on securities. Once again goods were traded against goods. In order to buy, one first had to produce and sell. Production had declined in a large part of Europe, and outlets were limited. By limiting or restricting credit, banks in England and the United States have put this axiom into sharper relief. Many buyers were taken by surprise. They had been buying without selling for the past five years. Yet the buyers themselves had been suffering. Without a doubt, consumers' reluctance had an influence on the reduction of domestic outlets, but the restriction of credit had slowed down exports to the United States and Great Britain.

Nevertheless, one had to stop sliding down this slippery slope. Europe ended up appearing to its creditors and bankers as a prodigal determined to keep on borrowing to its own ruin. At the beginning of 1920, American banks decided to apply the brakes and remind their customers that people could not live forever on credit. The banks in England and the United States came to an agreement on this point. By limiting credit, the banks forced American and English dealers to follow their example. In the United States and England, the credit crunch was at the root of the crisis. In France, the restriction of credit accompanied the crisis more than it caused it. France suffered the backlash of the American and English crises.

Consumers' reluctance and the restriction of credit caused market bottlenecks. Other factors were at play, however. From the beginning of 1921, Argentine products, which had accumulated in their country of origin because they lacked the means of transport, started appearing on the European markets. The production of some metals (copper in particular), which had been in great demand during the war, was 50 per cent greater than before the war.

Not all peoples equally needed the threat of restricted credit to remind them of the necessity of producing in order to rebuild. France in particular, thanks to a remarkable recovery, had for the most part restored its productive forces (with the exception of the coal mines), by the summer of 1920. From that time on, its textile industry in the North was largely reconstituted, and France's demobilized soldiers had brought in a mostly satisfactory harvest. France would reduce its imports and develop its exports. Competition was about to replace the monopoly of those countries which the war had left intact. Just as well, the drop in prices would be brutal and deep everywhere (see tab. 1.112).

Table 1.112 Price Index Numbers (July 1914 = 100)

	France	*Great Britain*	*United States*	*Japan*
April 1920	600	323	266	316
April 1921	354	206	154	200

No source given.

In countries with depreciated currencies, the improvement of the exchange rate following the restoration of the trade balance further intensified the fall in prices, without being the cause of it. The fall was all the worse due to the activities of dishonest speculators during the period of rising prices. Clandestine stocks had been accumulating. After the fall in prices, these were thrown onto the market. Banks then revised their credits on goods and other items. They were then blamed for doing this. Our criticism would rather be the reverse: they had been too generous with their credit during the period of increase. Credit's role should not be to skew the price of goods. The excesses committed during the price rise justified the exceptional severity and prudence after prices collapsed. While coming to the aid of honest industrialists and merchants, the Banque de France had to warn people practically of the storm ahead, using the traditional rise in its discount rate and its eclectic discount policy. The crisis had already been acknowledged when in April 1920 the Banque de France raised its rate by 1 to 6 per cent. The Banque was reproached for this attitude which was based on almost a century of experience. The same criticism had been levelled at the bank around 1860, after the crisis of 1857. This controversy has been settled for a long time. And only newcomers to business would be surprised by a moderate rise in the official discount rate.

The crisis of 1920 would indeed give central banks the opportunity to exercise their role in regulating credit. The US Federal Reserve Board and the Federal Reserve Banks were experiencing the first economic crisis since their creation in 1913. Until November 1919, the 'Board' confined itself to providing advice about the excesses of credit. But it was difficult to act on some 30,000 independent banks; from June to November 1919, bank loans increased to $5,800 million. Hence on 6 November, the Federal Reserve Board decided to raise the discount rate for the first time.[516] The Federal Reserve Bank in New York raised its rate to 7 per cent, maintaining it there until 15 May 1921. The rate on the open market followed the rise in the rates of the reserve banks. The average monthly discount rate in the United States developed as follows:

October 1919	5.98	January 1920	6.88
November	6.30	February	7.98
December	6.30	March	8.48

It was the same in England, where, on 6 November, the Bank of England raised its discount rate from 5 to 6 per cent, and then on 15 April 1920, to 7 per cent, a rate that was to be maintained until 28 April 1921. The Banque de France brought its rate up to 6 per cent on 8 April 1920 and kept it there until 28 July 1921. This was an indication of exceptional monetary pressure. For a long time in England and France, the official rate had never reached such a high level, especially for such a long period of time. The reaction this provoked was in direct response to the action that had been taken. The liquidation of the crisis proved particularly arduous.

An exceptionally violent crash on the stock exchange was to accompany the economic crisis, particularly in Paris, in May 1920. The rise in prices and profits realized in trade and industry had stimulated speculation on French securities. The dizzying drop in value of the franc had caused a parallel rise in transferable securities denominated in appreciated foreign currencies (in dollars, pounds, florins, etc.). In May, there was a drop in prices and, worse still, a fall in exchange rates. The collapse of rates was brutal. And one would have to go back to the crises of 1873 in Vienna and Berlin, or to the first periodic crises, to find such a significant panic. Whole fortunes were swallowed up in a few days. The daily press mentioned the case of speculators who arrived at the stock

516. R. G. Hawtrey, 'The Federal Reserve System of the United States', *Journal of the Royal Statistical Society* 85, no. 2 (1922): 224–69.

exchange in their motor cars and left with only a stick in their hand after having settled their debts in kind.

The Paris Stock Exchange was not the only one to have been severely tested, however; rates were down in New York and London. Bankruptcies likewise were recorded on the London and New York Stock Exchanges. French brokers, on the other hand, made it through the crisis without much difficulty. Although the brokerages crumbled, no one could claim the fault was theirs.

Bankruptcy, which had disappeared for a while from the economic scene, returned with a vengeance. In France, it was accompanied by its younger sibling, which has since disappeared: the voluntary settlement [*règlement transactionnel*].[517] In the United States, the number of bankruptcies and their liabilities rapidly increased.

C.) Depression

The 1920 crisis was the starting point for a period of intense depression. The metal industry, shipyards and shipping companies were all suffering particularly harsh effects. In effect, the crisis of 1920 signalled a chronic situation of overproduction; for real prosperity would return to the economically intact countries only after the economic reconstruction of the countries that had been economically weakened by the war.

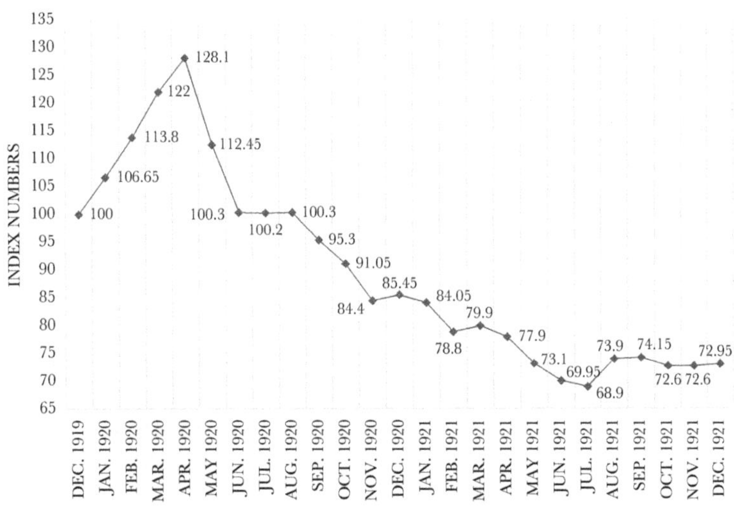

Figure 1.3 Monthly Price Index of Values on the Paris Stock Exchange, 1920–21. Source: 'La crise et la Bourse', *Revue d'économie politique* 36, no. 2 (1922): 248

For maritime shipbuilding, where the slowdown was one of the essential traits of the crisis of 1920, we possess figures from *Lloyd's Register*: in 1919 over 7 million tonnes had been built worldwide; in 1920, 5,860,000; in 1921, 4,341,000; and in 1922, 2,467,000.

517. André Trasbot, 'Le règlement transactionnel de la Loi du 2 juillet 1919' (JD thesis, Faculty of Law, University of Bordeaux, 1922).

Table 1.113 Ships Under Construction in the World

	Number	*Tonnage (gross)*
30 June 1920	2,195	7,720,000
30 June 1921	1,630	6,199.000
31 December 1921	1,126	4,457,000
31 December 1922	815	2,954,000

Source: *Lloyd's Register.*

Once again, the total on 31 December 1922 only gives us an incomplete idea of the situation; a large part of this tonnage (about 564,000 tonnes, 348,000 of which were for England) was composed of ships on which work had been suspended. Maritime transport also experienced one of the most critical periods in its history that saw the failure of many important firms. Shipping freight had diminished considerably. The index quotes 100 in January and 30 in October 1921 for Great Britain. Decommissioned tonnage reached several million tonnes worldwide.

Naturally, the metal industry also suffered the effects of the depression. At the beginning of 1922, the *Iron Trade Review* published statistics for cast-iron and steel production in the entire world. Table 1.114 shows the figures for cast iron. Steel shows similar figures.

Table 1.114 Cast-Iron Production (1,000s of tonnes)

	1913	*1920*	*1921*	*1922*
United States	30,600	36,401	16,606	26,500
Great Britain	10,260	8,035	2,611	4,865
France	5,126	3,380	3,308	4,900
Germany	19,000	5,563	6,098	6,500

Source: *Iron Trade Review*, 1922.

Some copper mines in the United States, after having reduced production by 50 per cent, were forced to suspend it altogether in 1921.

The textile industry had also suffered much – English textiles in particular. Yet it had been less affected than shipbuilding or the metal industry. American cotton mills were the principal consumer of this textile. Table 1.115 provides the amount of this consumption for the years from 1920 to 1923.

Table 1.115 Cotton Consumption of Mills in the United States, 1920–1923 (millions of bales)

	1920	*1921*	*1922*	*1923*
January	591	366	526	610
February	515	395	473	567
March	575	438	518	623
April	566	409	446	577
May	541	440	495	621
June	535	461	507	542
July	525	410	458	462
August	483	467	527	492
September	457	484	495	484
October	399	494	533	—
November	332	526	—	—
December	294	511	—	—

No source given.

Foreign trade, finally, had been seriously affected; the crisis had even started there. The countries left intact by the war lacked outlets; and as these countries had sound currencies, they also suffered in their exports because of the competition from countries whose currencies had depreciated. In the event of a decline in a country's national currency, equilibrium cannot immediately be restored between domestic prices, wages and exchange rates. An export premium and an import barrier were the temporary results of the progressive devaluation of exchanges. Great Britain and the United States had been particularly affected. France on the other hand, having reconstituted its productive forces, experienced a noticeable fall, especially in its imports, while its exports suffered less and were even able to develop. Monthly statistics on France's foreign trade reveal the gradual recovery in our country (see fig. 1.4).

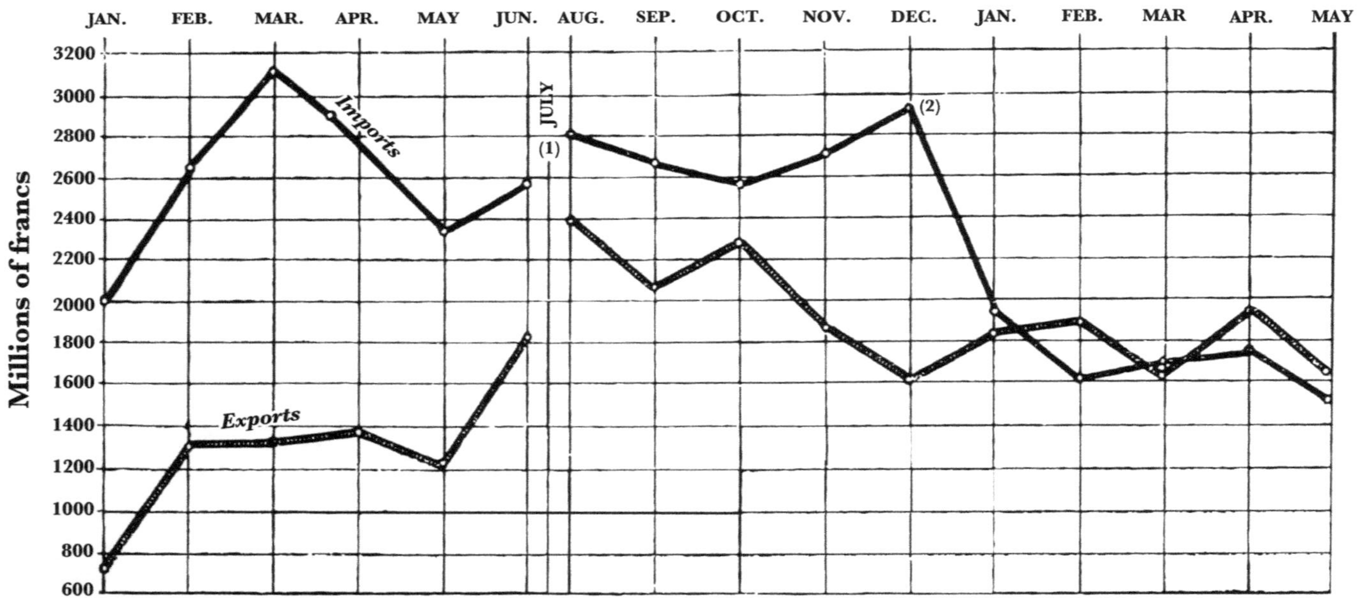

[(1)] **Figures for July 1920 are impossible to derive because of the change in the rate of valorization.**
[(2)] **This figure is artificially inflated by the inclusion of the Alsace-Lorraine trade figures for the whole year.**

Source: 'La crise et le commerce extérieur', ***Revue d'économie politique*** **35, no. 4 (1921): 495.**

Figure 1.4 Absolute Figures for Total Imports and Exports in France, 1920–21

The discount rate could finally be lowered in 1921 (see tab. 1.116).

Table 1.116 Discount Rates at the Banque de France, Bank of England and the Federal Reserve Bank of New York, 1920–1923

		Banque de France	*Bank of England*	*Federal Reserve Bank of New York*
1920	31 December	6 %	7 %	7 %
1921	28 April	"	6½	"
	15 May	"	"	6½
	16 June	"	"	6
	23 June	"	6	"
	21 July	"	5½	5½
	28 July	2½	"	"
	22 September	"	"	5
	2 November	"	"	4½
	3 November	"	5	"
1922	16 February	"	4½	"
	11 March	5	"	"
	13 April	"	4	"
	15 June	"	3½	"
	22 June	"	"	4
	13 July	"	3	"
1923	5 July	4	"	"

No source given.

The general depression caused a deflation of the portfolios of central banks of issue and deposit banks. Unlike previous economic crises, banks were experiencing difficulties in every country. For France, we will cite the Société Centrale des Banques de Province and the Banque Industrielle de Chine; for Italy, the Banca Italiana di Sconto; for Belgium, the Banque Transatlantique; and in the United States, we will cite the Fort Dearborn Trust Saving Bank and the Fort Dearborn National Bank, which were taken over by the Continental and Commercial National Bank, thus averting the most acute financial crisis that Chicago had faced in a decade.

The United States remained the only country where gold still circulated freely, and we will provide the essential data from the balance sheets of the 12 Federal Reserve Banks. The decrease in the portfolio and the reinforcement of cash holdings were very characteristic features; from 30 October 1920 to 15 November 1922, the portfolio fell from $3,351 million to $2,321 million; its gold reserves increased from $2,003 to $3,073 million. An influx of European gold did indeed augment the normal recovery of metal reserves after the crisis.

In France, the portfolio of the Banque de France shrank, and the current accounts receivable of our large credit companies decreased even more. The index numbers have been calculated for the main items on the balance sheets of our credit companies. Figure 1.5 shows their variations.

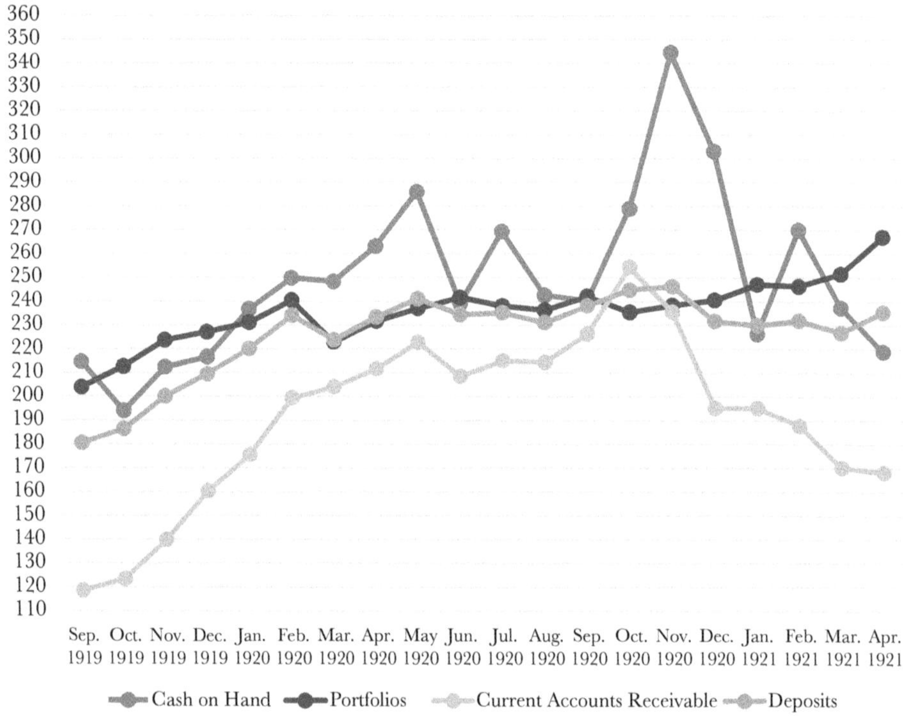

* The four credit institutions recorded are: Crédit Lyonnaise, Comptoir d'Éscompte, Société Générale, and Crédit Industriel et Commercial. The index value 100 = April 1914.

Figure 1.5 Principal Accounts of the Four* Large Credit Companies in France, September 1919 to April 1921. Source: Jean Lorin, 'La crise et les comptes des grandes sociétés de crédit', *Revue d'économie politique* 35, no. 4 (1921): 487–88

On the stock exchanges, the price of variable-income securities dropped considerably in 1921; while that of fixed-income securities increased. Interest rates were decreasing everywhere. But in France the interest rate remained very high, and the government was borrowing continuously. Thus, fixed-income securities were the exception, remaining stationary or decreasing. But it is interesting to study the drop in variable yield securities because they reflect the hierarchy of the major branches of production during the crisis. Marcel Bourbeau has compiled index numbers pertaining to the share prices on the Paris Stock Exchange. Here are our results. With the values on 31 December 1919 listed at 100, the securities most affected are, in order: maritime transport (indexed at 24 on 31 December 1921); naval shipyards (indexed at 41); the affected collieries (at 39); the metal industry, mechanical engineering and automobiles (at 53); and petrol values (at 56). Copper, lead and pewter values came next with index values varying from 60 to 70. The fall in prices varied from three-quarters to one-quarter depending on the categories, between 31 December 1919 and 31 December 1921.[518]

518. Marcel Bourbeau, 'La crise et la Bourse', *Revue d'économie politique* 35, no. 4 (1921): 489–93; 'La crise et la Bourse', *Revue d'économie politique* 36, no. 2 (1922): 245–48 tab. See also Marcel Lenoir's figures in the *Bulletin de la Statistique Générale de la France* (Jan. 1922).

Finally, the working classes – more specifically, those in countries left economically intact by the war – were hard hit by the depression. Workers in Britain, especially, endured intense and prolonged periods of unemployment and a drastic reduction in their wages. The *Labour Gazette* publishes monthly statistics that enable us to follow the effects of the depression on the labour market for all the workers in Britain. Let us provide some figures. For coal miners (1,122,000 workers), the total weekly wages declined from £2,590,000 in 1921 to £518,000 in 1922. Real wages, taking into account unemployment, in 1922 remained less than those of 1913. Similarly, in the cotton mills (500,000 workers), wages were reduced by 4 sh. 6 d. per pound in 1921, by 3 sh. 3 d. in March 1922 and by 10 d. in November, for a total decrease of 8 sh. 6 d. per pound in 1921 and 1922. However, the nominal wage remained double that of the pre-war figure. Yet unemployment and short-time work were affecting the overall nominal wage. Trade union funds suffered 'alarming' losses.[519]

In the merchant marine, on 25 January 1922, sailors' wages were to be reduced by £2 per month, and officers' salaries by the same proportion. The wage reduction was to take place in two stages, from 1 March to 1 May. By the end of February, some 30,000 crewmen and officers in the merchant navy were unemployed.

In the United States, too, there were a great number of unemployed throughout 1921. Thus, workers supported the Immigration Act of 1921, which limited the number of immigrants allowed into the country. From June 1920 to the end of 1921, the number of workers employed in all industries declined by 35.8 per cent, with the most critical period being from December 1920 to July 1921. The most affected were the metal industry, the brick and tile industries, the chemical industry and the rubber industry.[520]

In France, which was less affected, the number of unemployed workers on assistance reached its highest level on 21 May 1921, with 84,810 registering for the unemployment fund. In 1922, the figure decreased only slightly, by a few thousand. Wages had been reduced, particularly in the coal mines and in the textile, car and metal industries. But the absence of unemployment was an obstacle to a significant reduction in wages. Placement offices had returned some 200,000 farmers uprooted by the war. Regions that had been liberated were able to provide jobs to workers affected by the crisis.

§15. – The crisis of 1929–1930

A.) General remarks

The period that followed the crisis of 1920 proved to be one of the most difficult and complex in economic history. It was essentially a period of reconstruction: regions devastated by the war were rebuilt, inventories that had been wiped out were replenished, currencies were revalued by the return to gold and public finances were reconstituted. It was no wonder that the alternation of periods of growth and depression ceased, that

519. 'Annual Commercial and Financial Review', *Times*, 30 Jan. 1923, 12–13.

520. 'Les salaires et la durée du travail dans l'industrie aux États-Unis', *Revue du Bureau international du Travail*, no. 6 (Dec. 1922) 1013–17.

world solidarity waivered at this time and that after the success of this immense reconstruction effort, the world suffered from the phenomenon of overproduction.

In the previous 10 years, Europe had displayed an exceptional vitality. Not only had the devastation of the war been repaired, but thanks to technical improvements, world production surpassed 1914 levels by nearly 50 per cent. Production increased much faster than the population did. Although the world was richer, it was not happier. For this abundance contrasted with the universal unemployment. In accentuating the universal restoration of production, the crisis of 1929 also renewed and resurrected the classic problems of the pre-war years: in particular that of overproduction.

However, two key features separate the 1929 crisis from those which preceded it. In the United States, where it had its original focus, the crisis was not preceded by a period of growth similar to those which had been experienced before the war. It struck like a bolt of lightning, taking the keenest observers by surprise; for the barometers had been unable to detect the gathering storm. In the rest of the world, the crisis did not follow a period of growth: in Great Britain and Germany, it aggravated an existing depression rather than being the cause of it. France was to escape the global cyclone for a long time (until the autumn of 1930).

The crisis of 1929 unfolded during a period of falling prices and global economic depression. The crisis was not preceded by the general rise in prices, which had been a classic warning sign up to this point and still clearly present in 1920. Here again, it differed from the crises before the war.

If it seemed imprudent, to say the least, to want to capture the course of economic life using the rigid framework of statistical graphs, it was much more foolish to hope to use post-war methods disconnected from pre-1914 observations. In order to comprehend and situate the 1929 crisis, we must first determine the most salient features of the decade that it brought to a close. Here we find a background tendency, one which statistical evidence cannot define or measure. By studying and clarifying these distinctive characteristics, we will succeed in understanding the crisis of 1929.

Traditionally, political economists distinguished between long and short periods of general increases and decreases in prices.[521] The 1929 crisis occurred during a period characterized by a general decrease in prices. After the collapse of 1920, the price index remained hesitant until 1925. By 1923, one might have foreseen a new increase in prices, but no such attempt was made. From 1925 onward, the price indexes in the United States and Great Britain showed a downward trend, without any jolts or any real crisis. This basic trend was to persist. The year 1920 appears to have initiated a long period of declining prices. This period was reminiscent of the period from 1873 to 1896, which also began with the end of the war that, from 1870 to 1873, had raised the general price index quite high and abruptly.

521. Jean Lescure, 'Hausses et baisses générales des prix', *Revue d'économie politique* 26, no. 4 (1912): 452–90.

The general price fall prompted by the general crisis seems to have had two main causes: the reconstitution of world production, which the war had seriously compromised, and the technical advances being made in all fields.

In 1924–25, the production of the major raw materials – corn, cotton, wool, copper, zinc, pewter, cast iron and coal – still remained lower than the production levels in 1914. It was only after 1925 that the statistics for 1914 were surpassed. This delayed recovery was due to the slow reconstitution of European production: six years after the war, Europe still had not restored its productive powers. But from this time onward, its machinery, its inventories, its fixed capital, its floating assets, its natural wealth and its workforce were being restored. European products flooded the world market in rapidly increasing quantities.

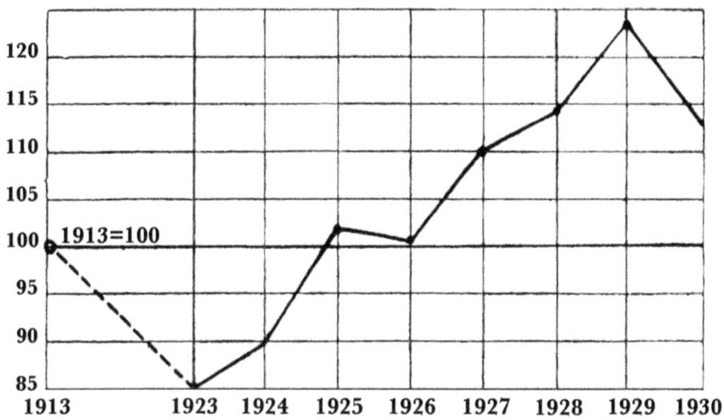

Figure 1.6 Production Index for Europe, 1923–1930 (Foodstuffs and Raw Materials). Source: Société des Nations (SDN), *Memoranda sur la production et le commerce 1913 et 1923–1927* (Geneva and Paris: Librairie Gamber, 1929), (calculated by the author with the help of the indexes of the League of Nations for 1923–1930, in connection with those of 1913); 'Die Weltproduktion an wichtigen Grundstoffen vor und nach dem Kriege', *Vierteljahrshefte zur Konjunkturforschung* 1 (1926): 35–68

European production coincided with production from outside Europe which had been stimulated by the war, by the high prices obtained during the war and immediately afterward. Supply exceeded demand. Markets would become 'sellers' for almost all products. Prices were trending downward.[522]

But the technical progress made in production and in all domains of agriculture and industry could also explain how producers were able to cope with the drop in prices. In agriculture, the more general use of fertilizers, selected seeds and 'combines' in the United States, Canada and Argentina; and in industry, the adoption of 'Taylorism' and 'Fordism', the more widespread recourse to automation and machines and a more rational and systematically economical organization of production allowed for a

522. Jean Lescure, 'La crise du blé', *Bulletin de l'Institut international de commerce,* Brussels (April 1931); *Europe nouvelle,* special issue devoted to gold, no. 688, 18 April 1931.

significant reduction in costs. In Canada, corn was being produced at 40 cents a bushel, or 30 francs per quintal. Some economists did not hesitate to speak of a second industrial revolution in light of the growing 'efficiency' of capital and labour.[523]

This tendency for wholesale prices to go down was to have the same effect on producers' incomes. However, a new phenomenon, to our mind most essential, was to aggravate the downward trend of prices and incomes. Retail prices seldom followed the downward movement of wholesale prices; or if they did, they followed at a much slower pace. Producers' incomes did not allow them to purchase goods in sufficient quantities at retail. The failure of retail prices to go down hindered the circulation of goods and compromised the equilibrium between production and consumption. A very serious under-consumption resulted that further increased the tendency for wholesale prices to drop. Of all the problems likely to retain economists' attention, the 'viscosity' of retail prices strikes us today as the most decisive. The fact that there was a 30 to 50 per cent gap in the increase between wholesale and retail prices worldwide in comparison to 1914 is an unprecedented anomaly. The underconsumption that resulted from that gap could explain the unemployment which in turn provoked further under-consumption and unemployment. Here was a vicious circle that had to be broken as soon as possible.

Yet the crisis of 1929 did not just occur in a period of generally falling prices. It broke out in a world that was still in recovery. No sooner had the ruins been rebuilt than overproduction appeared. And nowhere was the crisis preceded by a period of expansion comparable to those periods before the war. No doubt the United States was able to return to a normal situation more quickly than Europe. But after 1920, Europe was focussed on the immense task of rebuilding from the ruins, restoring its currencies and re-establishing its public finances. Political problems further added to its economic troubles. The disorder in this respect was universal. And the world had stopped advancing at the same pace: the solidarity and uniformity of the past had disappeared.

Before the war, price indexes were at the same level from country to country. After the war, the differences were enormous, with very high indexes in the countries that had participated in the war and lower indexes in the others. The gaps between the price indexes for agricultural products and raw materials and the price indexes for manufactured goods were considerable.[524]

Similarly, wage levels and working hours had changed profoundly in comparison to 1914.

523. H. Stanley Jevons, 'The Second Industrial Revolution', *Economic Journal* 41, no. 161 (March 1931): 1–18.

524. Filippo Carli, *Teoria generale della economia politica nazionale* (Milan: Ulrico Hoepli, 1931), 427–74; SDN, *Le cours et les phases de la dépression économique mondiale* (Geneva: Secrétariat de la Société des Nations, 1931); R. Courtin and P. Fromont, 'Essai sur la crise agricole: Production et population', *Revue d'économie politique* 44, no. 4 (1930): 1084–1123; Ernst Wagemann, *Struktur und Rythmus der Weltwirtschaft* (Berlin: Hobbing, 1931), 313; and Bertrand Nogaro, *La crise économique dans le monde et en France: Symtômes, causes et remèdies* (Paris: Librairie générale de droit et de jurisprudence, 1936).

We have already mentioned the worrying gap that persisted between wholesale and retail prices. There were so many obstacles to restoring a satisfactory economic equilibrium. Purchasing power no longer adjusted as it had in the past. The farmer who sold grain at lower prices purchased fewer industrial products. The disturbance of values since the war was at the root of the economic disorder. It caused a parallel imbalance in the volume of imports and exports and in exchanges.

The League of Nations established statistics for comparing present price levels with those of 1913. It distinguished between the prices of imported and exported goods. It calculated the volume of foreign trade for the different countries by eliminating the influence of price fluctuations since 1913: it applied 1913 prices to the statistics on the quantity of imports and exports. In this way, it obtained comparable figures on their volume.[525] The comparison of these statistics was conclusive: Agricultural countries were selling cheaply and in large quantities. Industrial countries were selling at high prices and in smaller quantities until very recently.

During the inflation, an analogous phenomenon was produced in the countries with debased currencies: they were selling cheaply and in large quantities, while buying at high prices and in smaller quantities.

These price shocks account for much of the global disruption and the unemployment in industrialized countries after the war.

Let us consider the case of Argentina (tab. 1.117), a country that exports wheat, corn, wool and meat and imports manufactured industrial goods. And the result: Argentina sells cheaply and sells a lot, and it buys at high prices and buys little.

Table 1.117 Argentina's Price Levels at Import and Export and Volume of Foreign Trade, 1923–1930

Price Levels at which Argentina Imports and Exports									
	1913	*1923*	*1924*	*1925*	*1926*	*1927*	*1928*	*1929*	*1930*
Import	100	193	185	175	157	155	131	130	130
Export	100	127	136	150	115	116	132	122	105
Volume of Imports and Exports									
	1913	*1923*	*1924*	*1925*	*1926*	*1927*	*1928*	*1929*	*1930*
Import	100	91	90	101	105	112	128	133	114
Export	100	117	144	112	132	167	154	151	113

No source given.

But Argentina was not an isolated example. The situation was similar in India (tab. 1.118), China (tab. 1.119) and Uruguay.

525. 'This index is obtained by dividing the recorded value of trade by the price index, and by converting the quotient into a percentage based on the trade done in 1913.'

Table 1.118 India's Price Levels at Import and Export and Volume of Foreign Trade, 1923–1930

Price Levels at which India Imports and Exports									
	1913	*1923*	*1924*	*1925*	*1926*	*1927*	*1928*	*1929*	*1930*
Import	100	180	178	172	165	136	133	128	105
Export	100	149	155	146	137	130	127	118	94
Volume of Imports and Exports									
Import	100	66	75	78	85	100	104	103	86
Export	100	98	102	101	93	101	106	108	96

No source given.

Table 1.119 China's Volume of Trade, 1923–1930

	1913	*1923*	*1924*	*1925*	*1926*	*1927*	*1928*	*1929*	*1930*
Import	100	108	108	107	129	107	122	122	110
Export	100	133	—	127	137	133	143	142	118

No source given.

The growth in trade volume moved in inverse proportion to the increase in prices. The balance was thus maintained. Yet purchasing power and selling power were turned upside down.

This phenomenon can also be found in the statistics for the countries using paper money, notably in Italy (tab. 1.120) and in France until 1928 (tab. 1.121). At the time of the inflation and fall in the value of currency, one sold cheaply and sold a lot; one paid dearly and bought little. This manner of deception which has been known for a long time as the export premium should more accurately be called exporting at a loss.

Table 1.120 Italy: Price Levels and Volume of Foreign Trade, 1923–1930

Price Levels									
	1913	*1923*	*1924*	*1925*	*1926*	*1927*	*1928*	*1929*	*1930*
Imports	100	509	523	615	614	494	454	444	384
Exports	100	493	481	533	594	479	439	409	342
Volume of Imports and Exports									
Imports	100	93	102	117	116	114	135	134	124
Exports	100	90	119	136	125	130	136	148	141

No source given.

Table 1.121 France: Price Levels and Volume of Foreign Trade, 1923–1930

	1913	*1923*	*1924*	*1925*	*1926*	*1927*	*1928*	*1929*	*1930*
Price Levels									
Imports	100	442	529	572	594	539	535	506	428
Exports	100	406	464	502	593	505	501	484	468
Volume									
Imports	100	88	90	92	111	109	116	193	143
Exports	100	111	133	135	134	146	148	147	131

No source given.

The counterexample is self-evident. Industrial or almost exclusively industrial countries were selling at high prices, selling little, but were buying cheaply and in large quantities.

This is particularly striking in the case of Great Britain (tab. 1.122).

Table 1.122 Great Britain: Prices Levels and Volume of Imports and Exports, 1923–1930

	1913	*1923*	*1924*	*1925*	*1926*	*1927*	*1928*	*1929*	*1930*
Price Levels									
Imports	100	149	155	155	142	135	137	134	117
Exports	100	190	189	184	173	163	163	159	152
Volume of Trade									
Imports	100	96	107	111	114	117	113	119	116
Exports	100	77	81	86	72	83	84	87	72

No source given. [Likely calculated in part from the League of Nations (SDN) sources cited in this section.]

In Germany, a less exclusively industrial country, the phenomenon was less obvious (see tab. 1.123). But it was noticeable once the mark returned to gold. During the inflation in 1922 and 1923, it was the reverse.

Table 1.123 Germany's Volume of Trade, 1923–1930

	1913	*1922*	*1923*	*1924*	*1925*	*1926*	*1927*	*1928*	*1929*	*1930*
Imports	100	59	45	63	84	73	108	103	99	89
Exports	100	61	53	51	65	73	76	86	95	91

No source given. [Likely calculated in part from the League of Nations (SDN) sources cited in this section.]

These observations were confirmed by the case of Sweden, where the volume of imports increased much more than that of exports. The price of imports rose much less than that of exports.

In order to remedy their unemployment, industrial countries would have to sell more cheaply to countries producing agricultural products or pay much more for agricultural products if they wanted to increase the sales of their industrial products, while maintaining the current prices. President Roosevelt has understood this need.

On the other hand, in the countries where the war had not provoked an imbalance between the selling price and the purchase price, the volume of trade had not been disturbed. And the growth in the volume of imports corresponded to that of the volume of exports. For instance, the United States, Switzerland and Norway only showed very slight gaps between the price levels of imports and exports (tabs 1.124–1.126). The volume of imports and exports expanded at roughly the same pace. Whenever the equilibrium was re-established between the price levels of imports and of exports, equilibrium was also restored between the growth in their volumes.

In 1929 and 1930, however, a significant gap opened up in the price indexes that was reflected in the trade volume, particularly for the United States (tab. 1.124).

Table 1.124 The United States: Price Levels and Volume of Imports and Exports, 1922–1930

	1913	*1922*	*1923*	*1924*	*1925*	*1926*	*1927*	*1928*	*1929*	*1930*
Price Levels										
Imports	100	113	132	129	142	139	130	126	119	97
Exports	100	138	146	143	144	133	124	125	125	113
Volume of Trade										
Imports	100	154	160	156	166	178	180	181	206	176
Exports	100	112	115	129	137	145	157	164	169	137
Difference between the Volume of Imports and Exports										
	0	42	45	27	29	33	23	17	47	39

No source given.

Table 1.125 Switzerland: Price Levels and Volume of Imports and Exports, 1925–1930

	1913	*1925*	*1926*	*1927*	*1928*	*1929*	*1930*
Price Levels							
Import	100	154	143	148	146	143	130
Export	100	162	152	147	151	150	142
Volume							
Import	100	87	89	91	98	101	105
Export	100	91	88	99	102	101	90

No source given.

Table 1.126 Norway: Price Levels and Volume of Imports and Exports, 1925–1929

	1913	*1925*	*1926*	*1927*	*1928*	*1929*
Price Levels						
Imports	100	233	187	152	148	142
Exports	100	233	175	144	140	135
Volume						
Imports	100	107	106	117	125	136
Exports	100	112	118	121	124	142

No source given.

The cases of Norway and Switzerland were typical. The case of Norway was especially so, as price fluctuations had been very considerable from 1925 to 1927. However, the fluctuations had been of the same order, as were the increases in the volume of imports and exports.

It was the same in Japan and New Zealand, where the price levels for imports as well as for exports shifted together, showing proportional increases in the volume of imports and exports. The case of Japan was particularly convincing in this regard because its volume of foreign trade had increased more than any other country since the war. And price levels for imports rose as much as those for exports, and the increase in the volume of imports was of the same order as that of exports. After 1931, a drop in price levels was accompanied by an imbalance in volumes.

Table 1.127 Japan: Price Levels and Volume of Imports and Exports, 1923–1934

	1913	*1923*	*1924*	*1925*	*1927*	*1931*	*1932*	*1933*	*1934*
Price Levels									
Imports	100	184	205	192	100	64.6	83.4	93.1	96.3
Exports	100	204	200	201	100	57.2	68.3	67.4	68.4
Volume									
Imports	100	146	162	178	100	100.4	104	111	116
Exports	100	110	140	176	100	125	138	163	185

No source given. [Likely calculated in part from the League of Nations (SDN) sources cited in this section.]

Thus, one principle emerges from these observations: the volume of imports or exports of a country increases in inverse proportion to the price levels at which it imports or exports. The disruption of prices since the war best explains the imbalance in the volume of foreign trade in some countries. This imbalance needs to be corrected. It accounts in no small measure for the unemployment suffered in Europe and, most notably, for the unemployment in Great Britain.[526]

Another anomaly: before the war, periods of prosperity (i.e., of increasing prices, profits, wages, growth and production) occur at the same time in the United States, Germany, England and France. From 1920 to 1930, the pattern changed. In 1923, 1924 and 1926, the prosperity of one country was the cause of distress in another. In 1923 and 1924, Great Britain benefitted from the disruption of German industry. In 1926, German industry found a source of prosperity in the general strike in the collieries of Britain. Furthermore, we observed that prices dropped from 1920 to 1930; but in Germany, the return to gold was accompanied by a rise in wholesale prices from 1925 to 1928.

526. For the statistical part of this analysis, see SDN, *Memorandum sur le commerce international et sur la balance des paiements, 1927–1929* (Geneva, 1930); and *Aperçu du commerce mondial, 1936* (Geneva, 1937), 87.

Finally, prior to the stabilization of currencies, the exchange-rate movements and the general price fluctuations that accompany them provoked the kind of excitement or paralysis that had occurred in response to overproduction crises before the war. The currency disruption in Europe, which only ceased in 1928, counteracted the repetition of alternating periods of growth and depression that had been observed before the war.[527]

The United States, having triumphed very quickly over the economic and financial disorders resulting from the war, was the only major industrial country able to return fairly rapidly to normal levels of activity.

The crisis of 1929 was to emerge quite naturally in the United States. However, the American crisis of 1929 differed in many ways from the crises before the war. And if historically economic crises had resembled each other without ever having been identical, this was especially true of the 1929 crisis. The original aspects of the crisis were the prosperity period that preceded it, the industry that became its focus and the symptoms and excesses that accompanied it, not to mention the attempts made to prevent it (the policies of the Federal Reserve Banks).

Finally, since statistical observation has become more careful and precise, we will be able to apply a more focussed methodology in our analysis: we will follow the path of the crisis from industry to industry, from country to country and from month to month with even greater precision than was possible in our study of the 1920 crisis.

Despite the intensity of the 1920 crisis, all the signs of an economic recovery could be seen in the United States from the beginning of 1923 onward.[528] But the period that preceded the 1929 crisis was not one of continuous growth. Indeed, the statistical methods introduced in the United States since the war have allowed us to observe the regularity of the periods of growth and depression as never before. The elimination of the long-term movements, and of the 'trend', has amplified and disfigured the oscillations of economic phenomena. With the method of calculating deviations from the mean, all statistics have been given the shape of a regular sinusoidal wave. But this constant extrapolation is arbitrary. It presupposes a deep underlying bias toward short-term movements. However, nothing has been demonstrated; one has not even attempted it. Better still, the shape of the curves varies very significantly according to the length of the period being used to calculate the average. And these new methods have the disadvantage of giving the impression of a regularity in the movements that in no way corresponds to reality.

By basing forecasts on such arbitrary methods, we run the risk of miscalculations. At the end of this book, we will specify the procedures that we prefer to use in these matters. But these remarks were necessary before we could begin the description of the period of growth which ended in 1929–30 in the United States.

527. Jean Lescure, 'La théorie des crises et l'anarchie économique contemporaine', *Scientia*, 2nd ser., 18, no. 10 (Oct. 1924): 253–60.

528. See the third edition of the present work, p. 253, and Jean Lescure, 'La reprise', *Revue économique internationale* 15, no. 1 (Feb. 1923): 213–33.

From 1923 to 1929 the United States itself did not experience a period of uninterrupted prosperity. The indexes synthesizing the movement of production show two very characteristic periods of depression, in 1923–24 and in 1927. The depression in 1923–24 was particularly harsh. At that time, the United States exhibited all the classical features of overproduction crises, albeit in a weaker form. The recovery that began in 1922 came to an abrupt halt in the spring of 1923.[529] Steel, cast-iron and automobile production experienced a sudden and significant reduction in 1923–24. Unemployment increased very rapidly in the United States. On Wall Street, share prices dropped. The price index declined very significantly.

This false start of the recovery was not without precedent in economic history. The careful study of alternating periods of growth has established that there was only one well-defined point in the economic cycle: it was the one that first drew our attention to the crisis in all its brutal manifestations. For the rest, the phrase alternating periods of growth and depression is sufficient to define the ever-changing, somewhat irregular ups and downs of economic life.

Nevertheless, the interruption of the growth in 1923 and 1924 deserves our attention because it was not to our mind the result of one of those coincidences that govern economic life as they do a man's health.

In 1923, the Federal Reserve Banks introduced the policy known today by the name 'open market' or managed monetary policy [*monnaie dirigée*]. It was claimed that a more systematic practice of varying the official discount rate, a new policy of direct intervention on the credit market by limiting or augmenting short-term capital available to the market, and the practice of 'open market operations' would act to stabilize the price levels and thereby stabilize the economic movement. There appears to be an antinomy between these terms and claims. We will be surprised by the results.

By tightening credit from the start of the recovery, the Federal Reserve Banks were about to trigger a 'pseudo-crisis', which we would like to call a 'para-crisis'. Instead of moderating the rise, a decline was precipitated in all areas of the economy. We find conditions that are roughly close to the levels of 1921. The curves from the *Annalist* of Harvard in particular clearly reflect a general economic depression, analogous to that which characterizes crises but less intense. It differed simply in the magnitude of the drop, which would be more brutal and pronounced in the event of a crisis. But apart from this difference, we find in 1923–24 all the traits of economic crises. The growth that began in 1922 was interrupted in 1923–24. The restriction of credit appears to us to have played a leading role here. Yet, even so, the depression would not survive the granting of new credit facilities. And one may trust in the effectiveness of the monetary policy initiated by the Federal Reserve Board. From 1925, moderate growth resumed. It was to be interrupted in 1927. The closure of the Ford factories for

529. Jean Lescure, 'Krisenlehre', in *Die Wirtschaftstheorie der Gegenwart*, vol. 4, *Konjunktur und Krisen*, ed. Hans Mayer et al. (Vienna: J. Springer, 1928), 42–45.

a 15-month period played a decisive role here. In fact, the United States did not experience a period of very clear prosperity until 1928: it then progressed rapidly. However, the wholesale price index was going down; while the price index of metals and minerals was trending upward, as it is constant in periods of prosperity. The growth of 1928–29 was to develop amidst general agricultural overproduction and a decline in agricultural products (foodstuffs and raw materials). Despite the difficulties of agriculture, American industry was to enjoy the most prosperous times for which policy makers did not hesitate to take the credit, whether deserved or not.

This growth period was to be characterized by the use of new methods of production, thereby increasing the output of the workforce. Cost prices were being reduced. Thanks to the greater 'efficiency' of production, wages were raised, and the length of the working day was reduced.[530] For some, business was a public service: the secret of its success was reducing selling prices and increasing wages. More was being produced, sold and consumed. The pace of economic life was accelerating. Profit itself was rising. Let us stop pitting wages against profit. Wages were the measure of the volume of sales. The volume of sales defined profit. One took this a step further. But it was a step too far to hope these practices would allow us to escape crises and eliminate overproduction. The crisis of 1929 buried such high hopes, without, by the way, refuting the reasoning behind them. But life is not reasonable. Like the crises of the past, the 1929 crisis was born of excesses and exaggerations. These excesses were such that the crisis of 1929 was one of the easiest to foresee in history. It was initiated by a violent crash on the stock exchange.

B.) Growth

1.) The United States.

The growth period that preceded the crisis of 1929 was short lived. Following the downturn of 1927, the US economy was to experience a great deal of prosperity.[531]

No doubt the movement of prices reflected less clearly than it had in the past the scale of transactions and the feverish activity in production and exchanges. It is customary to claim that the period from 1927 to 1929 was already one of falling prices. The general index for wholesale prices was clearly tending toward a downward movement. Yet during the expansion that preceded the crisis, some prices were showing fairly significant increases: metals and metal products. This index thus remains valuable. The growth period saw the prices of metals rise. (See figure 1.7.)

---

530. National Bureau of Economic Research (NBER), *Recent Economic Changes in the United States: Report of the Committee on Recent Economic Changes of the President's Conference on Unemployment*, ed. Edward Eyre Hunt, 2 vols. (New York: McGraw-Hill, 1929).
531. *Federal Reserve Bulletin.* See *National Bureau of Economic Research Bulletin*, especially nos. 50, 55 and 61.

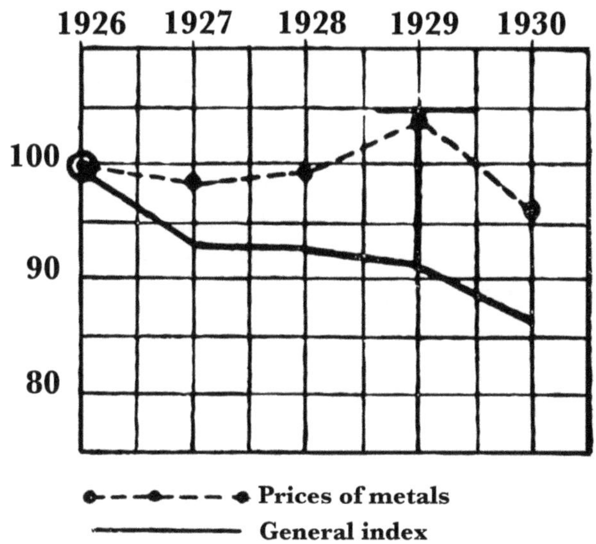

Source: Indexes of the *Federal Reserve Bulletin*

Figure 1.7 Prices of Metals and General Index Figures for the United States, 1926–1930

The same applied to the index prices of construction materials, which were slightly up in 1929.

The expansion period was also characterized by very strong issues of transferable securities. The year 1929 was the year of the 'investment trusts' the abundance of which led to many excesses.[532] The magnitude of share issues was of particular significance in 1929 (tab. 1.128).

Table 1.128 Issue of Transferable Securities (New Titles) in the United States, 1927–1930

	American Securities (millions of $)				*Foreign Securities (millions of $)*
	Shares	*Bonds*	*Public Funds*	*Total*	
1927	1,460	3,182	1,423	7,489	1,337
1928	2,900	2,378	1,387	7,979	1,251
1929	5,868	2,068	1,398	10,005	671
1930	1,503	2,980	1,441	6,918	905

No source given.

It was even out of proportion to the progress of production and trade. However, the stimulus in production came from a recently developed industry that had until then played a secondary role in times of crisis: the car industry.[533] Between 1927 and 1929,

532. Statistics from the *Commercial and Financial Chronicle* 129, no. 3343, 20 July 1929, 350.
533. Jaques Berruyer, *L'évolution récente de l'industrie automobile américaine* (Paris: Jouve, 1931).

the output of the American car industry increased by nearly 50 per cent, from 3.6 million cars in 1927 to 4.6 million in 1928 and 5.6 million in 1929. From this time on, the car industry was to occupy a dominant position in the United States. The railways, whose progress and setbacks had determined the course of business activity during the nineteenth and early twentieth centuries, were supplanted in this role by the car industry. The production curve of the car industry made its mark on the curve of industrial production in general. The annual publication of the American 'National Automobile Chamber of Commerce' entitled *Facts and Figures* affords us some insights, by measuring the car industry's share in the consumption of the products of the various large industries, the key industries in 1929 (see tab. 1.129).

Table 1.129 The Consumption of Key Materials by the Car Industry in the United States in 1929 (%)

Iron and Steel	18	Nickel	26
Glass	73	Tin	23.6
Leather	57.8	Lead	31.2
Wood	17.7	Rubber	84.2
Aluminium	37.4	Cotton	9.9
Copper	15.7	Petrol	80

Source: National Automobile Chamber of Commerce, *Facts and Figures*.

Better still, if it was in competition with the railways, it also proved to be one of its best customers. The transport of cars or materials intended for use in the car industry represented 10 per cent of the total number of loaded freight wagons in the United States. In this regard, a comparison of the indexes of the car industry's production and those of steel and cast-iron production is very significant.

Table 1.130 Total Industrial Production in the United States, 1926–1932 (1923–1925 = 100)

	1926	*1927*	*1928*	*1929*	*1930*	*1931*	*1932*
Jan.	106	105	105	116	103	82	71
Feb.	109	111	111	120	109	87	71
March	110	113	112	121	106	89	68
April	108	110	110	123	107	90	64
May	107	112	110	125	105	89	61
June	106	107	108	125	100	83	59
July	103	102	105	119	91	80	56
Aug.	109	109	110	121	90	78	59
Sep.	113	107	116	123	93	77	68
Oct.	114	105	118	120	90	75	68
Nov.	110	101	**115**	**108**	84	72	65
Dec.	101	96	108	95	77	68	60

Yearly Totals

1919	*'20*	*'21*	*'22*	*'23*	*'24*	*'25*	*'26*	*'27*	*'28*	*'29*	*'30*	*'31*	*'32*
83	87	67	85	101	95	104	108	106	111	118	97	81	64

No source given. [Index values in boldface mark the decline in production for the month of November in 1928 and 1929.]

Table 1.131 Production Index for Manufacturing in the United States, 1926–1932 (1923–1925 = 100)

	1926	*1927*	*1928*	*1929*	*1930*	*1931*	*1932*
Jan.	108	104	106	116	103	81	70
Feb.	111	110	114	120	110	88	70
March	111	113	115	125	109	91	66
April	110	112	113	127	110	91	63
May	108	113	111	127	106	90	60
June	106	107	104	126	99	82	59
July	102	102	103	119	90	79	55
Aug	108	104	110	121	89	77	58
Sep.	112	106	116	122	91	76	67
Oct.	112	104	117	119	88	72	66
Nov.	108	100	**115**	**107**	84	70	63
Dec.	99	95	109	92	76	66	58

Yearly Totals

1919	*'20*	*'21*	*'22*	*'23*	*'24*	*'25*	*'26*	*'27*	*'28*	*'29*	*'30*	*'31*	*'32*
84	87	67	87	101	94	105	108	100	111	119	96	80	63

No source given. [Index values in boldface mark the decline in manufacturing for the month of November in 1928 and 1929.]

In 1929, the *Wall Street Journal* provided the following breakdown of steel consumption in the United States: the railways represented 16 per cent, cars 18 per cent, construction 16.5 per cent, mining and gas 9.5 per cent, agricultural machinery 6.5 per cent, boxes and containers 5 per cent and others 25 per cent. From then on, the car industry enjoyed first place. Thus, we may measure the profound change in the structure of the American economy that resulted. During the crisis of 1907, the railway had absorbed the lion's share of steel production (see tab. 1.73). Yet, if the car industry was now the largest industry in America, then the growth period presented the normal features of growth periods in the past: an increase in production and demand and a rise in the prices of metals and metal products.

The construction of new factories would be accompanied by a parallel growth in the construction industry. Here, however, a distinction must be made. For, from 1928, the construction industry was showing a significant slowdown. Ernst Wagemann has established that housing construction does not increase at the end of a growth period. In the *Vierteljahrshefte*, he established indexes measuring the activity of the construction industry from 1925 to 1930 in the major industrialized countries. Wagemann's statistics for the United States are given in table 1.132.

Table 1.132 The Construction Industry in the United States, 1925–1930 (1928 = 100)

	Total Contracts	*Residential Buildings*	*Industrial and Office Buildings*	*Public Buildings*
1925	90.6	98.6	89.7	—
1926	96.3	95.8	106.6	—
1927	95.1	92.3	93.9	84.6
1928	100	100	100	100
1929	86.8	68.7	111.2	107.2
1930	68.3	39.5	72.4	74.8

Source: *Vierteljahrshefte zur Konjunkturforschung* 4, no. 4 (1931): pt A, p. 28. See also the *Frankfurter Zeitung*, 24 May 1931.

The growth in the construction industry was based on the statistics related to buildings for industrial use. But, from 1928 onward, the housing crisis neutralized and escalated beyond the positive influence of the industrial expansion.

Hence, it follows that the car industry essentially sustained and prolonged the prosperity, and its satisfactory performance was maintained until the autumn of 1929. This progress in production was accompanied by the development of rail traffic, which was measured by the number of wagons loaded per week (tab. 1.133), by the gross profits of the large companies, because the gross receipts were driving net profits (see table A2).

Table 1.133 Freight Wagons Loaded (Monthly Index Numbers for Loaded Wagons) (1923–1925 = 100)

	1928	*1929*	*1930*	*1931*	*1932*
Jan.	92	95	89	74	58
Feb.	94	99	92	74	59
March	97	98	90	75	58
April	96	102	93	77	57
May	104	110	97	79	53
June	103	109	95	77	52
July	105	111	95	78	51
Aug.	109	114	96	76	53
Sep.	119	121	99	78	61
Oct.	**119**	**118**	97	78	65
Nov.	108	102	86	70	58
Dec.	95	90	74	61	52

Source: *Federal Reserve Bulletin*.

Apart from the dominant position held by the car industry in the American growth, the extent of the development of short-term credit, stock market speculation and the surprising progress of a new form of credit, consumer credit, also deserves our further attention.[534]

534. Charles E. Persons, 'Credit Expansion, 1920–1929, and its Lessons', *Quarterly Journal of Economics* 45, no. 1 (Nov. 1930): 94–130; Edwin R. A. Seligman, *The Economics of Instalment Selling*, 2 vols. (New York: Harper, 1927).

Short-term credit was to develop along with trade and stock market speculation. But the Federal Reserve Banks, faithful to the policy of regulating the course of business, tried in vain to moderate the obvious excesses. They would try in vain to make a distinction between credit justified by business development and credit used in stock market speculation. The latter is easily hidden under the guise of commercial credit. The discount rate would be cautiously raised. The recourse to credit was to exceed any reasonable limits, without the Federal Reserve Banks managing to curb certain abuses, despite the lessons of the past. The past was too distant and easily forgotten. In the United States, for a variety of reasons, the prosperity had a sort of mystical quality that was to encourage the most flagrant abuses in the realm of credit and speculation.

From the start of 1929, the Federal Reserve Banks were restricting credit. They were to raise their discount, but ordinary banks would not obey the impulse from on high. The director of one of the most powerful American credit institutions would criticize and contradict the Federal Reserve Board's advice to be cautious.

Moreover, credit was being paid at such high prices that capital was soon flowing toward New York from all parts of the world.

This phenomenon was to manifest itself with a singular force at the stock exchange. An unusual, abnormal rise in American share prices was accompanied by a parallel rise in the money rate from one day to the next, and call money would draw available capital from all over the world to New York. Shipments of gold to New York became necessary to cope with such a large-scale transfer of capital.

The banks affiliated with the Federal Reserve System would show a certain reserve toward the stock exchange in the summer; however, the rates on call money (15 to 20 per cent) were such that money was streaming in from every direction: other lenders (the 'others') would take over from the banks, and the rise on Wall Street was to last until the autumn – an unprecedented rise in the prices and an unheard-of scale of the buying of securities on credit at prices that were clearly inflated.[535] (See figure 1.8.)

---

535. The following figures are based on *La conjoncture économique et financière*, the monthly journal edited by Jean Dessirier.

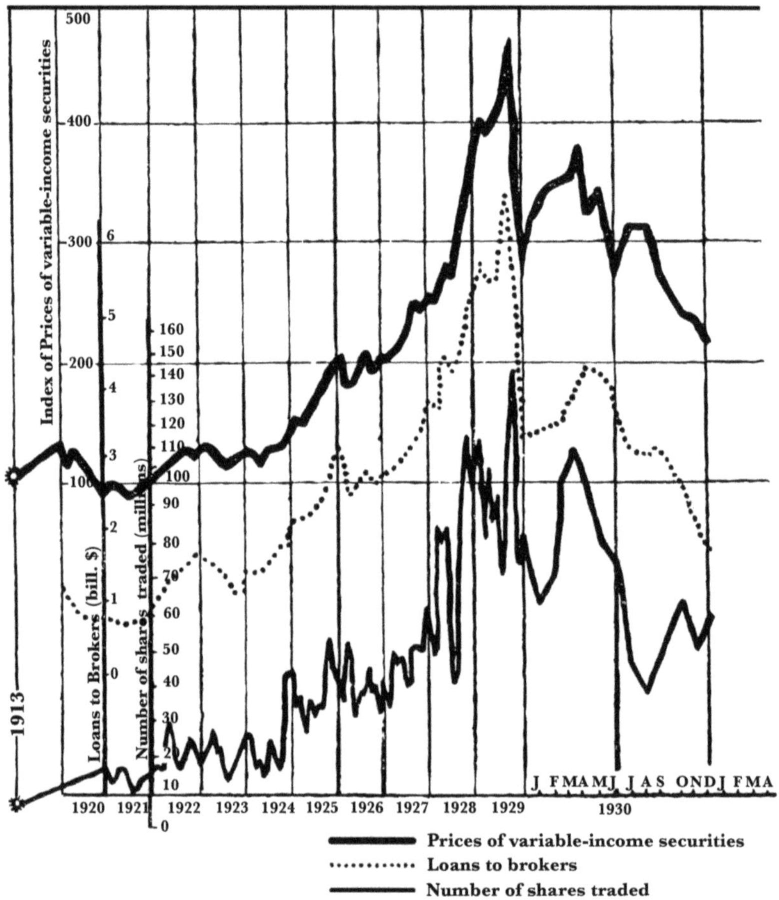

Source: Jean Dessirier, *La conjoncture économique et financière* (monthly review).

Figure 1.8 New York Stock Exchange

Table 1.134 Advances to Brokers (millions of $)

By:	*2 Oct. 1929 (maximum)*	*18 Nov. 1931*
Member Banks	1,071	775
Foreign banks to New York	1,826	623
Other banks or institutions	3,907	12

Source: The monthly review/index, edited by Jean Dessirier, *La conjoncture économique et financière.*

What was serious and disquieting about the situation of the stock exchange and what announced the crash without any hesitation was the difference between the index of share prices and the indexes that represented economic activity (prices, production and goods circulation). Until 1929, the graph of rates on the stock exchange had always presented movements on a scale proportional to those used in the graphing of the other indexes of business movement. From the end of 1928, the myth of prosperity had caused

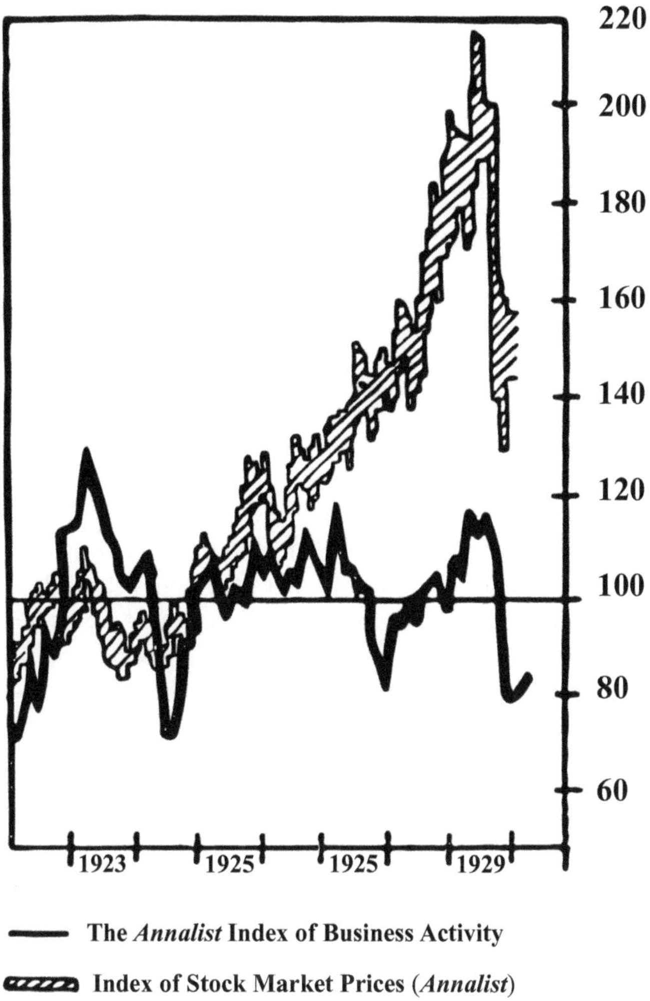

Figure 1.9 Graph Showing Wall Street's Excesses

a gradual divergence between the index of rates on Wall Street and the characteristic indexes of general economic activity.

Yet it goes without saying that the stock exchange must be supported by economic activity; for the reverse would be counter-intuitive. Stock market speculation, by allowing capital gains to be realized and dispersed by its faithful adherents without measure, will provoke additional demand for goods and particularly for luxury or semi-luxury products such as cars, radiophones and gramophones. But speculation 'in the air' is doomed to collapse. It will burst like a soap bubble. Before it bursts, however, it may give rise to artificial activity.

Speculation was also helped in this respect by the unprecedented development of a fairly new type of credit (new at least in its progression and scale), consumer credit and instalment selling. The easy, enormous capital gains on the stock exchange and the extension of consumer credit overstimulated consumption.

Table 1.135 Monthly Index of Retail Sales, 1928–1932 (1923–1925 = 100)

	1928	*1929*	*1930*	*1931*	*1932*
Jan.	91	90	88	79	64
Feb.	88	91	89	80	64
March	97	107	93	92	70
April	105	103	110	101	76
May	107	109	105	97	73
June	102	108	98	90	67
July	80	79	71	65	47
Aug.	81	84	77	67	50
Sep.	113	117	103	87	73
Oct.	118	122	112	93	77
Nov.	125	125	113	95	74
Dec.	192	191	165	142	109
Yearly Averages	108	111	102	91	70

Source: *Federal Reserve Bulletin.*

Of the $45 billion in total retail sales in 1926, $6.5 billion were made on credit. The most diverse goods were sold off in this way, but the record belonged to car industry, where $2.794 billion in credit sales represented 70 per cent of the total car sales. The United States Department of Commerce has been keeping monthly statistics since 1929. These figures represent the 369 companies selling on credit (car financing companies).

Table 1.136 Number of Cars Sold on Credit in the US in 1929 (Before the Crisis)

	Total Cars Sold (1,000s)	*New Cars Financed (1,000s)*
Jan.	147	76
Feb.	177	101
March	290	164
April	363	203
May	381	210
June	369	202
July	363	205
Aug.	323	177
Sep.	282	155

Source: *Commercial and Financial Chronicle* 129, no. 3361, 23 Nov. 1929, 3239.

If we total up the capital gains on the stock exchange measured fairly exactly by the progression of capital advanced in call money and the amount of the sales on credit and compare this with the total revenue of the United States: $90 billion, we can measure the extent of the 'overconsumption'. It is easy to appreciate how the production and sale of cars had almost doubled between 1927 and 1929, and the great danger inherent in such a situation.

Yet, the rise in wages, which was normal and constant in times of growth, also increased the demand for all things. This was especially the case in the United States, which had been practising the policy now known as the high wage policy since 1922.[536] This policy has already been discussed too often for us to belabour it here. Labour productivity had been increased through the introduction of the assembly line, Taylorism and the war on waste, and wages were calculated in such a way that this increase in productivity was accompanied by a wage rise. These methods caused some unemployment. But wage rates were increasing quickly enough for the majority of workers' income to rise significantly.

Two indexes enable us to follow this dual movement: the index of the number of workers employed (employment) and the index of the total amount of wages paid (payrolls). We have reproduced them in tables 1.137 and 1.138 for the period from 1926 to 1931 [*sic*].

Table 1.137 Factory Employment in the United States, 1926–1932 (1923–1925 = 100)

Yearly Index Values

1919	*'20*	*'21*	*'22*	*'23*	*'24*	*'25*	*'26*	*'27*	*'28*	*'29*	*'30*	*'31*	*'32*
107	108	82	90	104	96	100	101	99	97	101	88	74	62

Monthly Index Values

Year:	*1926*	*1927*	*1928*	*1929*	*1930*	*1931*	*1932*
Jan.	101	99	94	97	93	76	66
Feb.	102	105	96	100	93	77	67
March	103	106	97	101	93	78	66
April	102	105	96	102	93	78	64
May	101	104	96	102	91	77	61
June	101	102	96	101	89	75	59
July	99	99	96	101	86	74	57
Aug.	101	102	98	102	85	74	59
Sep.	103	102	98	103	86	75	62
Oct.	103	103	100	102	84	71	62
Nov.	101	98	**99**	**98**	81	69	61
Dec.	100	99	98	95	79	68	60

No source given. [Index values in boldface mark the drop in employment for November 1928 and 1929.]

536. Sumner H. Slichter, 'The Current Labor Policies of American Industries', *Quarterly Journal of Economics* 43, no. 3 (May 1929): 393–435; Hyacinthe Dubreuil, *Standards: Le travail américain vu par un ouvrier français* (Paris: Grasset, 1929); André Fourgeaud, *La rationalisation: États-Unis – Allemagne* (Paris: Payot, 1929); NBER, *Recent Economic Changes.*

Table 1.138 Majority of Wages (Payrolls) in the United States, 1926–1932 (1923–1925 = 100)

Yearly Index Values

1919	*'20*	*'21*	*'22*	*'23*	*'24*	*'25*	*'26*	*'27*	*'28*	*'29*	*'30*	*'31*	*'32*
98	118	77	81	103	96	101	104	102	102	108	87	66	45

Monthly Index Values

Year:	*1926*	*1927*	*1928*	*1929*	*1930*	*1931*	*1932*
Jan.	101	93	96	101	94	68	52
Feb.	106	105	101	108	97	73	54
March	107	106	103	111	98	75	52
April	105	105	100	111	96	74	49
May	104	104	101	111	94	72	46
June	104	102	101	109	90	68	43
July	99	99	98	105	83	64	40
Aug.	104	102	103	109	82	64	40
Sep.	105	102	104	111	83	62	42
Oct.	108	103	107	110	81	59	44
Nov.	105	98	104	**102**	75	56	41
Dec.	104	99	104	99	74	56	41

No source given. [Figure in boldface indicates the drop in the payroll index for November 1929.]

2.) Europe

The great nations of Europe were going through a unique period in their history, one characterized by the revival of their economies that had been shattered by the war. Until 1928, the instability of exchange rates dominated Europe's development, causing upheavals in economic life that prevented any normal development of the economy and any large-scale cyclical movements.

Political and social factors were weighing on the recovery of international trade and the restoration of production. The occupation of the Ruhr for a year and a half-weakened production in the most industrialized region in Europe. France, its most industrialized zones devastated, was absorbed by the slow, long work of reconstruction, which it had to complete with its own resources. Great Britain had to contend with unprecedented strikes. The attempted general strike of 1926 was unique in the social history of England, which had to face simultaneously the difficulties resulting from the return to par of the pound sterling in 1925. Germany was forced to reconstitute its currency after the collapse of the mark and to place its businesses back on solid footing. In fact, Europe did not return to a relatively normal economic situation until 1927 or 1928. (See fig. 1.6) From this date, production, currencies, credit and public finances were reconstituted. France completed the recovery of its industry and agriculture. Between 1925 and 1927, Germany was more or less successful in reorganizing its production methods: they were rationalized.

In short, Europe was barely emerging from the hardships caused by the war when the crisis of 1929 struck. However, it did to some extent partake in the economic growth enjoyed by the rest of the world in 1928–29; but here it must be repeated that Europe had ceased to be the focus of economic crises.

Neither Great Britain nor France, nor even Germany, had experienced any period of significant prosperity in 1928 and 1929. Great Britain was affected less severely by the chronic depression that began in 1920. And that was all. France, after experiencing a false crisis in 1927 (as a result of the stabilization of the franc), returned to normal economic conditions. Excesses were being committed particularly on the stock exchange.

Despite its more or less successful efforts, Germany was to endure the consequences of a monetary catastrophe without precedent in its history. Its working capital had been wiped out by inflation and had to be reconstituted. And more than ever before, savings were lost. After quite a brief period of economic growth in 1925 and 1926 and at a moment when its industries were reorganized with the assistance of foreign capital (American in particular), Germany would come to know a period of depression. And the crisis of 1929 would merely amplify these existing difficulties, mainly due to the lack and high cost of capital.[537]

As the United States had been the centre of the economic growth, it naturally became the focus of the crisis.[538]

C.) Crisis and depression

1.) The United States

The crisis of 1929 was to defeat the automatic forecasting method, the so-called barometer method. The speculation curve rose again in 1929 at a time when some indexes (metal prices and the profits in some industries) were showing a very clear sluggishness. Moreover, the crisis started with the crash on the stock exchange; but production and exchanges experienced a *simultaneous* decline. There was to be no interval in the reversal of the curves. On the contrary, a reaction, almost a recovery, occurred at the beginning of the year 1930, and the depression began to worsen only in the second half of 1930: a systematic response to the consequences of the crash (industrial orders placed by the railways, an intensification of public building construction) under the auspices of the highest authorities in the United States appeared to have been successful in postponing the most serious consequences of the crisis, without having averted them altogether.

Moreover, in the autumn an unforeseen political event, the German elections of 14 September 1930, was to disturb the international capital market. Economic recovery became more uncertain. The worsening depression was to spread gradually to all neighbouring countries: France in particular, until then almost completely unscathed, experienced a financial crisis at a very troubling moment.

537. See the experts' report from the conference at Basel, 1931, and the report of the Wiggin-Layton Committee, reproduced in full in 'La Conférence de Bâsle 1931 et le rapport Layton', *Bulletin mensuel de la Société de Banque suisse*, no. 5 (Sep. 1931).

538. See the NBER's study of the American crisis cited by Pelletier, *Information*, 5 Sep. 1931; J. Joyce Broderick (British commercial attaché) and Arthur J. Pack, *Economic Conditions in the United States of America, March 1931* (London: Department of Overseas Trade, 1931); and the accounts by Pierre Meynial in the *Revue d'économie politique*, 1929–1931.

One of the original features of the 1929 crisis seems to us to lie in the scale and intensity of the stock market crises that characterized it, with brutal price deflation on the order of 30 to 40 per cent, sometimes even more (especially in the United States).

The Wall Street crash that initiated the depression broke out suddenly in an atmosphere full of optimism. In mid-September, Professor Irving Fisher, responding to Roger Babson's guarded statements, indicated the reasons why American prosperity, caused and sustained by new methods of factory organization, would have no end.[539] On 14 October 1929, despite Wall Street's hesitations and the Hatry crash on the London Stock Exchange at the end of September 1929, the secretary of commerce, Robert P. Lamont, was still affirming his confidence in the future: 'Industrial and commercial activity during the first nine months', he declared, 'continued on the same high level which has characterized American business during the past few years.'[540] He then proceeded to provide statistical details.

As the gap was widening between the price levels at the stock exchange and the level of general economic activity, however, a crash became inevitable.[541] And as the reaction, here as elsewhere, was a direct result of the action, the drop was to be all the more brutal and intense. The 1929 crash was a remarkable specimen of its kind, a classic example, like the debacle of Law's system or the crash on the Vienna Stock Exchange in 1873. It surpassed even the Wall Street crash of 1907.

The American portfolio (securities listed on the New York Stock Exchange) suffered a loss of $32 billion between 1 October and 1 November 1929 (Colonel Ayres).

But did the stock market crisis usher in the depression, or did other symptoms precede it? Did the crash cause the depression or was it the consequence of industrial uncertainty? Despite the recent progress in statistics on the 'business cycle' [*la conjuncture*], our observations remain incomplete, and finding answers to these questions seems tricky, though not altogether impossible.

We are inclined to believe that the misgivings about the prosperity in the car industry preceded the crash. Yet the crash played a decisive role in the evolution of the industrial crisis by eliminating an essential component of 'overconsumption': the capital gains of the stock market.

Up to this point, periods of prosperity had been fuelled by the construction of railways, tramways and power plants and had naturally lasted for long periods of time. A prosperity period sustained by the rapid, abnormal development of car consumption was necessarily much shorter. The factors that had provoked artificial levels of consumption and production (capital gains on the stock market, credit purchases) enable us

539. See also his statements of 21 and 23 September, *Commercial and Financial Chronicle*, 129, no. 3357, 26 Oct. 1929, 2618.

540. *Commercial and Financial Chronicle* 129, no. 3356, 19 Oct. 1929, 2450.

541. André Siegfried, 'Vue d'ensemble des États-Unis en 1930', *Revue politique et parlementaire*, no. 427, 10 June 1930, 357: 'In July, August and September 1929, the general impression was still that this regimen of continuous increase was to persist.' See 'The Business Outlook as Viewed by Roger W. Babsen', *Commercial and Financial Chronicle* 129, no. 3350, 7 Sep. 1929, 1505–6; 'Roger Babsen and Prof. Fisher on the Speculative Situation', *Commercial and Financial Chronicle* 129, no. 3351, 14 Sep. 1929, 1645–46.

to understand the relatively brief duration of the growth period. Crises may be similar but cannot be identical.

Some would like to date the crisis to the spring of 1929, particularly to the copper crash of April–May 1929. But the May crash merely corrected obvious excesses, and the level of copper prices after the crash remained higher than the level before the peak plotted on the price graph for May (see fig. 1.10). It was to remain so until the beginning of 1930. This index in our opinion should be discarded.

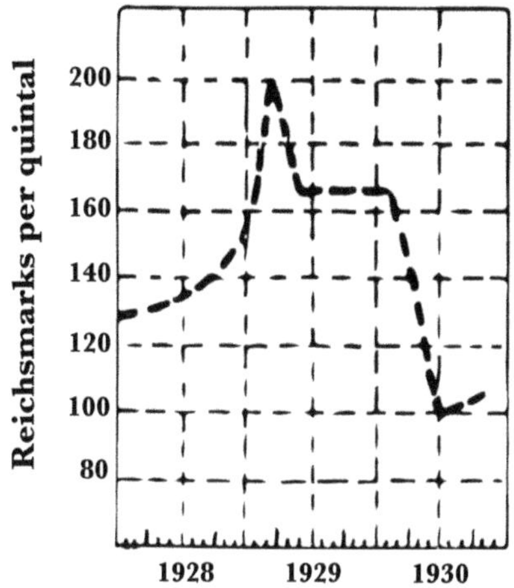

Source: *Vierteljahrshefte zur Konjunkturforschung* (1931): pt A, p. 18.

Figure 1.10 Electrolytic Copper Prices in Germany, 1928–1930

If we look at the prices for other key metals, such as cast iron and steel, and consult American periodicals, we find the situation was still satisfactory at the end of September and the beginning of October, on the eve of the stock market crash. Without a doubt, prices had hit their highest levels in April and May 1929. But in the autumn of 1929, they remained at a satisfactory level, only slightly different from that of the spring. The *Iron Age* provides price statistics for a variety of cast-iron and steel products, which are as follows:

Steel		*Cast Iron*	
Highest (2 April 1929)	2,412 c.	Highest (14 May 1929)	18.71
24 Sep. 1929	2,398 c.	24 Sep. 1929	18.29

Such a slight drop may have been seasonal.

The reviews remained very optimistic about the metal market until the beginning of November 1929.[542] The price index for metals provided by the Federal Reserve System

542. *Commercial and Financial Chronicle* 129, no. 3355, 9 Oct. 1929, 2302; no. 3356, 19 Oct. 1929, 2450; no. 3357, 26 Oct. 1929, 2597; and also no. 3358, 2 Nov. 1929. However, the pessimism

confirmed this.[543] It was only in December 1929 that the monthly index figure fell below that of the corresponding month in 1928 (see tab. 1.139).

Table 1.139 Monthly Price Index for Metals and Metal Products in the United States, 1927–1932 (1926 = 100)

	1927	*1928*	*1929*	*1930*	*1932*
Jan.	98.8	98.1	103.6	101.2	81.8
Feb.	—	98.3	104.4	100.9	80.9
March	—	98.4	106.4	100.6	80.8
April	—	98.4	106.4	98.8	80.3
May	—	98.6	105.2	96.8	80.1
June	—	98.7	105.1	95.4	79.9
July	—	98.6	105.0	94.3	79.2
Aug.	—	100.4	104.3	92.7	80.1
Sep.	—	100.5	104.1	91.8	80.1
Oct.	—	101.0	103.6	90.4	80.3
Nov.	—	101.7	102.3	90.2	79.6
Dec.	98.4	102.9	**102.1**	90.0	79.4

Source: Arthur B. Adams et al., 'The Business Depression of Nineteen Hundred Thirty – Discussion', supplement, *American Economic Review* 21, no. 1 (March 1931): 185. [The figure in boldface indicates December 1929 as the first month in which the index fell below the figure for the corresponding month in 1928.]

In fact, it was the car industry that was at the centre of the crisis. The crisis in this industry dated from the third quarter of 1929 and was characterized by the reduction in profits due to the rise in costs.

The statistics for profits realized by the large car companies were recorded quarterly. We would have preferred for them to have been recorded monthly. But they are most instructive. The decline in profits was already very noticeable for the large car companies from the fourth quarter (July–Sep. 1929) onward: it was very significant, either when comparing successive quarters in 1929, or when comparing the profits of the corresponding quarters in 1928 and 1929.[544]

The *Survey of Current Business* publishes the profit statistics established by the Federal Reserve Board of New York (tab. 1.140).

Table 1.140 Profits of 18 US Car Companies, 1928–29 (millions of $)

	1928	*1929*
2nd Quarter	90	94
3rd Quarter	123	103
4th Quarter	109	94

Source: Department of Commerce, *Survey of Current Business*.

was apparent in the issue (no. 3359) of 9 Nov. 1929, 2919.

543. *Federal Reserve Bulletin* 17, no. 3 (March 1931): 137.

544. Arthur B. Adams et al., 'The Business Depression of Nineteen Hundred Thirty – Discussion', supplement, *American Economic Review* 21, no. 1 (March 1931): 185.

From the fourth quarter of 1929, the drop in profits in the car industry was considerable. Yet was this decline in profits due to the rise in costs? The prices of metals and metal products rose in 1929, and such a rapid increase in manufacturing must have been accompanied by a rise in costs. Was the drop in profits the result of fewer sales or lower selling prices?

In the absence of overall statistics, we shall proceed by the monographic method, by questioning data provided by the major American companies, and in particular by the main car company General Motors, which manufactures 40 per cent of all cars produced in the United States. General Motors' profits declined from the third quarter in 1929. The available balance per common share reached the following:

	1928	*1929*	*1929 Compared to 1928, plus or minus*
3rd Quarter	$2.06	$2.01	– 0.05
4th Quarter	$1.77	$1.58	– 0.19

But the drop in profits and in available balances were not attributable to a reduction in sales. During the fourth quarter of 1929, car sales reached 594,000, compared to 544,000 during the corresponding quarter in 1928. And the drop in profits was not more attributable to the drop in selling prices. Yet, after we deduct production costs, net profits were down (see tab. 1.141).

Table 1.141 Sales Figures for General Motors

First 9 Months (Jan.–Sep.) of:	*Number of Vehicles Sold*	*Value of Sales*	*Net Profits after Production Costs*
1928	1,606,902	$1,210,408,566	$312,402,217
1929	1,675,964	$1,287,477,542	$291,384,676

Source: *Commercial and Financial Chronicle* 129, no. 3359, 9 Nov. 1929, 3007 [see p. 3006].

This drop in profits in the car industry beginning in the third quarter of 1929 was bound to have a decisive impact on Wall Street, when the figures were published at the end of October and the beginning of November 1929. While sales increased, gross profits increased, and net profits decreased: rising costs had reduced profits.

An examination of the other large car companies' balance sheets (Chrysler, Packard, Studebaker) confirmed the data from General Motors.[545] The *Commercial and Financial Chronicle* of 19 October 1929 provides the figures for Chrysler, a much smaller company than General Motors, but of some importance, nonetheless. If one considers the first nine months of 1929, net profits were rising:

545. For the Packard Company, see the *Commercial and Financial Chronicle* 129, no. 3359, 9 Nov. 1929, 3027; for Studebaker, see the *Commercial and Financial Chronicle* 129, no. 3358, 2 Nov. 1929, 2874. In the fourth quarter of 1929, Studebaker's net profits had dropped by half in comparison with those of the fourth quarter of 1928.

First 9 Months (Jan.–Sep.)	1928	$21,786,276
	1929	$24,730,419

But in the fourth quarter, net profits were considerably down:[546]

4th Quarter	1928	$10,095,797
	1929	$6,635,179

The car companies' drop in profits signalled and preceded the crash on Wall Street. Costs were increasing faster than prices and sales.

Moreover, another index shows the same movement of profits: the net profits of the American railways. From October 1929, net returns were less than those in 1928. For the remainder of the year 1929, the net profits remained below those of 1928 (see tab. 1.142).

Table 1.142 Net Profits of US Railways (millions of $)

	July	*Aug.*	*Sep.*	*Oct.*	*Nov.*	*Dec.*
1928	137.4	173.9	180.3	216.5	157.1	138.2
1929	168.4	190.9	181.4	**204.3**	127.1	106.3

Source: *Commercial and Financial Chronicle* 129, no. 3365, 21 Dec. 1929, 3877 [see p. 3955].

The profit data appear to us to be more instructive and precise than the statistics for production which, by the way, confirm the first data set, though with some delay. It was only in October 1929 that the statistics on car production from the Department of Commerce showed a figure that was less than that of 1928. In its issue from 26 October, the *Commercial and Financial Chronicle* prefaced its statistics relating to the month of September 1929 with the statement: slower growth in car production. On the other hand, in its issue of 23 November, the figures for October were given the title: production lower than a year ago.[547] Therefore, the fall in profits did precede the reduction in production if one compares the number of cars produced from month to month.

If we were to examine the consecutive months in 1929, we would arrive at a slightly different result: maximum production levels would have been reached in May 1929. But here, seasonal variations may have influenced the results. A month-by-month comparison appears more conclusive to us. Besides, the *Commercial and Financial Chronicle* also preferred to use this comparison, which we present in tab. 1.143.

546. *Commercial and Financial Chronicle* 129, no. 3356, 19 Oct. 1929, 2541 (Chrysler).

547. Cf. 'Automobile Production Seasonably Lower', *Commercial and Financial Chronicle* 129, no. 3357, 26 Oct. 1929, 2603; 'October Automobile Production Lower than a Year Ago', *Commercial and Financial Chronicle* 129, no. 3361, 23 Nov. 1929, 3239.

Table 1.143 Total Monthly Car Production in the United States (in thousands)

	Jan.	*Feb.*	*March*	*April*	*May*	*June*	*July*	*Aug.*	*Sep.*	*Oct.*	*Nov.*
1928	231	323	413	410	425	396	392	461	415.3	397	257
1929	401	466	585	621	604	545	500	598	415.6	**380**	217

Source: *Commercial and Financial Chronicle.*

If we examine the statistics for cars registered with the tax authority, we find that the maximum number was reached in August 1929. In comparing figures month-by-month, we note that it was only in November 1929 that the number of registrations fell below the figure for 1928 (see tab. 1.144).

Table 1.144 New Vehicles Registered Monthly with the US Tax Authority

	1928	*1929*
Jan.	135	219
Feb.	165	235
March	254	378
April	332	481
May	351	454
June	317	386
July	324	432
Aug.	329	376
Sep.	271	**304**
Oct.	284	288
Nov.	212	**183**
Dec.	154	323

No source given. [Boldface figures mark the first month of decline after the monthly maximum in Aug. 1929 and the first month in which the number of registered vehicles dropped below that of the corresponding month in 1928.]

Neither Harvard, nor the *Federal Reserve Bulletin*, nor the *Vierteljahrshefte* of the Institut für Konjunkturforschung in Berlin produced profit indexes. However, reports from companies allow us to establish indexes of profit movements, as they are the essential data for the movement of business. Here, improvement was needed. W. L. Crumb attempted to fill this gap by grouping the profits of 165 American companies for the period from 1926 to 1932 (see fig. 2.4).[548]

No doubt the crash had other causes, but the drop in profits in the car industry appears to be the decisive symptom. The seasonal tightening of credit in the autumn, the spread of the smaller London crash (the Hatry crash) at the end of September, the rise of discount rates in London, the return of British capital invested in call money, and the sale of American securities by British or American speculators did the rest.

548. W. L. Crum, 'The Course of Corporation Profits', *Review of Economics and Statistics* 16, no. 3 (1934): 61–64.

The obvious exaggerations in stock market prices were to be corrected by a panic, which occurred precisely at the moment when the car companies' earnings reports were published in the press at the end of October and beginning of November 1929.

Within ten days, from 18 to 29 October, some 70 million securities changed hands. From the end of September to the end of October, the value of securities listed on the New York Stock Exchange dropped by $32 billion. The drop in stock exchange values was to persist into November and December.[549] (See figs. 1.8 and 1.9.)

The *Financial News* has traced the trajectory of the 10 'black' days in October. Here is their chronology of events.

Date	*Main Events*	*Number of Securities Exchanged*
18 Oct.	A substantial increase in loans to brokers causes a sudden drop.	3,498,600
19 Oct.	Small speculators lose confidence. Unprecedented turnover on Saturday	3,484,000
21 Oct.	Massive liquidations. Large pools of bearish traders form. Bankers make reassuring statements	6,084,100
22 Oct.	Important recovery following bankers' declarations	4,110,700
23 Oct.	New weaknesses arise. Fears about loans to brokers	6,368,600
24 Oct.	*Black Thursday.* Record turnover. The ticker is on a 4-hour delay. Banks' intervention powerless to stop sales	12,880,900
25 Oct.	The formation of a pool of banks with capital of $1 billion restores confidence. Large drop in loans to brokers	5,910,900
26 Oct.	Stronger trend. Industry conditions in general are considered healthy	2,081,900
28 Oct.	Deluge of selling and large decreases. Business in chaos	9,199,700
29 Oct.	Banks' support proves useless. Sales pick up. Unprecedented turnover; large price gaps	16,388,700
Total number of securities traded:		70 million

The stock market crash inaugurated a period of depression that displayed all the classic features: price decreases, limited production and unemployment.

Depression. – The issuing of shares decreased. Bonds issues were preferred to shares. Thanks to monthly statistics, it is possible to determine the precise month in which the depression of production began, following the convulsions of the stock exchange crisis.

549. Colonel Ayres has explained the role played by investment trusts in the stock exchange crisis. The trusts make securities public. In order to subscribe, the public sells its shares. Instead of creating a securities portfolio with the funds obtained from their issues, the investment trusts place them in call money. Hence the fall of the supervisor of public sales on the stock exchange. We do not find this explanation very convincing. For call money encourages bullish speculation. And although investment trusts do not buy the securities directly, they buy them *indirectly* by making their funds available to the carry-over market. 'Col. Ayres of Cleveland Trust Advances Opinion that Investment Trusts may have Caused Stock Market Crash', *Commercial and Financial Chronicle* 129, no. 3361, 23 Nov. 1929, 3254–55.

The 1929 monthly index values fell below those of 1928 for the following areas of production on the following dates:

Cars	October 1929
Industrial production in general	November 1929
Production of manufactured goods	November 1929
Mining and metal industry	November 1929
Textiles	November 1929

For other industries, the decline came a bit later:

Leather	February 1930
Shoes	February 1930

Oil was to be hit later in November and December 1930 – much later[550] than other products, as had been the case during the post-war economic crisis in 1921. The drop was then continuous. The crisis spread gradually to most industries. The reduction in production was accompanied by a general drop in prices, a marked fall in wholesale prices and a less dramatic one in retail prices. In fact, retail sales experienced a later and less significant decline than wholesale sales and production in the most affected industries.

Wage rates had not been reduced, and the amount of the sums distributed as dividends and interest in 1930 exceeded the amount in 1929: $683 million per month against $621 million in 1929.

In the case of metals, errors were made, as the Coppers Export Association (copper trust) attempted to maintain high prices in spite of the crisis and depression and the rapid increase in inventory.

Table 1.145 Stocks of Metals (1,000 tonnes)

End of:	*Copper*	*Tin*	*Zinc*
Jan. 1930	184	29	85
Feb.	211	34	88
March	232	33	91
April	273	37	93
May	280	40	100
June	287	43	109
July	292	42	119
Aug.	315	44	124
Sep.	327	40	133
Oct.	331	40	141
Nov.	335	41	143
Dec.	332	43	142

Source: *Vierteljahrshefte zur Konjunkturforschung*, no. 1 (1931): pt A, p. 17 and no. 2, pt A, p. 25.

550. *Federal Reserve Bulletin* 17, no. 4 (April 1931): 194.

At first, however, the depression was not very severe. At the beginning of 1930, some indexes even recovered. The statistics for orders received by the steel trust even contradicted those for production. It was only in April 1930 that orders fell off (tab. 1.146).

Table 1.146 Open Orders of the Steel Trust and US Steel Production (1,000s of tonnes)

	Open Orders from the Trust			*Production Statistics for Steel in the United States*		
	1928	*1929*	*1930*	*1928*	*1929*	*1930*
Nov.	3,670	4,930	—	4,259	**3,513**	—
Dec.	3,980	4,420	—	4,018	2,893	—
Jan.	—	4,110	4,470	—	4,490	3,847
Feb.	—	4,110	4,480	—	4,326	4,068
March	—	4,410	4,570	—	5,058	4,358
April	—	4,430	**4,350**	—	—	4,142
May	—	4,600	4,050	—	—	4,089

No source given. [Boldface figures indicate the first month in which orders and production dropped below that of the corresponding month in the previous year.]

The United States attempted to implement the policies recommended by the president's Conference on Unemployment in 1921. President Hoover, who wrote the preface to the reports published in 1923 on the remedies to unemployment,[551] had obtained the railway companies' assurances that they would place new orders with the metal industry. He recommended that the public authorities revive the construction industry by undertaking new construction projects. The optimism of the official declarations restored confidence. Production indexes were much more favourable in the first half of 1930 than in the second. By the end of December 1929, as a result of the conference convened by President Hoover attended by representatives of the railways, heads of industry, agricultural leaders, key bankers and financiers, new orders were placed: $1 billion with the railway companies and almost $100 million with the electrical industry.

In addition, it was hoped that a policy of cheap and abundant credit would revive the spirit of enterprise very quickly. Yet, we must not forget that credit is only one element of the cost price and that the cheapness of credit is not sufficient to ensure the movement of considerable stocks of unsold products, to restore the broken balance between supply and demand and to revive the market for the means of production compromised by the lack of sales of manufactured goods. With such reservations, the official discount rate and the money rate on the open market experienced a rapid and considerable drop, falling to 1.5 per cent in May 1931 at the Federal Reserve Bank of New York. Yet the demand for credit did not match the banks' good will. And as had traditionally been the case in other periods of depression, the banks' portfolios were decreasing everywhere. This credit crunch was described in the *Federal Reserve Bulletin* as follows:

551. Herbert Hoover, forward to *Business Cycles and Unemployment: Report and Recommendations of a Committee of the President's Conference on Unemployment* (New York: McGraw-Hill, 1923).

> Taking the fifteen-month period from October 4, 1929, prior to the break in the stock market, to the present time [...] loans and investments of the member banks [...] decreased in all by $1,130,000,000. This liquidation of member bank credit was accompanied by an even larger liquidation of nonmember bank credit. [...] [T]he total decrease in bank credit outstanding for the 15-month period is in the neighborhood of $3,000,000,000. A part of this decrease in bank credit has been due to bank suspensions during the period and represents the elimination from the aggregate resources of active banks of such resources of failed banks as have not in one way or another been transferred to other banks.
>
> The reduction of about $3,000,000,000 in outstanding bank credit [...] was accompanied by a liquidation of about $5,500,000,000 of loans made by non-banking lenders to brokers and dealers in securities. Consequently, the total liquidation of credit extended by banks and the others through the banks has amounted to about $8,500,000,000 for the fifteen-month period.[552]

Table 1.147 Balance Sheets of the Federal Reserve Banks (millions of $)

	Gold Reserves	*Other Reserves*	*Portfolio*	*Bills Bought in Open Market*	*US Government Securities*	*Notes*	*Deposits*
1929 (Av.)	2,855	162	942	243	205	1,766	2,419
1930	3,000	166	253	213	565	1,488	2,448
1931 (Aug.)	3,429	165	188	66	680	1,772	2,510

No source given.

Loans made by 'others' to the brokers, which included much of the European capital, had been in large measure returned. As early as October 1929, large shipments of gold from the United States to Europe were required to meet these transfers of capital. By January 1930, imports were again outpacing exports (see tab. 1.148).

Table 1.148 Imports and Exports of Gold to and from the United States in 1929

	Imports (1,000s of $)	*Exports (1,000s of $)*
Oct.	21,321	3,805
Nov.	7,123	30,289
Dec.	8,121	72,547
Jan.	12,908	8,948

No source given.

What was new about the 1929 crisis, however, was the absence of sensational bank failures that had been common in the United States before the creation of the 'Federal Reserve System'. To be sure, a great many banks were to fail; however, there were nearly 30,000 banks across the United States, many of which were of little importance. The absence of a 'run' on the major banks is worth noting. To help banks in difficulty,

552. *Federal Reserve Bulletin* 17, no. 2 (Feb. 1931): 55–56.

the National Credit Corporation and then the Finance Credit Corporation were created at the end of 1931.

Table 1.149 Number of Banks and Amounts on Deposit in the United States, 1928–1931

	Number of Banks	*Amount on Deposit (millions of $)*
1925 (31 Dec.)	28,257	—
1928	25,576	56,766
1929	24,630	55,289
1930	22,769	53,039
1931	19,966	45,821

No source given.

At the stock exchange, brokers in trouble were also the exception. At the beginning of 1931, the bankruptcy of the major firm Pynchon and Co. is worth mentioning.

What was new was the duration of the depression and the crash on the stock market, the attempt to restore prices at the beginning of 1930 and the uninterrupted decline in prices that followed, which brought them back to their natural level, one that reflected the state of production and exchanges. A kind of abscess had formed on the stock exchange in 1928–29 that was slowly being drained. The indexes of stock exchange prices returned to the level of the other indexes of economic activity.

Foreign trade declined for both imports and exports, without causing an unfavourable trade balance for the United States. As the crisis intensified, the US increasingly turned to protectionism. The Haley-Smoot Tariff, the most draconian of customs tariffs, came into force in 1930, despite unanimous protests from Europe, which was also becoming more and more protectionist. The revival of protectionism is a classic response in times of depression.

Table 1.150 US Foreign Trade, 1928–1931 (monthly averages in millions of $)

	Imports	*Exports*
1928	340	427
1929	366	437
1930	260	315
1931	174	198

No source given.

A decline in the profits of industrial firms accompanied the depression. However, profits were not affected to the same degree in all industries. Companies supplying electricity and gas and the telephone companies were relatively unaffected; whereas the car industry, the metal industry, the railways and, a little later, the oil companies were hit very severely.

The drop in the interest rate was to accompany the depression. And the increase in fixed-income securities contrasted with the decrease in variable-income securities. The *Federal Reserve Bulletin*'s index of fixed-income securities (1926 = 100) went from 96.5 in January 1930 to 100.2 at the end of March 1931. The index of variable-income securities fell from 156 in January 1930 to 113 at the end of January 1931, although companies had maintained their dividends in 1930 at 1929 levels.

Yet, the depression was to hit the working classes particularly hard, and they would suffer less from a reduction in wages than from unemployment on an exceptional scale. The crisis triggered an 8.5 per cent decline in the number of marriages in 1930. Although immigration was not as important as it had been in the past, the crisis brought it down to the lowest figure recorded since the War of Independence (with only 97,139 immigrants).[553]

Once the crisis struck, many American companies were to remain faithful to the high wage doctrine. Maintaining wages was to ensure that production had an outlet. Wages, which were traditionally lowered in times of crisis, were largely maintained in the United States in 1930. Ford even increased its workers' wages and lowered the selling prices of its cars in order to moderate the effects of the crisis and increase sales. It was a partial success. In a conference with the president of the United States at the end of November 1929, William Green, the president of the American Federation of Labor, opposed any reduction of wages.[554]

This did not mean that the purchasing power of the working classes would be safeguarded, however. For the reduction in production demanded unemployment, which was to cause a decline in working-class incomes. The 'payrolls' index provides evidence of an even more serious decline. It was one of the first indicators of the scale of unemployment, since rates had been somewhat generally maintained.

Unemployment insurance as it was practised in Europe was unheard of in the United States. And, during the crisis, Mr Green declared the American Federation of Labor's hostility to unemployment insurance. On the other side of the Atlantic, the insurance was viewed as a form of charity contrary to the worker's dignity.[555] The Federation formally rejected any form of compulsory unemployment insurance at its annual conference held in Boston at the end of October 1930. The winter of 1930–31 was harsh for unemployed workers severely, who were often forced to resort to soup kitchens and employers' assistance.[556]

Due to the lack of unemployment insurance, the statistics on unemployment in the United States are very imprecise. An official survey was conducted in 1930, but nothing is more difficult to count than the number of unemployed workers. The most divergent figures have been produced. The optimism of the official statistics was counterbalanced by the pessimism of the data from the American Federation of Labor. Figures of 2, 3, 5 and even 7 million have been simultaneously advanced by so-called competent officials from various sides of the debate. Moreover, the figure varies according to whether

553. *Revue internationale du travail* (Nov. 1931): 644–47.
554. *Commercial and Financial Chronicle* 129, no. 3362, 30 Nov. 1929, 3361–62.
555. 'Letter from the United States', *The Times, Trade and Engineering Supplement*, 1 Nov. 1930.
556. Maurice Lewandowski, 'La lutte contre le chômage aux États-Unis', *Revue des deux mondes*, 8th ser., 4, no. 4 (Aug. 1931): 913–27; Meredith B. Givens, 'Statistical Measures of Social Aspects of Unemployment', *Journal of the American Statistical Association* 26, no. 175 (Sep. 1931): 303–18.

one simply counts the unemployed who are not working at all or includes those who work half or three-quarters time.[557]

The Federal Census of 30 April 1930 estimated the number of unemployed seeking work at 2,508,000. The British commercial attaché believed the figure to be over 5 million at the end of 1930. Mr Green estimated it at 5,600,000 at the end of September 1931[558] and at 11 million at the end of 1932. The sheer scale of the unemployment was incontrovertible. Table 1.149 gives the index of employment, which should give us an idea of the extent of unemployment in the United States.

Table 1.151 Employment Index for the United States, 1930–1932 (1923–1925 = 100)

	Jan.	*Feb.*	*Mar.*	*Apr.*	*May*	*Jun.*	*Jul.*	*Aug.*	*Sep.*	*Oct.*	*Nov.*	*Dec.*
1930	93	93	93	93	91	89	86	85	86	84	81	79
1931	76	77	78	78	77	75	74	74	75	71	69	68
1932	66	67	66	64	61	59	57	59	62	62	61	60

No source given.

The persistence of the crisis cast doubt on the doctrine of high wages. The railways in particular experienced enormous drops in their net returns at the beginning of 1931. Even some of the most important ones, such as the New York Central, suffered losses in the first quarter of 1931. Facts were shattering doctrine. Already in June, some wages were reduced.[559] The movement intensified during the summer and autumn of 1931. Wage reductions of 10 to 30 per cent were ordered, sparking protests from the American Federation of Labor and threats of strikes. In fact, the doctrine of high wages rests upon an ambiguity that confounds nominal and real wages. A nominal wage cut is able to allow projects to be carried out that would otherwise be postponed. Economic equilibrium is achieved around a level of values that must be respected by prices and revenues. Ruptures of equilibrium and crises arise precisely from a kind of 'mismatch' or disproportion between the price levels and income levels in various branches of production. From there, bottlenecks develop in circulation and production, thereby creating unemployment. Wages, which define the workers' purchasing power, also determine the cost price. The cost price cannot exceed the selling price without causing a slowdown in production, unless the cost price can be reduced to at least the level of the selling price through improved efficiency. The experience of a whole century seems to establish that a common level of wages and selling prices does constitute an essential element in

557. On the unemployment statistics in the United States, see NBER, *Recent Economic Changes*, 2: 462–78.

558. Broderick and Pack, *Economic Conditions*, 92; H. B. Butler, 'Les répercussions sociales de la crise économique en Amérique du Nord', *Revue internationale du travail* 24, no. 3 (March 1931): 309–33; and Butler, *Le problème du chômage aux États-Unis* (Geneva: Bureau Internationale du Travail, 1931).

559. *The Times, Trade and Engineering Supplement*, 6 June 1931, 257; E. M. Burns, 'Die nichtlandwirtschaftliche Arbeitslosigkeit in den Vereinigten Staaten, 1930–1932', *Weltwirtschaftliches Archiv* 37 (April 1933): 529–59.

maintaining the equilibrium. Some reduction in the nominal wage in the event of a crisis would then appear to be a part of recovery and, therefore, a remedy for unemployment and a means of raising the purchasing power of the working class as a whole. Producing more, we distribute and consume more.

Still, it is true that the drop in production prices should be accompanied by a corresponding reduction in retail prices.[560] The divergence between the level of wholesale prices and that of retail prices has constituted a serious factor in under-consumption in the United States, as in the majority of the countries in the world.[561]

In order to alleviate unemployment, grand public works projects were undertaken in the United States. But this policy was only palliative; while the real cure was to come from the recovery of industries, through the reawakening of the spirit of enterprise.

In the case of many products, the real remedy had been neglected: the drop in prices and the limitation of production in order to liquidate inventory and give new life to circulation. In 1930 and 1931, stocks were still building up. Supply had not been reduced to the level of demand. No attempt was made to revive demand by resolutely lowering prices. The cartels of the trusts persisted in a regrettable policy of resistance to price reduction.

2.) Other countries

The effects of the American crisis reverberated in Europe, Asia and South America.

In Asia, American crises often have an immediate impact on Japan, due to the drop in the price of silk, its primary export, and the decline of its silk exports to the United States in particular. Whereas a drop in the prices of metals and a build-up of stocks of copper, tin and lead would have an impact on the European metal industries.

Table 1.152 Chronology of the Global Crisis, 1929–30

	Start of the Crisis
United States	3rd Quarter 1929
Great Britain	4th Quarter 1929
The Netherlands	4th Quarter 1929
Czechoslovakia	4th Quarter 1929
Japan	1st Quarter 1930
France	3rd Quarter 1930
Switzerland	3rd Quarter 1930
Denmark	4th Quarter 1930

Source: *Vierteljahrshefte zur Konjunkturforschung* 6, no. 2 (1931): pt A, p. 36. [Here, Lescure uses the French convention of referring to 'trimestres', and illogically, to a '4e trimestre'. We have imperfectly rendered these as quarters, even though they do not correspond to fiscal quarters.]

560. Georges de Leener, 'La disparité des pouvoirs d'achat de l'or', *Revue de l'Institut de Sociologie Solvay* 10, nos. 3 and 4 (1930).

561. Jean Lescure, 'Les difficultés de la Grande-Bretagne', *Revue de France* (Nov. 1927).

Although the United States was not a very big customer on the European markets, the American crisis had to have an impact. And in Europe the industrial depression had already started: in Great Britain, chronically since 1920; in Germany, starting in 1927 (after a very short period of prosperity from 1925 to 1927), the American crisis was to worsen the pre-existing depression. During the winter of 1931, unemployment reached a very high level.[562] (See chap. 3, sec. 3.)

With the statistics of the London and Cambridge Economic Service and the Institut für Konjunkturforschung in Berlin,[563] we may dispense with a detailed study of the depression in Germany and Britain. In addition, extra-economic factors appear to us to have exerted a very significant influence both in Great Britain and Germany. In Germany, the general elections on 14 September 1930 had provoked a massive exodus of capital (both national and foreign) that greatly exacerbated the existing depression. Ahead of the crisis of June 1931 in Germany, long-term money had already reached a rate that made any new enterprises almost impossible. Thus, efforts were made to disguise long-term credit operations as significantly cheaper short-term credit operations.[564] This was to set the stage for an unprecedented monetary and banking crisis.

France had remained unscathed for quite a long time. It would take until the second half of 1930 for the first symptoms of the economic depression to be recorded. Still, the difficulties were serious only on the stock exchange and the financial market. Thanks to the stabilization of the franc, our country enjoyed an exceptional abundance of short- and long-term capital, which had been largely recovered after the monetary reform. In two years' time, the interest rate had dropped from 7 per cent to 4.5 per cent. This drop was eminently favourable to the issuing of fixed-income securities and was accompanied by very substantial orders placed with industry. Thus, at the beginning of 1931, French industry was still recording satisfactory production figures. France had not yet been seriously affected by unemployment: and where orders were down, the workday was reduced without having to sack the workforce. The number of unemployed receiving assistance grew beyond an initial peak, on 11 April 1931, to 55,814. But increased rapidly in November and December 1931, exceeding the maximum recorded during the crisis of 1927, which had accompanied the improvement of the franc, of 86,916, on 10 March 1927.

An initial crisis on the French stock exchange occurred in the autumn of 1930 in response to an external and unexpected event: the German elections which

562. *Vierteljahrshefte zur Konjunkturforschung* 6, no. 2 (1931): pt A, p. 17.

563. See also the columns by Henry Laufenburger, 'La vie économique en Allemagne', and by Henri Pouyanne, 'La vie économique en Angleterre', *Revue d'économie politique* 44–45 (1930–31). For Italy, see the annual volumes of Giorgio Mortana, *Prospettive economiche*, 15 vols. (Milan: Università Bocconi Editore, 1921–1937).

564. A chronology of the German financial crisis can be found in the *Bulletin de la Banque Nationale de Belgique*, 10 Aug. 1931, 76–86 and 10 Sep. 1931, 170–75 and the first report of the experts in Basel, published in full as 'La Conférence de Bâle 1931 et le rapport Layton', *Bulletin mensuel de la Société de Banque suisse*, no. 5 (Sep. 1931). See also the *Frankfurter Zeitung*, 20 and 25 Dec. and 1 Jan. 1931, on the crash of 1931.

had prompted a significant repatriation of French capital in Germany, and which made debtors proceed, 'for the sake of the franc', with massive sales of French securities in Paris. The selling provoked a rapid and considerable fall in prices, which caused liquidations of credit buyers (pensions). These liquidations had precipitated the collapse.

A slight mistrust spread among the public, causing sudden withdrawals of deposits, and even real 'runs' that were quickly stopped, with very rare exceptions.

A second stock market crisis in the summer of 1931 resulted from Germany's default and Britain's temporary abandonment of the gold standard. This crisis then spread to all of the stock exchanges in the world. On 21 September 1931, the only stock exchanges that remained open were Paris, New York and Prague. Several markets (Stockholm and Berlin) remained closed for some time. Exceptional measures were taken elsewhere: suspension of futures trading in London, very strict regulation of futures trading in Paris,[565] suspension of futures trading in Brussels and in Amsterdam and the close monitoring of margin trading in New York. The fall in the course of share values left the banks shaken.

The production indexes, the number of freight wagons loaded and the yield from the tax on turnover revenue each indicated an increasingly worrisome economic slowdown. French exports declined, since our cost prices and selling prices had not suffered the same compression as the prices of our competitors. The prices of imported goods in particular were significantly lower than the prices of French products, which were maintained at an excessively high level by a very aggressive protectionist policy in which quotas play an inordinate role. France, in turn, was selling high and buying cheaply. It was natural for her to sell in smaller quantities. Great Britain's return to protectionism in 1932 was to seriously worsen these difficulties. Lastly, reparations and the reconstruction of devastated regions, which had for so long supplied our heavy industries with orders, were complete. In 1922, we wrote:

> In the aftermath [...] of the reconstruction, important changes in the economic equilibrium are to be expected [...]
>
> Despite our best efforts, we cannot prevent the termination of orders placed under reparations from influencing the industrial situation [...] In any case, we must see this as a kind of industrial demobilization.[566]

565. From 30 September on, forward sales had to be covered by a margin deposit [*couverture*] equal to 40 per cent of the amount of the transaction and ¼ of the securities sold. For contracts settling at the end of September, very high backwardations [*déports*] were quoted: 100 francs on the Compagnie Générale d'Electricité where the price was: 2,220. The backwardation was still fixed at 300 francs on the day of settlement. It was reduced the next day.
566. Jean Lescure, *Le problème des réparations: Comment le résoudre* (Paris: Plon-Nourrit, 1922), 81.

Table 1.153 Monthly General Production Index for France, 1929–1931 (1913 = 100)

	1929	*1930*	*1931*
Jan.	137	144	133
Feb.	136	143	133
March	138	144	132
April	139	144	131
May	139	144	129
June	141	**144**	126
July	139	141	123
Aug.	139	139	121
Sep.	138	**137**	118
Oct.	141	136	115
Nov.	143	135	117
Dec.	144	134	115

No source given. [Boldface numbers for 1930 indicate the last month the index remained stable and the first month production fell below that of the previous year.]

Table 1.154 Monthly Wholesale and Retail Prices for France, 1929–1931

	Wholesale Prices				*Retail Prices* (in Paris)*		
	National		*Imports*				
	1930	*1931*	*1930*	*1931*	*1929*	*1930*	*1931*
Jan.	**606**	567	**621**	364	599	609	649
Feb.	**611**	557	**514**	375	602	598	650
March	600	560	501	370	607	591	647
April	595	566	495	365	615	586	641
May	590	552	485	350	626	590	634
June	585	539	470	365	624	593	632
July	598	532	461	347	606	601	615
Aug.	599	521	444	335	606	626	595
Sep.	595	504	428	316	602	637	588
Oct.	581	484	408	314	612	637	571
Nov.	565	475	395	313	618	647	555
Dec.	565	471	377	308	614	649	557

* The *Comité technique de l'alimentation* recently published an index more specific than that of the *Statistique générale*. 'Le coût de la vie à Paris', *Bulletin du Comité technique de l'alimentation*, no. 101, 15 April 1931. [Boldface figures mark the dramatic drop in wholesale import prices in comparison to national wholesale prices at the beginning of 1930.]

Table 1.155 The Paris Stock Exchange

	Share Prices				*Fixed-Income Securities*		
	1928	*1929*	*1930*	*1931*	*1929*	*1930*	*1931*
Jan.	345	544	493	366	83.6	97.6	95.9
Feb.	—	548	481	372	—	96.4	96.9
March	—	535	478	359	—	95.6	97.9
April	—	518	479	338	83.0	94.9	98.9
May	—	512	455	322	—	95.2	98.5
June	—	491	448	329	—	95.6	98.8
July	397	497	438	309	84.6	95.5	98.9
Aug.	—	501	427	304	—	96.0	99.5
Sep.	—	489	396	269	—	96.7	97.7
Oct.	—	518	421	249	86.6	97.7	94.8
Nov.	—	461	385	243	87.7	94.8	94.4
Dec.	483	462	340	221	91.6	94.4	90.8

No source given.

However, these troubles would have probably become less acute were it not for the German default. From June 1931 onward, there were two overlapping crises: the periodic crisis and the international credit crisis.

D.) The global monetary crisis

In the summer of 1931, the crisis of 1929 was to give way to a crisis of a completely different scale. Crises of public finance, banking and currency, of production, prices and trade: all these crises compound and aggravate each other reciprocally.[567]

An energetic policy was put in place everywhere to combat it, in the United States, Great Britain, Germany, Italy, France, Belgium and elsewhere, and it did so successfully.

A period of growth was to follow the depression. Its success would depend upon the extent to which capital could be reinvested. The size of these investments would depend upon the profit outlook, particularly in the wake of the 'devaluations'. Our most recent history confirms quite vividly the experience of the past and the data of economic science. The efficacy of the devaluations derives from the restoration of profit margins.

The question has been raised whether this long, intense and violent crisis that caused unprecedented unemployment was not a crisis of the capitalist system.[568] For our part, we did not think so.[569] But with hindsight, we may better understand and explain it. It seems crystal clear to us today that this severe depression was the consequence of the

567. Jean Lescure, 'La crise: causes et remèdes', Communication to the Association française pour le Progrès social, 5 Feb. 1932, *Les documents du travail* (1932): 30.
568. Ferdinand Fried, *La fin du capitalisme*, trans. Jean Brunnen (Paris: Grasset, 1932); Pierre Lucius, *La faillite du capitalisme* (Paris: Payot, 1932); Moritz Julius Bonn, *La destinée du capitalisme*, trans. Mathilde Schindler (Paris: Dalloz, 1932); and Gaëtan Pirou, *La crise du capitalisme* (Paris: Recueil Sirey, 1934).
569. See the fourth edition of the present work, p. 348.

gigantic upheavals caused by the war in the realms of production, trade and credit – credit having played a very major role here, especially in the United States. The credit excesses of the war and post-war reconstruction explain this crisis, which is almost identical in date to the periodic crisis, but quite different from it. Born of the war, it could only recur in the event of another world conflagration. The abuse of credit and the collapse of currencies were the most salient features. Its severity and characteristics varied from country to country. The crisis was sometimes external, sometimes internal, and sometimes both, if we consider its monetary and banking dimension to be the essential aspect.

1.) Europe

In Germany, the credit crisis was both domestic and foreign. It can be dated from 1931. The crisis began in Central Europe with the collapse of the Kreditanstalt in Vienna.

Like the previous crises, the last crisis in Germany was marked by the classic mistakes often denounced and carefully studied following the crisis of 1900. The German banks had largely tied up their deposits, thereby creating a most dangerous situation should massive withdrawals occur, which was precisely what happened in June and July 1931.

Yet, the violence of the 1931 crisis can be explained by the banks' policies in times of prosperity. Remaining faithful to the doctrine, according to which Germany was expected to reconstitute its pre-war productive power within its new borders, the banks were complicit in a formidable industrial expansion that worked alongside new methods of production encompassed by the term 'rationalization'. The new methods surpassed even those of Taylor and Ford. In order to succeed, banks had to borrow from foreign sources. The German crisis was firstly an 'external' credit crisis. Once foreign investors began withdrawing their capital, national investors very quickly followed suit. By July 1931, the total collapse would be complete.

The Reichsbank raised its rate to 7 per cent on 13 June, to 15 per cent on 1 August, 10 per cent on 12 August and 8 per cent on 2 September.

A general moratorium was declared following the defaults of two very large banks, the *Danatbank* (Darmstädter Bank) and the Dresdner Bank, whose operations could only be resumed with the support of the state. The internal moratorium would be lifted fairly quickly, but German banks were to obtain renewed moratoria from their foreign creditors for a six-month period under the stillstand agreements.[570]

This credit crisis was to result in the complete restructuring of the German banking system with the state's support, whereby the *Reich* would assume the dominant role in the organization and distribution of credit. The Hoover Moratorium (on reparations

570. Léon Proskourovsky, *La crise des banques de crédit en Allemagne depuis 1931*, thesis, Faculty of Law, University of Paris (Paris: Pedone, 1931); Rudolf Stucken, *Deutsche Geld- und Kreditpolitik* (Hamburg: Hanseatische Verlagsanstalt, 1937), 93–118.

debts) at the end of June 1931 was unable to save such a fragile banking system destined to collapse at the first 'run' by national and foreign depositors.

This cleaned-up and reorganized system would later serve as the backbone for Dr [Hjalmar] Schacht's audacious policies and the recovery of the German economy through a programme of public works projects and rearmament, with the Reichsmark ceasing to be convertible and becoming a currency as new as it was original in the abundant variety of different denominations.

English banks figured prominently among the creditors of Germany. The German crisis could not fail to have repercussions in England. The events that followed, however, have demonstrated, in our view, that England could have faced this situation if the ground had not already been prepared for a very serious crisis by Britain's large budget deficit (public debt, social spending weighed heavily on the budget) and by the revelation in an official report about the considerable sums held by foreigners in London. The two official reports by May and Macmillan bore a very heavy responsibility for the crisis of the pound sterling because the crisis in England was an external one: British depositors did not withdraw their deposits. But foreign investors holding more than £400 million in London withdrew their deposits *en masse*. The gold reserves of the Bank of England were reduced to £120 million.

On Wednesday, 16 September, £5 million in gold were withdrawn from the Bank of England; on Thursday, £10 million; on Friday, almost £18 million; and on Saturday, £10 million in one-half day. In August and September, the withdrawals reached £200 million, making Franco-American aid (£130 million) insufficient. The Chancellor of the Exchequer blamed this crisis of confidence on the persistent opposition of the Labour Party, on the suggestions of economists favouring inflation, on the mutiny of the sailors at Invergordon highlighted in the foreign press and on a political atmosphere full of uncertainty (meeting of the Commons on Monday, 21 September 1931). The pound sterling was no longer convertible to gold according to the Gold Standard Amendment Act of 1931. The convertibility has not been restored since. In vain, the Bank of England raised its rate to 4½ per cent on 21 September and to 6 per cent on 30 September. Raising the rate proved ineffective in this case.

Until 1931, 'runs' could be controlled by the re-discount at the central bank, because the massive withdrawals were being made by nationals. In 1931 a different type of 'run' appeared. Deposits had to be reimbursed in gold because the withdrawals were being made by foreigners. The storm came from outside.

In order to safeguard the gold reserves of the central bank, the convertibility of banknotes into gold had to be suspended. Lacking a 'gold point', foreign exchange became erratic. To reduce fluctuations, an Exchange Equalisation Account was created by the Finance Act of 1932 (16 June, pt 4), which has since served as a model for many countries. The new type of 'external run' was accompanied in the domain of monetary policy by a new institution: the exchange stabilization funds.

The fall of the pound sterling was to be accompanied by the fall of some 30 satellite currencies (in the Dominions, Scandinavian countries and many others). A 'sterling bloc' was created through a tacit monetary agreement between most of the countries in the world. In opposition stood the bloc of countries who had remained faithful to the gold convertibility of their currencies, which included France, Belgium, the Netherlands, Switzerland and Italy (before its expedition to Ethiopia) in the 'gold bloc'. The currencies of the gold bloc were a bit like satellites of the French franc. In September 1936, the French franc was to bring the other currencies of the gold bloc down with it, with the exception of the Belgian Franc, whose devaluation had already caused the first crack in the gold bloc in 1935.

The Belgian franc was a victim of both a domestic and a foreign crisis, but mainly a domestic one. The budget was in deficit due to the enormous debt. Belgian banks, acting both as deposit and investment banks, had frozen their deposits. A liquidation was becoming urgent. Depositors were withdrawing their deposits; yet, as was already the case in other countries at the time, notably in France in 1925 – and more recently in 1935–37 – Belgian capitalists were exporting their capital and hoarding gold, two actions that provoked a sudden and massive drop in the gold reserves or foreign currency holdings of the issuing bank. It was a new type of monetary crisis and run. The crisis was domestic: the mistrust was national.

However, this mistrust caused a serious depletion of the gold reserves: nationals were exporting their capital or hoarding gold. Gold convertibility had to be suspended, as in the case of massive withdrawals by foreigners (like the sterling crisis). Like England, Belgium had to resort to an exchange stabilization fund. It chose to reduce the weight in gold of the Belgian franc and to maintain convertibility. Nationals who had exported their capital or had hoarded gold returned their capital or their gold to the Banque de Belgique in order to obtain a quantity of Belgian francs larger than that which they had used to acquire the gold or currency. They bought back Belgian francs before the rise of domestic prices or the increase in the prices of Belgian shares on the stock exchange. 'Devaluation', that old acquaintance of our French kings exemplified by the name Philip the Fair, was capable of causing a massive return of gold and currencies to the coffers of the central bank and of acting on the discount and interest rates. It was thus able to support the economic recovery in Belgium.

The other countries of the gold bloc did not follow Belgium's example. But the crisis of the French franc in September 1936 caused the devaluation of the other currencies in the gold bloc (including Italy). Faced with the collapse of the pound sterling and the dollar, the French franc had remained resistant, despite the budget deficit, difficulties in agriculture and the industrial and trade crises. The French franc had even formed a pole of attraction for migrating capital in 1931, 1932, 1933 and 1934. The gold reserves of the Banque de France had reached an unprecedented level: over 80 billion francs Poincaré. Hence, the franc was in a very strong position. And it would take many setbacks and mistakes to compromise it. The economic recovery that began to take shape at the end of 1935 and the beginning of 1936 seemed for a moment to prove wrong those who claimed that a devaluation of the franc was desirable and inevitable.

Like the Belgian franc, the French franc had succumbed to a domestic crisis. However, the crisis of the French franc differed from that of the Belgian franc because of a feature that merits greater attention: the French banks were healthy. Their assets were not being 'frozen'. The budget deficit, the threat of draconian taxation and particularly the threats directed at capital owners had provoked the classic responses of exporting capital and hoarding gold. With the banknote remaining convertible, the gold reserves of the Banque de France fell victim to such sudden withdrawals that, despite the strongest assurances voiced in the *Journal Officiel*, a first devaluation of the franc was announced. It was a unique devaluation – accompanied by a tripartite monetary agreement between the United States, Great Britain and France, which fixed a higher gold point of 49 milligrams of gold and a lower gold point of 43 milligrams for the French franc by the law of 1 October 1936. These gold points had to be respected and defended by an exchange stabilization fund, inspired by the British [Exchange Equalization] account. The fund still exists today but operates under different conditions: a second devaluation of the franc occurred in June 1937, transforming the franc into a so-called 'floating' currency, the rate of which depended on supply and demand, under the supervision of the 'Stabilization Fund'.

The gold points have disappeared. In theory, the situation of the franc is the same as that of the pound sterling, which is also a floating currency. However, the franc has not been incorporated into the sterling bloc, and its value against the sterling has depreciated significantly. There are all the practical differences between the sterling and the franc that separate a floating currency firmly controlled by a stabilization account richly endowed with gold and currencies from a floating currency defended by a stabilization account whose endowment cannot frighten speculators on floating currencies empowered by the budgetary imbalance in the balance of accounts. The elimination of this double imbalance requires the stability of the franc.

Our main focus here must be on the franc crisis and its characteristics. The crisis was original in that it occurred at a time when agricultural and industrial difficulties were getting resolved. It broke out in a country with a healthy banking system. It merits being classified under the category of domestic crises: foreign involvement in the suspension of the franc's convertibility was completely secondary. The export of capital and the hoarding of gold did the essential work in the crisis, as they had in Belgium. And this had been the work of French nationals. The budgetary imbalance, aggravated by the railway deficit, caused inflation that put new francs into circulation, which were almost immediately converted into gold at the Banque de France. The economic depression, largely alleviated, played a secondary role in the fall of the franc.

The enormity of the public debt (war, reparations, armaments, railway deficit, public works), the impossibility of reducing it by conversion, the resulting tax needs, the draconian tax burdens and the threats made against capital caused the fall of the franc, the export of capital, hoarding and then a new fall of the franc. In circumstances such as these, any recovery would have been chimerical. Thus, France will be absent from our study of the recovery; for the most significant indices, including the general index of production, all remain unfavourable.[571]

The United States fared better after a more serious economic crisis.

571. SDN, 'Rapport au Conseil' (Sep. 1937).

2.) The United States

Credit has a reputation for working miracles; however, these miracles have a painful aftermath. The American crisis was a crisis of credit.[572]

But it was also an overproduction crisis. For through credit and thanks to it, America was able to develop its productive forces beyond what was necessary.

This situation, probably unique in history, can be explained by the war, by the post-war period and by the role that America played at that time, from 1914 to 1927. We choose the year 1927 because it was the date when European production was reconstituted after having been severely curtailed by the war (see fig. 1.6).

At that time, America would be forced to resolve the unprecedented situation in which the war and the post-war period had placed her, without her knowing it: a situation of bankruptcy, overproduction, massive unemployment and the threat of revolution.[573]

For almost 20 years, from 1914 to 1927, the United States had supplied the world. The war had very seriously compromised the production of the belligerent countries that were forced to purchase from America the products that they were no longer producing themselves. The rest of the world, which had depended on Europe for its supply of industrial products, had to turn to the United States to satisfy the demand for industrial products that Europe was no longer able to deliver. The war therefore exerted a profound influence on the economic situation of the United States, transforming it into the world's supplier of agricultural and industrial goods. It was a situation without precedent in history.

In response to this almost limitless demand, America had to develop its productive forces beyond measure: its agricultural as well as its industrial production. It was successful beyond all expectations, thanks to the magnificent progress made in the cultivation of cereals and industrial manufacturing (Taylorism), and thanks to the remarkable extension of the areas cultivated with wheat, cotton and maize. The accomplishments of the creative genius of science and the efficiency of capitalism can be measured in the *Statistical Abstract of the United States*: wheat production grew from 763 million bushels in 1913 to 952 bushels in 1919; steel production increased from 26 million tons in 1910 to 42 million in 1923. This phase in economic history singularly refutes the copious literature devoted to the decline of capitalism, to its ageing and impotence. Evidence of its vitality was clearly revealed in the war itself, where economic factors played a role comparable to that of armies.

During the war, America supplied the Allies with food, raw materials and ammunition. The statistics on American foreign trade, the enormous excess of exports over imports, reflected this phenomenon: US exports went from $2.5 billion in 1913 to $8 billion in 1919, while imports increased from $1.8 billion to $5 billion over the same

---

572. T. E. Gregory, *Gold, Unemployment and Capitalism* (London: P. S. King, 1933), 146–61 (on 'The great American panic of 1933').

573. Bertrand de Jouvenel, *La crise du capitalisme américain* (Paris: Gallimard, 1933). Edmond Chassery, *Les illusions de l'Amérique en matière de crédit, de 1914 à l'éxperience Roosevelt*, thesis, Faculty of Law, University of Paris (Paris: Librairie technique et économique, 1937).

years. The United States presented all the appearances of the greatest prosperity: rising prices, increased production, an increasingly favourable balance of foreign trade, and high wages.

At first sight, the end of the war appeared to bring an end to this prosperity. The United States was severely impacted by the crisis of 1920, which was marked by massive overproduction, a sudden and steep fall in prices and much unemployment. The trade balance became less favourable by 1922, when imports were $3.112 million, and exports were $3.831 million.

It could be believed that the end of the war marked the return to a normal situation, that the United States was, from then on, reduced to its pre-war outlets, and that the crisis would be deep and long-lasting for the United States. But this would be to misunderstand the situation. The world was to remain dependent on the United States for another seven years. With the peace concluded, the restored freedom of navigation favoured international trade. America would retain very large outlets for its exports.

If the belligerent countries were to be rebuilt, they had to rely largely on the United States.

Table 1.156 US Exports to Europe, 1922–1932 (millions of $)

1922	2,083	1928	2,374
1925	2,600	1929	2,340
1926	2,310	1932	784
1927	2,312		

Source: *Statistical Abstract of the United States* 55 (1933): 412, tab. 467.

For France, whose richest provinces had been devastated, the evidence was clear: it spent 100 billion francs on reconstruction. Yet the other belligerent countries also had immense needs.

England, less affected than others, had to rebuild its stocks and industries. Famine and misery reigned over Central Europe. The Revolution was raging in Russia, which stopped supplying Europe. Germany had been drained of its raw materials and livestock by the war and had to rebuild its stocks and rejuvenate its industries. In addition, Germany, its territories severed, tried to restore its pre-war productive powers within the limits of its new borders. It had to rationalize its industries. It needed machinery and food, which it imported mainly from the United States, whose methods Germany would try to emulate.

It was only in 1926 that European production returned to its 1913 levels. The League of Nations has established a statistical index of considerable importance (see fig. 1.6); for it demonstrates that it took almost ten years for European production to recover. However, the population of Europe had increased compared to 1913. We can therefore assume that Europe only returned to a more or less normal economic situation by 1927–28. At that point, the index of European production clearly surpassed that of 1913. Although it would be interesting to follow, country by country, the slow recovery of European agriculture (cereals, livestock) and industry, this is not our task here. Limiting ourselves to the United States, we will emphasize that until 1927–28, the

United States enjoyed almost limitless outlets in the world. The United States maintained its monopoly, supplying the world with agricultural and industrial products (see tab. 1.157).

Table 1.157 US Exports, 1923–1932 (billions of $)

1923	4.1	1927	4.8
1924	4.5	1928	5.1
1925	4.9	1929	5.2
1926	4.8	1932	1.6

Source: *Statistical Abstract of the United States* 55 (1933): 400, tab. 456.
Note: It was exports to Europe which accounted for the decline from 1929 to 1932 (see tab. 1.156).

The war and post-war period provided the impetus for the development of productive forces unique in history. And the capitalist system made it possible to solve the problem by creating the capital and the necessary enterprises. But by the same token, the world was unwittingly moving toward an unprecedented crisis of exceptional severity – the crisis from which we are emerging, and which was reflected in particular by an excessive development of the forces of production, principally and above all in the United States, which was equipped to supply the entire world with food and industrial products.

Once Europe had been reconstructed and could once again compete with the United States, an unprecedented economic shock took place, a shock which became all the more violent over time as Europe restored and improved its agriculture and industry. Two productive powers, two forms of capitalism, were clashing more and more violently: American capitalism and European capitalism, and finally, more recently, Japanese capitalism. The shock of these two or three blocs would cause an explosive fall in prices, which, after 1929, was to become catastrophic. Prices, which naturally tended to fall immediately after the war, experienced a tremendous drop with the usual consequences but intensified from 1929 onward.[574] Why was this date significant?

Between 1927 and 1929 the United States experienced a classic period of prosperity, one which resulted from the development of new industries. According to this hypothesis, the United States, which until 1927 was rebuilding the world, extended its prosperity by developing its car industry, aviation, radio, refrigeration industry and so on.

In 1929, a classic cyclical crisis was affecting the American car industry. We have explored this in detail above. The period of prosperity had been stimulated by car production. Yet this cyclical crisis in the United States broke out in a world ill-prepared to respond to it. The European market was closed. Europe was again in competition with the United States and was a formidable competitor thanks to its lower wages, the push to rationalize its production and its devalued currencies. This was to result in an exceptionally severe overproduction crisis in the United States.

574. Jean Lescure, *Hausses et baisses des prix de longue durée* (Paris: Domat-Montchrestien, 1933).

American agriculture had been extended during and after the war in order to supply Europe. Industry had developed for the same reason. However, in 1929 European production was almost 30 per cent greater than its pre-war levels.

A state of chronic crisis and depression ensued, characterized by a profound drop in prices, agricultural prices in particular. For despite the narrowing of its outlets, American agriculture maintained the same production levels:

Table 1.158 Corn Production in the United States (millions of bushels)

1929	812
1930	857
1931	900

No source given.

Corn production was being increased in Europe (France, Italy and Germany). Whereas industrial production adapted with a massive reduction of supply, agricultural production remained unaffected by the drop in prices. The general price index for agricultural products collapsed, falling more significantly than the general index. The price of wheat fell from $1 per bushel in February 1929 to 35 cents at the end of 1932. The United States was suffering from an excessive development of its productive forces because it no longer enjoyed the same outlets. It was necessary to adapt.

Yet, some maintain that the development of the forces of production in the United States was inexplicable. Europe bought from the United States, but from 1914 to 1926, it provided nothing in exchange, since it did not produce anything. How does one explain the economic growth in the United States? By credit: its miracles or its abuse, if you will. Credit had also made this immense development of the global forces of production possible.

Short-term credit. – We must now describe how this pyramid of credit was built. It could not have occurred at any other time in history. Capitalism, a master of building credit, was capable of feeding the prosperity, the illusion.

On the eve of the 1914 war, powerful issuing banks were to be found everywhere: the creation of forced exchange banknotes [*billets de banque à cours forcé*] gave states great purchasing power. However, the procedure was not new; it had already been used in the nineteenth century. One would do better by resorting to bank money.

Powerful deposit banks existed everywhere, and they now created purchasing power much like banks of issue. It was a major revolution. For a long time, deposit banks had received deposits and consented to loans with the amounts deposited. Nowadays the situation is somewhat reversed: a state or an individual brings treasury bills or promissory notes to these banks, and the bank credits the state or the individual with a current account for the corresponding amount. Next to banknote inflation, there was now deposit inflation. Paper money and bank money combined their efforts and effectiveness. The League of Nations provides us with the figures for bank deposits in North

America.[575] From 1914 to 1927, they had tripled from $8.732 billion in 1913 to $25,800 billion in 1927. The number of banks rose from 8,548 in 1913 to 28,218 in 1929.

Long-term credit. – Moreover, in the United States, the deposit banks held government securities against their deposits and credited the treasury in current accounts. They would buy government securities and credit private individuals, who then subscribed to further government bonds. A circuit was established. Securities were subscribed to by the billions, and loans were given on mortgages by the billions. The state's debt grew from $1,193 million in 1912 to $25,482 million in 1919. Companies issued shares and bonds in massive quantities. From 1927 to 1929, some $18 billion were issued. Mortgages grew at a similar pace. In 1933, the amount of mortgage debts was as follows:

(billions of $)

Cities	27.0
Countryside	8.5
Total	35.5

Everywhere during the war, such credit practices had been used and abused. Billions of banknotes and bank deposits were created, securities were issued (government securities and bonds), and mortgage loans were granted. And it was thanks to credit that the American farmer and American industries were able to increase production. The American farmer went into debt to acquire his land, cultivate it and purchase modern equipment (agriculture is a true industry in the United States). Through the issue of shares and bonds American industry expanded. The American state paid for its purchases and those of its allies with government borrowing. Production, which developed thanks to credit, found an outlet thanks to this same credit.

This resulted in states becoming indebted to each other: the indebtedness of European states to the United States amounted to tens of billions of dollars. The indebtedness of individuals also reached tens of billions of dollars.

During the war, debt had been primarily the debts of nation states. But after the peace, the debts were of individuals or municipalities (in Germany), and the railways which were borrowing money. France and Germany were borrowing from the United States to pay for materials used in reconstruction, mainly raw materials (copper, cotton, crude oil). Germany, which still inspired confidence, obtained vast amounts of credit in the United States. The United States made unsecured advances to Germany; American banks held enormous debt-claims on German industrialists and merchants in 1931, at the time of the crisis of the German mark.

575. SDN, *Deuxième rapport provisoire de la Délégation de l'Or du Comité financier* (Geneva, 1931), 123.

In short, the war had built a house of cards in receivables and debts, especially in the United States.

Credit had sustained many illusions in the world and in the United States especially. It created the illusion of unprecedented prosperity in the United States. It hid the essential truth that the credit granted by the United States was largely consumer credit. The US sold on credit to Europe for the war effort and to reconstitute its productive forces.

The US granted billions in credits to Europe, without Europe's production increasing significantly, that is, without Europe's ability to pay being increased. Moreover, American production power had increased so much that America became more and more self-sufficient and had little to import from Europe: at most, American tourism was to provide Europe with some means of repayment. The United States was lending without hope of being repaid; it could not be reimbursed. And whether it liked it or not, the United States' credit policy had turned into a magnificent bit of charity work: the American economy worked at full strength and on credit for nearly 20 years to enable Europe to go to war and then to reconstitute its productive forces initiated by the war. But these credits have by and large been lost. It was impossible for Europe to make the necessary transfers for reimbursement. This situation by itself was not catastrophic for the United States, since it was rich enough to carry on without receiving interest and depreciation from Europe. Although the United States could survive, the edifice of credit was collapsing. This collapse was to momentarily shake the whole economic structure and the capitalist order, which was itself based upon credit. The United States was doomed to go through an unprecedented credit crisis, which was to take hold in 1932–33. The talk then was of frozen credit, but it would be more accurate to call it lost credit. Let us distinguish between credit on foreign accounts and internal credit.

Foreign accounts receivable were largely irrecoverable because the United States had closed its borders to imports through their almost prohibitive tariffs; because it had its own large merchant fleet since the end of the war; because it had repatriated American securities held by Europe during the war; and because it had developed its international money market and pretended to be the world's banker. The only way in which Europe could free itself from the United States was by developing tourism.

Yet the trade balance remained favourable to the United States vis-à-vis Europe; the other elements of the balance such as capital were too. The spending of American tourists in Europe was insufficient to provide Europe with the means to settle its debt.

Europe could probably have also sent gold. But Europe would have fallen back into the erratic system of exchange rates; and gold would have been insufficient for Europe to pay off its enormous debts to the United States. Besides, the United States believed it had too much gold and fought against further gold imports. This was why the European states were forced to suspend their payments to the United States. This was why arrangements had to be made with private debtors in Germany. England and France fully honoured their commercial commitments to American banks and settled government loans other than those owed to the US Treasury as loans from the Treasury.

Lacking sufficient transfer possibilities, Europe was unable to settle its debts to the United States. There were two consequences: the first, for the US Treasury, and the second, for the banks. The first consequence was not too serious for the United States:

America had largely settled its public debt in 1914. The US government's debt was not catastrophic for its budget.

However, the banks affected by the default of foreign debtors were seriously threatened from 1931. President Hoover proposed a moratorium on reparations to save American banks threatened by the German crisis. Yet the difficulties that America was facing also stemmed from the domestic credit crisis. The federal budget and those of the states and cities were in deficit.

Farmers, the railways and companies of every sort were heavily in debt. Mortgage lending allowed the cities to make up for time lost during the war by building new houses. Long-term debts were considerable. Although the banks did not suffer any losses on their government bonds portfolios (the US government regularly paid its public debts), the same did not apply to municipal debts and all other debts. Yet the reason for the deficiency was different from that which motivated the default of foreign debtors. It would be the clash of two production rivals, America and Europe, once the latter recovered, that ignited the spark. The collapse of selling prices of goods rendered debtors insolvent.

Let us summarize. The taxes coming in were poor; municipalities were failing here and there. The railways and industrialists whose business had declined and whose selling prices had dropped considerably often suffered losses. American securities went through an unprecedented crisis: shares failed to pay dividends, bonds failed to pay interest and were depreciating. Mortgage loans reached considerable sums. Yet mortgages were in the hands of the banks and even of deposit banks. Rural banks in particular, which were very numerous in the United States, were lending mortgages to farmers. Facing price rises and growing agricultural gains, farmers took on heavy debt to increase their production and purchase land. As a result of the fall in prices, these farmers' debt obligations became largely irrecoverable.

In the cities, the 1929 crisis had caused massive unemployment. Houses had no tenants, or else rent prices were reduced. Homeowners, heavily burdened by local taxes, were unable to pay the interest and depreciation on their mortgages. This disruption of urban mortgage credit was threatening the life insurance companies, which were so powerful in the United States, and which – in the absence of compulsory social insurance – provided for a very great number of Americans in their old age.

After a period of euphoria, the exaggeration of credit during the war and post-war period placed the United States in a tragic situation in which it ran the risk of a possible social revolution. The shock of production and overproduction left 12 million workers unemployed. Despite imperfect statistics, the extent of the unemployment is undeniable. Poverty was apparent in the United States in 1931 and 1932: beggars were a common sight in the cities. Yesterday's high-earning worker had to rely on charity and public assistance. If we count five people per family, 12 million unemployed breadwinners represented as many as 60 million Americans in distress, in a population of 120 million inhabitants.

Does one liquidate the defaulting debtors, farmers and homeowners? It was tried. Serious disturbances resulted in the countryside. No successful bidders could be found for the goods on sale. Other Americans were themselves threatened by the credit crisis, or they abstained in protest against these forced auctions. Not to mention losses on shares, bonds, taxes and lost rents, all Americans were threatened by the banks' suspension of payments. Between 1929 and 1933, thousands of banks were liquidated. Depositors' losses were considerable. General mistrust prevailed in the banking sector. The banks had to endure the withdrawal of deposits. The insolvency of banks and companies of all kinds increased with the drop in prices. Yet the cheque was the primary instrument of exchange, the real currency. Around 1933, the entire American population – unemployed or not – felt threatened, and the insecurity was general. Hence the literature in America[576] which denounced poverty in the midst of plenty and the calls for a surgical operation to remedy an economic situation capable of shaking the whole social order should it be allowed to persist.

President Hoover tried in vain to restore the economic situation, engineer a recovery and support failing businesses (banks and railways) through the construction of public works, the purchase of cereal crops from the Farm Board, the creation of a National Credit Corporation and then the Reconstitution Finance Corporation. The fall in prices grew worse. The mistrust was general. Businesses were recording losses, and businessmen abstained from investing in new enterprises.

In vain the Federal Reserve Banks systematically degraded the credit rate: the discount rate at the Federal Reserve Bank of New York was at 1.5 per cent on 7 May 1931. In vain the banks placed increasing sums at the disposal of the market through the policy of the 'open market'. Credit was almost free. Yet nobody was asking for it. Prices continued their uninterrupted decline. The capitalist order was experiencing a crisis of confidence which was reflected in the collapse of securities issues. The capitalist machinery ground to a halt.

Table 1.159 Issues of Transferable Securities in the United States, 1911–1932

Stocks and Bonds (billions of $)							
1911	1.7	1916	2.1	1921	2.3	1926	5.2
1912	2.2	1917	1.5	1922	3.0	1927	7.3
1913	1.6	1918	1.3	1923	3.2	1928	7.8
1914	1.4	1919	2.7	1924	3.8	1929	10.0
1915	1.4	1920	2.9	1925	4.7	1932	0.6

Source: *Statistical Abstract of the United States* 55 (1933): 273, tab. 295.

Although not all were ruined, all Americans were affected. Farm owners were burdened with debts. Industrialists who had suffered losses refused to invest in new enterprises. Factories producing the means of production were short of orders, and steel production declined from 56 million tonnes in 1929 to 13 million tonnes in 1932.

576. See the essays by Stuart Chase, Rexford Tugwell and Adolph Berle in the *New Republic*.

Private property, private initiative and private enterprise were ruined. The richest and most prosperous country in the world now appeared to be the most tragically destitute. The crisis was so serious, so widespread, such a challenge to public authority and a threat to law and order that the president of the United States attempted to overcome it by resorting to entirely new methods. He chose to act instead of letting it happen. His policies were inspired by the work of American economists, who had elaborated a policy capable of alleviating the crisis, unemployment and the insolvency of the banks.

The crisis presented a dual aspect: the law of supply and demand had triggered the collapse of prices. The shock of increased production as a result of the war and the reconstituted production [of other countries] rendered part of the American productive forces unuseable and useless. A liquidation was necessary in the field of production. Production had to be limited to stem the fall in prices and restore the equilibrium between supply and demand.

However, the extension of production had only been possible thanks to an unprecedented exaggeration of credit (banknotes, deposits, transferable securities, mortgages, etc.). A settlement of these immense credit operations (during and just after the war) was imperative. It was a liquidation – that is to say, a reduction of debts sufficient for the surviving claims to be paid. Here two methods were conceivable: the simple reduction (cutting it by one-half, one-third or one-quarter); or a reduction by artificially raising prices and the use of monetary sorcery.

A reduction by one-half, one-third or one-quarter would have required settling all of the debts one by one – a liquidation of all the banks, all the businesses, of the farmers in debt and of mortgages. This would mean revising millions of dollars in debts. The president hesitated in the face of such a formidable, lengthy and possibly impractical undertaking. Where was one to find the courts, the bankruptcy trustees and liquidators capable of correctly carrying out this revision of debts and receivables? This would have prolonged the poisoned atmosphere of mistrust, bank closures and the immobilization of deposits. The president opted for monetary bankruptcy, for devaluation.

In order to appreciate the president's policies, one must examine the economic situation of the United States at the time when the president took office. America was on the verge of suffocating for lack of instruments of exchange. The banking system was threatened from all sides. Moratoria followed one after the other. Banks were closing in several states. Gold was being hoarded; capital was being exported. In a country where the cheque functioned as the main instrument of exchange, the situation could not last without becoming extremely dangerous. Exchanges, the lifeblood of the economy, were in danger of becoming paralysed, or, in any case, stifled. Facing such a threat, the president would try: first, to rebuild credit by a policy of rehabilitating the banks and a monetary policy designed to raise prices; second, to reduce agricultural production and reorganize industrial production; and third, to provide industries with new orders and assistance to the unemployed. Unemployment is a social consequence of an economic crisis. By fighting against the economic crisis, unemployment could be tackled. Public assistance alone was no cure-all; it purports to give work to workers who have none.

From there, a three-pronged approach was taken: first, acting on the currency and credit; second, acting on agricultural production (Agricultural Adjustment

Administration) or on industrial production (National Recovery Administration); and third, fighting unemployment through the creation of public works and assistance for the unemployed.

Currency crises have been accompanied by the flight of capital in the face of the national currency. International gold movements, unique in history, were the consequence (see tab. 1.160). The massive return of capital from abroad greatly contributed to the drop in short- and long-term rates, thus preparing the path to the recovery which we are about to examine.

Table 1.160 International Movements of Gold, 1931–1934

Surplus Imports/Surplus Exports	
Great Britain	
1931	– $143,729,000 at $20.67 per ounce
1932	+ $84,585,000
1933	+ $677,405,000
United States	
1931	+ $459,104,000 at $20.67 per ounce
1932	– $446,216,00
1933	– $173,455,000
1934	+ $1,131,934,000 at $35 per ounce
France	
1931	+ $718,176,000 at $20.67 per ounce
1932	+ $828,178,000
1933	+ $243,944,000
1934	+ $406,949,000 at $35 per ounce

Source: *Federal Reserve Bulletin*, 1934 and 1935. See also 'Statistics of International Capital Transactions of the United States, April–July 1937', *Federal Reserve Bulletin* (Oct. 1937): 998–1001, which provides very detailed figures.

The trends have since been reversed to the detriment of our country.

Table 1.161 Gold Reserves at the Banque de France

End of 1932	82 billion francs
End of 1936	60 billion francs

No source given.

In 1937, the influx of gold into the United States and in Great Britain was such (new gold production and exported or 'de-hoarded' capital) that gold was to become 'sterilized'.[577]

577. *Travaux du Congrès international de sciences économiques*, vol. 1, *Économie politique: L'étalon or et son avenir* (Paris: Domat-Montchrestien, 1937).

§16. – The economic recovery of 1933–1937

The recovery from 1933 to 1937 has defied an abundant literature devoted to the crisis and the end of capitalism. However, the current recovery presents many original features, even if we find at its root the essential feature of previous recoveries: the return of profit margins and the increasing investment of savings.

In detailing the crisis of 1929, we noted the specific circumstances under which it occurred: a downward trend in prices, a massive and growing gap between the prices of agricultural products or raw materials and the prices of manufactured goods, a massive gap between wholesale and retail prices, a significant gap between wage rates and selling prices (the high level of retail prices acting as a barrier to the reduction of wages), and a symmetrical disruption of foreign trade and the volumes of exports and imports.

Under the influence of a depression like no other in history, these imbalances were gradually corrected. Production and exchanges, which had been made difficult or even paralysed by these serious disruptions of incomes and prices, were recovering. Capital was reinvested. The spirit of enterprise was renewed. Although the depression was exceptionally long and abnormally intense, natural laws have corrected these burdensome imbalances. The world has experienced a new era of prosperity. The severe disequilibrium of prices and incomes, which we view as essential to crises, can be compared to the warping of rails on a train track due to the expansion of metal. Trains run with difficulty. The gaps in the prices of goods and services which preceded the crisis caused a slowdown in trade and production. As a result of the war, they exhibited an intensity unique to history, but they were gradually corrected, after having caused unprecedented monetary troubles, prompting governmental interventions comparable to the surgeon's operations in human pathology. Harmony was restored between price levels on the indexes, between the volumes of imports and exports, and between costs and prices. Initiatives that would have been considered dangerous in the past had become 'viable'. Growth had resumed.

The publications of the League of Nations, the indexes of wholesale and retail prices, and the indexes of import and export prices establish this reorganization of price indexes (wholesale, retail, raw materials, manufactured goods, agricultural and industrial products) around a common standard. This regrouping was fundamental to the equilibrium of markets and trade. For 'values are traded against other values'. Economic equilibrium is a balancing of values. And the value equilibrium regulates and dominates equilibrium of quantities.

As we see in table 1.162, plant products and textiles in particular rose far more than animal and mineral products.

Table 1.162 Sauerbeck-Paish Index of Commodity Prices

Products:	*Plant*	*Animal*	*Mineral*	*Textile*
1933	60	105	107	67
1936	76	109	118	83

Source: See translator's source note to table A1.

Wholesale prices rose more than retail prices. The unfortunate gap between wholesale and retail prices was greatly reduced, particularly in France, Belgium, England and the United States.[578]

The League of Nations calculated gold price indexes which completely confirmed this global recovery of prices in the largest categories (see tab. 1.163).

Table 1.163 Movement of the Gold Price in the Major Commodity Categories, 1933–1936 (1929 = 100)

	1933	*1934*	*1935*	*1936*
Foodstuffs	45.5	41.5	40.5	42.5
Raw and Semi-Manufactured Products	40.0	39.5	39.5	41.5
Finished goods	56.0	50.0	48.0	48.0
Aggregate	46.5	43.5	42.5	43.5

Source: SDN, *La production mondiale et les prix, 1936–37* (Geneva, 1937), 103. The gap between import and export prices has been reduced. The account balances returned to equilibrium. SDN, 'Aperçu du commerce extérieur', in *Revue de la situation économique Mondiale, 1936–1937* (Geneva, 1937), 149–50.

However, the growth, like the depression and the crisis before it, presents original features. The recovery was not spontaneous everywhere. State intervention was necessary. We live in a time of 'experiments'. Massive rearmament in the European states has largely absorbed capital and supplied heavy industries with orders. It would be most imprudent to not take this into account when formulating prognoses, the prerogative of any scientific inquiry, whose role is to enable us to know in order to predict [*savoir pour prévoir*].

These observations, however, do not have the same importance in all the countries. In some, such as Britain, the British Empire, Belgium, Holland, Switzerland and Sweden, the recovery has been largely spontaneous. Elsewhere it was *managed* [*dirigée*], and we want to stress the important or dominant role of government intervention. There are subtle differences between the countries in which the recovery has been directed by the state. In Germany, the role of the state has been quite dominant. In the United States, government intervention has been more modest. And the managed recovery [*reprise dirigée*] only has the ambition to prepare for a spontaneous recovery for which it merely paves the way. Private initiative is expected to take over from public initiative.

But everywhere, the growth has been expressed by the upward trend in the most significant graphs: the production indexes, trade, employment and short- and long-term credit. Unemployment, the extent of which has been such a preoccupation of governments, is declining everywhere and even disappearing. An improvement in the political climate would do even better.

578. See especially the indexes gathered by the *Federal Reserve Bulletin* (Oct. 1937): 1053–54.

A.) Great Britain[579]

It had been expected that the fall of the pound sterling would lead to a recovery of exports and, through spill-over effects [*par contagion*], to a general economic recovery. But as the pound fell, so did most of the world's currencies. The sterling bloc brought together almost 30 currencies. Recovery in England was first and foremost a domestic recovery. A sudden and unprecedented drop in interest rates (significantly reducing the costs of new enterprises and even those of older ones); a protectionist policy reserving the English market for domestic producers; and a preferential policy (under the Ottawa Agreements of 1932), which substantially improved export conditions in the countries of the Empire, provided the initial push that 'kick-started' the growth. After that, the growth fuelled itself, as it had always done at other points in British history. However, foreign investments and the corresponding export of goods and equipment did not play the same role as they had in previous periods of prosperity.

The fall in interest deserves the highest priority in our study of the recovery. It found expression in the gigantic conversion, the most colossal in financial history, of 'war loans' at 5 per cent to 3.5 per cent, which involved capital of nearly 200 billion francs Poincaré. The sudden and considerable drop in interest must hold our attention: for out of all the factors which contribute to economic recovery, the lowering of interest has always been one of the most effective. The size of the decrease has further increased its effectiveness.

The budget balance, which recovered thanks to a successful combination of tax and savings policies, very quickly restored the international credibility of the pound sterling. Capital which had flowed out in August and September 1931 by hundreds of millions of pounds very quickly returned to the city of London, and this abundance created cheapness.

This classic factor, the abundance of available assets, was not alone in causing this remarkable drop in interest rates, however.[580] Normally their influence has been, first and foremost, on the short-term money market and the discount rate. This action has manifested itself. Yet simultaneously, thanks to the balancing of the budget and the removal of the threat of massive state borrowings, the interest rate has also been significantly reduced. A new development has occurred that is particularly noteworthy: the banks, through their policy of buying government securities, have encouraged the rise in prices on the stock exchange, prepared the conversion, and strongly supported the drop in long-term money. This 'open market' policy has proven singularly effective and very opportune for promoting and intensifying the fall in interest. To be practicable, banks have traditionally used their deposits to purchase government securities.

---

579. London Economic Service; the *Economist* (Trade Supplement); and the *Times, Trade and Engineering Supplement.*

580. Robert Lasson, *La baisse de l'intérêt en Grande-Bretagne de 1932 à 1936*, thesis, Faculty of Law, University of Paris (Paris: Pichon & Durand-Auzias, 1936).

In France, transactions of this kind would be considered immobilization by our credit companies and are therefore impossible. Only savings bank deposits can be used for government securities in France.

Yet we must stress the novelty of the practice. Open market operations had up to this point been used to bring about the decrease in discount rates, to act on the money market by placing at its disposal larger quantities of money, or even to cause prices to rise by applying the quantitative theory. The policy practised in Great Britain since 1931, which has been imitated in the United States, is in our view very different: it has resulted in the increase in government securities and the decrease in interest, that is to say, in long-term money. However, it was the rate of long-term money that was most effective in encouraging the spirit of enterprise, when it coincided with the drop in raw materials (mineral ores, metals, textiles, construction materials) and machinery. This was precisely the case in Great Britain in 1932.

But another original factor helped the economic recovery: Great Britain's adoption of a protectionist policy. Customs revenue not only facilitated the balanced budget, indirectly contributing to the monetary recovery and to the drop in the money rate, but also, by reserving the domestic market for national industry and by creating privileged outlets for it in all the countries of the British Empire though the Ottawa Agreements, supported the recovery and encouraged the spirit of enterprise. The numerous and comprehensive production indexes that we now have at our disposal, in particular those found in the *Economist* or the publication of the London Economic Service, have allowed us to confirm that the industries producing for the domestic market were the first to successfully put their unemployed back to work.[581]

Export industries made progress later, as the economic growth spread globally. The rise in the prices of agricultural products and raw materials gradually restored the purchasing power of the population in that half of the world which depended on agriculture or the production of raw materials to survive: South America, Australia, New Zealand, Canada, India, Egypt and the Balkans. These countries bought more products manufactured in Great Britain, and conversely, Great Britain bought more agricultural products and raw materials from them. The recovery of foreign trade in England was due to this factor, far more than to the devaluation of the pound sterling.

More recently, in 1937, the significant armament production undertaken by the government amplified the growth, as it had done in Germany during the period of economic expansion from 1876 to 1900 (see chap. 1, §11, on the 1900 crisis).

The recent economic recovery in Britain, however, displayed the general characteristics of previous growth periods. The reduction of costs (particularly through the drop in money rates) while selling prices remained stable or even rose (thanks in particular to protectionism, whose effects are impossible to quantify) re-ignited the spirit of enterprise. Profits increased, and issues of transferable securities, which had fallen to an all-time low, intensified (see tab. 1.164). Factories sped up production.

---

581. Maurice Byé, 'La reprise britannique et ses causes', *Revue d'économie politique* 49, no. 2 (1935): 247–84.

Table 1.164 Issues of Securities in Britain, 1929–1936 (New capital in millions of £)

1929	253	1934	150
1931	88	1935	182
1932	113	1936	217
1933	132		

Source: Figures according to the Midland Bank; cf. the *Economist*.

Statistics taken from companies' balance sheets now provide us with a better picture of profits. From 1933 onward, companies' profits made progress; however, the balance sheets for 1933 recorded the previous year. Thus, in 1933 the results from 1932 were released. In its annual review of economic and commercial history, the *Economist* publishes data on the balance sheets of nearly 2,000 companies. The improvement in profits had preceded and signalled the economic recovery (see tab. 1.165). We cannot emphasize enough the fact that, as early as 1932, companies' directors were informed of this improvement which became public knowledge in 1933.

Table 1.165 Quarterly Net Profits for 1,945 Companies in England

	Number of Companies	*1932 (1,000s of £)*	*1933 (1,000s of £)*
1st Quarter	562	57,105	52,046
2nd Quarter	612	51,164	**52,871**
3rd Quarter	307	16,284	15,394
4th Quarter	464	16,101	21,116
Total	1,945	140,756	141,428
1933–34			
	Number of Companies	*1933 (1,000s of £)*	*1934 (1,000s of £)*
1st Quarter	547	52,922	55,751
2nd Quarter	642	56,970	67,334
3rd Quarter	318	13,425	17,139
4th Quarter	468	21,520	28,611
Total	1,475	144,839	168,837

Source: The *Economist*. [The figure in boldface marks the quarter in which net profits first surpassed those of the corresponding quarter in the previous year.]

The improvement has continued through 1935, 1936 and 1937. An increase in the issues of securities accompanied the improvement in profits.

The improvement in profits has overtaken the increase in production, the rise in prices and the expansion of foreign trade. We can follow the development of these phenomena closely, specifying their beginning and their sequence, as we have done for the American crisis in 1929 (and for the United States in the recovery of 1933).

However, as in other periods of prosperity, the construction industry led the way. Refuting the Marxist theories of excess capital and the impossibility of using new savings without further aggravating overproduction, and denying the often-refuted theories of the 'general glut', Great Britain was to rebuild its house, raze its slums and replace them with cottages, transforming the physiognomy of its major manufacturing cities.[582]

Out of all the industries, construction was the one most liable to be stimulated by the fall of interest rates. During the depression, with the almost complete halt of construction, the cost of materials had dropped considerably. The construction industry was at the centre of the recovery in Britain (see tab. 1.166). If we look at the unemployment figures and the decrease in the number of unemployed, we find that, out of all the large industries in England, the construction industry put the most people back to work: around 182,000 between 1932 and 1935.[583]

Table 1.166 The Construction Industry in Britain, 1931–1936*

	Number of Buildings Constructed	*Private Residences*	*Public Buildings*	*Cost of Construction (1,000s of £)*
1931	194,944	131,656	63,288	63,010
1932	201,976	133,486	68,490	66,254
1933	218,313	169,100	49,213	83,682
1934	363,669	260,327	53,342	95,563
1935	318,644	275,299	43,345	114,308
1936	339,528	274,654	64,874	117,032

* These figures need to be compared with the amount of the securities issued. The importance of the construction industry in the economic recovery becomes clearer.

No source given. [See the special issue devoted to the construction industry in the *Times, Trade and Engineering Supplement*, Dec. 1935.]

The British car industry, which had been lagging behind for so long, gave this growth period one of its defining features (tab. 1.167). Together with the construction industry, it appears to be one of the leading industries, along with the aviation industry.

Table 1.167 British Car Production, 1929–1932 (in 1,000s)

1929	241	1933	296
1930	241	1934	355
1931	226	1935	417
1932	248	1936	481

Source: Society of Motor Manufacturers and Traders in League of Nations, *Monthly Bulletin of Statistics* 18, no. 6 (June 1937): 244.

The other industries were soon to follow: the metal industry, machine manufacturing, shipbuilding and even textiles. Exports picked up again. The armaments industry, which had been neglected for so long, was to drive the iron and steel industries to near exhaustion by 1937. Thanks to the progress of statistics, we can sketch the general lines of this growth in the following table, which is characteristic of economic activity as a whole (see tab. 1.168).

582. See the special issue devoted to the construction industry in the *Times, Trade and Engineering Supplement*, Dec. 1935.

583. *Labour Gazette* (Dec. 1935): 456.

Table 1.168 The Recovery in Great Britain, 1931–1936

	1931	*1932*	*1933*	*1934*	*1935*	*1936*
Employment (1,000s of insured)	9,421	9,348	9,681	10,139	10,377	10,896
% Unemployed in Great Britain and Northern Ireland	21.3	22.1	19.9	16.7	15.5	13.2
Cost of Living (July 1914 = 100)	147	144	140	141	143	147
Retail Price of Foodstuffs (July 1914 = 100)	131	126	120	122	125	130
Industrial Production (incl. mining) (1930 = 100)	90.8	90.4	95.5	106.1	113.6	124.7
Industrial Production (Manufacturing) (1930 = 100)	91.2	91.7	98.0	108.5	117.1	129.4
Total Buildings Constructed	194,944	201,976	218,313	313,669	318,644	339,528
Amount Spent on Construction	63,010	66,254	83,682	95,563	114,308	117,032
Imports (1,000s of £	861,253	701,670	675,016	731,414	756,041	848,936
Exports (incl. re-exports) (1,000s of £)	454,489	416,045	416,990	447,229	481,137	501,135
Cast Iron (1,000s of tonnes)	3,772	3,574	4,136	5,969	6,424	7,685
Steel (1,000s of tonnes)	5,202	5,261	7,024	8,849	9,858	11,698
Coal (1,000s of tonnes)	219,459	208,733	207,112	220,726	222,235	228,525
Shipyards (tonnage launched, gross)	502,500	187,800	133,100	459,900	499,000	856,300
Electricity Produced (millions of units)	11,413	12,241	13,562	15,462	17,568	20,220
Rayon Production (thread) (1,000s of £)	54,600	72,500	84,000	93,000	124,000	145,300
Railway Earnings (1,000s of £)	156,992	143,965	143,925	149,715	151,757	157,807
Company Profits as % of Capital (from the *Economist*)	7.2	5.8	6.1	7.2	8.9	10.6
Bankruptcies	7,999	8,654	7,383	6,431	6,038	5,647
Great Britain's % Share in Commerce of Empire	26.7	27.5	28	29.2	30.1	31.3

Ed. note: Lescure provided no source information; however, employment and cost-of-living statistics were likely taken from the Ministry of Labour, *Twenty-Second Abstract of Labour Statistics of the United Kingdom (1922–1936)* (London: HMSO, 1937).

The most substantial profits were made by the heavy industries, the car industry and aviation. The consumer goods industries' profits were much less favourable. Table 1.169 provides some very interesting figures on profits as a percentage of capital for a variety of companies.

Table 1.169 Profits as a Percentage of Capital in Various Industries in Great Britain, 1933–1937

	1933	*1934*	*1935*	*1936*	*1937*
Heavy Industry	1.6	3.8	8.3	10.3	13.6
Electricity (lighting and power)	8.9	8.6	8.5	9.4	9.6
Cars and Aviation	10.7	16.2	16.2	17.7	20.8
Cotton	0.9	0.7	0.25	1.15	3.5
Shoes	7.4	7.7	8.5	7.8	8.6
Mineral Oils	7.5	8.3	10.4	12.5	21.9
Breweries	12.2	14.6	15.7	14.7	15.9

Source: *The Times, Trade and Engineering Supplement*, May 1938.

Unemployment has decreased considerably (see fig. A2). Wages have increased (see *Labour Gazette*).

B.) Belgium

Much like the recovery in England, the Belgian recovery was largely spontaneous. The Belgian devaluation caused a massive return of exported or hoarded national capital back into Belgian circulation and a parallel increase in metal reserves at the Banque Nationale and some other balance sheet items (hidden gold reserve).[584] Short-term money decreased: the discount outside of the bank went from 2 to 1 per cent, rounded to the nearest whole number. But the most remarkable fact was the more or less free conversion of the public debt and the considerable drop in the interest rate from 5 to 3.5 per cent.

The Belgian recovery can be explained by the movement of costs and of prices which caused a return of profit margins, by an abnormal factor – the Brussels Exhibition and the business activity that resulted from it – and by the global recovery. After considering the various factors in the economic recovery, the latter appears to have been the most important: the Belgian recovery was not confirmed in the production figures, prices or exports until 1937. Devaluation was not immediately followed by a recovery. Out of all the industries in 1935 and 1936, construction was the only truly prosperous industry in Belgium. The reduction in unemployment was clear, particularly in the branches of activity linked to the Brussels Exhibition. Exports had remained for a long time

584. See Mr Baudhuin's speech in *Travaux du Congrès des économistes de langue française* (Paris: Domat-Montchrestien, 1937), 166; *Bulletin de la Banque Nationale de Belgique* (in particular, year 12, vol. 2, no. 6, 25 Sep. 1936, 211–21); *Bulletin de l'Institut des Sciences économiques* (Louvain).

indifferent to the possible effects of the devaluation. But as profit margins increased, the recovery was confirmed.

The gap between costs and prices became positive at first and then grew under the influence of the respective cost and price movements. Prices rose, as did costs. But prices rose faster than costs because an important element of costs had decreased: the interest. Wages grew much less rapidly than the selling prices of industrial products. The Belgian National Bank's circular listed and reproduced the prices of potatoes, butter and eggs, three popular consumer items. In 1935, 1936 and 1937, the increase was insignificant. The price of potatoes was even lowered. The rise in wages was modest, clearly lagging behind wholesale prices. The general index of wages (average hourly wage), which had reached 91 in April 1935 (1933 = 100), only reached 107 in March 1937. In the metal industry, the wages of skilled workers rose from 93 in April 1935 to 127 in June 1937 (1933 = 100). But the price of cast iron, which was still at 330 francs in June 1936, went to 825 in June 1937, and that of steel billets was at 555 and 960, respectively. At export, the price of steel billets went from £2 7 sh. in June 1936 to £4 7 sh. 6 p. in June 1937 and to £5 7 sh. 6 p. in July 1937.

Little by little, Belgium was showing all the signs of an economy in recovery from 1935 to 1936 (see tab. 1.170).

Table 1.170 The Recovery in Belgium, 1929–1936 (monthly averages)

	1929	*1933*	*1934*	*1935*	*1936*
Industrial Production	100	69.1	71.4	72.3	83
Imports (millions of fr.)	2,961	1,347	1,235	1,142	1,426
Exports	2,649	1,234	1,169	1,128	1,317
Unemployed (1,000s)	27.2	338.0	349.1	284.2	213.7
Price of Industrial Shares	100	36.4	30.8	37.4	47.0
Wholesale Prices	100	58.9	55.6	63.1	69.1
Retail Prices	100	82.6	79.4	79.9	84.7
	Issues of Securities (mill. of fr.)		*Profits of Limited Liability Companies (1,000s of fr.)*		
1936	3,700		4,216		
1937	6,498		8,289		

Source: *Bulletin de la Banque Nationale de Belgique*, 10 March 1938.

C.) The United States[585]

With the American recovery, we reach the study of *dirigiste* recoveries truly worthy of the name. The crisis had been so violent, the unemployment so disastrous and the banking system so badly shaken by the fall in prices, so threatened by the immobilization of deposits (mortgages) and the hoarding of gold that the *vis medicatrix naturae* [natural healing powers] would not be enough to restore the economy. President Hoover's modest

585. Institute of Economics of the Brookings Institution, *The Recovery Problem in the United States* (Washington, DC: Brookings Institution, 1936).

interventions were followed by President Roosevelt's energetic policies, his 'experiment', the partial success of which is no longer disputed.

The results should not surprise us, because the president's policies have corrected the fundamental imbalances responsible for the American depression. And the success of his policies in the United States lies, as in England or Belgium, in the restoration of the balance between costs and prices. Here again, it was necessary to restore the balance between town and country, between agricultural and industrial prices. In doing so, America prepared the way for the global recovery that we have benefitted from for the last three years: by correcting agricultural overproduction, it has prepared the way for growth in that half of the world whose livelihood depends on agriculture, and consequently, it has stimulated growth in the entire world.

Table 1.171 Issues of US Securities, 1931–1936 (millions of $)

	Total, Foreign and Domestic	Domestic						Foreign
		Total	State and Municipal	Federal Agencies	Corporate			
					Total	Bonds and Notes	Shares	
A. New Capital								
1931	3,089	2,860	1,235	75	1,551	1,239	311	229
1932	1,192	1,165	762	77	328	305	20	19
1933	720	708	483	64	101	40	120	12
1934	1,386	1,386	803	405	178	144	35	6
1935	1,457	1,409	855	150	404	334	68	48
1936	1,972	1,949	735	22	1,192	839	352	23
B. Conversions and Refunding								
1931	949	893	21	51	821	789	32	56
1932	557	498	87	93	319	315	4	59
1933	343	183	37	26	219	187	32	60
1934	774	765	136	317	312	312	0	9
1935	3,242	3,216	365	987	1,864	1,782	81	26
1936	4,242	4,123	382	353	3,387	3,187	200	119

Source: *Federal Reserve Bulletin* 23, no. 10 (Oct. 1937): 1027–28.

President Roosevelt has created three large credit organizations to issue bonds guaranteed by the treasury to take over bad mortgages. Table 1.172 shows how they performed.

Table 1.172 Newly Formed Federal Lending Corporations in the United States (millions of $)

	Total	Federal Farm Mortgage Corporation	Home Owners' Loan Corporation	Reconstruction Finance Corporation
Dec. 1933	180	—	—	180
June 1934	681	312	134	235
June 1935	4,123	1,226	2,647	250
June 1936	4,718	1,422	3,044	252
Aug. 1937	4,643	1,410	2,937	296

No source given.

President Roosevelt placed large public borrowings directly, particularly in the banks, to meet his public works expenditures.

Table 1.173 Public Debt in the United States (millions of $)

June 1932	19,487	June 1935	28,701 (+1,748)
June 1933	22,529 (+ 3,052)	June 1936	33,779 (+ 5,078)
June 1934	22,053 (+ 4,514)	Aug. 1937	37,045 (+ 3,266)

No source given.

He gave the United States a stable currency and cleaned up the banks. He restored agriculture and industry and curbed unemployment. Using a policy we cannot fully endorse – far from it – he nonetheless managed to restore confidence to a great people who had become discouraged and almost lost in despair. To his opponents who reproach him for being untraditional, we say that his policy remained traditional in its major result: he has re-established a common price level for all products, agricultural and industrial, and he has restored profit margins. He thus laid the foundations for a healthy currency, prepared the way for the decline in interest, the revival of the spirit of enterprise and the growth of securities issues. His policies prepared the ground on which private enterprise would be able to build. Armaments production played an insignificant role here. The same is not true for public works.[586]

Production and domestic and foreign trade have returned to their highest levels or even surpassed them with astonishing speed. The growth has silenced the grotesque fantasies of the 'technocrats', the society builders, the reformers who proclaim that to produce means very little and that the most important thing is to redistribute – hence the need for government assistance, substantial pensions for all, ever-higher salaries and ever-shorter working days.

We could not describe in detail the policies of President Roosevelt without departing from our subject (we are dealing with periodic crises). We will only discuss what is essential to understanding the American recovery. If the National Industrial Recovery Act (NIRA), declared unconstitutional by the Supreme Court in 1937 [*sic*], appears to have played a secondary role in the recovery, and perhaps even to have impeded it, the Agricultural Adjustment Act (AAA), on the contrary, seems to us to have exerted a major influence, as did the Public Works Administration (PWA). By raising agricultural prices, which had been so deeply depreciated compared to industrial prices, and by

586. See *Travaux du Congrès des économistes de langue française* (Paris: Domat-Montchrestien, 1938), on 'La réforme économique aux États-Unis' [it was in fact the 1935 meeting of the Congrès des économistes de langue française which dealt in part with this topic; the publication of the 1938 Congrès, for which Lescure wrote the preface, had the themes 'La reprise allemande: Méthode et résultats' and 'Hausse des prix et réorganisation des entreprises']; Lewis L. Lorwin, 'Il primo anno della N. R. A.', in *Nuove esperienza economiche* (Florence: Sanson, 1935); Georges Bouvard, *L'agriculture dirigée aux États-Unis: Essai critique sur l'économie autoritaire*, thesis, Faculty of Law, University of Paris (Paris: Librairie technique et économique, 1935).

providing large orders to industry through his public works projects, the president managed to stabilize the banks and consolidate the dollar. Costs and prices have returned to a positive balance: the spirit of enterprise has reappeared. In this return to equilibrium, the systematic devaluation of the dollar does not seem to be of prime importance. Relief for the unemployed, too, played only a secondary role: the president aimed to give work to the unemployed by recovering economic prosperity. Government assistance was incidental. The thought of receiving welfare is repugnant to the American worker.

The president initiated the recovery by restoring a common price level for agricultural and industrial products. He claimed to have achieved these crucial results both by a devaluation of the dollar and by a policy of stock reduction and limited production. In our opinion, it was through these restrictions that he brought the two blades of the scissors closer together, since the devaluation affected the prices of both agricultural and industrial products. The devaluation was unable to bridge the gap between agricultural and industrial prices by itself. On the other hand, the credit facilities granted to farmers, by allowing them to carry forward their stocks and by paying premiums intended to encourage a reduction of cereal and cotton crops, contributed to limiting the supply of agricultural products. Certainly, poor harvests also contributed to the president's policy, although it would be impossible to weigh the respective influence of these factors exactly; yet, the restriction of production, a kind of 'blockage' of stocks, favoured the rise in the prices of agricultural products and made it possible to close the gap between agricultural and industrial prices. The indicators here are very convincing. As the rail gauges have returned to a normal, trains were able to run properly again. Farmers have been excellent consumers of industrial products, particularly those of the car industry. A fair vision combined with adequate policies has yielded considerable results.

In making farmers solvent again, the rise in prices enabled them to meet their obligations to the banks more effectively. When Roosevelt took office, the 'country banks' aroused the most suspicions. The rise in the prices of agricultural products have restored credit and the currency. Yet this considerable success was insufficient to restore the economy. The issues of securities had fallen to nothing. Heavy industry was lacking orders and was no longer productive. Public intervention was needed to replace failing private initiative.

The Roosevelt administration gave billions of dollars' worth of orders to industry: for bridges, roads, dams, power plants and buildings of all kinds, transforming the United States into one immense construction site. The activity spread, as always, like an oil stain. The prosperity was gradually gaining ground. And from 1934 onward, the United States consolidated its currency, stabilized its banks and sometimes reached the production figures of 1929. An exchange stabilization fund controlled the dollar's value, according to section 10 of the Gold Reserve Act of 30 January 1934.

Railway companies which had been in deficit were again making profits. There was no doubt that the depression had given way to the recovery.

The American government was able to pursue these massive public works projects thanks to the decrease of the interest rate, which in our view has been one of the most significant traits and one of the most decisive factors of the current recovery.

As in Britain, and following its example, American bankers widened the open market policy, transforming it into a means of precipitating the fall of interest rates.

To meet the enormous expenditures (the extraordinary budget having reached the same figure as the ordinary budget), the US Treasury invested billions in short-, medium- and long-term government loans to the banks at ridiculously low rates. Thanks to the fall in interest rates, the American government was able to convert its public debt, which had been swollen by the war but had by and large been written off subsequently during the periods of prosperity before the 1929 crisis. Thus, with interest being very low, the state borrowed billions of dollars for its public works projects without putting a severe strain on its budget. The debt swelled, but the arrears hardly increased at all, considering the total.

It is interesting and telling to compare the extraordinary expenses of the American budget with the dollar amounts of securities (shares and bonds) issued in previous periods of economic prosperity (tab. 1.174). In this way, we can capture one of the essential features of Roosevelt's policy in action.

Table 1.174 US Budgetary Expenses for Relief and Recovery Compared with Issues of Securities

Recovery and Relief (millions of $)*		*Issues of Securities (millions of $)*	
30 June 1934	4,004	1925	4,700
" 1935	3,366	1926	5,200
" 1936	3,341	1927	7,300
" 1937	3,079	1928	7,800

No source given.

* This category of treasury accounts comprises the expenditures for public works, relief, subsidies to agriculture, to homeowners, and to the Reconstruction Finance Corporation (monthly figures in the *Federal Reserve Bulletin*). As the project has progressed, the share of public works has become greater and that of relief and subsidies has decreased.

Table 1.175 US Treasury Expenditures (millions of $)

Financial Year Ending in June:	*Relief*	*Public Works*	*Other Expenditures*
1934	1,844	645	1,515
1935	2,342	7,020	294
1936	985	2,092	213

Source: *Federal Reserve Bulletin* 23, no. 1 (Jan. 1937): 63.

President Roosevelt gave public works precedence over relief and other expenses and put savings into circulation, thus providing the construction industry and heavy industries with orders at a time when private initiative, discouraged by the drop in prices and the reduction in the orders, was refusing to invest in new enterprises until such time as the recovery initiated by this policy of massive spending on large public works projects, by restoring profit margins, money, banks and confidence, led to a resumption of the issuing of shares and bonds. Little by little, private initiative was replacing public initiative. By the autumn of 1937, one contemplated handing over the reins definitively and completely to private interests. But making the hand off would be difficult. Negotiations continued between President Roosevelt and the business world. For better or worse, the president had all the power. The United States would experience a depression if public works were abandoned without private initiative picking up the slack from public initiative.

The construction industry played a significant part in the American recovery (see tab. 1.176).

Table 1.176 The Role of the Construction Industry in the American Recovery, 1932–1936

Value of Buildings Constructed (millions of $)			
	Private Buildings	*Public Buildings*	*Total*
1932	583	768	1,351
1933	573	683	1,256
1934	568	975	1,543
1935	837	1,007	1,845
1936	1,341	1,334	2,675

Source: Estimates of the E. W. Dodge Corporation for the 37 states east of the Rocky Mountains.

Just as in the period before the crisis of 1929, the car industry has fed American growth. In 1937, it surpassed its previous maximum production (tab. 1.177).

Table 1.177 US Car Production, 1933–1936 (1,000s)

1933	1,920
1934	2,753
1935	3,947
1936	4,454

Source: SDN *Bulletin*, June 1937.

However, in general, production never reached the maximum of 1929, as we see in table 1.178.

Table 1.178 Index of Business Activity for the United States (1923–25 = 100)

	1933	*1934*	*1935*	*1936**	*1929*
Industrial Production:	76	79	90	105	119
Manufacturing	75	78	90	105	119
Minerals	82	86	91	104	115
Employment (factories)	72	83	86	92	105
Mass of Wages	49	63	71	82	109
Wagons Loaded	58	62	64	75	107
Commerce:					
Exports (millions $) average	140	178	190	205	437
Imports (millions $) monthly	121	138	171	202	367
Retail Sales (1923–25 = 100)	67	75	79	88	88
Credit:					
1. Portfolio of Federal Reserve Bank, daily average (millions $)	2,429	2,502	2,476	2,481	1,459
2. Member Banks (Loans and Investments, average weekly balance) (millions $)	17,505	18,672	19,997	22,064	22,599
Money Rate:					
Commercial paper	1.72	1.02	0.76	0.75	5.85
Treasury Bonds (long term)	3.31	3.10	2.70	2.47	3.60
Interest on Industrial Bonds	4.49	4.00	3.60	3.24	4.73
Prices:					
Wholesale (1926 = 100)	66	75	80	81	95
Farm Products	51	65	65	81	105
Foodstuffs	61	71	71	82	100
Other Products	71	78	78	80	92
Retail (1923–25 = 100)	66	74	80	82	105
Stock Exchange:					
Share Prices	63	72	78	111	190

* The aggregation of the price indexes is remarkable in 1936.

Source: *Federal Reserve Bulletin*.

D.) Germany

The German recovery was so managed [*dirigée*] that it is impossible to regard it as a traditional kind of recovery. It was the first recovery in economic history entirely brought about and maintained by the state. Whereas in the United States the government confined its ambitions to ensuring smooth transitions, in Germany, the government dominated and directly intervened in the economy. Considerations of cost, price and profit were secondary. Profits were regulated and limited. The impetus no longer came from private initiative. The state played the essential role through its industrial orders, its financial policy (which imitated the policy practised during the war of 1914) and its two five-year plans.

However, the German economic growth bore similarities to traditional periods of expansion. First, a policy of grand public works projects, and then rearmament, supplied heavy industry and construction with orders, which had vanished after the 1931 financial crisis and the general crash of the banking and financial system.

As in England and the United States, the German government caused an artificial drop in the interest rate; but it initiated and caused the drop through forced conversions of public and private debts.[587] The open market policy would not have been practicable in Germany, where investment in government securities was regarded as a fixed asset [*immobilization*]. Moreover, the drop in interest rates cannot explain the German recovery, which was fuelled above all by treasury bonds or labour bills [*traites du travail*]. These two forms of credit played a very similar role in the recovery and the development of the growth, with treasury bonds replacing labour bills.

Up to this point, growth was fuelled and maintained by 'fresh' capital being invested in industry and trade. Savings played an important, formative role. In Germany, savings were virtually non-existent. Recently, savings have returned and are being absorbed by the redemption of the labour bills and short-term bonds with the aid of proceeds from the issue of medium-term Reich bonds.

German industry was 'fired up' thanks to a very original policy, which we must now trace by comparing it with the typical development of growth periods.

The German crisis, like previous crises, derived its essential characteristics from the shutdown of heavy industry – those industries delivering means of production – and from the collapse of financial markets and the issuing of securities. But one feature was new: the financial catastrophes of 1931 had wiped out enormous amounts of capital. In 1923, Germany had experienced a complete debasement of its currency and a total default on its public debt. Why save? Therefore, the German recovery could not have resulted from a return of entrepreneurial spirit, nor from an influx of capital into new businesses. Interest reached prohibitive rates of 6 and 8 per cent. In these circumstances, Germany resorted to methods that until then had been reserved for times of war. Germany had 6 million unemployed. Facing such distress, the government did not hesitate to resort to the most heterodox of financial measures, previously reserved for desperate situations.

The German state gave billions of Reichsmarks in orders to commerce and industry. The scale of the works undertaken was reminiscent of the magnitude of capital invested during traditional periods of economic expansion. The state initially undertook major public works projects and, as soon as the political situation allowed it, made enormous expenditures on armaments. The German '*Konjunktur*', to use a term currently in fashion across the Rhine, was a conjuncture defined by public works and armaments. Industrial orders from the government were abundant, and factories again resumed full production. Table 1.179 provides the official figures for Germany's public works expenditures – a total nearing 5.5 billion marks.

---

587. The 1935 conversions converted some 8 billion marks worth of *Pfandbriefe* (land loans and mortgage bonds) and municipal debts and some 2 billion in government borrowings into 4.5%. Stucken, *Deutsche Geld- und Kreditpolitik*, 144.

Table 1.179 German Public Works Expenditures under the Plans of the 1930s (millions of Reichsmarks)

The von Papen Plan (1932)	367
The Gereke Program (1933)	500
The Hitler Plan (Jan. 1933)	600
The Reinhart Plan (June 1933)	1,000
The Autobahn Plan (law of 27 June 1937)	1,400
The Second Reinhart Plan (buildings)	500

Sources: Karl Schiller, *Arbeitsbeschaffung und Finanzordnung in Deutschland* (Berlin: Junker & Dünnhaupt, 1936); Henry Laufenburger, 'La vie économique en Allemagne: Dix-huit mois d'expérience nationale-socialiste', *Revue d'économie politique* 48, no 4 (1934): 1286–89.

To this must be added 960 million marks for the railways, 110 million marks for the post office and nearly 2 billion marks for the autobahn.

The Reich was more discreet about its armaments production.[588] It has even stopped publishing its budgets. However, the information on the floating debt and its consolidation gives us an idea of the considerable scale of its arms spending.

However, the new feature was not spending without having money, since prodigies resolved this problem long ago. Rather, it was a matter of spending money without breaking the bank. In Germany, the first orders were paid for up front; new ones were spread out and others further still. The recovery that began in 1934 lasted into 1937. It was a typical recovery in both its duration and its dynamism. The recovery in the construction industry and the heavy industries has spread like an oil stain.

However, it has lasted because payments have been made. The 'financing' of public works projects and arms production constitutes the most novel aspect of the German recovery. Inflation, or the increase in banknote circulation, played a secondary role in this policy; whereas labour bills, *Sonderwechsel* [special bills of exchange], and treasury bills played the crucial role. More recently, the Golddiskontobank has put into circulation a significant amount of *Solawechsel* [i.e., 'single' bills of exchange or promissory notes]. Therefore, we must follow the trail of these vast financial operations through the balance sheets of the German deposit banks. The task is a delicate one since there are now a great number of banks and a distinction between the private and public sectors, which are both equally important. Nevertheless, it is possible to establish the pattern of these operations and the policy of financing great public works and armaments without savings and without long-term capital.

The operations were somehow reversed. Savings were used for the consolidation of floating debt or the withdrawal of drafts; yet the spending preceded the saving and not the other way round. The Reich has successfully drawn drafts on future savings and with considerable results. The political regime played its role, particularly in the floating debt consolidation, which was not totally spontaneous. Let us clarify.

588. Mr Churchill in his resounding speeches to the Commons has suggested the colossal figure of over 100 billion of our French francs. But this seems inflated.

To get its factories up and running again and provide work for the unemployed, the Reich developed plans for public works and arms production. It placed orders with industrialists. This got the ball rolling; however, the orders had to be paid for, and the bosses had to pay the wages. Billions of marks were needed. Banknotes could have been demanded from the Reichsbank, but the German people, well aware of the dangers of inflation, would not have consented to this. Limited liability companies were created for the large works (public works, railway lines, motorways, post offices, etc.). Suppliers drew drafts on them which were accepted.[589] These drafts were discounted by credit companies. The usual portfolio, consisting of commercial drafts, was replaced by a new type of portfolio composed of these bills drawn for financing major public works, or '*Arbeitsbeschaffungswechsel*'. Bank deposits were used in the completion of large public works projects. Entrepreneurs were, after discount, credited in current accounts with the amount of the discounted drafts. This original paper replaced drafts and current accounts receivable in the banks' assets. The published balance sheets of the banks give us information about these discount operations and the development of the balance sheets.

The amount of these labour bills has not been published officially. At the end of 1934, they were estimated at 3 billion Reichsmarks,[590] compared to 1.5 billion at the end of 1933.

However, this method was quite unsuitable for arms spending. While it is true that armaments companies could have been set up, this would have posed difficult challenges. Orders placed by the Reich were filled thanks to massive issues of the *Sonderwechsel*. Companies sometimes accepted these bills as payment. But more frequently these bills were discounted at the Reichsbank, credit companies and state-owned banks. The government was credited the same amount in current accounts. It then paid its suppliers by cheque. This method had been widely practised during the war of 1914.[591] However, the Reichsbank initiated a new policy in collaboration with its subsidiary: the Golddiskontobank. The Reichsbank could have re-discounted in the credit companies to lighten its portfolio, which had become overburdened by the *Sonderwechsel*, and would have thereby reduced its banknotes in circulation or current accounts. But this measure seemed unusual and inelegant. The Reichsbank was a re-discounting bank, and it could not resort to re-discounting in the credit companies without reversing roles, upsetting hierarchies and discrediting itself. The Reichsbank lightened its burden by signing over the *Sonderwechsel* to its subsidiary, the Golddiskontobank, thereby transferring them from its portfolio to that of the Golddiskontobank. The latter issued an entirely new kind of paper: the *Solawechsel*, which as accepted for re-discounting at the Reichsbank and for that reason was easily placed in the credit companies, where they were considered a very liquid use of their available assets.[592] In return for its *Solawechsel*, the Golddiskonto

589. Among these companies, veritable acceptance banks, we will mention the Deutsche Gesellschaft für öffentlichen Arbeiten (Oeffa), the Bau- und Bodenbank, the Rentenbank-Kreditanstalt and so on Stucken, *Deutsche Gold-und Kreditpolitik*, 125.

590. Ibid., 127.

591. See Lescure, 'La situation financière de l'Allemagne', *Revue de Paris*, 15 June 1915. Albert Rivaud, *Les crises allemandes, 1919–1931* (Paris: Colin, 1932), 28.

592. Stucken, *Deutsche Gold- und Kreditpolitik*, 134.

received banknotes from the Reichsbank or cheques. And, in return for the *Sonderwechsel* put under its control by the Reichsbank, the Golddiskonto handed over banknotes to the Reichsbank (deflating circulation) or a cheque (decreasing the Reichsbank's current accounts). The *Solawechsel* were issued for extremely high sums: 1 billion marks or more. This new paper was in some ways reminiscent of the *Reichskassenscheine* [imperial treasury notes] issued during the war[593] because it lightened the Reichsbank's portfolio; however, the *Solawechsel* differed from the latter in that they were not legal tender and were placed in banks, where they drained cash assets.

Yet while it may be fairly easy to conceive of a first string of large public works or armaments 'financed' by this method, it is less easy to perceive the basis for those that followed; for the banks inundated with this paper would lack the deposits and liquid assets to discount what amounted to irregular commercial paper [*cavalerie*]. In order to function, the pump needed to be primed again: in other words, the drafts and treasury bills had to be withdrawn from the banks in ready cash settlements. For this to succeed, the Reich was to issue consolidation loans. After issuance, the drafts would be withdrawn, and the treasury bills reimbursed. The *Solawechsel* would be taken out of circulation. And the banks would again achieve liquidity: consolidation loans would be taken out with savings, with long-term liquid assets. The money stock set in motion by the implementation of major public works or arms spending would partly crystallize in the form of savings which would then be induced to subscribe to the consolidation loans. The savings would have been built up in the savings banks and the insurance companies who would subscribe. They would appear in the current accounts of company banks. The companies' profits above a certain amount would even have to be compulsorily invested in government securities. The Reichsbank was allowed to purchase government securities (open market). Following the resounding bankruptcies, first domestic (1923), then foreign (1931), the Reich reduced its public debt to a very modest amount. As in the United States, public debt could be increased within reasonable limits. The economic prosperity and the orders placed with industry would be matched by the state's debt. From March 1933 to August 1937, the Reich's internal debt grew by 7,747 million marks, rising from 4,231 million on 31 March 1933 to 11,978 million on 31 August 1937.[594]

The composition of this short- and long-term debt was most original. A detailed monthly account can be found in *Wirtschaft und Statistik*. Non-interest-bearing treasury bills are listed at 2,478 million marks in August 1937. Thanks to this spending, the citizens' income was increased. The fiscal returns had improved, and the budget was balanced.

The consolidation operations have so far concerned some 10 billion marks.[595] But the massive public works and arms production have absorbed far greater sums. German banks have been inundated with government paper and labour bills. On the other hand,

593. François Sauvaire-Jourdan, 'La verité sur les caisses de prêt allemandes (Darlehenskassen)', *Revue d'économie politique* 29 (1915): 15–23.

594. *Wirtschaft und Statistik*, 1933–1937, provides the monthly status of the public debt. See also the supplement *Auswirkungen der unmittelbaren Arbeitsbeschaffung* 13, no. 21 (1933).

595. *Frankfurter Zeitung*, no. 174, 4 April 1938.

the government cannot pursue this policy indefinitely without increasing the public debt beyond measure. Arms spending is unlikely to continue at the same pace. The savings absorbed by the consolidation operations have been used up in advance and cannot be directed toward the creation of new businesses. Germany could face difficulties in this regard. Nevertheless, Germany plans to extend public works and arms spending through an autarkic economy [*conjoncture de l'autarcie*]. A four-year plan aims to provide Germany with all the products it lacks and must import.[596] But the four-year plan now underway is meant to be financed as much as possible by private initiative (companies and banks).

In any case, one cannot deny the originality of this gigantic experiment. And of all the novelties which we have seen emerge everywhere in the past years, the German growth and its financing deserve particular attention.[597] Traces of this financial policy can be found in the annual balance sheets of the credit companies. The current accounts receivable were reducing (i.e., sums loaned to private businesses), while discounts (in particular, of labour bills and treasury bills) were increasing. As long as the state placed orders and paid for them, industrialists repaid their debts to the banks. The number of debtors was reduced. The banks' balance sheets looked healthier, and discounting (the discounting of government drafts only!) replaced the 'debtors'.

At the present time, the German public banking sector (Reichskredit Gesellschaft, Golddiskontobank, Rentenbank und Kreditanstalt) is of comparable importance to the private sector (Deutsche Bank, Diskonto, etc.). We will distinguish between these two large banking categories in following the development of their annual balance sheets from 1932 to 1934 (see tab. 1.180).

Table 1.180 Balance Sheets of Germany's Public and Private Banks (millions of marks)

	30 Oct. 1933	*30 Oct. 1934*	*+ or – from Oct. 1933 to Oct. 1934*
Private Banks			
Accounts Receivable	5,029	4,762	– 267
Cheques and Drafts	1,299	1,744	+ 445
Non-Interest-Bearing Treasury Bills	642	603	—
Securities Portfolio	697	823	+ 126
Public Credit Institutions			
Accounts Receivable	2,449	1,463	– 986
Cheques and Drafts	430	697	+ 267
Non-Interest-Bearing Treasury Bills	489	1,062	+ 573
Securities Portfolio	297	1,066	+ 769

Source: See the report by the Reichs-Kredit-Gesellschaft AG, *Deutschlands wirtschaftliche Lage an der Jahreswende 1934–35* (Berlin, 1934), 59.

596. Henry Laufenburger, 'La vie économique allemande', *Revue d'économie politique* 51, no. 4 (1937): 1263–99. See the review of the *Vierjahresplan* in the *Frankfurter Zeitung*, 25 Dec. 1937, and 1 Jan. 1938 (review of the year 1937).

597. 'La reprise allemande: Méthodes et résultats', in *Travaux du Congrès des économistes de langue française*, 1938.

In 1935 these credit transactions were repeated. The *Frankfurter Zeitung* estimates their amount at between 2.5 and 3 billion for short-term credit operations.[598] Under the influence of this policy, the portfolio of bank drafts showed the following:[599]

(millions of marks)

1932	6,170	1934	7,950	1936	11,800
1933	6,410	1935	9,970	1937 (Oct.)	13,400

Thanks to this method, the usual indexes present the same signs as periods of prosperity (tab. 1.181).

Table 1.181 The German Recovery, 1933–1936 (monthly averages)

	1929	*1933*	*1934*	*1935*	*1936*
Production					
Industrial Production (I K.) (1929 = 100)	100	60.7	79.8	94.0	106.3
Production Goods Industry	100	43.6	72.6	99.4	113.2
Consumer Goods Industry	100	82.6	92.4	88.2	98.7
Coal (1,000 tonnes)	13,620	9,160	10,418	11,918	13,198
Lignite (1,000 tonnes)	14,538	10,566	11,437	12,282	13,445
Steel (1,000 tonnes)	1,354	634	993	1,344	1,598
Machines (orders) (I K.) (1929 = 100)	100	37.9	41.5	63.1	81.0
Cars (1929 = 100)	100	27.7	53.9	90.3	128
Commerce					
Imports (millions of marks)	1,120	561	389	350	371
Exports	1,124	800	478	406	347
Index of Retail Trade (I K.) (1929 = 100)	100	62.4	59.4	65.9	68.9
Transport					
Railways, Wagons Loaded per Day	152.1	104.9	117.5	124.3	135.2
Stock Exchange					
Variable-Income Securities	100	57.7	57.9	67.5	74.6
Employment, Wages					
Number Employed Workers (1,000s)	17,869	13,016	15,041	15,949	17,106
Unemployed (1,000s)	1,892	4,804	2,718	2,151	1,593
	July 1937: 563				
Wages. Tariff Rates (1929 = 100)	100	81.7	79.2	79.1	79.1
General Index of Wholesale Prices	100	68.0	71.7	74.2	75.9

No source given.

Unemployment in particular has almost completely disappeared: the number of unemployed has dropped from 6.5 million to 500,000. We have attempted to take stock of this reduction. Compulsory labour and military service has drawn 1,100,000 young people. The *Landhilfe* (agricultural aid) has directed around 160,000 unemployed to the countryside. Loans are granted to young couples on the condition that the wife does not

598. *Frankfurter Zeitung*, no. 662, 29 Dec. 1935.
599. *Frankfurter Zeitung*, 1 Jan. 1938.

work. The administration discouraged marriages between civil servants. These measures have thinned the labour market by 500,000 individuals; the economic recovery has taken the rest. In 1934, public works (motorways, railways) have employed 350,000 workers. Statistics by profession allow us to estimate that 200,000 people employed in construction and related industries were back to work by 1935. The number is considerably higher in the metal industries: from 1933 to 1935, the number of people employed increased by 400,000.

From 1935 onward, the armaments industry employed a large part of the workforce; although it is impossible to say how many. The second four-year plan involved the creation of new factories, producing substitutes (textiles, rubber, petrol) or new quantities of iron and steel (Goering forges). The remaining unemployed represented to a large extent a workforce difficult to employ – or what is nowadays called inevitable unemployment (resulting from job changes). With regard to reducing unemployment, the success has been complete. It is remarkable.[600] There is even a shortage of skilled labour and agricultural workers.

However, these positive statistics cannot hide Germany's difficulties. To carry out these plans, to repay certain debts, the Reichsbank has had to export its remaining gold. Germany's trade balance has raised many concerns for the Reich. Imports have become difficult due to insufficient exports, making it precarious to properly supply this population of 65 million, which now depends to a large extent on its domestic harvest for subsistence, and the crop yield is sufficient only in good years. Germany's prosperity finds greater expression in the activity of its factories, the intensity of labour and the disappearance of unemployment than in the comfort and well-being of its population, who are told by their government that guns must come before butter, that a strong people is better than a fat one.

E.) France

We would include France among the countries in which the recovery was managed by the government if the policies followed from June 1936 onward had been successful. But a country in which production was in decline, the trade balance showed an enormous deficit, the currency crumbled and then collapsed, and interest was at 6 or 7 per cent cannot be ranked among prosperous countries. Certainly, the number of unemployed receiving assistance was reduced by around 100,000 in 1936–37. However, in the absence of precise data, it would be difficult to say whether this reduction was not the result of much stricter controls over unemployed workers registered in the unemployment funds, the longer duration of the military service and the 40-hour work week.

However, this justified pessimism must be qualified by the following remark: our great country was not as profoundly affected by the crisis. Its soil, subsoil and climate

---

600. The *Reichsarbeitsblatt* records unemployment statistics and includes reports by the Reich Office of Employment and Unemployment Insurance [Reichsanstalt für Arbeitsvermittlung und Arbeitslosenversicherung].

are imperishable, and it would take very little for it to regain the taste for and joy of work, the abundance of savings and capital, and the lowest interest rate. Sooner and faster than most would think, France could again count herself among the prosperous nations.

We must recall one feature from the last economic crisis in France that was accompanied by a sharp drop in wages and unemployment. The magnitude of the crisis and the long duration of the depression have, as in other countries, strengthened the socialist movement for over a century. The 1936 elections saw significant gains for the Socialist Party and the Communist Party. These gains were measured in votes (3.5 million), and the increase in votes in comparison with previous elections (1 million). But it was nonetheless 3.5 million out of 10 million voters.

F.) Italy

The command economy [*économie dirigée*] and autarky inspired Italy's economic policies. The expedition in Ethiopia and the sanctions that resulted from it placed Italy in a very unique situation. The recovery in Italy can only be examined with precision after the end of the abnormal period it has just gone through and from which it is only now emerging. A primarily agricultural country, Italy depends more on its domestic harvest than on the global economy [*conjuncture mondiale*]. Lacking in coal, iron and heavy industries, it follows other rhythms and laws than the great industrial nations.[601] Its balance of accounts is heavily in deficit.

***

The undeniable global recovery resembles the periods of recovery we have already studied in many ways: price increases, growth in production and trade, reduction in unemployment and a rise in wages. Nevertheless, it has some original features.

Undoubtedly, the recoveries after the Napoleonic wars were marked by a drop in the interest rate and massive conversions of public debts inflated by the wars and the revolutions (see our accounts of the crises of 1825 and 1836). But the recent recovery was preceded by a more substantial drop in rates, and the colossal public debt has transformed the conversion operations into gigantic and unprecedented conversions. Moreover, the completely new open market policy prepared and maintained the fall in interest, giving the lowering of rates pride of place as a major recovery factor; while wages have resisted the decline and are rising in several countries under the direction of the public authorities.

---

601. We will not mention Russia here for similar reasons: Russia is dependent on its domestic harvest and agricultural production. The plans policy has failed completely in the domain of agriculture. On the other hand, it has met with substantial successes in the industrial sector. But the Russian industrial boom is of little interest to the rest of the world, given its autarkic policy, economic isolation and monopoly on foreign trade. On this point, see Jean Lescure, *Le bolchevisme de Staline: Le régime des plans* (Paris: Domat-Montchrestien, 1934).

In many countries, the devaluation of currencies has helped to lower the money rate and to restore the margin between costs and prices without which history shows us there can be no economic recovery. However, one country, Germany, owes its recovery to the government's policy of substituting its own initiative for that of private businesses, restoring the national economy through large public works and arms production. But elsewhere public works and armaments have also been an important part of the economic recovery.

But we believe we must point out that the recent economic growth will not last forever. In order to predict the arrival of the next depression and to assess the chances that the growth period will last, it is important to know the factors of the recovery and to weigh their importance. The dominant role of government intervention in some countries may significantly transform the alternating periods of prosperity and depression which continue to govern the economic world and its dynamics. Already in the United States, signs of a slowdown are evident. Profits have declined.[602] President Roosevelt has discouraged the resurgence of private initiative in his speeches. His resolutions will weigh heavily on the economic evolution of the United States and the world.

Appendix: Crises and public finance[603]

An initial observation is necessary: the coincidence between years of surplus and years of prosperity, between years of deficit and years of crises and depression.

Table 1.182 Public Revenue and Expenditures in France, 1878–1913. Surplus of revenue over expenditures: +; Surplus of expenditures over revenue: – (millions of francs)

1878	+ 79	1888	+ 47	1897	+ 4.5	1903	+ 79
1879	+ 167	1889	+ 24	1898	+ 92	1904	+ 105
1880	+ 166	1890	+ 87	1899	+ 67	1905	+ 50
1881	+ 169	1891	+ 105	1900	+ 67	1906	+ 10
1882	– 42	1892	– 9	1901	– 121	1907	+ 88
1883	– 62	1893	– 84	1902	– 110	1908	– 54
1884	– 89	1894	– 21			1909	– 45
1885	– 146	1895	– 17			1910	– 48
1886	– 124	1896	– 8			1911	+ 141
1887	– 17					1912	+ 113
						1913	+ 24

No source given.

This law is verified in other countries, in Germany, England and the United States. The *Statistical Abstract* for Britain opens with a rather suggestive statistic, which we will cite for the period from 1897 to 1912 (tab. 1.183). This observation can be verified in previous years. Revenue gains or losses, surpluses and deficits, alternate very regularly.

602. Bertil Ohlin, 'Can world prosperity be maintained? The Task of France and the United States', supplement, *Index Svenska Handelsbanken* 12, no. 142 (Oct. 1937).

603. Marcel Marion, *Histoire financière de la France*, vol. 5, *1819–1875*, and vol. 6, *1876–1914* (Paris: Rousseau, 1928 and 1931).

Table 1.183 The British Budget, 1897–1912 (millions of £)

	Revenue + or – in Comparison to Estimates	*Surplus + Deficit –*
1897–1898	+ 3.9	+ 3.6
	+ 1.5	+ 0.1
1899–1900	+ 9.2	– 13.8
1900–1901	+ 2.9	– 53.2
1901–1902	+ 0.4	– 52.5
1902–1903	– 0.5	– 32.9
1903–1904	– 2.7	– 5.4
1904–1905	+ 0.09	+ 1.4
1905–1906	+ 1.6	+ 3.4
1907–1908	+ 2.4	+ 5.3
1908–1909	– 1.5	– 0.7
1909–1910	– 30.0	+ 5.6
1910–1911	+ 4.0	+ 5.6
1911–1912	+ 3.4	+ 6.5

Source: *Statistical Abstract for the United Kingdom.*

In 1930–31, the English budget showed a deficit of £25 million and £75 million in 1931–32.

In the United States, in the period between 1890 and 1913, the deficit years were 1894 to 1899, 1905 and 1908, 1909 and 1930, all years of economic depression. The other years were surplus years. In 1930–31, the deficit reached $900 million. A much higher deficit was predicted for 1931–32: $2,123 million.

Table 1.184 The Budget of the United States, 1925–1932 (millions of $)

	Revenue	*Expenditures*	*Surplus or Deficit + or –*
1925–1926	3,962	3,585	+ 377
1926–1927	4,129	3,493	+ 635
1927–1928	4,042	3,643	+ 398
1928–1929	4,033	3,848	+ 184
1929–1930	4,177	3,994	+ 183
1930–1931	—	—	– 900
1931–1932	—	—	– 2,885

Source: *Statistical Abstract of the United States* 55 (1933): 159, tab. 161.

In Germany, the *Statistisches Jahrbuch* allows for similar observations. In 1930 the budget showed a deficit of 1.5 billion marks. In Italy in 1930–31, the deficit amounted to 1 billion liras.

Periods of crisis were periods of deficit; periods of prosperity were periods of surplus (see tab. 1.185). Why?

Table 1.185 The Crisis of 1929 and National Budget Deficits in 1930–31

United States (1930–31)	$900 million
Great Britain	£25 million
France	2.6 billion francs
Germany	1.5 billion marks
Italy	1 billion liras

No source given.

A.) Expenditures

In times of prosperity, states allow themselves to get carried away by surpluses. In the period from 1895 to 1905, Germany greatly increased its credits for war and for the navy. In his general budget report for 1903, A. Dubost was already complaining of the extravagance of the French legislature. Likewise, in the prosperity period from 1905 to 1907, the expenditures of the United States went from $578,360,000 for the fiscal year of 1906–7 to $659,552,000 for the 1907–8 fiscal year.

In France, the prosperity period from 1928 to 1930 was marked by extravagance. A full treasury had created an illusion and masked the budget deficits. Onerous laws for public finance have been approved – laws which often weigh heavily on the future.

Germany had given itself over to extravagant expenditures that upset the balance of its public finances.

B.) Revenue

However, this increase in spending was not the sole cause of the deficit. The reduction in resources further aggravated the increase in spending.

1.) Public domain [Domaine]

In a country like France where the public domain is composed mainly of forests, economic crises have no influence on this source of revenue, which in any case is insignificant. It is not the same in countries where the railways and the mines are the property of the state.

Before the war, the German railways provided essentially variable resources to the state budget. Our study of crises has shown the alternating rise and fall in the railways' net receipts. In the countries where the railways are operated by the government, this movement of net revenue exerts a direct pressure on the budget. The Prussian budget in particular was especially sensitive to this kind of fluctuation. The forecasts by the finance ministers in these matters were often disproven by the facts.

In France, although the majority of railways were operated by companies, there was a close relationship between the results of railway operations and the national budget, as a result of the interest guarantee. Under the provisions of the Conventions of 1883, as net revenues declined, the demand for the guarantee increased. In periods of growth, the companies reimbursed the government for part of the advances.

The P.-L.-M. (Paris-Lyons-Marseilles) and the Eastern lines had been relieved of their security debts [*dettes de garantee*] before the war.[604] Under the terms of the Convention of 28 June 1921, a common railway fund was created to ensure that companies' budgets were balanced. In the case of a deficit, the convention provided for an increase in tariffs, a questionable arrangement because one would have to raise tariffs during a period of crisis and depression. And this increase would not always be accompanied by an increase in revenue. During the recent depression, tariffs were not raised, and the railway deficit weighed heavily on the public finances and on the French currency. The common fund, which had shown a surplus during the period of prosperity, subsequently suffered increasing losses, covered by borrowing and by very expensive loans (see tab. 1.186).

Table 1.186 The French Common Railway Fund, 1928–1936 (millions of francs)

	Surplus	Deficit
1928	592	—
1929	302	—
1930	—	1,297
1931	—	2,624
1932	—	3,681
1933	—	3,978
1934	—	3,570
1935	—	4,012
1936	—	4,250

No source given.

If the recovery had manifested itself in France, the deficit of the common fund would undoubtedly have disappeared, since in 1928 and 1929 there had been substantial surpluses. In September 1937, the companies were replaced by a national company (Société nationale des Chemins de Fer), with the aim of absorbing the deficit.[605]

2.) Taxes

The return on direct taxes was once less significant than that of indirect taxes. Today, the situation is different.[606]

Direct taxes. – When we examine the net revenue from the income tax before the war, we grasp the influence of economic crises on income taxes. The phenomenon was

604. Georges Villain, *Notice sur la périodicité des crises économiques et ses rapports avec l'exploitation des chemins de fer français* (Paris: Imprimerie nationale, 1908), 49n1, 59; Douglas Campbell, 'Cyclical Fluctuations in the Railway Industry', quoted in 'Current Notes', *Journal of the Royal Statistical Society* 93, no. 2 (1930): 312–13.

605. Louis Marlio, 'Le nouveau régime des chemins de fer', *Revue des deux mondes*, 8th ser., 43, no. 4 (15 Feb. 1938): 864–82.

606. Henry Laufenburger, 'La réforme des systèmes fiscaux', in *Travaux du Congrès des économistes de langue française* (Paris: Domat-Montchrestien, 1934); Fritz Neumark, *Konjunktur und Steuern* (Bonn: Schroeder, 1930); Harald Fick, *Finanzwirtschaft und Konjunktur* (Jena: Fischer, 1932).

masked for the economic depression period from 1900 to 1904 by variations in the tax rate. But it was very clear for the periods of growth and the subsequent periods of crisis during which the income tax remained stable. The net revenue from the income tax swelled during the periods of growth; it remained stationary or decreased during periods of depression.

If the income tax is sensitive to economic variations, it resists them well, and often the amount of taxable income does not decrease simply because of the arrival of a crisis. This was the case even for the incomes most sensitive to the influence of crises: the commercial and industrial profits that comprise schedule D. Being taxed on the basis of the average income of the past three years, bad years are close to the best or less bad years, thus mitigating the fluctuations in the tax base.

Provided it does not give in to excessive optimism during the period of growth, the treasury can count on the yield from the tax, even in times of economic depression.[607] The period of great financial need in England following the Boer War is proof of this, and the war of 1914–1918 even more so. And it was the same for the long period of depression from 1920 to 1931.[608]

If one examines the behaviour of the Prussian *Einkommensteuer* [income tax] in times of crisis, we are led to similar conclusions. But it enables us to draw another one: the progressive income tax leads to miscalculations in times of crisis.

The crisis does not always cause a reduction in the number of taxpayers, nor does it reduce the total amount of taxable income, but it does result in a reduction of the total tax yield. Since the *Einkommensteuer* is a progressive tax, the three aspects – maintenance of the number of taxpayers, maintenance of the taxable income and decrease in yield – mean a 'downgrading' of taxpayers, a reduction in the number of high-income taxpayers hit by the highest rates on the progressive scale and an increase in the number of middle-income taxpayers at a more moderate rate. The crisis causes an abrupt redistribution of wealth and income; it reduces to the level of the middle class those who during the boom had been elevated to the ranks of the great capitalists by a particularly profitable activity or lucky speculations. A decline in large incomes decreases the percentage of the rates applied to taxable income and, by the same token, the tax yield.

This observation, already possible before the war (see the first and second editions of the present work), has recently become a prominent issue, especially in France. The yield from the income tax and, more specifically, the progressive general tax has literally collapsed, causing the most worrying budget deficits. The yield from our local taxes (real and proportional) has been maintained, however, without fail.

---

607. 'Histoire du système fiscal anglais, 1914–1929', *Bulletin de Statistique et de Législation comparée* (Feb. 1930) and the *Statistical Abstract of the United Kingdom*. Comparisons are very difficult due to the frequent modifications in tax rates.

608. Ernst Huncke, 'Die Entwicklung von Einkommensteur und Einkommen in England in den letzten zwanzig Jahren', *Finanz-Archiv* 22, no. 1 (1905): 138–209.

Table 1.187 Amounts of Tax Rolls Issued and General Income Tax in France, 1929–1936* (millions of francs)

1929	8,708	1933	5,837
1930	8,158	1934	5,672
1931	7,880	1935	4,438
1932	6,669	1936	4,415

* For further details see the yearly publications of the Ministère des finances, 'Renseignements relatifs aux impôts indirects', from 1933 to 1937.

The great sensitivity of indirect taxes to the state of trade and industry is too obvious to mention. The onset of a crisis indicates a slowdown of imports, consumption and hence of customs revenues, indirect taxes per se and monopolies.

In England, in his budget statements, the Chancellor of the Exchequer never stopped complaining from 1900 onward about the reduced customs and excise returns. Alcohol, wine, tobacco and beer have the cruellest consequences for him.

In France and in the United States, the situation was the same. Following the crisis of 1907, the yield from customs tariffs, after increasing during the growth period, decreased after the arrival of the crisis. In the United States, customs revenue fell from $333,230,000 in the 1906–7 fiscal year to $285,681,000 in 1907–8. In France, the figures fell from 482.6 million francs in 1907 to 467.3 million in 1908.

During the 1920 crisis and since, indirect taxes have been a disappointment to the French Treasury. The yield of the turnover tax in particular, which its adherents had estimated at an inflated figure, was seriously influenced by the crisis and depression during the first period of its enforcement (see tab. 1.188). During the year 1922, the yield from customs and this new tax brought monthly disappointments to the French Ministry of Finance. On the other hand, enormous surpluses had been collected in 1928–29, but were followed in 1930 by revenue losses after the gains of the period of prosperity.

Table 1.188 Yield from Indirect Taxes in France, 1929–1936 (millions of francs)

	Turnover Tax	*Indirect Taxes (wine, alcohol, transportation, etc.)*
1929	9,874	6,583
1930–31	8,708	6,538
1931–32	7,524	6,366
1933	6,854	5,941
1934	6,384	5,186
1935	5,857	5,121
1936	6,123	5,169

No source given.

However, it is important here to distinguish between *ad valorem* taxes and the specific taxes. The *ad valorem* tax, the base of which varies with commodities prices, will be far more sensitive to crises than specific taxes (wine, alcohol).

As we see in table 1.189, the yield from the principal tax categories in Germany from 1926 to 1930 confirms these observations.

Table 1.189 Yields from the Main Tax Categories in Germany, 1926–1930* (millions of marks)

	1926	*1927*	*1928*	*1929*	*1930*
Taxes on Wages and Salaries	1,094	1,348	1,414	1,396	1,300
Income Tax	1,064	1,301	1,524	1,441	1,270
Taxes on Companies	381	477	608	558	445
Taxes on Transactions	875	877	1,000	1,013	1,005

* Rates have been modified several times. See the corrected graphs in the *Vierteljahrshefte zur Konjunkturforschung* 5, no. 4 (1931): pt A, p. 78.

With the return of prosperity, the yield on all taxes has improved. Income tax, being progressive, has provided flexible revenue, particularly after the 1934 reform.[609]

Table 1.190 German Tax Revenue during the Recovery, 1932–1936 (millions of marks)

	1932	*1933*	*1934*	*1935*	*1936*
Total Revenue	6,647	6,846	8,222	9,654	11,492
Income Tax	1,332	1,292	1,720	2,497	3,202
(incl. Tax on Wages)	749	730	899	1,362	1,544
Tax on Companies	106	209	320	592	1,046
Tax on Transactions	1,354	1,516	1,872	2,020	2,389
Customs and Taxes on Consumption	2,624	2,783	3,253	3,478	3,630

No source given.

3.) Government borrowing [*Emprunt*]

No topic seems more alien to the theory of crises than government borrowing. It is not. Until the onset of industrial recovery, government bonds serve as a refuge for capital. Interest falls. The rates on government annuities increase. It is in the state's best interest to borrow at the point when this rise reaches its maximum, and this moment coincides with the end of periods of depression.[610]

Hence, this has an impact on the manner in which the government offsets deficits in periods of depression. It is in the government's interest to borrow in the short term during the first years of the depression and, to the extent that consolidation is necessary, to

609. *Frankfurter Zeitung*, no. 512, 24 Oct. 1937, 11. The tax on transactions (*Umsatzsteuer*) is the equivalent to the tax on turnover in France.

610. In 1903, a year of depression, Imperial Germany's borrowing at 3% of 290 million marks was covered 47 times. In 1905, which was already a year of growth, the imperial borrowing of 300 million marks was covered only 15 times. In April 1906, a year of decisive growth, the German government raised the rate of its arrears to 3½, and yet, its borrowing of 260 million marks was covered only one and a half times. See *Berliner Tageblatt*, nos. 187 and 188, 12 April 1906.

resort to this consolidation only three or four years after the crisis, when conditions are more advantageous. But a government must also amortize and convert.

The growth period offers it the opportunity to amortize; for the capitalist abandons government securities for industrial values, the rate on annuities falls, and at the same time, a period of surplus begins. The government covers its deficits in times of depression by means of short-term borrowings that it consolidates three to four years after the crisis; it uses the surpluses of the growth period for amortization. In this way, the government makes a profit on the stock exchange: with 3 per cent, it gets 100, and it buys back at 97 what it sold at 100. In 1885, the German Empire could get 100.30 with 3 per cent arrears; in 1900, it could then buy back at 84.90 what it had sold for 100.30; and in 1904, it could again with 3 per cent get 92.20. On 8 November 1907, the state could purchase with the German 3 per cent at 82.10, and on 3 August 1909, with 3 per cent it could get 86.60. A constant amortization each year therefore seems irrational, particularly if it forces a state to borrow in order to amortize, as is too often the case in periods of crisis and depression. Amortization funds frequently succumb in the face of such phenomena and the budget deficits they generate. In France, we spend 3.5 billion francs on debt repayment, while we borrow more than 20 billion. This is an error that can easily be corrected without violating the constitutional law on the amortization fund.

When should a state convert? The capitalization rate on an annuity reaches its maximum at the end of a period of depression; this is the moment the government will choose to offer the annuitant a repayment at par or a lower rate. If the state violates this principle, it runs the risk of a failure of its conversion. Many annuitants preferred their repayment at par to a reduction in their income when the German and Prussian 4 per cent was converted in 1897.[611]

France and England have never failed to follow these principles, and if at times they have not waited for the most favourable moment – the culmination of a depression – to convert, they have never chosen a period of economic growth either. Barely two years after the crisis of 1900, France proceeded to convert its 3.5 per cent with complete success. And very fortunately so, because soon after, serious political unrest erupted: the Russo-Japanese War; later still, the Moroccan dispute; and state funds were depleted. France would have probably reached the growth period of 1905 before it could convert.

In 1931, France saw its first conversions. It is regrettable that the government hesitated in May–June 1931 to proceed with all possible conversions.[612] In September 1932, however, the damage was successfully repaired with the greatest conversion in our history (the Germain-Martin-Palmade conversion), transforming our 5–6 and 7 per cent into 4.5 per cent. The bulk of the conversions represented 85 billion francs. The resulting savings from the conversion came to nearly a billion francs. The calls for repayment have been almost negligible.

611. See Bernhard Rost, *Über das Wesen und die Ursachen unserer heutigen Wirtschaftskrisis* (Jena: Fischer, 1905), 40–41.

612. On possible conversions in France, see *Rapport Palmade* on the budget of the Ministère des finances; Maurice Kellersohn, *Les conversions des rentes devant la technique et l'équité* (Paris: Stock, 1931).

For its part, Great Britain converted its 5 per cent (War Loan) into 3.5 with great success. The operation entailed a total of 170 billion francs in capital (Neville Chamberlain conversion, July 1932).

Thus, let us derive a few principles. A progressive tax is less resistant to crises than a proportional one. Incomes more closely related to commercial and industrial activity – industrial sector, indirect taxes, customs, excise duties, stamps, monopolies and so on – are particularly sensitive to fluctuations in the economy. This is why a period of growth and surpluses is followed by one of depression and deficits. During a growth period, budgetary surpluses inspire extravagant spending by the legislators; this increase in spending will be met with decreased revenue during the depression, which will thus have consequences for the forecasting of revenue and the preparation of the budget.

It goes without saying that the government should prepare the budget as close as possible to its vote; and the theory of crises lends new confirmation to this principle. But it calls into question the value of the antepenultimate rule. The application of this rule proves dangerous to the preparation of the budget, such as those of 1901, 1907, 1921 and 1931. In these cases, the antepenultimate coincides with a year of growth, and the yield in a growth year serves as the basis for forecasting revenue for a crisis year. The minister of finance is susceptible to miscalculations. The deficits that we see in times of crisis and the surpluses that we record in times of growth are in part a consequence of the antepenultimate rule. Its result in almost every year is to use the revenue in years of growth as a basis for estimating revenue in years of crisis and vice versa.

If the antepenultimate rule is worth keeping, since a finance minister cannot summarily present the budget to the Parliament at his pleasure, it must be applied with caution. French governments in the most recent period have renounced strict adherence to the antepenultimate rule, particularly in their revenue assessments for the budgets of 1931, 1932, 1933, 1934, 1935, 1936, 1937 and 1938, and not only for indirect taxes but for direct taxes too. The usual indexes of economic movement make it possible to correct the revenue estimates made according to the antepenultimate. So do the results from the penultimate period, which are already known at the time the budget is submitted in September.

In terms of borrowing, it is in the state's best interest either to borrow or convert during periods of depression, particularly in the final years of depression; on the other hand, it is in the government's interest to amortize during the years of growth, especially during the final years of the growth period. It will amortize on surpluses and buy back at lower rates on the stock exchange.

Section Two

Theoretical Outline of the Alternating Periods of Growth and Depression[613]

In societies such as ours where the development of capital constitutes the necessary condition for the increase or improvement of production, it is natural for the production of the means of production to take pride of place. It acquired this place at the beginning of the nineteenth century and has retained this position and even expanded it into the twentieth century.

Hence the multiple consequences. Marx noted one essential consequence: the concentration of production. There is another: the alternation of periods of growth and depression.

The production of capital, of capital equipment, presupposes previous savings ready to be employed in the work of production. The role of savings is transformed, and if it remains deferred consumption – that is, a specific aspect of consumption – modern discoveries have made it possible for savings to be used in the work of production. The flow of savings into industry constitutes the driving force of the contemporary economic machine. Savings are a creative force.[614]

D. H. Macgregor calculated an 'enterprise' index for new businesses created in England. He compared this index with that of prices and unemployment. This index is a good indicator of recoveries and crises. The reawakening of the spirit of enterprise from its previous slumber indicates the onset of growth or depression. Table 1.191 conveys the essence of his demonstration for the period from 1860 to 1913.[615]

613. See the graph of such an outline in Ernst Wagemann, *Einführung in die Konjunkturlehre* (Leipzig: Quelle & Meyer, 1929), 100–101. This diagram, which is more complex than the three Harvard curves, is worth recommending. It summarizes well the main stages of the economic movement. But it must be seen as an outline and nothing more; for the length of the stages and the intensity of the movements are extremely variable. Robert von Keller, *Die Kausalzusammenhänge in der Konjunkturbewegung* (Leipzig: Meiner, 1934).

614. Charles Rist, 'Quelques definitions de l'épargne: Essai de critique', *Revue d'économie politique* 35, no. 6 (1921): 729–52; Jean Lescure, *L'épargne en France, 1914–1934*, 2nd ed. (Paris: Domat-Montchrestien, 1934).

615. D. H. Macgregor, 'Enterprise and the Trade Cycle', in *Economic Essays in Honour of Gustav Cassel* (London: Fank Cass, 1933), 419–34.

Table 1.191 Years of Maximum and Minimum Index Values for Enterprise, Employment, and Prices in England, 1862–1909

Maximums			*Minimums*		
Enterprise	*Employment*	*Prices*	*Enterprise*	*Employment*	*Prices*
1865	1865	1864	1862	1862	—
1873	1872	1873	1868	1868	1870
1881	1882	1882	1878	1879	1879
1889	1890	1891	1885	1886	1886
1897	1899	1900	1893	1893	1895–96
1906	1906	1907	1902	1904	1904
			1908	1909	1909

Source: D. H. Macgregor, 'Enterprise and the Trade Cycle', in *Economic Essays in Honour of Gustav Cassel* (London: Fank Cass, 1933), 419–34.

When savings are abundant and it is difficult to find profitable investments for them, they are likely to be used in industry. When savings are employed in industry, the sum of industrial consumption increases, and with it, prices, and with prices, profits, and with profits, savings, and consequently, available capital. As savings flow into industry, an industrial boom takes shape. What does this mean?

§1. – Growth

The first type of production to be affected will be that of the means of production. At the beginning of the nineteenth century, this included the weaving and spinning looms, all of the machinery of the textile industry; a little later, all the formidable machinery of the railways and their equipment, and that of the iron steamship which replaced the wooden sailing ship; and nowadays, electrical power, together with its many industrial applications: the tramways, railways, furnaces, lighting and so on not to mention the car and aircraft industries.

Economic growth, with its variety of sources, has always been based on the satisfaction of new or more intense needs, and satisfying these needs requires the production of new means of production. The railways provide orders to the mining and metal industries, which in turn represent one of the railways' best customers through the transport of their heavy products. Or better still, the electrical industry orders its machines from the metal industry, which in turn receives lighting, fixtures, dynamos and so on.

Therefore, the health of the mining and metal industries is a barometer of the general state of a country's industry. Prosperity in these industries reflects an active production of machines, of capital – that is to say, an expansion of industry. Every boom period is marked by the development of mining and metal production: coal, oil, coke, cast iron, formerly iron, now steel, copper, rolled products and machines. Produced in large quantities, these goods demand a large workforce; the number of workers employed in these industries is growing, as are their wages. And since factories concentrate the workforce in limited spaces, there is increased demand for new housing. The construction industry prospers as a result (see fig. 1.11).

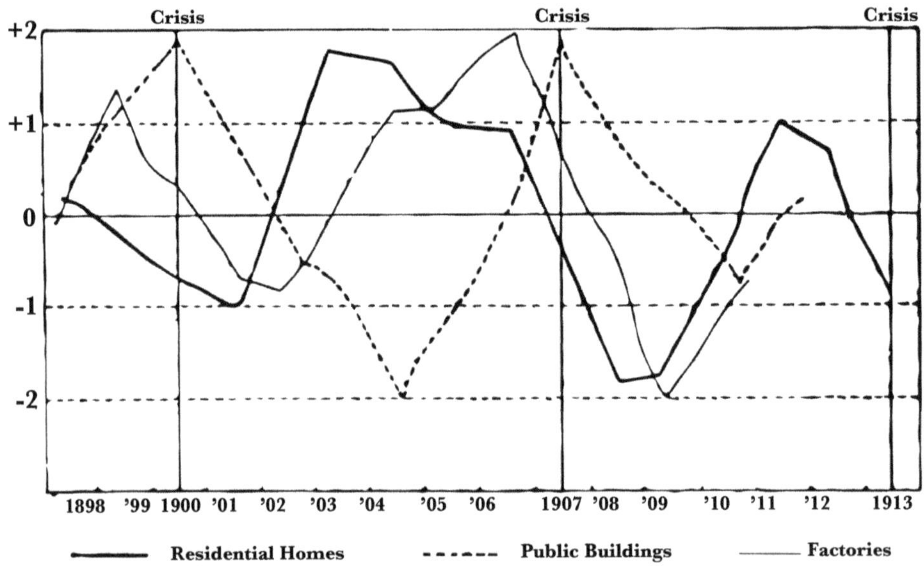

Source: Wagemann, *Einführung in die Konjunkturlehre*, 125.

Figure 1.11 The German Construction Industry, 1898–1913

The consumer goods industries, especially textiles, insofar as the fluctuating cost of its raw materials is not prohibitive, will also experience favourable years in which the demand for textiles increases, and with it, production.

The situation is similar for agricultural products, but with one difference: the unpredictable effects of seasonal variations on the harvest.

Besides, production and consumption are not the only areas to experience growth. Prices are also increasing, and as the most pressing demand is for iron and steel products, and more recently, for copper – in a word, for capital – the prices of these products rise to the greatest extent. The price of cast iron is, together with its production figures, one of the most reliable indicators for assessing the level of prosperity in a capitalist economy. Yet by association [*par solidarité*], the price of textiles and supplies increases, provided that the whims of the seasons or those of fashion do not interfere with this law.

Trade expands in quantity and value. Foreign trade and railway profits increase, foreign trade in particular, when the growth depends on foreign investments: foreign securities will be issued on the market of a given country, and the national industry will fulfil its orders for the means of production corresponding to the issues of marketable securities. The means of production are then exported. With this increase in trade, the need for money, either metal or paper currency, will also increase.

Nowadays metal money is far from being the principal instrument of exchange, yet it remains the support for fiduciary money. In the past during periods of growth, the need for metal money increased with the rise in wages and the development of the retail trade. The cash on hand at the large banks of issue declined to the benefit of the country's circulation.

The number of bills of exchange drawn will increase, as will their average amount. The entrepreneur of the joint-stock company in the process of equipping itself moves thousands upon thousands of tonnes first of coal, then coke, then cast iron, then steel, then rolled steel and finally machines. Each transfer of prosperity from one producer to another, from the coal producer to the coke producer, from the coke producer to the cast-iron producer, from the cast-iron producer to the steel producer and so on, causes a bill of exchange to be issued.

Thus, a period of growth is always marked by an increase in the portfolios of the banks, that is, in the discounted bills of exchange; and with the increase in demand for the discount, the discount rate rises.

Is the same true of banknote circulation?

Very often in a period of expansion, the banknote circulation of the banks of issue (Banque de France, Bank of England, Reichsbank) decreases. Just as one objects to Ricardo and the supporters of the quantitative theory that the speed of the circulation of money can compensate for the increase in the need for money resulting from the increase in exchanges and, hence, prevent the drop in prices which would normally result from the increase in the demand for money in the face of a constant supply of goods, so too can one object in the case of discounts that a given quantity of banknotes will be able to satisfy a growing demand for discounts. It is sufficient that the average maturity time of bills of exchange and their stay in the bank's portfolio decreases. The ebb and flow of banknotes will be faster, and the total amount of expected bills of exchange will be greater, though the amount of banknote circulation may have decreased.

As for cheques, their number and value increase. Clearing-house operations expand. On the stock exchange, capital moves into industrial shares, which increases their price. Often this rise causes more or less feverish speculation that sometimes produces crashes. If we look at the state of production and prices and everything seems to be in order, then we see it as an isolated stock market crisis. Exaggerated optimism on the stock exchange necessitates a drop in prices, but only on the stock exchange. Thus, a stock market crisis is a poor criterion for assessing the condition of a nation's economy.

The distribution of wealth and its evolution are more reliable indicators. The capitalist's income increases, as do workers' wages. The landowner realizes surplus profit because of the concentration of the population around the factories, in the cities and in the country. Often speculation arises encouraged by mortgage financing. In short, large profits appear, luxury spending grows, the crime rate drops, and the number of marriages increases until a crisis occurs.

§2. – Crisis and depression[616]

Most generally, the crisis begins by affecting new businesses created in the last year of the growth period. The highest hopes had been founded on them. No sooner had they come into operation than they suffered losses, or their profits were far lower than

616. W. C. Mitchell, 'Business Cycles', in *Encyclopaedia of the Social Sciences*, ed. Edwin R. A. Seligman, 15 vols. (London: Macmillan, 1930–35), 3: 100–106. See Jean Lescure, s.v. 'Crises', in ibid., vol. 4.

expected. Optimism and the spirit of enterprise had gone too far too fast, and a step backwards was necessary. Savings flow back into more secure investments.

Does this mean that savings are weaker than in the years of economic growth? Maybe. One cannot be entirely certain because government securities are issued in periods of depression.

Yet savings move further and further away from industrial investments and are then used to cover budget deficits, as was the case in Germany in 1907–8 and in France from 1932 to 1937, or to consolidate the securities issued during the growth period, as in the United States in 1908 and 1930. Savings accumulate in banks as deposits and current accounts payable and are used on the stock exchange in the form of deferred transactions [*reports*; i.e. call money], which become very cheap. Capitalists regain confidence in safe investments and fixed-income securities, raising their prices. Industrial investments are abandoned, industrial output declines and all incomes drop. And, with this drop in incomes, the amount of savings is also likely to fall. If savings seem more abundant than in times of growth, it is because they are less in demand, not because they are in greater supply.

Thus, the industries that are affected first and foremost are the mining and metal industries. As savings move away from industry, a crisis is certain in the metal and mining industries. It is more intense, however, in the metal industry than in mining. Coal mines, which have the unique quality of being used in the construction of the means of production and, once constructed, in their operation, are always less affected by a crisis than ore mines or the steel industry. The same is true today of oil or electricity. Cast-iron production is particularly characteristic: it drops abruptly and fast. Nowadays, new organizations have intervened aiming to regulate this drop in production. It is difficult to say whether they have slowed the process down or accelerated it; what is certain is that they do not prevent it. In any case, they make it possible to observe it better.

The first outbreak of the crisis results from a crisis in a particular branch of production and is soon followed by that of the machine industry, the iron industry, steel, mining and so on – in short, by all the factories involved in the production of modern machinery and equipment.

When production stops, unemployment starts, and workers are dismissed. The country mouse who had momentarily become a city mouse becomes a country mouse again. The immigrant who had been attracted by the high wages of industry returns to his native soil. A rent crisis occurs in the construction industry, which has already been affected by the high cost of materials and labour and the rise in interest rates on mortgage loans. With the construction crisis, real-estate speculation on land and houses collapses; mortgage banks see their operations significantly reduced. Skilled workers in the building trades, locksmiths, painters, masons, are hit by unemployment, when they are not victims of their customers' fraud or bankruptcies.

The crisis marks an intensification of the process of capitalist concentration; prices fall, and with them, profits; the crisis can only be dealt with in two ways:

1. by reducing production costs;
2. by lowering the value of business capital; the percentage of profits will increase in this way, making a return to normal more likely. Sometimes a factory very hard hit by the crisis will go under.

A production and consumption crisis are therefore the signals of:

1. a revision of production costs;
2. a reduction of capital;
3. bankruptcies.

An intensification of capitalist concentration is the result.

Bankruptcy hits weakened companies, which after having been rendered inactive during the preceding crisis, resumed business during the prosperity only to be hit once again by another crisis. Larger businesses are more resistant to the drop in prices. But reducing capital and production costs has a similar effect. By reducing its capital, the struggling business is more likely to be acquired by a larger firm. The integration of businesses will allow for a reduction in production costs which in turn triggers further concentration: the 1893 crisis in the United States, the 1900 crisis in Germany and the 1907 crisis in the United States were marked by a general movement toward concentration in the mining and metal industries, the electrical industry, the transport industry and the banking trade.

Thus, a crisis is usually the sign of a decline in the production of the means of production and a crisis in the construction industry, as well as a drop in selling prices, a reduction in the cost of production and, subsequently, an intensification of the process of industrial concentration.

This crisis of the industries producing the means of production and of the construction industry often spreads to the consumer goods industry and to agriculture. When such an important sector of production experiences a period of inactivity, its purchasing power declines, and with it, the demand for products from other branches of industry. As a result, the textile industry and agriculture find their products in less demand and often depreciated in value. Nevertheless, this depreciation may be offset by lower crop yields and an increase in the prices of raw materials.

The existence of the crisis implies a decrease in demand and production, that is to say, a drop in prices. The decrease, like the increase, will not affect all products to the same degree. Certainly, it is sometimes possible for forward and future contracts to distort the process of decline; however, the decline will only be delayed for a while, only to hit later with greater intensity. Economic laws govern human will, and even cartels and trusts, despite the power of their monopoly, cannot contravene them. In spite of its best efforts, the cartels in Germany were unable to avert the fall in prices made necessary by the crisis of 1900; in 1907, the trusts did not prevent it either. The steel trust tried in vain to resist the necessary decrease in prices in 1907 and 1908. It was also useless when the copper trust tried it in 1929–30. Thus, the crisis leads to a succession of decreases in product prices, which vary according to the categories under consideration. The drop is especially strong and constant for the products of the metal industry. For those products whose supply is subject to seasonal variations, a decline in the harvest can distort the law of falling prices. But the trend will definitely be downward.

The volume and value of trade decrease. The need for instruments of exchange is reduced. However, although this observation is generally true, it is not the case at the beginning of a crisis.

The rupture of the equilibrium between production and consumption leads to a disruption of trade, whether national or international, which will increase the need for money (metal or banknotes).

Normally, the debts of a trader, a commercial or industrial company, or a country are settled with its own commercial paper [*créances*]. When a crisis occurs and renders a whole series of products unsaleable, it upsets the normal equilibrium of commercial and industrial trade credit and debts [*créances et dettes*]. A host of traders and industrialists have bought but find it impossible to sell; at times it is totally impossible because there is no longer any demand; at times it is only relatively impossible, as prices have dropped. The individual, the corporation or the nation must nevertheless repay their debts; and if they can no longer do so by selling products, then they must resort to a medium that is always in demand: metal currency or banknotes convertible into metal.

This intense need for metal will have the effect of creating an abnormal demand for credit. However, to rely on credit is to discount, to borrow against collateral or on margin [*à découvert*]. This increase in credit will lead to an increase in the discount rate, an increase in the portfolio, a decrease in the cash on hand and an increase in banknote circulation or current accounts payable.

Yet banks discount by means of the deposits entrusted to them, and a crisis has the effect of reducing deposits. One begins by paying with one's own money before resorting to someone else's. The credit fund is depleted as the need for credit increases, and the discount rate rises rapidly. A time comes when it is so high that it is in the merchant's or industrialist's best interest to sell their products, even at a very great loss, rather than to resort to the discount. The crisis then reaches the moment of resolution, and the slowing down of trade results in a reduction of the portfolio, a drop in the discount rate and the return of metal and banknotes to the banks' coffers.

The theory of raising the discount rate in times of crisis should not be linked, as is often done, to the theory of the exchange crisis. This would be too narrow an application of the phenomenon of raising the discount rate. The phenomenon is also related to the law of value; as its use grows in intensity, the value of the discount increases. The exchange crisis is not the only kind of crisis to have this effect. In times of general economic crisis, there is also always a domestic credit crisis; for the exchange crisis is at bottom nothing more than a foreign credit crisis, and these two crises have a common origin: the sudden disruption of the normal equilibrium between purchases and sales, the interruption of trade, as a consequence of the disappearance of the spirit of enterprise, and the fall of prices. In the first case, that of an exchange crisis and foreign credit crisis, one imports and no longer exports or exports less; in the second example, one purchases and no longer sells. Let us note the character of the two formulas: to import is to buy, to sell is to export. Thus, the basis of the crisis is the same, and the increase in the discount rate has the same basis: an increased demand for the discount. It can be explained by the same law.

However, the effect of the two different crises on the rise in the discount rate is not the same in both cases. In the first case, metal and nothing but metal is needed, and banknotes are accepted only to be immediately exchanged for metal. In the second case, banknotes serve as well as metal; and the banknote, in spite of its high production cost,[617] is faster and easier to produce than metal. The increase in the discount rate necessary to resolve the first crisis will therefore be higher than the rise needed to remedy the second; for there will be the difference between the difficulty of obtaining gold and the cost of issuing a banknote.

Thus, the policy of the gold premium, which makes it possible to discern and separate the two crises, appears to be an excellent solution. Thanks to the gold premium, banks protect their reserves; once its gold reserve is protected, it can then satisfy the domestic demand for credit by increasing banknote circulation. In the past, the United States had to resort mainly to metal in the absence of central banks of issue. But the available metal was barely sufficient to defend against the exchange crisis. Thus, there was the possibility of supplying the domestic crisis with a means of payment other than metal by using an original type of fiduciary money, the clearing-house certificate.

More recently, the exchange stabilization funds have built up massive gold reserves, particularly in Britain and in the United States, which allow them to supply gold in the event of an exchange crisis without the central bank raising its discount rate.

Credit transactions quickly decrease once the crisis is liquidated, and they gradually decline until the next growth period. Clearing-house clearings show a similar result until the next growth period arrives.

General economic crises are always accompanied by a stock market crisis. The decline will affect variable-income securities in particular. This will often take the form of a crash. The more limited the production, the more prices will drop and the greater the fall in shares.

The capitalist will therefore suffer an initial decrease in his industrial values; he will also experience a decrease in incomes: dividends and interest decline with the fall in prices and profits. Bankruptcies follow, sometimes reducing the millionaire to his former existence as a valet. Fortune becomes a hated stepmother to her former worshippers. The ranks of the middle class, after having thinned out, swell again, while the upper class is reduced. The crisis exposes the often dishonest speculations of politicians, who are compromised by the shady dealings to which they had lent their name and influence. The working class is not spared. Unemployment develops with its dreadful consequences: begging and vagrancy. Wage rates decrease, as do working hours, the annual wage, the nominal wage and real wages; but real wages decrease much less than nominal wages. And, along with the decrease in wages, the number of marriages declines, and frequently there is an increase in the number of suicides[618] and deaths.

617. See Francesco S. Nitti, 'Essai sur les variations du taux de l'escompte', 3 pts., *Revue d'économie politique* 12, no. 5 (1898): 368–98; 12, no. 10–11 (1898): 789–826; and 13, no. 3 (1899): 278–320.

618. For a discussion of the influence of the economic situation on the number of suicides, see: Émile Durkheim, *Le suicide: Étude de sociologie* (Paris: Félix Alcan, 1897), 264; and Maurice Halbwachs, *Les causes du suicide* (Paris: Félix Alcan, 1930), 355.

There is also a greater reliance on public assistance. Finally, serious political unrest often erupts.[619] France in 1936 confirmed this century-old observation.

Such is the picture of the development of our modern economies. The economic world passes through alternating periods of growth and depression under the influence of savings, an ancient force, whose contribution to the work of production in the form of orders for machines, houses and capital goods of all kinds is essentially new. This ebb and flow of savings is the reason why our modern societies progress through periods of growth and depression. The former are characterized by an increase in production, consumption, prices, rates on the stock market, the circulation of wealth and recourse to credit, the rise in dividends, interest, land rents and wages; while the latter are characterized by the opposite phenomena.

Were we to examine the problem more closely, it would remain for us to investigate the cause of this ebb and flow of savings, of this rise and fall, that is to say, the cause of general overproduction crises. The alternating periods of growth and depression stem from variations in the production of the means of production. The formula is rather vague. What machines were created in the nineteenth and early twentieth centuries?

619. Jean Lescure, 'Quelques influences sociales des crises économiques', *Bulletin de l'Institut de Sociologie Solvay* (Jan. 1922).

Section Three

The Role of Various Industries in the Alternating Periods Growth and Depression

The alternatives of strong and weak production of the means of production and the flow of savings toward industry and their ebb into other investments are the essential characteristics of the alternating periods of growth and depression. The crisis begins with the drop in the prices of metals and is marked by a reduction in the orders sent to the metal industry. But we must express this more precisely: a certain customer of the metal industry abandons it. Our historical study enabled us to conclude that this customer was the transport industry, mainly in the nineteenth century, and also the construction industry.

The railways, tramways and maritime transport absorbed the largest share of savings in the nineteenth century, followed by the mining and metal industries.

Originally steam powered, the railway has more recently become electric. From 1890 onward, large amounts of capital were invested in electrical industries and also in the car industry. But make no mistake, we encounter mechanization primarily in transport, mining and the metal industry; elsewhere it plays a secondary role.

Whether we consider the statistics for horsepower or for securities, we arrive at the same conclusion. Of the 14,741,000 horsepower (hp) used in France in 1912, 11,516,000 were used in the railways and tramways, 1,117,000 in the mines and metal industry and 568,000 in electrical industries. The machines and equipment of other industries accounted for much less by comparison: 1,540,000 hp.[620]

If we go back in history to 1878, the disproportion was even more obvious and pronounced.

The statistics on securities confirm this point of view. The billions in savings invested in industry have essentially served to create transport, to equip mines, metalworks and electric power plants. Table 1.192 was drawn up by [Clément] Colson, according to the documents from the Securities Congress of 1900.

Table 1.192 Securities Listed on the Paris Stock Exchange (nominal values in millions of francs)

Public debts	29,800
Rail and tramways (in France)	18,419
Rail and tramways in the colonies	652
Mines	516
Metal industry	237
Maritime transport	390
Water, gas, electricity distribution	736
Various other industries	1,928
Banks and insurance companies	4,128

No source given.

620. See the detailed statistics in the *Annuaire statistique de la France.*

We could cite similar figures abroad. In the United States, the capital invested in the railways reached $21 billion!

But since the beginning of the twentieth century, a change has taken place which has placed investments in electricity, petroleum, chemical products and cars alongside railway shares.

The statistics for shares listed on the New York Stock Exchange allow us to clarify this transformation:

Table 1.193 Shares Listed on the New York Stock Exchange, Estimates as of 1 October 1929 (millions of $)

Cars	5,671
Chemicals	6,705
Petroleum	7,405
Iron and Steel	4,023
Gas and Electricity	5,849
Communications (cables, telephones, radios and telegraphs)	5,139
Railways (shares only)	11,945

Source: *Commercial and Financial Chronicle* 129, no. 3365, 21 Dec. 1929, 3896.

It is natural that the ebb and flow of the production of the means of production mainly results from the construction of railways, tramways, electric power plants and car factories.

And in fact, history demonstrates that the transport industries, the electrical and metal industries and, more recently, the car industry have played the essential role in these alternating periods of progress and retreat. The crises of the nineteenth and twentieth centuries have mainly been railway crises. The other industries (cotton, wool, silk, etc.) follow only imperfectly these starts and stops. Their interdependency [*par solidarité*] means that, in the event of a very clear and lively boom period, they will also be caught up in the expansion. But the fall in prices in the middle of a growth period often catches them off guard. The German survey of the crisis of 1900 indicates why the textile industries rarely took part in the good fortune. The expansion of production through the creation of new machines and equipment is too rapid in times of exceptional profits for competition not to moderate prices and check the increase. And in fact, among all the industries, the textile industry is the one which produces the lowest industrial profits. The textile manufacturer profits more from his commercial skill and speculations on raw materials than from his technical operations. The fact is well-known: the technical increase in production almost immediately follows the price rise.

The period of growth from 1905 to 1907 in the British textile industry confirms this point of view. From 1906, the creation of new operations slowed down. Similarly, in the crisis of 1920, growth had been very brief in the textile industry. The drop in prices followed very quickly, one year after the rise. Yet it was necessary to reconstitute most of the equipment of our powerful operations in Roubaix, Tourcoing and Lille. A few months sufficed. Denuc's recent work on company dividends confirms this observation for a period of almost a century (1857–1932), as far as France is concerned.[621]

The equipment of the textile industry is too light for their haphazard production to have a serious effect on the economic development of the metal industry. *A fortiori*, the production of metal consumer goods (metal hardware) is quite secondary. And apart from textile equipment, what other types of large machinery have our modern societies created?

Basically, the metal industry has four major customers: transport, electricity, cars and construction. The metal industry is also its own customer. If the crux of the problem of crises lies in the production of metals, the means of production and their alternatives, it is best to look at these four large customers. Why do they place orders at a given time, only to suspend them at another? For the history of crises demonstrates that the stop in orders placed with the metal industry, the decline in production and drop in the prices of metals constitute the best indexes for general crises.

No doubt, companies founded before a crisis (railway companies and others) are sometimes completed after its resolution. The production of the means of production will not always reach its minimum immediately after a crisis. But a crisis is a slowdown in orders, a decline in the production of cast iron, steel and copper. And explaining this slowdown is essential to explaining a crisis because that which triggers the drop in prices and the limiting of production will influence credit, banks and the stock exchange. It is this drop in the prices of cast iron and steel that through interdependencies [*par solidarité*] causes the general decrease in prices. The crisis in the metal industry affects all other branches of economic activity. Abandoned by one or another of its main customers, it suffers a crisis. The crisis which was initially partial becomes generalized. For a long time, the problem of crises was not so narrowly construed, and countless theories emerged.

Even today, new theories arise independent of any positive study of the phenomenon. They do not deserve to be taken into consideration. A theory of crises must be preceded by a historical and statistical study of the facts. Otherwise, it is worthless, or has at most the value of a hypothesis. There is, however, broad agreement on our understanding of the phenomenon; and the differences between theorists are no longer such that a synthesis of the main positive explanations of crises cannot be successfully attempted. We shall endeavour to do so in a study of the causes of economic crises.

Editorial Notes

i In his review of the fourth edition, R. G. Hawtrey points out that 'The British Government did not advance £28,000,000 or any other sum to the Bank of England in 1818', *Economic Journal* 44, no. 173 (1934): 111. As this figure also appeared in the first edition of 1906, Lescure may have misinterpreted a statement in Andréas Andréadès, *Essai sur la fondation*

621. Jules Denuc, 'Dividendes, valeur boursière et taux de capitalisation', *Bulletin de la Statistique générale de la France* 23 (July–Sep. 1934): 691–767.

et l'histoire de la Banque d'Angleterre (1694–1844) (Paris: Rousseau, 1901), 346, which has the Bank's directors imprudently advancing £28 million to the government.

ii Although 'cost price' is considered a somewhat outdated term in Anglophone (but not Francophone) corporate accounting today, it best captures the sense in which Lescure applied the term '*prix de revient*' generally to represent the sum of all direct and indirect costs incurred in the production and distribution of a product or service, which he juxtaposes with the '*prix de vente*', or 'selling price', when describing the effects of these variable costs on the margin of profit. Lescure outlines this relationship most precisely in the analytical discussion in chapter two, sec. two, §2. Organic Theories, part G.) 'Theories explaining [crises] through variations in potential profits'.

iii The more common term used in English today would be 'credit rollover'.

iv Lescure describes these transactions as 'opérations de report sur les valeurs des sociétés industrielles nouvellement créées'; in this sense, these were more like 'call options', as the purchaser could default on subsequent instalments and not complete the purchase, thereby losing the money already put in. Lescure's description of the *Raten- und Rentenbanken* and the *Maklerbanken* closely follows Schäffle, 'Der "grosse Börsenkrach"', 14, 27–30.

In France, 'Operations de report', or simply reports, worked much like call money, in that the broker would be advanced sums 'on call' for one day and pay only a percentage of the transaction up front, with the chance of renewing (deferring) repayment with a new loan on the next day. Although Lescure does not mention the role of call money in the context of the 1882 crash and the Union Générale failure, this later case is more illustrative of the role of call money in the stock market manias that often lead to financial crises. See Robert Z. Ailber, Charles P. Kindleberger and Robert N. McCauley, *Manias, Panics, and Crashes: A History of Financial Crises*, 8th ed. (Cham, Switzerland: Palgrave Macmillan, 2023), 82–84.

v See S. MacLean Hardy, 'The Quantity of Money and Prices, 1860–1891', *Journal of Political Economy* 3, no. 2 (March 1895): 145–68.

vi *Sic.* The last of the five companies should undoubtedly read Hamburg-Südamerika.

vii '*Politique dite de fusion*' refers to integration clauses in fixed-price contracts, which would allow economic price adjustments, or in this specific context, allow German coke and pig iron cartels to fix their prices for the next two years.

viii Lescure expresses tonnage here in *tonneaux* – i.e., 'casks', the old English unit of carrying capacity, equal to one English long ton.

Volume II

CAUSES AND REMEDIES

Chapter Two

THE CAUSES OF GENERAL OVERPRODUCTION CRISES

Among the theorists of crises, some focus their observations on the state of circulation and credit and claim to show that the crisis is a monetary phenomenon. Others prefer to consider production, distribution and consumption.[1] We must consider these factors as a whole. The open market policy constitutes quite an interesting novelty.

---

1. Eugen von Bergmann, *Die Wirtschaftskrisen: Geschichte der nationalökonomischen Krisentheorien* (Stuttgart: Kohlhammer, 1895); W. C. Mitchell, *Business Cycles: The Problem and its Setting* (New York: NBER, 1927); Warren W. Persons, 'Theories of Business Fluctuations: I. A Classification of Theories', *Quarterly Journal of Economics* 41, no. 1 (Nov. 1926): 94–128; Alvin H. Hansen, *Business Cycle Theory: Its Development and Present Status* (Boston: Ginn, 1927); Simon Kuznets, *Secular Movements in Production and Prices: Their Nature and their Bearing upon Cyclical Fluctuations* (Boston: Houghton Mifflin, 1930), as well as Kuznets, 'Monetary Business Cycle Theory in Germany', *Journal of Political Economy* 38, no. 2 (April 1930): 125–63; Alec L. Macfie, *Theories of the Trade Cycle* (London: Macmillan, 1934); Wilhelm Röpke, *Die Konjunktur: Ein systematischer Versuch als Beitrag zur Morphologie der Verkehrswirtschaft* (Jena: Fischer, 1922), and Röpke, *Crises and Cycles*, trans. Vera C. Smith (London: Hodge, 1936); Francesco Vito et al., *Cicli economici: Contributi dell'Instituto di Scienza sociali* (Milan: Società editrice 'Vita e pensiero', 1937); Hans Mayer, *Die Wirtschaftstheorie der Gegenwart*, vol. 4, *Konjunktur und Krisen* (Vienna: Springer, 1928); Ernst Wagemann, *Einführung in die Konjunkturlehre* (Leipzig: Quelle & Meyer, 1929), 20; Rolf Wagenführ, *Die Konjunkturtheorie in Russland* (Jena: Fischer, 1929); Tihomir J. Markovitch, *Les théories modernes de la sous-consommation* (Paris: Rivière, 1938); and see also the compendium, Gottfried von Haberler, *Prospérité et dépression: Étude théorique des cycles économiques* (Geneva: Société des Nations, 1937).

Section One

Theories Explaining Crises as Monetary Phenomena

Among the theorists of crises, some focus on the drop in prices, following Juglar's classic definition. For them, it is this termination of the price increase that needs to be explained.

As the rise is general, and also the drop, it is tempting to invoke the quantitative theory. But by 'money', one could understand metal money, banknotes or deposits. All three have been offered as the basis for the rise and fall of prices.

§1. – Metal money

This explanation of crises was based on facts and doctrine.

The 1857 crisis, which was preceded by a colossal level of gold extraction and an enormous price rise,[2] suggests that general economic crises can be explained by an increase in the stock of metal currency. Schäffle, among others, viewed the rise in prices from 1850 to 1857 as a monetary phenomenon and nothing more.

But because this theory was unable to explain subsequent crises, it was abandoned and seemed to have fallen into oblivion when it was taken up again by Sombart. For him, the crisis of 1900, which occurred after the exploitation of the Transvaal mines; the crisis of 1857; and finally the crisis of 1873, which followed the influx of the five-billion-franc French war indemnity, were confirmation of the causal relationship between the increase in the stock of metal money and general crises.

But how can an increase in the stock of metal cause general or, more precisely, generalized overproduction?

It is a well-known fact that the increase in metal stock leads to a price rise, which in turn stimulates the spirit of enterprise and feverish attempts to benefit from this price rise. The working class, largely employed, receives high wages; the capitalist class nets large dividends. Speculation occurs, and prices climb, thereby stimulating production. However, the time comes when production has expanded so much that the relationship between the quantity of existing money and that of goods to be exchanged is reversed; instead of an excess of metal compared with goods, there is an excess of goods in comparison to metal. We have overproduction. Since metal is in high demand, as evidenced by the diminished cash on hand at the banks of issue, the purchasing power of metal grows, the value of goods in relation to metal decreases and prices drop. This is the

---

2. See Werner Sombart, 'Referat über die Störungen im deutschen Wirtschaftsleben während der Jahre 1900 ff.', presented at the general meeting of the Verein für Socialpolitik, Hamburg, 15 Sep. 1903, in *Verhandlungen des Vereins für Socialpolitik über die Lage in der Seeschiffahrt beschäftigten Arbeiter und über die Störungen im deutschen Wirtschaftsleben während der Jahre 1900 ff.*, Schriften des Vereins für Socialpolitik 113 (Leipzig: Duncker & Humblot, 1904), 121–37; and Sombart, 'Versuch einer Systematik der Wirtschaftskrisen', *Archiv für Sozialwissenschaft und Sozialpolitik*, n.s., 1, no. 1 (1904): 1–22.

crisis. Growing demand is followed by decreasing demand; after the rise in profits and wages comes the decrease; and the fever of enterprise is followed by calm and stagnation.

Some objections must be taken into consideration.

In order to establish the causal link between the increase in the stock of metal currency and crises, every growth period would have to be preceded by an increase in money stock. However, if this was indeed the case in the 1851–1857 and 1895–1900 periods, it was not so in 1844–1847 or 1862–1866, or even in 1870–1873, because only an insignificant part of the five-billion indemnity was paid in money.[3] The first relationship therefore appears to us to be too accidental to allow one to establish a causal link.

That is not all. Logically, the increase should reach its maximum level in the country where the growth of the money stock is greatest and at the time of this growth. However, this is not the case: Germany saw its stock of gold increase to a far greater extent from 1890 to 1895, a period of decline, than in the growth period from 1895 to 1900. In the first case, it rose by 490 million marks, and in the second, by 170 million marks. In reality, the new gold production did not flow toward Germany; it helped to put a whole series of countries – Russia, Austria-Hungary, the United States and Japan – on the gold standard; and it was these countries that absorbed the new 8,150 million marks. The United States alone took 700 million marks from 1895 to 1900.[4] Not only did Germany receive a relatively small amount of gold during the prosperity period from 1895 to 1900, but it also received less in comparison to France and England. In France, the increase in the gold stock reached 670 million marks; in Britain, 1,100 million marks. Yet the growth was most noticeable in Germany.

Experience raises doubts as to the validity of Sombart's theory. However, the theoretical reasoning is not impeccable either. The quantitative theory thus formulated has nowadays been abandoned. The speed of money's circulation can compensate for the increase in the volume of exchanges to be made. Metal money plays a decreasing role in trade. It has many substitutes. And it is an exaggeration to take the word 'money' in the narrow sense to mean precious metals.[5] Sombart more recently abandoned this view, placing the primary emphasis on credit and paper money.

§2. – Paper money

Some authors have based their explanation of crises on a broadened quantitative theory. The generalization of the instruments of exchange, such as metal money, banknotes and deposits, has brought about a revision of this theory. Price would be a ratio between the exchangeable goods and the metal or paper currency.

---

3. Léon Say, 'Rapport fait au nom de la commission du budget de 1875 sur le paiement de l'indemnité de guerre et sur les opérations de change qui en ont été la conséquence', in Léon Say, *Finances publiques, liberté du commerce*, ed. J. Chailley-Bert (Paris: Guillaumin, 1896), 36–49.
4. Magnus Biermer, 'Die Letzte deutsche Wirtschaftskrise und ihre Ursachen', in *Sammlung nationalökonomischer Aufsätze und Vorträge*, vol. 1 (Giessen: Roth, 1905), 196–97.
5. According to Alfred de Foville, *La Monnaie*, 2nd ed. (Paris: Gabalda, 1907), 138–46. See also Rudolf Stucken, *Theorie der Konjunkturschwankungen* (Jena: Fischer, 1926).

A.) Theory explaining crises as an excessive issuing of banknotes

For some, the quantity of money which defines purchasing power is comprised of metal and banknotes. If the quantity of banknotes increases, demand increases, and with it, prices.[6]

At the beginning of the nineteenth century, economists were struck by the relationship that existed between the excessive issuing of banknotes and the price rise preceding every economic crisis. They also noted the coexistence of the drop in prices and the banknote crisis. They wondered whether the excessive issuing of banknotes might not be the cause of economic crises.

The proponents of the currency principle followed much the same line of reasoning as the gold stock theorists in terms of the mechanics of the price increase: rise in prices, drop in the discount, widespread use of credit, speculation. But the decrease seemed to them to arise less from overproduction than from a banknote crisis. In their minds, the crisis was to be considered a simple phenomenon of circulation. Unrestrained issues caused the public to lose confidence. The crisis is this loss of confidence as the banknote loses its value. This crisis is marked by the search for precious metals and by 'runs' on the banks. In this instance, the drop in prices was again seen as the consequence of a greater appreciation of precious metals. But this increase in the value of metals was thought to result from the crisis of the banknote, after excessive issues raised fears about its convertibility. This theory was very much en vogue around 1840–1844.[7] Its supporters were triumphant. The Bank Charter Act of 1844 regulating the Bank of England was inspired by the currency principle: it was essential that a banknote circulate at parity with gold for it to remain always convertible. In this way, every banknote issued had to be matched in the bank's cash on hand by a sum in gold equivalent to the amount of the note.

What to make of this theory?

It is not certain whether the excessive issues of banknotes had any influence on the crises of 1815, 1825 and 1836. By stimulating growth, they might have exaggerated the price increase and thereby intensified the severity of the crises, just as the excessive use of paper money had prepared the way for the violent crisis of 1920. Yet the abuse of credit exacerbated the crisis, without having caused it. Economic history demonstrates that economic crises are not always accompanied by abuses of this kind. No sooner had the Act of 1844 come into force than the crisis of 1847 broke out, and it was to be followed by many others. Those crises occurred independently of any banknote crisis.

---

6. See Andréas Andréadès, *Histoire de la Banque d'Angleterre*, 2 vols. (Paris: Rousseau, 1904), 2: 39–49; James Wilson, *Capital, Currency, and Banking*, quoted in Bergmann, *Die Wirtschaftskrisen*, 190; Samuel Jones Loyd, *Tracts and Other Publications on Metallic and Paper Currency by the Right Hon. Lord Overstone* (London: Longman, Brown, 1858).
7. We have proof that it was discussed in pamphlets, for example, Samuel Jones Loyd (Lord Overstone), *Reflexions suggested by a perusal of Mr. S. Horsley Palmer's pamphlet on the causes and consequences of the pressure on the money market* [London, 1837], quoted in Bergmann, *Die Wirtschaftskrisen*, 192. Charles Rist, *Histoire des doctrines relatives au crédit et à la monnaie* (Paris: Recueil Sirey, 1938).

Better still, the facts seemed to defy the theorists when, as early as 1847, they forced the authors of the Act of 1844 to violate the currency principle. Nowadays, while the 'currency principle' and the 'banking principle' are still being debated, there is no longer any question as to whether the issuing of banknotes causes crises.

Besides, already in the 1840s the shrewdest economists, Thomas Tooke among others, had set about refuting the currency principle.

Tooke had written the five volumes of his *History of Prices* to demonstrate that there was no connection between the rise in prices and the quantity of banknotes in circulation; he fought against the Act of 1844 and, during the parliamentary inquiry on the crisis of 1847, criticized the regulation of banknote issuance in England. He claimed, and history has since proven him right, that by inflaming public opinion, the Act of 1844 further aggravated the difficulties in times of economic crisis.

To the currency principle he opposed the banking principle. The issue of banknotes, instead of being the cause of exchanges and their activity, was simply the effect. The banknote was used to discount bills of exchange. The issuing of a note therefore presupposes a previous exchange, unless it is an accommodation bill of exchange [*lettre de change de complaisance*]. Attributing trade activity to excessive issues of banknotes would therefore be a real *petitio principii*. Only a prior circulation of wealth is capable of bringing about a greater recourse to credit and an increase in banknote circulation. And again, the speed of circulation can compensate for the importance of discount operations. A period of economic prosperity is not necessarily a period of increased banknote issuance.

But the inability of the Bank Charter Act of 1844 to prevent the crises of 1847 or 1857 has led some economists to question whether the regulation of issuance intended to avert the crises did not in fact cause them.[8] Thus, a school of economists formed in France that held the Banque de France's issuing monopoly responsible for economic crises. The Banque de France's monopoly,[9] by restricting discount facilities, led to an increase in the discount rate in the event of industrial and commercial growth. This increase in the discount rate placed heavy burdens on industry and commerce. The crisis was thought to occur at the moment when these burdens become too much for trade and industry to bear. These attacks on the Banque de France's monopoly had a considerable impact. This theory was welcomed in commercial and industrial circles, which eagerly awaited an increase in the discount rate at a time when the need for credit was most urgent. The course of general opinion was such that in 1865 the government

8. See J. Édouard Horn, *La liberté des Banques* (Paris: Guillaumin, 1866), 308–313, 440.
9. It was not clear which monopoly was meant. See Isaac Pereire, *Principes de la constitution des banques et de l'organisation du crédit* (Paris: Dentu-Guillaumin, 1865), 29–39; Horn, *La liberté*, 442; G. Poujard'hieu, 'Les crises financières et l'organisation du crédit en France', *Revue des deux mondes* 33, no. 3 (June 1861): 686–708; Charles Coquelin, 'Les crises commerciales et la liberté des Banques', *Revue des deux mondes*, n.s., 24, no. 3 (Nov. 1848): 445–70.

decided to open an inquiry into the Banque de France's monopoly. The Banque's privilege was upheld.[10]

This theory was in fact based upon multiple confusions: first, it confused the issuing monopoly with the discount monopoly. It also conflated the discount rate and the interest rate. However, the discount is subject to abrupt and intense variations which have no effect on the interest rate. Finally, this theory attributed a significance to the discount rate that it does not possess. The cost of raw materials and the wage rate have a more decisive influence on the economic prosperity of an industry or business. This theory, which was very successful, no longer has many adherents. The United States experienced crises throughout the nineteenth century despite the freedom to establish banks of issue.

Moreover, the banknote is not the only kind of paper currency, nor is it the main one. Credit will bear the responsibility for crises. But here we will discover two types of doctrines that are completely opposed. For some economists, the crisis is due to the exaggeration of credit; while for others, it has its source in the lack of sufficient credit, particularly in the scarcity of gold or its flawed and irrational distribution. The latter doctrine is close to the theories discussed in France around 1865 that we have just analysed.

B.) Theories explaining crises as the abuse of credit

Like the preceding theories, these base the crisis on simple monetary and credit relations. 'The crisis is the point at which the price increase stops', said Juglar. By money, they refer not only to metal money and banknotes but also to deposits and bills of exchange. The quantity of money is measured not so much by the quantity of precious metals produced than by the quantity of bills of exchange issued. Alongside the gold mine, the nineteenth century created a source of instruments of exchange and infinitely richer purchasing power: credit.

The mechanism of rising prices is more complex than the theorists of the currency principle or those of the gold mine have assumed. There comes a time when the economic depression that follows the appearance of any economic crisis has brought prices down to a level low enough for new demand to emerge, and a new price increase occurs. This quite natural increase is soon transformed into one created by pure speculation. The merchant or the industrialist no longer purchases or produces in response to demand, but in the hope of prolonging or intensifying the rise in prices. They make deals to deliver or to buy, not just with their own money but also on credit. In their feverish pursuit of profit, they even resort to credit accommodations.[i] Exchanges multiply in number and value, and with them, the discounted bills of exchange. In order to discern a period of growth, it is sufficient to know the amount of a country's discounts. And in fact, Juglar and his school predict crises by the increase in the portfolio of the banks of

10. *Enquête sur les principes et les faits généraux qui régissent la circulation monétaire et fiduciaire* (Paris: Imprimerie Nationale, 1866).

issue. They explain crises by the rapid growth of speculation, the abuse of credit and finally by the collapse of speculation and prices.

The rise in prices reaches its limit at the point when the bullish speculator can no longer find any speculator more optimistic than himself. One has purchased but can no longer find a buyer. Does one resort to credit in order to liquidate? Yet credit was abused during the growth period. Bills of exchange that come due must be settled. Either banknotes or gold are requested as payment. The cash on hand at the large banks of issue is reduced. The banks raise their discount rates in order to protect their cash. This increase in the discount rate slows down the demand for credit. People decide to sell, even at a loss, the goods in their warehouses and the securities in their portfolios. Prices fall, and the fall lasts long enough to allow demand to recover; then prices rise in a process similar in every respect to the previous increase.

This doctrine unites economists of all schools: Juglar, Block, Colson, Macleod, Wagner, Eberstadt, Oldenberg, Steinberg and many others still maintain that the abuse of credit is the primary cause of crises.[11]

Without disputing the significant role credit plays in our contemporary societies and without ignoring the fact that a crash can result from excessive speculation, the general overproduction crisis has a deeper cause. It is a crash, but it is also something more.

---

11. Clément Juglar, *Des crises commerciales et de leur retour périodique en France, en Angleterre et aux États-Unis*, 2nd ed. (Paris: Guillaumin, 1889), 29, 71–74 and 255; Juglar, 'Des crises commerciales et monétaires de 1800 à 1857', 2 pts, *Journal des économistes*, 2nd ser., 14, nos. 41–42 (1857): 35–60, 253–66; Juglar, 'Crises commerciales', in *Nouveau dictionnaire d'économie politique*, ed. Léon Say and Joseph Chailley, 2nd ed., 3 vols. (Paris: Guillaumin, 1900), 1: 641–50; Juglar and P. des Essarts, 'Crises financières et commerciales', in *Dictionnaire des finances*, ed. Léon Say, 2 vols. (Paris and Nancy: Berger-Levrault, 1889–1894), 1: 1348–55; Henry Dunning Macleod, *Theory of Credit*, 2nd ed., 2 vols. (London: Longmans, Green, 1893–1897), vol. 2, pt. 2: 938–54; Émile Levasseur, *La question de l'or: Les mines de Californie et d'Australie* (Paris: Guillaumin, 1858), 243–50; Maurice Block, *Les progrès des sciences économiques depuis Adam Smith: Revision des doctrines économiques*, 2 vols. (Paris: Guillaumin, 1890), 2: 15–16; Adolf Wagner, *Grundlegung der politischen Oekonomie*, 3rd ed., 2 vols. (Leipzig: Winter, 1894), 2: 144–48; Wagner, 'Krisen', in *Handwörterbuch der Volkswirtschaftslehre*, ed. Hermann Rentzsch, 2nd ed. (Leipzig: Klinkhardt, 1870), 525–37; William Fowler, 'Crises Commercial and Financial', in *Dictionary of Political Economy*, ed. R. H. Inglis Palgrave (London: Macmillan, 1894), 1: 455–61; Rudolf Eberstadt, *Die gegenwärtige Krisis: Ihre Ursachen und die Aufgaben der Gesetzgebung* (Berlin: Hoffmann, 1902), 15; K. Oldenberg, 'Zur Theorie der volkswirtschaftlichen Krisen', *Jahrbuch für Gesetzgebung, Verwaltung und Volkswirtschaft* 27, no. 3 (1903): 66–67 (850–51); Julius Steinberg, *Die Wirtschaftskrisis 1901: Ihre Ursachen, Lehren und Folgen* (Bonn: Cohen, 1902), 10; Georg Bernhard, *Krach, Krisis und Arbeitsklasse* (Berlin: Buchhandlung *Vorwärts*, 1902), 40; Clément Colson, *Cours d'économie politique*, 3 vols. (Paris: Gauthier-Villars and Guillaumin, 1903), 2: 723; Colson, *Cours d'économie politique*, vol. 4, *Les entreprises, le commerce et la circulation*, definitive ed. (Paris: Gauthier-Villars and Félix Alcan, 1920), 492; Knut Wicksell, *Geldzins und Güterpreise: Eine Studie über die den Tauschwert des Geldes bestimmenden Ursachen* (Jena: Fischer, 1898); Ludwig von Mises, *Geldwertstabilisierung und Konjunkturpolitik* (Jena: Fischer, 1928); and Friedrich A. von Hayek, *Geldtheorie und Konjunkturtheorie* (Vienna: Hölder-Pichler-Tempsky, 1929).

Certainly, growth can be accompanied by abuses: it provides a fertile ground for speculation; however, phenomena similar to those described by Juglar and his school can be found outside of the context of the general overproduction crisis. From a theoretical point of view, these authors take us back to the times of mercantilism when, according to Boisguilbert, the servant was made to play the role of the master.

Phenomena similar to those described by these authors, and by Juglar in particular, can be found outside of the general overproduction crises. Widespread recourse to credit, numerous futures markets, an increase in the portfolio at banks of issue, soon followed by an exchange crisis, a reduction in cash on hand and a raising of the discount rate can all be misleading when taken as signs of crises. Significantly abnormal imports can cause similar phenomena to appear, independent of any commercial crisis. Thus, at the beginning of 1847, following strong cereal imports into France and England, and in 1864, following the rise in cotton prices and circumstances we have previously described, we see in France and England all the crisis symptoms established by Juglar, and yet, the periodic crisis had not yet broken out. It is akin to the outbreak of war: the belligerents call in their claims on foreign countries, and this can also lead to an exchange crisis, the flight of gold and an increase in the discount rate; this was the case in France and England in 1861. In December 1899, the exchange crisis in Germany originated partly from England having realized its claims against foreign countries as a result of the outbreak of the Boer War. In 1911, it was France which realized its claims against Germany.[12]

On the other hand, some general economic crises occur independently of any reduction in cash on hand and any exchange crisis: in 1866 in France, 1873 in Germany and the United States, and 1882 in France.

Juglar's theory, despite the indisputable progress it made over previous crisis theories, also falls short of a sufficiently comprehensive study of the phenomenon. However remarkable the results of his research on the relationship between fluctuations in the balance sheets of large banks of issue and economic crises, however perceptive his analysis of the credit mechanism, it is nevertheless true that he has devoted too much attention to one side of the phenomenon. No doubt, price has an influence on production and consumption. But is price a pure and simple result of the relationship between the quantity of paper or metal (gold and silver) money in circulation and the quantity of goods produced? Does the bill of exchange cause production and consumption? Or is the bill of exchange not rather the record of a previous exchange, which has its own reason for being and its own explanation in the laws of production and of consumption? To accept Juglar's theory – which we would like to call the theory of credit-demand – would be to admit that the vast majority of credit agreements granted in our modern societies are simply accommodation credits [*crédits de complaisance*], corresponding to no actual transaction. If the crisis has its basis in the artificial demand caused by exaggerated credit and speculation, the fall will be even more abrupt and deeper, and the distress more

12. Jean Lescure, 'Les marchés financiers de Paris et de Berlin et la crise franco-allemande de juillet–octobre 1911', *Revue économique internationale* 9, no. 3 (Sep. 1912): 466–509.

intense than it actually is. The recovery, on the other hand, will be quicker. To imagine a similar crisis, let us extend it to include all branches of production, the stock exchange and the commodities market, like the one which struck in 1905 in France on the sugar market and the one in October–November 1920 on the New York Stock Exchange. The crisis would be more violent. But once the storm passed, the crisis would not degenerate into a slow economic depression. And just as the sugar market returned to normal within a few months, so too would the world market recover just as quickly. However, this is not in fact the case. Juglar's theory, questionable in its explanation of the period of growth, remains silent when it comes to the depression.

Juglar and his school find the cause of crises in the excesses of credit and the excessive price increases that discourage consumption, causing market gluts. Modern theories explaining crises by credit see the cause of crises in the lack of credit, the rise in discount rate and the resulting drop in prices. For Juglar, credit inflates prices, discouraging the demand for goods.

For contemporary economists, the credit crunch causes prices to decrease. This is a different conception. This is why we shall distinguish between them, adding that Juglar's conception seems to us to be more interesting and closer to the facts, albeit without getting to the bottom of things. The same conception is the inspiration for Maurice Ansiaux's recent book.[13] The exaggerations of credit, by inflating prices more than wages, would cause underconsumption.

C.) Theories explaining crises as the lack of sufficient credit

For these economists, the crisis is characterized by a drop in prices, which by cutting profits discourages the spirit of enterprise. For costs drop more slowly than prices. The decrease in prices itself is caused by a lack of credit.[14] Following a period of growth, depleted gold reserves force the central banks to raise the discount rate or even to control

13. Ansiaux, *L'inflation du crédit et la prévention des crises* (Paris: Dalloz, 1934).
14. Thorstein Veblen, *The Theory of Business Enterprise* (1904; repr. New York: Charles Scribner and Sons, 1915), 235; R. G. Hawtrey, *Currency and Credit*, 3rd ed. (1919; repr. London: Longmans, Green, 1928); Hawtrey, *Trade and Credit* (London: Longmans, Green, 1928); Henry Strakosch, 'Gold and the Price Level: A Memorandum on the Economic Consequences of Changes in the Value of Gold', supplement to the *Economist*, 5 July 1930, and 'The Road to Recovery', supplement to the *Economist*, 6 Jan. 1935; John Maynard Keynes, *A Treatise on Money*, 2 vols. (London: Macmillan, 1930), 2: 289; L. Albert Hahn, 'Grundprinzipien der monetären Konjunkturtheorie', in *Konjunkturforschung und Konjunkturtheorie: Wissenschaftliche Gutachten*, pt 2, *Beiträge zur Wirtschaftstheorie*, ed. Karl Diehl, Schriften des Vereins für Socialpolitik 173 (Munich and Leipzig: Duncker & Humblot, 1928), 153–64; SDN, *Rapports provisoires de la Délégation de l'or* (Geneva: SDN, 1930 and 1931); Werner Sombart, *Das Wirtschaftsleben im Zeitalter der Hochkapitalismus*, 2 vols. (Leipzig: Duncker & Humblot, 1927), 2: chap. 'Konjunktur'; Wicksell, *Geldzins und Güterpreise*; Friedrich A. von Hayek, 'Einige Bemerkungen über das Verhältnis der Geldtheorie zur Konjunkturtheorie', in *Konjunkturforschung und Konjunkturtheorie*, pt 2: 246–94; Royal Institute of International Affairs, *The International Gold Problem: Collected Papers* (London: Oxford University Press, 1931); and Baron Mourre, *Les fluctuations de l'activité économique: Les périodes de longue durée et les crises* (Paris: Félix Alcan, 1936).

credit. The equilibrium between the increasing quantities of products and the quantities of metal or paper money would thus be broken. A drop in prices results, and with it, the crisis. In 1930 and 1931, the influx of gold into the two creditor countries of the world, France and the United States, added something more to the classic and periodic cause of crises: the magnitude of the crisis of 1929–30.

It is a simple, seductive theory. We wish it was correct. For then the remedy would be easy. An opportune injection of sufficient money would either calm or cure the patient. Yet the facts establish that the abundance of credit is insufficient to remedy economic depressions. For the economists who explain crises by the abuse of credit appear to us to be far closer to the truth than the adherents to the doctrine of credit scarcity and insufficient stocks of gold. Wall Street would have avoided the crash of October 1929 if, by restricting credit, one could have curbed or stopped speculation. A cycle of growth or one of depression are otherwise complex. Credit is meant to sustain the growth and help overcome the depression. Money is made to play the essential role. Yet production and consumption, supply and demand, play a crucial role in economic life. To view money as the sole animator of economic life is to commit a sophism that is refuted merely by stating it.

The current doctrines relating to credit resurrect mercantilism, which economic science has correctly refuted and repudiated for over a century and a half. Certainly, a growth period requires an expansion of money circulation. But its elasticity is sufficient to be able to meet all needs. And the swelling stocks of money are insufficient to cause or create a period of prosperity.

A growth period presupposes new needs to be fulfilled and new industries to be created. This requires materials, labour, savings and entrepreneurs. It requires entrepreneurs to have confidence. Money alone is not enough to create and sustain this complex of conditions. The abundance of money alone is incapable of causing the rise in prices that can increase the profit rate and rekindle the spirit of enterprise.

Similarly, the abundance of credit at the end of a growth period is capable of provoking real anarchy in the price rise or in the increase in incomes. And it is anarchy: the imbalance in the price increase, the uneven development of various branches of production, the disequilibrium in quantity and value which cause the rupture – the crisis – and a drop in prices here or there, depending on the period and region.

During growth periods, the velocity of money circulation, of deposits in particular, increases.[15] This is proof that trade activity, not quantities of money, is the driving force behind the rise in prices. Trade activity causes a price rise, requiring the increase in the quantities of money and credit, and nevertheless, the velocity of their circulation increases.

15. W. Randolf Burgess, 'Velocity of Bank Deposits', *Journal of the American Statistical Association* 18, no. 142 (June 1923): 727–40; Burgess, 'The Money Market in 1929', *Review of Economics and Statistics* 12, no. 1 (Feb. 1930): 15–20.

To summarize, money and its movements are not the cause, they are the effect. It is the increase in prices that provokes the increased circulation, not the reverse. It is the drop in prices, the crisis and depression which cause circulation to contract, not the reverse.[16] In 1937 and 1938, the enormous increase in gold stocks was incapable of provoking an increase in prices. The law of supply and demand rules even general price variations.[17]

Thus, by way of conclusion, we must reject all of these theories that ascribe the dominant role to price considered as a monetary phenomenon, whether paper money or metals, in the formation of prices. Confined to the observation of only part of the economic phenomena, they are too narrowly focussed. Proponents of these theories have concentrated solely on identifying and describing the price rise mechanism and its conversion into the price fall mechanism, to the disadvantage of circulation. Some among them – Juglar above all – brought a remarkable level of depth to their analysis. Yet their analysis of the causes of the phenomenon remains fragmentary, insufficient and weak, particularly in comparison to their description of the reversing ebb and flow of the portfolio and the cash on hand of the large banks of issue. Attributing these alternating periods of growth and depression characteristic of our modern societies to pure monetary phenomena or to credit, while completely neglecting the relationship between production and consumption, is a bit like putting the cart before the horse. In fact, a greater reliance on credit comes from more active and numerous exchanges and not the other way around.

---

16. Cf. Charles Rist, *La déflation en pratique* (Paris: Giard, 1924); Dennis Holme Robertson, *Banking Policy and the Price Level* (London: P. S. King, 1926); A. C. Pigou, *Industrial Fluctuations*, 2nd ed. (London: Macmillan, 1929); Lionel Edie and Donald Weaver, 'Velocity of Bank Deposits in England', *Journal of Political Economy* 38, no. 4 (1930): 400 (graph); Achille Loria, *Corso di economia politica*, 4th ed. (Turin: Unione Tipografico-Editrice Torinese, 1934), 601.
17. Jean Lescure, *Hausses et baisses des prix de longue durée* (Paris: Domat-Montchrestien, 1933).

Section Two

Theories Explaining Crises through the Phenomena of Production, Consumption and Distribution

Thus, a number of authors have sought the cause of crises in the relationship between production and consumption and the influence of distribution on these two. Here we find before us a mosaic of opinions and theories, disconcerting at first sight. In this chaotic whole, we can nevertheless identify some distinct features.

The first essential distinction seems to result from the manner in which the crisis is considered. If the crisis is viewed as a phenomenon inherent in the organization of capitalist societies, we have before us what we shall refer to as an organic theory. It is based on the study of the modern economy as an organic whole. Otherwise, we have an inorganic theory. The first proceeds generally by way of observation, trying to find the source of crises in the economic characteristics of capitalist societies. The second combines, rather like the mathematician, the factors of production and consumption and attempts to formulate a general theory of crises that can be applied to any kind of exchange economy, as well as to a capitalist economy.

This fundamental distinction not only differentiates these two broad categories of crisis theory but also the history of their development. Whereas the inorganic approach has hardly been modified over the course of time, the organic theory has become more comprehensive and perfected, insofar as the facts have provided a broader basis for observation. From Lauderdale, Malthus, Sismondi and Ricardo to the present time, it has been expanded and refined.

§1. – Inorganic theories

All those theories based far more on *a priori* reasoning than on experience proceed from the same observation: the overproduction crisis is the result of an imbalance between production and consumption.[18] This explanation of crises comes down to this imbalance, and the appropriate name for these crises is not monetary or commercial crises, but sales crises

18. Joseph Garnier, *Éléments de l'économie politique: exposé des notions fondamentales de cette science*, 2nd ed. (Paris: Guillaumin, 1848), 204–5; Wilhelm Roscher, 'Zur Lehre von den Absatzkrisen' (1849), in *Ansichten der Volkswirtschaft aus dem geschichtlichen Standpunkte*, 3rd ed., 2 vols. (Leipzig: Winter, 1878), 2: 355–493; Roscher, *System der Volkswirtschaft*, vol. 1, *Grundlagen der Nationalökonomie*, 19th ed. (Stuttgart: Cotta, 1888); Clément, 'Des crises commerciales', *Journal des économistes*, 2nd ser., 17 (15 Feb. 1858): 161–91; A.-A. Issaïev, 'Les principales causes des crises économiques', 2 pts, *Revue d'économie politique* 7, no. 7/8 and 12 (1893): 654–92, 985–1011; Eugen von Philippovich, *Grundriss des politischen Oekonomie*, 3rd ed., 2 vols. (Freiburg: Mohr, 1899), 341–46; Edward D. Jones, *Economic Crises* (London: Macmillan, 1900), 21–39; Bernhard Rost, *Über das Wesen und die Ursachen unserer heutigen Wirtschaftskrisis* (Jena: Fischer, 1905), 2–15; Johannes Conrad, *Grundriss zum Studium der politischen Oekonomie*, 5th ed., 2 vols. (Jena: Fischer, 1905), 1: 256–64; and Camillo Supino, *Le crisi economiche* (Milan: Ulricho Hoepli, 1907). In the ninth edition of his *Grundriss*, vol. 1, *Allgemeine Volkswirtschaftslehre* (Freiburg: Mohr, 1911), 424–26, Philippovich analyses the theories of crises in the most recent works in the German language: Tugan-Baranowsky, Spiethoff and so on. He seems to follow these theories.

(*Absatzkrisen*). It is not in fact the relations between production and consumption that are distorted by the crisis, and what is lacking is not money but the sales outlet (*Absatz*). From here, one can easily envision the many circumstances that are liable to bring about a crisis.

Let us bring a little order to the chaos of factors which these authors cite as the causes of crises.

Since the crisis is an imbalance between production and consumption, its cause may be found either in production or consumption, or in a phenomenon likely to seriously affect one of these two. Moreover, this change in the equilibrium between production and consumption has to be abrupt.

With this in mind, this rupture can be either quantitative or qualitative: if quantitative, the crisis results in a sudden increase or decrease in production and/or consumption; if qualitative, one of the two factors changes its nature without diminishing, and one form of production or consumption gets replaced by another.

It goes without saying that these causes can exist in isolation, or they can co-exist; and if instead of offsetting one another they converge and intensify each other, the crisis will be all the more serious.

Thus, these theoretical givens enable us to distinguish between (a) quantitative crises of overproduction, underconsumption, overconsumption, underproduction or any combination of these factors and (b) qualitative crises of production and consumption. All that remains now is for us to classify under these headings the various phenomena that generate economic crises.

A.) Quantitative crises

1.) Overproduction crises

Among the many causes of overproduction are the division of labour, the opening of new markets and the subsequent speculation, the improvement of machinery and a protracted period of peace.

First, the division of labour: it is only natural, the proponents of this theory say, that the greater the division of labour, the more difficult it becomes to judge the extent of the market, the extent of production and consumption. The division of labour no longer remains at the local or even national level; rather, it is international. Thus, one can appreciate how isolated producers, working for a market they cannot comprehend because it is so large, will be vulnerable to simultaneously and unknowingly expanding production beyond demand.

This will prove especially true – and here we arrive at a second cause of overproduction – in cases where the increased division of labour coincides with the opening of new outlets. Eager to take advantage of the new windfall, each producer will expand his factories, order new machines and increase his output. New producers will come on line, and all this will be done in complete ignorance of what their neighbour is producing and the size of the market. Thus, they will continue to produce until an enormous drop in prices signals and reveals the market's saturation.[19]

It will be the same in the case of new improvements to the production process. Everyone will want to benefit from the profit that this new invention makes possible, and too many will end up exploiting the new discovery, and an overproduction crisis will be the result.

It would be very fortunate indeed if unbridled speculation did not aggravate the general blindness and hasten the inevitable appearance of overproduction and the collapse of prices. Finally, customs duties, by creating a Chinese wall around certain countries and by reserving the national markets for domestic producers, are also capable of causing an exaggerated sense of optimism, a false evaluation of the artificial increase in the market and, consequently, overproduction.

In periods of prolonged peace and international calm, societies will be led toward overconfidence and overproduction. And here we touch upon one of the most worrying aspects of this explanation of crises. For if a long peace is a factor in causing crises, its opposite, war, is no less so; and modern societies would struggle in the midst of these harrowing alternatives of peace or war, unable to avoid the overproduction equally implied by both!

2.) Underproduction

In effect, war leads to a decrease in production; the most productive part of the workforce is mobilized and sacrificed on the battlefield. Not only labour but also many other means of production – horses, railways, bridges and so on – are also wasted or destroyed. This decline in production results in diminished consumption, and hence, in overproduction. Yet the original cause is underproduction. The same could be said of revolutions, domestic unrest and epidemics. The same is true of a poor harvest, which reduces the buying power of rural consumers. The sectors of production that supply the rural population have neither the time nor the means to predict this sudden decrease in consumption and can fall prey to an outlet crisis [*crise de débouché*] and to overproduction.

But how then do we reconcile this apparently capricious cause of crises with their periodicity? This is what William Jevons attempted to do with his once famous but nowadays totally discredited theory of sunspots. He established a dual correlation: first, between bad harvests and excessive solar heat; and second, between the excessive solar heat and the appearance of sunspots. However, the appearance of sunspots would be periodic, occurring roughly every 10 years. Thus, the cycle of poor harvests would also recur every 10 years, as would crises. Since Jevons, it has been demonstrated: first, that poor harvests happen more often than every 10 years; and second, that sunspots do not appear every 10 years. Thus, the dual relationship on which the great economist built the fragile edifice of his theory has collapsed.

19. Marco Fanno, 'Cicli di produzione, cicli del credito e fluttuazioni industriali', *Giornale degli economisti e Rivista de statistica* 46, no. 5 (May 1931): 329–30, explains overproduction by the mistakes made by entrepreneurs, who during the expansion period exaggerate the increase in the number of new businesses created and the time needed for their creation.

It is no less true, however, that poor harvests continue to be invoked as the cause of crises and that they can and do deserve a place within a system of causes which is just as complex as that of the representatives of the inorganic school.[20]

3.) Overconsumption

Here, the disruption of equilibrium arises from the need for companies to quickly satisfy a sudden, but temporary, increase in demand. For a time, there will be much more demand; once it has been satisfied, a crisis will ensue, and there will be a lack of outlets. This can happen, for example, when new colonies or new countries are established. In the beginning, new plantations, roads, railways and houses will be built. Once this work is finished, however, a crisis will occur; after having produced great demand, the colony will not only purchase less but will produce less as well.

4.) Underconsumption

This last case can be boiled down to the second element: underproduction; for it is only in the event of a previous underproduction that one can speak of underconsumption in a theoretical study of the quantitative variations in the relationship between production and consumption. Production comes first, then consumption.

B.) Qualitative crises

The approach is different in the qualitative study of crises, where it is no longer a question of a decrease in production or consumption, but of a *change in direction* by one or the other. And it is here that distribution becomes a factor. Consumption will take different directions, depending on which social class benefits from the increase in income. So, here again, errors can be made in determining the direction of production or the sudden changes in the direction of consumption, which can upset the equilibrium between production and consumption.

An error in the direction taken by production will result from an increase in working-class income if the producer believes the income increase was among the wealthy classes. A crisis will then occur in the luxury industry. A crisis arising from a sudden change in consumption will have more diverse causes: fashion, war, the return of peace and saving income instead of spending it directly on consumption. Fashion is often

20. An American, H. L. Moore, has recently developed this idea, and so has William Jevons' son H. Stanley Jevons. D. H. Robertson grants a prominent place to this question. William Beveridge has published some interesting articles on this subject in the *Economic Journal*. In our view, this seems to open up a new field of economic research. Yet the general crisis evolves outside of this influence, although it is sometimes subject to it. There is thus a correlation between one phenomenon and another and nothing more. The coincidence of cause and effect is not consistent. See Vladimir P. Timoshenko, *The Role of Agricultural Fluctuations in the Business Cycle* (Ann Arbor: University of Michigan School of Business Administration, 1930).

cited as the cause of abrupt changes in consumption, and its whims have certainly been the cause of much embarrassment for the textile industry. The importance of this factor should not be exaggerated; for fashion is dictated more by the producer than the consumer. On the other hand, the industry most vulnerable to the whims of fashion, the textile industry, is endowed precisely with the remarkable ubiquity that allows its production to adapt quite easily to the whims of consumption.

The same does not apply to war; for not only does it lead to a decrease in production, but it can also cause an abrupt change in the direction of consumption. As Roscher rightly points out, war results in the creation of new taxes, war loans, as well as the establishment of extraordinary contributions and levies, and these sums do not receive the same allocation [*affectation*] they would have received had they been those of private consumers. In this respect, the *Chicago Tribune* of 31 December 1898 contains an interesting study on the economic influence of the Spanish-American War. War undeniably produced a shift in consumption and stimulated the production of pharmaceuticals, iron and steel, leather, packing cases, powder, brushes, agriculture, grain and flour; while shoemaking, construction and brewing were influenced in the opposite direction.[21] The war of 1914 allows for similar observations, but on a totally different scale.

The effects of changing the direction of demand will be even more noticeable when dealing with income that is saved (instead of being used in consumption) and its transformation into floating assets, followed by their immobilization into fixed assets. Clearly, there is a big difference between income spent on consumer goods and the investment of savings into building the means of production; in the first category are textiles and agricultural products, and in the second, the mining and metal industries.

Thus, for these theorists, crises have a common origin: the rupture of the equilibrium between production and consumption. The interdependencies [*solidarité*] of the industrial economy, arising from the ever-increasing division of labour and the expansion of credit, explain the general character of crises for the qualitative theorists. But their causes would remain extremely varied and multiple, making their occurrence very difficult or impossible to predict, and their prevention, an exercise in futility.

These theories also invoke experience. And while their proponents do not usually accept the periodicity of crises, they do, however, recognize the same years we have indicated as the dates for the onset of crises. Thus, for example, the 1814 and 1815 crises are attributed to the return of peace after many long years of war under the First Empire; that of 1825–26, to the opening of new markets and the speculation that ensued. Too many years of peace would have caused the 1839 crisis in America. In England, the transformation of income into circulating capital and then into fixed assets (railways) between 1846 and 1847, combined with poor harvests, would have caused the1847 crisis; in France, the crisis would have originated in the revolution of February 1848 and the poor harvests.[22] In 1857, the imbalance would have been caused by the discovery of gold

21. Jones, *Economic Crises*, 32–33.
22. Roscher, 'Zur Lehre von den Absatzkrisen', in *Ansichten der Volkswirtschaft*, 2: 416–17; Conrad, *Grundriss*, 1: 261; Issaïev, 'Les principales causes des crises', pt 2, 985; and Clément, 'Des crises commerciales', 184.

mines in California and Australia, which momentarily raised demand and prices.[23] In 1863, still more crop failures and destabilizing speculation would have led to the crisis.[24]

Finally, with the crisis of 1873, we would discover that this temporary increase in demand following a war caused the production side considerable embarrassment. In 1873, the payment of the war indemnity, which had to be settled within too short of a time frame, would further contribute to the crisis at the end of the conflict.[25] The 1882 crisis would be a consequence of speculation and the expansion of production, exaggerated by the risky manoeuvres of a new type of *crédit mobilier*: the Union Générale.[26] The American crisis of 1893 would stem from speculation and too rapid an expansion of railway construction, a bit like the crisis of 1847 in England. The crisis of 1900 in Germany would have its origin in and be caused by the shift in German customs tariff policy, the speculation of the banks and that of individuals,[27] though only a few branches of production (mining and metals) would have been affected. Germany would have even escaped any crisis truly worthy of the name.

The crises of 1920 and 1929 would be the result of the economic and monetary instability that followed the war of 1914. They are thought to be comparable to the crises of 1815 and 1818.

From a theoretical point of view, we do not deny the value of these doctrines or that they possess a certain logic; in fact, we do recognize that their evidence, however fragmentary and insufficient, is sometimes accurate and that there is a certain truth to their conclusions. Yet despite these concessions, we must address the numerous criticisms. For even if their claims are empirical, they are not sufficiently so; and if they are theoretical, they are too much so. The proponents of these theories most often classify crises according to their causes before providing a historical examination of crises and before empirically establishing their causes. On the other hand, despite listing a multiplicity of causes, there are some crises they still cannot explain.

There is no question that the division of labour, the improvement of machinery and the opening of new markets produce the effects indicated by the inorganic school. And if it were a question here of elaborating a general and *a priori* theory of economic equilibrium, perhaps we could follow Roscher, Clément, Jones, Conrad, Philippovich and their disciples. But the point is rather to explain the alternating periods of growth and depression. The object under investigation is not a hypothetical *a priori* phenomenon, a sudden disequilibrium between consumption and production; rather, it is a phenomenon *a posteriori*, constituted by experience and verified by history. These authors have not sufficiently narrowed down the economic phenomenon to be explained. And as we shall soon see, in studying the collectivist theories of crises, we must be careful not to explain the general crisis of overproduction with a general theory of overproduction.

23. Roscher, 'Zur Lehre von den Absatzkrisen', 415; Conrad, *Grundriss*, 1: 261; Clément, 'Crises commerciales'.
24. Conrad, *Grundriss*, 1: 261.
25. Ibid., 1: 262–63; Rost, *Wesen und Ursachen*, 13.
26. Conrad, *Grundriss*, 1: 263.
27. Rost, *Wesen und Ursachen*, 33–48.

Overproduction may happen suddenly or develop slowly. Can we give the same explanation in both cases? The starting point of these theories is open to criticism. So are the logical deductions that follow from it. Moreover, they could equally apply to both an exchange economy and capitalist economies. However, we hope to have demonstrated that the general overproduction crisis is a phenomenon that first appears with capitalism, and crisis theory must be grounded in the dominant features of the latter's mode of production. One should not reason *in abstracto* about the causes of an increase or decrease in production or consumption, trying to explain the facts in a way that fits the theories; rather, one should focus on drawing the explanation of the phenomenon from the study of facts. In place of a thorough historical study of general crises, these authors have merely assembled a motley assortment of causes.

These theories are weakest on empirical evidence. They must demonstrate a consistent simultaneity of wars, the opening of new markets, poor harvests, etc., and overproduction crises. This has not been demonstrated. From an accidental correlation, more often than not, these theorists have drawn a permanent relationship. Neither the crop failures of 1889 nor the Russo-Japanese War caused any sort of economic crisis. In 1900, the German crisis was not provoked by poor harvests, wars or the opening of new markets. We would be told that it was the result of speculation. But then we would come back to the hypothesis of the theorists who see crises as a consequence of speculation and credit abuse, and we have already explained this point. On the other hand, there are numerous cases where speculation intervened: in 1905, on the sugar market (crash of Jules Jaluzot and Ernest Crosnier); in 1905 and 1909 in the United States (speculation on corn); and yet, in these cases we do not see an overproduction crisis. In reality, in order for speculation to bring about, or appear to bring about, a general overproduction crisis, it must take place under a given set of circumstances; these circumstances alone can explain the crisis. This is what happened in New York in 1929.

In short, and by way of conclusion, theoretically these deductions would have a certain value if it were a question of giving a general view of the possible conditions of disequilibrium in societies with exchange economies. However, they are unable to account for a phenomenon with fixed boundaries, such as the general overproduction crisis. In effect, a whole series of causes are placed on the same level: wars, revolutions, peace, and so on, which are all irrelevant to the topic at hand. There are crises that occur in the absence of these causes. These causes have appeared throughout the course of history without provoking any overproduction crisis. Finally, and above all from an empirical point of view, these theories start with an insufficiently precise definition of the phenomenon, and they make the mistake of omitting that it develops with the advent of capitalism. Thus led astray, they ascribe to crises causes such as crop failures, which are just as likely to explain crises from the time of the Ptolemies as they are to shed light on our present day.

§2. – Organic theories

Theorists who view crises as a phenomenon specific to capitalist economies do not allow themselves to be as vague in their ideas. They always seek the cause of crises in some characteristic feature of modern economies.

Some theorists are attached to the notion of the anarchy of production and to the production fever in a society whose economic objective is profit; others focus on the expanded investment of savings in the work of production and on the production of capital equipment; others still look at the influence of distribution and wage labour on economic equilibrium and on consumption; and finally, others follow the length of the capitalist production process. We will attempt to retrace its historical development. This approach constitutes one of the best examples of the evolution of economic science toward ever more satisfactory results. In fact, we find that the principles taken up throughout the nineteenth century were already laid down from the beginning of the century. From Ricardo to Marx, the notion of the law of the tendential fall in the rate of profit; from Malthus to Tugan-Baranowsky, Pohle and Spiethoff, that of capitalist underconsumption; and from Sismondi to Rodbertus, that of working-class underconsumption, underwent remarkable transformations; but their starting point remained the same. We will retrace these transformations, this evolution of ideas, before laying out the theory that seems to us to be most in line with experience.

A.) The law of the tendency of the rate of profit to fall in David Ricardo and Henry George

The concept of rent guides Ricardo's theory concerning economic crises.[28] The normal play of the law of rent destroys profit, and with it, economic progress. Ricardo's hypothesis presupposes a society in the process of increasing development. In such a society, land rents increase, and production runs up against a contradiction: as a society develops, the cost of subsistence goods necessary to sustain the worker increases; the rent increases. Therefore, the minimum wage required for the worker's subsistence increases, and if wages increase, profit decreases. Thus, an economy in a dynamic state of development comes up against the following dilemma: either it continues to produce and sees a progressive decline in profit, or it slows down production – and still experiences a decline in profit. Certainly, by altering the normal play of the law of rent, technical improvements and the discovery and exploitation of new lands are also likely to alter that of the law of falling profit. But Ricardo reasons in the abstract, and having placed himself in the abstract, he does not fail to give chance and circumstances their place. As a result of the vagaries of history, these circumstances have undermined the law of rent. And the nineteenth century nonetheless recorded periodic overproduction crises. The facts belie the explanation.

Henry George, however, would attempt to explain crises on the basis of this law and by modifying Ricardo's ideas.[29] Instead of remaining attached to the idea of agricultural land rent, George considered what could be called urban land rent, or even mining land rent.

28. David Ricardo, *Des principes d'économie politique*, in *Œuvres complètes*, trans. Francisco Constâncio and Alcide Fonteyraud (Paris: Guillaumin, 1847), 92.
29. Henry George, *Progrès et pauvreté: Enquête sur la cause des crises industrielles* [...], trans. P.-L. Le Monnier (Paris: Guillaumin, 1887), 231–68.

He does not so much contrast the wage labourer with the entrepreneur as the wage labourer and the entrepreneur with the landowner. And he shows how the natural operation of the law of rent enriches the latter at the expense of the other two. As the population of a country grows and as large-scale industry is created, the law of rent comes into play. With the concentration of populations in large cities, the rent on urban land increases. Moreover, as industry develops, it must deal with the problem of mines becoming less and less profitable: here again rent plays a role. From the spontaneous generation of wealth that is rent, unhealthy speculation soon develops, inflating rents to such an extent that it becomes impossible for capitalists and workers alike to find remunerative activity – the first, for their capital, and the second, for their physical labour. No more houses are being built, as their construction would be ruinous for investors. No new mineshafts are being dug. A general halt in production occurs. Speculation pays dearly for its previous excesses. The artificial values created by repeated purchases and sales in the hope of an unlimited increase in rents are suddenly wiped out. Prices keep dropping until another round of urban population growth and industrial development enables the uptrend mechanism to begin again.

This theory is not without a certain level of rigour. Yet it is contradicted by the facts.[30] If the crisis were to result from a decrease in the share of the workers and capitalists in social production because the law of rent is at play, the period of increase would be characterized by a gradual decline in profits and wages. A time would come when they declined to such a degree that production would become impossible. This is not the case, however; for the capitalist's or worker's share, real as well as nominal, in the social wealth continues to grow. Moreover, if in theory the law of rent were capable of influencing the building and construction industry and if speculation were to paralyse the spirit of enterprise by driving up land prices, then the law of rent could not explain the stoppage of the mining and metal industries in times of crisis. No doubt the increase in production requires the exploitation of less and less productive mines. However, this is a long and slow process. And here again, the discovery of new technical improvements or of new, richer mines can counteract the effects of the law of rent. To give just one example, the discovery of the Thomas process in 1879 reduced the cost price of steel by enabling the use of cheap, phosphorous-rich ores in its production. Then, in 1890, the discovery of iron ore deposits at Mesaba, in the United States, compounded the effect of the first factor. Thus, the attempt to extend the law of rent to industry, however original it may be, is no less as imprecise as the mathematical and immediate application of the law of rent to agriculture.

We therefore reject George's theory. However, we do not reject it wholesale, and we acknowledge the sagacity of his analysis of the influence of urban rents on the building industry. His analysis was undoubtedly too narrow; for along with rent, the building entrepreneur must also take into account wages, cost of materials and interest rates. Nevertheless, land speculation plays an important role that we cannot overlook, and George deserves credit for bringing this to light. It is his contribution to a more comprehensive theory of economic crises.

30. The objections that we will address to George apply equally to Ricardo.

B.) Capitalist underconsumption and worker underconsumption

For Ricardo and George, the impossibility of realizing profits derived from the gradual increase in the cost of doing business; the crisis had its basis in the laws of production. The theories which we are about to discuss find the origin of the crisis in the facts of consumption and distribution.

Starting with the critiques of Jean-Baptiste Say's grand Law of Markets, according to which all production would be consumption, and all consumption, production, we must point out that not all production is always and necessarily consumption because, first, production can be savings instead of consumption; and second, production is consumption only if the producers have the power to consume or feel the need to consume an amount of wealth equal to their production. However, production does not always satisfy these two conditions. In fact, overproduction arises from the absence of one or the other of these conditions. In the first case, overproduction will result from an excess of savings; the producer will sell but will not buy. In the second case, the power to consume will belong to the one who does not feel the need to use it, and the one who has need of it will lack the power to do so. We shall call the first of these cases the theory of capitalist underconsumption, in which the capitalist saves too much; and the second, the theory of worker underconsumption, in which the capitalist has the power to consume but not the need to do so, while the worker has the need to consume but lacks the power.[31]

1.) Capitalist underconsumption

Malthus,[32] or more precisely Lauderdale[33] followed by Malthus, found the starting point for their theory in the criticism of an idea dear to Adam Smith, which holds that it is of no consequence economically whether an individual consumes his income or saves it. In both cases, the income is consumed. Only the consumer's identity and the nature of his consumption will vary, while the quantum of consumption remains the same. In the first case, the individual satisfies his needs directly; in the second, he uses his money to employ workers who in turn satisfy their needs. In total, consumption remains quantitatively the same.

It is this last point that is contested by Malthus. For if savings can be used as Smith supposes, it is not necessarily so, and overproduction can very well result from an excess of savings. Here is how. After telling us of a society at equilibrium, based upon normal exchanges between farmers and manufacturers, Malthus adds:

31. The latter theory is generally referred to as worker underconsumption. In fact, the underconsumption applies to both capitalist and worker alike.
32. Thomas Malthus, *Principes d'économie politique considérés sous le rapport de leur application pratique*, ed. Maurice Monjean, 2nd ed. (Paris: Guillaumin, 1846), 278–93 and 355–69. [Ed. – Quotations below are taken from the second English edition, *Principles of Political Economy*, 2nd, rev. ed. (London: Pickering, 1836).]
33. James Maitland, Earl of Lauderdale, *Recherches sur la nature et l'origine de la richesse publique, et sur les moyens et les causes qui concourent à son accroissement*, trans. E. Lagentie de Lavaïsse (Paris: Dentu, 1808), 154–206.

> While the farmers were disposed to consume the luxuries produced by the manufacturers, and the manufacturers those produced by the farmers, all would go on smoothly; but if either one or both of the parties were disposed to save largely with a view of bettering their condition, [...] the state of things would be very different. The farmer, instead of indulging himself in ribands, lace and velvets, would be disposed to be satisfied with more simple clothing, but by this economy he would disable the manufacturer from purchasing the same amount of his produce; and for the returns of so much labour employed upon the land, [...] there would evidently be no market.

Then, applying the same hypothesis of frugality to the manufacturers' camp, Malthus observes,

> There would evidently therefore be a general want of demand, both for produce and population; and while it is quite certain that an adequate passion for consumption may fully keep up the proper proportion between supply and demand, [...] it appears to be quite as certain that an inordinate passion for accumulation must inevitably lead to a supply of commodities beyond what the structure and habits of such a society will permit to be profitably consumed.[34]

Thus, for Malthus, excess savings are likely to lead to overproduction. The equilibrium between production and consumption freely assumed by Smith risks being destroyed by an exaggerated level of savings; such ruptures of equilibrium are the crises of overproduction.

Yet how do we explain the excess savings and insufficient consumption? Are they simply the result of the consumer's whim? Or, on the contrary, are they deeply embedded in the organization of our modern societies? Malthus refers here to Ricardo's law of the tendential fall in the profit rate. From the moment profit drops so low that the capitalist no longer has an interest in putting his capital into production, the saving of a part of his income becomes a source of overproduction. And this overproduction can very well be general. We have departed from Ricardo's theory and, by the same token, that of Malthus. There is no need to dwell on them any further.

We must reconcile Malthus's theory with the recent one put forward by Henry Strakosch, which suggests crises may be explained, at least in part, by capitalist underconsumption.[35] The drop in prices that accompanies the crisis is itself accompanied by an increase in the purchasing power of those with fixed incomes. The war of 1914 had increased this kind of income by inflating public debts. The crisis would increase the

34. Malthus, *Principles*, 323–25; cf. *Principes*, 287–89. A similar idea forms the basis for Carl von Manteuffel's theory of crises. Manteuffel sees the cause of crises in the difficulty of determining the portion of income allocated to savings. 'The producer cannot always predict what the national savings rate will be, and even small variations can distort his calculations'. Carl von Manteuffel, *Das Sparen: Sein Wesen und seine volkswirtschaftliche Wirkung* (Jena: Fischer, 1900), 108.
35. See Strakosch, 'Gold and the Price Level'; and publications by the Comité de l'Or of the SDN (Geneva, 1931).

purchasing power of rentiers at the expense not only of workers but also of shareholders. Strakosch maintains that rentiers were in no hurry to make use of the increase in their power to consume. There would be underconsumption. Available liquid funds would accumulate in the banks, as the balance sheets of the credit companies show.

The thesis is ingenious, but easily refuted. The distinction between the rentier and the shareholder is artificial; the capitalist is usually both a shareholder and a bondholder. What he would lose on the one hand (on his dividends) he would make up on his annuities and bonds. Compensation would occur, and the equilibrium would therefore be strengthened. As for the workers, since wages do not fall or fall only slightly in the event of a crisis, their purchasing power is in no way reduced to the benefit of bondholders. Real wages are not or only slightly affected in the event of a crisis.

Foster and Catchings have maintained that companies, by keeping too much of their profits in reserve (surplus), reduce the capitalist's purchasing power at the end of the growth period. Hence the overproduction. But the purchasing power remains at the disposal of the companies that make use of it. Overproduction is not implied by this shift in the means of consumption [*pouvoirs de consommation*].[36]

2.) Worker underconsumption under capitalism

The traditional doctrine of worker underconsumption in capitalism is otherwise logical and difficult to refute. Its proponents also admit that there is too much savings, too much production and not enough consumption. But their explanations differ as to why there is too much savings and production and not enough consumption. This is the result of the vicious way wealth is distributed in our modern societies, and not the law of non-proportional returns.

We already encounter the three fundamental ideas of this theory in Sismondi: the Iron Law of Wages – excess savings – which results in overproduction. As with Malthus, the crisis stems from excess savings, and according to Sismondi,

> nations can be ruined both by spending too much and by *spending too little*. A nation spends too much whenever it exceeds its revenue. For it can only do so by depleting its capital, and thus diminishing its future production [...] It spends too little whenever, in the absence of foreign trade, it fails to consume its production, or when there is foreign trade, and it fails to consume the surplus production over its exports.[37]

36. William Trufant Foster and Waddill Catchings, *Profits* (New York: Houghton Mifflin, 1925). See also the essay by Francesco Vito, 'Risparmio forzato e cicli economici', in Vito et al., *Cicli economici*, 9–115, which examines in great detail the theory of forced savings as a factor in underconsumption.
37. J.-C.-L. Simonde de Sismondi, *Nouveaux principes d'économie politique, ou de la richesse dans ses rapports avec la population*, 2 vols. (Paris: Delaunay, 1819), 1: 122. [Ed. – Cf. J.-C.-L. Simonde de Sismondi, *New Principles of Political Economy: Of Wealth in its Relation to Population*, trans. Richard Hyse (New Brunswick, NJ: Transaction Publishers, 1991), 105.] See Albert Aftalion, *L'œuvre économique de Simonde de Sismondi*, Doctoral thesis, Faculty of Law, University of Paris (Paris: Pedone, 1899), 90.

And this is what will happen when 'an economy creates more capital than the needs of industry can employ'.[38] Up to this point, one would think one was reading Malthus. When Sismondi turns to the examination of the creation of excess savings in capitalist economies, however, he diverges from Malthus. Here it is no longer chance or fantasy that causes the appearance of underconsumption, which soon turns into overproduction and crisis; these are the very laws according to which these economies function. After identifying two of their essential features – mechanized production and wage labour – he shows how crises necessarily result from this dual peculiarity.

Mechanized production has the effect of greatly increasing the stock of consumable wealth, while wage labour and the Iron Law have the effect of reducing the purchasing power and consumption of the working classes. The distribution of wealth in our modern societies has the following consequences: for some, the capitalists, their power to consume exceeds their needs; while for the others, the workers, their needs exceed their power to consume. This double absurdity results in double underconsumption: underconsumption of the capitalist, who has income at his disposal that he is physically unable to consume; and the underconsumption of the worker, who has the physical ability to consume, but lacks the means to do so.[39] Yet the overproduction crisis still results from the capitalist making use of that part of his income which he is unable to consume. He will save this part of his income. He will attempt to invest it in production in order to increase his already excessive income;[40] and the transformation of this savings into

38. Sismondi, *Noveaux principes*, 1: 381.

39. Simonde de Sismondi, *Études sur l'économie politique*, 2 vols. (Brussels: Société typographique belge, 1837), 1: 79–80.

Moreover, in Sismondi's work, this is not just a matter of the underconsumption of industrial workers but also that of agricultural labourers; for even if the concentration of property is proceeding rapidly in industry, it occurs no less rapidly in agriculture, and he demonstrates in passages of truly striking clarity how and why the small famer and the small landholder always give way to the large farmer and the great landowner in England. He views this as a new source of underconsumption. We would not have placed so much emphasis on this aspect of Sismondi's theory if subsequent authors had not neglected his study so much. Otto Karmin, a proponent of the theory of worker underconsumption, may have believed he was original in showing the concentration of agricultural property and the resulting worker underconsumption. Sismondi had already applied the theory of the concentration of production from which the concentration of property is more or less correctly deduced; and the latter did not fail to apply the theory of underconsumption to the agricultural classes. See Karmin, *Vier Thesen zur Lehre von den Wirtschaftskrisen* (Heidelberg: Carl Winter's Universitätsbuchhandlung, 1905), 45–47. It goes without saying that this theory, valid for England at the time Sismondi wrote and valid for Prussia in 1905 when Karmin published his book, is not applicable to France, where property has remained very fragmented. Moreover, Sismondi did not fail to make this distinction while explaining France's peculiar inheritance laws. See Sismondi, *Nouveaux principes*, 1: 225–35.

40. Brentano rightly points out that very often it is the opening of new markets which provokes this feverish production, and not the inability on the part of the capitalist to consume his income. Lujo Brentano, *Ueber die Ursachen der heutigen sozialen Noth* (Leipzig: Duncker & Humblot, 1889), 118.

machinery, housing and means of production of all kinds will only further increase the production of consumer goods, the excess of wealth over consumption – in a word, overproduction. Underconsumption on the one hand, and a rapid and progressive increase in production on the other, would be the key to explaining overproduction crises in capitalist economies.

This theory, already presented in this form by Sismondi in his *Nouveaux principes*, can be found in the writings of Proudhon, Louis Blanc, Rodbertus, Marx, Dühring, Herkner, Hertzka, Brentano, Vialles, May, Karmin, Bouniatian, and more recently in the United States, by Stuart Chase, Tugwell, Berle and the economists at the *New Republic*, and President Roosevelt himself; indeed, it has found adherents and seduced minds in all times and among all peoples.[41]

41. Louis Blanc, *L'organisation du travail*, 9th ed. (Paris: Nouveau-Monde, 1850), 58; P.-J. Proudhon, *Qu'est-ce que la propriété?* Vol. 1 of *Oeuvres complètes*, new ed. (Paris: Marpon & Flammarion, n.d.), 149–53 and 155–68; Karl Rodbertus, *Le capital*, trans. Émile Catelain (Paris: Giard & Brière, 1904); Karl Marx, *Le capital: Critique de l'économie politique*, vol. 3, pt 1, *Le procès d'ensemble de la production capitaliste*, trans. Julien Borchardt and Hippolyte Vanderrydt (Paris: Giard & Brière, 1901), 266 –67; and Marx, *Das Kapital: Kritik der politischen Ökonomie*, vol. 3, pt 1, *Der Gesamtprozess der kapitalistischen Produktion* (Hamburg: O. Meissner, 1894), 225–26; Eugen Dühring, *Cursus der National- und Socialökonomie einschliesslich der Hauptpunkte der Finanzpolitik* (Berlin: Grieben, 1873), see book 4, chap. 1, 'Normalität und Krisen', pp. 223–44; Charles Spinasse, speech before the Chambre des Députés, 2nd session, 27 Feb. 1931, in 'Débats parlementaires', *Journal Official de la Republic française*, no. 33 (28 Feb. 1931): 1298–1302; Henryk Grossman, *Das Akkumulations- und Zusammenbruchsgesetz des kapitalistischen Systems* (Leipzig: Hirschfeld, 1929); Rosa Luxemburg, *Die Akkumulation des Kapitals: Ein Beitrag zur ökonomischen Erklärung des Imperialismus* (Berlin: Vereinigung internationaler Verlags-Anstalten, 1923).

Theodor Hertzka, *Die Gesetze der sozialen Entwicklung* (Leipzig: Duncker & Humblot, 1886), 94–105; Otto Wittelshöfer, *Untersuchungen über das Kapital, seine Natur und Funktion* (Tübingen: Laupp, 1890), 228; Heinrich Herkner, *Die soziale Reform als Gebot des wirtschaftlichen Fortschrittes* (Leipzig: Duncker & Humblot, 1891), 65–74, and Herkner, 'Krisen', in *Handwörterbuch der Staatswissenschaften*, 2nd ed., ed. Johannes Conrad et al. (Jena: Fischer, 1898–1901), 5: 414–22; Lujo Brentano, 'Die Arbeiter und die Produktionskrisen', *Jahrbuch für Gesetzgebung, Verwaltung und Volkswirtschaft im deutschen Reich* 2 (1878): 110–76 (565–632); Pierre Vialles, *La consommation et les crises économiques*, Doctoral thesis, Faculty of Law, Université de Montpellier, 1902 (Montpellier: Montane & Sicardi, 1902); Raphaël Ernst May, *Das Grundgesetz der Wirtschaftskrisen und ihre Vorbeugemittel im Zeitalter des Monopols* (Berlin: Dümmler, 1902); Mentor Bouniatian, *Les crises économiques: Essai de morphologie et théorie des crises économiques périodiques*, trans. J. Bernard, 2nd ed. (Paris: Giard, 1930); Stuart Chase, *A New Deal* (New York: Macmillan, 1931); Rexford G. Tugwell, *The Industrial Discipline* (New York: Columbia University Press, 1933); Adolf Augustus Berle, *The Modern Corporation and Private Property* (New York: Macmillan, 1934). We find a new formulation of the theory of underconsumption in Émile Lederer, 'Konjunktur und Krisen', in *Grundriss der Sozialökonomie*, vol. 4, *Spezifische Elemente der modernen kapitalistischen Wirtschaft*, pt 1 (Tübingen: Mohr, 1925), 355–413, and in Foster and Catchings, *Profits* (companies do not distribute higher profits fast enough in a period of prosperity); Arthur B. Adams et al., 'The Business Depression of Nineteen Hundred Thirty – Discussion', supplement, *American Economic Review* 21, no. 1 (March 1931): 183.

Rodbertus and, more recently, May and Hobson have further consolidated this theory, lending its rigorous logic the appearance of empirical verification.

It could be objected to Sismondi, Proudhon, Kirchmann and the other early representatives of the worker underconsumption theory that the overproduction crisis was preceded by an increase in the rate of wages,[42] and consequently, that it was difficult to understand how overproduction could result from insufficient worker consumption at a time when wage statistics led us to presume an increase in this consumption. In his letters to Julius Kirchmann, Rodbertus refutes this objection.[43]

It is not the rate of wages that must be considered, but rather the share of wages in the total social product. For if a period of economic growth is a period of increasing wages, it is also a period of increased output. The question therefore is not whether wages increase, but whether they increase enough to absorb the increase in production output. And to this Rodbertus answered no, citing the rapid increase in the capitalists' earnings versus the slow rise in the workers' wages. Overproduction arises not because wages go up or down, but because they do not rise enough. May and Bouniatian supported Rodbertus' view by showing how prices rise faster than wages. From this price rise, they derived worker underconsumption. The nominal wage would increase, while the real wage would fall. Thus, this price rise, which explains a temporary increase in the rate of profits, eventually runs up against a crisis of underconsumption and, consequently, of overproduction. More recently, J. A. Hobson has demonstrated the divergence between the curve of the wage bill in the United States and the production curves. The increase in wages lags behind that of production.[44] Thus amended, the underconsumption theory is firmly grounded and difficult to critique. Nevertheless, we do not subscribe to it.

An equilibrium between production and consumption is possible, even in an economy where there is surplus value or profit and where a part of the income is consumed, and the other part is saved. Tugan-Baranowsky writes,

> One may spin the matter however one likes – one may assume not only the replacement of the worker by machines but also the decline in wages and in the incomes of small, independent producers – in an economy where there is a proportional distribution [*répartition*] of productive forces, the formation of a surplus product always remains fundamentally impossible. The misery of the masses can have an adverse effect on the circulation of goods only insofar as it hinders the proportional distribution [*répartition*] of social production.[45]

---

42. One encounters this objection notably in Marx, who at times agrees and disagrees with the underconsumption theory.
43. Rodbertus, *Le capital*, 58–59, 170–73, 283, 280–86, 292–93.
44. J. A. Hobson, *Rationalisation and Unemployment: An Economic Dilemma* (London: Allen & Unwin, 1930). Hobson cites statistics from the US Bureau of Labor Statistics comparing the sums paid to workers with production. The payroll index rises much more slowly than the index of production: if 1919 = 100, in 1928, the payroll index is 103 and the production index is 132.
45. Mikhail I. Tugan-Baranowsky, *Studien zur Theorie und Geschichte der Handelskrisen in England* (Jena: Fischer, 1901), 194. [Ed. – Lescure's translation has been altered slightly, using the German original to simplify the syntax in the English version produced here.]

Bourguin makes this same point more clearly:

> If at one moment the general overproduction caused by insufficient consumption is not theoretically implied by the makeup of the economic system, neither can it be in the moments that follow. It does not matter how much production has increased as a result of the reproductive savings made in the preceding period; nor even what the stationary state of the population is; the conditions of equilibrium between production and consumption are always the same; the whole social product, comprising at once a greater variety of consumer goods and a greater mass of means of production for reproductive savings, can always find investment by means of reciprocal exchanges. It is possible that producers may not know how to adjust to these different uses of the social income [...] But if they precisely observe the proportions between the consumer goods claimed for consumers and the means of production claimed by savings, they will avoid even partial crises of overproduction.[46]

Thus, the consumption-production equilibrium would be achievable even if the consumption of the poorer classes decreased. It suffices for the wealthier classes to consume more or to use a greater amount of their savings in purchasing means of production. Certainly, the production side may make mistakes in size or direction; it may even do so more easily since the division of labour and the complexity of economic relations make this equilibrium harder to achieve. But theoretically, the organization of capitalist societies by no means implies overproduction crises. In purely theoretical terms, the critique is decisive. However, the underconsumption theory alleges that at certain times the use of savings in the work of production becomes impossible without bringing about a corresponding overproduction. For Sismondi and his school, there is not only the workers' underconsumption but also capitalist underconsumption. Workers lack purchasing power, capitalists lack the need and physical capacity to consume. Should any portion of savings be applied to production, overproduction would necessarily follow.[47]

Our first criticism is therefore not yet sufficient, or it will only become so if we can demonstrate that the surplus [*saturation*] of the propertied classes is a pure hypothesis. This is simple enough to demonstrate. In fact, it is an economic axiom: needs are unlimited in number when they are limited in capacity. Luxury needs in particular are liable to expand indefinitely. How can one claim that the capitalist class is materially unable to consume its income? In reality, if the capitalist saves part of his income instead of purchasing consumer goods, it is because the savings provide a surplus value, a profit.[48]

---

46. Maurice Bourguin, *Les systèmes socialistes de l'évolution économique* (Paris: Colin, 1904), 320.
47. Recently, this thesis has been forcefully endorsed by Grossman, *Das Akkumulations- und Zusammenbruchsgesetz*, see esp. 78–278. Grossman returns to Marx's idea of the overaccumulation of capital and attempts to demonstrate the necessity of overproduction with aid of hypothetical statistical tables. But the author posits an annual accumulation of 10 per cent for constant capital and 5 per cent for variable capital (see tables, pp. 117–22). The statistics for securities issued renders this hypothesis untenable. The hypothesis conflicts with the facts. For crises are explained by the shortage of capital.
48. The most orthodox of Marxists recognize this implicitly when they claim that the accumulation of capital leads to imperialism. The need to equip the colonies creates a market for

With the opportunity for profit, we touch upon the decisive criticism to be addressed to the proponents of the worker underconsumption theory. For the contradiction upon which they base the necessity of overproduction in capitalist economies implies not only periodic and temporary overproduction but also chronic overproduction. One wonders how a society plagued by chronic overproduction – by a permanent excess of production over consumption – can still give profits to the owners of capital.[49]

This theory of worker underconsumption has recently inspired two 'experiments', the Roosevelt experiment in the United States and the socialist experiment in France. To remedy the crisis, it was said, wages and purchasing power had to be increased. In the United States, the Supreme Court put an end to this policy by ruling against the NRA. In France, the wage rise was quickly negated by price increases.

It is obvious that any rise in wages is followed by an increase in costs and prices.

But the reason for this policy's lack of success lies in an inaccurate conception of the structure of crises. Unemployment and overproduction are the consequences of capital and savings no longer being invested. Direct consumption (thanks to greater unemployment relief and as a result of the drop in prices) increased during the recent crisis in France. But heavy industries lacked orders. So did construction. Therefore, it is not a question of uniformly increasing purchasing power in order to alleviate unemployment. For prices will rise and quickly neutralize this increase. Rather, the problem is how to bring back orders to heavy industries and to construction. Only lower costs, an influx of savings into industry, the renewal of the spirit of enterprise and the initiative of industrialists can remedy crises. By increasing costs, we are turning our backs on solutions.

C.) Marx's theory of the tendency for the profit rate to fall

Marx, who alternated between being a supporter and an opponent of the underconsumption theory as we have presented it, answers this last objection, consciously or not, by connecting his law of the tendential fall in the rate of profit to underconsumption in his explanation of crises. The crisis takes on an original appearance here as the antidote to a continuous fall in profit. Since the continuous fall in profit has antidotes, profit persists in our societies.[50]

capital goods. On this point, see V. I. Lenin, *Der Imperialismus als jüngste Etappe des Kapitalismus* (Berlin: Verlag für Literatur und Politik, 1926); Nicolai Bucharin, *Der Imperialismus und die Akkumulation des Kapitals* (Berlin: Verlag für Literatur und Politik, 1926); and Grossman, *Das Akkumulations- und Zusammenbruchsgesetz*, 516–29.

49. It is sometimes objected to the worker underconsumption theorists that, in the event of a crisis, overproduction does not so much affect workers' consumer goods as it does iron, steel, cast iron and so on, and the means of production. In reality, this criticism does not hold; for every means of production has as its purpose the production of goods for consumption. And if the production of the means of production slows down, it is probably because the supply of consumer goods exceeds demand.

50. Grossman, *Das Akkumulations- und Zusammenbruchsgesetz*, 117–24.

Marx's originality lies in having attempted to combine the idea of overproduction and underconsumption with that of the progressive decline of profit, and in having tried to explain why this tendency does not translate into a continuous fall in profit.

Marx bases his law of the tendential fall in the profit rate on the very mode of capitalist production itself. For him, the development of production in capitalist societies has as its primary feature and precondition the previous production of certain machinery; this machinery tends to substitute itself more and more for labour. Expressed in Marxist terms, constant capital (machines, raw materials) tends to increase faster, either relatively or absolutely, than variable capital (wages). What will happen to the profit rate? For Marx, the terms 'profit' and 'surplus value' are synonymous; and for Marx, surplus value is that part of the workers' labour which goes unpaid and accrues to capitalist. The profit rate is the ratio of surplus value, of profit, to the total capital. Since constant capital tends to increase, the number of employed workers will decrease, either relatively, increasing less rapidly than constant capital, or absolutely, by being less than it was in the past. Marx will see this as one of the many contradictions with which the capitalist society must contend. In this fraction used to calculate the rate of profit, the numerator decreases, while the denominator rises; hence the rate of profit falls. If we represent surplus value by *pl* and the total capital (constant capital + variable capital) by *c*, then the rate of profit *t*, expressed by the fraction $\frac{pl}{c}$, decreases when *pl* decreases, while *c* increases. Now, this decrease in *pl* and increase in *c* are necessarily implied by the laws of development of capitalist economies.

To put it differently and more simply, in our modern societies a company needs to continually increase its capital in order to establish itself: 3, 4, 5, 6, 10 million and so on. In Marx's language, this is called the total capital, and this total capital is broken down into constant capital (machinery, raw materials) and variable capital (wages). As the role of constant capital increases, that of variable capital diminishes; as machinery becomes more important to production, the number of employed workers decreases; as the number of employed workers diminishes, so does surplus value, or profit. From then on, if capital increases and profit decreases, then the rate of profit must decrease. This is what Marx calls the law of the tendential fall in the rate of profit.[51]

Yet how are we to understand the notion that the fall in the profit rate is not continuous? This law encounters antagonistic factors, notably overproduction crises. And this crisis appears in Marx as an otherwise useless attempt by capitalist societies to escape the circle of contradictions in which they operate.[52]

The fall in profit will signal fiercer competition between producers. Very often the producer facing competition will try to compensate for the drop in the returns on each product by increasing his production and sales. Competitors will do the same. And this production frenzy will soon lead to as general an overproduction as possible; for all producers, when faced with the same fact of their falling profits, will resort to the same remedy: increasing their production. This increase in production will soon turn

51. Marx, *Le capital*, 3: 227–51; Marx, *Das Kapital*, 3: 191–212.
52. Grossman, *Das Akkumulations- und Zusammenbruchsgesetz*, 287–415.

into overproduction, into a crisis all the more intense because Marx accepts the link between worker underconsumption and this overproduction. Without being the cause of it, underconsumption intensifies overproduction. The crisis will be at the root of a process of destruction, or in any case, of the depreciation of a quantity of capital and products. The weakest producers will disappear. While the strongest – that is, those with the highest profits – will reduce their production costs (wages, overheads, etc.) in the face of overproduction and the drop in prices; and little by little, surplus value will increase. At the same time, overproduction will result in a depreciation of machinery and equipment, of all or part of the constant capital, leading many corporations to proceed with capital reductions. In the fraction $\frac{pl}{c}$, the denominator c decreases. The net profit, the surplus value as Marx would say, increases; the value of capital decreases; therefore, the rate of profit increases. And little by little, the capitalist economy regains momentary prosperity. A period of growth begins. The play of the tendency for profits to fall soon degenerates into a crisis. Marx succeeded in reconciling the idea of chronic underconsumption, of the law of the tendential fall in profit, with the reality of alternating periods of growth and depression. Marx's theory, although remarkable in its logical construction, clashes with experience; its argumentation is not beyond reproach.

Since in our view empirical criticism has much more decisive significance, we will begin with it. The overproduction crisis is not preceded by a fall in the profit rate but by its increase. On the other hand, the crisis, instead of being followed by the increase in the profit rate, is followed by its decrease. That the period of growth – of increased production and the development of machinery – is at the same time a period of increase for the profit rate is a fact that can be confirmed in the reports and on the balance sheets of joint-stock companies at the very beginning of the crisis. If production is feverish, this is not the result of an ever-intensifying competition, but of an ever-expanding market. Marx incorrectly characterized the growth period.

The same applies to his description of the depression period. According to Marx, the crisis would signal a depreciation in constant capital, manifested by reductions in the share capital of joint-stock companies. It would also cause a decline in wages, or an increase in surplus value. But in Marx's theory, depreciation of constant capital and the increase in surplus value mean an increase in the profit rate; pl increases, while c decreases. Now, it is indisputable that an economic crisis which marks the depreciation of constant capital also signals a fall in the profit rate.[53] Here again, Marx's theory runs up against the facts. Is it any more accurate in theory?

Does the increased role of constant capital in production imply a decrease in the profit rate? In his reasoning, Marx ignores: first, the decrease in variable capital, in so far as it consists of the wage fund, as a result of the reduction in the number of workers employed; second, the increase in labour productivity and, consequently, the depreciation of the labour contained in the constant capital that results. As the productivity of

53. Arthur Spiethoff, 'Die Krisentheorien von M. v. Tugan-Baranowsky und L. Pohle', *Jahrbuch für Gesetzgebung, Verwaltung und Volkswirtschaft im Deutschen Reich*, n.s., 27, no. 2 (1903): 332–33 (680–81).

labour increases, the amount of labour contained in a unit of output decreases, hence the value decreases; hence the value of the constant capital decreases. Why should this depreciation in the labour-value of constant capital not offset the purely hypothetical decrease in the remaining surplus value? Why should the increased productivity not amount to a real surplus value of mechanical labour-power, neutralizing the decrease in the surplus value of labour?

This is the starting point for Tugan-Baranowsky's critique of Marx.[54] Given a certain quantity of labour *a* used to produce a quantity of goods *b*, the value of the unit produced $= \frac{a}{b}$, and thus this ratio $\frac{a}{b}$ expresses the labour productivity at a given time; for the variations of *a*, labour applied to production, and those of *b* allow us to know very precisely whether labour efficiency is up or down. In other words, if, for example, *a* (the effort expended) decreases and *b* (production) increases, productivity would increase.

Given this, let us first assume there is production by means of labour and without capital. Labour would fall under what Marx and Tugan-Baranowsky call variable capital, which we will call *v*. In this particular case, supposing the surplus value *m* equals 100 per cent, the quantity of labour contained in the product can be broken down into variable capital and surplus value: $v = \frac{a}{2}$ and $m = \frac{a}{2}$. We have the following equation: $\frac{a}{2}v + \frac{a}{2}m = a$. Let us suppose that we introduce constant capital *c* into production and that in spite of this the labour-value of the product remains equal to *a*. The introduction of this constant capital will have the effect of reducing the labour employed, and as a result, the variable capital, the surplus value, remains equal to $\frac{a}{2}$. Since some workers have been dismissed, the wages paid only amount to $\frac{a}{4}$ and not $\frac{a}{2}$ as before, and the surplus value + the wage is therefore equal to $\frac{a}{2} + \frac{a}{4} = \frac{3}{4}a$. $\left(\text{In effect } \frac{a}{2} = \frac{2a}{4}.\right)$

Let us always refer to the quantity produced as *b*. In the first case, the surplus value was equal to $\frac{b}{2}$, and the variable capital to $\frac{b}{2}$. In the second hypothesis, the surplus value remains $\frac{b}{2}$; therefore, the share in production of variable capital and the surplus value is represented by $\frac{3}{4}b$.

Let us suppose that labour becomes more productive; the wage plus the surplus value cannot be $\frac{3}{4}b$ in the production process, but a smaller share, $\frac{b}{2}$ for example. But what then is the value of the unit produced? It is equal to the labour-power expended $\frac{3}{4}a$, divided by the product of this labour-power $\frac{b}{2}$. Now $\frac{3}{4}a : \frac{b}{2} = \frac{3a}{3b}$.

54. Mikhail Tugan-Baranowsky, 'Der Zusammenbruch der kapitalistischen Wirtschaftsordnung im Lichte der nationalökonomischen Theorie', *Archiv für Sozialwissenschaft und Sozialpolitik*, [n.s. of the *Archiv für soziale Gesetzgebung und Statistik* 19], 1 (1904): 273–306; and Tugan-Baranowsky, *Theorie und Geschichte der Handelskrisen*, 208.

The productivity of wages can be obtained by dividing the quantity of labour they represent $\frac{a}{4}$ by productivity $\frac{3a}{2b}$, $\frac{a}{4}:\frac{3a}{2b}=\frac{b}{6}$.[55]

Now, hypothetically, the constant capital has the same share in production as the variable capital, that is, $\frac{b}{6}$. Yet we know that the share in production of the variable capital and of the surplus value is represented by $\frac{b}{2}$. The surplus value is therefore equal to b minus the variable capital $\frac{b}{6}=\frac{b}{3}$.

In these circumstances the formula of total production is as follows:

$$\frac{b}{6}c+\frac{b}{6}v+\frac{b}{8}m=\frac{2}{3}b$$

Thus, we have the capital $\frac{b}{6}c+\frac{b}{6}v=\frac{b}{3}m$, or the surplus value.

So, as in the first case, the profit rate is 100 per cent because:

$$\frac{b}{6}+\frac{b}{6}=\frac{b}{3}$$

and

$$\frac{\frac{b}{3}}{\frac{b}{3}}=100\%$$

But Marx would say that this is precisely what he has always maintained, because the rate of the surplus value, which is the ratio of the surplus value, not to the total capital, but to the variable capital, has doubled; in the first case, the variable capital equals $\frac{a}{2}$, and the surplus value is $\frac{a}{2}$; the rate of the surplus value, which is here and only here confused with the rate of profit, is equal to 100 per cent. But in the second case, where surplus value is represented by $\frac{b}{3}$ and variable capital by $\frac{b}{6}$, the surplus value is equal to twice the variable capital, that is, to 200 per cent. Marx would argue this is what he is claiming: profit does not necessarily fall, but if it does not, it is because the surplus value, that is, the exploitation of the workers' labour, increases.

And although he was a Marxist, Tugan-Baranowsky nonetheless came to challenge Marx's theory of surplus value; surplus value was not the effect of manual labour alone. Machines, by increasing the productivity of manual labour, enabled this surplus to grow without any corresponding intensification in the exploitation of the workers. With the increasing productivity of modern equipment, the share of each of the co-participants

55. Note that there is a simpler way to find the productivity of $\frac{a}{4}$; in fact, we already have the equation $\frac{3}{4}a=\frac{b}{2}$, therefore $\frac{a}{4}=\frac{b}{2}:3=\frac{b}{6}$.

increases. It may be that capital's share increases faster than that of labour; however, as history has shown, the share of labour also increases. The increase in labour productivity is the main objection to Marx's law of the tendential fall of profit; this is the key to explaining the paradox that Levasseur describes in his *Traité d'économie politique* [*sic*], and which he formulates thus:

> Given that the selling price of a product is composed of the wages of workers, the cost of raw materials, the interest on capital, and the profit of the business, it is possible through science to create a cheaper product with more expensive materials, higher wages, more interest on capital and, ultimately, at *a considerably higher profit for the entrepreneur.*[ii]

Marx was wrong to ignore this economic paradox when he listed the series of factors that disrupted the free play of his law of the tendential fall in profit. He would have found it to be such a powerfully antagonistic factor that logic would have dictated that he sacrifice the law itself and, consequently, his theory of crises, at least in the form he presents it in this part of *Capital.*

D.) The theory of the anarchy and the irregularity in the production of the means of production

This was not the only theory found in Marx's *Capital.* And, after having critiqued Marx's theory of crises, Tugan-Baranowsky posed as a disciple of Marx himself. With very modest originality, he credited Marx with the creation of a new theory which Sombart could say he regarded 'as an extraordinary advance'.[56] If in volume three of *Capital* Marx had erred on the subject of crises, in volume two he had a stroke of genius that he was wrong not to have developed further in the third volume. Tugan-Baranowsky was to fill this lacuna as Marx's disciple.

The foundation of Tugan-Baranowsky's theory is twofold: the complexity of the economic equilibrium in a capitalist society and the anarchy in production that results and the importance of the production of means of production as an original and new factor in this equilibrium.

The notion of the complexity of economic equilibrium can already be found in authors prior to Tugan-Baranowsky, and the anarchy in the distribution of productive forces had already been cited as a cause of crises by the most diverse group of authors, belonging to a variety of different or opposing schools. Alongside liberals like J.-B. Say, we find more radical economists such as Louis Blanc, Herkner, Lexis and Brentano, or collectivists such as Marx, especially Engels and, more recently, Hyndman.[57] But we will not dwell on this point.

56. Sombart, 'Referat über die Störungen', in *Verhandlungen des Vereins für Socialpolitik*, 130.

57. Jean-Baptiste Say, *Traité d'économie politique*, 6th ed. (Paris: Guillaumin, 1841), 142–43; and J.-B. Say, *Cours complet d'économie politique pratique*, 2nd ed., 2 vols. (Paris: Guillaumin, 1840), 1: 345–47.

Herkner, 'Krisen', in *Handwörterbuch*, 2nd ed., 5: 414–22; Wilhelm Lexis, 'Ueberproduktion', in *Handwörterbuch der Staatswissenschaften*, 3rd ed., ed. Johannes Conrad et al., vol. 8, *Übergangsabgaben–Zwischenhandel* (Jena: Fischer, 1911); Brentano, *Ueber die*

In volume two of *Capital*, Marx emphasizes the importance of the production of means of production. He distinguishes between the material lifespan of fixed capital and its duration as a useable means of production. Technical improvements require a renewal of capital before its material turnover [*usure*]. And Marx believes, without saying why, that these transformations occur every 10 years. Here Marx finds, if not the causes of crises, then at least one of the factors capable of providing impetus to periods of growth and depression:

> This cycle of successive and interrelated [turnover] periods of several years' duration, during which capital is captive of its fixed element, furnishes a material basis for economic crises. As a result of these cycles of several years, in which concomitant changes in the fixed component of capital absorb the attention of the capitalists, we find a material basis for periodic crises and a succession of periods of depression, average activity, intense production, and crisis.[58]

Paul Cauwès finds the cause of crises in an outpouring of entrepreneurial spirit, in an excessive proliferation of the means of production.[59] In this he anticipates Tugan-Baranowsky, Spiethoff, Eulenburg, Pohle, Schmoller, Lexis and Feiler. In *Bau und Leben des sozialen Körpers*, Schäffle provides a remarkably precise description of the conditions of economic equilibrium in capitalist societies.[iii]

Ursachen, 22. But it was Engels in particular who emphasized the difference between the organization of production in the factory (teams of workers complementing each other in various and multiple ways) and the anarchy of production in society. Friedrich Engels, *Herrn Eugen Dühring's Umwälzung der Wissenschaft*, 2nd ed. (Zurich: Schabelitz, 1886), 260–61. H. M. Hyndman, *Commercial Crises of the Nineteenth Century* (London: Swan, Sonnenschein, 1902), 7–8, 12–13.

58. As the French translation is imperfect (cf. Marx, *Le capital*, 2: 197), we provide a translation that follows the German text, Marx, *Das Kapital: Kritik der politischen Ökonomie*, vol. 2, *Der Cirkulationsprocess des Kapitals* (Hamburg: O. Meissner, 1885), 156 [but see p. 164]; and see also Marx, *Le capital*, 2: 508; *Das Kapital*, 2: 432.

59. Cauwès, *Cours d'économie politique*, 3rd ed., 4 vols. (Paris: Larose & Forcel, 1893), 2: 390. Moreover, all the authors who have claimed to find the cause of crises in an excessive immobilization of fixed capital and insufficient circulating capital must be ranked among the precursors. For by 'circulating capital', they generally mean available capital. See in particular John Stuart Mill, *Principes d'économie politique*, 3rd ed., trans. Hippolyte Dussard and J.-G. Courcelle-Seneuil, 2 vols. (Paris: Guillaumin, 1873), 2: 283–84; Jean-Gustave Courcelle-Seneuil, *Traité théorique et pratique d'économie politique*, 2nd ed., 2 vols. (Paris: Amyot, 1867), 1: 329; Bonamy Price, 'One per Cent', *Contemporary Review* 29 (April 1877): 778–99, quoted in Bergmann, *Die Wirtschaftskrisen*, 205; Colson, *Cours*, vol. 4, *Les entreprises, le commerce et la circulation*, 492; Yves Guyot, *La science économique* (Paris: Reinwald, 1881); Baron Mourre, 'Les crises et leurs signes caractéristiques aux États-Unis de 1882 à 1921', *Journal de la Société de Statistique de Paris* 63, no. 1 (1922): 5–24, and comments of Y. Guyot, in minutes of the meeting of the Société de Statistique de Paris, in ibid., 2–3; Gustave Cassel, *Traité d'économie politique*, trans. Henry Laufenburger and Georges de Persan, 2 vols. (Paris: Giard, 1929); Keynes, *Treatise on Money*, 2: 95–147; and Vilfredo Pareto, *Cours d'économie politique*, 2 vols. (Lausanne: Rouge, 1896–97), 2: 287.

> [In] the balance between the share of national product due to the worker or to the owner and the production of consumer goods, either by workers or owners [...] One ought to know what part will be used for savings and what part will be used in luxury consumption by the classes accumulating part of their income; to which luxury needs and to what investments these different portions of the income will be allocated; direct consumption and reproductive consumption may thus be measured.
>
> The capital increase would not only make regular progress but should be regularly employed in the work of production, so that the producers employed with the influx of savings into industry would not be condemned periodically to unemployment and would continue to take part in the market as consumers.
>
> The needs of the unproductive classes would finally be known.

The new school seeks the cause of economic crises in these complex conditions of equilibrium and the rupture of this equilibrium.[60]

For Tugan-Baranowsky, Spiethoff, Pohle, Eulenburg and Schmoller, this rupture is connected to the role played by savings in our modern societies. The halt in the production of the means of production – the crisis – results from the lack of capital ready to be employed in industry. During the depression period, capital moves away from industrial investments, but savings continue to accumulate. Little by little a kind of reserve purchasing power builds up. The moment arrives when these savings are used in the work of production. This begins a period of increase that lasts until savings become insufficient to maintain production at the peak level reached during the growth period. Tugan-Baranowsky borrows a quite useful analogy from physics. He compares present-day society to a steam engine, where production is driven by a kind of economic steam in the form of savings. Like the piston of a locomotive engine, production moves forward until it reaches a point where its motive power can no longer maintain it, and then, like the piston, it will move in a retrograde motion.[61] In short, for these authors, the essential cause of crises lies in insufficient savings. Savings would accumulate in banks and would then be used in industry, but with such an intensity that the previous accumulation would quickly disappear. The current accumulation would soon become insufficient to maintain production at the peak level it had reached.[62]

Some have added to this theory. Marx had already spoken of the decennial turnover [*usure*] of fixed capital and of the need to resume its production every 10 years. This idea was incorrect. For even if fixed capital were to wear out in decennial cycles, nothing would imply the necessity of repairing or replacing all the fixed capital in the same year. An even distribution of the expenses over each year would be perfectly conceivable.

60. Bourguin, *Les systèmes socialistes*, 41–59; Arthur Spiethoff, 'Vorbemerkungen zu einer Theorie des Überproduktion', *Jahrbuch für Gesetzgebung, Verwaltung und Volkswirtschaft im Deutschen Reich*, n.s., 26 (1902): 267–305 (721–59), and Spiethoff, 'Krisen', in *Handwörterbuch der Staatswissenschaften*, 4th ed., ed. Ludwig Elster, Adolf Weber and Friedrich Wieser, 8 vols. (Jena: Fischer, 1923–29), 6: 8–91.
61. Tugan-Baranowsky, *Theorie und Geschichte der Handelskrisen*, 250.
62. See Arthur Spiethoff, comments at the general meeting of the Verein für Socialpolitik, Hamburg, 16 Sep. 1903, in *Verhandlungen des Vereins für Socialpolitik*, 219–20.

For example, fixed capital *a* produced in 1880 would be worn out and replaced in 1890, fixed capital *b* produced in 1881 would be worn out and replaced in 1891, and so on. Theoretically, the 10-year turnover of fixed capital in no way implies its erratic production.

Of course, Marx distinguishes between the material lifespan of fixed capital and the duration of its technical use.[63] Its wear and tear [*usure*] would be technical. Here Marx anticipates and predates Spiethoff,[64] although they do not conceive of the influence of technical discoveries and improvements in the same way. Marx confines himself to an assertion, and the facts contradict his theory. The same invention served as the turning point for several booms and crises: the railway, for example, and its construction were at the root of the crises of 1847, 1857, 1866, 1873, 1884 and 1907. Thus, Spiethoff corrects Marx's idea. For the former, the new invention, which he likens to the opening of an external market, provokes a temporary demand to which a permanent supply responds. The satisfaction of a temporary demand leads to the creation of complicated machinery that will stand idle once the demand is satisfied. No doubt, the means of production thus created could be adapted to the demand, perhaps by repurposing them. But Spiethoff would respond that such transformations of the production capital of commodity A into the production capital of commodity B are only valid in theory. This quality of ubiquity in no way corresponds to reality. In practice, very often the exploitation of a recent discovery or the opening up of new outlets will produce a temporary demand that will be met with a permanent supply.[65]

In theory, such reasoning has value only in the case of chronic overproduction. For if a temporary demand corresponds to a permanent supply, this supply will be permanent and the overproduction chronic. Yet crises are periodic. To explain the end of overproduction, we must assume either that a new invention has restored the machinery's utility, and then we are back to Marx's factually erroneous hypothesis about periodic technical improvements; or that the machinery has managed to adapt to the new circumstances resulting from the cessation of demand for the products that had motivated its creation, and this is the solution proposed by the optimistic school but rejected by Spiethoff. If inventions and the opening of new foreign markets are key to the progress of production in our modern societies, they are not the cause of the irregular course of this development. In practice, the answer given to Marx remains valid against Spiethoff. The railway, the same invention that gave rise to a very long-term and progressive demand, was nonetheless used in fits and starts. We cannot accept this correction, or rather addition, to Tugan-Baranowsky's theory.

---

63. Marx, *Le capital*, 2: 187; *Das Kapital*, 2: 156. Marx' concept had been developed by Mr René Bergerioux, *Un monde commence* (Paris: Grasset, 1932).
64. Spiethoff, 'Vorbemerkungen', 276–77 (730–31). See also Spiethoff, 'Krisen', in *Handwörterbuch*, 4th ed., 6: 8–91.
65. See this idea in Wilhelm Lexis's presentation on 'Les crises économiques', at the opening session of the 12th meeting of the Institut international de Statistique, 1909, p. 12, and Lexis's article 'Ueberproduktion', in *Handwörterbuch der Staatswissenschaften*, 3rd ed.

The same could be said of Pohle's theory, which attempts to locate an element of economic anarchy in population growth.[66] In a society in which the population is increasing, the production of means of production must provide employment not only for the existing adult population but also for those who will reach adulthood each year. The capital necessary for the use of these new productive forces must therefore be produced in advance. According to Pohle, the means of production allocated to this future need would exceed the present need, resulting in overproduction.

But even then, this economic 'layette' can only explain chronic overproduction. In Pohle's view, crises are a matter of temporary overproduction. Pohle's innovation could be presented in a more convincing way: the society that ignores the variable number of workers added to the workforce each year is liable to make mistakes. The means of production intended for this workforce could exceed future needs. But this hypothesis is incompatible with the periodicity of crises. Here chance would reign supreme. Crises, on the other hand, would be less intense than they actually are. They would not be characterized by unemployment – quite the opposite. The means of production would be left idle due to the shortage of labour. Finally, this refutation seems to us to be decisive: nations like France, whose population grows very slowly, are nonetheless affected by periodic crises.

From this collection of recent ideas and theories, a single one emerges: the development of capitalist economies through alternating periods of growth and depression stems from the irregular production of means of production and the ebb and flow of savings, sometimes toward industry and sometimes away from it. Yet, observing this phenomenon is not the same as explaining it.

Why do savings periodically flow toward industry and commerce and then away from them over a period of about five years? This is the crux of the matter. Because savings are lacking, the answer seems incidental. Spiethoff is even categorical on this point.[67] In contrast to Malthus, he sees the crisis resulting from a shortage of savings, rather than an excess of it. The demand for the means of production – for housing, railways, in short, for all those categories of economic goods whose production presupposes a prior accumulation of wealth – would be reduced to a standstill in the absence of savings sufficient to maintain production at the level previously achieved. The lack of capital would be reflected in a rise in the interest rate.

Is it certain that capital is insufficient in times of crisis? Is it accurate to offer this insufficiency as the real cause of crises? The lack of savings argument is at the very least doubtful. If we look at the statistics for industrial output as a whole, the demand for and

66. Ludwig Pohle, *Bevölkerungsbewegung, Kapitalbildung und periodische Wirtschaftskrisen* (Gottingen: Vandenhoeck & Ruprecht, 1902), 12; cf. August Lösch, 'Population Cycles as a Cause of Business Cycles', *Quarterly Journal of Economics* 51, no. 4 (1937): 649–62, and Lösch, *Bevölkerungswellen und Wechsellagen* (Jena: Fischer, 1936).

67. Spiethoff, 'Vorbemerkungen', 278 (732), 297 (751); Spiethoff, comments at the General Meeting of the Verein für Socialpolitik, Hamburg, 16 Sep. 1903, in *Verhandlungen des Vereins für Socialpolitik*; Pohle, *Bevölkerungsbewegung*, 29; and a similar idea in Y. Guyot, *La science économique*, 412–13.

supply of capital seem to have decreased little in the year that follows a year of crisis. Certainly, at the end of a growth period, the interest rate rises, and this rise would seem to indicate a tightening of the capital market. But interest is a part of profit,[68] and its increase may be a consequence of rising profits. With the prospect of increased profits, the entrepreneur agrees to a higher interest rate.

On the other hand, if the crisis stems from a lack of savings, the growth should resume as soon as savings are replenished. Yet the capital offered on the market is most abundant as soon as the monetary phase of the crisis has been resolved.[69]

No doubt, the supporters of this theory would respond with the argument that savings are not used in industry in times of depression because prices fall. But why do prices not rise as soon as savings are abundant? In fact, there is no shortage of savings in times of depression; the statistics on bank deposits or even the overall statistics for the issuing of securities lead us to think that there is. Nor is there any accumulation of savings. For one would search in vain for any significant trace of these savings in the deposits or credit accounts of the banks. Indeed, the interest rate decreases, but only because capital is finding less profitable uses (issues of government securities, bonds, cities, etc.) or because there is less demand for capital. Profitable investments will only be possible later. But when will savings flow toward industry, and why? This is the key to the problem.[70]

Recently Moulton has tried to re-assert this theory by arguing that at the end of a growth period, savings are used on the stock exchange instead of being invested in production. This would leave a gap in the demand for products. But this is to forget that the purchase of securities on the stock exchange is equivalent to a shift in purchasing power, not to its elimination. Hoarding alone reduces demand. And hoarding is a recent phenomenon, appearing in 1931.[71] It has disappeared in the United States.

In reality, this theory ignores consumption in its explanation of crises. As Kautsky objects to Tugan-Baranowsky, 'To produce means producing consumer goods for human needs. This fact can only be obscured by the division of labour, but not eliminated or simply limited by it.'[72]

Tugan-Baranowsky, Spiethoff and Pohle came to separate too radically the production of the means of production from that of consumer goods, and the consumption of savings from that of income. The aim of all production is consumption, and if there is nowadays

68. Alcée Dugarçon, *Le problème économique de l'intérêt*, thesis, Faculty of Law, University of Bordeaux (Bordeaux: Cadoret, 1905), pt 3.
69. Maurice Ansiaux, 'L'épargne au cours des phases d'essor et de dépression', *Bulletin d'information et de documentation de la Banque Nationale de Belgique* 6, vol. 1, no. 7 (10 April 1931): 229–34.
70. Albert Aftalion, 'La théorie de l'épargne en matière de crise périodique de surproduction générale et sa critique', *Revue d'histoire des doctrines économiques et sociales* 2 (1909): 229–62; Aftalion, *Les crises périodiques de surproduction*, 2 vols. (Paris: Rivière, 1913), 1: 297.
71. Harold Glenn Moulton, *The Formation of Capital* (Washington, DC: The Brookings Institution, 1935); and Moulton, *Income and Economic Progress* (Washington, DC: The Brookings Institution, 1935).
72. Karl Kautsky, 'Krisentheorien', *Die Neue Zeit* 20 (1902): 117–18.

an increasingly large distance between production and consumption, all production, even that of the means of production, finds its *raison d'être* and its measure in consumption.

E.) The theory of the length of the capitalist production process

This last criticism appears to have been the starting point for Bouniatian and Aftalion. For them, the crisis comes down to an imbalance between production and needs, which in a capitalist society must be preceded by a more or less intense development of the means of production industry. The appearance of a new, more intense need is insufficient to cause an immediate expansion of production. Any expansion of production presupposes the creation of new means of production. At the root of any expansion period is the insufficiency of production in relation to needs. In order to rectify this deficiency and satisfy its needs, a society must create new means of production, which leads to prosperity in the industries producing the means of production. As long as they are being created and installed, general economic activity is intense. From the moment the new means of production are brought online, overproduction appears. The production of consumer goods, which was initially insufficient to meet demand, now exceeds it. The crisis is triggered: the depression will last until the lack of the means of production or new needs require the production of new capital goods.

This theory of crises rests upon the irregular expansion of capital goods and of needs. Every four or five years, one would witness a shortage of existing capital in relation to needs; and once these needs are met, a crisis would arise.[73]

After having formulated the theory as a hypothesis, its verification was attempted in practice. But this explanation seems unsatisfactory both in theory, as a hypothesis, and in its substantiation by the facts.

Particularly in theory, it carries the same reservations as Marx's doctrine of the periodic turnover of capital. Assuming that the technical lengthening of production is a possible factor in overproduction, this alone cannot explain general overproduction crises. For a crisis is characterized by widespread malaise. However, the technical lengthening of the production process cannot explain how industries are to feel these effects simultaneously. A lag from one industry to the next would be inevitable because the technical timespan for the production of capital equipment varies fundamentally according to the industry. For example, the machinery used in the textile industry can be expanded very rapidly (one year at most); whereas a ship requires eighteen months to two years to build, and an underground mine takes two years or more to equip. Overproduction would have an essentially variable periodicity from one industry to the next. Yet all industries are affected by the crisis in the same year. Why this simultaneity? A common cause is needed to explain this quasi-unanimity. And since we like to use the term 'rhythm' to describe our phenomenon, it needs a conductor. Otherwise, each instrument can play its own tune with no regard for its neighbour. And overproduction

73. See Bouniatian, *Les crises économiques*; Aftalion, *Les crises périodiques*, and Aftalion's articles in the *Revue d'économie politique*, 1908 and 1909.

will be spaced out according to the time needed for the creation of additional equipment. The crisis would be periodic, but not general; for the periodicity would vary from one industry to the next.

Moreover, the lengthening of the technical production process would explain a six-month overrun in the production of equipment and a one-year overrun in years of crisis, but not a three- to four-year one. Could it be argued that two, three or four years are necessary to equip textile mills, deliver wagons or steam engines, and that the equipment under construction in years of crisis will require another three to four years to be completed, flooding the market with a growing quantity of products for the three or four years? Obviously not.[74]

In addition, for these theorists, the crisis is defined by supply exceeding demand. We have no statistics on demand. Unless we consider the production of other goods as demand for a product. But then the overproduction would not be general. Moreover, on the eve of a crisis, production levels are very high everywhere, and demand is very strong. In fact, demand is assumed to be constantly rising, while supply alone is subject to fluctuations and alternatively greater or less than this demand. In reality, like supply, demand is subject to fluctuations; the demand for a product depends on production, on the prices of other goods and on incomes. All these factors are subject to interdependent fluctuations [*fluctuations solidaires*]. A rectilinear demand curve is an assumption contradicted by the facts. During the boom period, production, prices and incomes increase, and demand increases. During the depression period, production, prices and incomes decrease, and demand decreases. It would be necessary to establish the superiority or inferiority of supply in relation to demand thus defined.

It would prove an arduous task. For supply thus appears in its true form, closely linked [*solidaire*] with demand and vice versa. For the demand for one good depends on the production and supply of others. One would have to establish the decline in demand in one given branch of production, which would drag the others down with it.

In fact, there are centres of crisis: certain countries, particular industries. The contagion spreads from one to the others.

Strong production does not necessarily result in overproduction. This is demonstrated by a period of growth. For years, more is produced every year without any glut in the markets. On the contrary, decreasing production coincides with a market glut. Using statistics, it is possible to establish overproduction during a period of depression, as production declines everywhere. Supply diminishes; and if demand were to increase constantly as is assumed, prices would have to rise everywhere. This is not the case.

74. Dennis Holme Robertson, *A Study of Industrial Fluctuation: An Inquiry into the Character and Causes of the So-called Cyclical Movements of Trade* (London: P. S. King, 1915), 14–15.

In a recent in-depth study, Pierre Jéramec writes: '[...] nowadays, due to constant technical improvements, the turnaround times are extremely short, considering the length of the periods of growth and of crisis. New machines can be put into operation in a relatively short period of time'. Jéramec, 'Une théorie dynamique de la production et son illustration par l'étude de l'activité industrielle dans la région parisienne (1927–1931)', *Journal de la Société française de statistique de Paris* 72 (1931): 243.

In terms of theory, this doctrine appears quite fragile. But is its accuracy supported by the facts? Statistics here would relate to horsepower used in industry, railway equipment, shipbuilding and the production of consumer goods (houses in particular).

1.) Statistics on horsepower

These statistics apply to France only, and more specifically, to the period from 1849 to 1910. But we concede that the periods 1870–1880 and 1890–1900 were exceptions to the rule (20 years out of the 60 under examination, or one-third). The exception is close to becoming the rule.

But if we consider the evidence thus circumscribed, we notice that the year of crisis marks the inversion of the curve in the increase of the amount of horsepower used in industry. During the boom period, the amount of horsepower increases; the crisis marks a break. Undoubtedly, the decrease intensifies as the depression continues. However, the crisis constitutes a very clear caesura.

To produce another interpretation of this phenomenon, sometimes three, six or eight years are bracketed off in order to demonstrate that the increase in capital equipment is especially important during the years preceding and following the crisis. But by slightly shifting the brackets, we can make them say something else. The increase is especially significant during periods of growth, but much less so during periods of depression. And it is very natural that the minimum increase occurs at the peak of the depression, just as the maximum increase occurs at the peak of the growth.

If we go into detail, we note that additional equipment enters the scene after and in spite of the crisis, which cannot be explained by the technical lengthening of the production process; the increase continues for three, four and five years in the textile industry. According to this reasoning, it would take three, four or five years to get spindles and looms up and running. Yet Robertson estimates the delay at one year. But even in the mines, where the time needed to dig the shafts is quite long, making the hypothesis more plausible, the evidence is contradictory: from 1850 to 1873, as soon as crises appeared, we entered a period of weak growth in the amount of new horsepower put into operation, and from 1873 until 1903, the period of strong growth continued for four years after the crisis. It does not take four years to dig a shaft. And what is more, the contradiction in the evidence is obvious.

If, on the other hand, we focus our attention on the points of maximum increase in horsepower in the mines, we find these peaks in years of crisis (1857, 1866, 1873, 1882, 1890, 1900 and 1901). The figures decrease thereafter.

In light of such results, we wonder whether the interpretation given to these statistics is consistent with reality. From the increase in horsepower in operation, we conclude that production and supply have increased. However, production and unemployment statistics contradict this result. We shall show why in a moment. How do we interpret the statistics for horsepower put into operation during the period of depression? Machinery is improved so as to reduce production costs. New machines operate alongside the old ones. And the statistics cannot distinguish between old and new machines, between active and idle equipment. The horsepower already in use is augmented by the horsepower newly brought into service. There is no way of knowing whether the purpose of this new equipment is to produce more or to improve the technical conditions of production, or whether it is the result of orders placed during the boom period and delivered after the crisis. Indeed, it is the latter interpretation that appears preferable to us in light of the growing unemployment experienced by all industries and the general decline in production.

Moreover, there is an index of the activity in the industries manufacturing machinery which is more reliable than that of horsepower put into operation in a less industrialized country (France), and that is the statistics for unemployment in the mechanical engineering industries in Great Britain, which employ over a million workers. (See figures A1 and A2 and table A3 in the Annexes.)

From the onset of the crisis, unemployment in these industries increased. The production of machines thus immediately contracted without any delay.

2.) Statistics relating to machines and equipment used in the railways

These statistics apply to the lengthening of the railways in France and the increase in the number of locomotives and wagons. 'Here again one discovers gaps between the phases of strong and weak growth over the periods of prosperity and depression. They are very common for the lines in operation and for the number of carriages and wagons, and represent the general rule, so to speak, for locomotives'.[75]

The same observation we made about horsepower applies here as well. The method of selecting time frames of two, three or eight years to find an average is a little arbitrary. By shifting the time frame that we bracket off, we change the result. If, on the other hand, we draw the curve of the lengthening of the railway and that of the increase in the number of locomotives and wagons, we notice that we reach a peak in each year of crisis, followed by a decline. The phenomenon is particularly clear in France for the crises of 1847, 1857 and 1882, which in this country were railway crises. The same is true for the United States (see below). It would be quite wrong to deny it.

Besides, even if the length of time needed for the construction of a railway line could explain the lengthening of the network after the crisis, the same is not true for the construction of locomotives and wagons. In some factories it takes no more than a month to manufacture a locomotive. We see no evidence of the lengthening of the production process here. For we note that this expansion does not require building new factories: around 1880, French factories delivered more locomotives than subsequently. If factories continue to produce locomotives in times of depression, the reason is not to be found in the lengthening of the production process. Long-term orders placed during the boom are fulfilled. As the growth continues, it becomes increasingly difficult for the railways to transport goods. Companies place large orders for equipment, which are filled during the depression. And this is very fortunate. It should be added that this observation is not valid for either England or the United States. Yet all the crises in the United States have been railway crises. The role of the railways in crises and depressions deserves to be studied in greater depth. And this is essential because the railways absorbed the bulk

75. Aftalion, *Les crises périodiques*, 2: 91.

of savings in the nineteenth century. We should not only consider the production of wagons and locomotives but also the extension of the railway network.

3.) Shipbuilding

The decline in tonnage launched reached its maximum one or two years after the crisis. The technical lengthening of ship production explains this delay of one to two years quite well. But we will add another reason: foreign trade – hit by the knock-on effects – does not suffer immediately in the event of a crisis. Sometimes it escapes the effects of the crisis altogether.[76] Still, we should not fail to note that when foreign trade is seriously affected, as in 1907 or 1920, the decline in maritime construction is immediate.

Finally, for Germany, which has not been mentioned and which nonetheless has had very large shipyards since 1895, the inquiry into the crisis of 1900 by the *Verein für Socialpolitik* has clarified the reasons why the decline in tonnage constructed was not immediate. Contracts signed in 1899 and 1900 were executed in 1901 and 1902. It was the same in 1913. Robertson is of the same opinion for Great Britain. Strong production was maintained – after the crisis – due to the fulfilment of orders placed before the crisis. The technical lengthening had nothing to do with it. Rather, the longer delay was legal. This is the reason why the depression does not reach its peak everywhere immediately following a crisis. Yet the crisis is there. Why? This is the problem.

Some industries are already severely affected, while the effect on others is delayed. The crisis does not strike everywhere at once, as the history of crises demonstrates, and the year-by-year observation here lacks precision. The sequence of events is neglected.

4.) Crisis and production of consumer goods

Yet let us accept the thesis of overproduction caused by an increase in capital goods. In order to substantiate it rigorously with statistical observations, one must demonstrate that during the depression the production of consumer goods increases in unison with the new equipment put into service. This increase characterizes overproduction and an overproduction aggravated by a growing supply. This has been attempted in the construction industry in France, and for the wool and cotton industries. Elsewhere statistics would be lacking.

For the construction industry, we refer to the tax statistics for new houses subject to property tax in France. If we recall that new houses are exempt from taxation for the first three years after being built, there is a three-year lag in the tax data. A house was built three years before it was taxed. The argument thereby collapses.

Moreover, we have seen the construction industry participate immediately in the crisis throughout the course of history. Statistics on building permits in the United States establish this. Wagemann has determined that the crisis in the German building industry preceded the general crisis by one or two years.[77]

76. As in the crisis of 1913 in Germany, for example.
77. Wagemann, *Einführung*, 125.

For cotton and wool, the statistics on the surplus of imports over exports of cotton or wool are considered. These statistics – customs statistics – are too imperfect for an opinion to be based on them. Yet can one establish here the increase in production during the depression?

For cotton, the import balances in France and England for the 1872–1911 period were considered. For, in the United States and in Germany, we 'no longer find a clear rhythm in the quantities of cotton that remained at the disposal of the spinning mills in each country'.[78] This is an important exception because, since 1870, crises have been particularly clear in the United States and Germany, where the cotton industry is highly developed.

But even in France and England, the peaks are reached in the year before the crisis, in the same year or in the following year. In fact, the cotton industry, which works with raw materials that are subject to the unpredictability of the harvest, takes part only imperfectly in economic cycles. However, in the event of a major crisis, production would immediately decline (1907). Besides, a crisis in the cotton industry would not be enough to bring about a general crisis. History often shows examples of crises in the cotton industry, without the other industries following suit (Germany in 1910, 1911 and 1912).

There can be other explanations for the slight delay that is sometimes observed in the decline of cotton consumption in France and England: France and England have suffered the aftershocks of the American and German crises since 1870, when they almost ceased to be the focus of serious crises. The silk industry in Lyon was only affected at the beginning of 1908, as America was purchasing less. Let us consider, moreover, the statistics following the characteristic crises: in Germany at the end of 1900, the decline in the production of cotton wares was still only restricted to individual mills; whereas the crisis had already begun in the electrical industries from 1899. But by 1901, the reduction was general in both the weaving and the spinning mills. Similarly, in 1913, the cotton industry was affected by the knock-on effects. Was the situation any different in other textile industries?

For the textiles wool, linen and hemp, one finds no regular increase in industrial consumption after a crisis. But quite often the crisis has an immediate effect on the wool or silk industries.

We have even been able to establish this immediate action for the wool industry in 1900 and 1913 in Germany and in 1907, 1920 and 1930 in the United States.

All in all, it has not been possible to establish for the textile industries, not even for cotton, a continuous increase in production – during the depression – that would explain the fall in prices as the result of increasing production.

Furthermore, unemployment statistics indicate a general restriction of production after the crisis.

The contraction of production following a crisis (instead of its increase) is derived from traditional indices: the statistics on the tonnage of goods transported at low speed

78. Aftalion, *Les crises périodiques*, 2: 141.

(strong increase during the growth period, decline during the depression), statistics on the volume of foreign trade, the movement of ships (in and out) and the number of bills of exchange drawn in each country.[79]

If prices are down despite the steady decrease in trade and output in quantitative terms, it is undoubtedly the fall in prices that causes the decrease in production; and it is not the increase in production through the introduction of additional equipment that explains the fall in prices. The facts seem to contradict this explanation.

Moreover, if this thesis concerning the strong increase in capital equipment were correct, the metal industry would experience its best years shortly before and after the crisis. The facts belie this interpretation: the prices and output of cast iron and steel drop significantly from the year of the crisis. This decline remains the best indicator of the onset of a crisis.

And on the whole, it seems to us that the excess of production over demand has not been statistically established, with production being greater during the depression than a regularly increasing demand (in theory).

Besides, a simultaneous increase in production in all industries would be the best antidote to overproduction.

The additional equipment put into operation after a crisis can aggravate or prolong the depression. However, the crisis precedes this. The crisis year must retain its character as a point of intersection: before the crisis, output and prices increase; capital equipment expands at a feverish pace. After the crisis, the opposite occurs: production declines, prices fall and the production of equipment gradually contracts.

The technical lengthening of the production process cannot explain these phenomena; for this lengthening, far from having the same impact on every industry, is essentially variable. And if the cause of overproduction lies in this lengthening, it would be spaced out from year to year for each industry according to the variable timespan involved in this lengthening. Overproduction would not be general. It would be particular to each industry. And each industry would follow a unique rhythm according to the time necessary to create new equipment, which would shape any excess of production.

While this hypothesis may explain certain aspects of overproduction, it does not seem to us to be a satisfactory explanation for general overproduction crises.

In our view, the facts do not establish an increase in equipment before and after a crisis; rather, the increase in equipment occurs during the growth period, and its production declines after the crisis and during the depression. For the crisis is the starting point of a gradual, slow paralysis of the majority of industries, the most regularly affected industries being from the beginning those which produce the equipment. This is borne out by the statistics on prices, steel production, orders received by trusts and cartels and the statistics on unemployment in the mechanical engineering industry in Great Britain. It is in these industries that the increase in unemployment is greatest during and

79. We confine ourselves here to the statistical annuaries. See also the indexes and graphs for France, the United States and Great Britain from 1890 to 1911 in Wesley Clair Mitchell, *Business Cycles* (Berkeley: University of California Press, 1913), 230–77.

from the beginning of the depression. Jéramec has demonstrated this for France in the most recent period through very ingenious statistical calculations.[80]

F.) The disproportionate extension of production in different branches of industry

Without admitting the possibility of general overproduction, Sombart and Carli claim to have discovered a cause of periodic imbalances in one feature of economic progress.[81] Industrial production develops more easily than agricultural production. It is more fluid. However, products are exchanged for other products. At the end of a growth period, manufacturing output has increased faster than agricultural production. And agricultural production is no longer sufficient to provide a market for the rapidly increasing industrial production. Hence there is overproduction.

This explanation of crises could be accepted if we remain at the level of the hypothetical and generalities. But the historical study of crises does not support it. The 1929 crisis occurred in the midst of agricultural overproduction that undeniably preceded it. Statistics for corn, coffee and sugar show this.

Every crisis has a focus: railways, electricity, the car industry and so on. Can one claim that the electrical industry's customer is the farmer? The same holds for the car industry.

Moreover, equilibrium is a question of value: if agricultural production progresses less rapidly than industrial production, agricultural production can conserve, in value, the same purchasing power: an additional demand for agricultural products would trigger a higher than proportional rise in their prices.

Finally, the harvest has a decisive influence on the quantities produced by agriculture. And harvests are volatile and unpredictable. Crises are periodic, appearing whether the harvest is good or poor. While the state of agriculture can influence the general state of business, it cannot explain crises on its own.[82]

G.) Explaining [crises] through variations in potential profits[83]

If the crisis is characterized by a slowdown in the creation of new businesses, and by the diversion of savings from industrial investments, it is this slowdown and diversion that

80. Jéramec, 'Une théorie dynamique', 263–67. See also the volumes of the SDN on *Production mondiale*.
81. Sombart, *Hochkapitalismus*, vol. 2: chap. 'Konjunktur'; Filippo Carli, *Teoria generale della economia politica nazionale* (Milan: Ulrico Hoepli, 1931).
82. Timoshenko, *Role of Agricultural Fluctuations in the Business Cycle*, appears to us to have observed the necessary caution in his study of the influence of harvests on periodic crises. This research deserves to be developed further. But the cause of crises lies elsewhere.
83. Maurice Ansiaux, *Traité d'économie politique*, 3 vols. (Paris: Giard, 1920–1926), 3: 220; W. H. Beveridge, *Unemployment: A Problem of Industry (1909 and 1930)*, 2nd ed. (London: Longmans, Green, 1930); Henry Clay, *The Post-war Unemployment Problem* (London: Macmillan, 1929); Mitchell, *Business Cycles* (1913); Pigou, *Industrial Fluctuations*; Paul Reboud, *Précis d'économie politique*, vol. 2 (Paris: Dalloz, 1937); Joseph A. Schumpeter, *Theorie der wirtschaftlichen Entwicklung*,

we must explain. In our modern societies, profit is the driving force behind the spirit of enterprise. The entrepreneur ceases to create on the day on which the margin between the cost of production and the selling price seems to be shrinking. At the end of an expansion period, costs rise faster than prices in certain essential industries. An already established company can realize high profits at a certain selling price, whereas a new company of the same kind will incur losses. This will be the case if the new company is obliged to pay a high price for its equipment (machines, rails, wagons, steam engines, etc.), if it has to borrow at high interest and if the labour it may hope to recruit demands high wages for inferior work. The same applies to the construction of new buildings. This hypothesis is made plausible by the history of crises, which has been marked by the failure of new businesses to produce the expected results.

2nd ed. (Leipzig: Duncker & Humblot, 1926); Fritz Schmidt, 'Ein Rechenfehler als Konjunkturursache', *Vierteljahrshefte zur Konjunkturforschung* 1, supplement no. 4 (1926): 3–27; J. C. Stamp, 'The Effect of Trade Fluctuations upon Profits', *Journal of the Royal Statistical Society* 81, no. 4 (1918): 563–608; Otto von Zwiedineck-Südenhorst, *Beiträge zur Erklärung der strukturellen Arbeitslosigkeit* (Berlin: Hobbing, 1927), 75; Committee on Industry and Trade (Balfour Committee), *Survey of Industrial Relations*, vol. 4 (London: HMSO, 1928), 257–66; Robert Liefmann, 'Konjunkturforschung und Konjunkturpolitik', in *Konjunkturforschung und Konjunkturpolitik*, ed. Karl Diehl, 39–86; Rudolf Hilferding, *Das Finanzkapital* (Vienna: Wiener Volksbuchhandlung, 1923), 322–23; Alfred Lansburgh, 'Les crises mondiales', 3 articles published in the journal *l'Information*, 28 and 29 Aug. and 1 Sep. 1931, and see in particular the article of 28 Aug. on the causes of crises; Edwin R. A. Seligman, *Principes d'économique*, trans. George Lecarpentier, 2 vols. (Paris: Giard, 1927), 2: 232–36; Richard T. Ely, *Outlines of Economics*, 4th ed. (New York: Macmillan, 1923), 329–31; Robert von Keller, *Die Kausalzusammenhänge in der Konjunkturbewegung* (Leipzig: Meiner, 1934); Ugo Papi, *Lezioni di economia generale e corporative*, vol. 3, *Teoria delle fluttuazioni economiche* (Padua: Cedam, 1934), 1–32; Achille Loria, *Economia politica*, 4th ed. (Turin: Utet, 1934), 730–32; Sumner H. Slichter, *Modern Economic Society* (New York: Henry Holt, 1931), 466–71; Johan Åckerman, *Economic Progress and Economic Crises*, trans. Elizabeth Sprigge and Claude Napier (London: Macmillan, 1932); D. H. Macgregor, 'Enterprise and the Trade Cycle', in *Economic Essays in Honour of Gustav Cassel* (London: Fank Cass, 1933), 419–34; and Lionel C. Robbins, *La grande dépression*, trans. Pierre Coste (Paris: Payot, 1935).

Sumner H. Slichter, *Towards Stability: The Problem of Economic Balance* (New York: Henry Holt, 1937); R. F. Harrod, *The Trade Cycle: An Essay* (Oxford: Clarendon Press, 1936), chap. 2; Clark Warburton, 'Plateaus of Prosperity and Plains of Depression', in *Economic Essays in Honor of Wesley Clair Mitchell* (New York: Columbia University Press, 1935), 499–516; Gerhard Albrecht, 'Bemerkungen zum Problem des Überproduktion', *Jahrbücher der Nationalökonomie und Statistik* 146, no. 3 (1937): 306.

This explanation is the basis for recent monetary theories of crises (Strakosch, Sombart, Hawtrey); however, the increase in profits in periods of growth is said to be monetary in origin (price rise through credit expansion), and the fall in profits that causes the crisis is to be explained by the drop in prices and the restriction of credit (reduction of the central banks' cash on hand and the increase of the discount). Cf. Lescure, 'Hausses et baisses générales des prix', *Revue d'économie politique* 26, no. 4 (1912): 452–90, in which we formulated this hypothesis to criticize and reject it. See also Lescure, 'Hausse des prix et essor économique de la période 1895–1913', *Revue économique internationale* 11 (May 1914): 269–98; and *Hausses et baisses des prix de longue durée.*

In this explication, we are presenting a synthesis of the most recent theories of crises, especially those which hold that savings or available capital are insufficient to maintain output of the means of production at the same level: savings appear insufficient because the interest rate is rising. It is more difficult to find investors for securities issued: for bonds, if the interest offered is too low, and for shares, if future profits cause concern. Hence the appearance of a lack of available capital. In reality, investors are more in demand and more cautious, as shown by the statistics on issues. Investment often peaks in the crisis year if one looks at the overall figure that measures annual savings. Similarly, the restriction of short-term credit and the increase of the discount hinder the progress of the expansion and trading on the stock exchange.[84]

Finally, we will also allow that businesses created at the end of an expansion period are faced with less eager customers. This acts as a break on the price rise or the earnings of a railway, tramway or powerplant. But a theory of crises must invoke other elements that can rupture the equilibrium, other disruptive factors. The interest and discount rates, the quantities produced, are one side of the problem. The analysis and evolution of start-up costs and production costs are more complex: interest is one element here; it is not the only one. Similarly, the selling price must be observed more closely. Prices vary very little. Cost and price variations influence profits and the spirit of enterprise. Neither should be ignored; rather, their evolution must be observed in detail. In any case, we hope that this starting point will be accepted in both theoretical and practical circles: the decline in profit potential paralyses business; hence, it is capable of generating the kind of crisis we are dealing with here. It remains to be seen whether facts confirm this hypothesis, and whether the crisis is initiated by a more rapid rise in costs than in selling prices or in the profits of firms selling at the list price.

A company's profits depend on its start-up cost, cost price and selling price. At the end of a growth period, the increase in start-up costs and cost prices is no longer offset by the rise in selling prices in many industries.

1.) Start-up costs

For the crises of 1847, 1857, 1873, 1882, 1900, 1907, 1913 and 1930, we were able to cite typical characteristics. Start-up costs exceeded forecasts, resulting in disappointing returns.

But independently of these specific facts, the price curve for mineral and metal materials makes this explanation very plausible: it is an index of the variations in the start-up costs of new businesses.

A business created a year or two before the crisis will be burdened with more fixed costs than expected. The closer one comes to the crisis, the higher the cost. Only new forges would be able to offset the increase in their initial costs with the increase in the selling prices of their products. Yet tools are not an end in themselves; they are merely a means. And the general price curve of consumer goods, *a fortiori*, the rates of the railway, electricity, tramway, water and gas companies will be largely outweighed by this sudden and rapid rise in the initial installation costs.

---

84. Wicksell, *Geldzins und Güterpreise.*

This increase in start-up costs should not be considered as a whole or by looking at averages. The percentage rise or fall during growth or depression periods matters little. Timing matters more than the average. And here we observe a delay in the rise of mineral and metal materials during the general rise in prices; but soon the curve recovers abruptly, moving away from the general price curve. A new business would lose all hope of making normal profits. The gap between the general price average and the price of minerals and metals becomes too great. This extreme gap can be very clearly observed for the crises of 1873, 1900, 1907 and 1913, in 1872, 1899, 1906, 1912 and 1929 (i.e., one year before each crisis). Let us compare this observation with the statistics on industrial output: industrial output often declines before the crisis year. In spite of the wave of optimism that sweeps through the business world during a period of prosperity, the time comes when the spirit of enterprise is paralysed by rising costs. Right up to the eve of the crisis, during the first years of the prosperity, the general price curve and that of other goods move in unison; at the end of the prosperity period, one branch of production is out of step with the others: the mining and metal industry. The gap would be even more pronounced if we separated the general index of mineral materials and compared the two indexes thus obtained.

During the depression, the reverse is true. The drop in metals is more profound. No doubt it demands more or less time to reach its lowest point and adjust. The sooner the lowest point is reached, the sooner the recovery can take place. Depending on the period, mining and metals resist more or less energetically the drop which will bring their selling price closer to that of other goods. Yet this drop is necessary for them to recover their customers. These conclusions are valid for Europe.

However, Mitchell has produced a double index for the United States, comparing the index for goods that play an intermediary role in production (producers' goods) (73 products) and the index for goods directly consumed (consumer goods) (55 products). The first index is far less stable than the second. For the year 1907, he has compiled this double index from month to month. And the monthly index demonstrates that the fall in prices first affected producers' goods.[85]

The *Institut für Konjunkturforschung* has established similar indexes for the recent period that support the previous data.

The rise and fall of start-up costs are thus more pronounced than those of consumer goods.

But the initial costs are not the only thing to be considered. Cost prices still depend on the cost of raw materials, interest and wages.

2.) Cost prices

Mitchell has calculated a double index for raw materials: one index for the prices of raw materials, and one for the prices of goods manufactured with the raw materials. Raw materials present more marked upward and downward oscillations than manufactured goods. The gap between the prices of raw materials and their manufactured products

85. Mitchell, *Business Cycles* (1913), 98–99.

progressively decreases during the growth period and increases during the depression. Calculated on a monthly basis for the year 1907, this double index demonstrates how the drop first affected raw materials and, then later, manufactured goods.[86]

Indeed, trade journals consulted on a daily basis by Mitchell show that factories and wholesalers reduced their orders several weeks and even months before retail sales dropped off. The crisis is not, therefore, a consequence of the production of all consumer goods having exceeded demand. The retailer sells his products normally, while the crisis has already been registered in the wholesale trade and among manufacturers.[87]

Interest fluctuates less than the prices; however, superimposed on the rise in initial start-up costs and in the cost of raw materials, they can sometimes compromise profits. In some industries, such as construction, the interest rate exerts an undeniable influence, which we have noted in 1900, 1907, 1913 and 1922 (recovery).[88]

In addition, the discount itself is subject to much more intense fluctuations. The discount rate weighs upon the commercial cost price.

The index reproduced in table 2.1 clearly shows that the discount rate rises faster than the price of goods. The year in which the recovery begins is given the value of 100, and then the percentage of the rise is calculated.[89]

Table 2.1 Index of the Average Discount Rate at the Bank of England Compared to Sauerbeck's Price Index

	Average Rate of Discount at the Bank of England	*Sauerbeck's Index*		*Average Rate of Discount at the Bank of England*	*Sauerbeck's Index*
1870	100	100	1896	100	100
1873	154.5	114.8	1900	160.1	122.9
1879	100	100	1904	100	100
1882	164.2	101.2	1907	146.4	115.1
1887	100	100	1910	100	100
1890	133.6	105.8	1913	128.2	109

No source given.

86. Ibid., 99–102.
87. Ibid., 502.
88. Wicksell, *Geldzins und Güterpreise*, and Wicksell, *Vorlesungen über Nationalökonomie auf Grundlage des Marginalprinzipes*, vol. 2, *Geld und Kredit* (Leipzig: Fischer, 1922), 228; Mises, *Geldwertstabilisierung*; Cassel, *Traite d'économie politique*; and Keynes, *Treatise on Money*, 2: 381, insist upon the rise of interest as a factor of the crisis. But the problem is more complex. Interest is only one element in the cost price. See Sombart, *Hochkapitalismus*, vol. 2, chap. 'Konjunktur'; Irving Fischer, *The Purchasing Power of Money* (New York: Macmillan, 1911); Minnie Throop England, 'Fisher's Theory of Crises: A Criticism', *Quarterly Journal of Economics* 27, no. 1 (Nov. 1912): 95–106.
89. Robertson, *Study of Industrial Fluctuation*, 214, tab. (completed by author).

Finally, wages themselves, subject to less variation than the prices of goods, are an essential component of the cost price in some industries. This is the case for the construction industry, and even more so for the railways. On several occasions, we have seen how the movement of wages exerted a decisive influence on the net returns of the American railways. The rise in wages when added in with other cost elements triggered the drop in the net product. This element has played a very important role in Great Britain, Germany and even in the United States since 1925. Yet higher wages could be explained by the high cost of living, which resists the decline, despite the considerable reduction in wholesale prices.

Let us add finally that labour output declines as the growth continues.[90]

A comprehensive theory of crises cannot ignore any of the essential elements of the cost price.

This explanation has the advantage of bringing to the forefront the determining factors in the alternation of growth and decline: the interest rate, the discount rate and the prices of minerals and metals. Practical people would find it difficult to understand why the money rate should not play a role in the recovery or slowdown of business. And they would readily admit that the excessive price of coal and equipment and high labour costs are factors that discourage business.

For from now on, every industrial product sees its production cost influenced by the price of equipment or motive power, and if [one were to argue that] the price of cast iron or coal is not part of the price of raw cotton or of raw wool, having never met anyone wearing only raw cotton or raw wool, we believe we could claim that the price of equipment and coal influences the cost of industrial products. A spinning mill or weaving mill created at the end of a growth period would consequently have exceptionally high costs. Yet the textile industry takes part only irregularly in the alternating periods of growth and depression. In order to get at the problem, we must observe the railways, tramways, electric companies and the construction industry. This is where we find the billions in savings for some. Here we would see that rising costs weaken the net product and put a stop to extensions and improvements.

Certainly, costs increase from the start of the period of prosperity. But the expansion cannot be stopped by this increase. For the interdependency [*solidarité*] of industries explains why the recovery in a given branch of industry implies a recovery elsewhere. Expansion stops when the rise in cost exceeds the rise in selling price in certain essential branches of production, thus reaching the net product for these industries and even the general net product, given their preponderance in modern economic life. It is similar for the depression.[91]

In reality there is not one cost or one price; there are as many costs and prices as there are industries and even factories. The rise in cost or price is not general, it is *generalized*, as

90. Denis, *La dépression économique*, 84; François Simiand, *Le salaire des ouvriers des mines de charbon: Contribution à la théorie économique du salaire* (Paris: Cornély, 1907), 48.

91. L. Kotany, 'A Theory of Profit and Interest', *Quarterly Journal of Economics* 36, no. 3 (1922): 413–53.

are the recovery and the crisis. The reciprocal actions and reactions explain the course of the rise or fall. Costs fall in the railway industry, and the net product increases. The railway places orders with various industries, especially the metal industry, and the price of metals rises. Here the recovery will depend on the price increase. But the metal industry in turn becomes a better customer for other industries and for the railway itself. The upswing continues. And there is no vicious circle in explaining the recovery here by the drop in costs, and elsewhere by the rise in prices. Reality does not present us with one cost and one price, but rather with industries, costs and prices. It is the variation of costs and prices in the different industries, and their equilibrium, which must be studied in order to reach a conclusion. And this study leads us to the conclusion that a crisis can be anticipated by costs rising faster than selling prices, or in the gross receipts of enterprises subject to tariffs. Recovery is the result of costs falling more than selling prices or gross receipts.

3.) Selling prices

It is enough that the rise in selling prices lags behind the increase in costs. However, in industries which absorb the most capital – the railways, power plants and electric tramways, construction (and in others too, since dividends drop before a crisis) – the rise in selling prices is not sufficient to offset the rising costs at the end of an expansion period. Why is this so?

In our modern societies, the industries whose creation absorbs the most capital sell their production at an almost fixed price. Land transport (rail- and tramways) and electricity (power, light) are subject to a tariff. The increases in their profits, then, result from the increase in their sales.[92]

In maritime transport, shipping rates are not fixed like a tariff but are frequently determined by pools. The general index numbers established by the Board of Trade for the period 1893–1903 for British freight rates give an impression of great stability (except for the year 1900, when freight rates were influenced by the Boer War) (see tab. 2.2).[93]

Table 2.2 Index Numbers for British Shipping Rates, 1893–1903 (1900=100)

1893	83.6	(1900)	(100)
1894	79.9	1901	17.0
1895	75.3	1902	70.7
1896	79.4	1903	72.8
1897	82.9		

No source given. [See Board of Trade, *Statistical Abstract for the United Kingdom, from 1892–1906*, no. 54 (London: HMSO, 1907).]

92. Mitchell has included journals and periodicals for these industries selling at a tariff rate.
93. See also the graphs of freight in Robertson, *Study of Industrial Fluctuation*, 271, figs, for the period 1885–1913.

It was much more stable than the general price index for goods.

The situation is similar in the construction industry. Rents do not follow the same fluctuations as the prices of goods; rents are more stable. The supply of flats built previously at reduced cost will make it more difficult to increase the rent in newer buildings. The French inquiry into wages and the cost of living has accumulated evidence on this point: rent is relatively stable.[94]

Finally, as new factories come online, supply increases. Raising prices and maintaining sales become more difficult.

In our first edition we had already observed:

> As an enterprise is being set up, it must ask itself whether its selling price will allow it to recoup its production costs through its sales. Consequently, the impossibility of doing this can be found as often in an industry producing goods for direct consumption as in an industry producing means of production. [e.g., the transport industry, lighting, textiles].

We added:

> Where then does this impossibility of recouping production costs through sales originate? It can come from either the consumer or the producer. The consumer may be unable or unwilling to consume any longer; the producer may have produced too much. In fact, these two factors are usually combined: as he extends his production, the entrepreneur is faced with consumers who are less and less willing to consume his products. The urgency of the service provided, of the need satisfied, has a tendency to decrease. The first entrepreneurs were generally met by the most eager consumers [...]
>
> On the other hand, and at the same time, high profits have often led to an excessive multiplication of the number of producers [...] There comes a time when certain branches of production find themselves trapped in the following dilemma: either they stop pursuing new business or, if business is still undertaken, the chances of making a profit are greatly reduced because, first, production costs are very high, and second, *given the increasing saturation of demand, an increase in selling prices has become impossible* [emph. added]. This impossibility diverts savings from industrial uses.[95]

In terms of railways, tramways and electricity supply, the most productive businesses were created first. The general price curve shows a definite deflation at the end of the expansion period, while the price curve for mineral and metal materials or even for other raw materials picks up. In many key industries, the cost of raw materials is becoming impossible.

All preceding statistics lead us to assume, for the moment, that there is a tendency for profits to reduce at the end of a growth period.

94. *Enquête*, pp. 80–95.

95. Lescure, *Des crises générales et périodiques de surproduction* (Paris: Larose & Tenin, 1906), 517–18. See also the 2nd ed. (Paris: Larose & Tenin, J.-B. Sirey, 1910), 505–11, in which these ideas are developed further, and where we emphasize the fact that certain prices are fixed (in particular railway tariffs).

4.) Profit

However, the presumption can only be admitted as proof in the absence of other evidence. Is it possible to demonstrate that the decline in profits and *a fortiori* in possible profit precedes and signals the crisis?

In Great Britain, it is well known that industrial and commercial profits were used for a long time to assess income taxes according to the average profit for the previous three years. The elevated profits of the expansion period served as the basis for 'assessments' in the first years of a crisis and depression. Normally the maximum would be reached in the tax statistics in the year following the crisis or the year after. However, these records allow for a comparison of price and profit fluctuations. It is sufficient to calculate three-year averages of prices corresponding to the three-year averages of profits subject to tax. On this basis, J. C. Stamp has produced a graph comparing the movement of prices and profits in Great Britain by using the median and the calculation of the deviations above and below this median for each year. We reproduce this graph in figure 2.1, which establishes that profit movements occur before those of prices. In a growth period, profits decline before prices, and in a period of depression, they rise before prices.

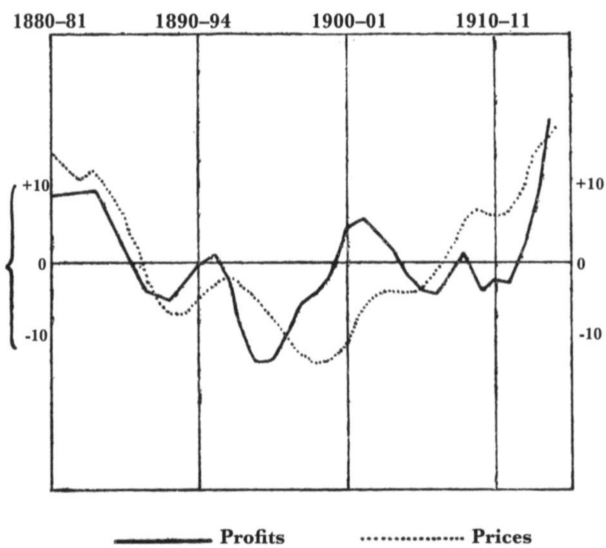

Source: Stamp, 'The Effect of Trade Fluctuations upon Profits', *Journal of the Royal Statistical Society* 81, no. 4 (1918): 588, fig. 8.

Figure 2.1 Percentage Fluctuations of Prices and Profits in Great Britain

However, figure 2.1 still indicates that profit variations are generally of the same order as those of prices, contrary to the conclusions we would arrive at by examining certain specific industries, notably the coal industry.

For the period following the war, statistics on profits in Great Britain are available to us based on dividends distributed by joint-stock companies. These statistics confirm Stamp's data relating to the pre-war period. In 1932, the profit increase preceded the rise in prices (fig. 2.2).

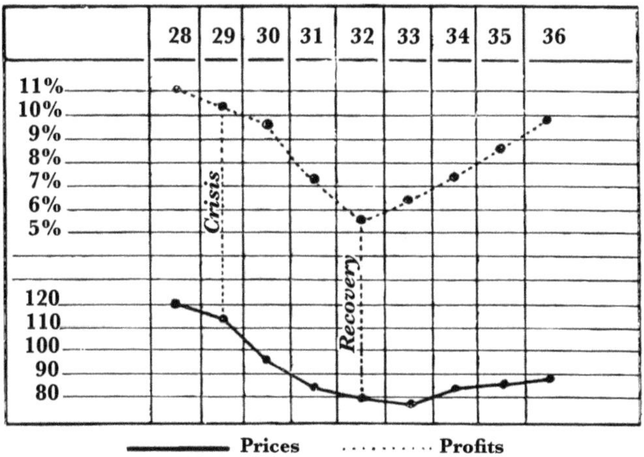

Sources: As profit index we have used the percentage of profits to capital for nearly 2,000 British companies (*The Economist*) and compared this to the Sauerbeck-Paish index (*The Statist*). See also above, chap. 1, §16, A.) Great Britain.

Figure 2.2 Prices and Profits, 1928–1936

The study of profits in a variety of industries also proves that profits decline in some industries before diminishing in others; for example, railway profits drop before profits in the coal industry. We will return to this example shortly.

For France, by using the same method, using the statistics on dividends, we will arrive at similar conclusions. The statistics on dividends subject to the income tax on securities can be considered as an index of profit: the influence of crises comes through very clearly. And the superimposition of the maxima and minima of the price index on the dividends curve demonstrates the upward or downward advance of profits over prices. This advance is obvious, if we note that the dividends distributed in a given year represent the profits realized in the preceding year. If we shift the dividend curve by one division, the priority of profit movements over prices is undeniable. The dotted line in figure 2.2 represents this transposition.

However, the graph of taxable dividends permits a further observation: whenever a country is the focus of a periodic crisis, the fluctuations upward and downward are particularly striking. France suffered a crisis in 1882 that was preceded by a considerable increase in dividends distributed and followed by a significant reduction. On the other hand, in 1890 France almost completely escapes the periodic crisis, and the dividend curve remains more or less stable. In 1900, 1907 and 1913, our country suffered the repercussions of serious foreign crises: dividends rose and fell, but much less than during the 1882 crisis. Finally, the fluctuations in dividends are of the same order as those in prices: all dividends are in fact affected by the creation of new businesses. This element changes the shape of the curve of dividends. If this correction is made, the overall rise in dividends does not seem to be much faster than the general price rise (fig. 2.3). We thus reach similar conclusions for France as Stamp has for Great Britain and Denuc has in a study devoted to the dividends of French companies from 1857 to 1932. Secondary railways and urban transport distributed their highest dividends in the periods of great-

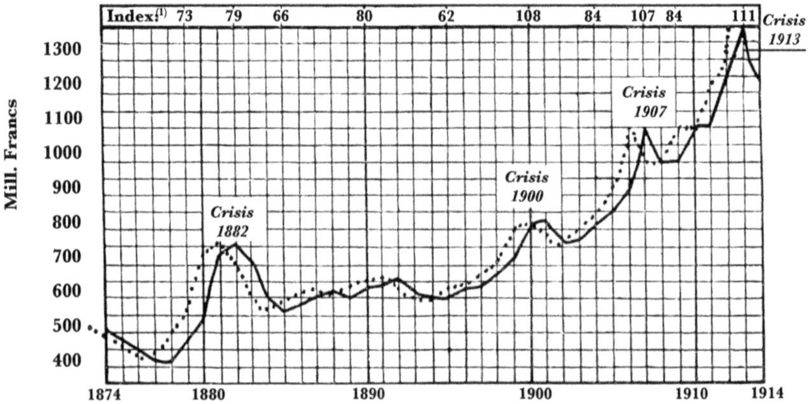

[(1)] **Index values represent the maximums and minimums of the Sauerbeck index for prices of mineral and metal materials. It is regrettable that the *Statisque générale de la France* has discontinued the publication of this numerical data. Cf. Jules Denuc, 'Dividendes, valeurs boursières et taux de capitalisation des valeurs mobilière français de 1847 à 1932', *Bulletin de la Statistique générale de la France* 23 (July–Sep. 1934): 691–767.**

Figure 2.3 Dividends of Share Companies Subject to Income Tax in France, 1874–1914

est prosperity: in 1881, 1890 and 1898, well before the years of crisis.[96]

For Germany, the work of Wagon and even more so that of Dermietzel confirm these observations.[97] They cover the 1890–1902 period and are based on the dividends of German joint-stock companies. From 1894 onward, dividends increased; from 1899 onward, they fall. The table drawn up by Dermietzel demands special attention: he calculates the percentage of German share capital receiving dividends varying from 0 to 35 per cent each year between 1890 and 1902 (see tab. 2.3). Thus, we see the proportion of share capital receiving a small or large dividend increasing or decreasing. The shift from year to year in favour of large dividends indicates the increase in profit and vice versa.

96. Denuc, 'Dividendes, valeurs boursières et taux de capitalisation', 734.
97. Eduard Wagon, *Die finanzielle Entwicklung deutscher Aktiengesellschaften von 1870–1900 und die Gesellschaften mit beschränkter Haftung im Jahre 1900* (Jena: Fischer, 1903); Otto Dermietzel, *Statistische Untersuchungen über die Kapitalrente der grosseren deutschen Aktiengesellschaften von 1876–1902* (Göttingen: Hofer, 1906), 61–63.

Table 2.3 Percentage Dividends of German Share Capital, 1890–1902

	Shares Receiving Dividends of							
	0%	*0–5%*	*5–10%*	*10–15%*	*15–20%*	*20–25%*	*25–30%*	*30–35%*
1890	1.6	5.4	54.8	31.4	4.9	1.9	—	—
1891	4.4	10.9	69.1	10.3	3.5	1.1	0.7	—
1892	3.5	19.5	66.2	8.5	1.6	—	0.7	—
1893	4.1	25.1	62.4	7.6	—	—	0.7	—
1894	7.5	13.3	65.9	12.6	—	—	0.7	—
1895	5.2	9.8	62.9	20.3	1.1	—	0.7	—
1896	3.2	5.0	66.9	21.2	3.1	—	0.5	—
1897	0.8	2.3	65.3	25.9	5.2	—	0.5	—
1898	0.7	2.0	61.1	29.8	5.7	0.7	—	—
1899	—	0.4	59.8	31.5	6.1	—	2.2	—
1900	1.4	8.0	62.1	22.4	3.3	2.3	—	0.5
1901	10.1	21.8	47.8	17.4	0.8	1.3	0.5	0.3
1902	9.4	16.9	54.9	15.1	2.0	0.9	0.5	0.3

Source: Dermietzel, *Statistische Untersuchungen über die Kapitalrente*, 61–63.

The index of the rates of variable-income securities on the Berlin Stock Exchange calculated by the *Jahrbuch für Nationalökonomie und Statistik* shows that, for the 1904–1913 period, the crisis was preceded by a decline in the prices of variable-income securities (see tab. 2.4). This is an index of the decline in real or potential profit in a number of businesses before the crisis.

Table 2.4 Index of Average Rates of Variable-Income Securities on the Berlin Stock Exchange, 1904–1913

1904	153.91	1909	156.96
1905	168.82	1910	162.77
1906	163.25	1911	162.45
1907 (crisis)	149.29	1912	158.78
1908	145.32	1913	157.59

Source: *Jahrbuch für Nationalökonomie und Statistik*, *Volkswirtschaftliche Chronik* (1913): 1067.

For the 1850–1930 period, the Statistique Générale de la France arrives at the same result. The drop in variable-income securities signals and anticipates the crises.[98]

In the United States, the Harvard curve has demonstrated that variable-income securities declined before crises in the 1903–1914 and 1918–1921 periods.[99]

For the 1929 crisis in the United States, we possess a particularly interesting statistic, concerning 163 American industrial and commercial companies. Net profits reached their peak in the second quarter of 1929, which we mark with a dotted line on the graph

98. See Marcel Lenoir, 'Cours des valeurs mobilières français', *Bulletin de la Statistique générale de la France* 11 (Jan. 1922), and the monthly indexes of variable-income securities prices. See also Jean Dessirier, *La conjuncture économique et financière* (monthly review).
99. See the *Review of Economics and Statistics* and the well-known A, B and C curves.

in figure 2.4. From the end of 1932 and the beginning of 1933, profits rose, signalling the recovery.[100]

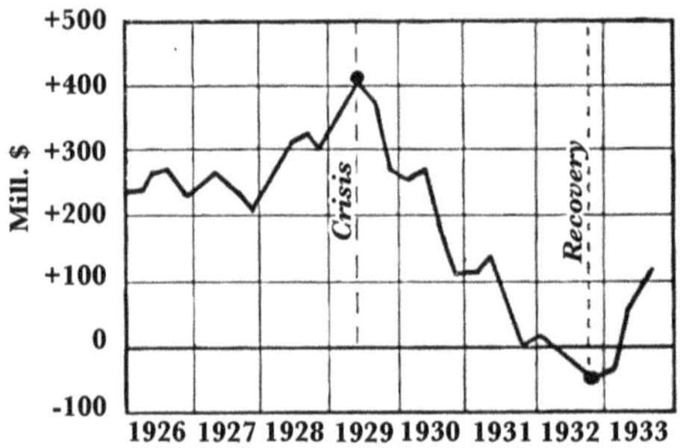

Source: W. L. Crum, 'The Course of Corporation Profits', *Review of Economics and Statistics* 16, no. 3 (15 March 1934): 61, fig. 1.

Figure 2.4 Quarterly Aggregate Net Profits of 163 US Industrial and Mercantile Corporations, 1926–1933

The National City Bank has produced a graph which compares the total amount of profits of 200 American companies with the *Annalist* general index of business activity (fig. 2.5).[iv] The importance of profit movements is very clear. The crisis of 1929 and the recovery of 1933 were preceded by profit movements, falling profits (third quarter of 1929) and rising profits (fourth quarter of 1932). The movements of decline or recovery in business follow changes in profit.

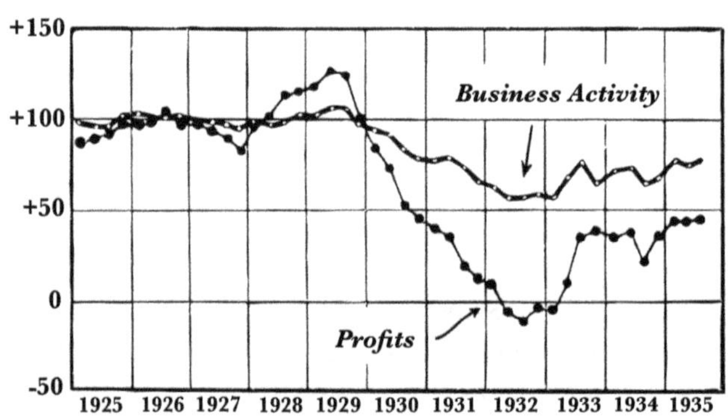

Source: National City Bank of New York, *Monthly Economic Letter* (Nov. 1935): 163.

Figure 2.5 Quarterly Index of Industrial Corporation Profits, and the *Annalist* Index of Business Activity, 1925–1935

100. See also Lescure, 'Les profits 1929–1935 (Grande-Bretagne, États-Unis, France)', *Journal de la Société statistique de Paris* 77 (1936): 192–200; Ralph C. Epstein, *Industrial Profits in the United States* (New York: NBER, 1934); H. Campion, 'Pre-war Fluctuations of Profits in the Cotton-Spinning Industry', *Journal of the Royal Statistical Society* 97, no. 4 (1934): 626–32.

However, as Stamp has remarked, the laws of profit vary from one industry to another; some move forward, while others lag behind. We must go into greater detail. For vital industries, those which have absorbed the most capital in the nineteenth and twentieth centuries, like the railways, tramways and electrical industries, and more recently the car industry, we can establish that the crisis is preceded by a decline in their profit or in their net product, considered as an index of their profit. Alongside this decline, we note a decrease in newly created businesses. If even well-established firms feel the effects of rising operating costs on their profits, a new company would be burdened with both enormous start-up costs and significantly higher operating costs simultaneously. In the United States, such firms regularly succumbed to bankruptcy in great numbers.

But if we neglect the rise in start-up costs and use only the operating costs, we can establish the decline in the railways' net product on the eve of the crisis. True, to establish this, it is not always enough to observe figures year by year; rather, we must look month by month.

And then, after having ranked the different industries in order of importance, assigning to each its proper place, we can verify our hypothesis for the principal industries and come closer to lending our explanation some degree of plausibility. For in order to interpret these alternatives correctly, we must not place all industries on equal footing; there are key industries. For the railways, the industry which has played an essential role in alternating periods of expansion and depression, we can establish this pre-crisis decline in profit. The decline in net receipts was followed by the slowdown of construction, by the crisis.

Table 2.5 Years of Maximum and Minimum Net Returns per Kilometre of French Railways

Maximums	*Minimums*
1847	—
1855–56	1849
1866	1858
1872	1868
1881	1877
1889	1886
1899	1893
1906	1901
—	1911

No source given.

The same is true in the United States. The decline in net returns precedes the decline in gross receipts, very often by a full year. But when net and gross receipts both appear to fall at the same time, because they fall in the same year, monthly statistics tell us that the drop in net returns precedes that in gross receipts. This was the case in 1907, 1913, 1920 and 1937. (See table A2 in the Annexes.)

And this decline in net earnings precedes and signals the drop in orders placed with the metal industry. The crisis in the metal industry exacerbates the problems of the railways. For the United States, where the rail network is still expanding very significantly, the extension of the railway before a crisis and the decrease in construction after a crisis were very evident between 1857 and 1913. This has been wrongly disputed.

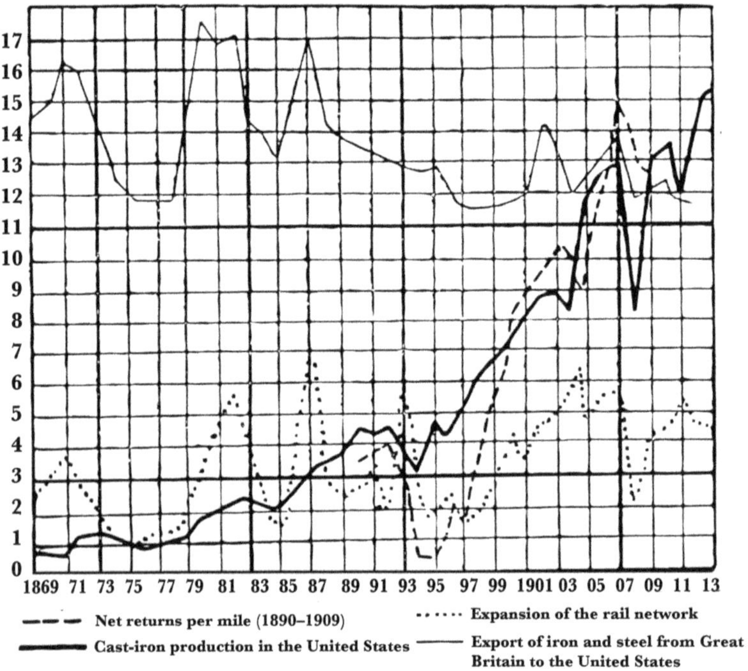

A.) Baselines for the graph in bold.
For the production of cast iron: horizontal 0.
For the extension of the railway network: horizontal 0.
For the net returns per mile: horizontal 3.
For the export of iron and steel: horizontal 11.

B.) Each unit-division of the graph [y axis] represents:
For iron production: 2 million tonnes.
For net returns per mile: 20 (horizontal 3 = 100).
For the extension of the railway network: 2,000 miles.
For the export of iron and steel: 200,000 tonnes.

C.) For the extension of the railway network up to 1890, see Poor's *Manual of Railroads*; from 1891 on, see *Statistical Abstract of the United States* 43 (1920): 344, table 238 (years ending on 30 June), and Interstate Commerce Commission reports.

D.) For net returns, see the index numbers in Mitchell, *Business Cycles*, 425. The index is established for the period 1890 to 1910 with the average 1890–1899 = 100.

See also John E. Partington, *Railroad Purchasing and the Business Cycle* (Washington, DC: Brookings Institution, 1929).

Figure 2.6 The Railways and the Metal Industry in the United States, 1867–1913

Figure 2.6 provides evidence of the close relationship between the net returns of the railways, the construction of railway lines and the progress or decline of the metal industry in the United States. However, before the prodigious expansion of the American metal industry, an acceleration of railway construction translated into parallel increases in iron and steel imports from England. This influence waned, tending to disappear almost entirely by 1890.

For the United States, however, we possess evidence that appears to lend great plausibility to our thesis: the statistics on railways placed under receivership (see tab. 2.6). Every crisis is signalled not only by the general decline in net earnings but also by the failure of a host of railway companies unable to meet their obligations.

Table 2.6 US Railways Placed Under Receivership, 1880–1914

	Number of Railways	*Mileage*	*Stocks and Bonds (millions of $)*
1880	13	885	140.2
1881	5	110	3.7
1882	12	912	39.0
1883	11	1,990	108.4
1884	**37**	**11,838**	**714.7**
1885	44	8,836	385.4
1886	13	1,799	70.3
1887	9	1,046	90.3
1888	22	3,270	186.8
1889	22	3,803	99.6
1890	26	2,963	105.0
1891	27	2,159	84.4
1892	36	10,508	357.6
1893	**74**	**29,340**	**1,781**
1894	38	7,025	395.7
1895	31	4,089	369.0
1896	24	5,441	275.5
1897	18	1,537	92.9
1898	18	2,060	138.7
1899	10	1,010	52.2
1900	16	1,165	78.2
1901	**4**	73	1.6
1902	5	278	5.8
1903	9	229	18.8
1904	8	744	30.0
1905	10	3,593	173.3
1906	6	204	55.0
1907	7	307	13.5
1908	24	**8,009**	**596.3**
1909	5	859	78.0
1910	7	735	51.4
1911	5	2,606	210.6
1912	13	3,784	182.1
1913	17	**9,020**	**477.7**
1914	22	4,222	199.5

Source: *Statistical Abstract of the United States* 43 (1920): 355, tab. 249. [Bold values indicate the rise in the number, length and value of railways placed under receivership in the years before a major crisis in the US, as well as the year (1901) with the fewest number of railway failures.]

For England, we have a set of particularly interesting figures: the length of lines granted and the number of concessions, which are indexes of entrepreneurs' state of mind. At the time when England constructed its railways (1830–1870), we found that crises were preceded by a decline in the length of concessions (1847) or marked by abandoned concessions (1857). As railways were absorbing the majority of capital in the nineteenth and twentieth centuries, we believe we have established the link between the decline in profits, the slowdown in construction and the drop in metal production.

Yet the metal industry has another important customer: maritime transport. It would appear that here also a decline in real profits, or in any case in potential profits, anticipates the crisis. Shipping companies sometimes distribute their highest profits during the growth period in the year before the crisis, as was the case for Hamburg-Amerika and Norddeutscher-Lloyd in 1906 (see tab. 2.7).

Table 2.7 Profits Distributed by the Major German Shipping Companies, 1906–1913

	1906	*1907*	*1908*	*1909*	*1910*	*1911*	*1912*	*1913*
Hamburg-Amerika	10%	6%	0	6%	8%	9%	10%	10%
Norddeutscher-Lloyd	8½%	4½%	0	0	3%	5%	7%	8%

No source given.

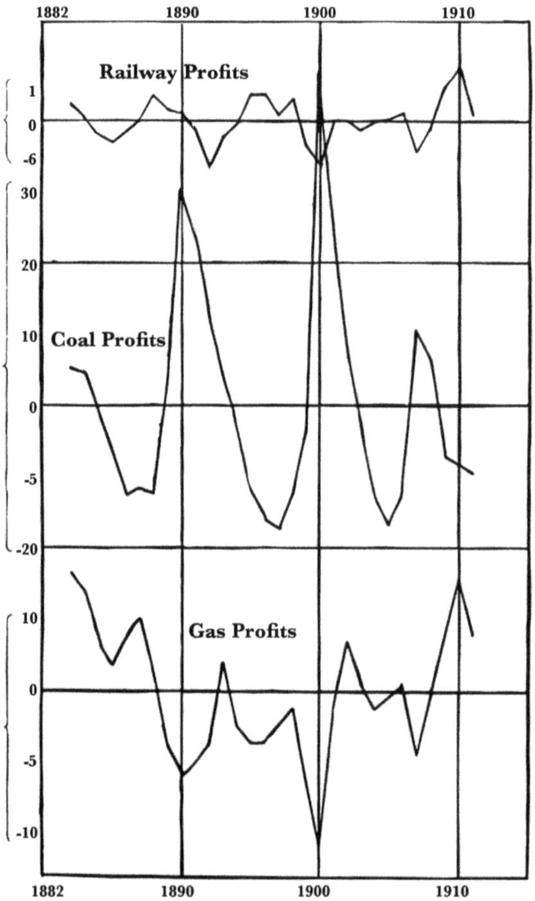

Source: Stamp, 'The Effect of Trade Fluctuations Upon Profits', *Journal of the Royal Statistical Society* 81, no. 4 (1918): 582, fig. 5.

Figure 2.7 Coal Prices and Railway and Gasworks Profits in Great Britain, 1882–1913

The decline in orders for ships seems to signal the crisis, much like the decrease in orders from the railways. Robertson suggests that a ship launched in 1901, for example, would have been ordered 18 months earlier. If we accept this discrepancy, we have to admit that the decline in orders anticipates and precedes a crisis.

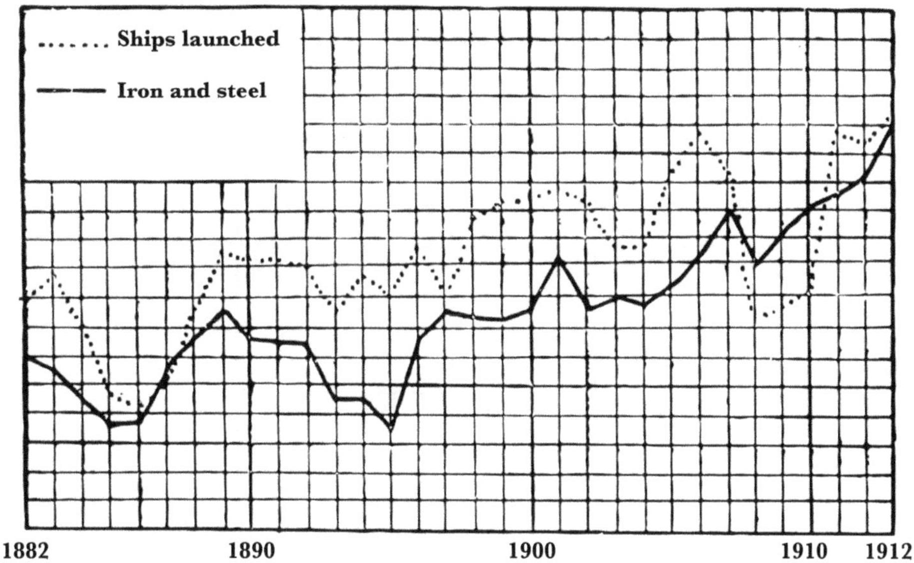

Note: With 1882 as the year of origin. During that year, iron and steel production reached 5 million tonnes, and each division of the graph represents 500,000 tonnes. The tonnage launched in 1882=950,000 gross tonnes, and each division represents 150,000 tonnes.

Figure 2.8 Shipbuilding and Iron and Steel Production in Great Britain, 1882–1912

Finally, the metal industry still has one other important customer. The construction industry is also one of the industries hit very early and very severely by crises. Unemployment statistics for Great Britain and the statistics on building permits in the United States in 1907, 1913, 1920 and 1929 demonstrate that the slowdown in the construction of houses or factories sometimes signals the onset of a crisis. And the recovery sometimes started with construction, in 1922 in particular, and in Britain in 1933.

Starting with the crisis, unemployment increased in the construction industry, and at the peak of the depression, the percentage of unemployed construction workers was reminiscent of the exceptionally high percentage in the metal and mechanical engineering industries. For the crises of 1873, 1882, 1893 (Australia), 1900, 1907, 1913 and 1929, we have been able to establish that the slowdown in construction was due to the increase in the costs of materials and interest, rising wages, the exaggerated price of land, the lack of new factories being constructed and a reduced demand for housing. The time when the building industry enters the crisis varies from case to case. In Germany in 1912, the crisis in construction anticipated the general crisis.

Yet for other industries, with the help of some monographs and surveys, we can establish a pattern: at the end of a boom period, new enterprises perform poorly; their initial costs and cost prices are too high.

The crisis of 1873 was the subject of an excellent monograph by Oechelhaeuser; the crisis of 1900 has been described in minute detail in the eight-volume survey of the Verein für Socialpolitik; and the 1913 crisis has been addressed in Feiler's work.[v] The

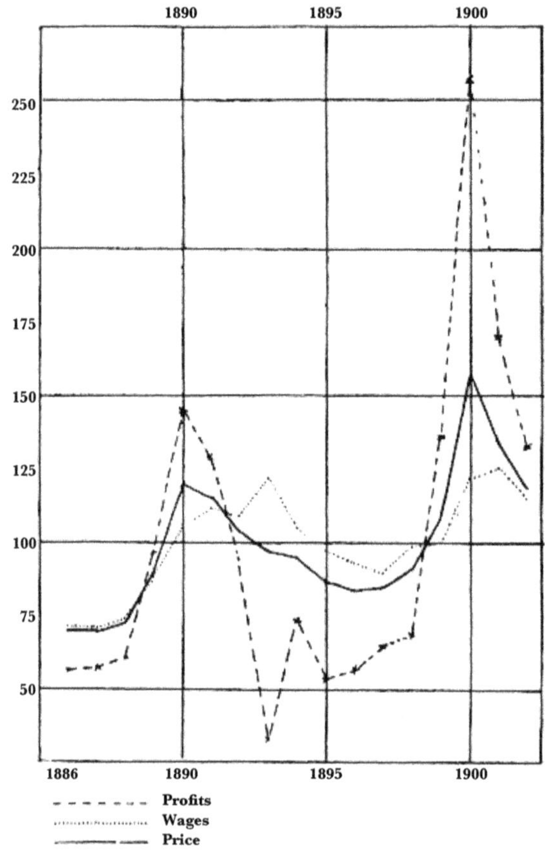

Source: Stamp, 'The Effect of Trade Fluctuations Upon Profits', *Journal of the Royal Statistical Society* 81, no. 4 (1918): 580, fig 4, according to the Parliamentary Return, no. 197, on 'Wages and Profits in Coal Mining', [in *Hansard*, HC Deb 10 June 1903, vol. 123, c. 440].

Figure 2.9 Coal Mining in Great Britain, 1886–1902

genesis and process of the crises could be observed in detail. With the help of these studies, which focus on the country that had been the main focal point of the crises in these three years, Germany, we believe we have demonstrated that the companies created at the end of the growth period do not produce the results expected by their promoters. Profits decrease here first or even disappear entirely.

The 1929 crisis was preceded and caused by the fall of profits in the car industry, which was due to rising costs.

In 1930, American railway traffic measured in gross earnings diminished by 14 per cent, whereas operating costs were down by only 12.8 per cent.[101] In 1937 [*sic*], the drop in the railways' net returns foreshadowed the depression (drop of June 1937).[vi]

101. J. Joyce Broderick (British commercial attaché) and Arthur J. Pack, *Economic Conditions in the United States of America, March 1931* (London: Department of Overseas Trade, 1931), 80–82.

In some industries, falling profits preceded the crisis; in others, they coincided with the crisis. This was the case in the coal mines, at least in England, and the French metal industry. The same applied to the oil industry.

In France, if we take the dividend distributed by the coal companies as an index of profit, the curve reaches its maximum in the first year of the crisis or in the year after. We would arrive at slightly different results if we were to consider net taxable income or the net profit per tonne of coal. But since both figures are calculated using tax statistics, the dividends are probably a better index of profits for the coal mines. The dividends curve for French mines resembles the profit curve for mines in Britain. In both France and Great Britain, the increase in profits is enormous from 1896 onward. And the variations in the price of coal have a significant influence on allotments [*répartitions*]. Yet the variations in profits have a much greater amplitude than the movement of prices.

As the share capital of French coal companies in relation to their facilities [*installations*] and the mining side [*domaine minier*] of the business is fairly low, an increase in profits results in a very substantial increase in dividends. Thus, from 1897 onward, our main coal companies were forced to split their shares: here they were divided by 30, there by 50, and elsewhere by 20. Needless to say, we have taken this division into account when plotting our curves (see fig. 2.10).

On the other hand, while there are industries (mainly tariff industries) where profits decline first, there are others where the fall in profits is delayed, as it is with coal mines, oil companies and cotton mills in England. The *Economist* publishes in its invaluable yearly reviews (Commercial History and Review) statistics on net profits, losses and dividends for 80 to 100 mills with shares since 1894. As the number of mills varies from year to year, we must look at the profits (or losses) of each company, or better still, the average dividend as a percentage of capital. In table 2.8 we provide the percentages from 1884 to 1908 (for the year ending on 30 November).

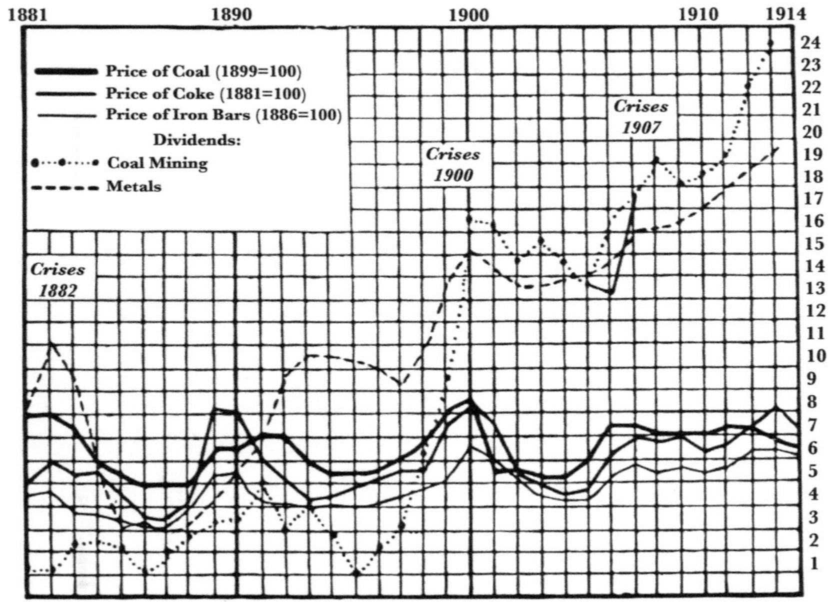

1. For prices, the baseline for the curves is horizontal 3, listed at 60; horizontal 4, listed at 80; horizontal 5, at 100, etc. The prices are those provided by the *Annuaire statistique de la France* (1919–20): 101–3.

2. For dividends of the coal mining companies, the baseline is horizontal 2, listed at 3,000 francs; each division represents 500 francs. Horizontal 4 is 3,500 francs; horizontal 5 is 4,000 francs, etc. The figures given are derived from the sum of the dividends of Courrières, Dourges, Lens, Marles, 70%, Vicoingne, as they appear in the *Annuaire des valeurs des agents de change*.

The Courrières disaster in 1906 led us to correct our graph accordingly. The solid line corresponds to the figures including Courrières.

3. We have added up the dividends of Chatillon-Commentre, Aciéries de la Marine, Le Creusot, Commetrey-Fourchambault, Longwy, and Denain-Anzin. We calculated an index of 100 for the dividends in order to make the prices and dividends comparable. But it would have crossed our framework. The comparison of price curves and dividend curves therefore gives an imperfect idea of the respective course of prices and dividends. However, that dividends rise faster than prices is very clear. In fact, it is even more pronounced.

Figure 2.10 Prices and Dividends of the Coal Mining and Metal Companies in France, 1881–1914

Table 2.8 Average Dividend as a Percentage of Capital for English Cotton Mills, 1884–1908

1884	5	1897	3
1885	2	1898	4⅓
1886	3	1899	6⅙
1887	4¾	1900	7¼
1888	5	1901	7⅙
1889	5	1902	4⅔
1890	7	1903	3
1891	5¼	1904	2½
1892	1¼	1905	7
1893	1	1906	9⅔
1894	1½	1907	15⅞
1895	1⅝	1908	11¾
1896	1¾		

Source: *The Economist*, Commercial History and Review.

However, there are industries in which the laws of profit are the opposite of the general law: the gas companies (tab. 2.9). Selling their products at a tariff rate and being subject to the consequences of variations in the price of coal, they make their highest profits in times of depression and their lowest in periods of growth.

Table 2.9 Index of Dividends for French Gas Companies, 1882–1932

1882	40	1899	92	1916	11
1883	57	1900	94	1917	5
1884	67	1901	94	1918	4
1885	70	1900	90	1919	18
1886	72	1903	91	1920	70
1887	77	1904	91	1921	99
1888	79	1905	100	1922	168
1889	81	1906	101	1923	242
1890	82	1907	105	1924	311
1891	87	1908	107	1925	424
1892	88	1909	109	1926	519
1893	89	1910	111	1927	927
1894	88	1911	117	1928	698
1895	90	1912	119	1929	933
1896	92	1913	101	1930	1,138
1897	92	1914	47	1931	1,165
1898	92	1915	41	1932	1,168

Source: Denuc, 'Dividendes, valeurs boursières et taux de capitalisation', 741.

All in all, there are branches of production where the fall in profits anticipates the crisis, others where the drop coincides with the crisis and others where the drop comes after the crisis.

Finally, the amplitude of the drop in profits varies greatly depending on the industry. In the branches of industry that provide for essential needs (food, water, gas, tramways, lighting, telephones, telegraph), the drop is much less significant than in an industry that has been the focus of the crisis or in industries producing the means of production. In this respect, the crisis of 1929 in the United States is quite typical.

Moody's Investors Service provides profit statistics for the United States based on the profit forecasts of 609 American companies. For the first quarter of 1931, the percentage reduction, when compared to the corresponding quarter in 1930, is as follows:[102]

Textiles	96.8%
Copper	94.9
Steel	91.4
Railway Equipment	69.7
Machines	63.7
Automobiles	49.9
Railways	39.3

On the other hand, in public utilities and foodstuffs the reduction is almost negligible:

Lighting, Power and Gas Companies	1.6%
Foodstuffs	6.6

It was the same in England in 1930–31. For the past 20 years, the *Times* has collected profit statistics for each half year using the data furnished by a very large number of share companies. Electricity and breweries were hardly affected.

We could make similar observations for France. Dessirier has calculated index numbers for net earnings on variable-income securities listed on the Paris Stock Exchange,

Table 2.10 Dividends as a Percentage of Capital in Great Britain, 1927–1931

	1927–28	*1928–29*	*1929–30*	*1930–31*
Coal, Iron and Steel	3	3.2	3.2	2.7
Mechanical Engineering	6.4	6.3	5.4	4.3
Electrical Engineering	6.8	6.2	6.8	6.3
Electricity	6.8	7.1	7.1	7.4
Cotton	8	7.8	6.2	3
Wool	7.1	6.6	5.4	3.9
Merchant Marine	5.8	5.6	5	2.6
Chemical Products	6.8	6.4	6.5	5.4
Petrol	12.5	13	14.9	10.7
Rubber	8.4	6.7	4.7	0
Breweries	14.9	14.3	14.5	14.4

Source: 'Industrial profits in 1930–1931', *The Times, Trade and Engineering Supplement*, 14 Nov. 1931, 201.

both in groups and as a general index (see tab. 2.11). The index reached its peak in June 1930 and its minimum in October 1931. However, all the groups were not affected to the same degree. Gas and electricity values contrasted with the others.

102. *Times*, 26 May 1931.

Table 2.11 Index of Net Earnings from Variable-Income Securities on the Paris Stock Exchange (1913=100)

	June 1930	*Oct. 1930*
General Index	384	310
Banks	267	235
Collieries (North)	398	335
Forges and Steel Mills	215	154
Textiles	640	200
Gas	439	486
Electricity	505	539

Source: Dessirier ed., *La conjoncture économique et financière* (Nov. 1931): graph no. 101. Cf. Jean-Marie Drappier, 'La conjoncture des cours des valeurs mobilières, de leurs dividendes et des taux d'intérêt en Belgique de 1830 à 1913', *Bulletin de l'Institut des sciences économiques* 8, no. 4 (1937): 391–449.

Denuc arrives at the same results in his study of the dividends of French companies from 1857 to 1932.[103]

But why would the prices of coal and metals fluctuate up and down more than the prices of other goods?

As the production of capital goods accelerates, metal factories will proceed to expand their operations. However, in order to create forges, steelworks and rolling mills and then put them into operation, steel and coal are needed. At the end of a period of expansion, the demand for minerals and metals is therefore exceptionally intense, more intense than the demand for other goods. This is why, despite the quickened pace of production, their prices nevertheless rise significantly. And herein may lie the key to the disequilibrium. We may compare industries to a marching troop. The tempo of the march remains steady, even when accelerating, provided all participants increase their pace at the same rate. If one of them gets ahead, the harmony is broken. It is the same at the end of a period of depression. The crisis restores the alignment. But it will take time for harmony to be restored. The breakdown will have led to general indecision. The industry that went ahead of the others will have to mark time. Its production and prices will drop. The graphs for coal, cast iron and steel production demonstrate this. It will take years, but how many? It all depends on the speed of this recovery.

However, one may wonder why the re-alignment did not take place sooner, why the depression did not reach its lowest point immediately after the crisis. It will be objected that as soon as costs fall, the recovery should take shape. Not so. Because the drop in costs is insufficient in the first place. The price index shows this (see tab. A1). As do the statistics on dividends and the net product of the railways (see tab. A2).

The resistance to the drop from the mining and metal industries after the crisis is quite natural. When they rise very high, they cannot drop too low without causing catastrophe. Cartels sometimes intensify this resistance. But the sooner the drop, the sooner the recovery appears. The period from 1903 to 1914 in the United States is of

103. Denuc, 'Dividendes, valeurs boursières et taux de capitalisation'. Dividends are studied in groups: banking, metal industry, textiles, etc.: 23 groups in total.

particular interest in this respect; so was the 1922 recovery. Moreover, orders placed before the crisis are filled after the crisis has begun. This means that the period of prosperity spills over into the period of depression. But from the start of the crisis, the downward mechanism is put into motion. With falling prices, capital flows away from industry. The fall here causes a drop there, and the downward trend spreads from one industry to the next.

Take the railways, for example, they reduce their orders. The metal and mining industries reduce their production. The quantities being transported by rail diminish. Gross returns decrease, and with them, net earnings. The railways reduce their orders even further. The prices of coal and steel fall.

There comes a time when the drop in costs is such that net profit increases. This is a fact. Economic recovery is again possible (see tab. A2).

Other industries follow the essential ones and are also affected: the shipping industry is short of freight. The textile industries lack orders; although in this case a variety of factors (credit, good or poor harvests in India, good or poor cotton harvests) can neutralize the influence of essential industries.[104]

Therefore, it is natural that the cost reduction should take some time, especially a reduction to the level of other commodities or the railways' gross receipts.

Yet even once the cost has fallen below the selling price, it is conceivable that it will take some time for new opportunities to emerge. Projects have to be set up. Estimates will have to be made, whether they be for railways, tramways or power plants, and plans will need to be drawn up for new housing. In the case of cars, it will take a number of years for them to wear out.

In any case, a reduction in the production of cast iron, steel and coal and an exceptional drop in their prices appear to be typical following a crisis. And despite the steady decrease in production, prices continue to fall. The price drop is not caused by an increase in production; rather, it is demand that is lacking. There comes a time when the harmony is restored between start-up costs, cost prices and selling prices. Capital is abundant and cheap. Savings flow back into industry. The recovery is at hand.

In conclusion, we will gladly admit together with Robertson that the crisis appears at the moment when a new expenditure of capital (investment) involves a short-term sacrifice greater than the enjoyment provided by the consumer good it will serve to create.[105]

This is our conclusion. If we have attempted a long demonstration of this thesis, it has not been simply for theoretical purposes but also to preserve the essential role of observations of the metals market in the forecasting of economic crises. We believe that one of the recent advances in our field has consisted in the observation of the thoroughly periodic alternations in the metal industry, and in establishing the relationship between crises and these alternations. The theory of crises should make it possible to explain this regular correlation (the only truly regular one). We may now add to this the net profit of

104. On this particular point, see the very interesting remarks in Robertson, *Study of Industrial Fluctuation*, 106.
105. Ibid., 243, and see also 180.

the railways and the dividends of newly created businesses. But in this last case, statistical observation must be fully organized. In the United States, railway returns appear to have already produced results as forecasting indexes of crises or recoveries.

All in all, at the end of an expansion period, profit in some industries is like being caught in a vice, one side of which is the considerable growth of costs, and the other, the fall, constancy or insufficient increase in selling prices. We emphasize the rise in cost. In 1929, the cost increase caused the decline in profit in the car industry. In the essential industries of the nineteenth and early twentieth centuries, prices are fixed (tariff), and the industries with less stable selling prices (textiles, among others) occupy a secondary place in comparison. Yet for the latter, we might accept that the rise is paralysed by the increase in production. However, increased production in these industries does not appear to be the key feature because production expands during the boom, without decreasing prices. Sometimes prosperity is even maintained after the crisis, whereas in essential industries (railways, electrical industries, mining, metal industries, mechanical engineering), production contracts, gross and net profits decline and prices drop along with profits. And during the depression and from the crisis onward, supply exceeds demand because demand contracts. Production is reduced in essential industries, and despite this reduction, prices fall.

In the core industries, a significant slowdown in production occurs from the onset of the crisis. It becomes more pronounced during the depression. Therefore, the fall in prices cannot be explained by an increasing production and the overproduction that results. It is demand that is shrinking. The cost increase is the crucial element here, while the production increase and its impact on prices are secondary. But when presented in this manner, the theory of crises is a synthesis of the explanations based on rising costs and those focusing exclusively on overproduction. At the end of a growth period, costs have increased more rapidly than selling prices. This is because selling prices increase with more difficulty when there is an increase in the quantities on offer. The margin for profit narrows, paralysing the spirit of enterprise. In industries producing means of production, orders already received are being filled, but no new orders are being placed, hence the fall in prices and the decrease in production. In short, a crisis is triggered.

H.) General overproduction or generalized overproduction?[106]

Therefore, overproduction is not general; rather, partial overproduction becomes generalized through the play of interdependent economic sectors [*solidarités économiques*]. It appears that J.-B. Say's Law of Markets must be maintained despite the criticisms which have been levelled against it. However, the law must be reformulated: instead of maintaining that products are exchanged against products, we would prefer to say that values are exchanged against other values. We also would suggest that the remedy offered by Say in the case of a partial overproduction – an increase in production everywhere

106. Leonhard Miksch, *Gibt es eine allegemeine Überproduktion?* (Jena: Fischer, 1929).

else – works better in theory than in practice. In fact, overproduction causes a generalized rupture of equilibrium. But, with this reservation, we hold that the thesis of the impossibility of general overproduction is well-founded.

In analysing the problem, we have shifted the focus onto the question of value. The economic equilibrium would be more complex than the purchase of products with other products. Trade also depends upon needs. Value would be measured by the intensity of the need. If we see in overproduction a decrease in the value of products, general overproduction is conceivable. It is enough that production increases in all branches, while finding a less intense need everywhere. A general fall in values is conceivable.[107]

The theory of generalized overproduction, however, seems to us to carry the most significance. General overproduction remains inconceivable for us because a general fall in values is not synonymous with general overproduction. Overproduction is in effect more than a decrease in values; it is a disruption of the economic equilibrium. But if the fall in values were the same for all products, there would be no break in equilibrium. Value is not something abstract, existing in a vacuum. Value is a relation – a relation of exchange.[108] There is therefore a break in exchanges only to the extent that the fall in the value of a product is proportionally greater than that of other products. At this point and only at this point can we speak of a rupture of equilibrium and say that products cease to be exchanged against other products. But if as a result of increased production the value of all products was to drop by 10 per cent, for example, this would not cause a break in equilibrium. For there to be a break in equilibrium, the fall in the value of a product or category of products would have to be particularly significant. This category of products no longer represents the same purchasing power as it did in the past.[109] A crisis of overproduction becomes conceivable. But it should be noted that this is only a partial crisis, due to a particularly sharp drop in values in one branch of production. Yet, because of their interdependence [*par solidarité*], the crisis will be passed on to the other branches of production – suppliers of raw materials and industries from which the overproducing industry used to purchase after having sold its production. The crisis is not general, but it is *generalized*. By placing ourselves on the firm ground of equilibrium in value, and by abandoning the notion of equilibrium in quantity, the theory of generalized overproduction is in our view more sustainable and preferable to the theory of general overproduction. Of course, values are exchanged against values, but only a particularly sharp decrease in the values within one branch of production can explain a break in equilibrium, a crisis. This partial crisis becomes generalized.[110]

107. Aftalion, *Les crises périodiques*, 2: 261–352.

108. Maurice Bourguin, *La mesure de la valeur et la monnaie* (Paris: Larose,1896), 56.

109. Carli, *Teoria generale*, 454.

110. In reference to the theory of generalized, partial overproduction, Aftalion writes: 'Of course, one would have to agree on its accuracy if it claimed to describe the genesis of a general crisis. However broadly the crisis may spread, it does not appear at the same time in a multitude of industries. It only becomes general after a number of partial variations and successive repercussions. And some industries escape the bad fortune almost entirely.' [See Albert Aftalion, 'La réalité des surproduction générales: Essai d'une théorie

The drop in the value of textiles in a crisis is not comparable to that of iron or steel products. The decline in manufactured goods differs from the decline in raw materials. If the effects of overproduction and of a general decline in values could be explained by a reduction in final utility, the reduced production during a period of depression should lead to an increase in the value of products. This is because the final utility, the intensity of the last need satisfied, would increase. However, this is not the case: the decline in values continues alongside the reduction in production.

This theory has the advantage of conforming better to reality and the genesis of economic crises. Born in a given branch of production, the crisis gradually spreads to the others. It also allows us to answer the objection derived from the Law of Markets against the theory of generalized overproduction. By virtue of the Law of Markets, overproduction in any given branch of production must imply underproduction in others because products are exchanged for products. Excessive production in one branch of industry therefore implies a very strong demand for the products of other industries and consequently the prosperity of those industries. Partial, generalized overproduction is therefore inconceivable because partial overproduction has as its necessary correlation the expansion of the other productive branches and not their state of crisis. However, the overproduction of products is not the same as an increase in value production. Value is the important factor from the standpoint of economic equilibrium. If a larger quantity of products has lower purchasing power than a smaller quantity, overproduction does not imply underproduction or, more precisely, an increase in value in other branches of production. Just as capital productivity must be assessed in terms of value and not quantity, so too in the case of overproduction and crisis one must consider the production of values and the value equilibrium. Partial overproduction – that is, a sharp drop in values in a given branch of production – far from implying prosperity in other branches, will rather lead to their crisis. Here one could invoke the theory of the elasticity of demand. If the demand for a product is inelastic, the fall in value is much more than proportional to the increase in supply. The producers' purchasing power is reduced by this decline in the overall value of production.[111] Values are exchanged against values.

We must seek the origin and explanation of crises in the break in equilibrium between created values. The equilibrium of values is indeed more complicated than the equilibrium of quantities produced. Yet it is also more complex than the intensity of needs; for value does not only depend on the intensity of needs but also on the production costs. We must note, however, that even so posed, the problem of general overproduction has no other solution than that of a generalized production. For as long as the increase or decrease in the intensity of needs and production costs are equal and move

des crises générales et périodiques', pt 1: 'Possibilité théorique et réalité des crises de surproduction générale', *Revue d'économie politique* 23 (Feb. 1909): 82; and cf. Aftalion, *Les crises périodiques*, 2: 262.]

111. Robertson, *Study of Industrial Fluctuation*, 198–205. On the elasticity of demand, see Ansiaux, *Traité d'économie politique*, 2: 52; Alfred Marshall, *Principles of Economics*, 4th ed. (London: Macmillan, 1898), 1: 177–91, and the French translation, *Principes d'économie politique*, trans. Françoise Sauvaire-Jourdan (Paris: Giard & Brière, 1906), 1: 234–54.

in the same direction, there is no need to fear a break in equilibrium. Such a rupture is only conceivable in the case of an exceptional rise or fall in either the intensity of needs or costs. Only variations of this magnitude and type can cause a disruption of value equilibrium. Thus, the theory of overproduction has the advantage of explaining both periodic crises and prolonged periods of falling prices.[112]

Lederer has objected to this conception of generalized crisis, observing that the downturn starts in one place and spreads little by little to others, that a decline here translates into an economy there and that the disequilibrium cannot be the result of the generalized decline. Corn prices drop, farmers' purchasing power is diminished, but corn consumers make a corresponding savings: their purchasing power increases. Purchasing power shifts without being diminished. The equilibrium is preserved. One might like to repeat here: 'Nothing is lost.'[113]

Such a theory clashes too much with observation and reality for it not to reveal cracks. The price of corn drops. Corn producers experience a reduction in their purchasing power. They consume fewer goods. The prices of other goods decrease. The purchasing power of the producers of other goods is diminished. And so on, step by step. One must situate oneself on dynamic terrain to observe and comprehend the course of a crisis. Let us add that cost does not immediately accompany the falling prices. And the erosion of the margin between cost and price causes, through its generalization, the generalization of the crisis. The crisis finds expression in the price imbalance much more than in the disequilibrium of quantities.

Editorial Notes

i *Crédit de complaisance* refers to unsecured lines of credit, which may be endorsed and can therefore circulate; however, as Lescure's usage suggests, here and above, such accommodations could be used for the purpose of fraudulently obtaining funds.

ii See Émile Levasseur, *Prècis d'économie politique* (Paris: Hachette, 1883), 34; and cf. Levasseur, *Elements of Political Economy*, trans. Theodore Marburg (New York: Macmillan, 1905), 42.

iii Lescure provides no edition, volume or page numbers for the lengthy quotation that follows, and it cannot be found in the German original: Albert Schäffle, *Bau und Leben des socialen Körpers*, 4 vols. (Tübingen: Laupp, 1875–78).

iv Lescure refers here to the *New York Times*, *Annalist* 'Index of Business Activity', which is graphed in figure 2.5, along with the *Quarterly Index of Industrial Corporation Profits.*

v See Oechelhaeuser, *Die wirtschaftliche Krisis*; *Störungen im deutschen Wirtschaftsleben*; and Feiler, *Die Konjunktur-Periode.*

vi A look at table A2 on the net earnings of US railways reveals that this obvious typographical error in the year should probably read 1907.

---

112. Lescure, *Hausses et baisses des prix de longue durée.*

113. Lederer, Konjunktur und Krisen, 376n2. We had anticipated such an objection and responded to it in Lescure, 'Hausses et baisses générales des prix'; and see our *Hausses et baisses des prix de longue durée*, 38, where this article is reprinted.

Chapter Three

REMEDIES FOR CRISES

Section One

Is the Crisis an Evil?

Before turning to an examination of the remedies for general overproduction crises, we will ask a preliminary question: Is the crisis an evil and why?

First, from an economic standpoint, economic activity is dominated by the principle of the economy of forces. The development of our modern societies through alternating periods of growth and depression results in a permanent violation of this law.

During the growth period, the increase in demand and the rise in prices allow the use of outmoded equipment and the reliance on inexperienced labour, overworked by overtime and hence less productive; so, the cost of production progressively rises. During the expansion period, more effort is expended on production than the current state of technology, the average efficiency of labour and the output of the labour force would normally have required.

The depression period is characterized by a steady decline in the cost of production, technical improvements and the elimination of producers using obsolete equipment. It appears at first glance as a period of the application of the least effort, but in fact, a large part of the equipment, even the equipment with the latest improvements, sits idle. Workers of average productivity are condemned to unemployment.

This development of our modern societies through alternating periods of expansion and depression is equivalent to a waste of energy, which has regrettable consequences from an economic perspective and above all from a social standpoint.

From a social perspective, the crisis originating from a sudden change in incomes has repercussions on all collective phenomena: moral, political and legal.

The boom period gives rise to dishonest speculation. Fortunes are quickly made. Such examples reach the regime itself. An honest merchant or industrialist will often fall victim to more unscrupulous traders. Yesterday's rich man becomes tomorrow's pauper; the crisis acts to violently eject the great capitalist of yesterday into the ranks of the middle class. The worker is condemned to unemployment, or his wages are reduced. A general social upheaval is the result. Gradually, this upheaval of purely economic origin turns into a social malaise. Crime increases. Not only does immorality increase but the legal, political and economic order itself is questioned.

From the point of view of the relations between capital and labour, the alternation of growth and depression is unfortunate. Strikes occur more frequently. The growth period is the source of an upward movement in wages and an improvement in the lot of the working classes, while the depression period is the starting point for the opposite phenomena. These shifts, in one direction or the other, are the source of incessant conflicts between employers and workers. In his work on wages, Simiand believes these alternating periods are beneficial: depressions can be occasions for technical and economic progress, but they are dangerous from a social point of view. Their political consequences are no less serious.

Therefore, many of the problems affecting the working classes should not be seen solely as problems of distribution. Unemployment and strikes would almost find a remedy in the suppression of the alternation of expansion and depression. This is particularly true of unemployment; for full insurance against unemployment could only become a reality at the moment when unemployment ceases to present itself as a daunting phenomenon originating in a disruption of the production equilibrium.[1]

States and governments cannot remain indifferent in the face of violent crises capable of threatening public order.[2] However, their policies must resemble doctors' prescriptions and be preceded by a thorough examination and a proper diagnosis. Government policies ought to be inspired by the maxim: help nature. This must proceed from a theory of crises, and for us, from a conception that views crises as the consequence of a disruption of the equilibrium between costs and prices. Effective policies will seek to remedy the imbalance by acting rationally on costs and prices. The present time is rich in lessons and even innovations in this regard. The fall in interest rates has played a crucial role in the recovery, and governments have initiated and encouraged it. States have influenced the movement of prices (both wholesale and retail prices).

Yet recovery *must* follow depression. The crisis cannot justify a total overhaul, which would be the surest way of worsening the disorder and unemployment.

1. John Maurice Clark, *Studies in the Economics of Overhead Costs* (Chicago, IL: University of Chicago Press, 1923), 386–415.
2. Henri Noyelle, *Utopie libérale, chimère socialiste, économie dirigée* (Paris: Recueil Sirey, 1934).

Section Two

Remedies

There is a wealth of therapeutic approaches, and there is no author writing on crises who has not made it a point of honour to propose his own 'special remedy', by which some claim to cure, others only to relieve, the suffering.[3]

§1. – Remedies aiming to alleviate crises

Remedies can be either preventative or curative.

A.) Preventative remedies

Remedies differ according to the causes assigned to the crises.

Statistics and legislation. – The proponents of the theory of disequilibrium between production and consumption have proposed the establishment of a comprehensive statistical service intended to enable industrialists to stop operating blindly. Thus informed about the extent of consumption and production, they would achieve a more and more perfect equilibrium between supply and demand.[4]

Concentration in all its forms: trusts, cartels and groups[5] will make it possible to improve production statistics and to better organize statistics on demand. Since 1907, we have been able to follow the onset and evolution of crises by using the statistics on orders of the steel trust and the large American companies.[6] Thanks to these statistics, stock market speculation, which played such a large role in the nineteenth century, would lose much of its importance. Up to the present, the stock exchange and stock market speculation have assumed the function of fixing prices, balancing supply and demand and adjusting production to consumption. Nowadays, with the development of concentration, the centre of price formation is shifting; supply and demand adjustments are more often decided in the offices of a trust, cartel or large corporation. Stock market speculation has ceased to play the leading role.

---

3. René Cortin, 'Essai sur la thérapeutique des crises', *Revue d'économie politique* 49, no. 4 (1935): 1256–1309.
4. Wilhelm Roscher, 'Zur Lehre von den Absatzkrisen' (1849), in *Ansichten der Volkswirtschaft aus dem geschichtlichen Standpunkte*, 3rd ed., 2 vols. (Leipzig: Winter, 1878), 2: 456–57; Gustav Schmoller, *Grundriss der allgemeinen Wirtschaftslehre*, 2 vols. (Leipzig: Duncker & Humblot, 1904), 2: 492; *Meyers Konversations-Lexicon*, vol. 8, *Glashütte–Hautflügler*, 6th ed. (Leipzig and Vienna: Bibliographisches Institut, 1904), s.v. 'Handelskrisen', p. 734.
5. François Perroux, 'La notion de groupe industriel', *Revue d'économie politique* 45, no. 5 (1931): 1377–1402.
6. Their publication was recently discontinued, which is regrettable because these included delivery statistics that provided information on the past, as well as statistics on orders that shed light on the future.

Nonetheless, stock market speculation still plays an important role. Legislators will try to limit its abuses in the form of the game of stock jobbing and cornering.[7]

The crisis and the stock market crash of 1929 have given this problem a singular relevance. Rarely have more blatant excesses been committed. When the crash occurred, we were unanimous in deploring them. But could they have been avoided or prevented?

Some have claimed to explain these exaggerations by the market's very organization: Wall Street ignores the forward market; and a stock exchange with fortnightly or monthly liquidation would not present the same dangers. The examples of London and Paris are often invoked. This is a fallacy. The crisis was less violent in Paris and in London for other reasons. A futures market would allow the same excesses as the overnight market in New York. The London futures market has even offered us a clear example of a crash in one commodity – copper – which was similar to the Wall Street crash of May 1929.

It seems more accurate to reproach the New York market for the inadequacy of the forward cover it demanded of margined sellers [*spéculateurs à découvert*]. These covers cannot be fixed, they should vary. The variation in the rate of the required cover would serve as a warning sign for the market. But Wall Street would then have to be provided with an advisory board similar to the Federal Reserve Board, an impartial and disinterested stock exchange committee, which would have the very delicate task of giving warnings to brokers and possibly the power to alter the rate of the cover or margin. However, this regulation should not be so strict as to discourage initiative, as was the case with the radical measures enacted under President Roosevelt with the Securities Exchange Act of 1934.[8]

One could also consider having a committee to regulate the call money rate. But the experience of 1929 suggests scepticism here. The stock exchange tolerated extremely high rates; and the inflated rates have rather fed, supported and encouraged speculators by providing them with the necessary capital to prolong their operations and to buy short.

We would venture to say that on a market such as the Paris exchange, where stockbrokers are ministerial officers with collective responsibility, and where the minister of finance retains a supervisory authority over the stock exchange, excesses are less to be feared than on a market organized by a simple syndicate. A stockbroker whose operations are of interest to other brokers is necessarily more cautious than one who is mainly concerned with his own commissions. It is remarkable that in New York the call for moderation came from the Federal Reserve Board or the government itself. But the brokers do not appear to have reacted in the same way.

One might then consider arming the Federal Reserve System or the government with the power to monitor and control Wall Street. But it is difficult to see how if the stock market continues to be regulated by a syndicate. The Federal Reserve System can

7. See Jean Lescure, *Le marché à terme de bourse en Allemagne: Titre IV de la loi du 22 juin 1896: Étude juridique et économique* (Paris: Recueil Sirey et du Journal du Palais, 1908).
8. For the text of the act, see the *Federal Reserve Bulletin* 20, no. 6 (June 1934): 396–410.

act upon affiliated banks, but this seems insufficiently effective. Undoubtedly, a massive increase in the discount rate could cause a general credit crunch. This tightening of credit would lead to corresponding difficulties in how business is conducted, and a crisis would dictate moderation on the stock exchange. The cure would then be worse than the disease. In 1928 and 1929, the excesses were limited to the stock market. This is in fact one of the features of this recent period of economic development: stable (and even falling) prices and moderate growth in production and trade contrast with the bold surge in stock market prices. In the past, a period of prosperity was characterized by exaggerations on all fronts. In 1928 and 1929, the excesses were largely confined to Wall Street. As a result of the development of trusts and the strict control of credit by the Federal Reserve Banks, the period of prosperity before the crash was not marked by any of the usual exaggerations, except on the stock market.

In conclusion, a unique problem emerges: how do we counteract the excesses of the stock exchange and how can they be remedied by procedures that influence the stock exchange and it alone? We are inclined to conclude where we started: by creating a supervisory committee with fairly extensive powers over the syndicate of brokers – particularly with regard to determining margins and covers. President Roosevelt went down this road, but he did so with such energy that by the spring of 1937, it had caused a real crisis on the stock exchange and in the metals market.[9] It is difficult to maintain the right balance.

What is true of sound stock exchange legislation also applies to legislation on joint-stock companies. In the nineteenth century, crises contributed to the improvement of legislation on joint-stock companies by exposing their flaws and shortcomings. In France, the crisis of 1930 led to the proliferation of a whole series of bills designed to protect savings. In Germany, the state asserted its control over credit companies by establishing a banking commissioner and a supervisory board charged with this very delicate mission (German Bank Act of 5 Dec.1934).

Banking policy. – Banks have a role to play in the creation of new joint-stock companies and the issuing of securities. With the concentration of credit, large banks' interests are increasingly aligned with the general interest; there is less temptation for a large bank to sacrifice the present to the future.

The German crisis of 1900, the American crisis of 1907 and the crises of 1920 and 1930 revealed many questionable practices. Mistakes that one might have believed belonged to the past were made again: the immobilization of deposits, the creation of new companies (maritime and others) with little chance of success and the trading in worthless securities. Significant losses were incurred and often handled poorly.

Let us recall the collapse of the Leipziger Bank in 1901, which was brought down by the *Trebergesellschaft*; that of the Knickerbocker Trust in 1907, engaged in copper speculations; that of the Industrial Bank of China in 1920, misled in speculations on

9. 'Securities Market in a Straight-Jacket', *Commercial and Financial Chronicle* 144, no. 3753, 29 May 1937, 3553.

the shares of maritime transport; that of the Banco Italiana di Sconto, brought down by the Ansaldo;[10] that of the Danat and Dresdner Bank in 1931; and that of the BNC in France. There are some rules the banks will never transgress with impunity, in particular those on the spreading of risks or the liquidity of the use of deposits.

Of course, monitoring this offers certain dangers. The spreading of risks will lead to a spread of bank operations and a multiplication of customers. It will become more difficult to monitor the various debtors, and if the crises of 1900, 1907, 1920 and 1930 have demonstrated the necessity of risk distribution, they have also underscored the dangers of a too varied and too numerous clientele. For a banker to know the exact circumstances of an industrialist, he would need to know all of his operations. However, by obtaining relatively moderate credits in relation to his business figures, a client can obtain credit from a large number of bankers and, by using this dodge, manage to exceed reasonable credit limits. Applying the principle of risk spreading must therefore be coupled with a certain concentration of credit operations. In 1904, Hecht proposed creating 'banking groups', a sort of association designed to keep bankers informed of the overall credit situation of a particular industrialist.[11] This is the system followed in the United States with banking chains.

With the concentration of banks in Europe, such groupings are becoming easier to organize. Credit insurance could help by condensing the documentation for each client.

In any case, by regulating the distribution of credit and by moderating speculation, the banks are the most powerful means of mitigating crises – of mitigating without curing, in fact.

Between 1920 and 1930, an abundance of scholarship was devoted to the possibility of preventing crises and remedying depressions through managed monetary policy [*politique de la monnaie dirigée*]. The excesses of speculation were to be moderated by credit rationing, raising the discount rate and establishing a legal ratio between the cash of deposit banks and the bulk of their deposits.[12] Banks of issue would 'control' credit. The results were clear in 1929–30. The reserve banks in the United States failed completely in their attempt to control credit. It has been argued for a century that banks have a part to play here; yet not all banks are capable. Rational moderation is not in the essence of human nature. The excesses have persisted. The massive loans made to brokers in 1929 and the resistance of American banks to the advice they were given invite a certain scepticism here. And we doubt even more the possibility of overcoming

10. Riccardo Bachi, *L'Italia economica nell'anno 1921: Annuario della vita commerciale, industriale, agraria, bancaria, finanziaria e della political economica*, vol. 13 (Città di Castello: Lapi, 1922), 52.
11. Felix Hecht, 'Lehren der Krisis', presented at the general meeting of the Verein für Socialpolitik, 15 Sep. 1903, in *Verhandlungen des Vereins für Socialpolitik über die Lage in der Seeschiffahrt beschäftigten Arbeiter und über die Störungen im deutschen Wirtschaftsleben während der Jahre 1900 ff.* Schriften des Vereins für Socialpolitik 113. (Leipzig: Duncker & Humblot, 1904), 139–66; Eugen von Philippovich, *Grundriss des politischen Ökonomie*, 3rd ed., 2 vols. (Freiburg: Mohr, 1899), 2: 279.
12. Maurice Ansiaux, 'Evolution du crédit et contrôle des banques', in *Travaux du Congrès des économistes de langue française* (Paris: Domat-Montchrestien, 1935).

a depression by an 'injection' of paper or metallic money – an 'injection' which should be called by its true name: inflation.

At most, one might consider separating merchant banks from deposit banks, expecting the real solution to come from the bankers themselves, from their competence and their concern for the public good. Perhaps this is too much to ask. The recent crisis has inspired legislation on banking supervision, the results of which will be interesting to observe in the future.

B.) Curative remedies

The measures advocated here will differ according to one's conception of the crisis.

Public works projects. – If the crisis is viewed as a break in the equilibrium between production and consumption, the state, the municipality and the public authorities in general are called upon to intervene.[13] Too much has been produced, while orders are lacking; they must be generated by starting up major public works projects: railways, canals, roads, public buildings and shipbuilding. The crisis is at the root of the fall in prices and interest: government and municipal borrowing enjoy public support; it is a favourable time to undertake great public works. Moreover, it would not only be industry that would benefit from the state's benevolent intervention but also the working class. In his 1901 report to the general assembly of the Verein für Socialpolitik, Jastrow went so far as to consider this remedy for crises as the solution to the problem of unemployment and unemployment insurance. If taken to such an extreme, government intervention would be excessive. However, this reservation aside, the state can and must intervene in this way. No doubt its intervention will take the form of assistance; for whatever the fall in prices and interest may be, from the beginning of the crisis onward, prices and interest will continue to fall. But this policy will stem unemployment.

In France, a commission was convened in 1908 by the *Ministre du Travail* to address the problem. In England, the parliamentary reports on unemployment of 1909 recommended the implementation of major public works projects in the event of a crisis. Following the crisis of 1907, this remedy was advocated by some of the members of the Reichstag in November 1908, and the minister of public works declared that he had sent orders to the factories for wagons, locomotives and so on. In 1922, the Bureau international du Travail passed a motion to this effect. Great Britain was even implementing a plan of this kind to alleviate unemployment. It would be desirable for all railway companies to follow this example. They could build up the capital equipment necessary to meet the abnormal needs of a boom period during the depression, taking

13. See Erwin Nasse, 'Ueber die Verhütung der Produktionskrisen durch staatliche Fürsorge', *Jahrbuch für Gesetzgebung, Verwaltung und Volkswirtschaft im Deutschen Reich*, n.s., 3 (1879): 166–69.

advantage of the more reasonable prices. This would thus avoid the congestion of the railways that marks any period of prosperity.[14]

The policy was successfully followed in the United States, Germany and France in 1930 and 1931. This was especially true in France, where the wagon-building workshops were still largely occupied with orders in the middle of the depression. In the United States, the railways relieved the burden on the metal industry, which had been badly hit by the crisis in the car industry. Unemployment was thus significantly alleviated, especially at the beginning of 1930.

More recently, President Roosevelt and Dr Schacht in Germany have applied these ideas on a much larger scale. (See chap. 1, §16.)

Some economists have denied the effectiveness of this policy and even advised against it, arguing that capital diverted to public works would be put to better use by private industry. There is a lack of capital, and public works projects cannot create it.[15] This view forgets that in times of depression, savings, however abundant, are reluctantly 'invested'. Public authorities and large companies therefore play an essential role in provoking the circulation of savings and in providing orders to the means of production industries.[16] Public works played a decisive role in the German and American recoveries after 1933.

Customs policy. – A sound customs policy can also help to resolve economic crises.[17] However, since crises are more often international, it is difficult to see how favourable export concessions can be obtained from states that are themselves beset by overproduction. Insofar as it is an industrial country, and especially an industrially developing country – that is, one purchasing more and more agricultural products from abroad – it would be possible to negotiate with a view to obtaining reduced tariffs on exports of

---

14. See Marcel Porte's 'Chroniques des transports et travaux publics', in the *Revue d'économie politique*; Clément Colson's quarterly chronicle, 'Questions de transport', in the *Revue politique et parlementaire*; and Georges Villain, *Notice sur la périodicité des crises économiques et ses rapport avec l'exploitation des chemins de fer* (Paris: Imprimerie Nationale, 1908).
15. Winston Churchill, *Budget's Speech*, 1929 and *Official Memoranda*, Cd. 3331, 1929 [Churchill's 1929 budget statement as chancellor of the Exchequer can be followed in *Hansard*, 5th ser., HC Deb 15 April 1929, vol 227]; Cassel, *Soziale Praxis* 36 (1927): 1057; Conversely, see *Vierteljahrshefte zur Konjunkturforschung* 1, no. 2 (1926): 48; Otto von Zwiedineck-Südenhorst, 'Beiträge zur Erklärung der strukturellen Arbeitslosigkeit', *Vierteljahrshefte zur Konjunkturforschung* 2, suppl. issue (1927); Herbert Hoover et al., *Business Cycles and Unemployment: Report and Recommendations of a Committee of the President's Conference on Unemployment* (New York: McGraw-Hill, 1923), 231; Henry Clay, *The Post-War Unemployment Problem* (London: Macmillan, 1929), 124–36; W. H. Beveridge, *Unemployment: A Problem of Industry (1909 and 1930)*, 2nd ed. (London: Longmans, Green, 1930), 414; Bureau international du Travail, *Le chômage et les travaux publics* (Geneva, 1931); *Travaux du Congrès international des Sciences économiques*, vol. 4, *Des programmes de travaux publics* (Paris: Domat-Montchrestien, 1938).
16. Along the same lines, see J. M. Keynes in the *Economist*, 17 and 24 Oct. 1936; and Keynes, *The General Theory of Employment, Interest and Money* (London: Palgrave Macmillan, 1936).
17. See Bernhard Rost, *Über das Wesen und die Ursachen unserer heutigen Wirtschaftskrisis* (Jena: Fischer, 1905), 49; Nasse, 'Ueber die Verhütung der Produktionskrisen', 169.

industrial products in exchange for reduced tariffs on imported agricultural products. But given the industrial character of large modern states, these views appear more theoretical than practical. The crises of 1920 and 1929 led to a revival of protectionism everywhere. Attempts to lower customs duties failed.[18] Great Britain abandoned free trade in 1931. France expanded the policy of import quotas.

A glance at the history of customs policies reveals that economic liberalism is only practised in times of prosperity. Protectionism grows everywhere in times of depression.

Currency devaluations. – By restricting imports and stimulating exports, currency devaluations exert an influence similar to that of customs protections. By influencing wholesale prices without having the same effect on costs, they enlarge or restore profit margins. They cause exported or hoarded capital to return, encouraging lower interest rates.

Yet unstable currencies have consequences too severe and frightening for devaluations to be listed among the remedies to crises. There can be no stable economic structure, nor any savings or long-term capital investment, with a floating currency.

Devaluation is an expedient, like a medical injection. Repeated use would kill the patient. Capital would no longer be invested. A rational credit and monetary policy must be inspired by other methods.

Banking and managed monetary policy [*monnaie dirigée*]. – The effectiveness of the policy of raising the discount rate and the need for it are no longer disputed today. The effect of raising the discount rate on the resolution of a crisis is one of the best and most well-known theories of political economy.[19] We shall therefore touch on this point very briefly, as we are more eager to get to the examination of the more interesting question of whether this policy as it has been practised up to the present requires further criticism and improvement.

As we have already seen in our historical study of crises, one of the regular features of crises is either a domestic or foreign credit crisis. The foreign credit crisis, commonly called an exchange crisis, like the domestic credit crisis, originates with the fall in prices. The resulting momentary cessation of trade leads to a corresponding disruption in the balance of accounts; liabilities are incurred that are not offset by new receivables. These have to be settled in money, and in the case of international debts, in metal, hence the increase in the portfolio and the decrease in the cash on hand of the major banks of issue. In order to protect their cash on hand, the major banks of issue raise their discount rate.

Raising the discount rate has the effect of drawing in available capital, attracted by favourable returns. Since it cannot migrate in the form of goods (for lack of buyers) or securities (for the same reason), it moves in the form of metal money. If, however, the

18. René Courtin, 'L'activité des institutions économiques internationales', *Revue d'économie politique* 45, no. 1 (1931): 136–82.

19. Maurice Ansiaux, *Principes de la politique régulatrice des changes* (Brussels: Misch & Thron, 1910); Otto Schwarz, *Diskontpolitik: Gedanken über englische, französische und deutsche Bank-, Kredit- und Goldpolitik* (Leipzig: Duncker & Humblot, 1911), see works cited pp. 462–66n11 and n13.

crisis proves to be of such intensity that an initial increase in the discount rate is unable to stop the outflow of gold, a second increase will take place. The rate of discount will rise until the merchant needing to make remittances finds it in his best interest to sell his securities or commodities, even at a loss, rather than having to resort to excessively expensive credit. The drop in the prices of securities or goods will entice foreign buyers to make purchases in the country where the crisis is taking place. New international debt-claims will thus be created to the benefit of the debtor country, which will pay for its imports during the expansion period with exports of depreciated securities and goods.

Thus, we can explain the phenomenon that appeared strange at first glance: the crisis, which is the starting point for a slowdown in production and consumption – that is, in either foreign or domestic trade – is not always, at least not immediately, the beginning of a reduction in the exports of the country affected by the crisis.[20]

These are well-known facts, and we will not belabour them further. But it is regrettable to impose a surcharge of 1, 2 or 3 per cent or more on all commercial paper indiscriminately because some merchants have to pay in gold abroad. How then do we lessen the burden of increases in the discount rate?

The formation of a portfolio of foreign commercial paper comprised of securities or bills of exchange appears to us as a first option. A long time ago, the Banque de Belgique employed a bill of exchange portfolio, and the securities portfolio has never been systematically used – wrongly to our mind, since it seems to be more practical and efficient.

In moments of crisis, if a bank has a large number of foreign bills, the supply of all these bills on the market will prevent the exchange rate from reaching the gold export point. The bank's cash on hand will be protected.[21] At first sight, this procedure is attractive. It is open to criticism, however. We will not object, as Juglar did, to its lack of success in Belgium during the crisis of 1857; for as Juglar himself admitted, the portfolio of foreign bills of exchange at the Banque de Belgique had dropped by 22 million francs by the time the crisis arrived (compared to 174 to 179 million in 1853–54), and it was practically non-existent at the time when its effectiveness was put to the test.[22] Nor will we object to how it fell out of favour for a time. For it appears to be gaining ground. It was advocated by almost all the members of the commission of inquiry into the renewal of the Reichsbank's privilege in 1908. Today it has become standard. Most issuing banks have a currency portfolio.

A bill of exchange is usually payable over a relatively short term; a bank that assumes the responsibility for maintaining a foreign bills portfolio is periodically a major buyer

20. Juglar observed this fact without really explaining it. See Clément Juglar, 'Des crises commerciales considérées dans leurs rapports avec les escomptes de la banque, la population, les importations et exportations, et le prix des céréales', *Annuarie de l'économie politique et de la statistique* 13 (1856): 578.

21. Nowadays, it is used by all the countries that have adopted the exchange stabilization fund.

22. Clément Juglar, *Des crises commerciales et de leur retour périodique en France, en Angleterre et aux États-Unis*, 2nd ed. (Paris: Guillaumin, 1889), 151–52, 173.

on the foreign exchange market. As the crisis approaches, at a time when the state of the money market is already very tense, a bank's purchase of a quantity of foreign exchange capable of warding off the crisis would, by intensifying demand, have the effect of causing the exchange rate to rise above the gold point, thereby hastening the arrival of the evil it was intended to remedy! This procedure rests upon a theoretical error. Just as credit does not create wealth, so too the creation of a foreign portfolio does not create new claims on foreigners. In times of crisis, however, new claims are needed.

Maintaining a securities portfolio does not raise the same objection. In practice, several examples confirm our point of view.

In 1847, the resolution of the first exchange crisis was greatly helped in France and England by the emperor of Russia's purchases of English and French annuities; these two countries paid for their imports of Russian corn with government annuities. More recently, in 1900, the German state issued a loan in the United States for 80 million marks in 4 per cent treasury bonds redeemable in 1904 and 1905. This operation was a complete success, and it had a favourable influence on the exchange rate. In 1907, the city of New York issued $40 million worth of 4½ per cent bonds in Europe to provide the money market with the available funds needed to move the harvest.[23]

During the war of 1914, Great Britain and France mobilized their portfolio of foreign securities, making it available to the central banks to support their currencies. But never before had a securities portfolio been used systematically during a period of prosperity in anticipation of a crisis.

At first glance, this presents some problems. This approach is advantageous only on two conditions: first, there is no depreciation of the portfolio at the time when its services are in use; and second, its realization does not trigger this depreciation. When the crisis is accompanied by a stock exchange crisis, there is a drop in the price of securities. The banks, unconcerned about bearing this depreciation in their values, will most likely pass their losses onto their clients; in this way, they will increase the price of their services and their discount rate. We are in a vicious circle.

This objection is unconvincing, since there are some securities whose rates are unaffected by the crisis, such as government securities and public funds. The crisis causes an increase in the rates of return on the latter. As for depreciation resulting from a mass realization, the multiplicity and diversity of government securities and the importance of public debts lead us to believe that it is possible nowadays to build up a significant portfolio of these securities under good conditions: comprised of a small number of each type of security, the realization of this portfolio would only involve a relatively small supply for each type [*compartiment*], and the prices of the securities would not be affected by this. Moreover, this realization would not occur in the same country or on the same stock exchange, and this is another reason for us to be confident in our optimistic forecasts. Finally, the realization of this securities portfolio on the stock exchange would not be indispensable. In the event of a crisis, if France needs trade credits [*créances*] on

23. *Commercial and Financial Chronicle* 85, no. 2201, 31 Aug. 1907, 490; no. 2203, 14 Sep. 1907, 622–23; no. 2204, 21 Sep. 1907, 681.

England, the French banks would send a portfolio of securities to England, and they would have access to an advance on securities from the Bank of England. This advance can be made either with banknotes or with the help of specie. But as the French banks merely need claims on England, they would be satisfied with banknotes. Yet banknote circulation is far more flexible than metal circulation. This policy would avoid the rush for gold that has until now accompanied any exchange crisis. This policy would mean that the cash holdings of the major banks of issue would no longer be the only reservoir for international claims drawn upon in times of crises. The defence of the cash on hand would require less energetic measures and a less considerable increase in the discount rate.[24]

A similar concern leads us to recommend a gold premium. But first, what does a gold premium entail? We have already had occasion to explain how gold flows out of the large issuing banks in times of crisis. Individuals needing gold to settle their foreign debts resort to discounting their securities or to advances on securities or goods; in this way, they obtain either banknotes or specie. If they receive banknotes, they only need to exercise their right to convert their banknotes into metal to obtain it. The gold premium consists of taking a percentage of the gold thus withdrawn either directly or indirectly from the bank's coffers. But some would say that the banks are violating their commitments, that they are bound to convert banknotes free of charge and on demand and that under no circumstances should there be a premium. This is only an illusion; for banks are free to deliver to the noteholder gold from any country. Now, if this noteholder needs to send gold to America, for example, it is in his best interest to do so in American currency. If he makes payment in French currency, he will have to bear the loss in weight due to excessive interest [*perte au poids provenant de l'usure*]. His American creditor will not be able to make his payments as conveniently in French currency as he would in American currency. For all these reasons, it is in the note bearer's interest to obtain a special kind of money from the bank. In these circumstances, the bank charges a premium for the service it provides in disbursing the gold specie requested by its customer at its counters. In this way, the bank manages a convenient settlement between the foreign debtor and the national debtor.[25]

This practice seems to us to have a real advantage. A feature of any economic crisis is an urgent need for money to settle purchases made prior to it and a recourse to credit.

---

24. This process was widely used during the war, particularly in France. Loans on collateral of foreign securities were opened to the French state.

    One could also envision a role for the Banque des règlements internationaux [Bank of International Settlements] as a re-discount bank for the central banks. This would have eased the credit crunch and the movement of gold, providing greater flexibility to international monetary circulation.

25. A common misconception consists in the belief that the Banque de France was offering to convert banknotes into silver money and charged a premium whenever gold was requested. This is incorrect. The gold premium was in use in France as we have explained in the text above. *Entretien de M. [Nelson] Aldrich avec M. Georges Pallain, gouverneur de la Banque de France, 26 septembre 1908* (n.p., 1908), 23.

The increase in the demand for credit originates sometimes from payments to be made abroad and sometimes from payments to be made at home. In the first case, the only acceptable form of currency is gold; in the second, payment can be made either in banknotes or metal. In the first case, the supply of credit is more limited than in the second and less elastic. It is therefore natural that the first service, which consists in providing gold, should be more expensive than the second and subject to a surcharge. This surcharge could take the form of a higher discount rate, but it is impossible to determine from the bill of exchange the destination of its sum. Therefore, the surcharge takes the form of the gold premium as we have previously defined it.

The gold premium seems to us to be perfectly equitable and economically justified. This is one of its advantages, but it is not the only or primary one. Its main advantage is that it allows for a slower and more moderate increase in the rate of discount. For insofar as the increase in the discount rate represents only the increased cost of a service in greater demand, it is infinitely lower in that it represents this increased cost plus the surcharge necessary to protect the bank's cash on hand. The best proof of this is the fact that in countries that do not use the gold premium policy, the discount is lowered despite the continuous growth of the portfolio and the increase in the demand for credit as soon as the outflow of gold has stopped. The portfolio swells, but banknote circulation increases at the same time; and as this form of credit is cheaper for the reasons we indicated above, the rate of discount nevertheless decreases. Therefore, by applying a *sui generis* and special remedy to the flight of gold, the gold premium policy allows for a more moderate and slower rise in discount rate. If the rise continues calmly and moderately, the resolution of the crisis will have the same characteristics.

Certainly, the foreign debtor overburdened by the gold premium will be forced into a more abrupt settlement. But the foreign market, especially in France, is not as important as the domestic market. The domestic debtor will enjoy the advantage of being able to postpone his situation by means of discounted bills of exchange and advances on securities and goods obtained under favourable market conditions. Thus, one avoids a sudden congestion of the domestic market, a sudden drop in prices, and perhaps even a certain number of bankruptcies. Is this not reason enough to recommend the gold premium policy as a happy complement to the policy of raising the discount rate?

However, the gold premium policy only really makes sense in a country that does not strictly adhere to the currency principle. Otherwise, the recourse to credit, either in the form of banknotes or metal, represents in all cases the same decrease in the credit reserve. In both cases, the increase in the discount rate has the same basis and must have the same measure. If I take banknotes against a bill of exchange, I tie up a corresponding sum in the bank's cash on hand; otherwise, the banknotes would no longer be exactly covered by metal; and the result is in fact the same as if I had taken out the metal from the bank's cash on hand, leaving the stock of banknotes intact. I have reduced the bank's reserves to the same extent. Thus, we are led to examine the policy of raising the discount rate in the countries adhering to the currency principle. The increase in the discount rate will be very dramatic there. In fact, England, whose Bank Charter Act of 1844 was inspired by the currency principle, is the country in the world with the most numerous and extreme variations in the discount rate.

Before the 1928 reform, the Bank of England could not issue notes above a certain limit unless they were covered by a corresponding amount in gold. Once this limit was reached, the bank was reduced to either refusing to discount or contravening the legal provisions which regulated it: issuing one more banknote was to exceed the maximum amount of uncovered notes allowed by law; reducing the cash on hand by one pound sterling would produce the same result, as the cover would become insufficient in relation to the amount of notes in circulation. Thus, the Act of 1844 had to be temporarily suspended during the periodic crises of 1847, 1857 and 1866. In 1890, gold was borrowed from the Banque de France, thus allowing banknote circulation to regain its flexibility. But in the period before the suspension of the act, the uncertainty about the future caused panics. The [Currency and Banknote] Act of 1928 partly remedied this problem by allowing the Bank of England the possibility of increasing its circulation without a corresponding increase in gold reserves. The Treasury has the power to give the necessary authorization.[26]

This option was used after the suspension of the gold standard in September 1931 and subsequently – notably following the hoarding of British banknotes in various countries in 1936 and 1937.

Very recently, in 1937, the great feudal lords of gold, the United States and England, inaugurated a policy inspired by the same concerns that caused the Banque de France to adopt its policy of the gold premium. Rightly alarmed by the influx of enormous gold stocks resulting from massive capital migration, they were concerned with protecting the money market from the rise in the discount rate that would be caused by the massive and sudden return of emigrated capital to its country of origin. With the help of the American and English treasuries, considerable stocks of gold were built up, capable of coping with a massive withdrawal of foreign capital emigrating to New York and London (hot money). Thanks to this wise precaution, British and American money markets were sheltered from the disruptions resulting from massive capital withdrawals. Any rise in discount rates would be avoided. This policy is thus similar to the gold premium in its motivation and consequences: to moderate or avoid the rise in rates.

The wisdom of this policy certainly deserves to be emulated by the countries that are victims of capital exports, and they should consider the monetary policy they will practise in the event of a massive return of emigrated capital. If France were to suddenly receive 20 to 25 billion francs in gold, would the Banque de France increase its banknote circulation or its current accounts by 20 to 25 billion francs? Would the state not have to absorb part of this mass by borrowing? Would we distribute this mass of metal to the credit companies, where they would increase deposits and current accounts by the same amount? So many problems arise and demand solutions. Under the influence of a massive return of capital, what would happen to the money rates? Would they remain remunerative? Our country cannot ignore these problems.

26. Gaston Leduc, 'La réforme monétaire anglaise', *Revue d'économie politique* 42, no. 6 (1928): 1595.

For a long time, it was assumed that money circulation could only achieve flexibility with the banknote. The circulation of cheques, in particular, lacked flexibility. England and the United States had mainly a cheque circulation. In the event of a crisis, it lacked flexibility. The re-discounting had to be matched by an issue of banknotes. Banks could not issue cheques against the discount. Cheques presuppose a deposit of money in the bank.[27] Discounting is the opposite of a deposit. Recently these conceptions have been criticized. Flexibility can be achieved with cheques. Originally, too, issuing a banknote presupposed a money deposit. Later the banknote was withdrawn during bank transactions and was guaranteed by them. Similarly, a current account at a bank presupposes an original deposit. However, a corresponding entry can be made in the current account against the discounted bills. Cheques can be drawn on these credits in the current account; so, cheque circulation can be expanded and enjoy flexibility. This is how the Bank of England operates today. Instead of delivering banknotes in return for re-discounting or advance transactions, it credits the client's current account with the amount of the discounts. A cheque drawn on the bank is worth one banknote. Cheques are also a substitute for banknotes.[28]

This very ingenious practice might not be as effective outside England. Where banknotes remain the predominant form of paper money, the flexibility of banknote circulation in times of crises is essential. For even in England, this policy is far from being the answer for everything: three times before the war the Bank of England had to borrow gold from the Banque de France, which thus became the bank of issue for all the other banks. Would the banknote not be a more efficient way of draining the country's gold reserves into the bank's coffers?[29] Besides, the United States made no mistake about it. Throughout the whole nineteenth century and at the beginning of the twentieth century, periodic crises signalled exceptionally violent monetary crises. Having to fill a gap in their banking systems – the absence of a reserve bank, a bank of banks in times of crisis – they created the 12 Federal Reserve Banks, both banks of issue and banks of deposit, providing circulation and credit with elasticity through banknotes and the current accounts and by draining the country's gold reserves with banknotes and deposits.[30]

The ideal bank in times of crisis now appears to be one that is both a bank of issue and of deposit, raising its discount rate in order to protect its reserves and avoid credit abuses, and moderating the rise through the policy of the gold premium, the foreign

27. Hermann Schumacher, *Le marché financier américain et sa récente crise monétaire*, trans. Jean Lescure (Paris: Giard & Brière, 1909).
28. Hartley Withers, *Qu'est-ce que la monnaie? Le marché monétaire anglaise*, trans. Cyrille and Joseph Rivière (Paris: Giard & Brière, 1920); René Delzangles, 'Étude comparée de la banque d'émission et banque de dépôt' (Doctoral thesis, Faculty of Law, University of Bordeaux, 1921).
29. Jean Lescure, 'Banques de dépôt, banques d'émission et banques de réserve: Contribution à la théorie des banques', *Revue d'économie politique* 35, no. 4 (1921): 420–31.
30. Hugo Bilgram and Louis Edward Levy, *The Cause of Business Depression* (Philadelphia: J. B. Lippincott, 1914), 362–80, even blame the lack of elasticity for the occurrence of crises in the United States. In fact, the lack of elasticity made the crises worse. Yet the cause of crises is different. American circulation has flexibility, and the United States is not free from crises.

securities portfolio and, more recently, by building up large reserves of free gold (or inactive gold), with the support of the treasury.

However, for the rise in the rate of discount to be effective, it must be followed by the open market, by the non-bank or private rate (market rate). Deposit banks have become powerful enough in some countries to comply only partially with the central bank's directives. The tightening of credit will not work well; the call for foreign capital intended to correct the exchange rate will be to no avail. Before the war, in Germany and England, there were concerns about how to force the free market to comply with the rise in the official market discount rate. The Bank of England had a portfolio of consolidated notes at its disposal. By dumping them on the market, it made the capital available on the open market scarcer and caused the discount rate to rise.

The Reichsbank discounted treasury bonds on the open market. With demand, the discount rate rose. Taking this a step further, the question was raised whether the central bank, in order to regain control over the discount activity, might not consider attracting deposits by paying interest on them, and by raising this interest when the discount rate rose; the available capital would have deserted the open market for the central bank, and the rate of discount would have risen on the open market. Or else the central bank, whenever it raised its rate without being followed by the market, could consider rediscounting part of its portfolio on the open market and thus force the discount upward.

Since 1923, the Federal Reserve Banks have systematically intervened in the credit market to moderate the rise or stimulate the recovery in the event of a drop: this policy is known as the open market policy.[31] In 1923 and 1924, it caused a halt in the business recovery, creating a moderate depression that was nonetheless similar to those which accompany crises.[32] In 1929, it did not manage to prevent Wall Street's excesses. In 1930–31, the rapid and massive lowering of the discount rate and the very broad assistance given by the central banks proved unable to revive business. This policy disappointed many hopes. It is currently the object of an official inquiry in the United States. We are speaking here of managed monetary policy [*monnaie dirigée*].

The cheapness of credit is undoubtedly an important factor in the resumption of transactions. But it is far from being the only one. The supply of credit is not enough; it must be complemented by demand. Businessmen will only take credit if the economic prospects seem favourable to them. If goods are piling up in shops, and if stocks of corn, coffee, silk, copper, tin or rubber are clogging up the warehouses, trade is paralysed. Banks will be faced with the classic problems of 'frozen credit', as their clients cannot pay them back if they are unable to sell their goods. Credit 'delays' inventories [*reporte les stocks*], it does not circulate them. On its own, it is incapable of circulating them.

31. See the *Federal Reserve Bulletin*'s general report for 1923; and Raymond Claoué, 'Le système bancaire des États-Unis de Amérique', in *Encyclopédie de banque et de Bourse*, ed. F. François-Marsal (Paris: Imprimerie Crété, 1930), 656–98.
32. Jean Lescure, 'Krisenlehre', in *Wirtschaftstheorie der Gegenwart*, ed. Hans Mayer, Frank A. Fetter and Richard Reisch, vol. 4 (Vienna: Springer, 1928), 32.

Nor would a change in the distribution of gold cause a business recovery.[33] It is not credit that is lacking, but the will to use it.

Moreover, credit cannot normally be used or requested in a world of political uncertainties. Security is the primary condition for credit. The distribution of gold is an effect, not a cause.[34]

The post-war period has also established that an unprecedented money glut is powerless to overcome a long depression. Instead of deflation, we would rather speak of inflation.

In a lecture given at the Institute of Bankers, Cassel advocated the purchase of securities by banks of issue in order to increase the funds available to the market. He expected this to lead to a resumption of purchasing, a halt in the fall of prices and a general price rise shortly thereafter. But it is to be feared that an operation of this kind would result in such an increase in the already excessive availability of funds, that the money rate would fall to ¼ or to ⅛, if not to nil. This would be the ruin of the banks, after that of industry and commerce. Cassel and the supporters of these doctrines forget that during a war the demand for goods precedes inflation and triggers it. It would be a question of reviving demand through inflation, an obvious error in this case. The consumer will not buy more bread or consume more corn or coffee, no matter how abundant the money supply is. For Cassel's thesis to be verified, an additional event would be necessary, one that would stop production and overstimulate demand. Inflation would be the result. Yet inflation is incapable of provoking demand where the need does not exist or exists only in a limited amount.[35] Should it be necessary to repeat once again that needs are limited in capacity when they are unlimited in number? In a crisis, there is too much of *some* goods in relation to needs. Inflation is powerless here. Even in times of war, inflation is an effect and, to a large extent, not a cause.

Here Cassel is guilty of the same *petitio principii* as the one relating to the distribution of gold, which is also an effect of the crisis and not the cause of it.

Statistics show, and the editor of the *Times* objected to Cassel's solution, that there is an overabundance of available funds; the world has never known such a monetary

33. Henry Strakosch, 'Gold and the Price Level: A Memorandum on the Economic Consequences of Changes in the Value of Gold', supplement to the *Economist*, 5 July 1930; and see *Europe nouvelle*, special issue on gold (*L'or*), no. 688, 18 April 1931; Robert Eisler, 'Un remède monétaire à la crise mondiale de chômage', *Revue d'économie politique* 45, no. 2 (1931): 333–51; Eisler, *La monnaie: Cause et remède de la crise économique mondiale* (Paris: Librairie Valois, 1932); and SDN, *Rapports provisoires de la Délégation de l'or* (Geneva: SDN, 1930 and 1931). Along the same lines, see the annual report of the Swedish company Kreuger & Toll for 1931.
34. See Henry Germain-Martin's article in *Le Capital: Dernières nouvelles financières et politiques*, 18 Nov. 1931; Charles Rist, 'La question de l'or', *Revue d'économie politique* 44, no. 6 (1930): 1489–1518; and Bertrand Nogaro, 'La question de l'or devant la Société des Nations: Méthode et résultats', *Revue d'économie politique* 45, no. 1 (1931): 1–36.
35. Eisler is more logical in proposing to undertake public works projects paid for with notes.

glut.[36] This glut has enabled the most regrettable abuses, notably the credits granted to Germany by the American and English banks.

The League of Nations has published statistics that very clearly refute the arguments of the economists inclined to view the recent economic depression as the result of an alleged deflation. Let us compare the statistics on the quantity of money with the indexes of global production and trade.[37] The growth of the money supply is far greater than that of production and trade.

Table 3.1 Index of Production Compared to that of Bank Deposits in Europe and North America

	Europe		
	Production Index	*Amount of Bank Deposits (mill. $)*	*Index of Deposits*
1913	100	9,304	100
1927	110	—	—
1938	114	15,705	168
	North America		
1913	100	8,732	100
1927	128	25,800	300

No source given.

The United States, however, remained faithful to these conceptions that claimed to regulate economic and price movements by the volume of credit. The Banking Act of 1935 created a committee charged with the systematic implementation of the open market policy on the money market. By buying and selling public funds on the market, the cash holdings (reserves) of the deposit banks were reduced or increased. This was even taken a step further. The Board of Governors of the Federal Reserve System has the right to modify the legally required ratio between the cash reserves and the deposits in the balance sheets of the deposit banks.[38] This power was used in 1937. By a deci-

36. *The Times*, 28 May and 3 June 1931; *The Times, Trade and Engineering Supplement*, 6 June 1931; and Maurice Ansiaux, 'De l'abus du crédit', *Bulletin d'information et de documentation de la Banque nationale de Belgique* 6, vol. 2, no. 8 (25 Oct. 1931): 285–91.
37. SDN, *Deuxième rapport provisoire de la Délégation de l'Or du Comité financier* (Geneva, 1931), 123.
38. 'Notwithstanding the other provisions of this section, the Board of Governors of the Federal Reserve System, upon the affirmative vote of not less than four of its members, in order to prevent injurious credit expansion or contraction, may by regulation change the requirements as to reserves to be maintained against demand or time deposits or both by member banks in reserve and central reserve cities or by member banks not in reserve or central reserve cities or by all member banks; but the amount of the reserves required to be maintained by any such member bank as a result of any such change shall not be less than the amount of the reserves required by law to be maintained by such bank on the date of enactment of the Banking Act of 1935 nor more than twice such amount.' Banking Act of 1935, Title II: Amendments to the Federal Reserve Act, sec. 207, sixth paragraph of section 19 as amended, in *Federal Reserve Bulletin* 21, no. 9 (Sep. 1935): 614.

sion of the Board of Governors on 30 January 1937, the amount needed in the reserves was increased from 19.5 to 26 per cent of the demand deposits in the member banks in central reserve cities, from 15 to 20 per cent in the member banks in reserve cities, from 10 to 14 per cent in the 'country banks', and uniformly from 4.5 to 6 per cent for term deposits. The increase proceeded incrementally from 1 March to 1 May 1937, the date on which it came into force.[39]

In the spring of 1937, the tightening of credit had effects similar to those observed in 1923 when the systematic use of open market policy was initiated,[40] and a kind of crisis arose on the market for raw materials and on the stock exchange. During the summer months of July and August, however, the situation was clearly improving. The metal industry was once again operating at 85 per cent of its production capacity, after using only 67 per cent at the beginning of July. President Roosevelt made official statements in September that worried the business world. The depression returned and worsened rapidly. To combat it, the proportion of reserves to deposits was reduced as of 16 April 1938 (see tab. 3.2).

Table 3.2 Percentage of Reserves (Cash on Hand) in Relation to Deposits Legally Required of Member Banks in the Federal Reserve System

	Demand Deposits			*Term Deposits*
	Banks in Central Reserve Cities	*Banks in Reserve Cities*	*Country Banks*	*All Banks*
Up to 15 Aug. 1936	13	10	7	3
15 Aug. 1936	19½	15	10½	4½
1 March 1937	22¾	17½	12¼	5¼
1 May 1937	26	20	14	6
16 April 1938	22¾	17½	12	5

No source given.

Finally, a policy inspired by the same principles was implemented with the aim of remedying depressions by means of credit. In September 1937, the US Treasury placed $300 million of 'sterilized' gold at the banks' disposal, thus increasing their cash on hand (reserves) and credit power. At the beginning of 1938, the Treasury went one step further, abandoning the policy of 'sterilizing' imported gold. In April 1938, it transferred $1,183 million of inactive gold into the coffers of the Federal Reserve Banks. The depression persisted, however, and it worsened, confirming our doubts about the accuracy of these conceptions and the effectiveness of this policy. The metal industry is now using only 25 to 30 per cent of its production capacity. Credit facilities are one, but not the only, element in economic recoveries. And the long-term money rate is more important than the short-term money rate, which is being addressed by increasing the volume of deposits.

39. *Federal Reserve Bulletin* 23, no. 2 (Feb. 1937): 95.

40. Lescure, 'Krisenlehre', 42–47.

The lowering of long-term money is indeed very effective in helping or triggering a recovery. And the open market policy takes on another function. The open market policy was initially intended to influence the monetary market. But more recently, it has been used to act on the long-term capital market. By purchasing government funds on the stock exchange, prices rise and the interest rate falls.[41] England and the United States have achieved remarkable results in this area and have seen the lowest interest rates in their history: 1.5 per cent in the United States!

However, other measures used in Germany and in Belgium have forced the interest rate down. Forced conversions prepared the way for the fall in interest. In Belgium, the reorganization of the banking system, the return to budgetary equilibrium and the stability of the franc have greatly supported the fall in interest initiated by the conversion operation. They have consolidated it. In Germany, strong government intervention succeeded in making the rate it had chosen triumph: 4.5 per cent. Thus Germany, which for a long time had suffered high rates (of 6, 8, 10 and 12 per cent), is now benefitting from much more moderate rates. All these observations confirm the past and the importance of lower interest in economic recoveries. Lower interest rates have prepared and consolidated the recovery in every country except France, where we are still waiting for it.

Will this new, effective policy produce such decisive results in the future? We are sceptical. The war had caused an abnormal and considerable rise in interest rates. In the absence of substantial amortization of the enormous debt, rates had remained very high. They have been corrected almost everywhere. It is doubtful whether the same policy of lowering interest rates can be used in the next depression.

The abundant literature devoted to monetary problems considered in relation to crises, which in our view is so full of illusions, errors or exaggerations, by claiming to be able to regulate prices with quantities of money, has it seems possibly or even probably unintentionally developed a means of lowering interest worthy of the greatest attention. But we would fall back into the realm of illusions and exaggerations were we to expect from it the disappearance of crises and depressions.

The synchronicity of wholesale and retail price movements. – The reservations we have just outlined about the effectiveness of monetary and credit policy find confirmation in the lack of concordance between wholesale and retail prices. If credit were the dominant factor in the rise and fall of prices, wholesale and retail prices would vary equally. The recent period of depression allows us to make the opposite observation. And the divergence between wholesale and retail prices has complicated and upset the equilibrium. Wholesale prices define and measure the extent of producers' income: profit, interest and wages. The level of retail prices determines the purchasing power of these incomes. If the retail price level is excessive compared to the wholesale price level, producers will no longer be able to purchase high-priced retail goods that were sold at low wholesale

41. See our study 'Une nouvelle thérapeutique monétaire: L'"open market"', forthcoming in *Mélanges dédiés à M. le professeur Henri Truchy* (Paris: Recueil Sirey, 1938).

prices. An abnormal and exceptional underconsumption, unheard of before the war, worsens the periodic crisis and the depression. Values are exchanged for values. The equilibrium in value is compromised. No doubt the middlemen are reaping profits that enable them to safeguard their purchasing power. But all the producers – that is to say, the vast majority of buyers – are no longer able to acquire the quantities of goods necessary for production to find an outlet.

This new, unprecedented problem urgently requires a solution. But is there a remedy for this evil? The facts seem to call for us to be especially cautious here. The medication is neither plentiful nor very effective.

The cause of the evil is fairly easy to see: monopolies have been resurrected almost everywhere. Small monopolies commit the same mistakes as large ones. They fix prices. As a result of the development of trade unions and simple agreements, or more simply, as a result of new habits developing from the scarcity of products or commercial premises, retail prices have become 'viscous'. The true remedy would be to revive competition. The corporation and its practices have reappeared thanks to the war and its aftermath. Three possibilities can be discerned to restore competition: action by public bodies, co-operatives and private initiative.

Public bodies can either tax goods or else organize retail sales at a fair price. These two policies have not produced great results. Taxation is poorly enforced. Only a country with a strong government is able to achieve anything by this method. As for state or local shops, experience condemns them: they are poorly managed. The war has provided us with fresh documentation on this point.

The same applies to co-operatives. At the very least, they could be assigned the role of regulating retail prices. However, except in certain branches of the retail trade, co-operation is difficult to evaluate against private trade. In the countries where it occupies the largest place, in Great Britain and Belgium, the divergence between wholesale and retail prices is as marked as elsewhere. In Germany, co-op prices are sometimes higher than those of commercial retailers.[42] Co-operation could play an essential role here; however, in this instance it has proven a disappointment. It has some uses. Yet it does not restore the equilibrium between wholesale and retail prices.[43]

It is therefore necessary to turn to private initiative. The level of retail prices determines wage levels. Industry is primarily interested in reducing the cost of living along with its selling prices. Could big businesses consider creating the necessary price-controlled shops? The experiment lacks scope. Yet Ford has successfully followed this policy. The rise in workers' wages had prompted Detroit merchants to raise their prices. By creating competing shops, Ford stopped the rise and caused prices to fall. More recently in Belgium, the administrator of a colliery has brought about a considerable fall in meat

42. In the Rhineland industrial region, co-operatives charge higher prices than the private retailers. See *Frankfurter Zeitung*, 10 July 1931.
43. Similarly, see Joseph Caillaux, 'Contradictions, Harmonies', *Le Capital: Dernières nouvelles financières et politiques*, 27 Nov. 1931. Commissary stores have reappeared in Russia under the name state factory co-operatives. They play a very important role in supplying the workers.

prices in his region by using this method.[44] *Multa renascentur…*[i] Could the old company store be reborn and revised under the guise of the price-controlling retail shop? In this area, in any case, the experiments tried in the United States and Belgium appear to have been the rare exceptions to meet with success. And economic equilibrium is primarily concerned with maintaining a significant gap between the levels of wholesale and retail prices.

After having enumerated and assessed the main remedies: the creation of national and international statistics on production, consumption, circulation and distribution; state intervention; action by the banks to curb speculation during periods of prosperity or the abuse of credit abuse after the onset of the crisis, we must examine the theories aimed at the suppression of economic crises.

§2. – On the suppression of economic crises

Among these theories, some invoke the monetary explanation of crises; others the theory of worker underconsumption and the overaccumulation of capital (Marx); and finally, still others the economic anarchy under the system of free-market competition.

Among the supporters of the worker underconsumption theory, some advocate establishing a constant relationship between the different categories of income: rent, wages and profit; others, a limit on profits.

Others conclude that the capitalist order must be destroyed and replaced by a collectivist economy; this is the theory of the collapse of capitalist societies after a succession of ever more intense and more frequently occurring crises. Finally, still others, inspired above all by the idea of the anarchical economy, see the need for the creation of new organizations to regulate production, cartels, trusts and industrial unions.

A.) Rational monetary policy

Not all proponents of the monetary explanation of crises go so far as to believe in the possibility of their elimination. Only a small number of contemporary economists, Strakosch in particular, have made this leap. The other supporters of this theory only suggest a mitigation of the phenomenon, albeit by using the same procedures.

If the boom – that is, the progress of production and trade – is being held back by an insufficient increase in gold stocks and by the lack of flexibility in gold production, then crises and cycles could disappear with better management of gold distribution and of credits. Money must accompany the extension of production and trade. Prices and profits will not fall.[45]

---

44. Fernand Baudhuin, 'Problèmes de distribution', *Bulletin d'information et de documentation de la Banque nationale de Belgique* 7, vol. 2, no. 10 (25 Nov. 1932): 358.
45. Henry A. Abatti, *The Unclaimed Wealth: How Money Stops Production* (London: Allen & Unwin, 1924); J. R. Bellerby and K. S. Isles, 'Wages Policy and the Gold Standard in Great Britain', *International Labour Review* 22, no. 2 (Aug. 1930): 137–54; and Henry A. Abatti et al., *The Economic Lessons of 1929–1931: The First Eleven Bulletins of the Unclaimed Wealth Utilisation Committee of Geneva* (London: P. S. King, 1932).

Strakosch merely asserts that a more rational gold policy may be able to suppress crises by eliminating the sudden and sharp drops in prices that cause them.

In a recent article, Eisler does not hesitate to advocate an increase in the circulation of banknotes in all countries of the world in order to remedy crises.[ii] He specifies quite a complicated monetary system, with the aim of stabilizing prices. This theory is similar to that of Fisher on the compensated dollar.[46] For the gold standard would be replaced by an index standard. Prices would be stable, while the value of claims [*créances*] would vary with the index (wages, interest, discounted capital debts). Hence, it is easy to imagine the complications which would arise in all accounting systems – hence, too, the disputes in the event the index standard would prescribe a sudden and deep drop in wages. In view of such complications and conflicts, traditional crises are probably better by comparison.

But having rejected the monetary explanation of crises, we are naturally sceptical about the ambitions of such a 'monetary' plan – about inflation as a remedy for crises. Moreover, how can it be claimed that the gold standard system counteracts an increase in money when the statistics show an unprecedented increase in money in circulation? McKenna has rightly pointed out the skill with which the banks have built up an impressive mass of fiduciary money (banknotes or deposits) on a relatively modest amount of gold.[47]

If the drop in profits and prices that marks the starting point of the crisis does not have a monetary origin, it is utopian to think that the crisis can be cured with monetary remedies. It would seem to us that the supporters of this doctrine are inverting the order of events. The fall in profits precedes the fall in prices. We believe we have established this with statistical evidence. It is the cause, not the effect. And the fall in profits is infinitely more complex than the high cost of credit at the end of the growth period. We have analysed this contraction of profit margins in great detail: the credit crunch seemed to represent an element of contraction – but it did not appear to be the only factor, or the main one. We therefore reject the complicated remedy and, to put it bluntly, world inflation, to which these economists would entrust the economic salvation of peoples. Wartime inflation is too close to us for these theories to have any chance of success.

B.) The theories of Rodbertus and May

Other economists pretend to be able to eliminate crises by legally fixing the wage earner's share of the total social product. This is Rodbertus' theory. We have already explained the meaning Rodbertus gave to the expression 'worker underconsumption'; it is not a question of absolute underconsumption, but of relative underconsumption;

---

46. Irving Fisher, *Le pouvoir d'achat de la monnaie*, trans. Roger Picard and Jean Boutroux (Paris: Giard, 1926); and for a critique of English monetary theories, see J. H. Jones, 'Exchange Stability Versus Internal Price Stability', *Journal of the Royal Statistical Society* 97, no. 3 (1934): 277–312. [Ed. – See also Irving Fisher, 'A Compensated Dollar', *Quarterly Journal of Economics* 27, no. 2 (1913): 213–35.]
47. Reginald McKenna, Speech to the shareholders of the Midland Bank, 1931.

wages would increase, but they would rise less quickly than labour productivity, and consequently, workers' consumption would grow more slowly than social production – hence the overproduction. How can this insufficient increase in the consumption of the working classes be avoided? By allocating to the working classes a certain share of production. The boss, the worker and the capitalist would always receive the same share of the social product: *a* per cent, *b* per cent, *c* per cent. Therefore, Rodbertus does not demand the entire product of labour for the worker, but rather an increase in his share of production.[48]

Having criticized the very foundation of Rodbertus' theory, we could dispense with an examination of the remedy he proposes: if there is an error in the diagnosis, there will be an error in the prescribed treatment. However, there is a series of objections that his theory raises, regardless of its imperfect foundations, which we will briefly address.

First, it is not enough to demand an increase in the worker's share to achieve equilibrium between consumption and production. The worker has the ability to use his income in two ways: in direct consumption or as savings. Yet it matters whether he uses it in one way or the other: the products in demand will vary. The government must therefore regulate not only the worker's share but also the division of his income between direct consumption and savings. The state will have to go even further and tell the worker which products he will buy for direct consumption and how he will invest his savings. Without this, the risk of an imbalance in the direction of production will remain. Moreover, these risks will be all the greater because, with the growth of his income, the worker may change his habits; instead of consuming more, he may consume products of higher quality, or even other products altogether: instead of drinking alcohol and going to the cabaret, he may choose the diversions of family life, reading and so on. This would risk producing for non-existent demand. And [by telling the worker how to use his income] would the government not then have effectively become a tyranny?[49]

Despite these common criticisms of Rodbertus' theory, May proposes a remedy for crises similar to that advocated by Rodbertus: limiting the rate of profit.

There would be a penalty[iii] for excessive profit as there is for interest. The maximum rate of profit would be fixed at 7 per cent.[50] With this limit in place, the entrepreneur

48. Karl Rodbertus, *Le capital*, trans. Émile Catelain (Paris: Giard & Brière, 1904), 283.

49. See in particular Wilhelm Lexis, 'Zur Kritik der Rodbertus'schen Theorien', review of *Das Kapital: Vierter sozialer Brief an von Kirchmann*, by Carl Rodbertus, in *Jahrbücher für Nationalökonomie und Statistik*, n.s., 9, no. 6 (1884): 473–76; and Georg Adler, *Rodbertus, der Begründer der wissenschaftlichen Sozialismus* (Leipzig: Duncker & Humblot, 1884), 51–60.

50. Raphaël Ernst May, *Das Grundgesetz der Wirtschaftskrisen und ihre Vorbeugemittel im Zeitalter des Monopols* (Berlin: Dümmler, 1902), 51, and his comments to the general meeting of the Verein für Socialpolitik, 16 Sep. 1903, in *Verhandlungen des Vereins für Socialpolitik über die Lage in der Seeschiffahrt beschäftigten Arbeiter und über die Störungen im deutschen Wirtschaftsleben während der Jahre 1900 ff.* Schriften des Vereins für Socialpolitik 113 (Leipzig: Duncker & Humblot, 1904), 249–56. In addition, May invokes as precursors to his theory, Geiler von Kaiserberg and Martin Luther, who had protested against the scandalous profits of monopolies in their time. May, *Grundgesetz*, 58; see *D. Martin Luthers Werke: Kritische Gesamtausgabe*, vol. 15 (Weimar: Hermann Böhlhaus Nachfolger, 1899), 279–322; [Ed. – See also the recent

with increased production would face the dilemma of either lowering his prices, so as to not realize profits above the amount prescribed by law, or increasing his workers' wages; in both cases, the increase in production would be matched by a corresponding increase in consumption.

One objection can be raised at the outset: limiting the profit rate carries the inherent risk of paralysing the spirit of enterprise, or even simple initiative, and any effort at technical improvement. The boss whose profit has reached the legal maximum of 7 per cent will care little about working either for the consumer or for the worker and will not improve his production process. The objection is too obvious for May not to have foreseen it. May imagines a kind of bonus for the vigilant boss and a method of punishment for the careless one. If a boss succeeds in increasing the productivity of his equipment, thereby managing to increase his profits, then the maximum profit limit will be raised by 1 per cent. On the other hand, if the careless boss is content with no more than his annual 7 per cent, the law will punish him by lowering the legal profit rate by 1 per cent. But here the objections arise: if the boss is content with 6 per cent annually, will his rate be lowered a further 1 per cent; and if so, at what point does this stop? This would be like the inquisition, and the remedy for crises would be worse than the disease. The application of such new limits [*usure*] implies permanent government interference in the affairs of commerce and industry. Where the joint-stock company exists as the dominant form, this incessant government intervention would still be conceivable; however, where private enterprises or any other form of company predominates, it is difficult to imagine the means by which the state could exert this control. How is the 7 per cent to be calculated for a private company? If the limit is exceeded, what kind of sanction should be imposed? A fine? But the fine would have to equal the excess profit. And since in modern companies 1 per cent of the profits sometimes represents millions, huge fines would have to be imposed. If we are to resort to imprisonment, the entrepreneur will soon find a frontman responsible for the legal violation and pay the latter for each day of imprisonment. It is difficult to understand how the sanctions of such a law will work.

On the other hand, no matter what May says, the spirit of enterprise would suffer: the lure of unlimited profit is a more powerful incentive than limited profit; the extra 1 per cent premium would not be enough to compensate for the restrictive effect of such a law.

Even if it were capable of being enforced and proved useful, it would be easy to circumvent. American trusts have 'wet' [*mouillé*] their capital.[iv]

Let us also reject the two remedies inspired by the theory of worker underconsumption: May's is impracticable; Rodbertus' is insufficient. After having allowed themselves to be seduced by a reorganization of our system of distribution, they might as well have proscribed our entire economic system. Marxists go so far as to assert that the

critical edition: Martin Luther, *On Commerce and Usury (1524)*, ed. Philipp Robinson Rössner (London: Anthem, 2015).]

existence of crises in our societies necessarily implies their transformation into collectivist economies.[51]

C.) The collectivist theory of collapse

The collectivist theory predicts a more frequent occurrence of ever more intense crises, based upon the theory of underconsumption and its threefold foundation: the growth of production, the Iron Law and capitalist concentration. According to the Iron Law, the wage-labourer's consumption is reduced to the bare minimum. Despite the increase in labour productivity resulting from concentration, workers' consumption remains constant. The evolution toward capitalism destroys the middle class. As production increases, social consumption decreases. Underconsumption worsens, as does the crisis. Workers affected by ever more frequent and intense crises will revolt and destroy the capitalist economies.[52]

This theory of collapse was for a long time one of the most cherished ideas and one of the most efficient means of propaganda for the socialist party. It is already very old, and no matter what Kautsky thinks,[53] it goes back to Marx himself. No doubt it takes on an original aspect in the latter, but for Marx also, 'overproduction, speculation, crises, surplus capital and surplus population' constitute proof 'of the merely historical, transitory character of the capitalist mode of production';[54] they demonstrate 'that it must necessarily be in contradiction with the very conditions of its development'.[55]

In 1929, Grossman published a volume devoted to the defence of this interpretation of Marx. He emphasizes capital accumulation and tries to show that this overaccumulation

---

51. Eduard Bernstein, *Socialisme théorique et social-démocratie pratique*, trans. Alexander Cohen (Paris: Stock, 1900); Karl Kautsky, *Le Marxisme et son critique Bernstein*, trans. Martin Leray (Paris: Stock, 1900).
52. Bernstein, *Socialisme théorique*, 119; Tugan-Baranowsky, 'Der Zusammenbruch der kapitalistischen Wirtschaftsordnung im Lichte der nationalökonomischen Theorie', *Archiv für Sozialwissenschaft und Sozialpolitik* [n.s. of *Archiv für soziale Gesetzgebung und Statistik* 19], 1 (1904): 273.
53. Kautsky, *Le Marxisme et son critique*, 85–98.
54. Karl Marx, *Le capital: Critique de l'économie politique*, vol. 3, pt 1, *Le procès d'ensemble de la production capitaliste*, trans. Julien Borchardt and Hippolyte Vanderrydt (Paris: Giard & Brière, 1901), 263–64; Marx, *Das Kapital: Kritik der politischen Ökonomie*, vol. 3, pt 1, *Der Gesamtprozess der kapitalistischen Produktion* (Hamburg: O. Meissner, 1894), 222–23.
55. Marx, *Le capital*, 3: 266–67; *Das Kapital*, 3: 225–26. On the conflict between the expansion of production and the difficulty in finding outlets, see also Marx, *Le capital*, 3: 269–73; *Das Kapital*, 3: 228–32.

    This theory still has supporters among the ranks of the socialist party. But the most respected theorists, either in Germany (Bernstein, Kautsky, Tugan-Baranowsky) or in France (see Jean Jaurès, *Études socialistes* [Paris: Éditions cahiers, 1900], 82–83), have abandoned the theory of collapse.

[*accumulation exagérée*] must lead to chronic overproduction and the impossibility of earning a profit from the capital in use.[56]

Otto Bauer, Hilferding, Kautsky, Tugan-Baranowsky and Jaurès abandoned this notion of overaccumulation [*accumulation excessive*]. They demonstrated that it was possible to conceive of a society in which savings developed and were employed in production without there being any overproduction. The consumption of capitalists and workers would increase. Their well-being would increase. Overproduction would be avoided. Otto Bauer in particular had drawn up a schematic table showing how capital could grow without causing overproduction or making it impossible to turn a profit.[57] Grossman critiqued Bauer on this point and created his own schematic table to replace Bauer's, in which the former covered a much longer period (35 years instead of 4), with the intention of establishing the necessity of the collapse of capitalist societies through the overaccumulation of capital. Starting from the assumption of an annual increase of 10 per cent in constant capital and 5 per cent in variable capital, and assuming that the surplus value is equal to the quantity of wages (a surplus value of 100 per cent), he maintained that over a period of 35 years, capital would absorb such a fraction of income and production that the capitalist would get nothing for the capital he invested in production. A developing capitalist society would require such an increasing quantity of capital that profit would become impossible. Capital growth would absorb almost all of production, leaving nothing for the capitalists.

This hypothesis clashes with reality: the capital increase does not have the magnitude Grossman assumed. It does not proceed in the manner of compound interest. Capital equipment does not grow at such a rapid rate. The statistics on industrial output establish this. Constant capital does not increase by 10 per cent per year. The crisis of 1931 did not differ significantly from previous crises, despite appearances to the contrary, despite the surplus of capital equipment and despite the excesses committed, especially in Germany and the United States. During periods of depression, outdated machinery is abandoned, written off and trimmed; supply and demand recover equilibrium. A new period of prosperity begins, and capital equipment expands anew. Despite the intensity of the depression, the complications arising from the global political situation and the recklessness of the American and English banks, there is no reason to assume an 'overaccumulation of capital' and the 'impossibility of profit', the collapse of

56. Henryk Grossman, *Das Akkumulations- und Zusammenbruchsgesetz des kapitalistischen Systems* (Leipzig: Hirschfeld, 1929), see esp. 216–25; and see Rosa Luxemburg, *Die Akkumulation des Kapitals: Ein Beitrag zur ökonomischen Erklärung des Imperialismus* (Berlin: Vereinigung internationaler Verlags-Anstalten, 1923); and Lucien Laurat, *L'accumulation du capital d'après Rosa Luxembourg* (Paris: Rivière, 1930).

57. Otto Bauer, 'Die Akkumulation des Kapitals', *Die Neue Zeit* 31 (1913): 872; Rudolf Hilferding, *Das Finanzkapital* (Vienna: Wiener Volksbuchhandlung, 1923), 300; Karl Kautsky, *Die materialistische Geschichtsauffassung*, vol. 2, *Der Staat und die Entwicklung der Menschheit* (Berlin: Dietz, 1927), 541; Jaurès, *Études socialistes*, 82–83; Tugan-Baranowsky, 'Der Zusammenbruch'; and Tugan-Baranowsky, *Studien zur Theorie und Geschichte der Handelskrisen in England* (Jena: Fischer, 1901), 24.

dividends. Facts contradict such pessimistic views (see chap. 2, sec. 2, §2, H). Capital accumulation would cease if profit was a utopian dream. An accumulation without profit is an antimony. The hypothesis is self-defeating.

Seeing things from above and from a distance, crises are neither multiplying nor intensifying.[58] The causes of our contemporary difficulties, the formidable scale of which cannot be disputed, are as much political as economic. And on economic grounds, the thesis of collapse cannot be accepted.

The decennial crises had taken on a benign aspect by the end of the nineteenth century. Many economists remained fixated on the economic depression that began in 1873 and often ignored the crises of 1882 and 1890. And if the crises of 1900, 1907 or even 1913 reminded optimists that the era of general crises was not over, the consensus was that these were of average intensity. They were in no way comparable to the crisis of 1873, for example. Some German economists have even claimed that the year 1900 deserves at most to be called a year of depression. The mitigation of crises is not in doubt; it is not disputed by anyone, not even by moderate collectivists like Bernstein or more radical collectivists like Kautsky.[59]

In fact, if we examine the curves of production, foreign trade, prices, the discount and interest – in short, all of the statistical curves we have at our disposal to judge the economic state of a country – they appear infinitely calmer than in the previous period. We have already noted the importance of cast-iron production as a characteristic indicator of the economic development of a capitalist nation. An examination of these figures for the period from 1873 to 1914 in France, England and Germany reveals a relatively calm trend. The same is true for the price curve: unlike the sudden jump in Sauerbeck's general index from 96 in 1870 to 111 in 1873 and a collapse to 83 in 1879, or even the more sudden and significant rise in the index for mineral materials from 85 in 1868 to 141 in 1873 and its collapse to 73 in 1879, we observe a completely measured rise in the general index from 83 in 1879 to 85 in 1881 and 84 in 1882; mineral materials, while remaining more sensitive to the boom, only increased from 73 in 1879 to 79 in 1882 but also fell only to 66 in 1885. The same phenomenon occurred in the expansion period preceding the crisis of 1890. During the growth periods from 1895 to 1900, 1904 to 1907 and 1910 to 1913, the pace became less steady: the general index rose from 61 in 1896 to 75 in 1900, and the index of mineral materials, from 62 in 1895 to 108 in 1900. The slump was then more profound, at 69 in 1904 for the general index and at 81 for mineral materials. Similarly, the general index rose from 70 to 80 between 1904 and 1907, and that of mineral materials from 81 to 107, only to fall to 73 and 89, respectively, in 1908. These indications from price statistics are confirmed by the statistics on the discount, the bank balance sheets, interest and dividends. From 1873 to 1895, the variations were weak, dominated by a largely downward trend; from 1895 until 1909,

58. Werner Sombart, *Das Wirtschaftsleben im Zeitalter der Hochkapitalismus*, 2 vols. (Leipzig: Duncker & Humblot, 1927), 2: 702; Edwin R. A. Seligman, *Principes d'économique*, trans. George Lecarpentier, 2 vols. (Paris: Giard, 1927), 2: 235; and for the opposing view, see Grossman, *Das Akkumulations- und Zusammenbruchsgesetz*, 256.

59. Bernstein, *Socialisme théorique*, 121; Kautsky, *Le Marxisme et son critique*, 255.

there was a marked upward trend and stronger oscillations, and the crises of 1900 and 1907 were in every respect more serious and distinct than those of 1882 and 1890.

From 1873 to 1895, economic crises decreased in intensity; on the other hand, in 1900, 1907 and 1913, we see an aggressive return of the crisis in Europe: Germany recorded very clear economic crises that were unquestionably much more serious than the French crisis of 1882 or the English crisis of 1890, which admittedly occurred during a long period of falling prices. In the United States, the crises of 1884, 1893, 1907, 1920 and 1930 were characteristic general crises of overproduction.

But, contrary to the collectivists' predictions, crises did not become increasingly violent. In fact, there is a contradiction between the theory of collapse and the law of capitalist concentration. For concentration, far from multiplying crises, tends to reduce economic anarchy and the risk of crises. The progress of concentration increases the probability that crises will be mitigated. Powerful organizations hold up better than small competitors. The crisis of 1930 crisis demonstrated this. And our present difficulties of unprecedented scale are political rather than economic in origin. They stem from the war and the exaggerations it caused in all areas: production, credit, consumption and so on (see chap. 1, sec. 1, §15, near the end), and which have now been largely corrected. The recovery from 1933 to 1937 demonstrates this.

D.) Concentration of business into cartels and trusts and the suppression of crises

Whether it is a question of predicting crises, avoiding the all too frequent abuses in periods of expansion (extreme price rises, starting risky business ventures), or, once the crisis has occurred, of warding off its effects, the large industrial and financial corporations appear to us to be more competent or more resistant. Thanks to the concentration of trusts and cartels, we will have at our disposal ever more precise and reliable statistics on production, prices and issues of securities. Orders may be carried over from the expansion period, when prices are high, to the depression period, when prices are low. Firms with a broad vision and concern for the future are likely to pursue a rational policy, capable of greatly mitigating the effects of alternating periods of growth and depression. Some progress has already been made. Reading the reports of certain corporations is significant in this regard because of the insights they provide into our phenomenon. Does this mean that with the progress of concentration any break in economic equilibrium can be avoided? Cartels and trusts have this ambition openly or tacitly. Have they achieved it? Certainly not. From the beginning of the twentieth century, cartels and trusts have been very widespread. Yet crises followed one after the other at regular intervals, in 1900, 1907 and 1913. Was this due to their incomplete development or because of some policy error? Probably both.

Cartels are powerful and numerous, but they do not exist everywhere. Where they do exist, their organization is not always efficient: their directives are not always followed. But more important still, we have many reservations about the doctrine that inspires them.

Certainly, it is possible to adjust supply and demand through the monopoly on production: by virtue of this monopoly, demand is concentrated in the offices of the cartel.

But production will nevertheless exceed demand. Today, national agreements are no longer enough. And international cartels are rare. The crisis of 1929–31 was characterized precisely by a continuous and abnormal swelling of the stocks of key raw materials (copper, zinc, tin, rubber, corn, cotton, coal, petroleum, etc.).

Moreover, the cartel's price policy is no more satisfactory than its production policy. The cartel's mission is to set prices, but its aim, according to many theorists, is to stabilize prices by moderating the rise during the expansion period and limiting the fall once the crisis has occurred.[60] Yet this is a mistake because moderating the price drop in the event of a crisis risks aggravating and prolonging the depression.

Cartels are particularly powerful in the mining and metal industries, which suffer most from the alternation of prosperity and crisis. But if moderating price increases during the boom is capable of prolonging the growth period and preventing the break in equilibrium between cost and selling price characteristic of crises, maintaining high prices during the depression impedes the recovery. Cartels, then, can intensify the depression and prolong it.

Before the war of 1914, German cartels went through three major crises: 1900, 1907 and 1913. In all three cases, they created the most serious difficulties for their buyers after the onset of the crisis. In 1900, the coal and coke cartels even imposed such strict conditions on their customers that an official enquiry was called for. This enquiry demonstrated the cartels' regrettable adherence to the policy of moderating the price rise and resisting the price fall. A comparison of cast-iron prices in Germany, a country with powerful cartels, and in Great Britain and France from 1895 to 1900 reveals the moderating influence of the cartel in Germany. But after 1900, the cartel's resistance to lowering prices placed the rolling mills in jeopardy and led to their collapse. In 1900–1901, some cartels even practised a particularly leonine policy.

Table 3.3 Price, Production Costs and Profits in the German Cast-Iron Cartel, 1896–1902 (in marks per tonne)

	1896	*1897*	*1898*	*1899*	*1900*	*1901*	*1902*
Price	55,266	58,681	60,285	61,914	72,430	83,972	66,785
Production Costs*	50,407	53,812	55,464	55,847	64,009	68,237	52,542
Profit per tonne	4,859	4,869	4,821	6,067	8,421	15,737	14,237

* Production costs do not include depreciation and interest payments.
No source given.

The price merger policy consisted of merging the 1900 contracts with those of 1901 and forcing buyers to commit themselves for a period of two years.[61] Originally – that is, at the height of the boom – this policy was to some extent understandable. However, the

60. Friedrich Kleinwächter, *Die Kartelle: Ein Beitrag zur Frage der Organisation der Volkswirthschaft* (Innsbruck: Wagner, 1883).
61. Cf. the deposition of Kaiser, in *Kontradiktorische Verhandlungen über deutsche Kartelle*, 5 vols. (Berlin: Franz Siemenroth, 1903–6), 3: 197.

decision to continue this policy once the crisis exploded must be severely criticized. If the cartel has an excuse for having concluded long-term contracts at high prices at a time when the future seemed brighter than ever, it has none for having maintained them once the crisis had begun. It was not very honest, and it was clumsy – not very honest, because the onset of the crisis should have inspired a more conciliatory policy; clumsy, because by demanding the strict fulfilment of long-term contracts, often half-imposed on its buyers, it precipitated their ruin, sacrificing the future to the present. It may be objected that contracts are inviolable.[62] This is pure abstraction. There are cases of force majeure, and there is no more clear-cut case than the onset of a crisis. The cartels were in any case less concerned with enforcing the principle of the inviolability of contracts than with slowing down and moderating the drop in prices.[63] Subsequent experience has proven this: the *Kohlensyndikat* [coal cartel] used it with its buyers from 1907 to 1909 and in 1913 as it had from 1900 to 1904.

In 1907, the coal cartel decided on a new price rise on 1 April; in October, it announced an increase for all deliveries to be made in 1908–9 and was imposing it on some grades. At that point, the Prussian state decided to acquire coal mines in the Ruhr to free itself from the demands of the *Kohlensyndikat*. The same was true for steel: cast-iron prices collapsed after the crisis of 1907; they fell again in 1908 and at the start of 1909. The steel cartel nevertheless kept its 1908 prices in 1909; true, it granted a premium of 15 marks per tonne to its buyers of semi-finished products to prevent their collapse, but despite an energetic reduction in their production costs, these buyers barely held on.

Similarly in 1913, the coal cartel maintained its prices throughout the year. It only consented to a reduction in coke prices on 1 January 1914 and in coal prices on 1 April. The cast-iron cartel did the same: despite the drop in the prices of manufactured products, it demanded the high prices of the boom period throughout 1913; it even raised its prices from 1 July onward. And for the first half of 1914, it reduced them from 2 to 4 marks per tonne only. The steel cartel was a little more reasonable: from the third quarter in 1913, it lowered its prices, and in the fourth quarter, it lowered them by another 5 marks (bars and girders).[64]

The case of the shipyards in 1913 is worth mentioning: with powerful shipping companies (Hamburg-Amerika, Norddeutscher-Lloyd) as customers and strong cartels as suppliers of raw materials (coal, steel), they were caught between the demands of both sides. Despite the importance of their orders, their profits were squeezed by the jaws of this vice.

---

62. Deposition of Kirdoff, in ibid., 1: 646–48.
63. The cartel, on the other hand, had among its members small producers who would have been ruined by too steep a drop in prices. In the enquiry into the cartels, Kirdoff points out how the *Kohlensyndikat* enabled a number of mines to survive the crisis. They did not close down, their equipment remained in good condition, their mineshafts were maintained and so on. They would be ready to respond to demand, once a new upswing took shape. See ibid., 1: 184.
64. Arthur Feiler, *Die Konjunktur-Periode, 1907–1913, in Deutschland* (Jena: Fischer, 1914), 25, 66, 142.

In addition, the cartel's requirements weighed unequally on its various members: more integrated firms could evade the production limitations prescribed by the cartel during the depression; while the non-integrated or 'pure' factories (*reine Werke*) bore the full burden. Some cartels were even dissolved on 1 May 1912, the so-called 'B-product' cartels: iron bars, sheet metal, piping and so on.[65]

In 1930 and 1931, the policies of the German cartels provoked the strongest protests. The contrast was striking between the monopoly prices (*geregelte Preise* [i.e., fixed prices]), which did not drop, and the competitive prices, which collapsed. The result was an imbalance in the purchasing power between the branches of production. Moreover, a country in which steel is expensive cannot undertake new business.[66]

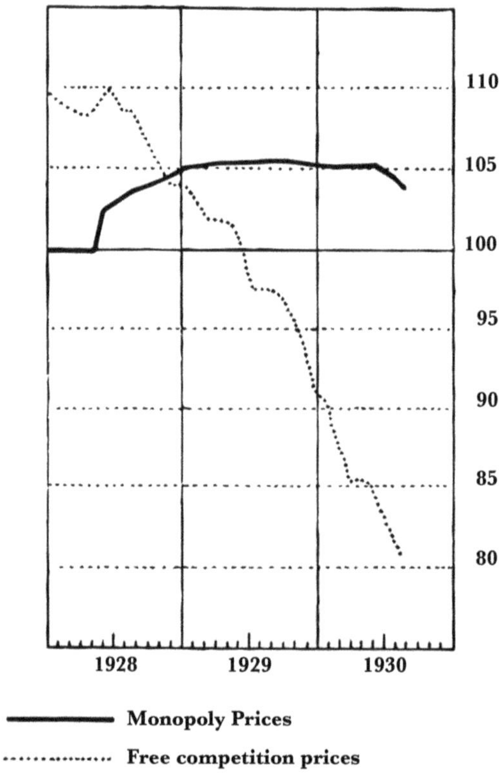

Source: ***Vierteljahrshefte zur Konjunkturforschung*** **5, no. 2 (1931): pt A, p. 62. The decree of 8 December 1931 prescribes a 10% price reduction for all German cartels. For the text of the decree, see *Frankfurter Zeitung*, nos 917–19, 10 December 1931, p. 6.**

Figure 3.1 Monopoly Prices and Free Competition Prices in Germany, 1928–1930

65. Ibid., 100.
66. *Vierteljahrshefte zur Konjunkturforschung* (1931); *Frankfurter Zeitung*, no. 935, 16 Dec. 1930; no. 963, 28 Dec. 1930.

All in all, the German experience – the insufficient organization of cartels and the errors of their pricing policies – may lead one to believe that the cartel is an ineffective means of remedying economic crises. This conclusion would be a bit hasty. When better organized and more powerful and inspired by a different price-fixing policy, mining and metal cartels have a role to play in alleviating crises. The policy of preferred pricing may seem onerous to them: moderating the price rise in order to prolong the boom, hastening the fall to precipitate the recovery. But in this way, they would avoid the intense depression of production and the unemployment that accompanies crises. Here they would find compensation for the compromises they made on their selling prices.

The best way to rekindle confidence in the buyer discouraged by an exaggerated rise in prices is to lower them significantly as soon as possible.

In this respect, the example of the United States seems particularly meaningful for us to consider. Either the steel trust immediately complies with the necessary price reduction, or it tries to resist it. Since the trust's formation in 1900, lowering prices seems to have been the best way to revive orders after crises occur. In 1903–4, its price policy quickly brought back buyers. In 1907–9, its resistance kept them away for a while. But immediately after the drop in prices, orders increased. The same occurred after the 1920 crisis. The steel trust quite rapidly consented to significant price reductions. Its order books, which had been empty since the end of 1920, began to fill up again from the beginning of 1922.

In 1930, Ford had managed to keep his markets open with a massive price cut. He maintained and revived demand by lowering prices. In the first half of 1930, Ford's sales increased compared to 1929. In the second half, they decreased. But in 1930, the reduction was 50 per cent in comparison to 1929 in the American car industry as a whole, yet it was barely 10 per cent at Ford.

We must also condemn the policy of 'dumping' that was widely practised during periods of depression. By keeping domestic prices high in order to encourage exports, the industry reinforces an essential feature of crises: excessive domestic prices for mineral and metal products. Selling at low prices abroad in a crisis is still acceptable; however, keeping prices high at home in order to sell cheaply abroad only strengthens the crisis. Even worse, dumping equips foreign industry at the expense of national industry, when the products being exported at a loss serve as raw materials: sheet metal, raw steel and so on. Following the crisis of 1900, Dutch steelyards worked with German sheet metal exported in this way, taking orders away from their German counterparts. The raw material cartels no doubt distribute export premiums to processing industries (e.g., rolling mills). But these premiums are most often ineffective.[67]

67. On premiums, see Leopold von Wiese, 'Die rheinisch-westfällische Eisenindustrie in der gegenwärtigen Krisis', *Jahrbuch für Gesetzgebung, Verwaltung und Volkswirtschaft im Deutschen Reich* 26, no. 1 (1902): 306; and Theodor Vogelstein, *Die Industrie der Rheinprovinz, 1888–1900: Ein Beitrag zur Frage der Handelspolitik und der Kartelle* (Stuttgart: Cotta, 1902), 98.

Following the crisis of 1900, the export of raw or semi-finished iron and steel products increased by 80 per cent from 1900 and 1901 and by 50 per cent from 1901 to 1902; that of manufactured products, by 9 per cent and 21 per cent over the same years.[68]

Premiums are not enough in fact. We will cite some examples.

At the beginning of 1901, the difference between the domestic price of a tonne of wire and its price abroad was around 30 marks, or the amount of the customs duty. Yet cast iron was worth 20 to 25 marks more on the domestic market than on the foreign markets; as one and a quarter tonnes of cast iron are consumed to produce each tonne of wire, the extra cost is around 30 marks, to which we must add one mark to account for the cost of coal. The domestic producer was thus burdened with a production cost 31 marks greater than the foreign producer. To what extent did the export premium counterbalance this artificial overcharge? From 1901 onward, the *Roheisensyndikat* (pig-iron cartel), together with the *Kohlensyndikat*, was paying a premium of roughly 10 marks per tonne of cast iron converted into wire and exported: that is, a premium of around 14 marks for each tonne of wire exported. The wire producer was therefore obliged to export at a loss of 17 marks on his production cost.[69]

After the economic crisis of 1907, during the whole of 1909, the steel cartel maintained 1908 prices for semi-finished steel and girders, but it distributed an export premium of only 15 marks per tonne to its buyers in order to avoid the ruin of the processing industries. In 1913 and 1914, the coal, cast iron and steel cartels resisted the drop in prices. At the end of May 1913, the steel cartel resurrected its export premiums, and the coal and cast-iron cartels followed suit in July. But the premiums were not enough, and once again, the processing industries fell victim to the cartels' policies.[70]

These policies of the cartels and trusts must be vigorously denounced. In a crisis, production monopolies can only keep prices high and sell cheaply abroad at great inconvenience. It is in their best interest to lower prices, even domestically, to revive the spirit of enterprise. The market for German industry in particular is national. In order to revive the market, domestic prices must be reduced. Cartels have followed the opposite policy. By reducing production, they increase overheads and production costs and worsen unemployment. By exporting at low prices abroad, they threaten the very existence of a whole sector of the national industry. Instead of the complicated system of insufficient export premiums arbitrarily distributed to buyers, they ought to pursue the only real stimulant to demand: a general, dramatic lowering of prices.

All in all, cartels and trusts seem to us to be effective at hasting the resolution of crises and prolonging periods of growth. But they will need to moderate price rises in

68. See the deposition of Gerstein, in *Kontradiktorische Verhandlungen*, 3: 439; Émil Lederer, 'Monopole und Konjunktur', *Vierteljahrshefte zur Konjunkturforschung* 2, suppl. no. 2 (1927): 16–32; Otto Conrad, *Absatzmangel und Arbeitslosigkeit als Dauerzustand* (Vienna: Hölder-Pichler-Tempsky, 1926).

69. See also *Kontradiktorische Verhandlungen*, 1: 167; and Gothein's comments to the general meeting of the Verein für Socialpolitik, Hamburg, 15 Sep. 1903, in *Verhandlungen*, ed. K. Diehl, 192–93.

70. Feiler, *Konjunktur-Periode*, 66, 142.

times of prosperity, hastening the drop in prices after the crisis.[71] Their profits will gain in stability and regularity what they lose in momentary magnitude. Production will be more stable, and unemployment will be kept to a minimum.

This, in our view, is the rational part to be played by organized production. The cartel can have the same effectiveness as the corporation, whose merits are so often touted.[72] But if this is taken a step further and a system of economic plans is suggested to us, we believe we must express our deepest reservations.

E.) The planned economy [Les plans]

Socialism has long argued that economic crises could be eliminated by substituting planning for free competition. In our time, these ideas have gained considerable ground.[73] Plans have ceased to be a figment of the imagination. They are in use in a considerable number of countries and in very advanced countries: not only in Russia but in Germany, Italy, Turkey and Japan. In many countries, economic recovery is entrusted to major public works plans: in the United States, France, Belgium and others still.[74] But the approaches vary quite significantly.

Sometimes planning is meant to tackle unemployment, to manage the transition from depression to prosperity. This concept is very old: the Freycinet Plan of 1879 already had this ambition. The public works plans of today are on a much larger scale, even if the approach is no different.

But elsewhere, planning has another goal: to regulate the development of this or that industry in preference to others. This is the case in Germany, where economic life is confined within the rigid framework of a plan.[75]

---

71. Abraham Berglund, 'The United States Steel Corporation and Price Stabilization', *Quarterly Journal of Economics* 38, no. 1 (Nov. 1923): 1–30; Berglund, 'The United States Steel Corporation and Industrial Stabilization', *Quarterly Journal of Economics* 38, no. 4 (Aug. 1924): 607–30; Émil Lederer, 'Le chômage en Allemagne', *Revue d'économie politique* 45, no. 2 (1931): 276–95; Lescure, s.v. 'Crises', in *Encyclopaedia of the Social Sciences*, ed. Edwin R. A. Seligman, vol. 3 (London: Macmillan, 1930); Arthur Salter, *Recovery: The Second Effort* (London: Bell & Sons, 1932), 295.
72. Jean Lescure, *Le nouveau régime corporatif italien (loi du 5 février): Cartels et trusts* (Paris: Domat-Montchrestien, 1934).
73. Lionel Robbins, *Economic Planning and International Order* (London: Macmillan, 1937); F. A. Hayek, ed., *Collectivist Economic Planning: Critical Studies on the Possibilities of Socialism* (London: Routledge, 1935); Charles Frederick Roos, *NRA Economic Planning* (Bloomington, IN: Principia Press, 1937); Henri Noyelle, 'Plans d'économie dirigée: Les plans de reconstruction économique et sociale à l'étranger et en France', *Revue d'économie politique* 48, no. 5 (1934): 1595–1668.
74. Jean Saint-Germès, *L'état capitaliste* (Paris: Recueil Sirey, 1937); and see the publications of the International Labour Office on public works and unemployment.
75. Henry Laufenberger, 'La vie économique en Allemagne', *Revue d'économie politique* 51, no. 4 (1937): 1263–99.

Elsewhere, plans are intended to promote a country's industrialization and economic development, while also eliminating the alternating periods of expansion and depression: this is the case in Russia.

Notions of the 'planned' economy solely preoccupied with suppressing crises have so far met with little practical success. Nowhere, except in Russia, have large administrations been established with the aim of regulating the country's economic activity through plans. Here, it is proposed that we entrust this role to corporations: we thus fall in line with the policy of national and international cartels.[76] Elsewhere, a large national or even international organization is proposed for the elaboration of economic plans. Yet these ideas are still in the realm of utopian fantasy.[77]

In reality, the advancement of the plans policy often proceeds from considerations far removed from the socialist conception of the suppression of crises. Planning policies can in fact be explained by the evolving political situation in the world. Politics takes precedence over and dominates the economy. Plans are designed to enable the country in which they are implemented to be self-sufficient in the event of war. Even demographic policies are dominated by political concerns. Thus, we see the reappearance of concerns that until recently had been considered obsolete and that had once dominated the policies of the kings of France. The desire for a strong state is the main preoccupation; while the concern for achieving progress with the least amount of effort takes second place.[78]

Even in Russia, the policy of five-year plans is guided by national and military concerns. The development of heavy industries takes priority and occurs far from the borders, where it can be protected from military strikes. Russia's aims are autarkic. Nationalism influences and dominates economic policy, even in Russia.[79]

It is therefore pointless to discuss in depth the drawbacks of this economic policy, which runs contrary to progress through a minimum of effort, and which leads to a situation in which private initiative ceases to yield the maximum results with the least amount of effort. Here one is less concerned with production and distribution than with strength through economic self-sufficiency. Some see this development as a regression; other more sinister signs point to a return to a bygone era and even to barbarism. But can we at least attribute to this novel approach and to these plans the suppression and disappearance of crises?

We have endorsed the policy and planning of large public works as a curative remedy above. But is the policy of having plans set the rules and directives for the whole of the national or world economy capable of eliminating crises? Our immediate answer is that it is capable of suppressing the alternating periods of growth and depression by which

76. Lescure, *Le nouveau régime corporatif italien.*

77. Salter, *Recovery*, 295; M. L. Fleddérus, ed., *World Social Economic Planning: The Necessity for Planned Adjustment of Productive Capacity and Standards of Living*, 2 vols. (The Hague and New York: International Industrial Relations Institute, 1932).

78. 'L'autarcie: La corporation devant la doctrine et devant les faits', in *Travaux du Congrès des économistes de langue française, 1936* (Paris: Domat-Montchrestien, 1936).

79. Jean Lescure, *Le Bolchevisme de Staline: Le régime des plans* (Paris: Domat-Montchrestien, 1934).

the forward march of humanity has proceeded for the past century, but it will slow down or stifle this forward progress. These alternations will be replaced by other more serious troubles: errors in the plans' implementation or design, or the failure to implement the plans, causing a decline in economic progress and general well-being. The experience that is unfolding before our eyes is too recent to allow us to make a positive, well-founded assessment. Yet the information we possess on the economies of the countries which have practised the plans approach most extensively, Russia and Germany in particular, does not inspire great confidence – from an economic perspective – in the merits of the system. In fact, in the case of Russia, it is difficult to determine what can be attributed to the plan method and what is the result of production by an improvised labour force, led by the managers chosen by the administration. But nowhere do we see economic and social results that would make countries regret not having adopted the system of plans. In Germany, there is a shortage of butter, margarine and textiles. The usual supplier has imposed an original, arbitrary form of rationing. Countries such as Great Britain, the United States and even France have no cause to be envious. And even if they have unemployment, their unemployed receive more assistance than the workers in countries with planned economies, and in particular, more than the Soviet worker.[80] Moreover, some countries that have not adopted the plans approach have long overlooked unemployment – notably France from 1921 to 1930. By virtue of a rational policy of the kind we have already specified, large, industrialized countries have largely been able to alleviate the worst effects of alternating periods of expansion and depression. They can alleviate them, without eliminating them, at least as long as their economies remain dynamic. There is a contradiction between perfect equilibrium and movement. And in dynamic countries, the plans method has proven incapable of ensuring a satisfactory equilibrium, notably in Russia.

No doubt Russian industry, taken as a whole, has been expanding from year to year since 1928. But Russia is still experiencing famine and scarcity in industry, as well as agriculture. History allows us to identify two periods and two types of crises in the evolution of societies and the study of crises. In the eighteenth century, France was still experiencing famines. It lacked all industrial products: its industry was developing continuously. Modern Russia, this bloc of 170 million inhabitants comprised mainly of peasants, is still at the stage where France was in the eighteenth century. A nation lacking in everything cannot be compared to one that has reached the plethoric stage of a mature economy. Above all, one cannot transpose and transport methods and systems from one country to another when there is such a wide gap between structures, ages and levels of development. The situation is radically different in countries where every inhabitant (including the unemployed) eats enough bread and begging has disappeared, and in a country where, in the event of a poor harvest, hunger still claims millions of lives. In the former, it is possible to produce too much grain; while in the latter, it is impossible to overproduce.

80. Walter Citrine, *I Search for Truth in Russia* (London: Routledge, 1936); translated into French as, Citrine, *A la recherche de la vérité en Russie* (Paris: Tisné, 1937).

It is the same with industrial products: the production of cast iron, steel, textiles and shoes per inhabitant in Russia is ridiculous in comparison to the production in the rest of Europe. Plans cannot be too ambitious. They will always fall short of demand over the long term. However, the absence of an overproduction crisis is the result of the practice of planning; it is due to the fundamental situation we have just described: in economic terms, Russia is more than a century behind the rest of Europe.[81]

Yet the practice of planning in Russia allows us to see the many drawbacks and imperfections of this policy. It even reveals its inability to achieve perfect equilibrium.

In agriculture, the failure up to now has been total: the difference between the figures included in the plans and the results of the harvests is enormous. In 1937, Russia did not publish the figures for its cereal harvest. But each year since 1928 has been marked by disappointments. Feeding the population remains precarious. Plans have failed completely in this respect, despite the number of tractors, combines, seeds and fertilizers made available to the Kolkhoz. The same failure can be observed in livestock farming. Yet in Russia, agriculture is the primary concern.

But in industry, where the achievements have been considerable, the plans approach has not prevented disruptions of economic equilibrium; it has transformed them, that is all. With great frankness, the government admits that production is insufficient, that its products are of poor quality, that the shops are irregularly supplied and that there are abuses in the retail trade. And if year after year the investment of funds has increased, it is thanks to a reduction in the real wages of the masses through taxes and profits. Much is made of the disappearance of unemployment in the cities. But highly qualified economists working with the Soviet government claim that the passport system played a major part in this.[82] There is no freedom of access to the cities. Moreover, in a country where industrial production is so clearly deficient, it would be natural to have a shortage of industrial workers. The Russian example will only become convincing once industry has developed sufficiently to meet the needs of production. And we doubt very much whether the plans will then be able to ensure a perfect equilibrium between production, demand and income.

Economic equilibrium through planning presupposes an exact knowledge of consumers' needs, their psychology, and of national and international statistics that are impossible to establish[83] – at least, if we respect the freedom of the consumer and of demand.

In reality, the plans method can, in our view, only produce the results it promises in a stationary economy,[84] where prices, incomes and the quantity and nature of the products consumed are determined and imposed by a sovereign authority. Germany

81. Paul Berline, 'Où va la Russie?' *Année politique française et étrangère* (1937): 120; W. Drabovitch, 'Le régime de l'U.R.S.S.', *Revue de Paris*, 15 Nov. 1937, 393.
82. A. Jugow, *Le Plan quinquennal* (Paris and Brussels: l'Eglantine, 1932), 179–88; Paul Haensel, 'Dangerous errors about Soviet Russia', *Contemporary Russia* (May 1937).
83. Robbins, *Economic Planning and the International Order.*
84. A. C. Pigou, *The Economics of Stationary States* (London: Macmillan, 1935).

is approaching this state. Otherwise, too much or too little will be produced, and the imbalances will reappear. The solution is utopian in agriculture, where the sun is not likely to abandon its dominion. Yes, plans may alleviate disequilibrium, but to eliminate it entirely: impossible.

Instead of the upheaval of a system of plans and the illusions it entails, we prefer the rational, more modest policy that we have already defined. Let us preserve the marvellous flexibility and the remarkable efficiency of an economy that has proven itself for more than a century. Rather than attempting to eliminate the alternations of growth and depression, let us focus on mitigating their effects as much as possible. Let us correctly ensure that unemployment is thus reduced to a minimum. In this way, we may reconcile progress with security, increasing production with periodic overproduction and well-being for all.

Section Three

Crises and the Working Class

A levelling of production would constitute the best remedy to the ills which the alternating periods of expansion and depression cause for the working class: strikes, unemployment, the dissolution of the trade unions or the reduction in their membership in times of crisis, as well as strikes in times of expansion to obtain an improvement in their wages. We cannot consider working-class action as a whole without going beyond the scope of our study. We shall confine ourselves to demonstrating how we may build upon knowledge of the development of capitalist societies through periods of expansion and depression in order to alleviate the consequences of crises for workers and perhaps even to improve their lot. The workers themselves, the government and the bosses can all play a role.

§1. – Crises and working-class action

Periods of growth are favourable to the development of trade unions and the increase in wages, even by means of strikes if necessary.

The trade unions have the best chance of peacefully obtaining wage increases and improved working conditions from the bosses during periods of prosperity. The bosses will consent to paying higher wages at the moment when they realize the greatest profits. But it is also at this moment that the union will appear to the worker as an effective means of improving his condition. The growth period will also be a favourable time to increase union dues, in order to support the unions' social programmes.

In effect, union membership swells especially in times of prosperity and often declines in periods of depression. The same applies to the resources of the trade unions. The crisis of 1920 made this particularly clear. Subsequently, from 1921 to 1931, under conditions of chronic depression, the number of trade unions decreased almost continuously. The number of union members also declined.

While during the nineteenth century the statistics on public assistance in Great Britain bear the clearest traces of the unemployment crisis, beginning in the twentieth century, the English worker substituted union funds for public assistance. In the statistics on unemployment benefits distributed by the unions, we discover traces of alternating periods of growth and depression. Relief increased steadily in times of depression and decreased in periods of growth.[85] (See tables 3.4 and A3 and figures A1 and A2.)

85. Tugan-Baranowsky is astonished to find that the statistics on public assistance in Great Britain ceased to be influenced by our phenomenon in the twentieth century. The reason for this is the one given in the text above.

Table 3.4 Unemployment Assistance Distributed by the Trade Unions in Great Britain, 1899–1910 (1,000s of gold francs)

	Total	*Construction*	*Mines*	*Metal Industry, Mechanical Engineering and Naval Construction*	*Textiles*
1899	4,792	612	262	2,017	666
1900	6,691	1,169	111	2,374	1,490
1901	8,146	1,680	443	3,300	1,090
1902	10,522	1,845	486	5,118	1,388
1903	12,605	2,020	450	5,601	2,812
1904	16,354	3,469	1,191	7,689	1,808
1905	13,074	3,574	889	5,693	610
1906	10,600	3,189	764	3,928	601
1907	11,641	3,987	377	4,985	1,239
1908	25,048	4,110	1,537	12,342	3,942
1909	23,591	3,571	2,160	11,220	3,572
1910	17,394	2,840	2,174	5,347	4,268

No source given.

More recently with unemployment insurance (Unemployment Insurance Act of 1920), the financial burden has shifted. The burden is now placed on the bosses, the workers and the state. Statistics on unemployment insurance reflect the state of prosperity or depression in the industries. The crisis of 1929 caused an enormous deficit in the finances of the unemployment insurance scheme, a deficit that subsequently worsened and contributed to the collapse of the pound sterling in 1931. But recently, thanks to the economic recovery, the unemployment fund in England recovered its financial balance (1937).[86]

Nevertheless, the trade unions may not always obtain concessions from the bosses peacefully; the resistance of the latter may sometimes have to be broken by strikes. Before the war, strikes occurred more frequently in times of prosperity.[87] They were more successful in periods of growth, and their failures were more frequent in periods of depression (except in France from 1901–1904 and 1911–1913). But the regularity of this pattern was remarkable in Germany and Great Britain, where industry dominates (see tab. 3.5).

86. 'The Unemployment Fund', *Labour Gazette* (March 1938): 89. Cf. figs. A1 and A2.
87. Charles Rist, 'La progression des grèves en France et sa valeur symptomatique', *Revue d'économie politique* 21, no. 3 (1907): 161–93; and Rist, 'Relation entre les variations annuelles du chômage, des grèves et des prix', *Revue d'économie politique* 26, no. 6 (1912): 748–58.

For the statistics relating to the number of unionized workers and the number of strikes in different countries, see the *Annuaire statistique de la France*.

Table 3.5 Average Percentage of Strike Failures

	France	*Great Britain*	*Germany*
Depression, 1890–1895	44.2	34	—
Growth, 1896–1900	43.5	33.7	—
Depression, 1901–1904	38.8	47.3	48.8
Growth, 1905–1907	37.6	41	38.9
Depression, 1908–1910	44.5	41.9	45.7
Growth, 1911–1913	47.9	29.1	39.1

No source given.

The strikes of 1908 and the general strike of the coal mines in Great Britain in 1921 and 1926 were economic mistakes, hence their lack of success. In periods of prosperity, however, strikes are more detrimental either to the owners or to the workers. Factories have many orders at profitable prices; workers are all employed and earning higher wages. The unions' efforts in these periods will be aimed at introducing the collective contract, and they will opt for collective bargaining without work stoppage in place of the strike. In Great Britain, the number of strikes decreased significantly from 1920 to 1934, alongside the practice of the collective bargaining (see tab. 3.6).[88] In Italy, strikes are forbidden; they are even considered a criminal offence under the terms of the compulsory contract and the labour law.[89]

Table 3.6 Strikes and Trade Union Membership in Great Britain, 1913–1937

	Strikes		*Trade Unions*	
	Number of Strikes	*Number of Strikers (1,000s)*	*Number*	*Number of Members (1,000s)*
1913	1,497	677	1,269	4,135
1919	1,352	2,401	1,360	7,916
1920	1,607	1,779	1,368	8,339
1921	763	1,770	1,258	6,624
1922	576	512	1,213	5,616
1923	628	543	1,173	5,421
1924	710	558	1,173	5,535
1925	603	401	1,156	5,497
1926	323	2,724	1,143	5,209
1927	308	90	1,137	4,908
1928	302	80	1,126	4,794
1929	431	493	1,114	4,839
1930	405	287	1,098	4,825
1931	420	490	1,114	4,841
1932	379	380	1,101	4,624
1933	357	136	1,074	4,443
1934	471	134	1,074	4,389
1935	553	271	1,056	4,570
1936	808	315	1,042	4,842
1937	1,122	595	—	—

Source: *Labour Gazette.*

88. Barthélemy Raynaud, *Une industrie sans grève: Les mines anglaises* (Paris: Rousseau, 1905).
89. Jean Lescure, 'L'État fasciste', *Revue de Paris* 36, no. 8 (15 April 1929): 762.

In Germany, an ordinance of 1923 had established a rather peculiar system of compulsory arbitration, which in fact resulted in wages and working conditions being determined by arbitration committees. In the event of a labour dispute, a committee would draw up a draft contract that the interested parties were free to accept or refuse. In the case of refusal by the parties, this draft, or if one prefers, this verdict, could be made compulsory (by the minister of labour in important conflicts), thus obtaining the legal status of a contract. Under this system, and since the stabilization of the mark (inflation and price rises had multiplied the number of disputes and labour conflicts), the number of disputes remained quite high. In terms of the number of workers involved, the lock-out was very similar to a strike (see tab. 3.7). Wages had risen until 1930. In the spring of 1930, a downward trend combined with a policy of reducing the cost of living had been initiated. In the event of a dispute, complete failure or success was very rare; deals were the usual outcome.

Table 3.7 Strikes and Lock-Outs in Germany

	Strikes		*Lock-outs*	
	Number	*Strikers Involved (1,000s)*	*Number*	*Workers Involved (1,000s)*
1911	2,798	356	—	—
1927	759	234	112	270
1928	691	328	72	451
1929	431	150	19	270

Source: 'Die Arbeitskämpfe in Deutschland', *Reichsarbeitsblatt*, no. 10 (5 April 1931): pt 2, p. 179 (labour disputes).

The Third Reich has introduced a system in which wages are determined by *Treuhänder der Arbeit* [Labour Trustees] or by the bosses under the supervision of the *Treuhänder*. Strikes have all but disappeared, and wages vary very little.[90]

In France, the crisis and depression led to an upsurge in the number of strikes in 1936 and to a new type of strike (with occupation of the workplace). But between 1920 and 1935, the number of strikes decreased significantly in France (see tab. 3.8). An extra-economic factor (the elections of 1936 and the socialists' assumption of power) played a decisive role.

A law on compulsory arbitration was passed (the law of 4 March 1938). The collective contract, which had more or less been abandoned between 1920 and 1930, became the general rule. And within a timespan that is difficult to specify, the trend toward a decrease in the number of strikes, which had characterized the 1920–1933 period in all countries, could well manifest itself again in our country. The stability in the cost of living would act very effectively here by allowing greater stability in wages.

90. *Wirtschaft und Statistik*, 15 Feb. 1938.

Table 3.8 Number of Strikes in France, 1910–1935

	Number	*Strikers Involved (1,000s)*		*Number*	*Strikers Involved (1,000s)*
1910	1,502	281	1926	1,660	349
1911	1,471	230	1927	396	110
1912	1,116	267	1928	816	204
1913	1,073	220	1929	1,213	239
1920	1,832	1,316	1930	1,093	581
1921	475	402	1931	261	35
1922	665	290	1932	330	54
1923	1,068	330	1933	331	84
1924	1,083	274	1934	361	61
1925	931	249	1935	412	89

Source: See the retrospective summary in the *Annuaire statistique de la France* (1937): 60.

In the United States as elsewhere, labour disputes, after having greatly diminished after the end of the war, have become very frequent in the recent period. As in France, politics have played a role in this upsurge in the number of strikes.

Table 3.9 Number of Labour Disputes in the United States, 1916–1937

1916	3,789	1924	1,249	1932	841
1917	4,450	1925	1,301	1933	1,695
1918	3,353	1926	1,035	1934	1,854
1919	3,630	1927	707	1935	2,014
1920	3,411	1928	604	1936	2,172
1921	2,385	1929	921	1937	4,613
1922	1,112	1930	637		
1923	1,553	1931	810		

Source: Bureau of Labor Statistics, 'Industrial Disputes', *Monthly Labor Review* 46, no. 4 (April 1938): 919–29.

§2. – *Government intervention*

The government, for its part, can remedy unemployment by undertaking public works. But this is a means that goes beyond the remedies for unemployment crises of the working class, and we have already considered it when dealing with the remedies for production crises.

In its approach to improving the workers' lot, the state must also take into account the alternating periods of growth and depression. Working hours will have to be reduced during periods of depression. In times of prosperity, bosses want to produce, and workers want to earn; the wage rate is elevated, and the workers are compensated very well for overtime. This is the moment when the free market for labour argument will make the strongest case against government intervention. The government must not expose itself to this objection. In this respect, our legislation in France of 20 March 1900, which came into force during a period of depression (an 11-hour day until 31 March 1902, a 10.5-hour day until 31 March 1904 and a 10-hour day from that date onward), was very well timed; and this coincidence, whether intended or not by our legislature, was certainly most fortunate. On the other hand, the eight-hour law was applied at an unfavourable time, in the middle of a boom period.

But it is in response to unemployment that governments have recently taken the boldest initiatives. Compulsory unemployment insurance, which became the general rule in Great Britain from 1920 onward, spread very rapidly to Austria, Czechoslovakia, Poland and Germany (law of 12 July 1927).[91] Under this system, governments combine the methodical organization of job placement with the payment of compensation for lost wages in the event of unemployment.

More than 46 million workers in 10 different countries had compulsory unemployment insurance, compared to 1 million in 1919. The expense of unemployment insurance was borne sometimes by employers and workers (Germany), and sometimes by employers, workers and the state (Great Britain).

Eligibility for the allowance begins after a certain period of time (usually one week), and it is exhausted once the insured person has been receiving the benefit for a certain period of time (quite often 26 weeks). In addition, a variable period of time (from 18 months to 2 years, depending on the legislation) is required before the insured person is entitled to the unemployment benefit.

Unemployment insurance is fraught with difficulties (definition of risk, benefit eligibility) and is open to many abuses. In the event of a crisis, revenues are no longer able to match spending; 'premiums' no longer cover 'claims', and public finances suffer the after-effects of this deficit. This is because almost everywhere unemployment insurance laws provide for government subsidies from the treasury to the insurance companies. In 1930, Great Britain and Germany had to disburse very large sums to the unemployment insurance. These laws need fine-tuning. Unemployment insurance is only a palliative. The true remedy for unemployment is to find work for the unemployed.

Compulsory unemployment insurance provides precise, detailed statistics on unemployment, which are very useful for studying economic trends. Employment agencies keep track of the number of workers seeking employment; the insurance services indicate the number of salaried workers receiving the benefit. Documentation is accumulating that will allow unemployment 'tables' to be maintained, applying the mathematical principles of actuarial science to unemployment.

The lack of precise statistical data led the French government to abandon compulsory unemployment insurance when it passed the Social Insurance Act of 1928, modified in 1930. But the French decrees organize compulsory assistance, which in many respects resembles compulsory insurance. The French unemployed person is entitled to daily allowances similar to the allowances of compulsory insurance (see the basic decree of 28 December 1926, art. 7, and the numerous decrees implementing it).[92]

91. On this point, see the publications of the International Labour Office, series and reports, series C (Employment and Unemployment), 'Report of the Director to the 15th Session of the International Labour Conference, 1931', in *Unemployment Problems in 1931*, pt 1 (Geneva, 1931), 36.

92. Georges Héreil, *Le chômage en France: Étude de legislation sociale* (Paris: Recueil Sirey, 1932).

Table 3.10 Total Number of Unemployed in France, 1934–1938 (1,000s)

	1934	*1935*	*1936*	*1937*	*1938*
January	332	479	474	426	403
February	350	503	487	410	412
March	345	484	465	388	401
April	334	452	445	371	394
May	323	428	422	345	380
June	310	402	419	321	—
July	320	381	425	313	—
August	325	380	413	311	—
September	323	373	407	305	—
October	343	380	406	319	—
November	369	409	407	332	—
December	419	439	410	357	—

Source: See *Journal Officiel de la République français*, on the last Saturday of each month.

For reasons of administrative simplicity, some suggest that 'insurance from the budget' [i.e., government insurance] should be substituted for insurance supported by the contributions of union members. British trade unions have recently advocated for this system.[93] They see the contribution as a tax that would be more rational to do away with, in order to request the necessary resources from the high taxes of the state. The worker who once preferred insurance to assistance would today accept 'insurance from the budget', which clearly resembles assistance. One should fear even greater abuses here than with insurance. And despite the complicated system of 'stamps' and 'cards', compulsory insurance seems preferable to insurance budgeted by the state.

The United States has long ignored compulsory unemployment insurance. Some companies organized, at their own expense, the payment of unemployment benefits: the Denisson Company in 1916 (the first to date) and General Electric in 1930.[94] An act of 1935 introduced compulsory insurance in the United States to be implemented in stages. Here, the United States imitates Europe.[95]

President Roosevelt distributed very extensive relief to the unemployed.[96]

93. *The Times*, 18 April 1931.
94. Lyle W. Cooper, 'Recent National Trade Agreements in the Silk Hosiery Industry', *Journal of Political Economy* 39, no. 1 (Feb. 1931): 69–75. See also J. Joyce Broderick (British commercial attaché) and Arthur J. Pack, *Economic Conditions in the United States of America, March 1931* (London: Department of Overseas Trade, 1931), 93–96; Dale Yoder, 'Some Economic Implications of Unemployment Insurance', *Quarterly Journal of Economics* 45, no. 4 (Aug. 1931): 622–39. See also four articles from the *Revue économique internationale*, August 1931.
95. On the Federal Social Security Act of 14 August 1935, see *Monthly Labor Review* 41, no. 6 (Dec. 1935): 1538; and 42, no. 1 (Jan. 1936): 134; and Paul H. Douglas, 'The United States Social Security Act', *Economic Journal* 46, no. 181 (March 1936): 1–20.
96. Tait, 'Le chômage aux États-Unis', in *Travaux du Congrès international des Sciences économiques*, vol. 2, *Économie sociale* (Paris: Domat-Montchrestien, 1938).

§3. – *Bosses' intervention*

Nowadays, bosses reduce the number of hours in the workday in times of crisis and, if necessary, the number of working days per week, but they do not dismiss workers, or dismiss very few. This system is known in England as 'short time' work. We have seen it regularly practised in France, Great Britain, Germany and the United States.

The crisis of 1929–30 has provoked quite a lively controversy about this remedy for unemployment. The workers' representatives demanded a legal reduction of the working week to 40 hours. Such a measure lacked flexibility: unemployment is neither general nor uniform. During a recovery, which is bound to come, new orders will undoubtedly require an extension of the working week, which legislation should not prevent. Moreover, any reduction in working hours must normally be preceded by an improvement in hourly output; otherwise, costs and prices will rise, while consumption declines. The rushed vote and implementation of the 40-hour week in France confirmed these observations.[97]

The bosses could also intervene in the event of unemployment resulting from economic crises by distributing relief to their workers, and perhaps even by setting up an unemployment fund in times of prosperity to be distributed in the event of a crisis, but these are all acts of generosity which in the present state of relations between capital and labour will become increasingly rare, even in the United States.

---

97. See the fourth edition of the present work, p. 554.

Conclusion

Despite the profound disruptions that have shaken the economic world since the war, the 1920 crisis and the 1929 crisis have demonstrated the persistence of our phenomenon.

No doubt the driving industries have changed: with the crisis of 1929, the car industry takes its place alongside the electrical industries and the railways. However, these industries are far from having achieved their full potential. The era of electricity and combustion engines that began in the nineteenth century is not over. Aviation is only just beginning. Steam networks have yet to be transformed into electrical networks, countries have yet to be equipped with power lines, hydraulic power has yet to be used and new countries have yet to be equipped. Housing must be rebuilt and improved everywhere. Large quantities of capital will be required. Their creation and use will be accompanied by alternating periods of growth and depression. Observation of the metal and machine industries will continue to bear fruit, with oil and electricity now having a place comparable to that of coal.

This is why we can still see the very keen interest of the industrialist, the merchant, the financier, the capitalist, the worker and even the politician, the criminologist or the sociologist, in recognizing the approach of a general crisis. The crisis often means the ruin of the merchant, the industrialists and the financier and a reduction of the capitalist's income. It signals unemployment, poverty, or at least a reduction in wages for the worker. Even the politicians are caught up in this kind of economic cyclone. Sometimes public opinion will blame the government; public finances will always be shaken.

How do we predict the onset of a crisis?

Since the time, already long ago, when the French *Ministère du travail* conducted the first study of the economic indexes that enabled the observation of economic trends and the forecasting of crises, considerable progress has been made. In almost every major country there is now a large service specializing in the creation and publication of these indexes and in their use as a tool for forecasting crises.

From 1908, the *Bulletin du Ministère du travail* and the *Bulletin de législation comparée du Ministère des finances* began publishing a selection of monthly indexes.[98]

The French example was followed much later in the United States with the creation at Harvard University of a similar, but materially better endowed, service in 1919: the Harvard Committee on Economic Research, which has more recently been succeeded by the Harvard Economic Society. The Committee publishes the *Review of Economic Statistics*, which attempts to track and forecast business activity. For its part, the Federal Reserve Board, created by the Federal Reserve Act of 1913, has organized a similar service and publishes the monthly *Federal Reserve Bulletin*, which is intended to inform

98. Commission des crises économiques, *Rapports présentés au nom de la Commission par MM. Georges-Cahen et Edmond Laurent sur les indices des crises économiques et sur les mesures financières propres à atténuer le chômage résultant de ces crises* (Paris: Imprimerie nationale, 1911); Lucien March, 'Le mouvement des prix et l'activité productrice', *Bulletin de la Statistique générale de la France* 1, no. 1 (1911): 63–103 (see numerous graphs of indexes). See also the first edition of the present work, p. 608.

American banks about business trends and in so doing to influence the policies of banks of issue. To this we should add the Department of Commerce's *Survey of Current Business*, the Babson indexes, the publications of the National Bureau of Economic Research, the *Annalist*'s curves and others still.

With the exception of France, Europe has been lagging behind for a long time but has very recently made up for lost time with the creation of the *Institut für Konjunkturforschung* in Germany, the London Economic Service, the Vienna Institute and the institutes in Moscow, Louvain and Rome.[99] However, in France, the service created in 1911 is the main centre of information, and the *Bulletin de la Statistique générale de la France* deserves its place as the best working instrument in the field of observation and forecasting of business trends.[100]

Political economy has been led to borrow the language of other sciences, and in particular, of the exact sciences. It speaks of periodic crises and cycles. But these terms cannot be taken in the strict sense. The period is not defined, and the cycle is even less so. In reality, there is only one clearly defined point in this back-and-forth phenomenon, and it is the one that first drew our attention: the crisis, or the sudden transition from growth to depression. The opposite pole (recovery) is always much harder to determine. A recovery is preceded by many hesitations, and it is very often interrupted before reaching the period of high tension that precedes and prepares the way for the crisis.[101]

By establishing curves, eliminating a so-called uniform and constant 'trend', we almost succeed in obtaining sinusoids. But by modifying the yearly average which serves as the basis for calculating the deviation from the average, the curves can be

99. See: *Review of Economic Statistics*; *Vierteljahrshefte zur Konjunkturforschung*; *Wirtschaftskurve* (*Frankfurter Gazette*); the quarterly *Bulletin de l'Institut de recherches économique* of the University of Louvain; Giorgio Mortara, *Prospettive economiche* (annual); the London and Cambridge Economic Service (monthly); Ernst Wagemann, *Konjunkturlehre* (Berlin: Hobbing, 1928), and Wagemann, *Einführung in die Konjunkturlehre* (and bibliographies); Geoffrey Crowther, 'The Economist Index of Business Activity', *Journal of the Royal Statistical Society* 97, no. 2 (1934): 241–76, and the supplement to the *Economist*, 21 October 1933; Constantino Ottolenghi, *Elementi di semiologia economica, parte generale: I segni della situazione economica di un paese* (Milan: Società editrice libraria, 1936) (and its observatory). The International Institute of Statistics has appointed a committee on economic fluctuations.

100. We may also cite the quarterly graphs by Huber and March. From 1930, Jean Dessirier has published a monthly review: *La conjuncture économique et financière*, which produces about a hundred graphs each month. At the Faculty of Law in Paris, we have recently created a *Service d'observation du mouvement des affaires*, which includes 15 associate professors and lecturers [*agrégés et chargés de cours*] from the faculties of law, each specializing in the study of one or more countries. Working sessions bring together the director and the contributors; the reports are compared and discussed, after which prognoses are formulated. Theory dominates and inspires these efforts. The Société d'études et d'information économique publishes a monthly review: *l'Observation économique*. The *Ministère de l'économie nationale* has just created an observation service directed by Alfred Sauvy.

101. Cf. Adolf Löwe, 'Wie ist eine Konjunkturtheorie überhaupt möglich?', *Weltwirtschaftliches Archiv* 24 (1926): 165–97.

given a very different form. Today, specialists are almost unanimous in recognizing the artificial nature of these procedures.[102] Professor Wagemann writes in his *Einführung*:

> The multiplicity of possible methods for calculating the trend underscores the difficulties here. It is to a certain extent arbitrary to assume that the trend is sometimes a straight line; sometimes a parabola of the first, second, third, or even higher degree; or an exponential curve. In addition, this results in a very different representation of the trend, depending on the time period taken as a basis. Even if it is extended to several decades, it remains an analytical model that is only ever applicable to the past; whereas the fundamental trend is always liable to change in the following years: it can slow down, stagnate or even reverse. The trend curve therefore does not represent the entire system [*système planétaire*]. It remains merely an estimated magnitude [*grandeur calculée*].
>
> By using these methods for calculating the various kinds of movements, we are basically dealing with pure abstractions, not to say fictions.[103]

This is why we have the most serious reservations about these methods. And we specify the one we prefer: the *complex historical method*.

First let us discard the so-called barometer method, which enjoyed widespread approval for four or five years, but which is now rightly considered obsolete.

The most well-known of these barometers were the Harvard curves. For two years, Germany constructed a barometer similar to this one. Recently – in light of the obvious ineffectiveness of this method – it abandoned it. The Harvard services themselves have abandoned this forecasting method for the same reasons. Three curves were drawn, *a*, *b* and *c*. Curve *a* indicated the pace of speculation on the stock exchange, curve *b* reflected the movement of prices and production and curve *c* charted the course of credit. Variations in curve *a* were meant to anticipate those in curves *b* and *c*. For isn't the role of speculation precisely to predict? The rise or fall of curve *a* could have made it

102. Warren F. Hickernell, *Financial and Business Forecasting*, 2 vols. (New York: Alexander Hamilton Institute, 1928)), which is reviewed in the *Journal of the Royal Statistical Society* 93, no. 2 (1930): 292–93; Otto von Zwiedineck-Südenhorst, 'Preislehre und Konjunkturforschung', *Zeitschrift für das gesamte Staatswissenschaft* 82, no. 2 (1927): 284; Wagemann, *Einführung*, 88; Oskar Morgenstern, *Wirtschaftsprognose: Eine Untersuchung ihrer Voraussetzungen und Möglichkeiten* (Vienna: Springer, 1928); Eugen Altschul, 'Die modern Konjunkturforschung in ihrer Beziehung zur theoretischen Nationalökonomie', in *Konjunkturforschung und Konjunkturtheorie*, ed. Karl Diehl, 165–84; Folkert Wilken, 'Wesenhafte und symptomatische Konjunkturerkenntnis', in *Konjunkturforschung und Konjunkturtheorie*, ed. K. Diehl, 37–152; Hans Stähle, 'Das Beobachtungsverfahren der wirtschaftlichen Wechsellagen des Harvard Committee on Economic Research', *Jahrbuch für Gesetzebung, Verwaltung, und Volkswirtschaft im Deutschen Reich* 52 (1928): 261–310, a penetrating critique of the three Harvard curves, which argues that crisis theory must be informed by the use of statistics; and Constantino Bresciani-Turroni, 'Considerazioni sui "barometri" economici', 3 pts, *Giornale degli economisti e Rivista di Statistica* 68 (year 43), nos. 1, 5 and 7 (1928): 1–26, 361–93 and 579–619.

103. Wagemann, *Einführung*, 88.

possible to foresee the rise or fall in prices and production, or the rise or fall of the rate of interest.

More recent evidence – and better still – a more extensive study covering a longer period (1873–1929) has established the inadequacy of this method. It had been thought that one could generalize from observing the results over a period of 20 years (1903–1920). However, observations of both the subsequent (1920–1929) and earlier (1873–1900) periods have invalidated this overly simplistic forecasting method. Nowadays, one can no longer adhere to this method, and it has been more or less abandoned.[104]

In fact, we must now return to the complex method. We need to multiply our observations, compare them and bring them together. Above all, we need to improve and extend our observations.

The Progress Still to Be Made

Despite the considerable efforts made and the imposing accumulation of figures and indexes statistics in our field present serious shortcomings.

In the business world, the profit potential generates movement. The status of orders received makes it possible to determine the future of production and forecast the prosperity of business enterprises. Yet in these two related areas, profits and orders, everything or almost everything remains to be done. Here, we can only arrive at results in roundabout ways: the status of the orders by way of the development of selling prices. But more often than not, the price rise lags behind the increase in orders. Similarly, realized gains remain a mystery until the annual – and more rarely, semi-annual or quarterly – publication of company profits. The increase in prices, which provides insight into the progress of orders, is still the only indicator that can shed some light on potential or probable profits. And this is incidentally why the observation of prices was initially given pride of place by the forecasting services. But today we must do better by observing profits and orders directly. It is in this twofold direction that the practical businessman can contribute more effectively to perfecting the observation of business trends and forecasting in the field of economics.

Very interesting monthly figures, such as the net profits of the American railways, are not even reproduced in the publications which claim to keep us informed of the latest business trends. Yet, this is a very interesting index of the gap between selling price and cost. (See table A2, in the Annexes.) For the selling prices here are fixed; they are set tariff rates. Profit increases either by lowering costs or by increasing traffic (or let us say orders and deliveries to keep our terminology consistent).

It would be beneficial if the railway companies published similar figures in every country. In France, we have statistics on the net product per kilometre, but they are only given annually. In addition to the number of freight wagons loaded, the railways

104. Jean Dessirier, 'Nouveaux essais de statistiques sur les mouvements boursiers', *Journal de la société statistique de Paris* 70 (1929): 50.

should provide us with at least the monthly figures for their net earnings, as they do in the United States.

By a concerted effort of theory and practice, it should be possible to establish statistics and indexes of profits. Of course, we would not go as far as to expect profit statements from this or that company, but the overall profit statistics for the enterprises in a given branch of production. Business secrets would be respected, and the observation of business activity would become more precise. In the United States, there are already quite a few publications of this kind, but they are seldom put to use.

In France, for orders, we already have very useful statistics: the statistics on the cotton industry. If we examine them closely, we can see that they provide a much better idea of the progress in this industry than production statistics. Despite the irregularity of orders, the businessman tries to regularize the output of his factories: production varies far less than orders. And the irregularity of orders is reflected in the fluctuations in the inventories of manufactured products, which can sometimes increase or decrease rapidly. But the statistics on orders are much more significant. They make it possible to predict a slowdown in production. For if the decline in orders persists, production must in turn be curtailed in the long run. The one implies the other. Orders above all deserve analysis and observation.

In the absence of statistics on orders, it is interesting to know the statistics on inventories. Significant progress has recently been achieved in this area. Jean Dessirier has published some excellent graphs in his *La conjoncture économique et financière* which have inspired other publications.

In short, we perceive a new field of observation to be organized and developed. We have established how this method is more instructive and more rigorous than the one which is limited to observing prices and production.

But it goes without saying that price indexes are very useful to know and to manipulate. If we lack statistics on orders or profits, the upward and downward movements of prices can inform us about the development of one or the other. But the movement in prices lags behind that of orders and profits. This instrument of observation is insufficient, imperfect and inadequate.

Likewise, when it comes to raw materials, price movements provide us with information on the development of costs. Prices indirectly provide insights into the possibility and probability of profit. But the observation of prices must be complemented by the observation of profits and orders themselves.

The method we prefer is a complex one. Just as the physician multiplies his observations, analyses and examinations, so too must the economist avail himself of as much information as possible before making his diagnosis. And in using the documents, one question must preoccupy him above all: will there be work? Will this work be remunerative?

Thus, we must also take into account the wage rates, the productivity of the workforce, the cost of money, depreciation, the cost of factories under construction, possible competition from substitutes, the existence of agreements and their renewal or modification.

The future of profits, the future of production, that is the goal. And the means: the future of profits can be determined by studying projected costs and selling prices; and the future of production, by relying on the development of orders.[105]

The Method of Grouping Statistics

After briefly establishing how we intend to go beyond current methods, we shall choose a rational grouping of already existing and regularly published statistics. Great progress has been made in this regard: we have a very large number of figures. If demand, which precedes and determines production, is poorly and insufficiently studied, the same is not true of supply and production. Economic life resembles the life of living organisms: production ensures the nutrition of the economic organism; circulation contributes to feeding its cells. When these functions are carried out harmoniously, there is very little waste: bankruptcies in particular are less numerous. Thus, observation can be general – by studying production and circulation as a whole and from above. It can then go into detail, studying the various branches of production, their evolution, their future, or even the most representative companies within a given branch of production. But the study of the general state of the economic organism must precede this detailed study of the particulars. The interdependency [*solidarité*] that unites enterprises, branches of production and economic functions implies a dominant tendency in the evolution of the economic world. In order to forecast the chances of a given enterprise, it is necessary to know the state of the environment in which it is meant to operate and whether the overall prospects are favourable or not. What is true of a business is also true of a simple commercial operation.

A regularly increasing production – and a corresponding increase in circulation – reflects the satisfactory state of the economic organism. We may then say that the *general health* is good. In the economic sphere, as in the living world, the general health is of primary importance. After that, we will delve into detail, to examine, as it were, specific industries such as mechanical engineering, textiles, coal and electricity, by the method

105. In a well-documented study, Pierre Jéramec proposes a novel index for predicting crises: the acceleration of the pace of production. This index, which can now be calculated, seems to us to be very interesting. But establishing good indexes for orders in the various industries is the most useful innovation for the observation of business life. The movement of orders, or if one likes, the acceleration of orders, is the most significant indicator of the vitality of an economy and its growth. Likewise, the elements which enable us to estimate the potential for and possibility of profit are no doubt more decisive than the production indexes.

The index of the demand for labour, which Jéramec calculates in the same study using advertisements (job offers) in the periodical press, is also very useful and fills a gap in the statistics. The variations in the labour market have so far been very imperfectly measured and observed in France. See Jéramec, 'Une théorie dynamique de la production et son illustration par l'étude de l'activité industrielle dans la région parisienne (1927–1931)', *Journal de la Société française de statistique de Paris* 72 (1931): 232–67.

we have already specified: by looking at the status of orders, profits and prices (selling prices and cost prices).

It goes without saying that the general situation must be of primary concern to the economist. It is in this area that he can provide insights to practical men, who better appreciate detail. But theorists and practitioners complement each other in this: one has a better view of the whole, while the other is better at noticing the details. They ignore each other at their own peril. In this area, great progress has been achieved in the United States, where the general state of business is now as much a concern for firms as the progress of their own businesses.

The General State of Business

§1. – Production

How should we observe the general state of business? In the recent period, significant results have been obtained thanks to the creation of general production indexes. In all major industrial countries, indexes are now being established, the calculation of which is similar to that of the price indexes and which, with one figure, give us an idea of the general state of production. A comparison of these monthly indices enables us to grasp very quickly the pace of production in the United States, France, Great Britain and Germany.

Yet this general index is of course the sum of the specialized indexes established for the various branches of production. After studying the general index, specialized indexes can be consulted and compared, and we can observe whether they move concordantly, or whether there may be a delay here or an exaggeration there. In short, the alignment of the indexes matters, as well as the parallelism in their progression. If the movement which animates the various branches of production is of the same order, if they advance at more or less the same pace, then there is a great chance that the trend will be durable and persistent. On the other hand, if one industry shows signs of sluggishness, there is a strong chance that it will spread, infecting the others. The interdependency [*solidarité*] of industries seems to explain how there can be a general state of the economy, and how a change in the general health of the economy can result from the poor health of a given branch of production. If, since J.-B. Say, there has been almost unanimous agreement on the impossibility of general overproduction, we must also concur, on the other hand, that a partial crisis tends to become generalized as a result of the linkages [*solidarité*] between industries.

The general production index can and should be compared with another index of the same order: the unemployment index. In all major countries, monthly unemployment statistics are compiled. The basis for these figures is not the same everywhere. In countries with compulsory unemployment insurance, the figures for placement and insurance are available; elsewhere, we are limited to less exact indicators, such as the percentage of unionized workers out of work. In France, there is little information on the number of unemployed. In the United States, the Federal Reserve Board compiles statistics, not on unemployment, but on employment. Thus, we have at our disposal a valuable piece of general information that corroborates, verifies and tallies with the information from the general production index.

In many countries, the general unemployment index is supplemented by an index of unemployment in the various branches of production. The use of these figures is similar to that of the production indexes compiled for each branch of industry.

§2. – Circulation

Products enter circulation to be consumed either domestically or abroad. The activity of circulation is as important as that of production. And one drives the other. We now have precise figures at our disposal that allow us to closely monitor the circulation activity, domestically and externally.

1. *Domestic circulation.* – Its activity is measured by the railway traffic, by the projected amount of tariff revenue. Everywhere today, statistics are published on the tonnages transported by rail, or the number of freight wagons loaded. The periodic balance sheets of the large credit companies – the tax statistics (tariff stamps) – make it possible to know the flow of commercial bills of exchange from month to month.

2. *Foreign trade.* – The ships entering and leaving the ports – the statistics on imports and exports are instructive in this regard.

3. *General index.* – In a number of countries, taxes based on the amount of turnover have been established since the war. The variations in the amounts taxed provide us with information about domestic trade activity and the intensity of imports.

The observation of these various indices, of these various statistics and their curves, allows conclusions to be drawn about the general business flow. Symmetries and parallels in their progression are essential to assessing the future. Breaks in equilibrium stem from the fact that disruptions can occur in this rather complex whole. Excessive prices, exaggerated money rates, too rapid an increase in production and an excessive reliance on credit are likely to provoke a slowdown in demand, a sudden drop in prices and a credit crunch, which can paralyse or compromise the normal course of demand, production and circulation. Here more than anywhere else, we must respect the ancient wisdom: Nothing in excess.

Yet all those familiar with economic phenomena know that there is no rule more difficult to observe than this one.[106] In a world where speculation – in the literal sense of forecasting – dominates the course of business, mistakes and excesses are becoming almost inevitable because of the complexity of the economic organism and the diversity of its interconnected [*solidaires*] functions. Psychology is useful here in explaining the

---

106. The excesses of Wall Street in 1928–29 are the best illustration of this principle (see fig. 1.9). A stock market crash seemed inevitable from the beginning of 1929. It occurred in the autumn, right at the moment of the usual credit crunch at this time of the year.

feelings of optimism or pessimism. However, there is no better remedy to these errors of excessive speculation than statistics – figures that allow us to support our views and correct the exaggerations of speculators. To this effect, the study of general business trends, with the help of a few well-chosen and well-established indexes, seems to be the best remedy to ill-advised entanglements; the best response to unwarranted disillusionment; and the best obstacle to bankruptcies, the statistics on which are the crowning achievement of the statistical observation of the general movement of business.

The State of the Main Branches of Production

The study of the general movement of business cannot dispense with the study of the main branches of production.

Until now the information has been rather imperfect. Some progress has nevertheless been achieved since the war. We now have at our disposal monthly production statistics for the main branches of production. But a rational approach would mean studying the selling prices, cost prices, profits, orders, stocks and production for each branch. This method has yet to be followed anywhere.

Here a problem arises: should such a survey be arranged by country or branch of production? For products with an international market, the statistics must combine data for each country. A first attempt at collecting global statistics could be made. On the other hand, for products with a more limited market, one could organize statistics by individual country.

The Selection of Statistics

Here there is too often the tendency to misuse index numbers. The figures themselves are in many ways more instructive than an index number. They suggest more to the mind by providing fuller information. For example, it is more useful to know that in a given year France produced 8 million tonnes of cast iron than to know that the index of iron production was 90 (with year *x* equalling 100).

The index number or index should be preferred to the real figures only when it is a question of totalling aggregate observations and expressing them as an overall figure: as in the general price index, the general production index or the general index for the course of values on the stock exchange. With the index method, we rise from the level of the particular to the general, which is the aim of all science. But in our view, this is the limited sense in which the index may be substituted for the figures themselves.

Certainly, the index method makes it possible to establish a series whose movement is comparable. With the help of the index approach, one can draw comparisons between the variations in cast-iron production (expressed in millions of tonnes), the movement of prices (in francs per tonne) and the rate of unemployment (expressed as the total number of unemployed). But the logarithmic scale graph is used in the same way and has the advantage of allowing comparisons, while also providing the raw figures themselves.

Therefore, indices are preferable only when it is a matter of giving a general idea of a phenomenon: price rises, increases or reductions in production, the general rising or falling of share values or specific kinds of securities on the stock exchange.

However, instead of the index numbers for a country's imports or exports, for example, we would prefer the statistics themselves in terms of the volume [*en poids*] or value of imports and exports. Here we have an overall figure informing us on a significant phenomenon. The statistical figures are more suggestive than an index number; they allow for reflections and comparisons (between countries) that an index number does not.

The index number should not be done away with altogether, however; and in the case of foreign trade, the index numbers for the volume of imports and exports are valuable to have (see tabs 1.117–1.127).

Similarly, it is common today to 'weight' or 'adjust' the indexes. We have the most serious reservations about this way of manipulating the figures. This is all the more problematic because the adjusted, weighted index is most often very close in appearance to the index, which it is not. However, what we are interested in is the movement; and we know very well that statistics only allow the forecasting of *trends*, not mathematical forecasting. A deviation, an upward or downward movement, never exactly reproduces a previous movement or deviation. Just as living beings never completely resemble each other, neither do economic phenomena repeat themselves identically. Like living beings, they are similar. They are not identical.

The disadvantage of these weightings and adjustments is that they make it much more difficult for those who use them to critique the documents and their interpretation. When an index number is adjusted, one is obliged to spend (or we should say, waste) many hours examining the method used for this adjustment. Otherwise, one cannot accurately work with the figure or use it.

Moreover, these methods, when taken to an extreme, run the risk of discouraging some from using statistics because they are put off by these often rather complicated calculations. They expose statisticians to easy criticism, which is still too common in many circles.

Adjustments or weightings should be used only when absolutely necessary. Whenever we can arrive at our results through simpler procedures, accessible to all, we must avoid recourse to adjusted figures. If I know the tonnage a country has produced, imported or exported, of coal, cast iron, woollens, cotton wares or sugar; the price at which it has sold or purchased; the number of its unemployed; the discount portfolios of its major credit companies; the number of loaded freight wagons, I will have a better grasp of this country's economic vitality, its growth, than if I am given the best adjusted index numbers in the world.

Rules for Using Statistics

After having grouped the figures around the centres or nuclei, so as to question the state of this or that part of the economic organism (production, circulation, consumption), we must consider their movement.

Economic life, like human life, is not uniform; it is diverse. Well-being follows malaise and vice versa. Just as the thermometer, radiography and chemical analysis come to the aid of the physician, so too do the great strides made in statistics enable the economist to gain a clearer picture of economic change. Thanks to recent improvements, we have at our disposal weekly and monthly information that sheds light on the vitality of a country and of the various countries in the world. In order to use all these figures, it is not enough to group them together, they must also be interpreted. As far as possible, this interpretation should be made accessible to everyone. The conclusions drawn from them must be presented with the utmost circumspection. In our field, the conclusions are very similar to the physician's diagnoses; just like their collection, their study resembles the medical auscultation.

Their study in the period before the war made it possible to identify long and short periods of growth and depression.[107] Finally, the seasons influence the economic life and vitality of a country.

It is possible to study any of these alternatives. In any case, if we study one of them, either a long-term, cyclical or seasonal variation, we cannot fail to ask ourselves what influence one may have on the other.

The course of the economic cycle is not the same when we are dealing with a long period of expansion (1857 to 1873 or 1896 to 1914) or a long period of depression (1873 to 1896 or 1920 to 1937). The essential observation here is to clarify that the cyclical variations are much more pronounced and wide-ranging in a long boom period than in a long period of depression.

Similarly, if the production of cast iron or coal is down in a given month compared with the previous month, one cannot assess this fall without asking at what time of the year it takes place. Production regularly drops in the summer. A drop during the summer months does not mean we may conclude that a long-lasting decline has begun.

Rather complicated methods have been devised which allow us to correct the statistics, to purge them in a way, in order to eliminate the influence of long-term and seasonal variations. We lack the space to go into detail about them here.[108]

We would, however, like to express some reservations about their usefulness. These methods only seem advisable if it were possible to apply the spirit of geometry to the observation of economic phenomena, if one cycle could be compared with another, as

107. Jean Lescure, 'Hausses et baisses générales des prix', *Revue d'économie politique* 26, no. 4 (1912): 452–90; and Lescure, *Hausses et baisses des prix de longue durée* (Paris: Domat-Montchrestien, 1933).

108. See the index of general business conditions compiled by Warren M. Persons in the *Review of Economic Statistics*, from 1919 onward; Warren M. Persons, William Trufant Foster and Albert J. Hettinger, eds, *The Problem of Business Forecasting* (Boston: Houghton Mifflin, 1924); Édouard Lacombe, *La prévision en matière de crises économiques* (Paris: Rivière, 1925); Pierre Ginestet, *Les indices du mouvement général des affaires* (Bordeaux and Paris: Cadoret/Recueil Sirey, 1925); Wagemann, *Konjunkturlehre*; Bradford B. Smith, 'A Forecasting Index for Business', *Journal of the American Statistical Association* 26, no. 174 (June 1931): 115–27; and Crowther, 'Economist Index of Business Activity'.

triangles and angles are compared. But the meticulous historical study of these phenomena has demonstrated that each cycle has its own physiognomy and that even when cycles are similar, they are never identical. The most important observation here is the need to draw a very clear distinction between the cycles in long periods of economic expansion and those in long periods of depression. Far from merging all the cycles together, as recent theories would like to do with statistical corrections and adjustments, it is necessary to clearly separate the cycles in the two periods of growth (from 1840 to 1873 and from 1886 to 1914) from the cycles of the periods of decline (from 1873 to 1896 and from 1920 to 1937). A significant, essential difference can be formulated simply: short periods of growth during long periods of depression; short periods of depression during long periods of expansion. To eliminate the so-called trend through calculations is to conceal one of the essential characteristics of economic development. It is a mistake similar to that of a physician who treats his patient without taking into account the latter's overall state of health.[109]

We therefore prefer the raw curves, as they emerge from the statistician's crucible, to the corrected, revised and sometimes even augmented curves of the creators of these improved methods. In the economic domain, nature is our master. Statistics must reflect real life and allow us to follow its movements. The statistician should provide us with photographs or, if one prefers, X-rays; we do not need his silhouettes or pastiches. The living being is preferable to the mannequin. In our opinion, there is a disproportion between the effort and the result of multiplying the number of additions and subtractions with the intention of correcting the immediate data of economic reality. Although these methods may be acceptable for demonstration purposes, we cannot recommend them for research and forecasting. And as for the observation of business activity, one should stick to statistics and indices that are as close as possible to reality, giving the observer the greatest amount of information – as frequent as possible and as detailed as necessary – emanating as directly as possible from the economic environment.

Monthly statistics (or possibly indices), properly grouped, are to be preferred. Yet the use of monthly statistics requires precautions due to the seasonal variations in economic activity.

Here again, the recent methods are striving to eliminate the influence of seasonal variations, allowing the basic trend of economic activity to appear. Yet, we must accept that certain unforeseeable variations, which we will describe as accidental, cannot be eliminated and should not be ignored. How are we to understand the statistical data for England in 1926 without taking into account the coal strike?

There is no doubt, however, that the monthly statistical observation of business trends must take into account seasonal variations.

109. For the shortcomings of this same method, which gives cycles too uniform a shape, see W. M. Persons, 'An Index of General Business Conditions, 1875–1913', *Review of Economics and Statistics* 9, no. 1 (1927): 20–29. See also Stähle, 'Das Beobachtungsverfahren'; Hickernell, *Financial and Business Forecasting*; Wagemann, *Einführung*; and George Paish's comments in the discussion of Crowther, 'Economist Index of Business Activity', 264–65.

But unlike the methods created with the aim of eliminating the influence of seasonal variations, which are complicated and always a bit arbitrary, we propose an infinitely simple method that avoids all the calculations and wasted time and that produces immediate results without any correction or manipulation of the raw figures. A suitable arrangement and grouping of monthly data are sufficient to eliminate the errors that can arise from the regular seasonal variations of economic activity. Monthly statistics, instead of being grouped in distinct series year by year, as is too often the case,[110] should be juxtaposed in series allowing month-by-month and year-by-year comparisons.[111] By comparing figures for the same months (or weeks) or series of consecutive years, seasonal influences are eliminated in the simplest and most universally accessible manner and the least questionable and most reliable way.

Having taken this precaution, the monthly figures can also be compared within a given year. This is a quick way for us to see at a glance whether there is progress or decline, without the seasonal variation distorting the result in any way. A figure in bold type (in the absence of a graph) draws the reader's attention to the month in which the increase follows the drop (and vice versa).[112]

A rise follows a fall when the monthly figure in a given year is greater than the figure for the same month in the previous year. When this observation is repeated for several months in a row, the conclusion is obvious: the recovery is underway. The same reasoning would apply in reverse in the case of a decline.

To get a closer look at the phenomena, we could calculate and compare the percentage increase or decrease from one month to the next. Using this method, we can then specify the month in which the upturn occurred for cast-iron production, railway earnings or unemployment, and ask ourselves which of these phenomena precedes the other and if this process is recurring.

Using this method, we were able to establish that in the United States during the crises of 1907 and 1913, the fall in the railways' net receipts, and during the 1929 crisis, the fall in profits in the car industry, both preceded the drop in gross returns. The decline in profits preceded the decline in economic activity.[113]

The rise in profits preceded and anticipated the 1933–1937 recovery. (See chap. 2, sec. 2, §2, G.)

Conclusion. – The methods of forecasting economic phenomena and business trends must in our view be simple, clear methods that can be used by everyone. The observer must

110. As in the *Federal Reserve Bulletin*; Société des Nations, *Bulletin statistique mensuel*; *Vierteljahrshefte zur Konjunkturforschung*, Berlin.
111. Weekly statistics on loaded freight wagons in France are published every Monday by *Le Temps*. Weekly statistics are available for the number of unemployed receiving assistance in Great Britain.
112. See chap. 1, sec. 1, §15, devoted to the crisis of 1929–1931.
113. Likewise, monthly indices for several consecutive years can be plotted on a single twelve-month field, giving the graph for each year a different line. In this way, very suggestive comparisons can then be made. See figs. 1.1 and 1.2.

be able to quickly assess the documents used and draw practical conclusions from them, immediately if possible.

Group together useful and well-chosen figures, as few as possible, but enough to encompass the complexity of economic life.

Group together figures that provide the maximum amount of information, engage the mind and are suggestive.

Group together figures month by month, or better still, week by week, using the method of horizontal series.

Then make a judgement on the course and future of business; in short, make a diagnosis.

This is the process we believe is to be preferred.

But there is still much to be done to improve these observations: monthly statistics on orders and profits earned will positively complement an already abundant and valuable body of evidence. We would more readily entrust the future of the very delicate task of forecasting business trends and crises to improvements in our methods of observation, rather than to the weighting and adjustment of figures.[114]

But whatever these improvements may be, nothing can replace experience itself. In order to predict and understand crises, it is essential to have 'observed' the day-to-day unfolding of these phenomena – to have 'lived' them, as it were, and to have practised, appreciated and manipulated the complex forecasting instruments at our disposal today.

Experience alone is capable of fine-tuning one's abilities in the practice of auscultation and diagnosis.

We believe our conclusion will justify the title of this book: On General and Periodic Crises of Overproduction. The crisis is general because it affects the whole of the economic organism; it is a crisis of overproduction because it is characterized by a sudden halt in trade, by a surplus of production, either actual or possible, over demand and consumption; it is moreover periodic, for up to the present day it has recurred with remarkable regularly in every decade in the economic life of the great capitalist nations. Because it is periodic, we believe it is predictable.[115] In conclusion, we have tried to specify as briefly as possible the means of predicting it. Let us hope that our conclusion, based primarily upon experience, will not be contradicted by experience, and that from now on, the great psychological principle brought to light by Guyau – that by becoming aware of a habit or instinct we can escape its domination – will be verified in the economic sphere. This would be an unexpected and most valuable reward for our modest efforts.

---

114. Cf. Arthur Balfour, et al., *Final Report of the Committee on Industry and Trade* (London: HMSO, 1929), 224–34; Gaston Cadoux, 'Compte rendu des travaux de la XVIIIe session de l'Institut international de statistique tenue à Varsovie au mois d'août 1929', *Journal de la Société française de Statistique* 70 (Nov. 1929): 317–18.

115. On periodicity in the natural sciences, see *Nature* (Sep. 1928): 2: 201. This periodicity is not stricter than that of economic crises. The periodicity of the seasons and the tides is not strict in fact. Seasons may come early or late.

Editorial Notes

i A reference to Horace's phrase 'Multa renascentur quae jam cecidere', 'Many terms that have fallen out of use shall be reborn' (*Ars Poetica*, 70).

ii See Eisler, 'Un remède monétaire', 348–49.

iii Here Lescure uses the phrase 'délit d'usure' – i.e., 'usury prohibition' – a play on the premodern Christian 'precursors' to May's theory mentioned in the next footnote.

iv In this context, to 'wet' capital means to invest at high risk.

ANNEXS

Table A1 The Sauerbeck-Paish Index for the Price of Commodities and Precious Metals, 1846–1937 (1867–1877 = 100)

Year	*Vegetable Food (corn, etc.)*	*Animal Food (meat, etc.)*	*Sugar, Coffee and Tea*	*Minerals (iron, cast iron, coal, copper)*	*Textiles*	*Grand Total*[*]
1846	106	81	98	92	77	89
1847	129	88	87	94	78	95
1848	92	83	69	78	64	78
1852	80	69	75	80	78	78
1857	105	89	119	108	92	105
1858	87	83	97	96	84	91
1862	98	86	98	91	123	101
1863	87	85	99	93	149	103
1864	79	89	106	96	162	105
1865	84	97	97	91	134	101
1866	95	96	94	91	130	102
1867	115	89	94	87	110	100
1868	113	88	96	85	106	99
1871	94	100	100	93	103	100
1872	101	101	104	127	114	109
1873	106	109	106	141	103	111
1874	105	103	105	116	92	102
1875	93	108	100	101	88	96
1876	92	108	98	90	85	95
1877	100	101	103	84	85	94
1878	95	101	90	74	78	87
1879	87	94	87	73	74	83
1880	89	101	88	79	81	88
1881	84	101	84	77	77	85
1882	84	104	76	79	73	84
1883	82	103	77	76	70	82
1884	71	97	63	68	68	76
1885	68	88	63	66	65	72
1886	65	87	60	67	63	69
1887	64	79	67	69	65	68
1888	67	82	65	78	64	70
1889	65	86	75	75	70	72
1890	65	82	70	80	66	72
1891	75	81	71	76	59	72
1892	65	84	69	71	57	68
1893	59	85	75	68	59	68
1894	55	80	65	64	53	63
1895	54	78	62	62	52	62
1896	53	73	59	63	54	61

(Continued)

Table A1 (Continued)

Year	*Vegetable Food (corn, etc.)*	*Animal Food (meat, etc.)*	*Sugar, Coffee and Tea*	*Minerals (iron, cast iron, coal, copper)*	*Textiles*	*Grand Total**
1897	60	79	52	66	51	62
1898	67	77	51	70	51	64
1899	60	79	53	92	58	68
1900	62	85	54	108	66	75
1901	62	85	46	89	60	70
1902	63	87	41	82	61	69
1903	62	84	44	82	66	69
1904	63	83	50	81	71	70
1905	63	87	52	87	72	72
1906	62	89	46	101	80	77
1907	69	88	48	107	77	80
1908	70	89	48	89	62	73
1909	71	89	50	86	64	74
1910	65	86	54	89	73	78
1911	70	90	61	93	76	80
1912	78	96	62	110	76	85
1913	69	99	54	111	84	85
1914	75	100	58	99	81	85
1915	108	126	70	126	92	108
1916	133	152	86	158	129	136
1917	177	192	113	172	192	175
1918	168	207	130	192	222	192
1919	179	213	147	220	228	206
1920	**227**	**263**	**198**	**295**	**262**	**251**
1921	143	218	83	181	140	155
1922	107	184	82	142	134	131
1923	98	162	101	155	140	129
1924	119	158	105	158	170	139
1925	118	162	89	154	165	136
1926	108	150	88	154	133	126
1927	108	138	83	141	131	122
1928	107	142	78	123	136	120
1929	99	146	72	126	122	115
1930	77	142	54	112	84	97
1931	68	119	50	100	63	83
1932	72	105	50	99	64	80
1933	60	106	47	107	67	79
1934	63	108	50	109	72	82
1935	66	107	42	112	80	84
1936	76	109	41	118	83	88
1937	93	117	49	142	93	102

Source note: Augustus Sauerbeck compiled statistical commodities indexes for the *Journal of the Royal Statistical Society* (London) from 1886 to 1912. Thereafter, his efforts were continued by Sir George Paish in the *Statist*, and Paish's tables continued to appear in the *Journal of the Royal Statistical Society*. See Sauerbeck, 'Prices of Commodities in 1912', *Journal of the Royal Statistical Society* 76, no. 4 (March 1913): 402. Lescure's somewhat inconsistent references throughout the text to Sauerbeck's Index, the Sauerbeck-Paish Index or the *Statist* Index are a consequence of this important index changing hands between the second and third editions of his book.

* Note: Headings have been taken directly from Sauerbeck. Lescure headed the last column '*Moyenne générale*'; but since Sauerbeck's tables also included various averages, Sauerbeck's heading, 'Grand Total', has been used to avoid confusion. Boldface values for 1920 mark the jump in the prices of consumer goods after the First World War.

Table A2 Monthly Gross and Net Earnings of US Railways, 1906–1937

	Jan.	*Feb.*	*Mar.*	*Apr.*	*May*	*Jun.*	*Jul.*	*Aug.*	*Sep.*	*Oct.*	*Nov.*	*Dec.*
Part 1: Net Earnings (millions of $)												
1906	38.6	33.4	40.3	31.5	37.3	31.0	42.8	48.0	48.3	51.6	48.0	43.9
1907	**36.2**	30.6	40.9	42.5	43.7	41.0	**41.8**	45.6	41.8	46.9	39.1	45.9
1908	29.6	26.1	39.2	37.4	38.0	41.8	67.1	75.0	81.6	88.5	74.5	51.5
1909	50.2	49.1	69.5	62.3	64.6	74.1	78.3	90.3	95.4	104.1	94.5	68.6
1910	57.4	56.9	78.3	66.7	70.0	77.1	**73.1**	89.5	91.5	93.6	83.9	67.8
1911	53.8	49.8	69.2	64.7	69.1	72.7	72.4	86.2	90.7	93.8	79.0	56.7
1912	**45.9**	57.4	69.0	57.9	61.0	76.2	79.4	99.1	96.8	108.0	93.0	72.9
1913	64.2	59.4	64.8	60.1	73.6	75.0	64.3	83.1	92.8	97.7	78.2	82.6
1914	52.7	39.6	67.9	59.3	57.6	66.2	75.3	87.7	111.7	87.6	67.9	68.2
1915	51.5	51.2	68.4	67.5	71.9	81.6	87.6	99.7	124.4	119.3	118.3	61.1
1919	36.2	27.6	29.5	44.8	58.2	69.3	96.7	112.2	98.3	104.0	48.1	38.5
1920	**28.4**	10.6	40.8	2.8	28.6	21.4	18.8	12.3*	102.3	117.9	85.7	51.3
1921	28.4	**20.7**	58.5	57.6	64.8	80.5	99.8	123.0	120.6	137.9	97.3	67.8
1922	57.4	76.7	113.4	80.5	92.9	109.4	102.2	86.5	91.3	120.2	113.6	111.9
1923	93.2	70.3	117.1	118.6	126.7	124.0	121.0	136.5	129.3	141.9	124.9	**106.2**
1924	83.9	104.1	114.7	101.6	96.0	101.5	112.6	134.6	159.1	168.7	135.1	124.4
1925	101.0	99.4	109.2	102.8	112.8	130.8	139.6	166.5	177.2	180.6	148.1	134.4
1926	202.2	99.4	133.6	114.6	128.5	149.4	161.0	179.4	191.9	193.9	158.1	**119.2**
1927	99.4	107.1	135.6	**113.6**	120.7	127.7	125.4	164.0	179.4	180.9	125.9	90.3
1928	93.9	108.1	131.8	110.9	128.7	127.2	137.4	173.9	180.3	216.5	157.1	138.2
1929	117.7	126.3	139.6	136.8	146.7	150.1	168.4	190.9	181.4	**204.3**	127.1	106.3
1930	94.7	97.4	101.4	107.1	111.3	110.2	165.5	139.1	147.2	157.1	99.5	80.4
1931	71.9	64.6	84.6	79.1	81.0	89.6	96.9	95.1	92.2	101.9	66.8	47.1
1932	45.9	57.3	67.6	56.2	47.4	47.0	46.1	62.5	83.0	98.3	63.9	57.8
1933	45.6	41.4	43.1	52.5	74.8	94.4	100.4	90.1	94.2	91.0	66.8	59.1
1934	62.2	59.9	83.9	65.2	72.0	74.5	67.5	71.0	71.7	80.4	59.1	62.1
1935	51.3	54.8	67.6	65.3	70.4	64.9	57.4	72.7	88.9	108.5	82.7	70.4
1936	67.3	64.6	71.7	78.3	80.7	88.8	101.3	104.2	108.6	130.1	40.2	114.8
1937	77.9	77.7	111.5	89.5	85.5	**86.0**	98.4	91.4	100.3	102.5	68.9	57.1

(Continued)

Table A2 (Continued)

	Jan.	*Feb.*	*Mar.*	*Apr.*	*May*	*Jun.*	*Jul.*	*Aug.*	*Sep.*	*Oct.*	*Nov.*	*Dec.*
Part 2: Gross Earnings (millions of $)												
1906	128.5	120.7	129.8	109.9	121.0	100.3	129.3	137.5	136.8	143.3	140.6	135.7
1907	133.8	123.9	141.5	142.8	144.2	132.0	137.2	144.9	141.2	154.3	**138.0**	132.1
1908	135.1	123.3	141.1	134.5	133.6	126.8	195.2	206.7	218.9	232.2	211.5	205.7
1909	182.9	174.4	205.7	196.9	196.8	210.3	219.9	236.5	246.9	261.1	248.0	222.6
1910	211.0	202.8	238.7	225.8	230.0	237.9	230.6	254.0	256.6	263.4	248.5	236.8
1911	215.0	199.0	227.5	218.4	226.4	231.9	224.7	243.8	249.0	260.4	241.3	233.6
1912	210.7	218.0	237.5	220.6	232.2	243.2	245.5	276.9	272.2	293.7	276.6	263.7
1913	246.6	232.7	249.2	245.1	263.4	259.7	**235.8**	259.8	285.0	299.1	269.2	254.2
1914	233.0	209.2	250.1	236.5	239.1	230.7	252.2	269.5	294.2	269.9	240.2	232.5
1915	220.2	210.8	238.1	237.6	244.6	248.8	262.9	279.8	301.2	311.1	306.7	295.2
1919	395.5	351.0	375.7	369.4	413.1	424.0	454.5	469.8	495.1	508.0	436.4	451.9
1920	494.7	421.1	408.5	388.6	387.3	486.2	467.3	554.7	594.1	633.8	592.2	539.1
1921	**469.7**	405.0	546.9	401.6	444.0	460.5	460.9	504.5	496.7	534.3	464.4	406.8
1922	393.8	400.4	473.4	416.2	447.2	472.3	442.7	472.2	498.7	545.7	523.7	512.4
1923	350.8	444.8	533.5	521.3	545.5	540.0	534.6	563.2	544.2	586.3	530.1	493.0
1924	467.8	477.8	**504.0**	474.0	476.4	464.7	480.7	507.4	539.8	571.4	504.5	**504.8**
1925	483.1	454.0	485.4	472.5	487.6	506.0	521.5	554.5	564.8	590.1	531.7	523.0
1926	480.0	459.2	528.9	498.4	516.4	538.7	555.4	577.7	588.9	604.0	559.9	525.4
1927	485.9	467.8	529.8	497.2	517.5	**516.0**	508.4	556.4	564.0	582.5	502.9	466.5
1928	456.5	455.6	504.2	473.4	509.7	501.5	504.1	556.9	554.4	616.7	530.9	495.7
1929	486.2	474.7	516.1	513.0	536.7	531.0	556.7	585.6	565.8	**607.5**	498.3	488.1
1930	450.5	427.2	452.0	450.0	462.4	444.1	456.3	465.7	466.8	482.7	398.2	377.4
1931	365.4	336.1	375.0	369.1	368.4	369.2	377.9	364.0	349.8	362.6	304.8	288.2
1932	274.9	266.8	289.6	367.4	254.3	245.8	237.4	251.7	372.0	298.0	253.2	245.7
1933	228.8	213.8	219.8	227.3	257.9	281.3	297.1	300.5	295.5	297.6	260.5	248.0
1934	257.7	248.1	292.7	265.0	281.6	282.4	275.5	292.2	275.1	292.4	256.6	257.1
1935	263.8	254.5	280.4	274.1	279.1	280.9	274.9	293.6	306.5	340.5	300.9	295.8
1936	298.7	300.0	307.8	312.4	320.4	330.2	349.2	350.0	356.6	390.8	357.9	371.6
1937	330.9	321.2	337.8	350.9	352.0	351.0	364.5	358.9	362.4	**372.2**	317.5	299.8

* Loss

Source: *Commercial and Financial Chronicle*, years 1907–1937.

Note: A comparison of these two tables shows that for a period of 30 years the movement of net earnings *in general* precedes that of gross earnings in a crisis or depression. The figures in boldface mark the reversals of the trend (see our conclusion at the end).

Figure A1 Unemployment in Great Britain, 1871–1914: Percentage of Union Workers Out of Work. Source: Board of Trade, *Seventeenth Abstract of Labour Statistics* [Cd. 7733] (London: HMSO, 1915), 2–3, table.

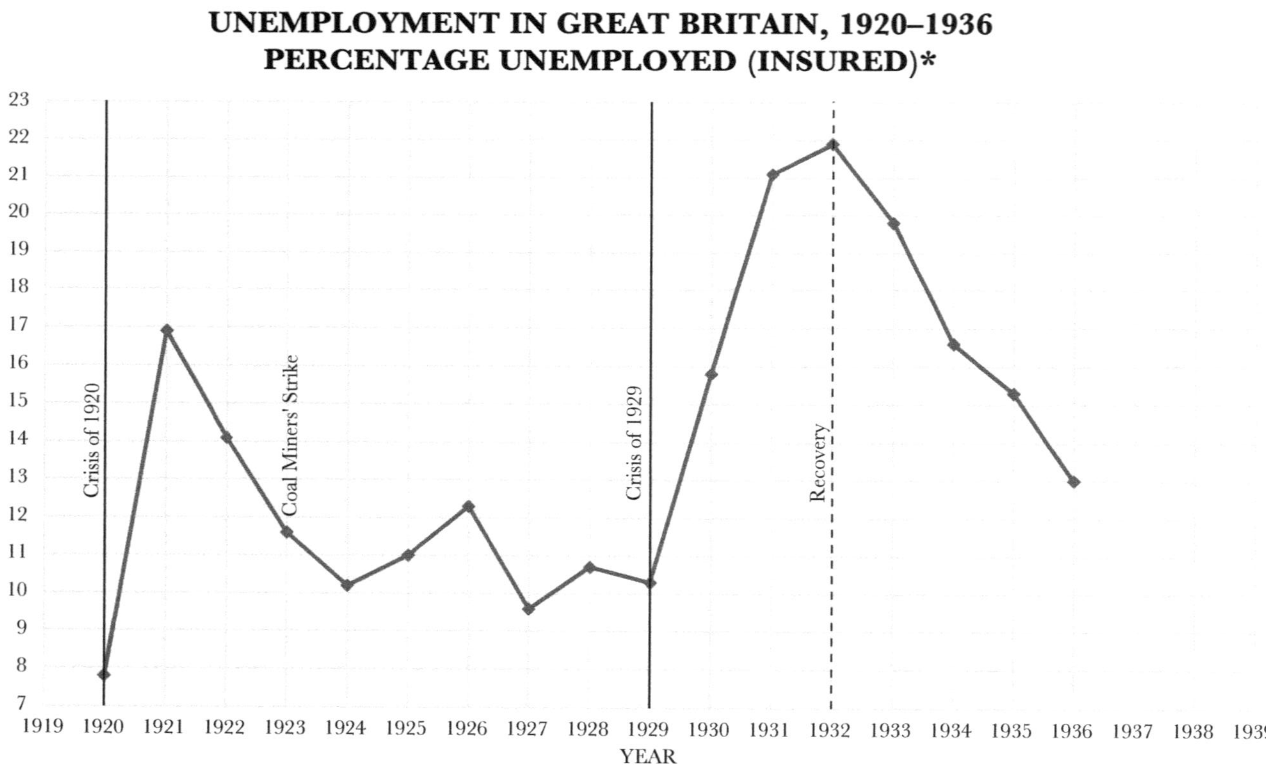

* Includes partially employed.

Figure A2 Unemployment in Great Britain, 1920–1936: Percentage of Unemployed (Insured).

Source note: Lescure provided no source information for this figure, or for the table below which deals with similar data. His graph has been recreated using unemployment figures from the Board of Trade, *Twenty-Second Abstract of Labour Statistics of the United Kingdom* [Cmd. 5556] (London: HMSO, 1937); and the *Eighteenth Abstract of Labour Statistics* [Cmd. 2740] (London: HMSO, 1926).

Table A3 Crisis of 1929–1933: Percentage Unemployed in Select Industries

	Quarter	*1929*	*1930*	*1931*	*1932*	*1933*
Coal	1st	15.9	13.5	23.1	27.3	19.4
	2nd	17.6	20.8	29.8	35.3	36.1
	3rd	16.7	24.9	33.0	40.6	36.7
	4th	14.8	22.4	26.9	32.5	29.4
Iron and Steel	1st	18.8	22.9	44.1	46.5	43.9
	2nd	17.8	29.1	45.0	48.2	40.9
	3rd	18.6	35.5	47.2	48.2	35.9
	4th	20.5	44.4	44.7	46.5	31.5
Engineering	1st	10.0	12.7	25.8	27.8	29.4
	2nd	9.1	15.1	27.4	28.3	26.1
	3rd	9.5	18.4	29.4	30.3	23.9
	4th	10.1	22.8	27.7	29.8	20.9
Shipyards	1st	23.5	22.4	46.8	57.2	59.6
	2nd	20.1	26.1	52.0	58.0	56.6
	3rd	20.5	31.9	55.8	60.9	55.0
	4th	21.0	40.2	57.7	60.4	51.8

Source note: *See figure A2 above.*

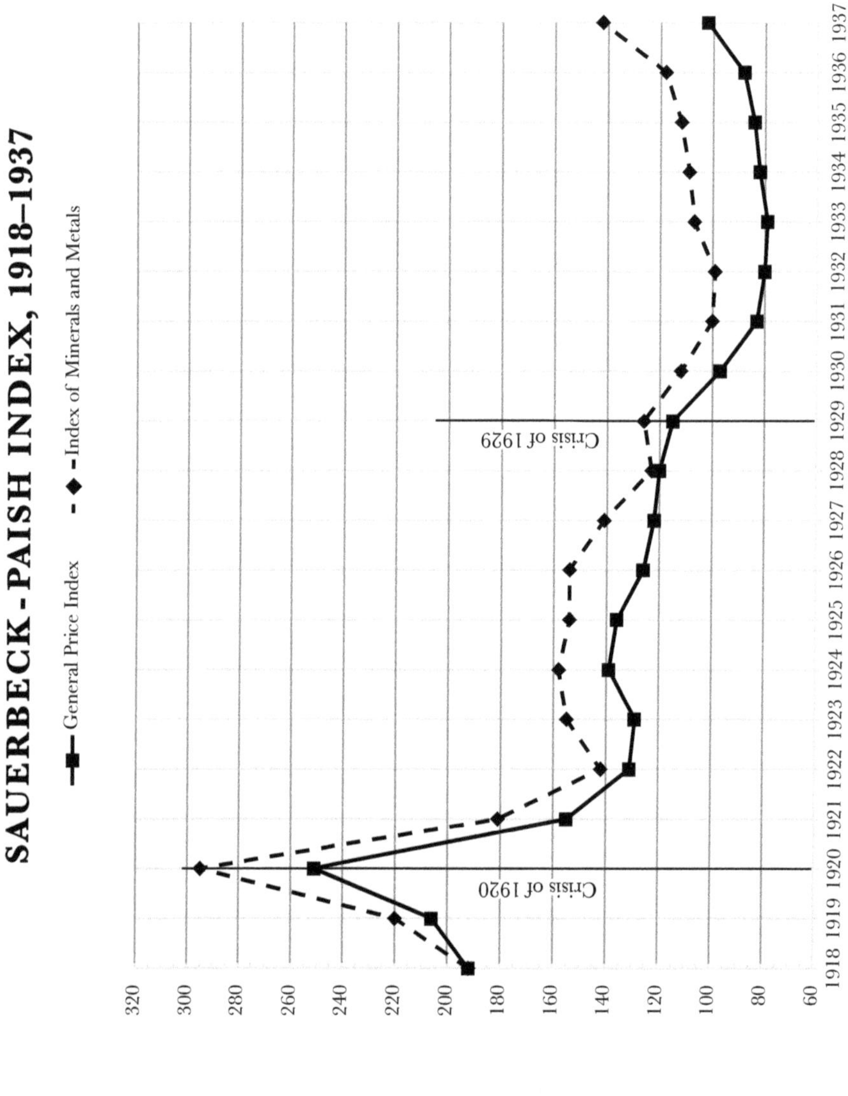

Figure A3 Sauerbeck-Paish Index, 1918–1937. Source: *See table A1.*

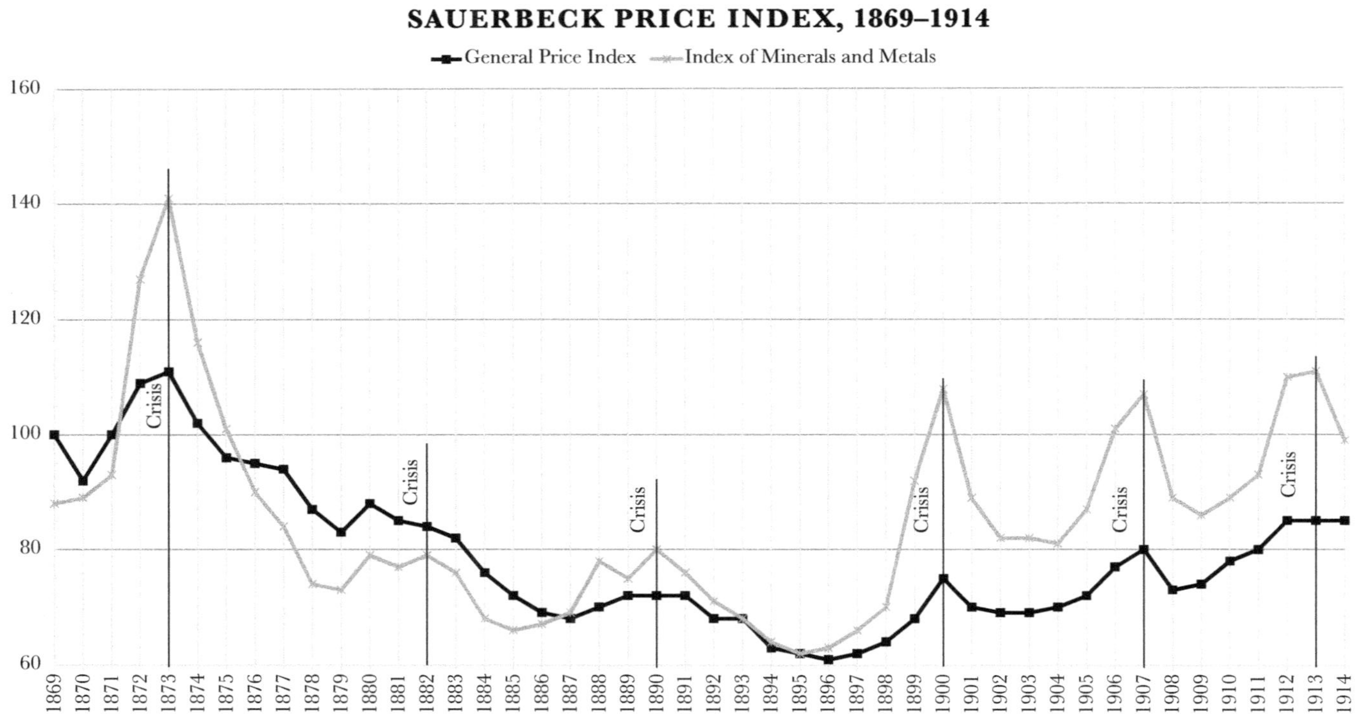

Figure A4 Sauerbeck Price Index, 1869–1914. Source: *See table A1*.

Appendix One

BIBLIOGRAPHY OF THE WORKS CITED BY JEAN LESCURE

The fifth edition of 1938 did not include a bibliography. The following has been prepared by the translator to assist the reader. This list includes all published sources cited in the text and footnotes. Following standard practice, it excludes most newspaper and magazine articles, statistical annuaries, most untitled or anonymous works and most encyclopaedia and dictionary entries, all of which are, whenever possible, given full references in the footnotes.

Abatti, Henry A. *The Unclaimed Wealth: How Money Stops Production.* London: Allen & Unwin, 1924.

Abatti, Henry A., ed. *The Economic Lessons of 1929–1931: The First Eleven Bulletins of Unclaimed Wealth Utilisation Committee of Geneva.* London: P. S. King, 1932.

Adler, Georg. *Rodbertus, der Begründer der wissenschaftlichen Sozialismus: Eine sozial-ökonomische Studie.* Leipzig: Duncker & Humblot, 1884.

Åkerman, Johan. *Economic Progress and Economic Crises.* Translated by Elizabeth Sprigge and Claude Napier. London: Macmillan, 1932.

Adams, Arthur B., Carter Goodrich, Joseph Demmery, Willard L. Thorp and Alvin H. Hansen. 'The Business Depression of Nineteen Hundred Thirty – Discussion'. In 'Papers and Proceedings of the Forty-Third Annual Meeting of the American Economic Association'. Supplement, *American Economic Review* 21, no. 1 (1931): 183–201.

Afanassiev, Georges. 'La crise actuelle des capitaux en Russie'. *La réforme sociale*, 4th ser., 10 (coll. vol. 40) (Oct. 1900): 577–86.

Aftalion, Albert. *L'œuvre économique de Simonde de Sismondi.* Doctoral thesis, Faculty of Law, University of Paris. Paris: A. Pedone, 1899.

______. 'La théorie de l'épargne en matière de crise périodique de surpoduction générale et sa critique'. *Revue d'histoire des doctrines économiques et sociales* 2 (1909): 229–62.

______. 'La réalité des surproduction générales: Essai d'une théorie des crises générales et périodiques'. Pt 1, 'Possibilité théorique et réalité des crises de surproduction générale'. *Revue d'économie politique* 23 (Feb. 1909): 81–117.

______. *Les crises périodiques de surproduction.* 2 vols. Paris: Rivière, 1913.

Albrecht, Gerhard. 'Bemerkungen zum Problem der Überproduktion'. *Jahrbücher für Nationalökonomie und Statistik* 146, no. 3 (1937): 285–308.

Andréadès, Andréas. *Histoire de la Banque d'Angleterre.* 2 vols. Paris: Rousseau, 1904.

Andrew, A. Piatt. 'Substitutes for Cash in the Panic of 1907'. *Quarterly Journal of Economics* 22, no. 4 (Aug. 1908): 497–516.

Ansiaux, Maurice. *Principes de la politique régulatrice des changes.* Brussels: Misch & Thron, 1910.

______. *Traité d'économie politique.* 3 vols. Paris: Giard, 1920–1926.

______. 'L'épargne au cours des phases d'essor et de dépression'. *Bulletin d'information et de documentation de la Banque nationale de Belgique* 6, vol. 1, no. 7 (10 April 1931): 229–34.

______. 'De l'abus du crédit'. *Bulletin d'information et de documentation de la Banque nationale de Belgique* 6, vol. 2, no. 8 (25 Oct. 1931): 285–91.
______. *L'inflation du crédit et la prévention des crises*. Paris: Librairie Dalloz, 1934.
Audiganne, Armand. 'La crise commerciale et la Banque d'Angleterre'. *Revue des deux mondes* 18, no. 1 (April 1847): 153–74.
Bachi, Riccardo. *L'Italia economica nell'anno 1921: Annuario della vita commerciale, industriale, agraria, bancaria, finanziaria e della political economica*. Vol. 13. Città di Castello: S. Lapi, 1922.
Baudhuin, Fernand. 'Problèmes de distribution'. *Bulletin d'information et de documentation de la Banque nationale de Belgique* 7, vol. 2, no. 10 (25 Nov. 1932): 356–59.
Bauer, Otto. 'Die Akkumulation des Kapitals'. *Die Neue Zeit* 31 (1913): 831–38 and 862–74.
Bellerby, J. R., and K. S. Isles. 'Wages Policy and the Gold Standard in Great Britain'. *International Labour Review* 22, no. 2 (Aug. 1930): 137–54.
Bergerioux, René. *Un monde commence*. Paris: Grasset, 1932.
Berglund, Abraham. 'The United States Steel Corporation and Price Stabilization'. 2 parts. *Quarterly Journal of Economics* 38, nos. 1 and 4 (1923): 1–30, 607–30.
Bergmann, Eugen von. *Die Wirtschaftskrisen: Geschichte der nationalökonomischen Krisentheorien*. Stuttgart: Kohlhammer, 1895.
Berle, Adolf Augustus. *The Modern Corporation and Private Property*. New York: Macmillan, 1934.
Bernhard, Georg. *Krach: Krisis und Arbeiterklasse*. Berlin: Buchhandlung *Vorwärts*, 1902.
Bernstein, Eduard. *Socialisme théorique et social-démocratie pratique*. Translated by Alexander Cohen. Paris: Stock, 1900.
Berruyer, Jacques. *L'évolution récente de l'industrie automobile américaine*. Paris: Jouve, 1931.
Beveridge, W. H. *Unemployment: A Problem of Industry (1909 and 1930)*. 2nd ed. London: Longmans, Green, 1930.
Biermer, Magnus. 'Die Letzte deutsche Wirtschaftskrise und ihre Ursachen'. In *Sammlung nationalökonomischer Aufsätze und Vorträge*, vol. 1, 171–212. Giessen: Roth, 1905.
Bishop, W. H. 'The Argentine Crisis'. *Economic Journal* 1, no. 3 (Sep. 1891): 533–38.
Blaise, Adolphe-Gustave. 'Les chemins de fer et le crédit'. *Journal des économistes* 18, no. 69 (Aug.–Nov. 1847): 44–53.
Blanc, Louis. *L'organisation du travail*. 9th ed. Paris: Bureau du Nouveau Monde, 1850.
Block, Maurice. 'La crise économique'. *Revue des deux mondes*, 3rd ser., 32, no. 2 (Aug. 1879): 433–59.
______. *Les progrès des sciences économiques depuis Adam Smith: Revision des doctrines économiques*. 2 vols. Paris: Guillaumin, 1890.
Bonn, Moritz Julius. *La destinée du capitalisme*. Translated by Mathilde Schindler. Paris: Dalloz, 1932.
Bouniatian, Mentor. *Les crises économiques: Essai de morphologie et théorie des crises économiques périodiques*. 2nd ed. Translated by J. Bernard. Paris: Giard, 1930.
Bourbeau, Marcel. 'La crise et la Bourse'. *Revue d'économie politique* 35, no. 4 (1921): 489–93.
Bourguin, Maurice. *La mesure de la valeur et la monnaie*. Paris: Larose, 1896.
______. *Les systèmes socialistes de l'évolution économique*. Paris: Colin, 1904.
Bouvard, Georges. *L'agriculture dirigée aux États-Unis: Essai critique sur l'économie autoritaire*. Doctoral thesis, Faculty of Law, University of Paris. Paris: Librairie technique et économique, 1937. (Thesis supervised by J. Lescure)
Bresciani-Turroni, Constantino. 'Considerazioni sui "barometri" economici'. 3 parts. *Giornale degli economisti e Rivista di Statistica* 68 (year 43), nos. 1, 5 and 7 (1928): 1–26, 361–93 and 579–619.
Brentano, Lujo. 'Die Arbeiter und die Produktionskrisen'. *Jahrbuch für Gesetzgebung, Verwaltung und Volkswirtschaft im Deutschen Reich* 2 (1878): 110–76 (565–632).
______. *Ueber die Ursachen der heutigen sozialen Noth*. Leipzig: Duncker & Humblot, 1889.
Broderick, J. Joyce, and Arthur J. Pack. *Economic Conditions in the United States of America, March 1931*. London: Department of Overseas Trade, 1931.
Bucharin, Nicolai. *Der Imperialismus und die Akkumulation des Kapitals*. Berlin: Verlag für Literatur und Politik, 1926.

Buret, Eugène. *Essai sur la misère des classes laborieuses en France et en Angleterre.* 2 vols. Paris: Chez Paulin, 1840.

Burgess, W. Randolph. 'Velocity of Bank Deposits'. *Journal of the American Statistical Association* 18, no. 142 (June 1923): 727–40.

______. 'The Money Market in 1929'. *Review of Economics and Statistics* 12, no. 1 (1930): 15–20.

Burns, E. M. 'Die nichtlandwirtschaftliche Arbeitslosigkeit in den Vereinigten Staaten, 1930–1932'. *Weltwirtschaftliches Archiv* 37 (April 1933): 529–59.

Butler, H. B. *Le problème du chômage aux États-Unis.* Geneva: Bureau Internationale du Travail, 1931.

Byé, Maurice. 'La reprise britannique et ses causes'. *Revue d'économie politique* 49, no. 2 (1935): 247–84.

Calwer, Richard. *Handel und Wandel: Jahresberichte über den Wirtschafts- und Arbeitsmarkt.* Vols. 1900 and 1901. Berlin: Edelheim, 1901–2.

Campion, H. 'Pre-war Fluctuations of Profits in the Cotton-Spinning Industry'. *Journal of the Royal Statistical Society* 97, no. 4 (1934): 626–32.

Carli, Filippo. *Teoria generale della economia politica nazionale.* Milan: Ulrico Hoepli, 1931.

Cassel, Gustave. *Traité d'économie politique.* Translated by Henry Laufenburger and Georges de Persan. 2 vols. Paris: Giard, 1929.

Cauwès, Paul. *Cours d'économie politique: Contenant, avec l'exposé des principes, l'analyse des questions de législation économique.* 3rd ed. 4 vols. Paris: Larose & Forcel, 1893.

Chase, Stuart. *A New Deal.* New York: Macmillan, 1931.

Chassery, Edmond. *Les illusions de l'Amérique en matière de crédit, de 1914 à l'éxperience Roosevelt.* Doctoral thesis, Faculty of Law, University of Paris. Paris: Librairie technique et économique, 1937. (Thesis supervised by J. Lescure)

Chevalier, Michel. 'Des forces alimentaires des états et de la crise actuelle'. *Revue des deux mondes* 18, no. 5 (June 1847): 874–919.

Citrine, Walter. *I Search for Truth in Russia.* London: Routledge, 1936.

______. *A la recherche de la vérité en Russie.* Translated by Marie Thérèse Génin. Paris: Pierre Tisné, 1937.

Claoué, Raymond. 'Le système bancaire des États-Unis de Amérique'. In *Encyclopédie de banque et de Bourse,* ed. F. François-Marsal, 656–98. Paris: Imprimerie Crété, 1930.

Clark, John Maurice. *Studies in the Economics of Overhead Costs.* Chicago, IL: University of Chicago Press, 1923.

Clay, Henry. *The Post-War Unemployment Problem.* London: Macmillan, 1929.

Clément, Ambroise. 'Des crises commerciales'. *Journal des économistes,* 2nd ser., 17 (15 Feb. 1858): 161–91.

Cochut, André. 'De la crise des chemins de fer'. *Revue des deux mondes* 18, no. 5 (June 1847): 925–39.

Cole, Arthur H. 'Cyclical and Seasonal Variations in the Sale of Public Lands, 1816–60'. *Review of Economic Statistics* 9, no. 1 (Jan. 1927): 41–53.

______. 'Statistical Background of the Crisis of 1837–1842'. *Review of Economic Statistics* 10, no. 4 (Nov. 1928): 182–95.

______. 'Statistical Background of the Crisis of 1857'. *Review of Economic Statistics* 12, no. 4 (Nov. 1930): 170–80.

Cole, G. D. H. *British Trade and Industry.* London: Macmillan, 1932.

Colson, Clément. *Cours d'économie politique.* 3 vols. Paris: Gauthier-Villars and Guillaumin, 1903.

______. *Cours d'économie politique.* Vol. 4: *Les entreprises, le commerce et la circulation.* Definitive edition. Paris: Gauthier-Villars and Félix Alcan, 1920.

Committee on Industry and Trade (Balfour Committee). *Survey of Industrial Relations.* Vol. 4. London: HMSO, 1928.

Comte, Auguste. *Cours de philosophie positive.* 5th ed. 6 vols. Paris, 1892–94.

Conrad, Johannes. *Grundriss zum Studium der politischen Oekonomie.* 5th ed. 2 vols. Jena: Fischer, 1905.
Conrad, Johannes, Ludwig Elster, Wilhelm Lexis and Edgar Loening, eds. *Handwörterbuch der Staatswissenschaften.* 2nd ed. 7 vols. Jena: Fischer, 1898–1901.
______. *Handwörterbuch der Staatswissenschaften.* 3rd ed. 8 vols. Jena: Fischer, 1909–11.
Conrad, Otto. *Absatzmangel und Arbeitlosigkeit als Dauerzustand.* Vienna: Hölder-Pichler-Tempsky, 1926.
Cooper, Lyle W. 'Recent National Trade Agreements in the Silk Hosiery Industry'. *Journal of Political Economy* 39, no. 1 (Feb. 1931): 69–75.
Coquelin, Charles. 'Les crises commerciales et la liberté des banques'. *Revue des deux mondes*, n.s., 24, no. 3 (1848): 445–70.
Courcelle-Seneuil, Jean-Gustave. *Traité théorique et pratique d'économie politique.* 2nd ed. 2 vols. Paris: Amyot, 1867.
Courtin, René. 'L'activité des institutions économiques internationales'. *Revue d'économie politique* 45, no. 1 (1931): 136–82.
______. 'Essai sur la thérapeutique de crise'. *Revue d'économie politique* 49, no. 4 (1935): 1256–1309.
Courtin, R., and P. Fromont. 'Essai sur la crise agricole: Production et population'. *Revue d'économie politique* 44, no. 4 (1930): 1084–1128.
'The Crisis of 1890'. *Economic Journal* 1, no. 1 (Mar. 1891): 192–96.
Crowther, Geoffrey. 'The Economist Index of Business Activity'. *Journal of the Royal Statistical Society* 97, no. 2 (1934): 241–76.
Crum, W. L. 'The Course of Corporation Profits'. *Review of Economics and Statistics* 16, no. 3 (15 March 1934): 61–64.
Crump, Arthur. 'The Baring Financial Crisis'. *Economic Journal* 1, no. 2 (June 1891): 388–94.
Delzangles, René. 'Étude comparée de la banque d'émission et banque de dépôt'. Doctoral thesis, Faculty of Law, University of Bordeaux, 1921.
Denis, Hector. *La dépression économique et sociale et l'histoire des prix.* Ixelles-Brussels: G.-J. Huysmans, 1895.
Denuc, Jules. 'Dividendes, valeurs boursières et taux de capitalisation des valeurs mobilière françaises de 1847 à 1932'. *Bulletin de la Statistique générale de la France* 23 (July–Sep. 1934): 691–767.
Depitre, Edgard. *Le mouvement de concentration dans les Banques allemandes.* Doctoral thesis, Faculty of Law, University of Paris. Paris: Rousseau, 1905.
Dermietzel, Otto. *Statistische Untersuchungen über die Kapitalrente der grosseren deutschen Aktiengesellschaften von 1876–1902.* Gottingen: Hofer, 1906.
Deschesne, Laurent. *La panique financière aux États-Unis, fin 1907.* Paris: Larose & Tenin, 1908.
Dessirier, Jean. 'Nouveaux essais de statistiques sur les mouvements boursiers'. *Journal de la Société statistique de Paris* 70 (1929): 35–94.
Diehl, Karl, ed. *Konjunkturforschung und Konjunkturtheorie: Wissenschaftliche Gutachten.* Vol. 2: *Beiträge zur Wirtschaftstheorie.* Schriften des Vereins für Socialpolitik 173. Munich and Leipzig: Duncker & Humblot, 1928.
Dolléans, Éduoard. *Le Chartisme.* 2 vols. Paris: Floury, 1911.
______. *Histoire du mouvement ouvrier, 1830–1871.* Paris: Colin, 1936.
Douglas, Paul H. 'The United States Social Security Act'. *Economic Journal* 46, no. 181 (1936): 1–20.
Drappier, Jean-Marie. 'La conjoncture des cours des valeurs mobilières, de leurs dividendes et des taux d'intérêt en Belgique de 1830 à 1913'. *Bulletin de l'Institut des sciences économiques* 8, no. 4 (1937): 391–449.
Dubreuil, Hyacinthe. *Standards: Le travail américain vu par un ouvrier français.* Paris: Grasset, 1929.
Dugarçon, Alcée. *Le problème économique de l'intérêt.* Doctoral thesis, Faculty of Law, University of Bordeaux. Bourdeaux: Cadoret, 1905.

Dühring, Eugen. *Cursus der National- und Socialökonomie einschliesslich der Hauptpunkte der Finanzpolitik.* Berlin: Grieben, 1873.

Durkheim, Émile. *Le suicide: Étude de sociologie.* Paris: Félix Alcan, 1897.

Eberstadt, Rudolf. *Die gegenwärtige Krisis: Ihre Ursachen und die Aufgaben der Gesetzgebung.* Berlin: Hoffmann, 1902.

Edie, Lionel D., and Donald Weaver. 'Velocity of Bank Deposits in England'. *Journal of Political Economy* 38, no. 4 (1930): 373–403.

Eisler, Robert. 'Un reméde monétaire à la crise Mondiale du chômage'. *Revue d'économie politique* 45, no. 2 (1931): 333–51.

______. *La monnaie: Cause et remède de la crise économique Mondiale.* Paris: Librairie Valois, 1932.

Elster, Ludwig, Adolf Weber and Friedrich Wieser, eds. *Handwörterbuch der Staatswissenschaften.* 4th ed. 8 vols. Jena: Fischer, 1923–29.

Ely, Richard T. *Outlines of Economics.* 4th ed. New York: Macmillan, 1923.

Engels, Friedrich. *Herrn Eugen Dühring's Umwälzung der Wissenschaft.* 2nd ed. Zurich: Verlags-Magazin J. Schabelitz, 1886.

England, Minnie Throop. 'Fisher's Theory of Crises: A Criticism'. *Quarterly Journal of Economics* 27, no. 1 (Nov. 1912): 95–106.

Epstein, Ralph C. *Industrial Profits in the United States.* New York: National Bureau of Economic Research, 1934.

Eulenburg, Franz. 'Die gegenwärtige Wirtschaftskrise: Symptome und Ursachen'. *Jahrbücher für Nationalökonomie und Statistik*, 3rd ser., 24, no. 3 (1902): 305–88.

Fanno, Marco. 'Cicli di produzione cicli del credito e fluttuazioni industriali'. *Giornale degli economisti e Rivista di statistica*, 4th ser., 46, no. 5 (1931): 329–70.

Faucher, Léon. 'Du monopole des fers'. *Journal des économistes* 14, no. 56 (July 1846): 301–3.

______. 'La crise financière dans la Grande-Bretagne'. *Journal des économistes* 18, no. 72 (Nov. 1847): 313–28.

Feiler, Arthur. *Die Konjunktur-Periode, 1907–1913, in Deutschland.* Jena: Fischer, 1914.

Fick, Harald. *Finanzwirtschaft und Konjunktur.* Jena: Fischer, 1932.

Fisher, Irving. *The Purchasing Power of Money.* New York: Macmillan, 1911.

______. *Le pouvoir d'achat de la monnaie.* Translated by Roger Picard and Jean Boutroux. Paris: Giard, 1926.

Fleddérus, M. L., ed. *World Social Economic Planning: The Necessity for Planned Adjustment of Productive Capacity and Standards of Living.* 2 vols. The Hague and New York: International Industrial Relations Institute, 1932.

Foster, William Trufant, and Waddill Catchings. *Profits.* New York: Houghton Mifflin, 1925.

Fougerousse, Auguste. 'La crise industrielle en France'. *La réforme sociale* 7 (1884): 200–26, 257–69, 306–20, 402–14.

de Foville, Alfred. *La monnaie.* 2nd ed. Paris: Gabalda, 1907.

Fried, Ferdinand. *La fin du capitalisme.* Translated by Jean Brunnen. Paris: Grasset, 1932.

Garnier, Joseph. *Éléments de l'économie politique: Exposé des notions fondamentales de cette science.* 2nd ed. Paris: Guillaumin, 1848.

______. 'Coup d'œil sur l'année 1852'. *Annuaire de l'économie politique et de la statistique* 10 (1853): 491–512.

George, Henry. *Progrès et pauvreté: Enquête sur la cause des crises industrielles et de l'accroissement de la misère au milieu de l'accroissement de la richesse, le remède.* Translated by P.-L. Le Monnier. Paris: Guillaumin, 1887.

Germain-Martin, Henry. 'Chronique sur les questions monétaires et le credit: La crise américaine'. *Revue d'économie politique* 22, no. 3 (1908): 203–25.

Ginestet, Pierre. *Les indices du mouvement général des affaires.* Doctoral Thesis, Faculty of Law, University of Bordeaux. Bordeaux: Cadoret and Paris: Recueil Sirey, 1925.

Giraud, Raoul. *Des banques hypothécaires allemandes.* Doctoral thesis, Faculty of Law, University of Paris, 1901. Paris: Rousseau, 1904.

Givens, Meredith B. 'Statistical Measures of Social Aspects of Unemployment'. *Journal of the American Statistical Association* 26, no. 175 (Sep. 1931): 303–18.

Glier, L. 'Zur neuesten Entwicklung der amerikanischen Eisenindustrie'. 3 parts. *Jahrbuch für Gesetzgebung, Verwaltung und Volkswirtschaft im Deutschen Reich* 27, nos. 3 and 4 (1903): 229–99 (1013–83), 43–127 (1223–1307); and 28, no. 1 (1904): 149–278.

Gregory, T. E. *Gold, Unemployment and Capitalism.* London: P. S. King & Son, 1933.

Grossman, Henryk. *Das Akkumulations- und Zusammenbruchsgesetz des kapitalsitischen Systems.* Leipzig: Hirchfeld, 1929.

Gutmann, Franz. *Das französiche Geldwesen im Kriege (1870–1878).* Strasbourg: Tübner, 1913.

Guyot, Yves. *La science économique.* Paris: Reinwald, 1881.

Haberler, Gottfried von. *Prospérité et dépression: Étude théorique des cycles économiques* Geneva: Société des Nations, 1937.

Hahn, L. Albert. 'Grundprinzipien der monetären Konjunkturtheorie'. In *Konjunkturforschung und Konjunkturtheorie: Wissenschaftliche Gutachten.* Vol. 2: *Beiträge zur Wirtschaftstheorie*, edited by Karl Diehl, 153–64.

Halbwachs, Maurice. *Les causes du suicide.* Paris: Félix Alcan, 1930.

Halle, Ernst von. 'Die wirtschaftliche Krisis des Jahres 1893 in den Vereinigten Staaten von Nordamerika'. *Jahrbuch für Gesetzgebung, Verwaltung und Volkswirtschaft im Deutschen Reich* 18, no. 4 (1894): 151–219 (1181–249).

Harrod, Roy Forbes. *The Trade Cycle: An Essay.* Oxford: Clarendon Press, 1936.

Hawtrey, R. G. 'The Federal Reserve System of the United States'. *Journal of the Royal Statistical Society* 85, no. 2 (1922): 224–69.

______. *Currency and Credit.* 3rd ed. London: Longmans, Green, 1928.

______. *Trade and Credit.* London: Longmans, Green, 1928.

Hayek, Friedrich A. 'Einige Bemerkungen über das Verhältnis der Geldtheorie zur Konjunkturtheorie'. In *Konjunkturforschung und Konjunkturtheorie.* Vol. 2: *Beiträge zur Wirtschaftstheorie*, edited by Karl Diehl, 246–94.

______. *Geldtheorie und Konjunkturtheorie.* Vienna: Hölder-Pichler-Tempsky, 1929.

Hayek, Friedrich A., ed. *Collectivist Economic Planning: Critical Studies on the Possibilities of Socialism.* London: Routledge, 1935.

Hearings before the Industrial Commission on the Subject of Trusts and Industrial Combinations. Washington, DC: Government Printing Office, 1899.

Hecht, Felix. 'Lehren der Krisis'. Report to the general assembly of the Verein für Socialpolitik, 15 Sep. 1903. In *Die Störungen im deutschen Wirtschaftsleben während der Jahre 1900ff.*, pp. 139–66. Schriften des Vereins für Socialpolitik 113. Leipzig: Duncker & Humblot, 1904.

Hennebicq, Léon. 'La crise des frets'. *Revue économique internationale* 6 (May 1909): 392–99.

Héreil, Georges. *Le chômage en France: Étude de legislation sociale.* Paris: Recueil Sirey, 1932.

Herkner, Heinrich. *Die soziale Reform als Gebot des wirtschaftlichen Fortschrittes.* Lepizig: Duncker & Humblot, 1891.

Hertzka, Theodor. *Die Gesetze der sozialen Entwicklung.* Leipzig: Duncker & Humbot, 1886.

Heymann, Hans Gideon. *Die gemischten Werke im Grosseisengewerbe: Ein Beitrag zur Frage der Konzentration der Industrie.* Stuttgart: Cotta, 1904.

Hilferding, Rudolf. *Das Finanzkapital.* Vienna: Wiener Volksbuchhandlung, 1923.

Hobson, J. A. *Rationalisation and Unemployment: An Economic Dilemma.* London: Allen & Unwin, 1930.

Hoover, Herbert (Forward) et al., *Business Cycles and Unemployment: Report and Recommendations of a Committee of the President's Conference on Unemployment.* New York: McGraw-Hill, 1923.

Horn, J. Édouard. 'Le commerce extérieur et la crise à Hambourg'. *Journal des économistes*, 2nd ser., 17, no. 2 (Feb. 1858): 215–53.

______. *La liberté des banques.* Paris: Guillaumin, 1866.

Hübener, Erhard. *Die deutsche Wirtschaftskrisis von 1873.* Berlin: Ebering, 1905.

Hull, George H. *Industrial Depressions: Their Causes Analysed and Classified with a Practical Remedy for such as Result from Industrial Derangements; or, Iron, the Barometer of Trade.* New York: Frederick A. Stokes, 1911.

Huncke, Ernst. 'Die Entwicklung von Einkommensteuer und Einkommen in England in den letzten zwanzig Jahren'. *FinanzArchiv* 22, no. 1 (1905): 138–209.

Hyndman, H. M. *Commercial Crises of the Nineteenth Century.* London: Swan, Sonnenschein, 1902.

Institute of Economics of the Brookings Institution. *The Recovery Problem in the United States.* Washington, DC: Brookings Institution, 1936.

Issaïev, A.-A. 'Les principales causes des crises économiques'. 2 parts. *Revue d'économie politique* 7, nos. 7/8 and 12 (1893): 654–92, 985–1011.

Jaurès, Jean. *Études socialistes.* Paris: Éditions cahiers, 1900.

Jeidels, Otto. *Das Verhältnis der deutschen Grossbanken zur Industrie, mit besonderer Berücksichtigung der Eisenindustrie.* Leipzig: Duncker & Humblot, 1905.

Jéramec, Pierre. 'Une théorie dynamique de la production et son illustration par l'étude de l'activité industrielle dans la région parisienne (1927–1931)'. *Journal de la Société française de Statistique de Paris* 72 (July–Aug.–Sep. 1931): 232–67.

Jevons, H. Stanley. 'The Second Industrial Revolution'. *Economic Journal* 41, no. 161 (March 1931): 1–18.

Jones, Edward D. *Economic Crises.* London: Macmillan, 1900.

Jones, J. H. 'Exchange Stability Versus Internal Price Stability'. *Journal of the Royal Statistical Society* 97, no. 2 (1934): 277–312.

de Jouvenel, Bertrand. *La crise du capitalisme américain.* Paris: Gallimard, 1933.

Juglar, Clément. 'Des crises commerciales'. *Annuarie de l'économie politique et de la statistique* 13 (1856): 555–81.

______. 'Des crises commerciales et monétaires de 1800 à 1857'. 2 parts. *Journal des économistes,* 2nd ser., 14, nos. 41–42 (April–May 1857): 35–60, 253–266.

______. 'La crise de New-York'. 2 parts. *Économiste français,* 16 Aug. 1884, 191–92, and 13 Sep. 1884, 315–17.

______. *Des crises commerciales et de leur retour périodique en France, en Angleterre et aux États-Unis.* 2nd ed. Paris: Guillaumin, 1889.

Jugow, A. *Le Plan quinquennial.* Paris and Brussels: l'Eglantine, 1932.

Jutzi, Wilhelm. *Die deutsche Montanindustrie auf dem Wege zum Trust.* Jena: Fischer, 1905.

Karmin, Otto. *Vier Thesen zur Lehre von den Wirtschaftskrisen.* Heidelberg: Carl Winter's Universitätsbuchhandlung, 1905.

Kautsky, Karl. *Le marxisme et son critique Bernstein.* Translated by Martin Leray. Paris: Stock, 1900.

______. *Die materlialistische Geschichtsauffassung.* 2 vols. Berlin: Dietz, 1927.

Keller, Robert von. *Die Kausalzusammenhänge in der Konjunkturbewegung.* Leipzig: Meiner, 1934.

Kellersohn, Maurice. *Les conversions des rentes devant la technique et l'équité.* Paris: Stock, 1931.

Keynes, John Maynard. *A Treatise on Money.* 2 vols. London: Macmillan., 1930.

______. *The General Theory of Employment, Interest and Money.* London: Palgrave Macmillan, 1936.

Kleinwächter, Friedrich. *Die Kartelle: Ein Beitrag zur Frage der Organisation der Volkswirthschaft.* Innsbruck: Wagner, 1883.

Kontradiktorische Verhandlungen über deutsche Kartelle: Die von Reichsamt des Innern angestellten Erhebungen über das inländische Kartellwesen in Protokollen und stenographischen Berichte. 5 vols. Berlin: Franz Siemenroth, 1903–6.

Kotany, L. 'A Theory of Profit and Interest'. *Quarterly Journal of Economics* 36, no. 3 (1922): 413–53.

Kreller, Emil. *Die Entwicklung der deutschen elektrotechnischen Industrie und ihre Aussichten auf dem Weltmarkt.* Leipzig: Duncker & Humblot, 1903.

Kühnert, F. 'Die Hypothekenbewegung in Preussen während der Rechnungsjahre, 1895 bis 1900'. *Zeitschrift des Königlich Preussischen Statistischen Bureaus* 43 (1903): 324–402.

Kuznets, Simon. 'Monetary Business Cycle Theory in Germany'. *Journal of Political Economy* 38, no. 2 (April 1930): 125–63.

______. *Secular Movements in Production and Prices: Their Nature, and Their Bearing upon Cyclical Fluctuations*. Boston: Houghton Mifflin, 1930.

Lacombe, Édouard. *La prévision en matière de crises économiques*. Paris: Rivière, 1925.

Lasson, Robert. *La baisse de l'intérêt en Grande-Bretagne de 1932 à 1936*. Doctoral thesis, Faculty of Law, University of Paris. Paris: Pichon & Durand-Auzias, 1936. (Thesis supervised by Lescure)

Lauderdale, James Maitland, Earl of. *Recherches sur la nature et l'origine de la richesse publique, et sur les moyens et les causes qui concourent à son accroissement*. Translated by E. Lagetie Lavaisse. Paris: Dentu, 1808.

Laufenburger, Henry. 'La vie économique en Allemagne'. *Revue d'économie politique* 51, no. 4 (1937): 1263–99.

Laurat, Lucien. *L'accumulation du capital d'après Rosa Luxembourg*. Paris: Rivière, 1930.

de Laveleye, Émile. *Le marché monétaire et ses crises depuis 50 ans*. Paris: Guillaumin, 1865.

Lederer, Émil. 'Konjunktur und Krisen'. In *Grundriss der Sozialökonomie*. Vol. 4: *Spezifische Elemente der modernen kapitalistischen Wirtschaft*, pt 1, 355–413. Tübingen: Mohr, 1925.

______. 'Le chômage en Allemagne'. *Revue d'économie politique* 45, no. 2 (1931): 276–95.

Leduc, Gaston. 'La réforme monétaire anglaise'. *Revue d'économie politique* 42, no. 6 (1928): 1587–1609.

Lenin, V. I. *Der Imperialismus als jüngste Etappe des Kapitalismus*. Berlin: Verlag für Literatur und Politik, 1926.

Leroy-Beaulieu, Paul. 'La liquidation de la crise de 1882 et l'état présent du marché financier'. *Économiste français*, 20 Sep. 1884: 345–47.

______. *Traité de la science des finances*. 6th ed. 2 vols. Paris: Guillaumin, 1899.

Leroy-Beaulieu, Pierre. 'L'Australie et la Nouvelle-Zélande'. *Revue des deux mondes*, 4th ser., 137, no. 2 (15 Sep. 1896): 409–42.

______. 'Mouvement économique et social aux États-Unis'. *Économistes français*, 11 March 1904.

Levasseur, Émile. *La question de l'or: Les mines de Californie et d'Australie*. Paris: Guillaumin, 1858.

______. 'Influence de l'or sur la condition des personnes'. *Journal des économistes*, 2nd ser., 17 (1858): 216–38.

______. *Histoire des classes ouvrières et de l'industrie en France de 1789 à 1870*. 2nd ed. 2 vols. Paris: Rousseau, 1901–1902.

Levi, Leone. *History of British Commerce and of the Economic Progress of the British Nation, 1763–1870*. London: John Murray, 1872.

Lévy, Raphaël-Georges. 'La crise économique en 1907 et les États-Unis d'Amérique'. *Revue des deux mondes* 42, no. 4 (Dec. 1907): 805–28.

Lewandowski, Maurice. 'La lute contre le chômage aux États-Unis'. *Revue des deux mondes*, 8th ser., 4, no. 4 (1931): 913–27.

Lexis, Wilhelm. 'Zur Kritik der Rodbertus'schen Theorien'. Review of *Das Kapital: Vierter sozialer Brief an von Kirchmann*, by Carl Rodbertus-Jagetzow. In *Jahrbücher für Nationalökonomie und Statistik*, n.s., 9, no. 6 (1884): 462–76.

Liefmann, Robert. 'Konjunkturforschung und Konjunkturpolitik vom Standpunkte einer dynamisch-individualistischen Wirtschaftstheorie'. In *Konjunkturforschung und Konjunkturtheorie: Wissenschaftliche Gutachten*, 39–86. Schriften des Vereins für Sozialpolitik 173. Munich and Leipzig: Duncker & Humblot, 1928.

Lindenberg, G. 'Die Ergebnisse der deuschen Kriminalstatistik'. Part 2. *Jahrbücher für Nationalökonomie und Statistik*, 3rd ser., 8, no. 5 (1894): 714–29.

Loria, Achille. *Corso di economia politica.* 4th ed. Turin: Unione Tipografico-Editrice Torinese, 1934.

______. *Economia politica.* 4th ed. Turin: Utet, 1934.

Lösch, August. *Bevölkerungswellen und Wechsellagen.* Jena: Fischer,1936.

______. 'Population Cycles as a Cause of Business Cycles'. *Quarterly Journal of Economics* 51, no. 4 (1937): 649–62.

Löwe, Adolf. 'Wie ist eine Konjunkturtheorie überhaupt möglich?'. *Weltwirtschaftliches Archiv* 24 (1926): 165–97.

Lucius, Pierre. *La faillite du capitalisme.* Paris: Payot, 1932.

Luxemburg, Rosa. *Die Akkumulation des Kapitals: Ein Beitrag zur ökonomischen Erklärung des Imperialismus.* Berlin: Vereinigung internationaler Verlags-Anstalten, 1923.

Macfie, Alec L. *Theories of the Trade Cycle.* London: Macmillan, 1934.

Macgregor, D. H. 'Enterprise and the Trade Cycle'. In *Economic Essays in Honour of Gustav Cassel,* 419–34. London: Fank Cass, 1933.

MacLeod, Henry Dunning. *Theory of Credit.* 2nd ed. 2 vols. London: Longmans, Green, 1893–97.

Malthus, Thomas. *Principes d'économie politique considérés sous le rapport de leur application pratique, suivis des définitions en économie politique.* 2nd ed., with unpublished remarks by Jean-Baptiste Say. Edited by Maurice Monjean. Paris: Guillaumin, 1846.

Manteuffel, Carl von. *Das Sparen, sein Wesen und seine volkswirtschaftliche Wirkung.* Jena: Fischer, 1900.

March, Lucien. 'Le mouvement des prix et l'activité productrice'. *Bulletin de la Statistique générale de la France* 1, no. 1 (1911): 63–103.

Marion, Marcel. *Histoire financière de la France depuis 1715.* 6 vols. Paris: Rousseau, 1914–1931.

Markovitch, Tihomir J. *Les théories modernes de la sous-consommation.* Paris: Rivière, 1938.

Marlio, Louis. 'Le nouveau régime des chemins de fer'. *Revue des deux mondes*, 8th ser., 43, no. 4 (15 Feb. 1938): 864–82.

Marshall, Alfred. *Principles of Economics.* 4th ed. 2 vols. London: Macmillan, 1898.

______. *Principes d'économie politique.* Translated by Françoise Sauvaire-Jourdan. 2 vols. Paris: Giard & Brière, 1906–9.

Marx, Karl. *Das Kapital: Kritik der politischen Ökonomie.* Vol. 1: *Der Produktionsprocess des Kapitals.* Vol. 2: *Der Cirkulationsprocess des Kapitals.* Vol. 3 (in 2 books): *Der Gesamtprozess der kapitalistischen Produktion.* Hamburg: O. Meissner, 1867, 1885, 1894.

______. *Die Klassenkämpfe in Frankreich, 1848–1850.* Reprinted from *Die Neue Rheinische Zeitung*, 1850. Berlin: Verlag der Expedition des *Vorwärts*, 1895.

______. *Le capital: Critique de l'économie politique.* Vol. 3: *Le procès d'ensemble de la production capitaliste.* Translated by Julien Borchardt and Hippolyte Vanderrydt. Paris: Giard & Brière, 1901.

May, Raphaël Ernst. *Das Grundgesetz der Wirtschaftskrisen und ihre Vorbeugemittel im Zeitalter des Monopols.* Berlin: Dümmler, 1902.

Mayer, Hans. *Die Wirtschaftstheorie der Gegenwart.* Vol. 4: *Konjunktur und Krisen.* Vienna: Springer, 1928.

Menger, Anton. *Le droit au produit intégral du travail: Étude historique.* Translated by Alfred Bonnet. Paris: Giard & Brière, 1900.

Miksch, Leonhard. *Gibt es eine allegemeine Überproduktion?* Jena: Fischer, 1929.

Mill, John Stuart. *Principes d'économie politique.* 3rd ed. Translated by Hippolyte Dussard and J.-G. Courcelle-Seneuil. 2 vols. Paris: Guillaumin, 1873.

Mises, Ludwig von. *Geldwertstabilisierung und Konjunkturpolitik.* Jena: Fischer, 1928.

Mitchell, Wesley Clair. *Business Cycles.* Berkeley: University of California Press, 1913.

______. *Business Cycles: The Problem and its Setting.* New York: National Bureau of Economic Research, 1927.

______. 'Business Cycles'. In *Encyclopaedia of the Social Sciences.* Vol. 3. Edited by Edwin R. A. Seligman. London: Macmillan, 1930.

de Molinari, Gustave. 'La crise financière et commerciale en Angleterre'. *Journal des économistes* 17, no. 67 (June 1847): 274–84.

Mondet, N. 'Les chemins de fer des États-Unis en 1913'. *Journal des économistes*, 6th ser., 42 (April 1914): 83–85.

Morgenstern, Oskar. *Wirtschaftsprognose: Eine Untersuchung ihrer Voraussetzungen und Möglichkeiten.* Vienna: Springer, 1928.

Moulton, Harold Glenn. *The Formation of Capital.* Washington, DC: The Brookings Institution, 1935.

______. *Income and Economic Progress.* Washington, DC: The Brookings Institution, 1935.

Mourre, Baron. 'La crise de 1920–1921 et ses causes'. *Revue d'économie politique* 35, no. 5 (1921): 545–67.

______. 'Les crises et leurs signes caractéristiques aux États-Unis de 1882 à 1921'. *Journal de la Société de Statistique de Paris* 63, no. 1 (1922): 5–24.

______. *Les fluctuations de l'activité économique: Les périodes de longue durée et les crises.* Paris: Félix Alcan, 1936.

Nasse, Erwin. 'Ueber die Verhütung der Produktionskrisen durch staatliche Fürsorge'. *Jahrbuch für Gesetzgebung, Verwaltung und Volkswirtschaft im Deutschen Reich*, n.s., 3 (1879): 145–89.

Neumann-Spallart, Franz Xaver von. *Übersichten der Weltwirtschaft, 1883–1884.* Stuttgart: Julius Maier, 1887.

Neumann-Spallart, Franz Xaver von, and Franz von Juraschek. *Übersichten der Weltwirtschaft, 1885–1889*, with additions by F. von Juraschek up to 1895. Berlin: Verlag für Sprach- und Handelswissenschaft, 1896.

Neumark, Fritz. *Konjunktur und Steuern.* Bonn: Schroeder, 1930.

Nitti, Francesco S. 'Essai sur les variations du taux de l'escompte'. 3 parts. *Revue d'économie politique* 12, nos. 5 and 10/11 (1898): 368–98, 789–826; and 13, no. 3 (1899): 278–320.

Nogaro, Bertrand. 'La question de l'or devant la Société des Nations: Méthode et résultats'. *Revue d'économie politique* 45, no. 1 (1931): 1–36.

______. *La crise économique dans le monde et en France: Symptômes, causes et remèdies.* Paris: Librairie générale de Droit et de Jurisprudence, 1936.

Noyelle, Henri. *Utopie libérale, chimère socialiste, économie dirigée.* Paris: Recueil Sirey, 1934.

______. 'Plans d'économie dirigée: Les plans de reconstruction économique et sociale à l'étranger et en France'. *Revue d'économie politique* 48, no. 5 (1934): 1595–1668.

Oechelhaeuser, Wilhelm. *Die wirthschaftliche Krisis.* Berlin: Springer, 1876.

Oldenberg, K. 'Zur Theorie der volkswirtschaftlichen Krisen'. *Jahrbuch für Gesetzgebung, Verwaltung und Volkswirtschaft im Deutschen Reich*, n.s., 27, no. 3 (1903): 49–78 (833–62).

Ottolenghi, Costantino. *Delle perturbazioni economiche.* Turin: Fratelli Bocca, 1901.

Overstone, Samuel Jones Loyd, Baron. *Tracts and Other Publications on Metallic and Paper Currency by the Right Hon. Lord Overstone.* London: Longman, Brown, 1858.

Papi, Ugo. *Lezioni di economia generale e corporative.* Vol. 3: *Teoria delle fluttuazioni economiche.* Padua: Cedam, 1934.

Partington, John E. *Railroad Purchasing and the Business Cycle.* Washington, DC: Brookings Institution, 1929.

Parvus. *Handelskrisis und Gewerkschaften: Gesetzentwurf über den achtstündigen Normalarbeitstag.* Munich: Ernst, 1901.

Pereire, Isaac. *Principes de la constitution des banques et de l'organisation du credit.* Paris: Dentu-Guillaumin, 1865.

Perroux, François. 'La notion de groupe industriel'. *Revue d'économie politique* 45, no. 5 (1931): 1377–1402.

Persons, Charles E. 'Credit expansion, 1920–1929, and its Lessons'. *Quarterly Journal of Economics* 45, no. 1 (Nov. 1930): 94–130.

Persons, Warren M. 'Theories of Business Fluctuations: I. A Classification of the Theories'. *Quarterly Journal of Economics* 41, no. 1 (Nov. 1926): 94–128.

______. 'An Index of General Business Conditions, 1875–1913'. *Review of Economics and Statistics* 9, no. 1 (1927): 20–29.
Persons, Warren M., William Trufant Foster and Albert J. Hettinger, eds. *The Problem of Business Forecasting.* Boston: Houghton Mifflin, 1924.
Picard, Alfred. *Les chemins de fer français.* 6 vols. Paris: Rothschild, 1884.
Pigou, A. C. *Industrial Fluctuations.* 2nd ed. London: Macmillan, 1929.
______. *The Economics of Stationary States.* London: Macmillan, 1935.
Pirou, Gaëtan. *La crise du capitalisme: Capitalisme et économie dirigée, néo-socialisme et capitalisme, capitalisme et nationalisme, l'avenir du capitalisme.* Paris: Recueil Sirey, 1934.
Philippovich, Eugen von. *Grundriss des politischen Ökonomie.* 3rd ed. 2 vols. Freiburg: Mohr, 1899.
Pohle, Ludwig. *Bevölkerungsbewegung, Kapitalbildung und periodische Wirtschaftskrisen: Eine Betrachtung, der Ursachen und sozialen Wirkungen der modernen Industrie- und Handelskrisen mit besonderer Berücksichtigung der Kartellfrage.* Gottingen: Vandenhoeck & Ruprecht, 1902.
Poujard'hieu, G. 'Les crises financières et l'organisation du crédit en France'. *Revue des deux mondes* 33, no. 3 (June 1861): 686–708.
Price, Bonamy. 'One per Cent'. *Contemporary Review* 29 (April 1877): 778–99.
Proskourovsky, Léon. *La crise des banques de crédit en Allemagne depuis 1931.* Doctoral thesis, Faculty of Law, University of Paris. Paris: Pedone, 1931. (Thesis supervised by J. Lescure)
Proudhon, P.-J. *Qu'est-ce que la propriété?* Vol. 1 of *Œuvres completes.* New edition. Paris: Marpon & Flammarion, n.d.
Raffalovich, Arthur. 'La crise de Londres en novembre 1890'. *Journal des économistes,* 5th ser., 4, no 12 (Dec. 1890): 321–32.
______. 'La crise et le protectionnisme en Australie'. *Journal des économistes,* 5th ser., 15 (1893): 87–91.
Raynaud, Barthélemy. *Une industrie sans grève: Les mines anglaises.* Paris: Rousseau, 1905.
Reybaud, Louis. 'Des ouvriers qui vivent du travail de la soie'. Pt 5. *Journal des économistes,* 2nd ser., 19 (Aug. 1858): 201–27.
Ricardo, David. *The High Price of Bullion, a Proof of the Depreciation of Bank Notes.* London: John Murray, 1810.
______. *Des principes d'économie politique.* In *Œuvres completes de David Ricardo.* Translated by Alcide Fonteyraud and Francisco Constãncio, 1–394. Paris: Guillaumin, 1847.
Riesser, Jakob. *Die deutschen Grossbanken und ihre Konzentration.* 3rd ed. Jena: Fischer, 1910.
Rist, Charles. 'La progression des grèves en France et sa valeur symptomatique'. *Revue d'économie politique* 21, no. 3 (1907): 161–93.
______. 'Relation entre la variations annuelles du chômage, des grèves et des prix'. *Revue d'économie politique* 26, no. 6 (1912): 748–58.
______. 'Quelques definitions de l'épargne: Essai de critique'. *Revue d'économie politique* 35, no. 6 (1921): 729–52.
______. *La déflation en pratique.* Paris: Giard, 1924.
______. 'La question de l'or'. *Revue d'économie politique* 44, no. 6 (1930): 1489–1518.
______. *Histoire des doctrines relatives au crédit et à la monnaie.* Paris: Recueil Sirey, 1938.
Rivaud, Albert. *Les crises allemandes, 1919–1931.* Paris: Colin, 1932.
Robbins, Lionel C. *La grande dépression.* Translated by Pierre Coste. Paris: Payot, 1935.
______. *Economic Planning and International Order.* London: Macmillan, 1937.
Robertson, Dennis Holme. *A Study of Industrial Fluctuation: An Inquiry into the Character and Causes of the So-called Cyclical Movements of Trade.* London: P. S. King, 1915.
______. *Banking Policy and the Price Level: An Essay in the Theory of the Trade Cycle.* London: P. S. King, 1926.
Rodbertus, Karl. *Le capital.* Translated by Émile Catelain. Paris: Giard & Brière, 1904.
Rodet, Matthieu. 'Le marché à terme et les jeux des Bourses'. *Journal des économistes,* 4th ser., 17 (Jan. 1882): 361–83.
Roos, Charles Fredrick. *NRA Economic Planning.* Bloomington, IN: Principia Press, 1937.

Röpke, Wilhelm. *Die Konjunktur: Ein systematischer Versuch als Beitrag zur Morphologie der Verkehrswirtschaft.* Jena: Fischer, 1922.

______. *Crises and Cycles.* Revised and adapted from the German by Vera C. Smith. London: Hodge, 1936.

Roscher, Wilhelm. 'Zur Lehre von den Absatzkrisen' (1849). In *Ansichten der Volkswirtschaft aus dem geschichtlichen Standpunkte.* 3rd ed., vol. 2: 355–493. Leipzig: Winter, 1878.

______. *System der Volkswirtschaft.* Vol. 1: *Grundlagen der Nationalökonomie: Ein Hand- und Lesebuch für Geschäftsmänner und Studierende.* 19th ed. Stuttgart: Cotta, 1888.

Rosenberg, Hans. *Die Weltwirtschaftskrisis von 1857–1859.* Stuttgart: Kohlhammer, 1934.

Rost, Bernhard. *Über das Wesen und die Ursachen unserer heutigen Wirtschaftskrisis.* Jena: Fischer, 1905.

Roulleau, Gaston. 'L'abus du crédit aux États-Unis et la théorie des crises'. 2 parts. *Journal de la Société de statistique de Paris* 49, nos. 3 and 4 (1908): 92–98, 115–22.

______. *Les règlements par effets de commerce en France et à l'étranger.* Paris: Dubreuil, Frèrebeau, 1914.

Royal Institute of International Affairs. *The International Gold Problem: Collected Papers.* London: Oxford University Press, 1931.

Saint-Germès, Jean. *L'état capitaliste.* Paris: Recueil Sirey, 1937.

Saint-Léon, Étienne Martin. *Cartels et Trusts.* Paris: Lecoffre, 1903.

Salter, Arthur. *Recovery: The Second Effort.* London: Bell & Sons, 1932.

Sauvaire-Jourdan, Françoise. 'La verité sur les caisses de prêt allemandes (Darlehenskassen)'. *Revue d'économie politique* 29 (1915): 15–23.

Say, Horace. 'Crise financière et commerciale'. *Journal des économistes* 20, no. 77 (April 1848): 15–24.

Say, Jean-Baptiste. *Cours complet d'économie politique pratique.* 2nd ed. 2 vols. Paris: Guillaumin, 1840.

______. *Traité d'économie politique, ou simple exposition de la manière dont se forment, se distribuent et se consomment les richesses.* 6th ed. Paris: Guillaumin, 1841.

Say, Léon. 'Rapport fait au nom de la commission du budget de 1875 sur le paiement de l'indemnité de guerre et sur les opérations de change qui en ont été la conséquence'. In *Finances publiques; Liberté du commerce*, edited by Joseph Chailley-Bert, 24–60. Petite bibliothèque économique français et étranger 17. Paris: Guillaumin, 1896.

Schäffle, Albert. 'Zur Lehre von den Handelskrisen'. Part 1. *Zeitschrift für die gesamte Staatswissenschaft* 14, no. 2 (1858): 402–70.

______. 'Der "grosse Börsenkrach" des Jahres 1873'. *Zeitschrift für die gesamte Staatswissenschaft* 30, no. 1 (1874): 1–94.

______. *Bau und Leben des socialen Körpers.* 4 vols. Tübingen: Laupp, 1875–78.

Schiller, Karl. *Arbeitsbeschaffung und Finanzordnung in Deutschland.* Berlin: Junker & Dünnhaupt, 1936.

Schmidt, Fritz. 'Ein Rechenfehler als Konjunkturursache'. *Vierteljahrshefte zur Konjunkturforschung* 1, supplement no. 4 (1926): 3–27.

Schmoller, Gustav von. *Grundriss der allgemeinen Volkswirtschaftslehre.* 2 vols. Leipzig: Ducker & Humblot, 1904.

Schumacher, Hermann. 'Die Ursachen und Wirkungen der Konzentration im deutschen Bankwesen'. *Jahrbuch für Gesetzgebung, Verwaltung und Volkswirtschaft im Deutschen Reich* 30, no. 3 (1906): 1–43.

______. 'Die deutsche Geldverfassung und ihre Reform'. *Jahrbuch für Gesetzgebung, Verwaltung und Volkswirtschaft im Deutschen Reich* 32 (1908): 1257–1388.

______. *Le marché financier américain et sa récente crise monétaire.* Translated by Jean Lescure. Paris: Giard & Brière, 1909.

Schumpeter, Joseph A. *Theorie der wirtschaftlichen Entwicklung.* 2nd ed. Munich and Leipzig: Duncker & Humblot, 1926.

Schwarz, Otto. *Diskontpolitik: Gedanken über englische, französische und deutsche Bank-, Kredit- und Goldpolitik: Eine vergleichende Studie.* Leipzig: Duncker & Humblot, 1911.

Seligman, Edwin R. A. *The Economics of Instalment Selling: A Study in Consumers' Credit, with Special Reference to the Automobile.* 2 vols. New York: Harper, 1927.

______. *Principes d'économique.* Translated by George Lecarpentier. 2 vols. Paris: Giard, 1927.

Simiand, François. *Le salaire des ouvriers des mines de charbon: Contribution à la théorie économique du salaire.* Paris: Cornély, 1907.

de Sismondi, J.-C.-L. Simonde. *Nouveaux principes d'économie politique, ou de la richesse dans ses rapports avec la population.* 2 vols. Paris: Delaunay, 1819.

______. *Études sur l'économie politique.* 2 vols. Brussels: Société typographique belge, 1837.

Slichter, Sumner H. 'The Current Labor Policies of American Industries'. *Quarterly Journal of Economics* 43, no. 3 (1929): 393–435.

______. *Modern Economic Society.* New York: Henry Holt, 1929.

______. *Towards Stability: The Problem of Economic Stability.* New York: Henry Holt, 1937.

Smith, Bradford B. 'A Forecasting Index for Business'. *Journal of the American Statistical Association* 26, no. 174 (1931): 115–27.

Soetbeer, Adolf. *Materialien zur Erläuterung und Beurteilung der wirtschaftlichen Edelmetallverhältnisse und der Währungsfrage.* 2nd ed. Berlin: Puttkammer & Mühlbrecht, 1886.

______. 'Materials Toward the Elucidation of the Economic Conditions Affecting the Precious Metals and the Question of Standards'. Translated from the second German edition by F. W. Taussig. In Edward Atkins, *Report made by Edward Atkins to the President of the United States, upon the present status of bimetallism in Europe.* Executive document 34. US Senate, 50th Congress, 1st session. October 1887.

Sombart, Werner. 'Versuch einer Systematik der Wirtschaftskrisen'. *Archiv für Sozialwissenschaft und Sozialpolitik* [n.s. of *Archiv für soziale Gesetzgebung und Statistik* 19], 1, no. 1 (1904): 1–22.

______. *Das Wirtschaftsleben im Zeitalter der Hochkapitalismus.* Vol. 3 of *Der moderne Kapitalismus.* 2 vols. Leipzig: Duncker & Humblot, 1927.

Spiethoff, Arthur. 'Vorbemerkungen zu einer Theorie des Überproduktion'. *Jahrbuch für Gesetzgebung, Verwaltung und Volkswirtschaft im Deutschen Reich*, n.s., 26 (1902): 267–305 (721–59).

______. 'Die Krisentheorien von M. v. Tugan-Baranowsky und L. Pohle'. *Jahrbuch für Gesetzgebung, Verwaltung und Volkswirtschaft im Deutschen Reich*, new ser., 27, no. 2 (1903): 331–60 (680–708).

Sprague, O. M. W. *History of Crises Under the National Banking System.* Washington, DC: Government Printing Office, 1911.

Stähle, Hans. 'Das Beobachtungsverfahren der wirtschaftlichen Wechsellagen des Harvard Committee on Economic Research'. *Jahrbuch für Gesetzebung, Verwaltung, und Volkswirthschaft im Deutschen Reich* 52 (1928): 261–310.

Stamp, J. C. 'The Effect of Trade Fluctuations upon Profits'. *Journal of the Royal Statistical Society* 81, no. 4 (1918): 563–608.

Steinberg, Julius, *Die Wirtschaftskrisis 1901: Ihre Ursachen, Lehren und Folgen.* Bonn: Cohen, 1902.

Die Störungen im deutschen Wirtschaftsleben während der Jahre 1900 ff. 7 vols. Schriften des Vereins für Socialpolitik 105–111. Leipzig: Duncker & Humblot, 1903.

Die Störungen im deutschen Wirtschaftsleben während der Jahre 1900 ff.: In ihrem Rückwirkungen auf die industriellen, Effekten- und Geldmarktsverhältnisse Österreichs. Schriften des Vereins für Socialpolitik 112. Leipzig: Duncker & Humblot, 1903.

Struck, Émile. 'Zur Geschichte des Pariser Börsenkrisis von Januar 1882'. *Jahrbuch für Gesetzgebung, Verwaltung und Volkswirtschaft im Deutschen Reich*, n.s., 7, no. 1 (1882): 241–72.

Stucken, Rudolf. *Theorie der Konjunkturschwankungen.* Jena: Fischer, 1926.

______. *Deutsche Geld- und Kreditpolitik.* Hamburg: Hanseatische Verlagsanstalt, 1937.

Supino, Camillo. *Le crisi economiche.* Milan: Ulricho Hoepli, 1907.

Taussig, F. W. 'The Crisis in the United States and the Repeal of Silver Purchase'. *Economic Journal* 3, no. 12 (Dec. 1893): 733–45.

Timoshenko, Vladimir P. *The Role of Agricultural Fluctuations in the Business Cycle.* Michigan Business Studies, vol. 2, no. 9. Ann Arbor: University of Michigan School of Business Administration, 1930.

Tooke, Thomas, and William Newmarch. *A History of Prices and the State of Circulation from 1793 to 1856*. 6 vols. London: Longman, Brown, Green and Longman, 1838–57. Reprinted by P. S. King, London, 1928.

______. *Die Geschichte und Bestimmung der Preise während der Jahre 1793–1857*. Translated by C. W. Asher. 2 vols. Dresden: Rudolf Kunze, 1858–59.

Tugan-Baranowsky, Mikhail I. *Studien zur Theorie und Geschichte der Handelskrisen in England*. Jena: Fischer, 1901.

______. 'Der Zusammenbruch der kapitalistischen Wirtschaftsordnung im Lichte der nationalökonomischen Theorie'. *Archiv für Sozialwissenschaft und Sozialpolitik* [n.s. of *Archiv für soziale Gesetzgebung und Statistik* 19], 1 (1904): 273–306.

Tugwell, Rexford G. *The Industrial Discipline and the Governmental Arts*. New York: Columbia University Press, 1933.

Veblen, Thorstein. *The Theory of Business Enterprise*. 1904. Reprinted, New York: Charles Scribner and Sons, 1915.

Vergeot, Jean B. *Le crédit comme stimulant et régulateur de l'industrie: La conception saint-simonienne, ses réalisations, son application au problème bancaire d'après-guerre*. Paris: Jouve, 1918.

Verhandlungen des Vereins für Socialpolitik über die Lage in der Seeschiffahrt beschäftigten Arbeiter und über die Störungen im deutschen Wirtschaftsleben während der Jahre 1900 ff. Schriften des Vereins für Socialpolitik 113. Leipzig: Duncker & Humblot, 1904.

Vialles, Pierre. *La consommation et les crises économiques*. Doctoral thesis, Faculty of Law, University of Montpellier. Montpellier: Montane & Sicardi, 1902.

Villain, Georges. *Notice sur la périodicité des crises économiques et ses rapport avec l'exploitation des chemins de fer*. Paris: Imprimerie Nationale, 1908.

Vito, Francesco, ed. *Cicli economici: Contributi dell'Instituto di Scienza sociali*. Second series. Pubblicazioni della Università Cattolica del Sacro Cuore, Scienze sociali, 17. Milan: Società editrice 'Vita e pensiero', 1937.

Vogelstein, Theodor. *Die Industrie der Rheinprovinz, 1888–1900: Ein Beitrag zur Frage der Handelspolitik und der Kartelle*. Stuttgart: Cotta, 1902.

Wagemann, Ernst. *Konjunkturlehre*. Berlin: Hobbing, 1928.

______. *Einführung in die Konjunkturlehre*. Leipzig: Quelle & Meyer, 1929.

______. *Struktur und Rhythmus der Weltwirtschaft: Grundlagen einer weltwirtschaftlichen Konjunkturlehre*. Berlin: Hobbing, 1931.

Wagenführ, Rolf. *Die Konjunkturtheorie in Russland*. Jena: Fischer, 1929.

Wagner, Adolf. *Grundlegung der politischen Oekonomie*. 3rd ed. 2 vols. Leipzig: Winter, 1892–94.

Wagon, Eduard. *Die finanzielle Entwicklung deutscher Aktiongesellschaften von 1870–1900 und die Gesellschaften mit beschränkter Haftung im Jahre 1900*. Jena: Fischer, 1903.

Warburton, Clark. 'Plateaus of Prosperity and Plains of Depression'. In *Economic Essays in Honor of Wesley Clair Mitchell*, 499–516. New York: Columbia University Press, 1935.

Webb, Sidney and Beatrice. *Histoire du trade unionisme*. Translated by A. Métin. Paris: Giard & Brière, 1897.

Wicksell, Knut. *Geldzins und Güterpreise: Eine Studie über die den Tauschwert des Geldes bestimmenden Ursachen*. Jena: Fischer, 1898.

______. *Vorlesungen über Nationalökonomie auf Grundlage des Marginalprinzipes*. Vol. 2: *Geld und Kredit*. Leipzig: Fischer, 1922.

Wiese, Leopold von. 'Die rheinisch-westfällische Eisenindustrie in der gegenwärtigen Krisis'. *Jahrbuch für Gesetzgebung, Verwaltung und Volkswirtschaft im Deutschen Reich* 26, no. 1 (1902): 299–323.

Wilson, James. *Fluctuations of Currency, Commerce and Manufactures Referable to Corn Laws*. London: Longman, Orme, Brown, Green and Longmans, 1840.

Wirth, Max. *Geschichte der Handelskrisen*. 2nd ed. Frankfurt: Sauerlaender, 1874.

Withers, Hartley. *Qu'est-ce que la monnaie? Le marché monétaire anglaise*. Translated by Cyrille and Joseph Rivière. Paris: Giard & Brière, 1920.

Wittelshöfer, Otto. *Untersuchungen über das Kapital, seine Natur und Funktion: Ein Beitrag zur Analyse und Kritik der Volkswirtschaft.* Tübingen: Laupp, 1890.

Wolowski, Louis. 'La crise financière de l'Angleterre'. *Revue des deux mondes*, 2nd ser., 64, no. 4 (Aug. 1866): 927–56.

Wright, Carroll D. *The First Annual Report of the Commissioner of Labor, March 1886: Industrial Depressions.* Washington, DC: Government Printing Office, 1886.

Yoder, Dale. 'Some Economic Implications of Unemployment Insurance'. *Quarterly Journal of Economics* 45, no. 4 (Aug. 1931): 622–39.

Zwiedineck-Südenhorst, Otto von. *Beitrage zur Erklärung der strukturellen Arbeitslosigkeit.* Berlin: Hobbing, 1927.

______. 'Preislehre und Konjunkturforschung'. *Zeitschrift für die gesamte Staatswissenschaft* 82, no. 2 (1927): 255–87.

Appendix Two

BIBLIOGRAPHY OF THE WORKS OF JEAN LESCURE

Books

Lescure, Jean. 'Des crises générales et périodiques de surproduction'. Doctoral thesis, Faculty of Law, University of Bordeaux, 1906.

Published as, *Des crises générales et périodiques de surproduction.* Paris: Larose & Tenin, 1907. [Russian translation, by N. I. Suvirov, St. Petersburg, 1908]

______. 'Le marché à terme de bourse en Allemagne: Titre IV de la loi du 22 juin 1896: Étude juridique et économique'. (Second) Doctoral thesis, Faculty of Law, University of Bordeaux, 1908.

Published as, *Le marché à terme de bourse en Allemagne: Titre IV de la loi du 22 juin 1896: Étude juridique et économique.* Paris: Recuil Sirey/Larose & Tenin, 1908.

______. *Trusts et cartels, leurs consequences.* Paris: Recueil Sirey, 1908.

______. *Des crises générales et périodiques de surproduction.* 2nd ed. Paris: Recueil Sirey, 1910.

______. *Les marchés financiers de Berlin et de Paris et la crise franco-allemande de juillet–octobre 1911.* Paris: Larose & Tenin, 1912.

______. *L'épargne en France.* Paris: Tenin, 1914.

______. *La baisse des prix et ses problèmes.* Paris: Tenin, 1921.

______. *Le problème des reparations: Comment la résoudre.* Paris: Plon-Nourrit, 1922.

______. *Des crises générales et périodiques de surproduction.* 3rd ed. Paris: Recueil Sirey, 1923.

______. *Les origines de la Révolution russe: L'ancien régime et le problème social.* Paris: Tenin, 1927.

______. *La Révolution russe: Le bolchevisme, communisme et N.E.P.* Paris: Gamber, 1929.

______. *Des crises générales et périodiques de surproduction.* 4th ed. 2 vols. Paris: Domat-Montchrestien, 1932.

______. *Hausses et baisses des prix de longue durée.* Paris: Domat-Montchrestien, 1933.

______. *Le nouveau régime corporatif italien (loi du 5 février 1934): Cartels et trusts.* Paris: Domat-Montchrestien, 1934.

______. *Le Bolchevisme de Staline: Le régime des plans.* Paris: Domat-Montchrestien, 1934.

______. *L'épargne en France, 1914–1934: Revue et mise à jour.* 2nd ed. Paris: Domat-Montchrestien, 1936.

______. *Des crises générales et périodiques de surproduction.* 5th ed. 2 vols. Paris: Domat-Montchrestien, 1938.

______. *Étude sociale comparée des régimes de liberté et des régimes autoritaires: Essai d'économie sociale comparée.* Paris: Domat-Montchrestien, 1939.

______. *Après la paix: La reconstruction économique (esquisses et réflexions).* Paris: Librairie générale de droit et de jurisprudence, 1943.

______. *Guerre et crises économiques: Face au chômage.* Paris: Librairie générale de droit et de jurisprudence, 1944.

______. *Étude sociale comparée des régimes de liberté et des régimes autoritaires: Essai d'économie sociale comparée.* 2nd ed. Paris: Domat-Montchrestien, 1946.

______. *Cours d'économie sociale comparée.* Paris: Les Cours de droit, 1947.

______. *Principes d'économie rationnelle: Essai de perspectives économiques.* Paris: Domat-Montchrestien, 1947.

Articles

Jean Lescure. 'L'évolution du cartel dans la grande industrie Allemande de la houille et du fer'. *Revue d'économie politique* 20, no. 5 (1906): 368–86.

______. 'La conception de la propriété chez Aristotle'. *Revue d'histoire des doctrines économiques et sociales* 1, no. 3 (1908): 282–300.

______. 'Aspects récents de la concentration industrielle: L'intégration dans la métallurgie'. *Revue économique internationale* 6, no. 3 (Aug. 1909): 256–94.

______. 'Esquisse de l'évolution du change et des théories relatives au change'. *Revue d'histoire des doctrines économiques et sociales* 3, no. 1 (1910): 48–69.

______. 'Surproduction générale ou surproduction généralisée?' *Revue d'économie politique* 24 (1910): 157–62.

______. 'La liberté du commerce des grains et le Parlement de Paris (1763–1768)'. *Revue d'économie politique* 24 (1910): 451–70.

______. 'Chronique des questions ouvrières'. *Revue d'économie politique* 25, no. 2 (1911): 219–51.

______. 'L'accroissement de la production de l'or et la hausse générale des prix'. *Revue d'économie politique* 25, no. 6 (1911): 729–44.

______. 'La puissance d'épargne de la France et les placements étrangers'. *Revue politique et parlementaire* 71, no. 212 (Feb. 1912): 303–17.

______. 'Chronique des questions ouvrières'. *Revue d'économie politique* 26, no. 1 (1912): 84–110.

______. 'Les marchés financiers de Berlin et de Paris et la crise franco-allemand de juillet–octobre 1911'. *Revue économique internationale* 9, no. 3 (Sep. 1912): 466–509.

______. 'Hausses et baisses générales des prix'. *Revue d'économie politique* 26, no. 4 (1912): 452–90.

______. 'Chronique des questions ouvrières'. *Revue d'économie politique* 27, no. 2 (1913): 210–40.

______. 'Chronique des questions ouvrières'. *Revue d'économie politique* 28, no. 2 (1914): 199–223.

______. 'Nouveaux progrès de la concentration dans les banques anglaises'. *Revue d'économie politique* 28, no. 4 (1914): 471–73.

______. 'Le trésor de guerre privé français au moment de la déclaration de guerre'. *Revue d'économie politique* 28, no. 6 (1914): 704–5.

______. 'Hausse des prix et essor économique de la période 1895–1913'. *Revue économique internationale* 11, no. 2 (May 1914): 269–98.

______. 'La réforme du système bancaire aux États-Unis (La Federal Reserve System)'. *Revue d'économie politique* 29 (1915): 59–79.

______. 'La situation financière de l'Allemagne'. *Revue de Paris,* 15 June 1915.

______. 'Le movement ouvrier depuis l'armistice jusqu'en mars 1920'. *Revue d'économie politique* 34, no. 3 (1920): 337–57.

______. 'Banques de dépot, banques d'émission et banques de réserve: Contribution à la théorie des banques'. *Revue d'économie politique* 35, no. 4 (1921): 420–31.

______. 'La reprise'. *Revue économique internationale* 15, no. 1 (Feb. 1923): 213–33.

______. 'Le marché des capitaux en France et ses particularités récentes'. *Revue d'économie politique* 37, no. 6 (1923): 863–68.

______. 'La théorie des crises et l'anarchie économique contemporaine'. *Scientia,* 2nd series, 18, no. 10 (Oct. 1924): 253–60.

______. 'Les sociétés allemandes par actions après le retour à l'or'. *Revue d'économie politique* 40, no. 4 (1926): 1060–63.

______. 'Le commerce mondial, d'après le mémorandum sur les balances des paiements et sur les balances du commerce extérieur (1911–1925)'. *Revue d'économie politique* 41, no. 3 (1927): 979–83.

______. 'Les assurances sociales en Angleterre: Leur influence sur le coût de la production'. *L'Europe nouvelle*, 27 Aug. 1927.
______. 'Réparations et dettes entre alliés'. *Revue d'économie politique* 42, no. 6 (1928): 1449–54.
______. 'Krisenlehre'. In *Die Wirtschaftstheorie der Gegenwart*, edited by Hans Mayer, Frank A. Fetter and Richard Reisch, vol. 4, 32–48. Vienna: Springer, 1928.
______. 'L'état fasciste'. *Revue de Paris* 36, no. 8 (15 April 1929): 748–67.
______. 'La production et le commerce dans le monde avant et après-guerre'. *Revue d'économie politique* 43, no. 4 (1929): 1143–48.
______. 'Crises'. In *Encyclopaedia of the Social Sciences.* Edited by Edwin R. A. Seligman. Vol. 3. London: Macmillan, 1930.
______. 'Die Zerrüttung der Wertsphäre'. *Weltwirtschaftliches Archiv* 38 (1933): 1–15.
______. 'Prix, monnaie et crédit'. In *Economic Essays in Honour of Gustav Cassel*, 387–98. London: Fank Cass, 1933.
______. 'Les prodromes de l'expérience Roosevelt'. *Revue économique internationale* (Dec. 1935).
______. 'Les profits 1929–1935 (Grande-Bretagne, États-Unis, France)'. *Journal de la Société française de statistique* 77 (1936): 192–200.
______. 'Une économie politique sans doctrines: Étude compare du capitalisme et du bolchevisme'. *Revue d'économie politique* 51, no. 1 (1937): 28–42.
______. 'Parité des pouvoirs d'achat et cours des changes'. *Journal de la Société française de statistiques* 86 (1945): 227–32.

Translation

Schumacher, Hermann A. *Le marché financier américain et sa récente crise monétaire.* Translated by Jean Lescure. Paris: Giard & Brière, 1909.

Select Book Reviews and Other Writings

Lescure, Jean. Review of *Wirtschaftskrisen und Ueberkapitalisation*, by Mentor Bouniatian. *Revue d'histoire des doctrines économiques et sociales* 2 (1909): 423–24.
______. Obituary 'Maurice Bourguin (1856–1910)'. *Revue d'économie politique* 24 (1910): 97–101.
______. Review of *Kartelle and Trust*, 2nd ed., by Robert Liefmann. *Revue d'économie politique* 24 (1910): 572–73.
______. Review of *Allgemeine Volkswirtschaftslehre*, by Wilhelm Lexis. *Revue d'économie politique* 24 (1910): 667–70.
______. Obituary 'G. de Molinari (1819–1912)'. *Revue d'économie Politique* 26, no. 2 (1912): 233–34.
______. Review of *Gold Prices and Wages*, by J. A. Hobson. *Revue d'économie politique* 28, no. 2 (1914): 252–53.
______. Review of *Les crises industrielles en Angleterre*, by [Mikhail I.] Tugan-Baranowsky. *Revue d'économie politique* 28, no. 1 (1914): 116–17.
______. Review of *Business Cycles* (1913), by Wesley Clair Mitchell. *Revue d'économie politique* 28, no. 1 (1914): 119–20.
______. 'Pour nos étudiants démobilisés: Une caisse de prêts sur l'honneur'. *Revue d'économie politique* 33, no. 5 (1919): 599–601.
______. Review of *Profits*, by Foster and Catchings. *Revue d'économie politique* 40, no. 6 (1926): 1403–4.
______. Review of *Industrial Fluctuations*, by A. C. Pigou. *Revue d'économie politique* 41, no. 3 (1927): 992–93.
______. Review of *Le capital étranger en Russie*, by Anton Crihan. *Weltwirtschaftliches Archiv* 42 (1935): 52–53.

______. Preface to *Les origines économiques et politiques du socialisme de Sun Yat Sen*, by Tsiang Kouen. Paris: Domat-Montchrestien, 1933.

______. Preface to *La gestion des bons de la defense nationale par la caisse autonome d'amortissement: Les bons a deux ans et le marche monetaire*, by Gustave Verdeil. Paris: Recueil Sirey, 1935.

______. Preface to *Guide à travers les panacées économiques*, by Fitz Machlup. Translated by R. Hadekel. Paris: Librairie de Médicis, 1938.

______. Preface to *La politique financière du Président Roosevelt*, by Francis Louis Closon. Paris: Rivière, 1938.

______. Preface to *La dévaluation du franc belge: Mars 1935–avril 1936*, by Jean Sylvestre. Paris: Librairie sociale et économique, 1939.

______. Preface to *L'expérience Roosevelt: La politique bancaire et monétaire postérieure à 1934*, by René Vincent. Paris: Librairie sociale et économique, 1939.

INDEX

Pages in boldface indicate material in figures and tables

Milton Keynes UK
Ingram Content Group UK Ltd.
UKHW022136010524
441892UK00001B/6

9 781839 988301